COMPARATIVE ANALYSIS OF NATIONS

COMPARATIVE ANALYSIS OF NATIONS

Quantitative Approaches

Robert L. Perry
Department of Behavioral Science
University of Texas—Permian Basin

John D. Robertson
Department of Political Science
Texas A&M University

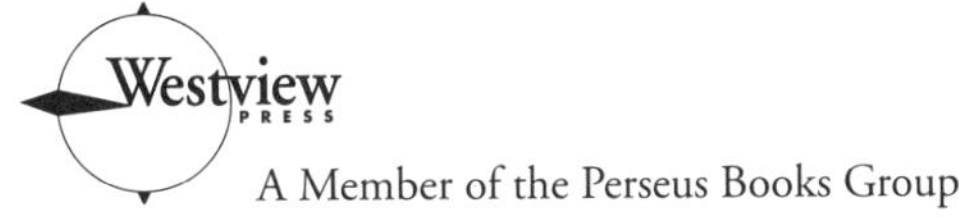

A Member of the Perseus Books Group

Westview Press books are available at special discounts for bulk purchases in the United States by corporations, institutions, and other organizations. For more information, please contact the Special Markets Department at The Perseus Books Group, 11 Cambridge Center, Cambridge MA 02142, or call (617) 252–5298.

Published in 2002 in the United States of America by Westview Press, 5500 Central Avenue, Boulder, Colorado 80301-2877, and in the United Kingdom by Westview Press, 12 Hid's Copse Road, Cumnor Hill, Oxford OX2 9JJ

Find us on the World Wide Web at www.westviewpress.com

Library of Congress Cataloging-in-Publication Data

Perry, Robert L.
Comparative analysis of nations : quantitative approaches / Robert L. Perry and John D. Robertson.
p. cm.
Includes bibliographical references and index.
ISBN 0-8133-9806-1
1. Comparative government. I. Robertson, John D. II. Title.

JF51 .P47 2001
320.3'01'1—dc21 2001024875

The paper used in this publication meets the requirements of the American National Standard for Permanence of Paper for Printed Library Materials Z39.48-1984.

10 9 8 7 6 5 4 3 2 1

To Our Parents

This is the second important duty of science in relation to national life. It is to develop our brainpower by providing training in method and by exercising our powers of cautious observation. It has to teach not only the leaders of our national life, but the people at large, to prepare for and meet the difficulties of new environments.

—Karl Pearson, *National Life from the Standpoint of Science* (1901)

What is now understood when we speak of an explanation of facts is simply the establishment of a connection between the single phenomena and some general facts, the number of which continually diminishes with the progress of science.

—Auguste Comte, *The Positive Philosophy* (1853)

I am afraid, my dear Watson, that most of your conclusions were erroneous. When I said that you stimulated me I meant, to be frank, that in noting your fallacies I was occasionally guided towards the truth.

—Sherlock Holmes (Sir Arthur Conan Doyle), *The Hound of the Baskervilles* (1902)

Contents

Application Demonstrations

Preface

To observe is to know; to compare is to understand. For Aristotle, to understand why tyranny was the corrupted form of monarchy, or why a polity was better suited to justice than democracy, required one to compare the differences and similarities across these different properties of authority and to weigh the advantages and disadvantages of their different conditions and circumstances. So it remains today as it was for the person to whom we assign the distinction of being the first student of comparative analysis in the Western world. For Aristotle, life for the rational person was one of wonderment and endless puzzles fed by the powers of observation. The intellectual order that humankind fashioned to comprehend and ultimately master the political world was constructed, sustained, and refined by the process of comparative observation. Comparison is the vital center in the activity we call "normal" science. Applying the principles of normal science to the field of political science highlights the central role of comparative analysis and, more specifically, cross-national analysis within the discipline.

Comparison is as crucial to our understanding of the contemporary political world as it was to Aristotle's. The United States, we know, is democratic—but how democratic is it, and in what sense? To understand the level and type of democracy in the United States, it is necessary to examine these questions through a comparative perspective. Similarly, we know that Germany is wealthy—but how wealthy? We know that Nigeria is ethnically complex—but how complex? Of course, we can empirically verify Germany's wealth and Nigeria's ethnic complexity. However, without a comparative framework we are unable to explain why these attributes are important within not only the German and Nigerian political systems but any political system. Without comparison, we can only describe what we see. We cannot explain because we cannot observe variance. Therefore, we cannot offer an accurate assessment of the true dimensions of what we observe within a specified context. Without comparison, we lack depth and perspective.

Comparison is a normal activity of our daily lives. In fact, most decisions we make require some comparison of our potential choices. For instance, the fact that you attended a certain university was most likely the result of a choice based on some comparisons that you made concerning such things as costs, prestige of degree, distance from home, availability of degree programs, availability of extracurricular activities, and so on.

When it comes to comparing countries, a more technical form of comparison is often employed in an effort to achieve a broader generalization. We call this approach cross-national analysis, and it is one of several means by which we come to understand our political world. It is also one member of the family of comparative strategies commonly employed in political science. As such, cross-national analysis is governed by the same logic as conventional comparison, with this crucial difference: In cross-national analysis we systematically explore data across as many different cultures and political systems as possible and feasible. Cross-national analysis is designed to subject our images and pictures of the political world to as demanding a test as possible. If we are to understand the various dimensions of countries or nations, we must think beyond national borders or capitals. We must be willing to complement our reliance on proper nouns when discussing political phenomena across the globe by a habit of mind that formulates questions and seeks answers in terms of general concepts, processes, and behavior and authority patterns that transcend specific regions or nation-states. We must strive to discover and confirm those principles of our political world that have relevance and consequence beyond the particular culture, political system, or nation-state. Our subjectivity, in other words, must be subordinated to a higher priority: that of a general theory of political behavior and institutional authority forged from the application of normal science, though necessarily contoured to the peculiar conditions of social science. Of course, most cross-national research cannot reasonably go as far as we might want; present methods, data, and technology, as well as our own powers of imagination and observation, still impose severe restrictions on our range and capacities. But the willingness to do so, indeed, the recognition that we must do so, is what separates cross-national analysis from more general comparison. It is, in short, the science of comparing nations, and it establishes the foundation for, and holds out the promise of, a general theory of political behavior and institutional authority.

WHAT IS THE SCIENCE OF COMPARING NATIONS?

Epistemologists (those who study the philosophy of knowledge and seek to discern the reasons and procedures we employ to come to know what we think we know to be true) inform us that in order to approximate the activity of normal science, which itself is the process of subjecting our assumptions about how the world around us operates to rigorous and systematically controlled observation, cross-national analysis must entail six basic steps:

1. Conceptualization
2. Operationalization

3. Specification
4. Measurement
5. Analysis
6. Evaluation

We shall explore each of these steps in more detail within Chapter 1. Suffice it to say at this point that to properly employ quantitative cross-national research, and to have it effectively serve as an instrument of theory building, we must consider the enterprise as a multidimensional activity requiring some familiarity with the philosophy and rules of normal science, the rules and logic of basic social statistical techniques, and the substantive content and conceptual inventory central to the subfield of comparative politics.

The What, How, and Why of Cross-National Research

Essentially, cross-national analysis is a *process* wherein we subject our concepts of the political world to systematic quantitative analysis, conditioned by the rules and guidelines of normal science. An introduction to the science of comparing nations need not entail the use of techniques that require the mastery of advanced matrix algebra or calculus. They can certainly help, but they are not necessary. Understanding and effectively applying the science of comparing nations does require, however, dedicated and careful attention to measurement and conceptualization. Such an introduction requires combining an appreciation of the philosophy of science, some awareness of the basic concepts that are commonly used in constructing our models, and an appreciation of how to appropriately apply the basic tools of social statistics to data analysis. To that end, this text is designed to specifically address three questions frequently confronting students of comparative politics:

- *What* do I do once I have identified a question (or puzzle) that I want to explore within a cross-national perspective?
- *How* do I address (conceptualize, operationalize, measure, sample, analyze, and evaluate) this question?
- *Why* should I do these things?

TO WHOM IS THIS TEXT DIRECTED?

This book is not a substitute for a basic text on comparative politics, but it is designed to be useful to any student who has had some exposure to either a basic political science course, an introductory comparative politics course, or an introduction to a basic methods course. It is, in short, a second course in comparative politics, intended to complement a conceptual foundation that the student has acquired already within a basic introduction to political science or comparative politics. It requires no previous training in statistics or math, and certainly no previous study of the philosophy of science, computer programming, or data analysis.

Organizational Issues

The goal of each chapter is to introduce the student to an integral component of cross-national analysis. Taken as a whole, the text combines concepts, measurement issues, data, and basic statistical analysis in such a way as to provide practical guidance and experience in the use and application of the cross-national strategy of comparative analysis. The text progresses from a simple introduction to the logic of quantitative cross-national research, through more advanced conceptual, measurement, and statistical issues. It remains at the level of bivariate analysis, for purposes of clarity and simplification. The logic that guides this text is simple: Before students can fully appreciate and effectively use the more powerful tools of analysis available to them in cross-national analysis, they must come to understand the role and utility of basic variance as a tool for discovery and clarification. While this may be similar to the role and utility of variance in American studies, or other domains of social science research, cross-national analysis is unique because its intent is to maximize variance across diverse national and cultural contexts and therefore it is particularly well-suited to the effective and rewarding application of basic tools of variance analysis. This process begins with explicit application and demonstration of the elementary steps in examining patterns of variance across nation-states and proceeds with acquired familiarity to more advanced and sophisticated tools and applications—tools and applications that carry more risk for the "supplier" and the "consumer," yet offer the promise of more precision. In short, once one has become comfortable with the basics discussed and demonstrated throughout the various chapters, the more advanced techniques are merely logical extensions with some technical considerations that are fundamentally not different from those governing simple bivariate analysis.

The seventeen chapters that compose this text can be logically broken into four parts:

Chapters 1 and 2 explore the logic and strategies of quantitative cross-national analysis

Chapters 3–5 explore various applications within quantitative cross-national analysis, including Central Tendency Statistics, Standardized Measures, and Inferential Measures

Chapters 6–8 address fundamental issues of measurement and hypothesis testing

Chapters 9–17 introduce the student to the basic techniques of hypothesis testing, including Tabular Analysis (using survey data), ANOVA, Scatterplots, Factor Analysis, and basic, bivariate regression

TO THE INSTRUCTOR

The concepts surveyed in this text are what one would consider the basic building blocks of comparative research. These include culture, democracy, economic organization, modernity, human development, prosperity, geographical and civilizational tradition, size, national power, political-economic ideology, and economic inequality. They are introduced in a necessarily abbreviated fashion for the student, with emphasis on measuring the concepts and effectively applying data to models that can bring the concepts to bear on our questions of political behavior and/or institutional authority. We have taken care to note for the student where these data can be found within the public domain, including on the web, should the enterprising student wish to extend the sample and modify the analysis on his or her own.

This text is intended to provide guidance and explanation to those students who want to go beyond their conceptual literature and enter the world of systematic comparative research. While the text does not include specific practice exercises for the student at the end of each chapter, instructors can utilize the data provided in the accompanying CD-ROM to devise such exercises, if they wish.

The principal database that contains the variables and data from which the demonstrations in the text are produced is CROSSNAT.50.SAV. It is an SPSS system data file that contains cross-sectional data on fifty of the largest countries of the world, as of 1997. There are four types of data within the variables contained within CROSSNAT.50: (1) variables based on *original* data (for example, POPULATE, which is the population of a country taken from the World Bank), (2) variables that have been *computed* from the variables based on original data (such as POWER, which is the sum of scores for each country based on the original data from three other variables, ZAREA, ZPOP, and ZGDP), (3) data that have been *recoded* from their original scale and format from the variables based on original data (for example, PARREG3, which is a three-category variable collapsed from the original five-category variable, PARREG), and (4) data that have been *derived* by the SPSS 10 statistical procedures (for example, ZAREA, which is the standardized value of the original data for the variable AREA, derived within the SPSS procedure *DESCRIPTIVE* and saved as a system file in CROSSNAT.50 for use in analysis and demonstrations).

In addition to CROSSNAT.50.SAV, we have included within the accompanying CD-ROM a more extensive cross-national database, CROSSNAT.181.SAV. This file contains fewer variables than CROSSNAT.50.SAV, but includes data for 181 countries, rather than fifty. The database also contains several variables reported across at least two different time points. This affords the student and instructor the opportunity to explore simple time-series comparisons. However, all the original variables recorded in CROSSNAT.50 are also included in CROSSNAT.181. Of course, with so many entries, many variables have missing data for several countries. The data in CROSSNAT.181.SAV are only *original* data—there are no recoded variables, no computed variables, and no program-derived variables. The file does, however, contain several variables that are not available in CROSSNAT.50.SAV. Therefore, the student and instructor are afforded the opportunity to extend, elaborate, and replicate the various analyses and demonstrations included within the body of the text itself.

A third data set, EFFICACY.21.SAV, which is used primarily in Chapter 10, has been included in the CD-ROM. This data file contains recoded variables based on survey data of twenty-one democracies of the world as of 1996. The recoded data in this file come from the International Social Science Project's "Role of Government" series (see Chapter 10 for more details). Also included on the CD-ROM is the data file ROG3, which reports the original survey data from which the data in EFFICACY.21 are derived.

Each data set comes with a complete codebook, indicating the variable's mnemonic identifier, its value, definition, and coding structure, as well as a complete list of sources from which these data were drawn. Indeed, many of these sources are on the web, and these sources' web addresses have been hyperlinked within the codebooks.

The codebooks are in four different formats for the user: Corel WordPerfect 8, Microsoft Word 97, Microsoft Rich Text Format, and PDF. The databases have been saved in five different formats: SPSS system date file (for example, CROSSNAT.50.SAV), SPSS portable file (such as CROSSNAT.50.POR), Microsoft EXCEL (CROSSNAT.50.XLS), Corel Quattro Pro 8 (CROSSNAT.50.WB3), and ascii format (CROSSNAT.50.DAT). The size of ROG3 is too large to be saved in *.XLS or *.WB3 format.

We have relied throughout the text on SPSS (Social Science Statistical Package, version 10 for the standard PC). We strive to effectively, though briefly, introduce the student to the various techniques in this package and to explain why one would use these techniques, how one would interpret their output, and what one must do to actually execute the various procedures introduced in the text. Indeed, we offer in footnotes at appropriate locations throughout the text detailed instructions as to how one may execute the steps in the demonstration within SPSS 10. While the instructor and student may prefer other statistical packages, the use of SPSS 10 nonetheless holds a number of strong and indisputable advantages to an introductory text on quantitative cross-national analysis. SPSS 10 affords the relatively less experienced student ease of access, user-friendly and clear documentation and assistance with the various programs, and the advantage of near-universal usage throughout academics and business. It is an excellent introduction to the basic techniques vital to an effective application of cross-national analysis. Nonetheless, as noted above, each of these data files has been saved in a variety of formats, which affords the student and instructor the opportunity to transport these data into different statistical software platforms, such as SAS, STATA, RATS, and LIMDEP.

Confronting Statistics and Data Analysis

There can be no escaping the fact that a major component of cross-national analysis is statistical manipulation of data. Thus, a major component of this text is an introduction to the role of the statistical technique as a vehicle to explore cross-national data in the quest for building general theory. In this sense, we adopt in our presentation of the various basic statistical principles and techniques the strategy that has been utilized by Richard Harris in his wonderfully thorough introduction to the mathematical principles of multivariate analysis. Like Harris, we try to make the distinction between *heuristic* presentations and *computational* presentations. The heuristic presentation of statistics focuses on the rationale that defines the logic of the statistic. Its primary purpose is to explain what (and why) the statistic is intended to accomplish as a tool of measurement and analysis. The computational approach, on the other hand, focuses primarily on the mechanics and steps involved in reaching an answer to a formula. The heuristic approach stresses the reasons why we use a statistic, and what it does (or does not do) for us in certain situations. The computational approach stresses the utility and application of a statistic as a tool of measurement designed to derive a solution to a problem.[1]

The data employed within the demonstrations and analyses throughout the text are cross-sectional. That is, we introduce the conceptual issues and present the statistical analysis in terms of country comparison across data at one point in time. The data in this study date from 1997, or as close to this date as possible. While time-series data offer perhaps more opportunities to directly and explicitly test causality, such models also confront instructors with the prospect of diverting attention from the fundamentals of the science and exploring in much more detail than they might like the technical aspects of sophisticated statistical and mathematical assumptions. Therefore, these more advanced time-series techniques have been avoided in order to maximize attention upon the more fundamental components and aspects of cross-national analysis. As noted above, the data file CROSSNAT.181 contained on the accompanying CD-ROM does, however, contain several variables that were recorded at several time points (for instance, 1990, 1995, 1999). From these variables, a simple cross-national time-series model may be utilized by the instructor or student to extend the cross-sectional models found in the text itself.

The sample, as noted above, consists of fifty countries. Again, this choice was made to facilitate ease of analysis and comparison for the beginning student. However, a sample of fifty is a broad sample and the conclusions we offer would not, in most instances, be affected by a significantly larger cross-national sample. A still-broader sample of 181 countries can be obtained from the file CROSSNAT.181 on the CD-ROM.

THE SCIENCE OF COMPARING NATIONS IN PERSPECTIVE

Traditionally, students of comparative politics, especially those who were interested in applying concepts to a cross-national test of data, were confronted by four individual approaches. The first may be labeled the "traditional textbook" approach. This remains the backbone of formal learning for students of comparative politics. In the context of quantified cross-national analysis, this approach is distinguished by systematic focus on concepts and a wealth of country-specific substantive information. This strategy, however, ordinarily entails only a limited and much less systematic consideration of data and samples. What data are offered are usually selected and presented merely to illustrate substance or concepts. Understandably, there is little concern for the rules of sampling or analysis in this strategy.[2]

The second approach may be labeled "philosophy of science." This strategy entails exposing the undergraduate or the beginning graduate student to the logic and rules of measurement and analysis. There is little systematic focus on concepts or on data (because philosophy of science has no immediate disciplinary boundaries that restrict its application to specific concepts or data). How we go about measuring our social world and what governs our statistical analysis of that world are the systematic focus of this approach, not the foundation concepts or relevant data of interest to students of cross-national analysis.[3]

The third approach may be labeled the "statistical cookbook." Data and tools of statistical analysis are the principal target of systematic discussion in this strategy. Too often, little attention is paid to concepts or to measurement issues, thus denying the student an appreciation for why certain tools are needed. Furthermore, the sample and data issues are frequently presented as if there is merely a rote process involved, thereby denying students exposure to critical decisions about the tools available as well as the results of the analysis, let alone the utility of the analysis to our conceptual understanding of our political world.[4]

Finally, the fourth approach may be labeled "advanced conceptual." This strategy is governed by the need to expose the undergraduate and the beginning graduate student to a more detailed and critical evaluation of the concepts originally presented in the textbooks. What data are ordinarily discussed are covered in an unsystematic fashion, designed, as in the textbook approach, to illustrate conceptual issues of more central concern to the strategy. Concepts and measurement issues are systematically covered by this strategy, with little attention necessarily given to the actual rules and strategy of statistical analysis.[5]

An introductory text to the more specialized strategy of cross-national research cannot adequately combine each of these four approaches and simultaneously match each approach in its basic mission. This text is designed, however, to integrate these four approaches and offer the undergraduate and/or the beginning graduate student a systematic exposure to the basics of each approach. It is designed, if you will, as a second course in either comparative politics or an introduction to the scope and methods of political science, with specific focus on applying basic and specific statistical tools to the cross-national analysis of data. With the four strategies combined within a single text, the student of cross-national analysis can more fully realize and, most importantly, apply the important and crucial lessons of each of these four approaches.

Our concern throughout is to expose the strategy and process of quantitative cross-national analysis to students who may otherwise assume that quantitative cross-national analysis is too challenging and intimidating. Ultimately, we hope to show why the science of comparing nations is the foundation upon which all political theory must rely. We hope also to show students that at the core of cross-national analysis lies the role of normal science. As such, comparative analysis is a strategy of ongoing discovery. The process of normal science is not a closed cul-de-sac. Rather, each new finding elicits new avenues along which lie new puzzles and within which there await new opportunities to wrestle with new and challenging ideas. Each new puzzle and idea requires a new round of measurement and additional analyses. Systematic, cross-national quantitative analysis must play a central role in our construction of general political theory. It is crucial if we are to avoid becoming prisoners of a complacency that slowly consumes our senses when we no longer wonder about that which lies beyond our vision, when we all too easily favor the familiar, and when we gradually come to prefer avoiding the aggressive pursuit of the inexplicable. To that bold end, this book is dedicated.

Robert L. Perry
John D. Robertson

NOTES

1. See Richard J. Harris, 1975, *A Primer of Multivariate Statistics* (New York: Academic Press), pp. 7–9.

2. The range of major texts within comparative politics is quite extensive. Leading texts using the traditional country approach, often in combination with a specified conceptual framework that organizes the presentation of the material, include Rolf H. W. Theen and Frank L. Wilson, 2001, *Comparative Politics: An Introduction to Seven Countries*, fourth edition (Upper Saddle River, N.J.: Prentice Hall); Michael G. Roskin, 2001, *Countries and Concepts: Politics, Geography and Culture*, seventh edition (Upper Saddle River, N.J.: Prentice Hall); Lawrence C. Mayer, et.al., 2001, *Comparative Politics: Nations and Theories in a Changing World*, third edition (Upper Saddle River, N.J.: Prentice Hall); and Mark Kesselman, Joel Krieger, and William Joseph, 2000, *Introduction to Comparative Politics: Political Challenges and Changing Agenda*, second edition (New York: Houghton Mifflin). Popular comparative politics texts that have relied on a strictly conceptual approach to an introduction to the subfield include Rod Hague, Martin Harrop, and Shaun Breslin, 1998, second edition, *Political Science: A Comparative Introduction* (New York: St. Martin's); James N. Danziger, 2001, *Understanding the Political World: a Comparative Introduction to Political Science*, fifth edition (New York: Addison Wesley, Longman, Inc.); and Jean Blondel, *Comparative Government: An Introduction*, second edition (Upper Saddle River, N.J.: Prentice Hall). Popular texts that have tried to offer a relatively balanced combination of a conceptual orientation as well as a country-specific introduction to the subfield of comparative politics include Gabriel A. Almond, G. Bingham Powell, Kaare Strom, and Russel J. Dalton, 2000, *Comparative Politics Today: A World View,* seventh edition (New York: Longman); and Gregory

S. Mahler, 2000, *Comparative Politics: An Institutional and Cross-National Approach*, third edition (Upper Saddle River, N.J.: Prentice Hall).

3. Of particular note here for students of political inquiry are Jarol B. Manheim and Richard C. Rich, 1995, *Empirical Political Analysis: Research Methods in Political Science*, fourth edition (White Plains, N.Y.: Longman Publishers); Alan S. Zuckerman, 1995, *Doing Political Science: An Introduction to Political Analysis* (Boulder: Westview Press); W. Philips Shively, 2001, *The Craft of Political Research*, fifth edition (Upper Saddle River, N.J.: Prentice Hall); and Stella Z. Theodoulou and Rory O'Brien, eds., 1999, *Methods for Political Injury: The Discipline, Philosophy, and Analysis of Politics* (Upper Saddle River, N.J.: Prentice Hall); and Louise G. White, 1999, *Political Analysis: Technique and Practice,* fourth edition (Belmont, Calif.: Wadsworth). Though it is designed as a basic introduction to a particular statistical package designed for classroom teaching and instructional use, rather than original research, an excellent introduction to the basic elements of empirical research can be found in Michael Corbett, 2001, *Research Methods in Political Science: An Introduction Using MicroCase®*, fourth edition (Belmont, Calif.: Wadsworth/Thomson Learning). For those who prefer more familiar spreadsheet software as the means of learning about and applying statistical analysis to social science data, see Gerald Keller, 2001, *Applied Statistics with Microsoft® Excel* (Pacific Grove, Calif.: Duxbury).

4. Included in this genre of particular note for students of political science are Alan Agresti and Barbara Finlay, 1997, *Statistical Methods for the Social Sciences*, third edition (Upper Saddle River, N.J.: Prentice Hall); Chava Frankfort-Nachmias and David Nachmias, 2000, *Research Methods in the Social Sciences*, sixth edition (New York: Worth Publishers); Earl Babbie, 2001, *The Practice of Social Science,* ninth edition (Belmont, Calif.: Wadsworth Publishing Company); and Jack Levin and James Alan Fox, 2001, *Elementary Statistics in Social Research*, eighth edition (Boston: Allyn and Bacon).

5. See, for instance, Lawrence Mayer, 1996, *Redefining Comparative Politics: Promise Versus Performance* (Newbury Park, Calif.: Sage Publications); B. Guy Peters, 1998, *Comparative Politics: Theory and Methods* (New York: New York University Press); Lawrence C. Mayer, 1972, *Comparative Political Inquiry* (Homewood, Ill.: The Dorsey Press); and Mark Irving Lichbach and Alan S. Zuckerman, eds., 1997, *Comparative Politics: Rationality, Culture, and Structure* (Cambridge, UK: Cambridge University Press).

Acknowledgments

We have been fortunate over the years to have had students—graduate and undergraduate—whose persistent curiosity, perceptive inquiries, and patient skepticism (not to mention, in many cases, superior intellect and aptitude) have served to both guide and enlighten us. That which is of value to those students who read this text is due primarily to the intellectual generosity and vigor of those who have gone before them in our classes and in various joint projects within which we have labored. They have been an indispensable component of a rich scholarly environment that has continually challenged and inspired. We remain forever grateful to our primary partners in scholarship, our students.

Many of our colleagues have also served to encourage us as we have proceeded through the various versions and revisions of this book. However, two have been truly steadfast and unrelenting in their patience, insight, and surprisingly, given how little we fear they have received in return, loyal friendship. Bob Harmel and Jim Dyer have articulated and explained in so many ways for so many years the bigger picture within which this text will ultimately be judged, and to which it must be welcomed if it is to be of any value to the field. They have also provided the more mundane but crucial task of clarifying and correcting some of our worst misconceptions. Whatever is lacking in this text, whatever is missing, and whatever may be wrong, is so not because our friends and colleagues have failed to warn and patiently prod us. Rather, it is so because we have not listened as carefully as perhaps we should have, and may well have allowed our stubborn pride to stand between their measured advice and our professional judgment.

We have been lucky to have had the opportunity to work with David McBride, David Pervin, Leo Wiegman, and Steve Catalano at Westview Press. Leo's encouragement and steadfast dedication to a vision, as well as his honest and professional judgment and his perceptive nature, have inspired and sustained us as we have worked our way through various drafts of this project. In no small way, we have learned much from Leo and most certainly would not have completed the project without his guidance.

Our project editor at Perseus Publishing Services, Kay Mariea, has been absolutely invaluable in carefully ensuring that our text be both accessible and comprehensible to the reader. And finally, Judith Serrin diligently labored to edit the style and presentation of our language, elevating it far beyond what we could ever hope.

We also acknowledge the invaluable role of the anonymous reviewers who so carefully and painstakingly read over the earlier drafts of this manuscript. Their insights and careful attention to detail as well as their astute knowledge of the field in general have served to strengthen our confidence, not to mention in many cases humble us as we have tried to diligently and faithfully incorporate their recommendations and suggestions into the text. We apologize in advance if we have fallen short in our efforts to build on their careful advice. In addition, we would like to express our deepest appreciation for the generous and continuing support of our respective departments and to our colleagues and staff of the Program for the Cross-National Study of Politics at Texas A&M University. At Texas A&M, Mi-Kyung Kim was an invaluable assistant in helping us compile various data and providing crucial and adept assistance in researching background literature. We would also like to thank Stanton K. Ware of the Information & Technology Exchange Center within the Texas Transportation Institute for his skillful and patient assistance in providing the world map that appears in Chapter 1.

Finally, of course, we owe a special thanks to those who have been the most supportive and devoted to us in all of our various endeavors. It is to them that we owe such a debt of immeasurable gratitude and loving appreciation for the constant source of energy and inspiration they offer, for the foundation of optimism and reassurance they provide, for all they have selflessly done for us for so long, and, most importantly, for simply, and always, being there—our wives, Sue and Irene, and our children, John, Brad, Jeff, Adam, Sean, and Aidan.

R. L. P
J. D. R.

The Elements of the Science of Comparing Nations

Terms: *Concepts, Specification, Evaluation, Analysis, Decision-Domains, Variables, Research Paradigms, Data Availability, Types of Data, Operationalization, Theory, Hypothesis Testing, Samples/Populations, Missing Data, Validity, Units of Analysis*

In 1944, a senior American foreign service officer stationed in the Moscow embassy composed a long telegram for his superiors in the State Department in Washington, D.C. The telegram outlined the officer's assessment of the domestic motivations he thought would influence Soviet policy toward Europe, the United States, and the world during the years immediately following World War II. The officer vividly described and astutely analyzed the unique historical, cultural, economic, and political forces that distinguished the Soviet Union from the United States and other democratic nations. He cautioned his superiors against the inclination to assume that merely because the Soviet Union was a formal military ally of the United States in its war with Hitler's Germany, Soviet leaders and the Soviet public would be motivated by many of the same fears, interests, and hopes as Americans.

Later, following his diplomatic assignment in Moscow, while the foreign service officer was on the faculty of the War College in Washington, D.C., the Secretary of the Navy, James Forrestal, asked the officer to expand upon his telegram. Concerned that his earlier telegram was not fully appreciated by his superiors and by those who had been privy to its contents, the officer wrote an article synthesizing many of the details he had included in the telegram, and expanded the analytic content of his thesis. The article was eventually published in one of America's premiere foreign policy journals, *Foreign Affairs,* under the pseudonym of "X" and became synonymous with America's foreign policy during the forty years of the cold war that followed. "The Sources of Soviet Conduct" became arguably the most influential and controversial comparative analysis of politics ever produced in the United States and catapulted its author, George F. Kennan, to the status of unofficial dean of Sovietologists in the United States and the Western world.[1]

What made his analysis so compelling was the scope and precision of his astute observations regarding the Soviet political system and the political behavior of Soviet policymakers. From this article, the United States fashioned a foreign policy strategy toward the Soviet Union that was labeled "containment." The article subsequently provided the rationale for the United States to form the North Atlantic Treaty Organization (NATO), the first military alliance with foreign powers in American history. It also served to shape domestic priorities in the United States by shifting vast sums of federal and state money into both military and educational expenditures in order to compete with and ultimately contain the spread of Soviet communism around the globe. American military involvement in Korea and Vietnam, the Cuban Missile Crisis of October 1962, low-level military confrontations with the Soviet Union or its allies in regional conflicts (in Berlin, the Dominican Republic, Iran, Africa, and Indonesia, to name a few), and less publicized efforts by the U.S. Central Intelligence Agency to use moneys to secretly influence elections in Australia, Italy, and Japan were all policies and actions that owe their existence in no small part to the analysis and implications of Kennan's comparative analysis of Soviet political behavior.

COMPARATIVE POLITICAL ANALYSIS: A "RISKY BUSINESS"

We leave to historians the task of deciding whether Kennan's "containment" thesis was misunderstood, or whether the American policy response was appropriate. For our purposes, this example—though exceptional in its circumstances—illustrates the potential power of analyzing political behavior and political institutions from a cross-national perspective. From Aristotle's systematic comparison of constitutions nearly twenty-five hundred years ago, through the analysis of government structure and political behavior offered by James Madison, Alexander Hamilton, and John Jay in *The Federalist,* to Alexis de Tocqueville's prescient analysis of the American political culture in the 1830s, and Kennan's compelling dissection of Soviet political behavior, students of political phenomena have labored to derive general theories of government and political behavior—theories that apply to political behavior and institutional authority regardless of the specific country or culture. It is a task fraught with error and requires discipline and care on the part of the student and the experienced scholar alike.

Despite the risks, the science of comparing nations and the cross-national study of political behavior and institutional authority is the only way in which political scientists can claim a credible theory of politics. Political science without the cross-national study of political behavior and government is analogous to the proverbial six blind men from Indostan, each describing a whole elephant according to the specific part he could feel.

Comparison is a risky business, as illustrated in the example of George Kennan's famous "X" article. His analysis relied on finely tuned powers of observation and skill of interpretation. The facts he presented to support his thesis were those he drew upon from his years of experience in the Soviet Union and his deep appreciation of Russian history. The telegram and the article were intended by Kennan to provide the informed public policy maker with clear direction in aligning American policy with American interests relative to the likely motivations and actions of the Soviet Union.

Kennan's case study of the Soviet Union, however, became a "model" from which scholars and policy makers drew many inappropriate conclusions and fashioned public policy toward other communist regimes, such as those in Eastern Europe and China. His study drew on data that were anecdotal (that is, data selected by Kennan to support his particular point) and it was taken solely from his observations of the Soviet Union and Russian history. As such, drawing inferences about Eastern Europe and China from Kennan's analysis was often careless and risky—especially if scholars or policymakers chose anecdotal data that were similar to those Kennan had used in his case study of the Soviet Union. Critical historical and circumstantial differences were missed and similarities often exaggerated. In short, his analysis was subjective, not inter-subjective.

As such, many of these subsequent cross-national studies failed to refine and sharpen our general understanding of politics, and policy for much of the 1950s and 1960s suffered from the delusion that most, if not all, communist states had the same motivations and aspirations as those derived from Kennan's case study of the Soviet Union. Gradually, political scientists came to realize that general theories of politics would require broader thinking drawn from the observation of data that were not taken solely from one unique country and/or time period.[2]

THE BUILDING BLOCKS FOR THE CROSS-NATIONAL STUDY OF POLITICS

Before beginning with the formal examination of cross-national data, it is necessary that we become familiar with various components of science as they apply to the comparative study of political behavior and institutional authority. These include concepts, variables, measurement, data, operationalization, and theory development. Together, these components precede any statistical analysis of data and provide the foundations for a general (rather than a subjective and idiosyncratic) understanding of our political world.

Concepts

To begin, you most likely have already formed a picture of the basic building blocks that comprise the analyzing of political behavior and institutional authority across several countries and cultures. These building blocks are called *concepts*. A concept is simply a mental image or label we have of some phenomena. We really cannot begin to understand something, or have any rational discourse about it, without these labels. While this may seem abstract, it is actually quite basic. Consider, for example, the task of purchasing a personal computer.

If you knew nothing about computers yet were contemplating buying one, you would seek out someone who did know something, or you would read some publication that would inform you of the important information you needed to know in order to most effectively spend your money. The first two concepts you would have to know would be "hardware" and "software." Hardware consists of those things such as keyboards, monitors, processor chips, motherboards, printers, and modems. Software refers to specific objects such as the word-processing code that allows you to write your term papers (for example, MS Word or WordPerfect), the statistical package that contains the code that computes complicated formulas in a problem-solving task (such as Lotus 1–2–3), and possibly the personal information manager you may want to have in order to schedule your appointments. Knowing that hardware is separate from software allows you to better organize your decisions and thereby reduce the time it takes to sort out individual pieces of information relevant to the demands of purchasing a computer and assembling the components necessary for it to do what you want. Concepts organize and simplify our world and allow us to formulate an idea of how certain objects or actions are related to one another.

For scientists, concepts work the same way, providing intellectual building blocks and allowing scientists to connect these building blocks to form a clear, yet often intricate, picture of the political world. With a conceptual picture of the political world in place, the political scientist is prepared to determine whether his or her expectations about the way political concepts should work in relation to each other are, in fact, accurate. This, then, is the essence of science: to test whether our ideas concerning the relationship of concepts are true.

In this text, we explore several basic concepts central to the cross-national study of political behavior and institutional authority. Among them are: political authority, political culture, modernity, political economy, economic and social development, and income inequality.

Variables and Units of Analysis

If hardware and software are concepts, the specific components of hardware (keyboard, modem, monitor) and particular packages of code (word processing, spreadsheets, statistical packages) are *variables*. What are variables? They are the specific representations of the broader concept and they are assumed to vary in their empirical representation across a sample of observations. Thus, an example of a concept may be political participation, and its variable representation may be the proportion of eligible voters who vote in a national election. While the concept does not vary across countries (the concept should have equivalent application and relevance to any country in the sample), the measurable representation of the concept—the properties of the concept itself—will vary from country to country. Some countries will have more political participation than others; yet, the concept is present (to some degree) in all the countries in the sample. Variables manifest themselves within specific *units of analysis.* These are the things or objects that we are observing in order to build our body of knowledge. For the student buying the computer, her unit of observation is the computer itself. Because she will look at several computers in her quest for the right one, she will soon discover that the way the concept of hardware is manifested, for instance, will indeed differ from computer to computer. Some computers will have sixty-four megabytes of random access memory (RAM), others only sixteen. In this case, RAM becomes a variable manifestation of the concept of hardware, and it is distinguished by a unique *attribute*, in this case, the number of megabytes. Attributes are the observed features or qualities of a variable. It is important to keep in mind that for a variable to be such, it must have *variation* in its attributes. Generally, if you can answer the question, "What is the unit of analysis's _______?" and the question makes sense, then you most likely have a variable. For instance, in reference to the variable RAM, the question "What is the computer's sixty-four megs of RAM?" makes little sense. However, the question "What is the computer's amount of RAM?" makes much more sense, and is illustrative of a variable.

In sum, the science of comparing nations entails careful specification and operationalization of variables. Cross-national analysis is therefore the systematic, quantitative exploration of variables drawn from a sample of data extracted from a diverse sample of countries and cultures for the purpose of testing and refining our assumptions of political behavior and institutional authority in order to better generalize our understanding of the political world.

This presents a major challenge to students of cross-national analysis—challenges that are generally different from and more challenging than those confronting students of American politics or students of specific countries. First of all, in cross-national analysis, the unit of analysis is usually—though by no means always—the country, for example, Germany, Russia, the United States. Herein lies one difficulty, because the student is immediately confronted with the challenge of finding a way to measure the attributes of variables across so many different units of analysis. It is difficult enough when, for instance, the student of American government requires data for all fifty states. Imagine the challenge to the researcher looking for data on fifty different nation-states. This underscores the importance of data availability, the first major challenge to those engaged in the science of comparing nations. This challenge, however, may be less daunting than the second major challenge to the student who wishes to apply the rules of science to the comparative study of nations. This second challenge requires the comparativist to balance the need to achieve measurement validity against the conflicting need to produce general findings for the process of theory building.

Measurement Validity

Perhaps the most challenging problem of quantitative cross-national research is *measurement validity*, which refers to the extent to which a variable can measure what it purports to measure. A simple example will illustrate the challenge of measurement validity in cross-national analysis of political data. Consider for a moment three simple concepts that are familiar to everyone: gender, race, and social class. These three concepts are manifested in certain ways: male and female for gender; black, Hispanic, Asian, and white for race; and lower and upper for social class. But what about the attributes? There are, obviously, some readily identifiable attributes that distinguish a female from a male, so little controversy is associated with measures of this concept.

The same generally holds for race, but it can be more difficult at times, especially when considering mixed races. For instance, it is common to separate race and ethnicity as different attributes. But are they? The problem is greatly compounded with social class. It is common to examine the attribute of income as a manifestation of the concept of social class. However, one's income may have little to do with the overall wealth of a person (especially in different countries or cultures), and thus income may be an inaccurate attribute of the concept of social class—at least in certain countries. Furthermore, one's wealth may still not be enough. In some countries, or to some scholars, educational level is another important attribute of social class; to others, the prestige and status of one's occupation is equally important to the concept of social class. Social class, in other words, may be best measured as a "multidimensional" concept, meaning that more than one dimension (reflected by more than one variable) is required to fully represent the concept accurately.

So, while we may all be familiar with the term "social class," and while we may further all agree that the concept "varies" across countries somewhere between low and high, we may not agree as to how we know what in fact is upper social class and what constitutes lower social class. We may assume that based on education, one country has a higher proportion of its adult population in a lower social class than another country, when in fact, social class may not have anything to do in either country with education. In both countries, the term social class may refer to wealth and nothing more. When you try to assign specific attributes to particular variables across several different countries, the risk that you might in fact be using inappropriate attributes for a given variable, as well as inappropriate variables for concepts, is greatly increased. This falls under the label of "concept stretching." This problem confronts students of American government as well when they consider different states within the union. However, the vast range of possible errors caused by data validity are not as great as that confronting the student of cross-national analysis. We will consider this problem in more detail in Chapter 6.

Earl Babbie suggests four types of measurement and data validity. *Face validity* implies that data conform to our commonly accepted mental images of the world.[3] In cross-national research, face validity is frequently relied upon to validate measures. For example, if our measure of democracy identifies Iraq as a democracy, the measure would most certainly be discredited as a valid measure.

When one measure predicts the values of another measure, we may assert that the predictive measure has *criterion validity*. For example, we might want to determine whether citizens living in more-democratic countries tend to be more satisfied with their governments than do those living in less-democratic countries. We would then develop two measures, one for level of democracy and the other for satisfaction with government. If we then found that the two measures were highly correlated, that level of democracy seemed to predict satisfaction with government, we would say that our measure for level of democracy had criterion validity.

Statistical analysis alone, however, cannot serve as a sufficient test for the validity of a measure. Statistical correlation between measures can occur even if our measures are invalid. One can generate a sample of random scores and frequently observe a strong statistical correlation. Furthermore, when our hypotheses (formally stated predictions) fail to materialize as we anticipated, we need not automatically discard the measures as lacking in sufficient criterion validity. Rather, it merely directs attention to this issue as part of the checklist of considerations the researcher surveys when assessing the results of a statistical analysis. Criterion validity is one of four types of validity assessments we use to evaluate our measures. It should not be the sole basis to validate or invalidate measures.

Measures are often evaluated in terms of their *construct validity*, which refers to the internal logic of a concept. In our example of social class, we assume that education should be related to the phenomenon of class. If we were to correlate the level of education attained by a group of people with the final measure we have devised for social class, and the correlation was very high, this would constitute evidence of the logical consistency of the measure of social class. We would conclude in this case that the construct validity of our measure of social class is credible.

Note that construct validity differs from criterion validity. The latter correlates the measure in question with another variable that is not considered part of the internal construction of the measure we are evaluating. For instance, suppose we rely upon social class to predict voting behavior of individuals. Voting behavior is believed to be associated with social class, but not part of the internal logic by which we construct the measure of social class. Construct validity, however, refers to correlations among variables that are both believed to represent internal attributes or properties of the principal concept. In Chapters 6–13, we will explore measures of democracy. In Chapter 13, we will devise a final, multidimensional index measure of democracy. We will utilize a particular technique—factor analysis—to verify the construct validity of the final measure. In subsequent chapters we will use the measure of democracy to test hypotheses. These tests will allow an assessment of the measure's criterion validity. The construct validity of social class would be verified if we could show education, income, and occupation—the internal components by which we construct the measure of social class—were all correlated in the expected direction with each other.

Finally, Babbie notes the importance of *content validity*. Content validity assumes your measure has subsumed the entire range of different meanings associated with a particular concept. If, for instance, we relied solely upon education as a measure of social class, by the standard of content validity our measure would be insufficient. By ignoring occupation and income, our measure of social class would be severely deficient in its coverage of the common meanings of social class.

Throughout this text, we will attempt to demonstrate to the student the importance and utility of using basic tools of statistical analysis, in conjunction with measurement and theory, to devise measures of political behavior and institutional authority that promise greater degrees of content validity. Indeed, in Chapter 6, we will consider the special problem of concept stretching in cross-national research. Concept stretching is generally introduced (unintentionally) into cross-national research when we attempt to extend the content validity of measures. It often arises because the student of cross-national analysis must balance precision in measurement with validity of measures. Unfortunately, this often means relying upon primary properties of our concepts that have limited construct or face validity within the sample. The ideal situation, of course, would be the luxury of sufficient amounts of valid quantitative data available to test the hypotheses across a cross-national sample. In such circumstance, we would have little difficulty in aligning conceptual clarity and measurement validity. In fact, with sufficient quantitative data more realistically limited to the student of cross-national analysis, we often settle for measures that fall short of the highest standards of validity. Thus, as Mayer laments, "The optimum solution for comparative political inquiry may entail [variables] that are imperfectly valid and theory that is less than universal in scope."[4]

Finally, when this text refers to measurement validity, it is understood to mean validity in its broadest sense—a combination of face, criterion, construct, and content validity–unless otherwise specified. Measurement validity will be more thoroughly explored within the context of cross-national research in Chapter 6.

Data

Within this text, all the variables you will need in your introduction to the cross-national analysis of political data are provided for you and formatted for use with statistical packages such as SPSS (Statistical Package for the Social Sciences). These are certainly not the only variables you could use. Indeed, each research project will dictate a new set of variables, given the research question and theory at hand. However, the variables contained in CROSSNAT.50 and EFFICACY.21 (the two basic databases used within this text) serve the purposes of introducing the student to the basic foundations of quantitative cross-national analysis. For additional variables and years, see CROSSNAT.181 on CD-ROM.

The basic data used in this text summarize attributes of a country. We call these type of data *ecological data*. In cross-national analysis, ecological data represent a country as the unit of observation within quantitative analysis. In addition, in Chapter 10 we will introduce you to the application of *survey data* within cross-national research. These data differ from ecological data in that survey data measure the attitudes and values of individuals within countries.

Data availability is not a problem within this text. Data availability problems are, as we have noted, never fully resolved. This is something all students of cross-national analysis must live with and come to appreciate. It is, in effect, a humbling experience to be a student of cross-national analysis—often the analytical imagination is well beyond our physical capacity to obtain valid data to measure the attributes we need in our quest for a general theory of politics. Nonetheless, as we shall see, if we understand this, and remain cautious in our analysis, data availability does not preclude the process of building a general body of knowledge about political behavior and institutional authority from cross-national analysis. It just makes it more difficult—and challenging.

Reliability

To minimize these obstacles to cross-national research, we must try to make sure that those who read and rely upon our findings know exactly how we measured the variables we are analyzing. A measure is reliable to the extent that it produces the same results under the same circumstances, no matter who is doing the measuring. You may recall that in 1989 researchers in Utah and Texas reported that they had achieved cold fusion (the generation of excess heat at low temperatures) in laboratory tests. Subsequent researchers, following the same measures and procedures, were unable to replicate these tests, hence, the original test results were considered unreliable. To the extent that any measure is unreliable, it is not valid.

A similar problem can occur in cross-national research. The measures that we develop must have properties that can be understood and quantified (for example, weight, height, color, age, length, name), and we must be able to isolate these properties in such a way as to monitor them and record any relevant changes.

Operational Definitions

One of the first steps in developing a measure (and in strengthening its reliability) is to define it. The particular definition that we provide is referred to as an *operational definition*: It allows us to measure a variable's attribute in such a way as to be clearly understood by others and to distinguish it *empirically* (that is, through measurement) from other variables.

We saw that one way of measuring the variable of memory in a computer is megabytes of random access memory included in the computer hardware. The operational definition here is megabytes of RAM (random access memory). In the example of social class, if we decide that class manifests itself in the wealth of a certain segment of the population, then we might operationally define wealth as the total dollar value of all forms of income received by a typical household in a country for a given year. This might be reported in a standard statistical yearbook. The yearbook should report this wealth for different groups of the population so that we can distinguish upper social class groups from lower social class groups. In this way we have, in effect, operationally defined social class. We still may disagree as to how much wealth constitutes upper social class and how much constitutes lower social class, but we have at least agreed upon how we intend to measure the concept of social class. Careful and clear operational definitions of our attributes also offer clues to others as to *what* and *how* to measure the concept of social class.

We shall see in later chapters, for instance, that the researcher may sometimes modify her operationalizations when sharp limitations in data demand such decisions. For instance, in Chapters 11 and 12, we will explore the relationship between gender empowerment and the competitiveness of political participation within countries. We define competitive political participation as the degree to which citizens within a country may wield their influence over public officials and thereby constrain the choice and options of elites with respect to public policy and authority. It is operationally defined (and measured) along a five-point scale ranging from a value of one (indicating a country with suppressed political competition) to a value of five (indicating a country with competitive and stable participation). Because of the limited number of countries within the various categories of the variable representing competitive political participation, we eventually decide to collapse, or in effect combine, two of the separate categories in the operationalized version of the variable. This has the effect of modifying the original operational rule governing the empirical representation of the concept. However, we do not modify the meaning of the concept itself. We merely change the metric of its representation. Of course, at some point, changes in the operationalization of a concept will stretch the meaning of the concept beyond any reasonable threshold. If such modifications are applied judiciously and with caution, stretching as a result of necessary adjustments to operational rules may be avoided.

Concepts, Variables, and Operational Definitions in Context

Conceptualizing information is as essential to shopping for a computer as it is in trying to understand how political behavior and institutions affect power and authority in the world around us. Once we have organized information around mental images and organizing principles—concepts—we are in a position to begin to build knowledge systematically—whether that knowledge pertains to the purchase of a computer or the political behavior of a society. No matter what computer store you chose to explore in your quest for a new computer, the concepts of hardware and software provide a common language that guides you through the maze of complex and complicated data. These data are the attributes that reflect these concepts. While these attributes may vary from computer to computer, if we operationally define the key variables that interest us, we can more efficiently determine what hardware or software to buy given our particular needs and wants—regardless of the particular computer brand name. We have, in other words, a general theory that guides our decision to purchase one computer rather than another.

So too with cross-national analysis. If we have a set of concepts, with corresponding variables that represent these concepts according to particular attributes, and if we can carefully observe, measure, and operationally define these attributes, we can more efficiently draw conclusions about the general (as opposed to particular) nature of political behavior and institutions of public power and authority.[5]

THEORY BUILDING AND CROSS-NATIONAL POLITICAL ANALYSIS

Our student of computers is now in a position to formulate a simple theory of computers. A theory constitutes a set of related concepts that together explain a part of our real world. While they may only be simplified mental constructs of the real world, theories are, nevertheless, powerful because they offer the student a way to reliably generalize about common phenomena or objects—such as computers.

Before actually purchasing the computer, the student has come to some preliminary conclusions, or propositions, about computers. First, she knows that her principal objective is obtaining a computer that will maximize her leisure for her social activity. Second, she knows that most of her needs are word processing—writing—all those term papers and book reviews. Third, she knows that the most efficient software for her needs requires a minimum of 128 megabytes of random access memory to work on a computer. Therefore, she concludes, she must find a computer that links the concept of hardware (random access memory) to software (for example, WordPerfect) in such a way as to maximize her leisure time. She has performed something quite basic, yet quite sophisticated. She has carefully specified, or connected, the relationships between several distinct concepts and in doing so, formed a theory of computers. Her reasoning is based on her previous personal experience when using a computer under different circumstances, or from her formal research, which has shown her the results of the tests linking RAM to computer efficiency, for instance.

The student of cross-national analysis builds theories of politics in a similar fashion. For instance, a political scientist interested in understanding why some countries exhibit less political violence than others may reason, first, that wealth is critical to satisfying the needs of people and that wealth is related to people's freedoms to own and use property as they wish. She might then conclude that in those countries where there has been a tradition of land concentration in the hands of the state, and not individuals, wealth declines, and that violent political acts are more likely in these types of countries.

This process of connecting concepts and their manifested attributes together in a logical structure is called *syllogistic reasoning*. Each of the components of a syllogistic argument is composed of propositions. *Propositions* are simply statements, usually made in declarative form, that are either true or false. For example, we could paraphrase Kennan's arguments concerning the Soviet Union with the following propositions:

A. The United States needs to protect its national life from external intrusions.
B. The Soviet Union inherently seeks to expand its influence.
C. The United States can protect its national interests by containment of the Soviet Union.

Connecting concepts and attributes ("national interests," "intrusions," "expand," "influence," and "containment") together in such a chain of logically connected propositions is the process of theory building. Keep in mind that propositions, as stated above, are either true or false. They require, therefore, that the student of cross-national analysis actually test and thereby validate these propositions by measuring operationally defined attributes across samples of units (for example, countries) to test the validity of his or her logical reasoning. In this case, the real world is represented by the actual data we collect to test our propositions. Scientists call these propositions *hypotheses*, and the process of validating logical reasoning, *hypothesis testing*.

This process never really stops—all logical constructs can be better refined and modified to bring our logical constructs closer to the real world of politics. *Through this ongoing process of hypothesis testing knowledge is built*. As old logical constructs are replaced with newer, modified ones, our knowledge base grows and broadens. And from this simple task of hypothesis testing through cross-national analysis of data, we are in a position to apply our findings to the practical world of politics.

From Kennan's logical reasoning and implied propositions about the relationship between communist regimes and power, democratic nations fashioned security policies. Arguably, there is nothing more practical to the daily lives of citizens everywhere than the process of cross-national political analysis, especially when that analysis presents such important policy implications.[6]

Research Paradigms

How do we choose the questions that guide cross-national analysis? How do we know which concepts to use, and therefore which variables to measure and theories to test? How is this elaborate process validated? After all, any number of concepts, variables, or theories may be relevant to our political world. The meaning and relevance of the concepts, variables, and theories that we use emerge only when we have a framework of reference within which to place these mental constructs. Our frame of reference in any field of scientific analysis is called the *research paradigm*. It is so basic that it is rarely discussed by professionals in their day-to-day research activities. Yet, it is essential to an appreciation of all that is done within the operational and analytical tasks of data analysis.

For students of cross-national analysis, the research paradigm is the comprehensive picture we hold in our mind's eye of how the individual elements of the political world come together to form one cumulative, extended, and integrated whole. It is, to use a German phrase, a *Gestalt*, or a broadly integrated configuration of connected units or parts whose relevance are strictly dependent upon their relation to each other. The research paradigm provides the framework for the questions comparativists ask. It provides the list of concepts that most scholars select for their analysis and therefore structures, however indirectly, the variables we measure. Ultimately it affords final validation of the theories we test. It is the research paradigm, in essence, that provides the meaning and importance of information for the political scientist. A quantitative analysis without the guidance of a research paradigm is equivalent to a collection of musicians without a symphonic score to coordinate their music; it is a cacophony of different sounds without harmony; it is a Supreme Court with no constitutional heritage.

Alas, paradigms present a real test of patience for the beginning student of cross-national political analysis because there is no dominant paradigm in political science, and therefore, no dominant paradigm in comparative political studies. The reasons for this need not concern us here. It is enough to know that the field of political science has several competing paradigms. There are Marxist paradigms, economic paradigms, rational choice paradigms, systems paradigms, and so on.[7]

Arguably, one of the traditionally dominant paradigms within comparative politics is the *structural-functional paradigm*. Proponents of this paradigm, as refined and elaborated by its two leading students, Gabriel A. Almond and G. Bingham Powell Jr., view the political world as consisting of specific functions performed within a system of regularly interacting parts.[8] These parts (for instance, political parties, executives, legislatures, families, schools, different levels of government) each contribute to the performance of specific tasks critical to the legitimate authority of government and its role in making policy and regulating behavior within a country. This interactive process, built around specific functions carried out by the various actors of the political system, provides an overarching structure to our political world.

The structural nature of the political world implies specific boundaries between different types of functional processes. For instance, the U.S. Congress performs specific functions, but is surrounded by an economic, cultural, and political environment domestically, as well as an international environment. Each influences how Congress performs its functions, and, importantly, how the policies, or outputs of congressional functions, will be received by the various domestic and international environments within which Congress operates. Regardless of the country in question, a structural-functional paradigm can identify the functions that must be performed within the context of the political system to ensure some semblance of legitimate governmental authority in the country. What differs is how important certain functions are within different cultures, what parts carry out certain functions, and the variety of parts allowed to contribute to the outputs of the political system.

Samples and Populations

Inference is the basic rationale for using statistical tools to analyze cross-national political data. Students of cross-national data analysis (that is, the testing of operationally defined hypotheses with data drawn from several different countries) want to infer from a sample of cross-national data they have collected across several different cultural settings to a population. What is a population? In a sense, a population is an abstraction. We envision a population, but ordinarily we can only imagine what it is; *we never really capture a population in our statistical analyses.*

In this text, we do not have a sample of all countries of the world, per se. Rather, we have a sample of a *target* population of countries—a population that in most regards is both practically and substantively more appropriate for the purposes of an introduction to quantitative cross-national analysis.

A sample is, simply, a subset of a population. In cross-national analysis, there are conceivably many populations from which we may sample. For instance, we may want to select a subset of countries from a population of *wealthy democracies*. Or, we may want to select a set of countries from a population of *African nations.* We may want to select a population of countries that begin with the letter *E*, or we may want to select a subset of a population of countries defined by particular latitudinal and longitudinal coordinates.[9]

What determines our choice? First and foremost, our particular theory and research paradigm directs our choice of sample. And a cross-national sample is driven by theory that seeks to generalize our understanding of the political world.

Very important to students of cross-national analysis is the matter of maximizing data validity, reliability, and availability. This "practical" consideration is a very real issue in cross-national analysis. If one wants to study the world's population of countries, one is likely to immediately run into some very severe obstacles. As we have noted above, one of the primary obstacles to the student of cross-national politics is data availability—many countries do not have the means to publish such things as basic demographic data. Before long, the student will also notice there may be some very inexplicable measures of attributes that appear for some countries. Thus, the problem of data availability is often compounded by the problems of reliability and validity. Because the student cannot use the entire population of countries, he or she must choose from a sample of countries. For many reasons, a random sample of the world's population of countries is usually not practical or even useful when exploring general questions of cross-national analysis. It is also unnecessary. What one wishes to maximize in any empirical endeavor involving inference is a sample that reflects the "typical" member of a *target population*. In our situation, that means finding a sample that reflects the typical country in the target population we are interested in exploring.

What is the target population from which the principal sample in this text has been drawn? In this text, the principal database used for cross-national analysis is CROSSNAT.50, consisting of *ecological* data. This database is composed of fifty countries selected according to: (1) the country's population as of 1997, (2) the availability of data for each country, and (3) the country's geopolitical/regional location. *The countries in CROSSNAT.50 are the fifty most populous countries as of 1997 for which we have complete data on all variables utilized within this text, and which allow us to reasonably approximate the distribution of countries according to geopolitical and regional locations.* Thus, three factors governed the selection of countries within our sample: (1) country population (as of 1997), (2) data availability (we want to avoid missing data), and (3) geopolitical/regional distribution.

Population. Why did we chose the attribute of population to select countries? Because of the basic questions we wish to explore throughout this text. Politics is ultimately a social phenomena: people interacting with each other through authoritative governmental institutions to shape the course and direction of a country and its people. Therefore, to analyze effectively the general political phenomena that are most commonly associated with political behavior and institutional authority across countries and cultures, we concentrate on that structural attribute of a country that best defines a country's relevance to universal political phenomena.

Data Availability. To ensure a sample large enough to accommodate adequate statistical analysis and inference, and yet remain selective enough to avoid the problems of data reliability, availability, and validity, we first considered the fifty *most populated countries* of the world as of 1997 for which we have complete data. In 1997, the World Bank included within its basic database 202 sovereign, independent countries, protectorates, and territories. Unfortunately, for many of the largest countries of the world the most important variables we will work with in this text are simply not available. For a variety of reasons, reliable and valid estimates of many of the most important political, economic, and social aspects of these countries are not at our disposal. Missing data is a common problem in social science, especially cross-national empirical analysis. It presents particular statistical problems and challenges that we wish to avoid for the moment in this introduction to quantitative cross-national analysis. More importantly, missing data need not, as in the past, severely restrict the ability of the researcher to utilize a sample that allows effective reflection of power distribution across the globe. Therefore, eight of the fifty most populous countries of the world (as of 1997) were excluded from the sample because of missing data. Of the next twenty-eight most populous countries of the world, seventeen more were excluded because of missing data. In addition, three more countries were excluded because of geopolitical/regional distribution issues. Thus, the smallest country in our sample, Tunisia, is actually the seventy-eighth most populous country of the 202 surveyed from the World Bank database as of 1997.[10]

Geopolitical/Regional Distribution. Of particular importance to any cross-national sample is the distribution of countries included in a sample according to the geopolitical and regional placements of the country. Researchers have a number of options at their disposal with respect to how they may wish to group and subgroup their countries according to the geographical region of the world within which a country lies; however, with a sample of fifty countries, we have limited our classification to broad regions. There are in effect four specific geographical regions to which countries have been assigned: *Asia* (including East Asia, South Asia, and North Asia); *Latin America* (including Central and South America); *Sub-Saharan Africa*; and the *Middle East/North Africa*, or Arab countries. This latter group is transcontinental in nature: it contains countries technically in Asia (such as Iran) and Africa. Furthermore, we have distinguished as a separate and distinct group those countries of the former Soviet Union or members of the Soviet Union's political empire as members of the CIS-EE (Commonwealth of Independent States and Eastern Europe), and those countries that are the most industrially advanced and established democracies of the world (designated as Industrial and Other West European Established Democracies). This latter group is also transcontinental. It includes Japan, Australia, Canada, and the United States, representing three different continents. This division of our sample into four distinct geographical (Asia, Sub-Saharan Africa, Latin America, and Arab/Middle East–North Africa) regions and three distinct geopolitical regions (Arab nations, CIS-EE nations, and Western Industrial and 0ther West European Established Democracies) reflects conventional geopolitical and regional demarcations for countries across the globe. As we will see in Chapter 2, such distinctions are essential in order to account for critical cultural and historical features of countries that influence their political and economic systems and must be taken into account when conducting cross-national research.

Taking geopolitical-political/regional location of a country into account requires us to ensure that we do not overrepresent our sample by having too many countries within one or more geopolitical-political groups. This would distort conclusions of the analysis, weighting results in a way that reflects not a "global" picture, but a "regional" or "geopolitical-political" picture. The table compares our distribution of countries in CROSSNAT.50 with that of the of the 181 sovereign nation-states in the World Bank's database for 1997 (excluding territories and protectorates), by geopolitical-political/regional classification.

From the table, it is clear that on the whole, there is close approximation within CROSSNAT.50 to the actual distribution of countries in the world, according to the conventional geopolitical-political/regional grouping of countries. However, there is some deviance, which is to be expected. Poverty and political turbulence in Africa

TABLE 1.1 Comparing Distributions by Geopolitical/Regional Classification

	Percent of Countries Included in Respective Samples	
Geopolitical Regional Classification	*World, based on World Bank database (N = 181)*	*CROSSNAT.50, based on systematic sample of populous countries of the world (N = 50)*
CIS-EE	14.4%	10.0%
Asia	15.5%	22.0%
Sub-Saharan Africa	24.9%	18.0%
Industrial–West European	16.6%	24.0%
Latin America	18.8%	16.0%
Arab/Middle East–North African	10.0%	9.9%

Chi-sq. = 4.859; ñ = .433

make it difficult to include countries in a cross-national sample when minimizing missing data is a criteria for including a country in a sample. Thus, CROSSNAT.50 underrepresents Sub-Saharan African countries by nearly 7 percent. Similar circumstances account for the slight underrepresentation of CIS-EE countries (4.4 percent). Vibrant economic growth, large populations, and stable political economies account for the overrepresentation of Asia (6.5 percent) and industrial–West European countries (7.4 percent). However, these deviations are not large enough to severely undermine our efforts to achieve a data-rich and representative cross-national sample.[11]

CROSSNAT.50 is, in effect, a particular kind of random sample. It is a systematic sample. Technically, as we will see later, a random sample assumes that within a population, each member of the population has an equal probability of being selected according to some rule. A systematic sample simply means that the selection process has a system to it—that is, it is not truly random in the strict sense of the word. Our system for selection is the population size of the country. Each country within a distribution range of country-population (the fifty most populous countries) has been systematically selected for inclusion in our sample. This, of course, has been further qualified by data availability and geopolitical/regional location.

In fact, CROSSNAT.50 is quite close to being a target population, and not a sample. Why? Because there were only about 150–190 countries existing at any time during the period between the late 1980s and early 1990s. A few come, and a few go, but the population of the *most populous* is very stable—though there have been, of course, some additions and subtractions with changing world events. The student of cross-national political analysis is always working within a much more restricted population than is a survey researcher. The latter has hundreds, thousands, or millions of people to sample from. The comparativist who specializes in comparing nations at the aggregate level has a much smaller group. Thus, when working with questions at a broad level, as we are throughout most of this text, the idea of a true sample is actually closer to a target population than would be the case in most other scientific settings. Nonetheless, our inferences and conclusions offered throughout this text are directed at a global sample—the world, so to speak. Because our geopolitical/regional distribution is reasonably reflective of the "world," and because the key political issues confronting the most populous nations of the globe for the most are the very issues confronting those of smaller populations (though of course, not entirely), we may reasonably assume our findings reflect the basic trends common to the population of countries in the world.

Statistics

What, then, are statistics? *Statistics are measures of attributes within a sample*. When we examine the sample, we do so with an eye to inferring to the population of all political systems, not just to those in our particular sample. We are, therefore, less interested in *describing* the attributes in the sample than in using the sample as a means to understanding the population. Furthermore, we are more interested in confirming our assumptions regarding the relationship between concepts in our political environment. To this end, we are also less interested in describing "current events" than understanding the fundamental nature of political behavior and institutional authority that characterize the global landscape.

Throughout this text, we will consider some of the special statistical measures common to cross-national analysis that help us determine how confident we may be in inferring from the statistics reflecting the sample to the population as a whole. For now, it is important to note the critical mission of cross-national analysis is to discern patterns and relationships among variables in a diverse sample in order to describe, but more importantly, to *explain* the patterns and relationships in the target population—a population we cannot actually measure and therefore must speak of in somewhat abstract terms. Statistics provide the confidence we need when inferring from our sample to a more abstract population; they legitimize and at least help to validate the very process of building general knowledge about the political world. But, statistics are no better than the building blocks and samples of data that precede the actual statistical analysis.

The Three Domains of Decisionmaking Within the Science of Comparing Nations

In a broader sense, the role of statistics is one of the three critical domains of decisionmaking within the enterprise of the science of comparing nations. This enterprise, as we have shown in this chapter, entails critical choices to be made by the student of comparative politics. These decisions fall into three separate domains, each with its own formal and informal rules, yet each related to the other two domains within the enterprise of comparing nations. These decisionmaking domains are (1) the epistemological, (2) the statistical, and (3) the conceptual. Epistemology is a field of philosophy that explores how we come to know what we think to be the truth, and the reasons we have come to know what we think we know. Epistemological decisions within the science of comparing nations require the student to select the particular comparative research strategy that best serves the intent of her research goal (we shall discuss the main strategies of comparative research in more detail in the next chapter) and from there to proceed with matters of conceptualization, operationalization, specification, and measurement. From these epistemological decisions one may ascertain the reasons *why we compare* phenomena across different cultures and nations, for the choices made at this stage by the student of comparative politics reveal the researcher's priorities and values with respect to theory building and expose the puzzles that the researcher believes to be essential in the quest for general theory.

Statistical decisions require the comparativist to select the appropriate tools by which to conduct the process of analysis and evaluation. She must either collect or select a sample, as well as decide upon the sources of data from which we ascertain the empirical values of key properties within the units included in the sample. The level at which these data are measured, the rules that govern the selection and collection of the sample, the sample size itself, as well as the judgment of the researcher pertaining to the reliability and equivalency of the data across different national and cultural settings are all critical factors in constraining the choices of the statistical techniques to employ in the analysis phase of the cross-national research enterprise. In addition, these decisions color the final evaluations of the findings which the statistics produce. From these statistical decisions made by the student and researcher, one may discern *how we compare* phenomena across different cultures and nations.

Finally, conceptual decisions require the comparativist to decide which concepts are in fact central to the research question at hand, how these concepts are best employed within the conceptualization phase of the cross-national research process, and how they might be refined and modified based upon the analysis and evaluation phase of the research process. These decisions require some knowledge of the substantive issues common to the field of comparative politics, as well as a familiarity with the literature in the broader field of political science (and related social science disciplines). From the decisions that have been made with regard to the concepts of comparative politics within the enterprise of the science of comparing nations, we learn *what to compare* across different cultures and nations. That is, from the decisions about which concepts to explore and which to consider in more detail as the research process continues, we know what segments of the broader political world are of greater interest and challenge to the comparativists who apply cross-national analysis. Figure 1.1 depicts the triangular structure that shapes the critical decisions within the enterprise of the science of comparing nations.

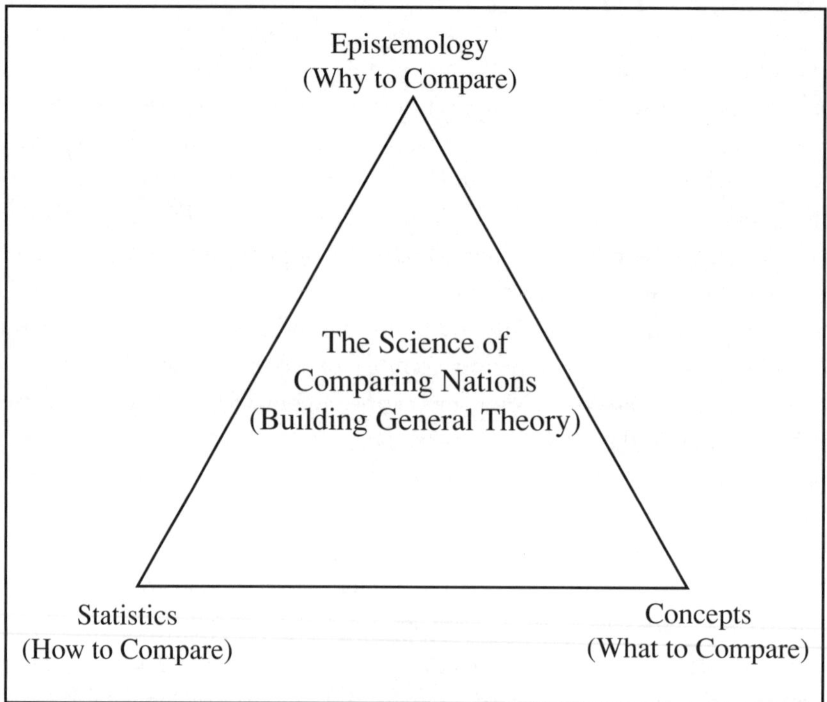

FIGURE 1.1 The Foundations of Cross-National Analysis

AN INTRODUCTION TO THE CROSSNAT.50 DATASET

As we indicated, the principal database used in this text is CROSSNAT.50. To reiterate one of the more important points raised throughout this chapter, it is very important to keep in mind that whenever students engage in cross-national data analysis they will very likely encounter problems with their data. That is, the data vary across countries in terms of the accuracy of the variable being measured, the exact year within which the data were actually collected by the countries, and, as we have noted, the availability of certain data. As mentioned previously, this is particularly troublesome when we rely on data from countries that are not very wealthy—collection of statistics is often spotty because this is not necessarily a high priority for their governments. Yet, it is often the case that even wealthy countries are reluctant to report some of the most basic and seemingly "innocent" data, such as employment figures, national economic growth figures, and trade figures. The CROSSNAT.50 database covers basic attributes of countries between 1992 and 1997. By the turn of the century, the most common year for which data for all fifty countries in the CROSSNAT.50 database is available is 1997; for some measures, it is earlier.

Table 1.2 lists the countries within the CROSSNAT.50 database alphabetically. It also lists four critical variables: the *code* for each country (an abbreviated form of the country's name that will be of important use later in the text), the *population* (in millions of people) of the country, the *area* (in square kilometers) of the country, and the *economic wealth* of the country (the gross domestic product, GDP, of a country, measured in billions of U.S. dollars, as of 1997). Note that these are in fact concepts and variables, along with their operational definitions. The concepts are *area, population*, and *economic wealth*. The respective variables are total land area, population, and gross domestic product. The corresponding operational definitions are (a) millions of people as of 1997, (b) thousands of square kilometers, and (c) total value of all goods and services produced in a country as represented in U.S. dollars, as of 1997.[12] Most of the data in CROSSNAT.50 are drawn from the World Bank's *World Development Report*.[13] In addition, the ordinal rank of each country (from one to fifty) for each of the three variables is indicated in Table 1.2. The most recent report from which data have been drawn is the 1999/2000 study, although earlier editions have also been the source of some of the data found in CROSSNAT.50. Another key source of data is the United Nations *Human Development Report*. This annual publication has been produced since 1990. The CROSSNAT.50 database draws most heavily from the 1999 *Report*.[14] While the fifty countries in CROSSNAT.50 constitute approximately 28 percent of the sovereign countries in the world as of 1997, they collectively represent the lion's share of political influence around the globe. For instance, these fifty countries comprise 81.6 percent of the world's population as of 1997, 74.2 percent of the land area (measured in square kilometers), and 88.4 percent of the world's wealth as of 1997. Additionally, Table 1.3 lists the countries contained in CROSSNAT.50, organized by the six geopolitical/regional groupings.

THE ROLE OF SCIENCE AND ITS UTILITY FOR COMPARING NATIONS SUMMARIZED

In summary, the science of comparing nations entails the application of the cross-national strategy of comparison, according to the rules and procedures dictated by the philosophy of normal science. In essence, this involves six basic steps:

1. Conceptualization
2. Operationalization
3. Specification
4. Measurement
5. Analysis
6. Evaluation

TABLE 1.2 Countries Included in CROSSNAT.50

COUNTRY	*CODE*	*POPULATE*	*Rank*	*AREA*	*Rank*	*GDP97*	*Rank*
Algeria	ALG	29183000	29	2381740	9	130700000000	31
Argentina	ARG	34673000	28	2780400	8	367500000000	19
Australia	AUL	18261000	40	7741220	6	374500000000	18
Bangladesh	BNG	123063000	8	144000	45	129700000000	32
Brazil	BRA	162661000	5	8547400	5	1060000000000	9
Canada	CAN	28821000	31	9970610	2	680900000000	12
Chile	CHL	14333000	44	756630	23	186100000000	27
China	CHN	1210005000	1	9596960	3	3838000000000	2
Colombia	COL	36813000	27	1138910	16	272800000000	22
Congo	CON	48200000	22	2344860	10	40880000000	43
Czech	CZR	10304100	49	78860	48	108298166272	36
Ecuador	ECU	11466000	46	283560	38	58980000000	40
Egypt	EGY	63575000	15	1001450	17	184000000000	28
France	FRN	58041000	19	551500	27	1291000000000	6
Germany	GFR	83536000	12	356980	33	1745000000000	4
Ghana	GHA	17698000	41	238540	41	29490000000	45
Greece	GRC	10539000	48	131960	46	131900000000	30
India	IND	952108000	2	3287590	7	1610000000000	5
Indonesia	INS	206612000	4	1904570	12	699800000000	11
Iran	IRN	66094000	13	1633190	13	108600000000	35
Italy	ITA	57661000	20	301270	36	1167000000000	8
Japan	JPN	123537000	7	377800	32	3035000000000	3
Kenya	KEN	23896000	33	580370	26	33920000000	44
Korea	ROK	42869000	23	99260	47	624900000000	15
Madagascar	MAG	11525000	45	587040	25	13110000000	50
Malaysia	MAL	17507000	42	329750	34	176400000000	29
Mexico	MEX	85121000	11	1958200	11	790000000000	10
Morocco	MOR	26164000	32	446550	30	90310000000	39
Nepal	NEP	19104000	38	147180	44	24270000000	47
Netherlands	NTH	14952000	43	40840	50	329500000000	20
Nigeria	NIG	86488000	10	923770	19	108000000000	37
Pakistan	PAK	113914000	9	796100	21	200000000000	26
Peru	PER	21841000	36	1285220	14	114100000000	33
Philippines	PHI	65037000	14	300000	37	258900000000	23
Poland	POL	38109000	26	323250	35	252100000000	24
Romania	RUM	22775000	34	238390	42	97100000000	38
Russia	RUS	148081000	6	17075400	1	644200000000	13
South Africa	SAF	41743000	24	1221040	15	299600000000	21
Spain	SPN	39181000	25	505990	29	626300000000	14
Sri Lanka	SRI	18553000	39	65610	49	46210000000	42
Tanzania	TAZ	29058000	30	945090	18	18090000000	49
Thailand	THI	58851000	17	513120	28	405600000000	16
Tunisia	TUN	9020000	50	163610	43	48860000000	41
Turkey	TUR	62484000	16	774820	22	404500000000	17
Uganda	UGA	20158000	37	241040	40	23620000000	48
Ukraine	UKR	50864000	21	603700	24	111100000000	34
United Kingdom	UK	58490000	18	244880	39	1224000000000	7
United States	USA	265563000	3	9363520	4	7765000000000	1
Venezuela	VEN	21983000	35	912050	20	201800000000	25
Zimbabwe	ZIM	11271000	47	390760	31	26930000000	46

TABLE 1.3 Countries in CROSSNAT.50, by Geopolitical/Regional Classification

Countries of Eastern Europe and The Former Soviet Union (CIS-EE)	*Advanced Industrial–West European Countries*
Czech Republic	Australia
Poland	Canada
Romania	France
Russia	Germany
Ukraine	Greece
	Italy
	Japan
	Netherlands
	Spain
	Turkey
	United Kingdom
	United States
Asian Countries	*Latin American Countries*
Bangladesh	Argentina
China	Brazil
India	Chile
Indonesia	Colombia
Korea	Ecuador
Malaysia	Mexico
Nepal	Peru
Pakistan	Venezuela
Philippines	
Sri Lanka	
Thailand	
Sub-Saharan African Countries	*Arab (Middle East–North African) Countries*
Congo	Algeria
Ghana	Egypt
Kenya	Iran
Madagascar	Morocco
Nigeria	Tunisia
South Africa	
Tanzania	
Uganda	
Zimbabwe	

Conceptualization

Conceptualization is the process of specifying the generic components of our political world. Political concepts are the pictures we hold in our mind's eye of how the political world functions. They are designed to simplify and clarify complex phenomena in such a way as to facilitate simple explanation of why things are the way they appear and how they come to be that way. Thus, they serve to establish for us reasonable expectations about what is likely to happen under certain circumstances. Concepts cover several different types of more specific political behavior and institutional authority.

Operationalization

To operationalize is to specify the precise measurable dimensions and properties of a concept. The process of *operationalization* requires that we specify precisely one con-

MAP 1.1 Geographic Location of Countries in CROSSNAT.50

cept from another and define the measurable dimensions of the properties within the concept in such a way as to enable one to accurately assess the degree to which the concept is present or absent across different circumstances and situations.

Specification

Specification connects, or links, concepts into a causal chain. That is, each concept (defined and operationalized, and thereby rendered distinct from other concepts) is logically tied to at least one other concept in a "cause-and-effect" sequence. Without such specification of the connection between a causal concept and a subsequently effected concept, explanation of our political world cannot proceed in a systematic and meaningful manner. The stated cause-and-effect linkages that connect our concepts are called hypotheses (or, in their more informal version, propositions). Once connected, we have a model of our political world. Such models are commonly referred to as theories.

Measurement

Measurement is the process of collecting the evidence to permit the testing of our hypotheses. It entails the careful and systematic assignment of values to those properties central to the definition of a concept. The values we attach to properties are specifically observed across a collection of similar units or objects, called a sample (the collection of selected persons, institutions, organizations, political parties, leaders, or countries that are likely to reflect the empirical properties of the specified concepts and that we observe under controlled and special conditions). The coding process assigns numeric values to the properties of the concepts found in the units we observe. This matching process follows carefully the defined properties specified by the respective operationalizations. Data, therefore, are the measurable representations of the operationalized properties within our sample. We shall see in Chapter 6 that measurement in cross-national analysis is often fraught with controversy and challenge.

Analysis

Within the process we call "normal" science, *analysis* of data involves measuring the variance patterns of specified properties across the sample. Ultimately, within the exercise of normal science, data analysis has as its principal goal the falsification of our specified hypotheses connecting operationalized concepts. Failure to falsify lends support to the ultimate validity and truth of the specified linkages. In the social sciences, such analysis most commonly entails the application of statistical analysis. In order to falsify, we must measure the observed impact of a causal variable upon a second variable (the effect) and compare this observed impact to the size of the effect we expected (and had specified in our hypothesis). The degree of fit between "observed reality" and our "predicted reality" allows us to measure more precisely the degree to which our expectations (specified in our model via connected concepts) match reality. If they do not match well and within a specified margin of error, our theory and its attendant system of hypotheses are falsified. In this manner, we are able to systematically and incrementally eliminate hunches (hypotheses) that simply do not align with empirical reality. In this phase of "normal" science, we are able to incrementally and systematically separate what is "thought" to be true from that which is "observed" to be true.

Evaluation

As we proceed from one such test to another in our efforts to falsify and clarify, we must subject the logic that initially directed our hypotheses and dictated our specification of linkages between concepts to careful and scrutinizing *evaluation*. General theory born from the enterprise of normal science assumes, however, that we do more than merely falsify or verify the truth of a specified hypothesis. Additionally, we must ask subsequent questions of our theory, its model, and the assumptions that have guided the design of our operationalizations, measurement, and sample collection and coding procedures. Such questions include: "Is the measurement logical and are the instruments appropriate?" Or, "Are our concepts carefully considered and clearly operationalized?" Or, "Are the countries we have selected for analysis in our sample appropriate for the concepts we are using?" Or, "Have we missed a connection, or have we missed a critical concept?" Finally, we may ask, "Have our operationalized properties been too broadly or too narrowly defined, thereby rendering our findings either too general or too refined for use with our sample and our theory?"

Above all, we must eventually evaluate whether we have offered something credible with respect to the goal of building general theory. It is, indeed, the desire to offer such evidence as free as possible from reliance upon national, cultural, or temporal qualifications that undergird the fundamental rationale for the cross-national strategy of comparison. We can approximate such powerful conclusions only when we measure and analyze data across as wide a sample of countries as possible.

It is important to remember that in the process of hypothesis testing, we often discover patterns that allow us to suggest important qualifications to our original hypothesis. Finding patterns among a subset of countries in a cross-national sample, or finding countries that exhibit attributes quite different from those of other countries we assume to be similar in all relevant aspects, helps us specify important qualifications to our theory. This only underscores the utility of cross-national analysis, for such discoveries eliminate false hopes of generalization that might lead us astray from our quest for general theory. Thus, such refinements as we may discover are not to be frowned upon but rather welcomed, for they strengthen our understanding of the world and help to calibrate more precisely the degree of generalization possible.

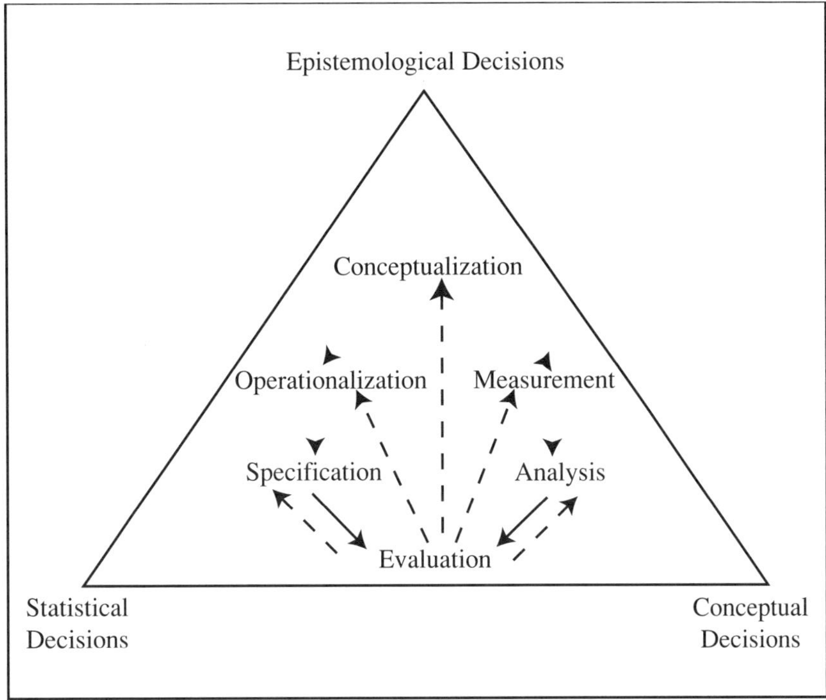

FIGURE 1.2 The Process of Cross-National Analysis Within the Context of Normal Science

Figure 1.2 summarizes the logic of quantitative cross-national research within the context of normal science. This figure serves to remind us that quantitative cross-national analysis is not merely governed by the rules and principles that underlie the philosophy of normal science, but that the enterprise of cross-national research itself is bounded by the three domains of decisions that structure the science of comparing nations. Statistical decisions bear upon the analysis and evaluation steps within cross-national analysis; conceptual decisions determine the conceptualization step within cross-national research, as well as color our evaluations of the analysis; and the epistemological decisions shape the operationalization, specification, and measurement steps in cross-national research.

As illustrated in Figure 1.2, the process of quantitative cross-national analysis involves moving back and forth between conceptualization, operationalization, specification, measurement, analysis, and evaluation. Thus, through evaluation, the student sharpens and elaborates her conceptual picture of the world, refines her measures, extends and/or transforms her original measurements (and perhaps sample), and supplements her tools of statistical analysis. The only element in this enterprise that distinguishes cross-national analysis from the "ordinary" empirical analysis of social science data is that the student of cross-national analysis relies on a sample of data from a variety of different political systems and cultures.

NOTES

1. For excerpts from the text of the original telegram and the circumstances surrounding it, see George F. Kennan, 1967, *Memoirs, 1925–1950* (New York: Pantheon Books), pp. 547–559 and 354–367.

2. Kennan's analysis may have been subjective, but it was not descriptive. A clear distinction should be made between the subjective, inter-subjective, and descriptive. Lawrence Mayer notes that "conclusions are subjective in the sense that they depend on the internal disposition of each individual drawing them." (Lawrence Mayer, ed., 1996, *Redefining Comparative Politics: Promise Versus Performance* (Newbury Park, Calif.: Sage Publications), p. 35). Science, as we shall see, demands stricter adherence to careful specification and operationalization so as to minimize the variance across different people with respect to their understanding of findings and conclusions emerging from cross-national research. This enhances the inter-subjective validity and value of comparative research, laying the foundations for universal interpretation of political phenomena, regardless of cultural, linguistic, or national differences across the consumers of the research. Why would it be inappropriate to consider Kennan's analysis, and others like it, as descriptive? Descriptive works fail to explain. While his analysis focuses exclusively on the Soviet context, Kennan nonetheless fashioned his conclusions in such a way as to offer generic conclusions regarding the conduct of Soviet-style communist countries. It was, in a sense, something akin to what we call a most-similar systems design, as we shall see in Chapter 2. This afforded a degree of extrapolation to other political systems, and from this, offered something in the way of a general theory of communist behavior. It would appear that in failing to operationalize more carefully, he left the door open to subsequent research to extrapolate to different national contexts that were not equivalent to the Soviet case in crucial properties. Thus, inappropriate extrapolations, unconstrained by more precise empirical specifications and operationalization terminology regarding key properties of domestic power and culture, led to expectations of others about the conduct of behavior beyond the Soviet context (something Kennan apparently did not intend). When these expectations did not materialize, the entire analysis of Kennan was brought into question and perhaps unjustifiably accused of bias. While eloquent and powerful as an explanatory analysis, his essay too readily contributed to a subjective interpretation and undermined inter-subjective clarity among readers at that point in history.

3. Earl Babbie, 2001, *The Practice of Social Science*, ninth edition (Belmont, Calif.: Wadsworth Publishing Company), pp. 143–144.

4. Mayer, 1996, p. 55.

5. For a superb and thoroughly accessible introduction to the foundations of science and their role within the study of social behavior, see Eugene Meehan, 1965, *The Theory and Method of Political Analysis* (Homewood, Ill.: Dorsey Press). Also see, Alan S. Zuckerman, 1991, *Doing Political Science: An Introduction to Political Analysis* (Boulder: Westview Press); Eugene J. Meehan, 1994, *Social Inquiry: Needs, Possibilities, Limits* (Chatham, N.J.: Chatham House Publish-

ers, Inc.); and Abraham Kaplan, 1964, *The Conduct of Inquiry: Methodology for Behavioral Science* (San Francisco: Chandler Publishing Co.).

6. For insights into the foundation of empirical theory within comparative politics, see: B. Guy Peters, 1998, *Comparative Politics: Theory and Methods* (New York: New York University Press); Lawrence C. Mayer, 1972, *Comparative Political Inquiry* (Homewood, Ill.: The Dorsey Press); Richard T. Holt and John Turner, eds., 1970, *The Methodology of Comparative Research* (New York: The Free Press); Richard Merritt, 1970, *Systematic Approaches to Comparative Politics* (Chicago: Rand McNally); and Mattei Dogan and G. Pelassey, 1990, *How to Compare Nations* (Chatham, N.J.: Chatham House); and Howard J. Wiarda, ed., 1991, revised edition, *New Directions in Comparative Politics* (Boulder: Westview Press). More detailed discussion can be found in Mattei Dogan and Stein Rokkan, eds., 1971, *Quantitative Ecological Analysis in the Social Sciences* (Cambridge, Mass.: Cambridge University Press) and Hans Keman, ed., 1993, *Comparative Politics: New Directions in Theory and Method* (Amsterdam: VU University Press).

7. For a brief but clear and concise discussion of paradigms within cross-national analysis, see Mark Irving Lichbach and Alan S. Zuckerman, eds., 1997, *Comparative Politics: Rationality, Culture, and Structure* (Cambridge, Mass.: Cambridge University Press) or Lawrence C. Mayer, 1996, *Redefining Comparative Politics: Promise Versus Performance* (Newbury, Calif.: Sage Publications). For more detail and a survey of the common traditional paradigms in cross-national analysis, see: Richard T. Holt and John Turner, eds., 1970, *The Methodology of Comparative Research* (New York: The Free Press); Ruth Lane, 1997, *The Art of Comparative Politics* (Boston: Allyn and Bacon); Jean Blondel, 1990, *Comparative Government: An Introduction* (Hemel Hempstead: Philip Allan); and Rod Hague, Martin Harrop, and Shaun Breslin, 1998, second edition, *Political Science: A Comparative Introduction* (New York: St. Martin's).

8. Gabriel A. Almond and G. Bingham Powell Jr., 1978, *Comparative Politics: System, Process and Policy* (Boston: Little Brown). Also see Gabriel A. Almond, G. Bingham Powell Jr., Kaare Strom, and Russel J. Dalton, 2000, *Comparative Politics Today: A World View*, seventh edition (New York: Longman), pp. 49–157. For a critical evaluation of the structural-functional paradigm, see James Gregor, 1968, "Political Science and the uses of Functional Analysis," *American Political Science Review* 42 (December): 425–439.

9. For a brief but excellent overview of the research design and the role of sampling in statistical analysis, see Stella Z. Theodoulou, 1999, "Starting From Scratch: the Research Process," in Stella Z. Theodoulou and Rory O'Brien, eds., 1999, *Methods for Political Inquiry: The Discipline, Philosophy and Analysis of Politics* (Upper Saddle River, N.J.: Prentice Hall), pp. 142–151.

10. The eight countries excluded from the sample because of missing data, which nonetheless are part of the fifty most populous countries of the world are: Vietnam, Ethiopia, Myanmar (Burma), Afghanistan, Uzbekistan, Democratic Republic of Korea (North Korea), Iraq, and Saudi Arabia. Additionally, seventeen countries were excluded between the fifty-first and seventy-eigth most populous countries of the world (as of 1997) because of missing data: Mozambique, Republic of Yemen (North Yemen), Kazakhstan, Syria, Cote d'Ivoire, Cameroon, Angola, Cuba, Yugoslavia, Guatemala, Cambodia, Burkina Faso, Mali, Malawi, Belarus, Niger, and Zambia.

11. In order to correct for even further overrepresentation of the industrial–West European countries within CROSSNAT.50, and to prevent further underrepresentation of Arab/Middle East–North African countries, Belgium, Hungary, and Portugal were excluded

from the sample selection process. European countries (especially the industrial Western countries) were adequately represented in the first seventy-three most populous (as of 1997) countries of the world. Thus, Tunisia was included in the sample, though technically Hungary, Portugal, and Belgium have complete data and have larger populations than Tunisia. Note the chi-square (chi-sq.) statistic (4.859) and the symbol $\tilde{n}$ ($\tilde{n} = .433$) in Table 1.1. This tells us the distribution of the two samples (the world-based sample and the sample of fifty countries in CROSSNAT.50) are not significantly different. We shall have more to say about such statistics and their utility in Chapter 5.

12. Actually, the technical measure of the gross domestic product (GDP) which is reported in Table 1.2 and used throughout this text is known as GDP-PPP. That is, the GDP for a country has been converted into a universal standard. The conversion corrects for inflation within each country. Thus, if a country has a huge GDP but very high inflation, its GDP is reduced accordingly to account for the fact that in dollar terms, a consumer will be able to buy a smaller basket of goods and services than a consumer in a country with a smaller GDP but a much smaller rate of inflation.

13. The World Bank is an international organization. It is officially known as the International Bank for Reconstruction and Development (IBRD). It was created in 1944 as part of the Anglo-American Bretton Woods plan for the post-war world. It counts over 180 countries as members and specializes in loaning money to poorer countries of the world. It has three divisions. First is the IBRD, which raises capital through advanced industrial markets in the world and loans to those poor countries that are less "risky" investments. Second is the International Development Association (IDA), which redistributes contributions from wealthy members to the very poorest of the world's countries. Finally, the International Finance Corporation (IFC) invests in the capital markets of the world's poor countries in an effort to stabilize markets and spur economic development. The World Bank is an invaluable source of data for the student of cross-national research. Each year it publishes the *World Development Report*, with analysis of world political and economic conditions, and tables of demographic, political, and economic data from its member countries. It publishes a CD-ROM for more complete time-series data, as well. The interested student may obtain some data and insights into the World Bank and its research by going to the World Bank's web page at http://www.worldbank.org/data/.

14. Some of the data from the various United Nations *Human Development Reports* may be obtained at the U.N.web site, http://www.undp.org/hdro/. The complete data from the *Human Development Reports* may be obtained from the United Nations at its web location, http://www.undp.org/hdro.

2

Strategies of Comparative Political Inquiry

Terms: *Case Study Strategy, Comparable Cases Strategy, Most-Similar Systems Design, Most-Different Systems Design, Statistical Method, Theory Building, Measurement Scales, Culture*

For many political science studies, comparison appears as the observation of events, behavior, or institutions exclusively drawn from the United States. As we saw in the last chapter, for political scientists to make significant strides toward building a general body of knowledge about politics, they must be able to observe events, institutions, and political behavior across more than one country, as well as across more than one culture. In political science the examination of data measuring political behavior or institutional authority in one country other than the United States, or in more than one country simultaneously, regardless of the nations involved, ordinarily falls within the subfield of comparative politics. However, when we test theories and hypotheses with quantitative data for the explicit purpose of formulating generalizations that extend beyond the particular countries and cultures included in the data set, we are employing a particular strategy of comparative political inquiry, namely, cross-national research. Understanding the strategies of comparative inquiry is essential to appreciating the epistemological principles of the science of comparing nations, and is necessary to properly orient one to the unique contribution of quantitative cross-national research. We begin with an overview of the three basic strategies of comparative political inquiry.

LOGIC OF COMPARISON: THREE BASIC STRATEGIES

In Chapter 1, we explained that nearly all knowledge of political behavior and institutional authority is based on some method of comparison. To this point, we have discussed only the cross-national strategy of comparison. It is the object of this textbook. The primary intent of cross-national comparative strategy is to systematically build general theory via comparative political inquiry. However, there is, as implied, more than one method of comparative inquiry in political science. Indeed, two other major strategies both complement and supplement the cross-national strategy: the *case study strategy* and the *comparable cases strategy*. Keep in mind though that quantitative cross-national analysis is the only strategy of comparative political inquiry that can effectively falsify our specified hypotheses. This is because the cross-national approach offers the greatest opportunity for the student of comparative inquiry to achieve sufficient variance across data drawn from different cultural and national contexts and thereby to satisfy minimal requirements of hypothesis testing in normal science. However, each strategy of comparative political inquiry plays an indispensable role in building our general knowledge of politics. Each employs a distinctly different logic of comparison, and as such, each is governed by unique rules pertaining to its use and role in the comparative research process.[1]

What then are the major differences between these three strategies of comparative political inquiry? The differences may be honed down to three:

- The number of variables and cases employed in their analysis.
- Their ability to offer general conclusions about political behavior and institutional authority.
- Their reliance on substantive detail specific to particular cultures and political systems.

The Case Study Strategy

The case study strategy of comparative political inquiry is employed by the student of comparative politics to study one country, or case, along one or several dimensions of political behavior or institutional authority. The purpose may be to apply the general knowledge of politics to a specific country in order to test crucial assumptions about politics within that country. Or, the purpose may be to derive new information from intense field research that often accompanies case studies. From this effort, the student may offer new information that can be incorporated into the general body of knowledge about politics.

The point to emphasize here is that knowing a great deal about one political system of government is useful in its own right, but it is of only limited value when one wishes to explore political phenomena outside that one system. The problem with case studies as strategies for comparative political inquiry is that they generate too little variance to falsify hypotheses, which requires cross-national variance. What variance is generated is solely internal to the country, or case, itself. As theories cannot be general if they apply only to one cultural and national context, case studies are very limited vehicles for building general theory.

Case studies in comparative politics may be logically grouped into two types: *descriptive case studies* and *analytic case studies*. The crucial distinction between descriptive and analytic case studies is the range of variance within the case study itself. The descriptive case study focuses solely upon one principal variable (for example, economic reform in Russia). In describing market reforms in Russia, it might be noted that other important changes occur within the country. For instance, suppose one observed that as market reforms were increasingly institutionalized within the legal structure of Russia, the public popularity of the president increased as well. The variance pattern of the institution is informally linked with the variance pattern seen in the process—that is, market reform. One would therefore be tempted to conclude that in general presidential authority increases with liberalized markets. One might further conclude that market reforms as a process had dramatic impact on the institutionalized policymaking and policy implementation process in Russia, thereby affecting in a real sense the legitimacy and effectiveness of government in Russia.

Yet, this, of course, would be speculation. The only reasonable and credible conclusion would be that in Russia, executive authority increased with market reform. The descriptive case affords no systematic evidence to support a more general conclusion such as market reforms' impact on any other institutional structure other than the executive. More importantly, a credible cross-national extrapolation or generalization to another system is impossible, as only one cultural and national context was observed. There is only one case, and one concept—the economic system—that is thoroughly explained within the case. The linkages to other concepts, let alone other countries, are informal and non-systematic. They lack proper conceptualization, operationalization, and measurement to allow falsification and extrapolation beyond the one case and one concept.

Without observing the pattern across a number of different institutional contexts within the case itself, you cannot be certain the pattern will repeat itself, thus offering broader and more generalized findings, even if limited to Russia alone. To refute the claim that what you have observed is not just an accident of unique circumstances in one country that cannot be replicated elsewhere (and therefore has no cross-national, or universal, validity), you must see the pattern appear in numerous cases in similar settings. Furthermore, to explain something requires that you see the predicted outcome occur under specified conditions in different national and cultural contexts, repeatedly. One case and one concept offer no basis for explanation. From a cross-national perspective, case studies are strategies of description. This said, it is rare to find a case study that does not imply some linkage between one concept and another within the case. Any good journalistic report will imply some degree of causality between more than one attribute or event and a subsequent effect. However, the distinguishing characteristic of a descriptive case study is unmistakable: It focuses almost exclusively upon one central concept within one country, either at one point in time, or longitudinally over several years.[2]

Analytic case studies, on the other hand, offer one advantage over descriptive case studies: They tie more than one concept together in a specified system of cause and effect. This affords the comparativist an opportunity to offer very preliminary, and extremely qualified, extrapolations beyond the particular cultural and national context within which the concept is developed, defined, and operationalized. Certainly, the spatial constraint is the same as in the descriptive case study (one country and one national culture). However, analytic case studies extend their focus to two or more concepts and therefore two or more variables.

For instance, let us imagine a hypothetical situation where one finds that the popularity of the French president consistently declines relative to the authority of the prime minister during periods of recession. This hypothetical analytic case study has more internal variance than the descriptive case study. The variance of prime ministerial authority and that of presidential authority has been linked to the variance in economic conditions within France. While extrapolation to other political systems is still quite questionable and lacking in credible evidence, the greater internal variance within the analytic case study model affords the researcher some basis upon which to explain the differences between French presidential authority and French prime ministerial authority, and from this, to lay the foundation for a general proposition that prime ministerial authority and presidential authority vary in opposition, depending upon the condition of the economy. The addition of a second concept affords the minimal requirement for some degree of internal variance from which at least some general conclusions can be suggested. Within the field of comparative political inquiry, the most fruitful case study research is of the analytic type.[3]

The great advantage of these two types of case study strategies is their attention to the substantive detail gathered within the specific context of a particular culture or political system. While the descriptive case study is clearly the weaker strategy for building general theory through comparative political inquiry, both approaches—descriptive and analytic—promise very limited opportunity for credible generalizations about political behavior and institutional authority beyond the specific cultural and national context.

Comparable Cases Strategy

The comparable cases strategy entails linking several case studies together in an attempt to test our assumptions of how various political phenomena relate to each other. This can be accomplished either with statistical analysis, or without. In this sense, the strategy is a step beyond the simple case study method, because data from several cases constitute the database from which conclusions can be made. Students of comparative politics commonly employ the comparable cases strategy of political inquiry when they are trying to extend case studies but have only a few countries or cultures from which to conduct their research.

As with case studies, comparable cases strategy entails two approaches. One type focuses upon one central concept but explores this concept in depth across several countries, usually common to a given geographical region of the world. The second type extends the conceptual range somewhat.[4] Both methods are important and indispensable to the study of politics. They serve to balance, in part, the accumulation of substantive detail about particular cultural and political contexts, with some attention to testing hypotheses through comparison. They remain, nonetheless, limited in their explanatory power.

The logic of comparison via a comparable cases strategy is a very popular and successful tool for comparative political inquiry. In general, the logic of the strategy is, in effect, to examine variance across either the dependent variable or the independent variable within a model. The dependent variable is the concept we wish to explain, and is universally denoted by the term *Y*. The independent variable is the phenomenon that we expect to impact, or affect, the dependent variable, and is universally denoted by the symbol *X*. The X variables are therefore held to be exogenous, or free of effects from the dependent variables (thus, their variance is independent of the values of the dependent variable). Two logically distinct approaches prevail within the logical application of comparable cases. One is known as the "most-similar systems design," while the other is known as the "most-different systems design."[5]

The most-similar systems design logically requires the student to select a sample of countries that have as many similarities as possible (such as culture, government structure, legal system) among the independent variables thought to have some effect on the dependent variable. Any variance in the dependent variable cannot, according to this approach, be explained by similarities among the countries, but must be explained by some important variance within one of the independent variables.

For example, suppose the student were examining economic performance across a sample of countries that were all advanced industrial democracies, with unitary forms of government. She would likely conclude that any variance in economic performance among countries is not owing to their being advanced industrial democracies, or to their being unitary, but must be caused by some other factor, perhaps level of international trade—a variable that likely has a fairly high degree of variance within it.[6]

The problem, of course, is that in the social sciences, we always encounter more explanations than we have countries. Comparable cases strategy draws on only a few of these. Yet, we have a seemingly infinite number of possible concepts from which we can imagine causal linkages designed to explain the properties reflected in the attribute Y.

Thus, the most-similar systems design can be used effectively when working with a limited number of countries to eliminate possible explanations for Y. It cannot, however, serve (in most conceivable situations) to logically offer a credible explanation of Y.

A useful alternative to the most-similar systems design is the most-different systems design. As a design for comparable cases, it requires the student to select countries that are very different in terms of their respective attributes. If the student finds that two or more countries have a similar value for the Y variable, then such similarity must be explained by similarity within one of the independent variables. For example, suppose the student were examining government corruption levels among countries and found that the United States, Costa Rica, and Ghana each had the same level of corruption. The constant Y value among these countries would not be explained by their many differences, but is explained by some variable whose value was common to each of the three.

The advantage of the most-different systems design is that it allows the researcher to avoid running out of cases as quickly as one does (ordinarily) when using a most-similar systems design. We are thus able to enjoy the benefits of a larger sample of countries and thereby utilize variance as a means of offering greater refinement to our possible explanations for the Y attribute.[7]

The drawback to the most-different systems design within a comparable cases strategy is that we cannot avoid the problem so common to any strategy of comparable cases. Namely, eventually, you end up with many more variables that can ultimately explain Y than you have countries. That point is not reached as quickly as with the most-similar systems design, but it is not long before the researcher confronts the problem of having more independent variables than countries. Once this point is reached, the student cannot manipulate the countries to effectively refine further the conclusions about which independent variables are more important than others in accounting for patterns of variation in attribute Y within the sample. Nonetheless, the approach allows one to maximize the size of a limited sample, and, within a restricted setting of sample size, offer greater refinements to our conclusions. Such refinements afford the scholar a greater likelihood of achieving a general theory. Yet, within the context of comparable cases strategy, even the most-different systems design offers something less in the way of credible evidence than the cross-national design. Only the cross-national design (employing, as it does, both statistical methods and the most-different systems design logic) can effectively accomplish the principal goal of normal science: falsification of hypotheses.[8]

The Statistical Approach Within the Cross-National Strategy of Comparison

The statistical method of comparison carries with it the mystique of having the accuracy and power of "hard" science. In fact, we should keep in mind that political science is a social science, and as such it is focused on patterns of human behavior. Consequently, it can be prone to many more errors of measurement and interpretation than those fields of study associated with the laws of nature. Yet, statistical methods, within reason and despite limitations, offer the most powerful means for building general bodies of knowledge about politics.

The logic of the statistical method is based first on the requirement that there be enough observations to appropriately use the tools of statistics for comparing patterns of political behavior and institutional authority. Second, there must be more than one variable from which to build credible explanations of these patterns. At the heart of the statistical method of comparison is hypothesis testing. Indeed, the key distinction between the statistical method and the case study method is that despite hypothesis testing activity within specific case contexts, case studies and comparative case methods tend to generate hypotheses rather than test hypotheses. On the other hand, cross-national research based on the statistical method can both generate and test hypotheses. With such power comes the responsibility to use the tools of analysis both widely and with caution.

The power of the statistical method, if applied appropriately, is that it allows the researcher to draw conclusions about political behavior and institutional patterns with minimal regard to specific national or cultural settings. It is ordinarily more important for the political scientist to say that legislatures play a certain role in the political process, than to say they play a specific role in a specific country, and yet another role in still another country. The former allows a generalized knowledge of politics; the latter informs with regard to a specific, though not generalized, context. In political science today, the statistical method (as well as more formal methods derived from many of the assumptions associated with the statistical logic) is the dominant method for building empirical bodies of knowledge about politics. The cross-national analysis of political behavior and institutional authority ordinarily implies the application of the statistical method of comparison.[9]

There is a caveat we have touched on briefly above: Case studies can also employ a statistical method. For instance, political scientists studying the American Congress often employ statistical methods to measure change or events within Congress. However, when a statistical method does not include more than one or even a few countries or cultures, it is not considered to be a cross-national analysis of legislatures. This important distinction is adopted throughout this text.

THE LADDER OF THEORY BUILDING

Undoubtedly, political scientists are better off in their quest for general knowledge if they combine all three strategies of comparison. Each strategy complements the others, and each allows a unique and important contribution to the process of building general knowledge. There is, however, no way of avoiding the statistical logic if one is truly interested in a general knowledge of either politics or computers, or for that matter, virtually any phenomena worth studying.

The logical relationship between these methods and their role in the comparative analysis of politics is depicted in Figure 2.1. The "Ladder of Theory Building" suggests that the process of comparison is repetitive, starting at Step 1 (Descriptive Case Studies) and extending up the ladder to Step 4 (Cross-National Statistical Method) with its reliance on formal hypothesis testing, and eventually extending back down the ladder to Descriptive Case Studies at Step 8. At Step 8 in Figure 2.1, the process conceivably repeats itself, refreshed with new insights and questions that became apparent to the student passing through the first eight steps. In short, the ladder simply suggests that we move back and forth between generalizations and detailed substance, refining and extending our ideas, questions, concepts, and theories, and employing different techniques and tools at each stage in a comprehensive activity of comparative research.

ELABORATING CROSS-NATIONAL RESEARCH STRATEGIES

The Ladder of Theory Building draws attention to the single most prominent feature of cross-national analysis: the sample. Do we select one, a few, or many countries to explore? This question stands as one of the most important decisions the student of cross-national analysis must make after he or she has identified the question, stated it within a theoretical framework, and distilled the theory to a few manageable concepts. It is, however, by no means the only factor influencing the research strategy of the student of cross-national analysis.

Spatial Scope

The careful student will observe that all attributes vary with respect to space and time. Countries occupy a unit of space within the global political environment. As we move from one country to another and compare various attributes across these countries, we are working within the spatial dimension of comparison. We are, in effect, comparing properties of space, in this case, properties of countries. Of course, not all cross-national research is limited to the nation-state. Comparative research often focuses on institutions, sub-national groups, or particular organizations as distinct elements of our political environment, devoid of particular country properties. Yet, it is rare to find a study that purports to be a comparative analysis that at some point does not reflect on the implications of the findings within the context of the nation-state's policies or properties.

Temporal Scope

The careful student will also observe that all properties vary across time, as well as space. All properties subject to quantification are also subject to the effects of time, which we describe as change and transformation. Therefore, the role of time itself is a

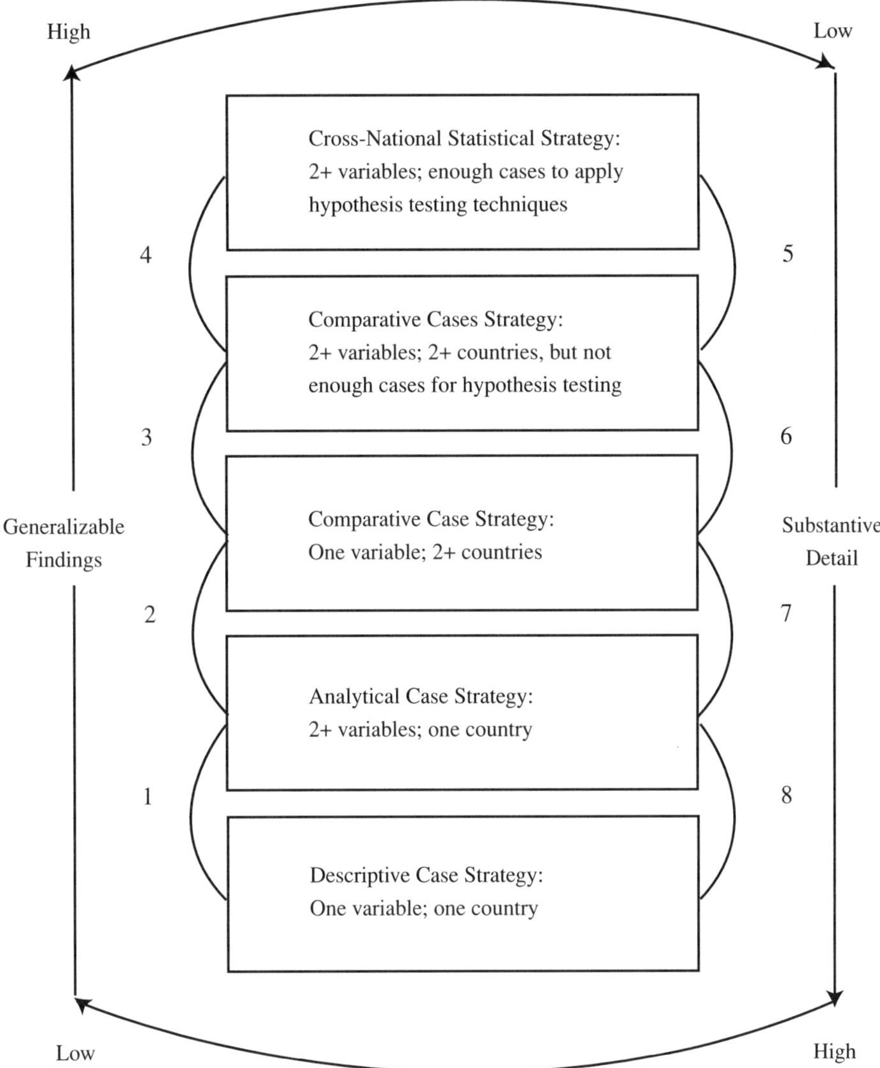

FIGURE 2.1 The Ladder of Theory Building in Comparative Politics

critical dimension that often plays a crucial role in devising a strategy for cross-national analysis. Specifically, we must decide the importance of including the effect of time into our research strategy when drawing our sample and operationally defining our variables. As we add the time dimension to our cross-national analysis, we extend temporal scope.

Moving beyond spatial scope to include temporal scope, however, is neither an easy move nor one without significant potential problems. The broader our research strategy, the greater the variance we obtain in our measures, and consequently, the more we may generalize our findings. However, as our net extends, we risk violating critical technical assumptions regarding our data (a topic we will leave for the most part to more advanced texts on statistics).

Of more immediate concern is the challenge posed to our measurement strategies. As we extend our reach for data further outward from a "simple" case study, we increase the likelihood that some, if not many, of our measures will no longer seem reasonable for our purpose. Very refined and specific definitions honed for a particular country (for example, the United States), become virtually useless as we build a broader database by including countries with experiences and histories vastly different from the United States. Even if we decide to remain within only one country, we must consider whether we want to extend the time frame within which we will collect valid data. If we reach backward and collect data covering a thirty-year period, for instance, we run the risk of incorporating data in the sample that have very different meanings and connotations across the specified time frame.

The time dimension to the research strategy defines the extent of temporal variance in our data selected for analysis. Temporal variance is constrained by the degree to which our data represent a specified attribute recorded at different chronological points. The advantage of extending temporal variance is twofold. First, we enhance our ability to generalize about our findings. If we limit our analysis to data that cover only one point in time, we run the risk that our data capture conditions that are very time specific. Second, with temporal variance, we are better able to assert true causality between variables in our analysis. Before we can credibly assert that something "causes" something else, we must demonstrate an antecedent effect of one attribute upon a subsequent condition within a second attribute. The research must isolate these "before and after" conditions and directly attribute them to the antecedent effect before causality can be determined. It is very important to note that in the social sciences, causality is almost never conclusively determined.[10]

Table 2.1 summarizes the various degrees of temporal variance and their relationship to the basic methods of cross-national analysis. For simplicity, we have summarized the range of temporal variance along the horizontal axis of Table 2.1 as extending from one point in time (or the absence of temporal variance) to "many" independent points in time. There is no particular number that defines "many." This depends entirely upon the unit of time appropriate for the particular research project. Data that are recorded by days (such as the stock market closing price) will have a different time scale than data recorded annually (such as GDP values). Twenty-five independent time points for annual data may be "many," while this would constitute only a "few" independent time points for data recorded daily.

The difficulty for researchers, of course, is that once they have made a decision regarding the unit of time over which the data will vary, all the data in the sample must be measured at this unit of time in order for any meaningful conclusions to be drawn from the results of the analysis. Obviously, there is some margin of variance that would

TABLE 2.1 Research Strategies, Combining Time and Space Dimensions

		Cross-National Research Strategies			
Spatial Scope: Extent of Cross-National Variance	Many Countries	Traditional Cross-National (CROSSNAT.50)	Extended Cross-Sectional/ Cross-National	Longitudinal Cross-National (Pooled Cross-Sectional)	Extended Longitudinal Cross-National
	Few Countries	Cross-Sectional/ Comparable Cases	Extended Cross-Sectional/ Comparable Cases	Longitudinal Comparable Cases	Extended Longitudinal Comparable Cases
	Two Countries				
	One Country	Restricted Case Study	Traditional Case Study	Longitudinal Case Study	Extended Longitudinal Case Study
		One Point in Time	*A Few Independent Time Points*	*Several Independent Time Points*	*Many Independent Time Points*
		Time: Extent of Temporal Variance			

be reasonably allowed (for example, one variable might vary over twenty-five years, another over only twenty-three of the full twenty-five-year period). However, you cannot combine daily units with weekly units, or weekly units with annual units in one sample without collapsing the smaller time units into comparable larger units. The largest unit of time will govern the final unit of time by which the data are measured.

A case study based on one point in time is labeled a "restricted" case study in Table 2.1. This is equivalent to the "descriptive" case study noted in Figure 2.1. It is restricted because there is no temporal variance by which to compare change and transformation over time. Indeed, a restricted case study has virtually no variance of any sort in the sample. It has, in effect, one country at one point in time. Such a design constitutes the classic descriptive study.

At the opposite extreme are research strategies that extend over many chronological points, as well as over many different countries: the extended longitudinal cross-national research design. Few cross-national studies fall into this category. The sheer volume of missing data across so many countries over such extended time renders this design risky for researchers. The effort required to gather these data in such a design (relative to the validity and reliability of the findings) often discourages students and professionals alike from proceeding with such a broad-based sample. There are, however, notable exceptions. We will draw on data from one such study, by Ted Robert Gurr and his colleagues, in Chapter 7 when devising measures of democracy.

The design explicitly employed throughout this text is the traditional cross-national research strategy. Within this approach, the researcher measures attributes at the national level, collected across several countries during one slice (that is, a cross section) of time. However, the overall strategy employed is the traditional cross-sectional design, limiting data points to, or as close as possible to, 1997. As a means of introducing the student to the measurement strategies and statistical tools and rules of cross-national analysis, the traditional cross-national strategy minimizes the extensive difficulties one encounters when extending data over many independent units of time. While most professionals extend their temporal variance at least to the midrange (for example, longitudinal cross-national, or longitudinal comparable cases designs), much of the basic research in comparative politics still rests on the traditional cross-national strategy.

As we move toward the top of Table 2.1, and especially toward the top right-hand corner (extended longitudinal, cross-national) we increase our opportunities for generalized findings. That is, with maximum spatial and temporal scope, we are in a better position to conclude that the results of our sample approximate a true population of countries and circumstances. Of course, we never manage to fully capture a population. Nonetheless, our scope is such that we are in a position to assume that most circumstances and countries have been represented in the sample. Whatever results we obtain in subsequent statistical analysis are more likely to be "true" than if we simply selected one slice of time, or once small slice of space (that is, countries).

On the other hand, as we move upward in Table 2.1, we also greatly increase the risk of rendering our measures invalid across so many different countries over increasingly extended, and therefore, different, time periods. This particular phenomenon is referred to as "concept stretching," and will be discussed in detail in Chapter 6.

Cultural (Geopolitical) Scope

Beyond the two more common features of space and time is a third dimension critical to cross-national research: culture. It reflects the geopolitical scope of our analysis, and is generally understood to be the unique collection of symbols, attitudes, values, and beliefs held by a population and how members of that particular population relate to authority and power. This dimension of a society is universally viewed as a major factor in shaping the political environment of countries.

Culture is also perhaps the most elusive and challenging property to adequately quantify at any point in time, much less over time. Identifying reliable and valid measures of national culture is too often beyond the reach of current technology; such efforts to explore national culture have generally limited their analysis to one or a few similar countries. Of course, within each nation-state, many subcultures can exist. Robert Putnam, for instance, has shown that in Italy, deeply rooted regional variations in political culture account for important differences in crucial attitudes toward power and government among Italians.[11] We will explore the concept of subculture in more detail in Chapter 11.

These limitations have not prevented students of comparative politics from recognizing and indeed recording important differences across groups of countries comprising "families" of a particular broad political culture. As noted briefly in Chapter 1, region plays a crucial role in many cross-national studies; the pattern of political behavior and institutional authority can be traced to unique historical patterns within certain geopolitical regions of the world. Recently, Samuel Huntington refocused attention on classifying global cultures. His widely discussed classification scheme divides the globe into nine broad cultural groups, or civilizations, which closely approximate the geopolitical regional classification traditionally offered by students of cross-national analysis.[12] These civilizations are: Western, Slavic-Orthodox, Sinic (Confucian), Buddhist, Japanese, Hindu, African, Latin American, and Islamic.[13] Therefore, when working with broad national-level cultural patterns across the global landscape, we capture cross-cultural variance when we maximize the range of geopolitical regions covered in the cross-national analysis.[14]

Cultural scope offers the researcher the opportunity to account for differences across broad cultural groups when exploring particular political attributes in comparative research. As with space and time dimensions, the cultural dimension incorporated into a cross-national research strategy may range from one through many. When combined with the temporal and spatial scope of the cross-national research strategy,

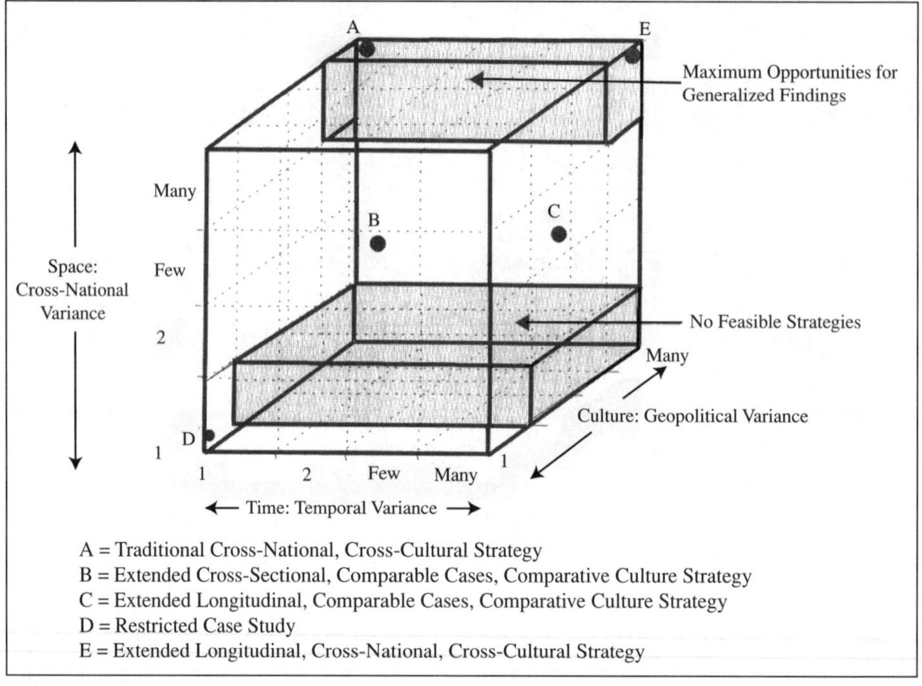

FIGURE 2.2 Three-Dimensional Schematic Representation of Cross-National Research Strategies

we obtain a three-dimensional representation of the various cross-national strategies open to students of comparative analysis. Figure 2.2 summarizes this three-dimensional scheme.

Figure 2.2 identifies two important outcomes of the choice made regarding the cross-national research strategy. If the student selects the single case-study method (point D in Figure 2.2), he or she has, in effect, closed out the option of cross-cultural analysis (broadly defined) because the student has no possibility to account for more than one geopolitical region. This limits the student's analysis strategy to a two-dimensional approach: space and time. This is reflected in Figure 2.2 by specifying the region of the box labeled "No Feasible Strategies."

In selecting cross-national and cross-cultural strategies, the student enters the region of the box in Figure 2.2 where the opportunities for generalized findings are maximized. Of course, the most general findings can be achieved if the students limit their strategy to an extended longitudinal, cross-national, and cross-cultural analysis of comparative data (point E in Figure 2.2). Nonetheless, the relative gains achieved in cross-national, cross-cultural strategies in terms of generalized findings are greatly improved as we move from single cases to cross-national strategies.

As with temporal scope, culture (or, geopolitical) scope significantly increases the difficulties of achieving valid and reliable measurement. Data are more difficult to obtain as we stretch our analysis across different geopolitical regions, as well as over several independent time points. Our measurement precision declines accordingly, all things being equal. As a result, most cross-national studies limit their scope to one country or culture.

MEASUREMENT SCALES

The principal objective of the statistical method of comparative analysis is to measure quantified attributes of a sample of countries and to infer generalizations with reference to these attributes to a population of countries. This strategy requires that the student of comparative politics be familiar with the most basic rules of statistical analysis, as well as with the most common tools of comparative analysis.

The most basic rules of statistical inference begin with the matter of measurement. Measurement is the process of systematically assigning or coding numbers to objects, events, or persons. In other words, measurement ultimately involves some type of categorization of the values within each variable. It is the most basic activity of students of comparative politics, regardless of whether students are employing the case study method, the comparable cases method, or the statistical inferences method. Thus, while it is one of the most basic activities in analysis, it is one of the most important. It requires as much precision on our part as possible. Assigning numbers (which is usually nothing more than quantifying attributes, such as age, income, area, and population) to countries in a sample determines the subsequent types of tools we can use to analyze the measured attributes. The reader must be able to understand clearly the decision rules the researcher is applying in measuring his or her variables. Any ambiguity on the part of the researcher will reduce the study's validity.

Generally, there are four basic levels of measurement, or scales, that we can use in assigning data:

the nominal scale
the ordinal scale
the interval scale
the ratio scale

Typically, the last two scales, interval and ratio, are treated as if they were the same scale, because the difference between them and the former two—nominal and ordinal—is so large. Furthermore, the restrictions on the tools we may use with interval and ratio-level variables are generally the same, but are quite different from those we must employ when we include variables measured at the nominal or ordinal level in our analysis.

As we move from nominal and ordinal scales of measurement scales to interval/ratio scales, we gain precision in our ability to make exact measurements of an attribute; therefore, we say that we are moving "up" the levels of measurement. The more precise the measurement, the "higher" the level of measurement. Nominal is the lowest level of measurement, ordinal is higher, but still lower than interval, which technically is even lower than the ratio level, which is the most precise scale of measurement.

Nominal Scale

When we measure an attribute at the nominal scale, we simply categorize or code countries according to mutually exclusive labels that do not imply an ordering of the values along an implied continuum ranging from "more" or "less." For example, you are no doubt familiar with such demographic variables as "sex" and "religion." Each of these is typically measured on a nominal scale. A researcher might code each female in a data set as a "1," and each male as a "2." Similarly, a Catholic might be coded as a "1," a Jew as a "2," and a Muslim as a "3." Once again, there is no intrinsic value in these codes. Male isn't "more" than female, and Muslim isn't "more" than Catholic.

Also, while it is pertinent to all levels of measurement, it is particularly important in assigning values to nominal variables that we pay attention to two things: First, we must make sure that all categories within a variable are *mutually exclusive*; each value must fit into one, and only one, category. Second, we must make sure that categories are *collectively exhaustive*, that is, that every unit of analysis will fit into a category within our variable.

Within the CROSSNAT.50 data set, REGION is a nominal variable: Each country is labeled according to the geopolitical region within which the country is located (see Table 1.3). We do not assume that a value of 1 (CIS-EE, those countries that were former republics within the Soviet Union, and East European countries) is more or less than a value of 4 (advanced industrial and other West European countries). The value of the variable simply identifies a country as part of a mutually exclusive regional group. Similarly, for the variable CIVIZ, a value of 1 (those countries that are of the Orthodox civilization) implies a mutually exclusive set of countries, different from those that have a value of 3 (Hindu civilization). Whatever defines a country as Orthodox in the variable CIVIZ is assumed to be entirely absent in a country defined as Hindu.

As should be immediately obvious from these two examples, nominal variables are both important and commonly used by students of comparative political analysis. One important aspect of a nominal variable is that it cannot assume the character of transitivity. Transitivity holds that if $1 < 2$ and $2 < 3$, then $1 < 3$. But with nominal variables, if one country is Orthodox and assigned a value of "1," a second is Sinic and assigned a value of "5," and a third is Western and assigned a value of "7," it cannot be assumed that the country with the value of "1" has less of something than the country assigned a value of "5," or that "1" < "5" (other than the exclusive attribute of an Orthodox civilization). Furthermore, a country assigned a value of "7" cannot be assumed to have more of something than the country assigned a value of "5" (or, "7" > "5"). Rather, the country assigned the value of "7" has something different than a "5"—a political culture rooted predominately in Western values and civilizational history, not a Confucian culture and history.

One other important feature of nominal variables relates to their very practical value. They allow us to divide our sample into various groups of countries according to the unique values across the countries, thereby allowing us to further refine and sharpen our focus of analysis.[15] Thus, if we wish to compare GDP values by "civilization/culture" attributes, we may do so if we have coded our countries by the measure CIVIZ.

Ordinal Scale

Ordinal scale measurement assigns values to countries based on a rank-ordering logic. These values are arrayed along a scale ranging from "less" to "more" according to the attribute that the variable represents. The values assigned cannot be assumed to be precise measures of distance. Rather, they reflect the researcher's assessment of the relative ordering of the attributes. For instance, if a researcher asks you whether you favor a particular policy, and then asks you to select one of three categories that best describes your attitude toward this particular policy—(1) unfavorable; (2) indifferent; (3) favorable—the researcher would in essence be employing the ordinal scale of measurement. The numerical value you give to the researcher reflects the degree to which you favor that policy. The common attribute shared by all values (in varying degrees, as specified by the order of the values 1, 2, and 3) is policy, and one's attitude toward that policy. Here, there is a rank order to the values given—a person answering "3" is more favorable towards that policy than a person who answers "1." The values in the ordinal measure are not indicative of a mutually exclusive category, as with REGION or CIVIZ. However, as stated above, these measures are not precise. In other words, you know that every person who answers "3" to the question favors the policy, but you cannot know the degree to which all those who answered "3" actually favor the policy. A person answering "3," for instance, is not exactly three times more favorable than someone answering a "1." The higher value simply means there is more of a disposition to be favorable, but how much more is left unspecified. It is highly unlikely that each person in that category feels exactly the same way towards the policy.

Survey data are not the only data that are measured at the ordinal level. Frequently, students of comparative politics who employ ecological data also require ordinal scale measurements. For instance, in CROSSNAT.50 is the variable CODEFREE. This variable is an alphanumeric variable (it is reflected within CROSSNAT.50 not in terms of numeric codes, but rather in words, or alphabetic characters) measuring whether a country is "Free," "Partly Free," or "Not Free." This measure is drawn on codes produced by Freedom House.[16] A "free" country has extensive free political institutions (not dominated by one political party or a single dictator, or a group of dictators, such as in an oligarchy), a free press, extensive civil liberties and rights guaranteed to individuals, among other attributes. A "partly free" country has fewer of these empirical traits than a "free" country, and a "not free" country has even less—indeed, it is virtually absent any basic freedoms and liberties afforded even a "partly free" country. Many of the individual attributes that the coders of Freedom House evaluate for each country require some degree of "judgment." Thus, this measure is not as exact as measuring the size of a country in thousands of square kilometers.[17]

Actually, Freedom House provides two different measures of the degree of freedom, or democracy, within a country. One is a seven-point scale for both the two basic dimensions of democracy: the civil libertarian dimension, and the "political institutional" dimension. Each measure ranges from 1 to 7. This, too, is technically an ordinal measure, but its greater variance (seven values rather than just three) affords the researcher the opportunity to treat the variable as if it is something slightly more "exact" than a simpler ordinal variable.[18]

The other measurement of democracy offered by Freedom House is the more classic ordinal measure, indicated as CODEFREE in CROSSNAT.50. It assumes much less precision and exactitude than does the other measure, and as such, affords us an excellent example of a common ordinal variable, based on ecological data (and not just survey data). It exhibits all three common and classic traits of an ordinal variable: (1) the numbers or codes reflect a rank order indicating "more" or "less" of something, (2) which, itself, means that the variable does not have a mutually exclusive assumption associated with each of its different values (each value assumes a common underlying attribute—freedom), and (3) the variable assumes transitivity (a country that is "Partly Free" has more freedom than a country that is "Not Free," and a "Free" country has more political and civil freedoms than a country that is "Partly Free" and than a "Not Free" country). We shall revisit these measures in Chapter 7 when discussing various measures of democracy.[19]

The third reason comparativists rely upon ordinal data is more technical and also introduces the second set of rules that govern statistical inference. Namely, data must reasonably approximate a "normal distribution" before certain tools of statistical inference can be properly applied. We will consider this point in more detail in Chapter 5. For now, it is important to note that when the sampling distribution of interval/ratio level data departs sharply from certain assumptions, the researcher has the option of moving down to a lower scale of measurement, to the ordinal scale. This is accomplished by simply grouping the original interval data into ordinal categories and "smoothing" out the variance of a variable, thereby minimizing the effects of distributional problems. If the data are originally measured at the ordinal level, there is very little researchers can do: They cannot readily move to the nominal scale, nor can they move to the interval/ratio scale.

Interval and Ratio Scales

Exact measurement (that is, ratio-level measures) is maximized when we have values that assume equal distance between adjacent values on a scale and have an absolute, real zero point. An absolute zero point means that the zeros in a sample are not arbitrary—they are in fact the total absence of an attribute. An example of a "true" ratio-level scale commonly employed in cross-national analysis is any variable reflecting a value less than zero, such as the annual rate of growth in a country's urban population (URBANRT), or a variable that can have a value of zero, such as the total value of the agriculture sector of an economy as a proportion of the nation's Gross Domestic Product (AGRI, in CROSSNAT.50), or the proportion of the total population in a country who hold a higher educational degree (EDU3, in CROSSNAT.50).

The interval scale assumes equal distance between adjacent values, but lacks an absolute zero point. You can measure the distance precisely between two objects or persons, but your reference is distorted because you lack an absolute zero point. An example of an interval measure is LIFEEXP (or the years an adult within a country can expect to live). In Uganda, it is 42.5 years, while in Japan it is 80 years. We know that the typical Japanese will live 46.9 percent longer than the Ugandan, who will have a life span that is 53.1 percent of that expected by the typical Japanese.

In sum, once researchers have a research question, they must confront the real constraints placed on their research options by the data themselves. Obtaining data that can readily accommodate assumptions of interval- or ratio-scale measurement would be ideal in most circumstances. This, unfortunately, is not always possible or practical. Frequently, researchers cannot obtain the data necessary to explore their question at the more precise scale of measurement. Therefore, they must improvise and rely on measures that step down from these higher scales of precise measurement. In later chapters, we will introduce variables that indeed may allow us to measure them at the interval or ratio scale. However, to accommodate the illustration of various statistical techniques of cross-national analysis, we will often initially measure these attributes at the ordinal level.

Table 2.2 summarizes the logic and practice of applying scales of measurement in cross-national research. For instance, whenever your data were originally measured at interval/ratio level, you have the option of modifying them to allow a rank-ordering, ordinal scale of measurement. One of the most common examples would be test grades. Typically, scores between 90 percent and 100 percent become "A" grades, while scores between 80 percent and 89 percent become "B" grades, and so on.

Ratio-level data can be modified to conform to interval-level data. However, in practice, the most common transformation is to move from interval or ratio level to the ordinal scale. Indeed, as indicated in Table 2.2, you really cannot move to the nominal-level scale if your data were originally measured at interval/ratio or ordinal level. Why? Because when your data were originally measured as ordinal, interval, or ratio, you cannot easily "categorize" these measures into mutually exclusive groups devoid of assumptions of at least "more" or "less" of an attribute. There may be exceptions, but in practice, it is rare. As we will see, it is frequently the case where one must come down from interval/ratio level to ordinal scale. You cannot go up to interval/ratio from data originally measured as ordinal or nominal.[20]

TABLE 2.2 Summary of Optional Treatment of Data at Various Levels of Measurement

	Different Ways of Assigning Numbers to Data			
Levels of Measurement Achieved in Original Data	*Label Scores as Categories*	*Rank Order Scores*	*Equal Distance Between Adjacent Scores (scores of zero are arbitrary)*	*Scores May Assume Absolute Zero (scores of zero are not arbitrary)*
Ratio	Not Possible	Optional	Optional	Definitive Treatment
Interval	Not Possible	Optional	Definitive Treatment	Not Possible
Ordinal	Not Possible	Definitive Treatment	Not Possible	Not Possible
Nominal	Definitive Treatment	Not Possible	Not Possible	Not Possible

The means by which we move down scale to ordinal from interval/ratio levels is referred to as recoding, or collapsing, or computing new measures from existing measures. We will discuss these procedures in Chapters 11 and 17.

CHAPTER SUMMARY

In this chapter, we have explored strategies for comparative political inquiry. We have explored three basic strategies: the case study strategy, the comparable cases strategy, and the cross-national strategy. We have shown how theory, concept formulation, methods, scope of analysis, and sample selection combine to establish the overall research strategy for cross-national research endeavors.

Our primary focus in this regard has been to prepare the student for learning the statistical method and its role in cross-national research as a tool of comparative political inquiry. While case studies and comparative case methods are essential to a well-rounded understanding and appreciation of political behavior and institutional authority, only statistical analysis employed within a cross-national design can provide the necessary degree of comparison that will allow us to significantly advance our generalized understanding of our political world. As we will see in Chapter 3, the statistical method, in combination with a cross-national, cross-cultural analysis, offers the greatest possibilities for generalized findings in political science research.

NOTES

1. See Lawrence Mayer, 1996, *Redefining Comparative Politics: Promise Versus Performance* (Newbury Park, Calif.: Sage Publications); Rod Hague, Martin Harrop, and Shaun Breslin, 1992, *Political Science: A Comparative Introduction* (New York: St. Martin's Press), pp. 23–44; Arend Lijphart, 1971, "Comparative Politics and Comparative Method," *American Political Science Review*, 65: 682–693; Mattei Dogan and G. Pelassey, 1990, *How to Compare Nations* (Chatham, NJ: Chatham House); and Charles C. Ragin, 1987, *The Comparative Method: Moving Beyond Qualitative and Quantitative Strategies* (Berkeley: University of California Press).

2. For an example of a rich and insightful descriptive case study, see Margaret Popkin, 2000, *Peace Without Justice: Obstacles to Building the Rule of Law in El Salvador* (University Park, Pa.: Penn State University Press).

3. For a standard source on the utilities of the case study within comparative politics, see Bernard E. Brown, 1976, "The Case Method in Comparative Politics" in Bernard E. Brown and James Bernard Christoph, eds., *Cases in Comparative Politics* (Boston: Little, Brown), pp. 3-16. For examples of compelling and widely cited analytic case studies, see T. J. Pempel, 1982, *Policy and Politics in Japan: Creative Conservatism* (Philadelphia: Temple University Press); Arend Lijphart, ed., 1981, *Conflict and Coexistence in Belgium: The Dynamics of a Culturally Divided Society* (Berkeley: Institute of International Studies, University of California); Arend Lijphart, 1975, *The Politics of Accommodation: Pluralism and Democracy in the Netherlands* (Berkeley: University of California Press).

4. For two classic examples of the first type of comparable cases strategy of comparative political inquiry, see Gabriel Almond and Sidney Verba, 1963, *The Civic Culture* (Princeton: Princeton University Press) and Arend Lijphart, 1977, *Democracy in Plural Societies* (New Haven: Yale University Press). A more recent example is Scott Mainwaring, 1992, "Presidentialism in Latin America," in Arend Lijphart, ed., *Parliamentary Versus Presidential Government* (Oxford: Oxford University Press), pp. 111–117. As an example of the more expansive approach, see Ronald Inglehart, 1977, *The Silent Revolution* (Princeton: Princeton University Press).

5. Adam Przeworski and Henry Teune, 1970, *The Logic of Comparative Social Inquiry* (New York: Wiley).

6. For an in-depth analysis of the "most-similar" and "most-different" system logic in comparative political analysis, see Theodore Meckstroth, 1975, "'Most Different Systems' and 'Most Similar Systems,'" *Comparative Political Studies* 8 (July): 132–157; and John P. Frendreis, 1983, "Explanations of Variation and Detection of Covariation: The Purpose and Logic of Comparative Analysis," *Comparative Political Studies* 16 (July): 255–272. For an example of applied most-similar systems design within a comparable cases strategy, see John D. Robertson, 1984, "Economic Performance and Transient European Cabinet Administrations: Implications for Consociational Parliamentary Democracies," *International Studies Quarterly* 28 (December): 447–466.

7. For an example of applied most-different systems approach within the comparable cases strategy, see Stein Rokkan, 1973, "Cities, States and Nations: A Dimensional Model for the Study of Contrasts in Development," in S. N. Eisenstadt and Stein Rokkan, eds., *Building States and Nations: Models and Data Resources* (Beverly Hills, Calif.: Sage), pp. 562–600; and Edward C. Page, 1995, "Patterns and Diversity in European State Development," in Jack Hayward and Edward C. Page, eds., *Governing the New Europe* (Durham, N.C.: Duke University Press), pp. 9–43.

8. See Rod Hague, Martin Harrop, and Shaun Breslin, 1998, *Political Science: A Comparative Introduction* (New York: St. Martin's Press), pp. 280–284, for further discussion of the "focused" approaches to comparative political inquiry (that is, case studies and comparable cases).

9. The risks and rewards of the statistical approach to comparative politics, especially when we employ aggregate, ecological data, are considered in Robert W. Jackman, 1985, "Cross-National Statistical Research and the Study of Comparative Politics Systems," *American Journal of Political Science* 29 (January): 161–182; John P. Frendreis, 1983, "Explanations of Variation and Detection of Covariance: The Purpose and Logic of Comparative Analysis," *Comparative Political Studies* 16 (March): 255–272; and John Ravenhill, 1980, "Comparing Regime Performance in Africa: The Limitations of Cross-National Aggregate Analysis," *Journal of Modern African Studies* 18 (March): 99–126.

10. We should note, however, that time-series measurement strategies (not discussed directly in this text) offer greater opportunities for demonstrating causality than strategies devoid of temporal variance. While time series offer the opportunity for more direct tests of causality, they also present problems for most studies of cross-national analysis. The most common approach to time-series analysis in cross-national analysis is to "pool" the variance across both space and time. In other words, you have several time points from which you have collected data for a country. These times points are then added to a sample of other country-time points. Thus, you may have data for 1950, 1955, 1960, 1965, 1970, 1975, 1980, for fifty

countries. However, these types of pooled time series common to cross-national analysis require that special provisions be made to ensure that the results of the analysis are not inaccurate because of compounded error that comes with pooled time series. The issue is technical and beyond the scope of this text. However, the interested student may consult Nathaniel Beck and Jonathon N. Katz, 1995, "What To Do (And Not To Do) With Time Series Cross-Section Data," *American Political Science Review* 89 (September): 634–647; and/or, Nathaniel Beck, Jonathon N. Katz, R. Michael Alverez, Geoffrey Garrett, and Peter Lange, 1993, "Government Partisanship, Labor Organization, and Macroeconomic Performance: A Corrigendum," *American Political Science Review* 87 (December): 945–948. For an example of a pooled time-series model within the cross-national analysis strategy and the special treatment of data required, see Robert L. Perry and John D. Robertson, "Political Markets, Bond Markets, and the Effects of Uncertainty: A Cross-National Analysis," *International Studies Quarterly* 42 (1998): 131–60.

11. Robert D. Putnam (with Robert Leonardi and Raffaella Y. Nanetti), 1993, *Making Democracy Work: Civic Traditions in Modern Italy* (Princeton: Princeton University Press).

12. Samuel P. Huntington, 1996, *The Clash of Civilizations and the Remaking of World Order* (New York: Simon & Schuster).

13. Within CROSSNAT.50, the variable CIVIZ codes the civilization membership for each country in our sample. The value "other" refers to those four countries in which no one of the nine civilizations is dominant. CIVIZ is an "alphanumeric" variable: its values are actual alphabetic characters—words—not numbers. The variable CIVCODES provides numeric values for the formal names listed in CIVIZ. The data are based on Samuel Huntington's analysis (1996) and are obtainable for all countries of the world, since 1800, at Richard Tucker's web page at http://www.vanderbilt.edu/~rtucker/data/clash/.

14. The concept of civilization as proposed by Huntington has been met with both admiration and scorn. Admiration because of its power, simplicity, and effectiveness as a tool to explain the post–cold war world. Scorned, because to many, it is too simplistic, overlooking key cultural differences within broader civilizations (for example, is American culture the same as British, though both are members of the Western civilization?), and because it invites simple but careless stereotypes about the differences that separate different peoples. To Huntington, a civilization is a cultural entity—the broadest cultural entity to which all humans identify in a very meaningful and concrete way. Certainly within each civilization differences in cultural values diverge. Yet, when we look for the broader commonalities, the world seems, to Huntington anyway, divided into nine distinct civilizations, or megacultures. A megaculture influences the way nation-states interact with each other and carries with it important implications for how people of one civilization are likely to act with respect to people of a different civilization in an age of labor mobility and globalization. "Civilizations are differentiated from each other by history, language, culture, tradition, and most important, religion. The people of different civilizations have different views on the relations between God and man, the individual and the group, the citizen and the state, parents and children, husband and wife, as well as differing views of the relative importance of rights and responsibilities, liberty and authority, equality and hierarchy. These differences are the products of centuries. . . . They are far more fundamental than differences among political ideologies or political regimes." (Huntington, 1996, p. 3). For an extended historical comparative analysis of civilizations and culture, see Fernand Braudel, 1994, *A History of Civilizations*, translated by Richard Mayne (New York: Penguin Books).

15. Other nominal variables of interest within CROSSNAT.50 are ELECTSYS (that is, the technical type of electoral system governing national elections in each country), FROMCODE (indicating from which country/empire, or under what circumstances a country originally evolved), and TYPE1950 (indicating the type of authority structure, such as democratic or authoritarian, that characterized a country in 1950).

16. Freedom House was formed in 1948 and is a nonprofit/nonpartisan organization committed to promoting democracy and freedom around the world. It offers a wealth of insight and analysis on the changing shape and nature of democracy around the world. More information on Freedom House and its data can be obtained by visiting the web site at http://www.freedomhouse.org/.

17. It is important to keep in mind two basic fallacies in the social science. One is the *ecological fallacy*, and is particularly relevant to the use of ecological data. The ecological fallacy holds that one cannot infer to individual units of analysis when working from data computed from groups. For students of cross-national analysis, this means we cannot infer that *individual citizens* within a country we code as "democratic", for instance, are in fact democratic in their political personal disposition. Nor can we say that a particular American, for instance, is richer than a particular Ukrainian, just because the United States has a much higher per capita income than Ukraine. These are examples of inferring from data based on grouped, or ecological data, to the individuals within the units from which the data have been aggregated. The second fallacy common within social science research is the *individualistic fallacy*. This fallacy is the opposite of the ecological fallacy. This fallacy is crucial to students of comparative politics when working with survey data—that is, data based on public opinion surveys of citizens within a country. We will explore the use of such data in comparative politics in detail in Chapter 10. For now, however, we can familiarize ourselves with this crucial fallacy. For instance, if we find that 51 percent of respondents polled in Hungary express support for democracy, we cannot infer that Hungary is a democratic country. We cannot use data drawn from individuals to construct an ecological measure. Ecological data must be constructed properly from units at the level at which all conclusions will be directed. Thus, if we wish to infer to countries, we must collect data across the nation-state unit. If, however, we wish to measure attitudes across countries, we must collect data at the level of the individual (that is, opinion polls). This would be an individualistic fallacy. For more detail, see Chava Frankfort-Nachmias and David Nachmias, 2000, *Research Methods in the Social Sciences*, sixth edition (New York: Worth Publishers), pp. 48–49.

18. The variables POL97 and CIV97 within CROSSNAT.50 are the seven-point measures of civil liberties and political freedoms for each country, as of 1997.

19. Within CROSSNAT.50, the variable CODE2000 reports the ordinal values of freedom for each country as of the year 2000. This measure is also taken from Freedom House, as are the variables PRESS (an ordinal measure of press freedom as of 1997), TYPE1900, TYPE1950, and TYPE2000 (nominal measures of the type of political authority in a country as of 1900, 1950, and the year 2000, respectively).

20. One must be careful in using ratio-level data. Important variance might be masked in one of the variables used to construct the ratio. This, in turn, can lead to very misleading measures within a cross-national sample. For example, in Chapter 11 we will consider the variable GENDEV, or the degree to which women in a country have achieved equal social development status with men, as determined by measured degrees of literacy, life expectancy, educational

attainment, and so on among women in that country. This measure is drawn from the United Nations, which labels it the *Gender Development Index* (GDI). The United Nations also computes a *Human Development Index* measure (HDI), which combines social development for both men and women. This variable is in CROSSNAT.50 as HUMDEV. From these two development measures, the organization computes a third measure, the *Gender Equality Index* (GENEQ in CROSSNAT.50). This is simply the ratio of the *Gender Development Index* to *Human Development Index* for each country. However, by computing this ratio measure, the original variance in the Gender Development Index is radically transformed. Why? Because its variance is now standardized, in effect, to the variance in the *Human Development Index*. As the *Human Development Index* is based on values drawn from the *Gender Development Index* itself, virtually all countries in the sample will assume scores near 1.00 as a ratio score for gender equality (GDI). Thus, as a measure of the extent to which different countries have achieved comparative rates of development for women, the Gender Equality Index would offer an inaccurate representation of gender development itself, thereby offering a slightly misleading cross-national assessment of the nature of social, economic, and political differences across genders in a cross-national sample. For example, Canada records a value of .932 for HDI and a value of .928 for GDI, for a Gender Equality score of .9957. However, Uganda records an HDI score of .404 and a GDI score of .397, for a Gender Equality score of .9827. If one were to argue that social development among women were equal to that among men, they would be correct. This is also the case with Canada. However, it would be inaccurate to conclude that based on the Gender Equality ratio measure, Uganda's social development for women was equal to that found in Canada.

3

The Role of Univariate Analysis in the Science of Comparing Nations

Terms: *Statistical Method, Basic Rules of Statistical Analysis, Central Tendency Statistics (relative frequencies, cumulative frequencies, percentiles, mean, median, variance, standard deviation), Normal Distribution, Histograms*
Concepts: Nation-State Longevity
Demonstrations: Histograms, 3.1; Treating Sharp Departures from Normal Distributions, 3.2

In this chapter, we will consider how the statistical approach, beginning with the most basic "univariate" techniques, can be applied to the cross-national analysis of political phenomena. In doing so, the student may also highlight the individual country or groups of countries that stand apart on one or more of the important political attributes explored. Specifically, we will demonstrate how descriptive statistics are used to summarize four basic variables within our sample CROSSNAT.50: POPULATE (population), AREA (area), GDP97 (wealth), and AGE1800 (sovereign duration in years since 1800). Because we will be working with ecological data measured at the interval/ratio level, we will focus on frequency distributions, percentiles, medians, means, variance and standard deviations, skewness, standard error, confidence intervals, and histograms.

CENTRAL TENDENCY MEASURES

The most common statistical tool employed by students of comparative politics is univariate analysis. Such analysis is generally the first step in the statistical presentation of your cross-national analysis. The object of such analyses is the description of data. In other words, if we had a sample with only a few cases, we could examine the data in their entirety. We could easily describe each case and how each compares to the others. However, if our sample includes hundreds of cases, such a method of describing the data would be far too cumbersome. We must, therefore, use statistics that summarize the data. Such descriptive statistics are developed by applying such methods as frequency distributions (relative and cumulative), percentiles (deciles, quartiles, quintiles), bar charts, modes, medians, means, standard deviations, skewness, standard errors, confidence intervals, and histogram analyses.[1]

Frequency Distributions

We begin with frequency distributions. These statistics are quite simple: they are employed for the purpose of exploring the distribution of scores within our sample. If we assume we have a random sample and have not biased the selection of cases included in the sample, we may reasonably infer from these sample statistics to the target population of populous countries. From frequency distributions, we can gain a sense of the sampling distribution and also determine whether we have any extreme outliers within our sample. We shall discuss these technical terms in more detail below. Knowing something of the frequency distribution will facilitate a clearer understanding of these terms. For purposes of a simple demonstration, we will focus on AREA within CROSSNAT.50. Table 3.1 shows the frequency distributions for this variable.[2]

The first column of numbers in Table 3.1 corresponds to values of AREA within the sample (CROSSNAT.50). Frequency tables list the scores in the sample for the particular attribute in ascending order (from lowest value to highest value). Thus, the smallest value for AREA is 40840 (40,840 square kilometers); the largest value in the sample is 17075400 (17,075,400 square kilometers).

The second column in Table 3.1 represents the *relative frequency* of the value for the attribute reported in the first column. A relative frequency is the proportion of cases in a sample of a respective score. Because AREA is an interval-level variable, and because the likelihood of two or more countries having exactly the same size is extremely remote, we should not be surprised to see that the relative frequency for each value is the same: in this case, 2 (one country comprises 2 percent of a sample of 50). There is, in other words, one country (or case) per value of AREA.

The fifth column is the *cumulative frequency* for the values in the first column. The cumulative frequency represents the total proportion of the sample falling between the lowest score recorded in the sample for that attribute, and any particular score in the sample. We note, for instance, that only 4 percent of the sample falls between 40840 and 65610. However, 24 percent of the sample falls between a value of 40840 and a value of 244880. When you reach the highest value in the sample (17075400),

TABLE 3.1 Frequency Distribution, AREA (SPSS10)

AREA Area in Square Km. (WDI)				
Valid	*Frequency*	*Percent*	*Valid Percent*	*Cumulative Percent*
40840	1	2.0	2.0	2.0
65610	1	2.0	2.0	4.0
78860	1	2.0	2.0	6.0
99260	1	2.0	2.0	8.0
131960	1	2.0	2.0	10.0
144000	1	2.0	2.0	12.0
147180	1	2.0	2.0	14.0
163610	1	2.0	2.0	16.0
238390	1	2.0	2.0	18.0
238540	1	2.0	2.0	20.0
241040	1	2.0	2.0	22.0
244880	1	2.0	2.0	24.0
283560	1	2.0	2.0	26.0
300000	1	2.0	2.0	28.0
301270	1	2.0	2.0	30.0
323250	1	2.0	2.0	32.0
329750	1	2.0	2.0	34.0
356980	1	2.0	2.0	36.0
377800	1	2.0	2.0	38.0
390760	1	2.0	2.0	40.0
446550	1	2.0	2.0	42.0
505990	1	2.0	2.0	44.0
513120	1	2.0	2.0	46.0
551500	1	2.0	2.0	48.0
580370	1	2.0	2.0	50.0
587040	1	2.0	2.0	52.0
603700	1	2.0	2.0	54.0
756630	1	2.0	2.0	56.0
774820	1	2.0	2.0	58.0
796100	1	2.0	2.0	60.0
912050	1	2.0	2.0	62.0
923770	1	2.0	2.0	64.0
945090	1	2.0	2.0	66.0
1001450	1	2.0	2.0	68.0
1138910	1	2.0	2.0	70.0
1221040	1	2.0	2.0	72.0
1285220	1	2.0	2.0	74.0
1633190	1	2.0	2.0	76.0
1904570	1	2.0	2.0	78.0
1958200	1	1.0	2.0	80.0
2344860	1	2.0	2.0	82.0
2381740	1	2.0	2.0	84.0
2780400	1	2.0	2.0	86.0
3287590	1	2.0	2.0	88.0
7741220	1	2.0	2.0	90.0
8547400	1	2.0	2.0	92.0
9363520	1	2.0	2.0	94.0
9596960	1	2.0	2.0	96.0
9970610	1	2.0	2.0	98.0
17075400	1	2.0	2.0	100.0
Total	50	100.0	100.0	

you have consumed 100 percent of the sample. Therefore, the *cumulative* frequency corresponding to the value of 17075400 is 100.00.

The cumulative frequency allows you to gain a sense of proportion and more readily reveals interesting and potentially important information about the sampling distribution. For instance, note that 48 percent of the sample falls between 40,840 and 551,500 square kilometers in size. Yet, this range constitutes only 3.2 percent of the total range of values in the sample. This is determined by computing the range—which is the difference between 40,840 (the lowest value) and 17,075,400 (the highest value), or, 17,034,560 square kilometers. In other words, while we have covered 48 percent of the countries in our sample (in ascending order of area from the lowest to the twenty-fourth largest country), we have only accounted for 3.2 percent of the total area of all the countries in our sample. This is our first indication that AREA is skewed—a term we will turn to in more detail later in this chapter.

Percentile Analysis

Another means of describing a sample distribution is to rely on percentiles. A percentile represents the proportion of scores that fall at or below a given score for an attribute within a sample. Commonly, researchers use a particular percentile to describe distributions. This is the quartile. A quartile reports the scores that divide the sample into quarters. Thus, the First Quartile is the score that separates the smallest 25 percent of the scores in the sample from the largest 75 percent of the scores for an attribute in the sample. The Second Quartile is the score that separates the sample into two exact halves—50 percent of the cases in the sample fall below this value for a particular attribute, and 50 percent of the cases in the sample are above this value. The Second Quartile has a more common name—the median. The Third Quartile reports the score that separates the 75 percent of all cases that fall at or below the score from the 25 percent of cases in the sample that fall at or above this score.

There are other percentiles that researchers may use to describe a sample. Quintiles divide the sample into fifths, deciles into tenths, and so on. When computing percentiles with interval/ratio-level data, finding the exact value of a score corresponding to the First Quartile, or even the median, is not as direct as it may seem. Indeed, different statistical programs use different procedures for dealing with the inexactness of using these percentiles with interval/ratio-level data. When using ordinal data, there are very specific equations that can be employed to compute the percentiles (see Chapter 12). However, these equations do not always work as neatly for interval/ratio-level data. Consequently, when using ecological data measured at the interval/ratio level (such as most of the variables found in CROSSNAT.50), it is important to note that the exact values of a score corresponding to particular percentiles will vary depending on how a program or researcher deals with the inevitable inexactness associated with these statistics. Nonetheless, one need not exaggerate the issue. Generally, a very clear

TABLE 3.2 Basic Central Tendency Statistics, AREA (SPSS 10)

Statistics

AREA Area in Square Km. (WDI)

N	Valid	50
	Missing	0
Mean		1932531.00
Std. Error of Mean		482334.29
Median		583705.00
Std. Deviation		3410618.44
Variance		1.163E + 13
Skewness		2.793
Std. Error of Skewness		.337
Kurtosis		8.148
Std. Error of Kurtosis		.662
Range		17034560
Minimum		40840
Maximum		17075400
Sum		96626550
Percentiles	25	273890.00
	50	583705.00
	75	1701035.00

and reliable assessment of the sample distribution can be confidently gained from the use of percentiles in cross-national analysis.

Let us consider the variable AREA in CROSSNAT.50. What would be the score corresponding to the twenty-fifth percentile (or First Quartile) with respect to AREA in CROSSNAT.50? Within SPSS 10, one may merely specify in the FREQUENCIES command an option for quartile breakdown, or for any other percentile breakdown you desire.[3] Table 3.2 notes the statistical output associated with the frequency analysis obtained from SPSS 10 for the variable AREA. This table specifies all of the basic central tendency measures one would ordinarily require for a thorough initial examination of a variable. Focusing solely on the percentile analysis (see bottom of Table 3.2 where the quartiles are reported), we note that 25 percent of the sample lies between 40,840 square kilometers and 273,890 square kilometers. The second quartile, or those countries whose size places them between the twenty-fifth percentile and the fiftieth percentile (or, the *median* value), range in value between 273,891 square kilometers and 583,705 square kilometers (583705 is the sample median, or the value that divides the sample in half, indicating that exactly half the sample is smaller than 583,705 square kilometers, and half the sample of countries is larger than 583,705 square kilometers). The third quartile (those countries between the fiftieth percentile and the seventy-fifth percentile) consists of those countries whose size varies between 583,706 square kilometers and 1,701,035 square kilometers. This means that the fourth and final quartile (those countries between the seventy-fifth percentile and the hundredth percentile, or the largest value in the sample for the variable) of countries

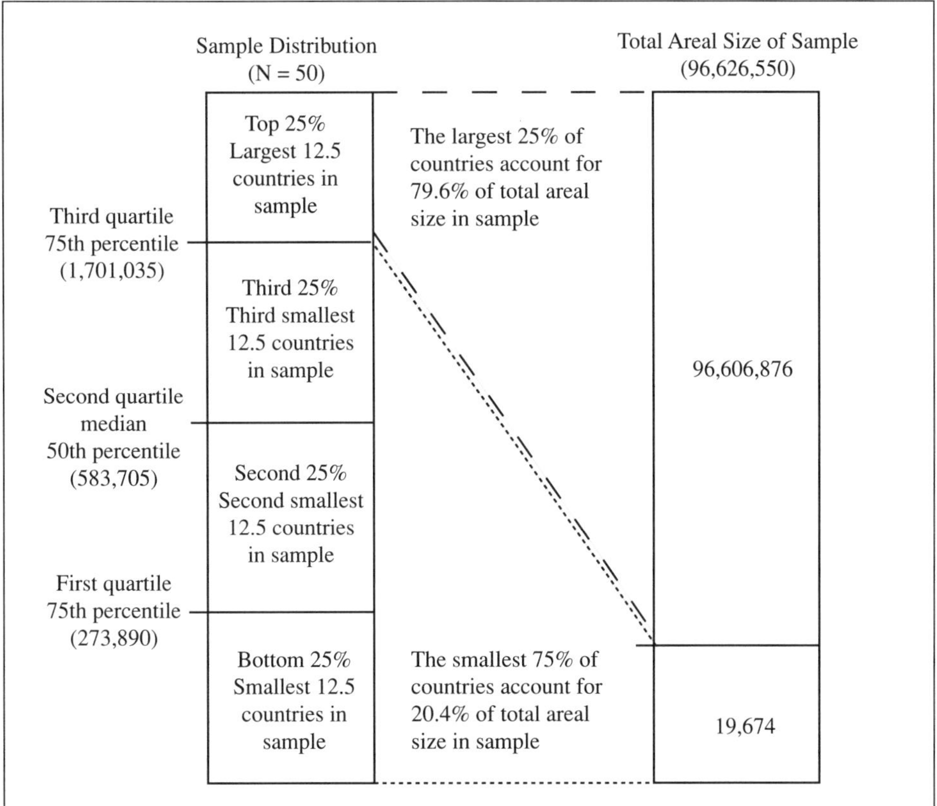

FIGURE 3.1 Illustration of Percentile Analysis of AREA

within our sample are those countries whose size lies between 1,701,036 square kilometers and 17,075,400 square kilometers.

With percentiles, we may elaborate on our earlier assessment of the skewed nature of our sample (with respect to the attribute, AREA). If we were to sum the total size of all fifty countries in CROSSNAT.50, we would find the total land size to be equal to 96,626,550, or 96,626,550 square kilometers.[4] If we sum the areal size (AREA) for those countries in ascending order up to and including the seventy-fifth percentile (all those countries whose size is less than or equal to 1,701,035 square kilometers), we note that thirty-eight countries account for a total of 19,674,080 square kilometers.[5] This constitutes 20.4 percent of the total areal size of all fifty countries in the sample (96,626,550). In other words, 79.6 percent of the total areal size of the sample still lies within the largest 25 percent (or, to be exact, 12.5) countries of the sample. Once again, we have evidence of something we call skewness—something we will discuss in detail shortly. *In other words, a few countries are extremely large, while most are, relatively speaking, rather small.* Figure 3.1 illustrates this observation. Table 3.3 presents the distribution list in CROSSNAT.50 for the variable AREA. The table lists the values of AREA for each country in the sample, in ascending order.[6]

TABLE 3.3 Distribution List, AREA (SPSS 10)

		Country	AREA
1		Netherlands	40840
2		Sri Lanka	65610
3		Czech	78860
4		Korea	99260
5		Greece	131960
6		Bangladesh	144000
7		Nepal	147180
8		Tunisia	163610
9		Romania	238390
10		Ghana	238540
11		Uganda	241040
12		United Kingdom	244280
13		Ecuador	283560
14		Philippines	300000
15		Italy	301270
16		Poland	323250
17		Malaysia	329750
18		Germany	356980
19		Japan	377800
20		Zimbabwe	390760
21		Morocco	446550
22		Spain	505990
23		Thailand	513120
24		France	551500
25		Kenya	580370
26		Madagascar	587040
27		Ukraine	603700
28		Chile	756630
29		Turkey	774820
30		Pakistan	796100
31		Venezuela	912050
32		Nigeria	923770
33		Tanzania	945090
34		Egypt	1001450
35		Colombia	1138910
36		South Africa	1221040
37		Peru	1285220
38		Iran	1633190
39		Indonesia	1904570
40		Mexico	1958200
41		Congo	2344860
42		Algeria	2381740
43		Argentina	2780400
44		India	3287590
45		Australia	7741220
46		Brazil	8547400
47		United States	9363520
48		China	9596960
49		Canada	9970610
50		Russia	17075400
Total	N	50	50

This detailed discussion illustrates the importance of using a percentile analysis. If we have a random sample, and we have no reason to assume that our sample is biased in its selection of countries, we can draw the reasonable conclusion from the analysis of percentiles and frequency distributions that size is skewed not only in the sample, but skewed in the target population as well. Because skewness renders some statistics misleading, it is often more appropriate to rely on the percentiles (including the median) when reporting summary statistics of skewed variables.

The Sample Mean

The mean (denoted as $\bar{X}$ is commonly known as the "average" value of a score in a sample. Technically speaking, the mean is an appropriate summary of the sample only if the data are measured at the interval/ratio level, though in very large samples of ordinal-scale data, such as with survey data, the mean will be used occasionally (see Chapter 12 for an illustration). Technically, when we are working with samples that are small (certainly samples of less than 120 observations) and contain ordinal-level data, the appropriate summary measure of the sample is the mode or median, but not the mean. If we are working with nominal data, we rely only upon the mode to summarize the central tendency of the data in the sample.

The power of the mean as a tool for analysis lies in the fact that unlike the median and mode, the mean takes all scores directly into account. The mean is simply the best prediction we have of what an individual score in a sample would be if we knew nothing else about the country (or case, if not a cross-national sample). For instance, if we knew nothing else about Indonesia, we would predict that the size of Indonesia would be the mean value of AREA within our sample.

What makes the mean the best predictor of a country's score within a sample? The mean is the point in the sample around which the individual scores for a variable in a sample are "balanced," or, in other words, the point around which the variation of scores is minimized. The variation of a score is the difference between the actual score of a country and the expected score of a country. The actual score is what we observe, or, what we have entered in the database. The expected score is the reference point by which we compare all actual scores in the sample. In univariate analysis, this reference point is the mean. When we subtract the value of each score in the sample from the mean, and sum these individual differences, the sum will always total 0; in other words, the sum of individual variations in a sample is always equal to zero. We say that the mean is an efficient measure of a sample because it takes into account the actual values of each case in the sample. In this sense, the mean offers a simple and meaningful statistical summary of all scores in the sample. This is, of course, much more useful and potentially powerful information than that which we would have with the median or the mode alone. The mean allows us to make a "reasonable" estimate of the "typical" score in a sample (assuming we have a random sample and a sampling distribution that does not sharply depart from a normal distribution)—something neither the median nor mode can provide.

To summarize, the mean considers each score, the difference between each score in the sample, and the size of the sample. Neither the median nor mode take each of these facts into account. The formula for the mean $\bar{X}$ is:

$$\bar{X} = \frac{\Sigma (X_i)}{N} \qquad \text{Formula 3.1}$$

where X_i is each individual score in the sample, ΣX_i signifies the summing of each of the individual scores in the sample, and N represents the number of cases in the sample (excluding any missing values for individual cases, if there are missing data).

We see from Table 3.2 that the mean of AREA is 1,932,531. From this output we can conclude that, knowing nothing else about a country, we would expect a typical country's size to be 1,932,531 square kilometers. Of course, as our sample is a systematic sample based on the largest countries in the world, this would be a hazardous guess. Actually, it would be more appropriate to say that among the most "populous" seventy-five countries of the world, the mean size would be 1,932,531 square kilometers. If we were to include the remaining 140 or so countries, the average would drop significantly, as the remaining countries of the world are increasingly smaller in size than those included within our systematic sample.[7]

The Mean and the Sample Distribution

The mean, in conjunction with the median and standard deviation (a term we shall explain shortly) and other statistics of univariate analysis, can be used to derive a summary assessment of the sampling distribution. In the case of CROSSNAT.50, we can compare the mean to the percentiles already computed to confirm what we already know: The sample distribution of AREA is certainly not a "normal" distribution. How do we know this? First, we already know from Table 3.2 that the median score for AREA in our sample is 583,705 square kilometers (this, recall, is also the fiftieth percentile). The mean in this sample is far larger than the median (1,932,531 > 583,705). If the median represents the value that divides the number of countries in the sample into equal halves, we can see clearly that the value of the mean lies well down the list of countries that are included (Table 3.3) in the "top" 50 percent of scores for AREA in the sample.

In a perfect normal distribution, the mean, median, and mode are identical. In reality, we rarely find this in cross-national samples. However, a difference of this magnitude (583,705 versus 1,932,531) is a sharp departure from a reasonable difference that might ordinarily occur in most cross-national samples. Thus, the *typical* score for AREA is estimated to be well into the largest 25 percent of the sample (or Fourth Quartile). This would hardly constitute a *typical* score for an empirical attribute in a sample that is normally distributed. Because the sample is skewed with a disproportionately small number of very large countries, the mean actually represents a misleading picture of the "typical" country's size. These very large countries are "pulling" the mean toward them, and away from the much more numerous smaller countries—countries that actually come closer to reflecting the "typical" size of "populous" countries. This underlines the fact that the mean is highly sensitive to extreme values (that is, the size of the mean is being determined by a few very, very large countries in the sample; to be exact, Russia, China, the United States, and Canada, as can be seen in Table 3.3).

In summary, we see that first, means are very sensitive to scores that are quite different (either much smaller or much larger) than the majority of scores in the sample, and second, that the mean can be a very misleading summary statistic for univariate analysis if it is used by itself, and if the sample distribution is skewed (as is the distribution for AREA). If we concluded that the typical populous country had a size of 1,932,531 square kilometers, we would be correct. However, we would be remiss if we did not also report the standard deviation (to be explained below) and relevant statistics from the frequency distributions and/or the percentile analysis. These additional statistics common to univariate analysis would provide the necessary reference with which one could evaluate the mean relative to the sampling distribution (see Table 3.2). By comparing the mean to the median we have confirmed what frequency distributions have already revealed to us: The sample is skewed. We will have much more to say about skewed distributions. For now, these illustrations should make it clear that the mean is a powerful tool, and like all such powerful tools, it must be used cautiously and in its proper context. The utility of this statistic is vast (as we will see as we proceed through subsequent chapters). For this reason, extra care should be taken when applying the mean as a summary of a sample. It must always be evaluated in the context of the sampling distribution.

The Sample Variance (s^2)

As should be clear from the discussion of the mean, the variance of a sample is closely related to the sample mean. Ultimately, the variance is more useful in combination with the mean than are the percentiles and medians. Indeed, the mean without the variance is as useful to students of cross-national analysis as is an automobile without tires to a racecar driver. The potential power is there, but to effectively use this power, students must be able to transfer the power from a potential capacity to an actual effect. In cross-national analysis, as in all statistical analysis of data, we must be able to demonstrate with a reasonable degree of confidence and credibility that our sample accurately reflects what we will find in the target population—again, within reason.

As we know, the mean cannot tell us anything about the sample distribution. This prevents us, therefore, from making any assessment of the accuracy of the sample as a reasonable reflection of the population. In this sense, the mean alone prevents us from knowing whether we can be reasonably confident about our inferences from the sample to the population—the principal purpose of undertaking quantitative cross-national analysis in the first place. After all, without this inferential capacity, we cannot generalize from our findings and cannot test nor develop theory. Such confidence comes only when we can estimate the variance in the sample. There are two basic measures of a sample's variance. One is the nominal variance in the sample, labeled the *variance*. The second is the *standard deviation*, which is a standardized measure of variance. Because the standard deviation is derived from the variance, we will turn our attention first to the variance of a sample, then proceed to the more important, and commonly applied, standard deviation.

The variance statistic is a measure of the aggregate deviation of scores in the sample from the mean of the sample. It is, therefore, derived from the variation of individual scores from the mean. Specifically, the variance for a sample (s^2) is computed according to the following formula:

$$s^2 = \frac{\Sigma (X_i - \bar{X})^2}{N - 1} \qquad \text{Formula 3.2}$$

Thus, to calculate the variance for a sample (s^2), we (1) subtract from each score in the sample (X_i) the sample mean ($\bar{X}$), (2) square each of these differences, (3) sum these squared differences, across the sample, (4) subtract the value of 1 from the total number of observations in the sample (N–1), and (5) divide the sum of the squared differences by the degrees of freedom (N–1).

Step 4 determines the degrees of freedom for the sample. This determines how free any hypothetical score is to vary in size. The fewer the restrictions on any hypothetical score to vary, the larger the degrees of freedom. The greater the degrees of freedom in a sample, the more confidence we have in our estimates of the population drawn from the sample. A common restriction is the actual size of the sample itself. Thus, the larger the sample, the smaller the restriction, and the greater the degrees of freedom, and the more confidence we have in our statistical estimates. We will return to the concept of the degrees of freedom in more detail beginning in Chapter 5.

Subtracting 1 from the sample size (N–1) is not necessary with very large samples (because large samples very likely approximate the population). However, it is customary that we always set the denominator for the computation of the variance to N-1 for any cross-national sample of ecological data, such as CROSSNAT.50.You will remember that in a fraction, when the denominator decreases (as in N-1) and the numerator remains constant, the numerical value of the entire fraction increases. When we employ cross-national ecological data, we are using data that are typically few in number; hence the variance is restricted, especially when using countries as the unit of analysis (after all, there are only a limited number of countries in the world at any given time). When working with survey data, however, you will find that most statistical packages relax the degrees of freedom restrictions and do not set the denominator to N-1, but rather leave the denominator set to simply N. Many statistical packages such as SPSS 10 customarily set the denominator to N-1, unless the sample size is over 500.

The larger s^2, the greater the dispersion of scores around the mean; the smaller s^2, the more clustered and tight the range of values around the mean of the sample. The sample variance (s^2) is a crucial statistic in calculating more powerful measures of association, which we will begin considering in Chapter 9. The variance has limited practical application. Of much greater utility is the standard deviation, which is based on the variance.

As is reported in Table 3.2, the variance of the sample of AREA is 1.163E+13, which is scientific notation for 11630000000000 (or, 11,632,318,160,201.02, to be exact). When numbers become quite large, SPSS 10 and other advanced statistical programs will use shorthand notation, or the scientific notation, for purposes of convenience. We cannot attach any meaningful interpretation to this number. What we need is a standard deviation, which places the variance back into a scale corresponding to the original data.

The Sample Standard Deviation (s)

Variance, as we have seen, has little intuitive meaning, and is therefore of limited applied value for students of social statistics. The central drawback to the variance statistic is that it does not "standardize" its scale to make comparisons across samples easy. By squaring the individual deviations in the computation of the variance statistics, we have removed the variance statistics from the scale of the variable itself. To put the variance back to the scale of the variable, we simply take the square root of the variance. By doing so, we compute the *standard deviation*. This statistic is critical for interpretation of samples and dispersion.

The standard deviation (s) is the typical deviation of a score from the sample mean. Thus, its formula:

$$s = \sqrt{s^2}$$ Formula 3.3

$$s^2 = \sqrt{\frac{\Sigma (X_i - \bar{X})^2}{N - 1}}$$ Formula 3.4

The standard deviation of AREA in CROSSNAT.50 is 3,410,618.44 (see Table 3.2). Therefore, in our sample, the typical country deviates by 3,410,618.44 square kilometers from the statistical mean. The larger the standard deviation—*relative to the mean*—the larger the spread of values in the sample for a particular variable. The smaller the standard deviation—*relative to the mean*—the more concentrated are the values across a sample for a particular variable.

We must always evaluate a standard deviation in the context of the variable's scale of measurement, and with specific reference to the sample mean for that variable. Therefore, with a smaller standard deviation, *relative to the mean*, we know we have a greater probability of reducing our error in predicting the value of any individual score of a variable based on the sample mean for that variable. The larger the standard deviation—*relative to the mean*—the greater the error we can expect in trying to estimate accurately a particular score from the mean of the sample.

We also know that when the standard deviation is quite different from the mean, we have a sampling distribution that is skewed. The larger the difference between the mean and standard deviation, the greater the departure from a "perfect" normal distribution. Note that the standard deviation for AREA is *larger* than the mean. This indicates a sample with great variability of scores, suggesting sharp skewness in the distribution of AREA.

The mean and the standard deviation are the workhorse statistics for statisticians and for students of cross-national analysis. More often than not, more credible and reliable information can be gleaned about a sample and a particular attribute from the mean and standard deviation than from many more "sophisticated" statistics employed by social scientists. Because all of the most sophisticated measures of hypothesis testing (employing interval/ratio-level data) are based on an analysis of variance and estimates of typical scores for an attribute within a sample, all of the most sophisticated tools of hypothesis testing and analysis are derived from the mean and the standard deviation (or the variance). We will return to the standard deviation in Chapter 4 when we consider standardized scores (z-scores) and their utility to cross-national analysis.

Recapping Frequencies, Percentiles, Means, Medians, and Standard Deviations

To summarize our discussion of univariate analysis to this point, recall that we drew an important distinction between a sample and a population. Assuming that our sample in CROSSNAT.50 is a reasonably accurate reflection of the population of the *most populous countries* over a defined space and time, we can conclude from our initial examination of the central tendency analysis that:

- Fifty percent of the sample of countries fall at or below 583,705 square kilometers in areal size.
- The largest 25 percent of populous countries (with respect to areal size) account for over 79 percent of the total areal size within our sample. This is a clear indication of a skewed sample distribution for AREA.
- The typical populous country is 1,932,531 square kilometers in size ($\bar{X}$ = 1932531.00). Given the skewness in sample distribution, it would be misleading

to assume that one can easily predict any individual country's areal size in the population based solely on the mean.

- The typical country in our sample deviates 341,618.44 thousand square kilometers from the mean (standard deviation = 341618.44)—a relatively large deviation when we consider the sample mean is only 1,932,531 thousand square kilometers.

The most important conclusion to draw from the univariate statistics to this point is that the size of the standard deviation relative to the mean, as well as the size of the median relative to the mean, indicate quite vividly that the sample is *skewed*. There are some countries that are substantially *larger* in size than others, and therefore are distorting the mean as an accurate reflection of the typical areal size of our sample. This does not mean that the mean is wrong, but rather that the mean is simply a misleading estimate of what we would describe as the "typical" size for populous countries. This brings us to that part of univariate analysis where we focus exclusively on the *shape of the distribution*, an essential aspect of central tendency analysis.

Finally, to highlight the calculations lying behind the mean, variance, and standard deviation, Table 3.4 demonstrates the computation of each statistic for AREA in CROSSNAT.50. The first column lists the fifty countries in the sample (in alphabetical order). The second column lists the actual value of AREA, the third column reports the residual deviation of the score from the sample mean. The fourth and final column lists the residual deviations, squared. The sum of the squared deviations, divided by N-1 (or, 49 in this case) represents the basis upon which the variance (s^2) and the standard deviation (s)—the square root of s^2— are computed, in accordance with Formulas 3.3 and 3.4.

SAMPLE DISTRIBUTION

Sample distributions refer to the proportional distribution of scores for an attribute within a sample. A "perfect" normal distribution assumes the shape of a symmetric curve with respect to proportional distribution of scores for a variable within a sample. Exploring the sample distribution is an essential aspect of univariate (also known as central tendency) analysis. Comparing a given sample distribution to the "normal distribution" is a habit that all students should develop before proceeding to more sophisticated techniques of cross-national data analysis. In this section, we will consider the specific aspects of a sample distribution's shape, how to recognize common patterns concerning the shape of a normal curve, and how to interpret these different shapes. Before we do so, however, it is important that we keep four points in mind when considering the shape of sampling distributions.

First, a "perfect" normal distribution is not likely to occur very often in a cross-national sample wherein the unit of analysis is the country (such as in CROSSNAT.50).

TABLE 3.4 Example of Basic Central Tendency Measures (AREA)

COUNTRY	*AREA*	*Residual (AREA - mean)*	*Residual²*
Algeria	2381740	449209	201788725681
Argentina	2780400	847869	718881841161
Australia	7741220	5808689	33740867898721
Bangladesh	144000	-1788531	3198843137961
Brazil	8547400	6614869	43756491887161
Canada	9970610	8038079	64610714010241
Chile	756630	-1175901	1382743161801
China	9596960	7664429	58743471896041
Colombia	1138910	-793621	629834291641
Congo	2344860	412329	170015204241
Czech	78860	-1853671	3436096176241
Ecuador	283560	-1648971	2719105358841
Egypt	1001450	-931081	866911828561
France	551500	-1381031	1907246622961
Germany	356980	-1575551	2482360953601
Ghana	238540	-1693991	2869605508081
Greece	131960	-1800571	3242055926041
India	3287590	1355059	1836184893481
Indonesia	1904570	-27961	781817521
Iran	1633190	-299341	89605034281
Italy	301270	-1631261	2661012450121
Japan	377800	-1554731	2417188482361
Kenya	580370	-1352161	1828339369921
Korea	99260	-1833271	3360882559441
Madagascar	587040	-1345491	1810346031081
Malaysia	329750	-1602781	2568906933961
Mexico	1958200	25669	658897561
Morocco	446550	-1485981	2208139532361
Nepal	147180	-1785351	3187478193201
Netherlands	40840	-1891691	3578494839481
Nigeria	923770	-1008761	1017598755121
Pakistan	796100	-1136431	1291475417761
Peru	1285220	-647311	419011530721
Philippines	300000	-1632531	2665157465961
Poland	323250	-1609281	2589785336961
Romania	238390	-1694141	2870113727881
Russia	17075400	15142869	229306481551161
South Africa	1221040	-711491	506219443081
Spain	505990	-1426541	2035019224681
Sri Lanka	65610	-1866921	3485394020241
Tanzania	945090	-987441	975039728481
Thailand	513120	-1419411	2014727586921
Tunisia	163610	-1768921	3129081504241
Turkey	774820	-1157711	1340294759521
Uganda	241040	-1691491	2861141803081
Ukraine	603700	-1328831	1765791826561
United Kingdom	244880	-1687651	2848165897801
United States	9363520	7430989	55219597518121
Venezuela	912050	-1020481	1041381471361
Zimbabwe	390760	-1541771	2377057816441
Sum:	*96626550*	*Sum:*	*569983589849850*
N:	*50*	*Variance (s^2):*	*11632318160201.00*
Mean:	*1932531.00*	*Standard Deviation (std):*	*3410618.44*

The small size of the sample we generally work with when undertaking cross-national research (N < 500) reduces the variance of our samples, and as such, sharply reduces the probability of achieving a "perfect" normal distribution. Of course, not all cross-national samples are small, and even small samples might take on the characteristics of a "perfect" normal distribution. The important point is that the absence of a "perfect" normal distribution does not preclude the researcher from undertaking meaningful cross-national quantitative analysis. Even when a sample is small, we can rely upon the Central Limit Theorem to justify our use of the sample, all things being equal. We will discuss the Central Limit Theorem later.

Second, it is more important to have a sample that reasonably approximates an accurate depiction of the target population than to have one that conforms to the shape of a normal distribution. This requires that your sample selection process does not arbitrarily include or exclude groups of countries from the target population in your sample. A sample that departs from a "perfect" normal distribution, but is a reasonable approximation of a random, non-biased sample, must be interpreted as an accurate depiction of the target population.

This leads to the third point: Target populations can be and often are characterized by non-normal distributions. Therefore, the presence of a non-normal distribution should not immediately be interpreted as evidence of serious error in your sampling selection process. Assuming you have selected your sample of countries in accordance with prudent attention to your target population, and have ensured a reasonable approximation of a random, unbiased choice of countries in your sample, you must further assume that a non-normal distribution in the sample reflects a non-normal distribution in the target population.

Finally, judgment regarding the degree of the severity of departure from a normal distribution is acquired through practice and experience. We will consider examples of what would ordinarily be considered a severe departure from "perfect" normal distributions. However, others might reasonably find that what you might consider a minor departure from a "perfect" normal distribution is in their judgment a severe departure. It is therefore essential that you become comfortable with those basic tools of univariate analysis that allow you to diagnose any potential problems in the sampling distribution, as well as to report the statistics central to a univariate analysis that clarify the sampling distribution for your audience.

Properties of the Normal Distribution

A sampling distribution allows one to estimate the probability that a particular score will occur within a sample of a particular size (N). A sampling distribution assumes a particular shape, referred to as a curve. The curve reflects the proportional distribution of scores of a variable. A "perfect" normal distribution has precise symmetry with respect to the "peak" and the "tails" of a curve. Assumptions about the "normality" of a

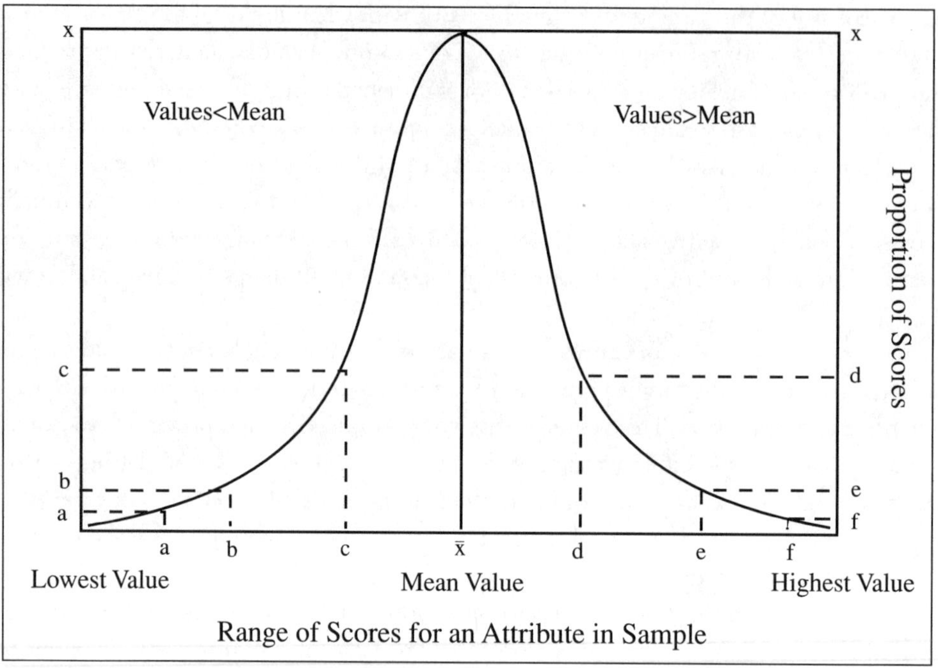

FIGURE 3.2 The Characteristics of the Normal Distribution

sample distribution lie at the heart of all statistical analysis. These assumptions become critical in hypothesis-testing techniques. Figure 3.2 depicts the shape of a nearly "perfect" normal distribution. What empirical properties dictate this shape?

The main empirical properties of a "perfect" normal distribution relate to the proportional distribution of scores in a sample relative to the mean value within the sample. For instance, we find in a "perfect" normal distribution that 68.26 percent of the sample of scores for a variable lie within a specific standard range of the mean; 95.44 percent of the scores lie within a larger specified standard range from the mean; 99.72 percent of the scores lie within an even larger specified standard range from the mean; and so on. The larger the specified standard range of scores from the sample mean, the smaller the proportion of scores within a sample that will fall inside this standard range. Statisticians have specified the exact proportion of scores that fall within the standard ranges from the mean in a normal curve. The size of these standard ranges (in terms of the proportion of scores expected to fall within the respective standard range) are the same for all samples, regardless of the variable or data. We shall explore these sample ranges in more detail in Chapter 5. These ranges are referred to as the "areas under the normal curve" and are illustrated in Figure 3.2.

Let us consider the empirical properties of a "perfect" normal distribution in more detail. The mean is the essential statistic in determining sampling distributions. Pinpointing the mean and then comparing the proportional distribution of scores along the value range of the attribute with reference to the mean allows the researcher to ascertain how closely his or her sample approximates a normal distribution.

The proportional distribution of scores for a particular attribute relative to the mean value of that attribute will take on the properties of a curve, when graphed. The curve in Figure 3.2 approximates a "normal" curve. The two critical components of this curve are its peak and its tails. It is *unimodal*, meaning there is only one peak to the curve. This signifies a clustering of scores around a particular value of the variable. The peak in a "perfect" normal distribution lies at the midpoint of the range of scores for the attribute: thus, the peak lies in the middle of the curve.

The lowest scores in the sample (and by inference, the lowest scores in the target population) lie to the far left end, or "tail" of the curve, while the high scores of the attribute (and by inreference, the high scores of the target population) lie to the far right end of the curve in Figure 3.2. Tails can be "light," indicating few cases located at the tail, or "heavy," indicating a large proportion of scores located at the tail. Tails in a "perfect" normal distribution are equally light.

This midpoint of a "perfect" normal distribution also corresponds to the mean value of the sample (represented by the center line beginning at $\bar{X}$ on the horizontal axis in Figure 3.2). *In a "perfect" normal distribution, the mean, median, and mode all have the same value*. Therefore, in a "perfect" normal sample distribution, the mean divides the sample of scores in half. Fifty percent of the scores are below the mean, and 50 percent of the scores lie above the mean. The proportion of scores that fall between ordinates $\bar{X}$ and c on the horizontal axis is equal to 34.13 percent of the total scores in the sample; as is the proportion of scores falling between ordinates $\bar{X}$ and d on the horizontal axis in Figure 3.2. The proportion of scores between ordinates c and b and ordinates d and e on the horizontal axis each equal 13.59 percent. Finally, the proportion of scores falling between ordinates a and b on the horizontal axis, as well as ordinates e and f on the horizontal axis is equal to 2.14 percent of the sample of scores. The distance between each of the contiguous ordinates in Figure 3.2 is equal to a specific proportion of the total area under the curve. Therefore, for instance, the distance between ordinates $\bar{X}$ and c consumes 34.13 percent of the total area under the "normal" curve.

Kurtosis

Kurtosis is the name given to the properties of the peak within a sampling distribution. A peak may be either *mesokurtic* (distinguished by a moderately curved peak near the center of the range of scores in the sample—the shape of an ideal "normal" curve), *leptokurtic* (distinguished by a sharp peak), or *platykurtic* (distinguished by a flatter peak). When the tails are heavy, the peak will be flat, reflecting a platykurtic peak. When the tails on a sample distribution are extremely light, the peak will be very sharp, indicative of a leptokurtic distribution. Kurtosis focuses only on the shape of the "main" peak within a sample. It has nothing to do with the shape or symmetry of the tails. Kurtosis alerts you to distributional problems that may arise when an unusually large number of scores have the same value in a sample (characteristic of a leptokurtic distribution), or when there is an absence of any clustering in your sample. Extreme kurtosis occurs when all the scores have the same value (maximum leptokurtic), or when all the scores are extremely diverse in their in values (very platykurtic distribution).

Skewness

Whereas kurtosis is expressed by the shape of the peak in a distribution, skewness is expressed when the distribution is characterized by a disproportionate number of scores occurring on either side of the mean. Specifically, skewness occurs when one tail in the distribution contains a disproportionately large number of the scores (labeled, the "heavy" tail), and the other tail holds a disproportionately small number of scores (the "light" tail). Note that in Figure 3.2, both tails are symmetrically shaped, and each contains an equal number of the scores; both tails are "light." A sample is skewed in the direction of the tail with the disproportionately small number of scores. Scores located on the "lighter" tail are known as "outliers": they fall outside the range of values where the vast majority of scores are located within a sample. The mean is always pulled toward the "lighter" tail; the median is always located toward the "heavier" tail in a skewed distribution. Larger values for scores are located to the right in a graphical depiction of a sample distribution; smaller values are located to the left of a graphically displayed sample distribution (see Figure 3.2).

A right-skewed sample means there are a few scores that have values much *larger* than most of the cases in the sample. We refer more technically to a right-skewed sample as a *positive skew.* It is positive because the skew (or, light tail) is in the direction of the larger values in the sample distribution. A sample skewed to the left is distinguished by a few outlier cases that have very small values relative to the majority of scores in the sample. A left-skewed sample is referred to as a *negative skew.* It is negative because the skew (or, heavy tail) is in the direction of smaller values.

Generally speaking, in cross-national samples, skewness is a much more serious problem than kurtosis; at least, it receives much closer examination and attention than kurtosis. Skewness is also a much more common problem with sampling distributions. Leptokurtic and platykurtic distributions can still approximate a reasonably normal distribution, so long as there are no major distortions to one of the tails. Distortions in tails of the curve indicate the presence of outliers, which has the effect of distorting the mean as an accurate estimate of the "typical" score in a sample. The ramifications of this distortion are far greater than the peakedness of the curve (unless you have very extreme platykurtic or leptokurtic distributions). Nonetheless, examining the shape of the peak presents the researcher with an excellent opportunity to describe accurately the distribution of an attribute within a sample. Skewness, however, more readily lo-

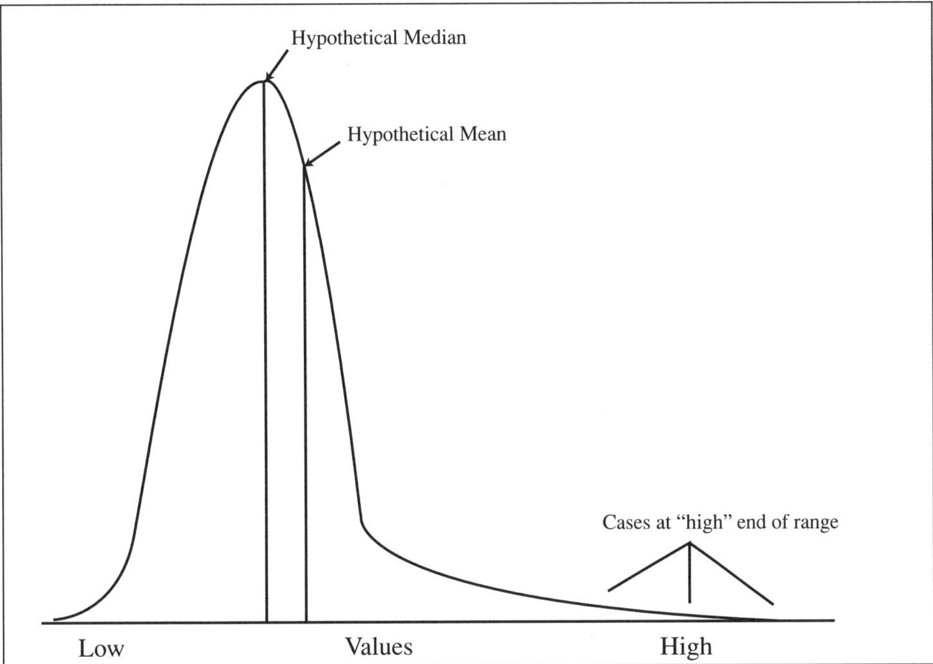

FIGURE 3.3 Representation of Positive Skewness

cates outliers, which have, all else being equal, more significant implications for both substantive and analytical applications of cross-national data analysis.

Figures 3.3 and 3.4 graphically display the two types of skewness—positive and negative, respectively. To summarize skewness:

Positive Skewness: The light tail is to the high scores in the sample. The mean is therefore larger than the median (or skewed to the right, as in Figure 3.3). The larger the mean relative to the median, the larger the positive skewness. $\bar{X} > Md.$)

Negative Skewness: The light tail is toward the low scores in a sample. The mean is therefore smaller than the median (or skewed to the left, as in Figure 3.4). The larger the median relative to the mean, the larger the negative skewness. $\bar{X} < Md.$)

Statistical Estimates of Kurtosis and Skewness

The statistical expressions for the kurtosis and skewness of samples are rarely applied in cross-national analysis. Rather, as we shall soon see, histogram analysis is usually re-

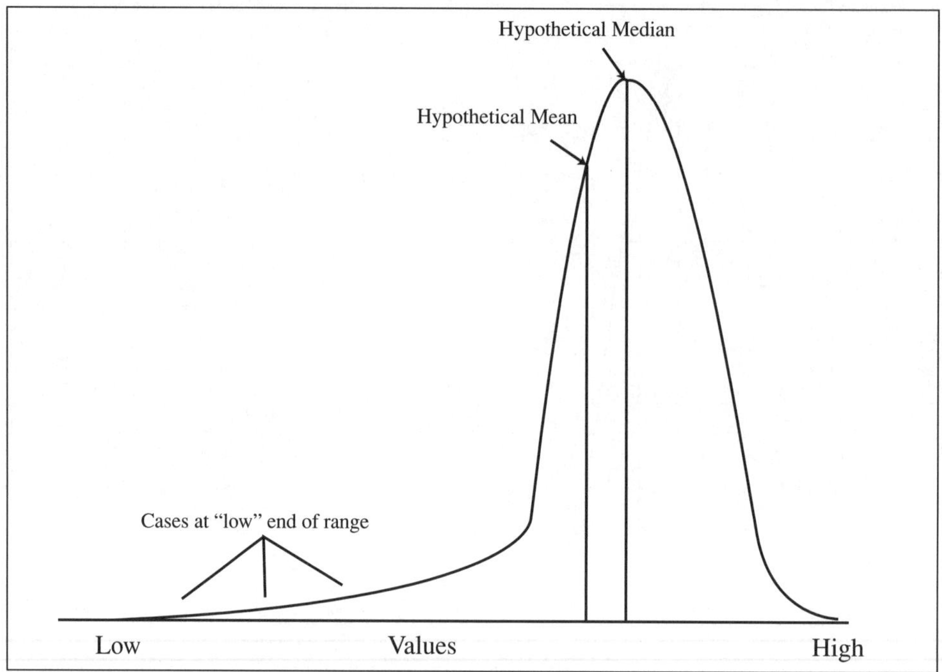

FIGURE 3.4 Representation of Negative Skewness

lied upon to explore the potential kurtosis and skewness of a sample. Nonetheless, advanced statistical software packages and spreadsheets afford you the option of producing a statistical measure of kurtosis and skewness. For example, within SPSS 10, the formula employed sets a normal distribution to 0: Both kurtosis and skewness statistics would equal 0 for a variable that had a normal distribution of scores within a sample. A kurtosis statistic larger than 0 ($k > 0$) would indicate a leptokurtic distribution; a negative kurtosis statistic ($k < 0$) would indicate a platykurtic distribution. A positive skewness statistic would indicate a positive skew to the sample distribution ($sk > 0$); a negative skewness statistic would indicate a negative skewness to the distribution ($sk < 0$). Most samples will have deviations from zero in their respective skewness and kurtosis statistics. Exactly how much of a deviation is "too much" depends on the sample. That is why the examination of a histogram (when using interval/ratio-level data) is always recommended as an initial part of a univariate analysis.

For AREA within CROSSNAT.50, skewness is 2.773; kurtosis is 8.153. These two statistics (computed by SPSS 10) confirm our earlier conclusion that AREA is both sharply positively skewed and leptokurtic. These statistics only specify with more precision what the examination of frequency distributions, percentiles, and means and median comparisons have already revealed.

Skewness in Perspective

The sample distribution of AREA sharply departs from a normal distribution in our sample of populous countries. The mean and standard deviations of the sample depart from assumptions of normality, as discussed above. The shape of the distribution does not conform to that shown in Figure 3.2. Virtually all samples—especially in cross-national analysis—deviate from perfect normal distributions. If this is true, why do we bother with skewness? There are two reasons it is important to know the skewness of the sample.

The first has to do with our substantive interpretation of the data. If we believe, as some comparativists do, that areal size plays a significant role in constraining political authority and influencing political behavior within a country, then knowing that the distribution of areal size is sharply skewed helps us understand why some countries may not easily conform to our assumptions and expectations about political and institutional authority. We might have to adjust our predictions and expectations about those countries that are so much more different than the rest of the sample.

The second, and more technical, reason the skewness is an important piece of information is because it affects our ability to include this variable in any subsequent analysis that relates areal size to a second attribute of a country. If the value of AREA is so much larger than the rest of the sample, any analysis based on AREA may lead to a distortion in the findings, such as exaggerating the true size of a measured relationship between AREA and a second attribute (such as GDP97). More importantly, skewness raises the specter of *some unintended error.* For instance, perhaps you have selected a country very different from others with respect to the attribute of AREA. This country is so much different from other countries that you cannot and should not make any inferences based on data that include that country in the sample because such conclusions will distort the sample mean and standard deviation, thus resulting in misleading conclusions regarding the typical country within your sample of populous countries. Or, perhaps you have simply incorrectly entered the value of a score in your database. Perhaps the authors of the original database from which you have drawn these figures made a mistake in entering the values of the variable.

An examination of the sampling distribution is one of the many steps we undertake in cross-national analysis to expose the "unexpected" and make a decision as to the substantive and statistical implications of these "deviations" or "outliers" for our analysis. Of course, it is not only outliers or deviations that are important. Knowing where most countries fall in regard to AREA, for instance, is as important as knowing that a few depart from this mean by quite large margins. It is the outliers though that are unexpected, by definition, since the mean predicts scores will fall within reasonably close proximity to its value. And as we shall see beginning in Chapter 9, it is critical in hypothesis testing to be alert to these deviations and to use them as critical bits of information in assessing the validity of our hypothesis tests.

THE CENTRAL LIMIT THEOREM

Statisticians have developed a theorem—the Central Limit Theorem—which allows researchers to remove the restrictions of normality from their sample—if, and only if, the sample is large (and assuming you have reasonably approximated a random, unbiased sample). The Central Limit Theorem states generally that as you draw more and more samples of size N, you will accumulate a sample of means (one mean for each new sample). Eventually this sample of means itself will approach a normal distribution—at least in theory. Thus, if your individual sample size is large and your sample is random and unbiased, even if it is not precisely distributed according to a normal curve, you can assume that the mean and standard deviation reflect the true population mean and standard deviation—within reason. There will always be deviations, but these will not be so great as to render your sample invalid (unless you have not reasonably approximated a random sample). Therefore, we are safe in assuming the mean and standard deviation computed from a sample accurately reflect the target population's actual mean. However, if the sample is not random and is in some way biased in its selection of cases, disregarding the assumptions of normality in sample distributions will be very dangerous and lead to seriously flawed inferences to the target population. In this instance, our ability to credibly test our assumptions and hypotheses will be sharply undermined.[8]

DEMONSTRATION 3.1: HISTOGRAMS

The actual statistical measure of skewness is less important than a visual examination of the distribution itself. Indeed, this is the most common means by which researchers determine whether their sample deviates from a normal distribution. How does one obtain a visual depiction of the sample distribution? The easiest technique is the *histogram*. A histogram looks like a typical bar chart, with which most students are familiar. A histogram is very different though. A bar chart simply reports the number—or frequency—of countries that occur for *every value* of the variable in the sample. A histogram, by contrast, reports frequencies (or proportional distributions) of countries within a specified *range* of values in a sample. In essence, the histogram *groups* several groups of scores into equal-sized ranges and reports the number of cases (or countries) that fall within each range. Histograms are useful for assessing the shape of a sample distribution when using interval/ratio data. When working with ordinal data, the bar chart may serve as the histogram.

Figure 3.5 illustrates a bar chart, plotting interval/ratio-level data. Note that every value in the sample for AREA is different. Consequently, each bar is the same height, because each value of AREA in the sample has the same number of cases, or frequencies, associated with it: one.[9]

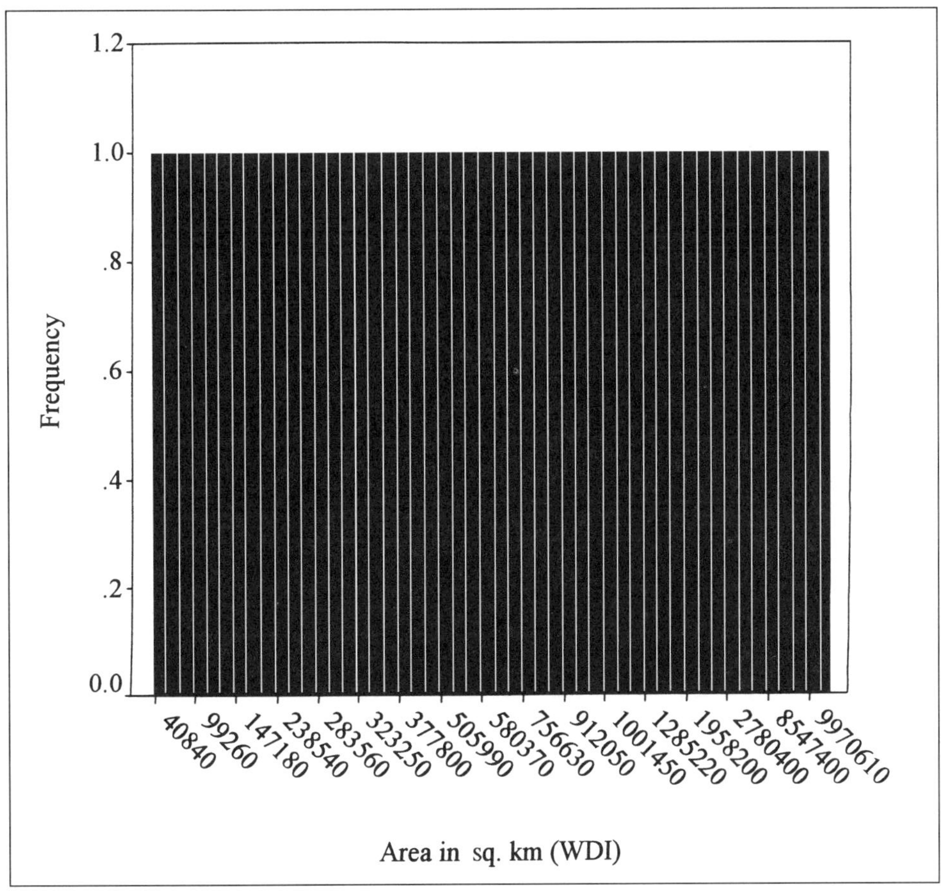

FIGURE 3.5 Bar Chart, AREA

Other than visually confirming that all but two countries have different values for AREA, there is nothing a bar chart can really do if one has ratio/interval-level data.

Figure 3.6 reproduces a histogram (developed by SPSS 10), with some additional editing included. This figure graphically underscores what we already know merely by comparing the mean and median: The sample is severely skewed to the right—a positive skew. Several countries trail off toward the right side—or high end—of the scale on AREA. This trailing effect produces a light tail. It would be prudent to exercise extreme caution when using AREA in any analysis. Should we, however, conclude from this that our sample is flawed and that we must assume that the target population has in reality a different distribution pattern than that shown in Figure 3.6? The answer is no.

In all likelihood, the distribution pattern shown in Figure 3.6 reflects the actual distribution of AREA across the target population. However, such a severe skewed leptokurtic distribution would distort subsequent hypothesis testing if the test were to include AREA. The histogram has confirmed skewness (and leptokurtic peakedness)

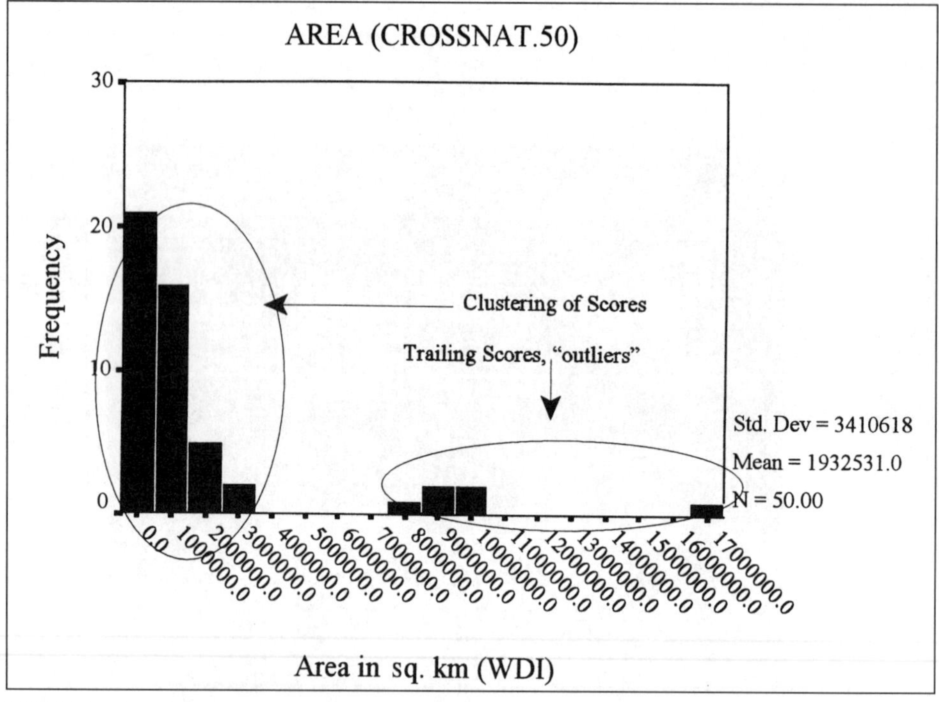

FIGURE 3.6 Histogram

and has drawn attention to the fact that a few countries are very large. These "trailers"—or outliers—will act to distort any hypothesis-testing technique based upon assumptions of normally distributed values for AREA.[10]

Bimodal Distributions

Figure 3.6 is unimodal (that is, its curve has only one "hump"), despite being sharply skewed and leptokurtic. Sometimes, however, histograms depict sample distributions that alert the student to another very serious problem in the distribution of values within a sample: *symmetrical bimodal* distributions. A symmetrical bimodal distribution has two peaks of roughly equal size at opposite ends of the range of scores in the sample. Each peak is located toward the extreme tails of the curve and each is approximately equal distance from the mean. Finally, within the groups of scores between the peaks are a disproportionately small number of scores. Consider, for example, the variable AGE1800 in CROSSNAT.50. This reports the number of years since 1800 a country has been an independent nation (with 1800 set as the baseline, and 1997 as the last year for independence).[11] Robert Jackman has shown that the capacity of a country to realize important outcomes associated with power, such as security, wealth, and prosperity, is related to how long a country has been an independent nation.[12] You will

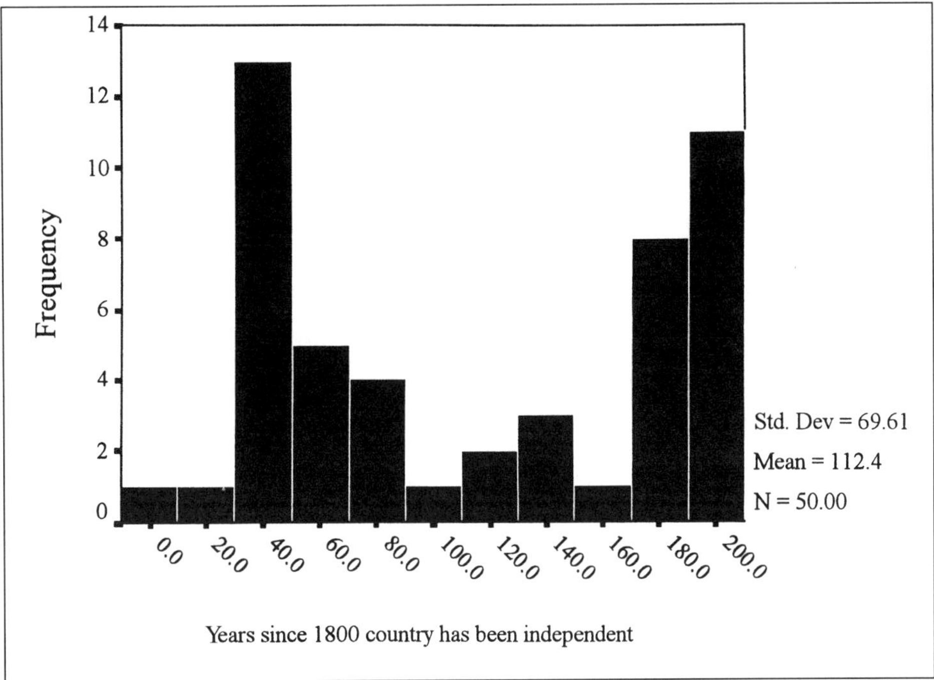

FIGURE 3.7 Histogram

find that for this variable, the mean for AGE1800 is 112.4, with a median value of 106 and a standard deviation of 69.61. The distribution is only slightly skewed to the right (sk = .059) and is somewhat platykurtic (k = -1.786). These univariate statistics would not indicate any particular problem with the sample distribution.

The histogram produced in Figure 3.7 reveals that the sample approximates a symmetrical bimodal distribution. There are two large peaks of approximately equal size. Each peak lies at or near the opposite end of the value range for AGE1800. Lying between these peaks is a "valley" where few countries reside. The shape of the distribution confirms a sample that is not skewed, but is bimodal. It is platykurtic because the peaks contain approximately equal numbers of scores and the two peaks together hold a disproportionately large number of scores in the sample.

Thus, we can see that it is sometimes difficult from basic univariate statistics alone to obtain an accurate picture of the sampling distribution. An examination of the frequency distributions and percentiles would have alerted the student to the possibility of a symmetric bimodal distribution. However, only a histogram vividly confirms this. Finally, because the mean is the most important univariate statistic, relying exclusively on the mean as an estimate of the typical score in a sample is risky. In this example, the mean would suggest the typical country was approximately 112.44 years old. Yet, this score hides the fact that the mean actually falls within a region of the sample distribution that is occupied by very few countries (that is, the "valley"). There are two more "typical" ages of a country's sovereignty in CROSSNAT.50, each falling within two clusters of scores at opposite ends of the range of values for AGE1800. Therefore, the mean is of little value if we wish to accurately describe (and predict) the typical age of a country in our sample.

DEMONSTRATION 3.2: TREATING SHARP DEPARTURES FROM NORMAL DISTRIBUTIONS

In the examples of AREA and AGE1800, we are confronted by severe deviations from assumptions of normally distributed samples. Indeed, while some deviation from normality is almost always the case with cross-national data, the severity of these deviations is so great they cannot be overlooked. The reason is simple: Any analysis linking one variable to another when one (or both) is sharply skewed or symmetrically bimodal would produce extremely misleading results. The data must therefore be modified in order to produce credible results. Statisticians have a number of sophisticated and advanced techniques for treating variables that severely violate assumptions of normal distributions. The most basic, and simple, is to merely convert the data from interval/ratio-level data (if our original data are interval/ratio) to ordinal data. By doing so, we move down the scale of measurement and relax our assumptions about the normality of sample distributions. However, we cannot use the same techniques that we would ordinarily employ if our data were still at the interval/ratio level. In this sense, we trade a degree of precision that we achieve with interval/ratio-level measures and techniques, for the credibility we require but would be denied if we failed to treat the severe violations of normal sample distributions.

Departures from normal distributions pose no problem when applying univariate analysis. If we can reasonably assume we have a random sample of cases that has not been afflicted by a systematic bias in the selection of countries to the sample, reporting skewness does not mislead anyone. In fact, it is highly important and useful information. It must be assumed to be an accurate description of the real world (because, of course, the real world can be afflicted by skewed distributions). This information is vital to our comparisons across countries. It is important and useful to know, for instance, that China is larger than 94 percent of the sample of populous countries (and therefore, we expect it to be larger than approximately 94 percent of the population of populous countries). It is even more useful to know that China stands very far apart from other countries with respect to size. This may help to bring into clear relief a number of important and quite unique characteristics of Chinese political behavior and institutional authority.

However, if we move beyond simple descriptions of one attribute to the correlation of two attributes, as we do when we test hypotheses in cross-national analysis, sharp skewness in the sample of one of these attributes will present major challenges to the researcher. We will consider hypothesis-testing techniques and strategies in subsequent chapters. For now, we must consider the most basic and reasonable strategies to treat the matter of sharp deviations from assumptions of normal distributions.

As mentioned previously, the procedure for converting data from interval/ratio level to ordinal level is referred to as *recoding* or *collapsing*. This entails assigning ordinal values to a range of interval/ratio values for a specific variable. A new variable—an ordinal variable—is created from the original interval/ratio variable. The process necessarily reduces the precision and accuracy of measurement. However, it also reduces the variance within a sample. There is more variance across a sample of fifty unique scores than a sample with only two to five unique values for a particular attribute. This presents the student with a challenge when recoding or collapsing interval/ratio-level data into ordinal measures. The fewer ordinal categories there are, the less the variance, and therefore, the less accurate and precise our measure of the attribute in a cross-national sample.

As we increase the number of categories for the new ordinal-level variable, however, we run the risk that some of the categories will have a very different number of cases (or countries) associated with a particular score. This imbalance will introduce its own degree of distortion into our measures and subsequent conclusions. For instance, we can see from Figure 3.6 that the vast majority of cases in CROSSNAT.50 are clustered at the left (low) end of the distribution range of the scores for AREA. If we were to create a new ordinal-level variable with five categories (1 = very small countries and 5 = very large countries), we would in effect replicate the same skewed, leptokurtic sample distribution as we have with the interval/ratio-level measure. Most of the scores would be concentrated at the low end of the new ordinal categories (categories 1 to 2), with only a very few countries found at the ordinal scores of 4 to 5. The reason is simple: The skewness and clustering of the original sample is so severe that a multiple-category ordinal variable will still reflect extreme cases at the high or low end. These extreme cases, while important information when applying univariate analysis, can still produce misleading results when applying statistical analysis to hypothesis testing.

An Example: AREA

Let us consider a simple example. Table 3.2 confirms that the range of values for AREA is 17,034,560 square kilometers (17,075,400 – 40,840). If we decide to collapse AREA into a new ordinal-level variable with three ordinal categories (for example, 1 = small, 2 = moderate, and 3 = large), we must make a decision as to which values of AREA are assigned to each of the respective ordinal categories in the new variable. Because the new variable is ordinal, we assume a rank ordering to the values in the sample. Therefore, a value of 1 in the new variable would be low scores in AREA, a value of 2 in the ordinal variable would be the "middle" range of scores in

AREA, and the value of 3 would be the higher values in AREA. The exact cutoffs that assign scores in AREA to the new ordinal variable are critical. An arbitrary decision should be avoided. Therefore, absent any substantive justification for dividing the original sample into three groups for the new ordinal-level variable, you must divide the sample into three ranges of *equal distance* between the ordinal values in AREA.

To do so, you divide the range (17,034,560) by 3. This produces your *base interval* (5,678,187). You then begin by subtracting the base interval from the highest value in AREA (17,075,400 – 5,678,187 = 11,397,213). From this value you then subtract the base interval (11,397,213.3 – 5,678,187 = 5,719,026.3), producing the cutoff for the moderate range of scores in your new ordinal variable. Because we have only three categories in the new ordinal variable, you now have computed your cutoff ranges for the three values in your new ordinal-level variable: "Large" (score = 3, or those scores ranging between 17,075,400 and 11,397,213.3 in AREA); "Moderate" (score = 2, or scores ranging between 11,397,213.2 and 5,719,026.3 in AREA); and "Small" (score = 1, or scores ranging between 5,719,026.2 and 40,840 in AREA). However, the relative frequency distribution of this new ordinal variable is highly skewed: the value 1 ("small" countries) has forty-four countries, the value 2 ("moderate" sized countries) has five countries, and the value 3 ("large" countries) has only one country. With three categories, you have gained very little in terms of eliminating the effects of the skewness and disproportionate clustering.

Therefore, because of the extreme skewness and clustering of AREA, the only option is to divide the sample into two equal parts at the median value (583,705). This has the advantage of providing a sufficient number of cases within each category (twenty-five) and of avoiding skewness and clustering. There would not, however, be a normal distribution to the new variable (there are no tails to the new variable, though the sample would be symmetric). For this reason, statisticians and more experienced researchers often prefer to use different techniques to "adjust" distributional problems with interval/ratio-level data. These techniques convert the original data into a form that more closely approximates a normal distribution. This decision, however, can legitimately be made only when the researcher assumes his/her sample *deviates* sharply from assumptions of both randomness and unbiased selection of cases. In that instance, the conversion is simply correcting the sample to more accurately reflect the "real world" population, which is assumed to be normally distributed. If, however, you cannot assume the sample is flawed—that is, if you must assume the distributional problem is in fact reflective of a skewness and sharp clustering in the population—forcing a conversion that approximates a normal distribution is questionable. Because we must assume our sample is not afflicted by severe departures from randomness and unbiased selection (assumptions that are easier to make when working with a very finite number of countries in the world), we are safer simply defining a new measure at a lower level and accepting the loss of accuracy in our conclusions. We must, however, keep in mind that the actual values from which the ordinal-level variable were created are, in fact, highly skewed and clustered. This information is critical background coloring any final conclusions the student may wish to make about the attribute under investigation.

You cannot rely upon the new ordinal variable to verify that China, for instance, is larger than 94 percent of the population of populous countries in the world. Nor will the new variable confirm that China stands far apart from other countries with respect to areal size. Your new variable serves a different purpose. It merely distinguishes "large" countries from "small" countries. Thus, you can now say only that China is a "large" country. Precision has been severely reduced. However, if later on, as we will see in subsequent chapters, you wish to undertake a hypothesis test using areal size as a concept, you will achieve more credible, if less accurate, results if you avoid AREA (because of its sharp departure from assumptions of normal distribution) and rely instead on the new, two-category, ordinal-level measure.

Finally, we must ask the question: Are we misleading the reader if we eliminate the skewness of the interval/ratio-level variable by creating a new variable that is measured at the ordinal level? The answer is: *It depends*. We are misleading the reader if we do not report the original negative skewness. We are also doing a great disservice if we do not examine the countries associated with the extreme cases reflected by the sharp skewness in the original variable. We will explore at length in subsequent chapters the importance of examining outlying countries in samples. However, we are not misleading readers if we report the original data and, when using the lower-level variable, report our conclusions with some qualification. Recall, however, by moving to the ordinal level of measurement, we cannot draw as precise and accurate conclusions as when we remain at the interval/ratio level of measurement. Consequently, we cannot mislead the reader as severely at the ordinal level of measurement because we do not have the same assumed degree of precision and accuracy associated with such measures. Our conclusions are necessarily less refined. We do not mislead the reader therefore, we simply offer less precise and accurate conclusions—conclusions that may nonetheless suggest important information and implications for our cross-national analysis.[13]

Considerations when Dealing with Non-Normal Distributions. From the previous section, we know that before we convert data to a lower scale of measurement, we need to carefully consider two questions. The first is whether there is *substantive* explanation why the non-normal distributions would occur. Second is whether this substantive explanation is important enough to warrant consideration in our decision governing the assignment of new values measuring the attribute. In the example of AREA, political and historical reasons have certainly dictated why some countries have legitimate claims to very large geographical space, while others are limited to much smaller confines. However, there is no obvious single explanation for this phenomenon that is vividly revealed in simple univariate analysis of AREA. Consequently, we are left with a decision about how to assign ordinal values to these interval/ratio-level data without having to consider a specific substantive explanation that might govern this decision.

Another point to consider is whether the sample is sharply skewed and severely clustered. If so (as in the case of AREA), we are wise to avoid multiple categories in our new ordinal variable, and simply opt for a two-category ordinal variable. In this circumstance, the most prudent and statistically defensible choice is to divide the sample at the median value (that is, 583,705). All countries with a value at or below this score are assigned an ordinal value of 1 (identifying them as "smaller" countries). Those countries in the sample that are larger than 583,705 square kilometers are assigned a value of 2 (identifying them as "large" countries). By dividing the sample at the median value for the attribute, we essentially divide the sample into equal parts: twenty-five "smaller" countries, and twenty-five "larger" countries. In this sense, we eliminate the extreme scores of AREA. The score of 17,075,400 (Russia) is now simply converted to "2." The new variable (consisting of only two values, 1 and 2) is now named AREA2: AREA for the original variables from which the new variable was derived, and 2 indicating it is a dichotomous variable, one that assumes only two values. Thus, the variable has two clusters to its distribution, one cluster consisting of the countries assuming the value of 1, and the second cluster consisting of the countries assuming the value 2. Table 3.5 lists each country by its value of AREA and its value for the converted variable, AREA2. The listing is by rank order, in ascending order.[14]

A Second Example: AGE1800

We have constructed one new variable: AREA2. Let us consider one more example, AGE18002. Table 3.6 reports the frequency distribution for AGE1800. As we have seen in Figure 3.7, with AGE1800 we have a particular problem: a bimodal distribution. As such, an important substantive explanation lies behind the symmetric bimodal distribution. A simple cursory examination of Figure 3.7 suggests that we could divide the historical period between 1800 and 1997 logically into two parts: one group being those countries that had their independence before or during 1917, and the second, those countries that obtained their independence after 1917. Actually, it makes perfect sense that this variable would be divided into two camps: those that were sovereign and independent before the end of the First World War (before 1918), and those that were sovereign and independent only after the First World War (from 1918 on). We know from univariate analysis that the median for AGE1800 is 106. The year that corresponds to this median value is 1891 (1997 – 106 = 1891). The First World War (1914–1918) signifies a major historical point. At that time four of the great modern empires—German, Austro-Hungarian, Russian, and Ottoman—collapsed as a result of the war and its consequences. The end of the war freed a number of the empires' former colonial holdings in Europe and elsewhere.

Therefore, we would be justified in selecting a different criteria to divide the sample and thereby convert the data to an ordinal scale. Rather than using the median

TABLE 3.5 AREA, by Dichotomous Grouping

Small Countries			*Large Countries*		
COUNTRY	AREA	AREA2	COUNTRY	AREA	AREA2
Netherlands	40840	1 Small	Madagascar	587040	2 Large
Sri Lanka	65610	1 Small	Ukraine	603700	2 Large
Czech Republic	78860	1 Small	Chile	756630	2 Large
Korea	99260	1 Small	Turkey	774820	2 Large
Greece	131960	1 Small	Pakistan	796100	2 Large
Bangladesh	144000	1 Small	Venezuela	912050	2 Large
Nepal	147180	1 Small	Nigeria	923770	2 Large
Tunisia	163610	1 Small	Tanzania	945090	2 Large
Romania	238390	1 Small	Egypt	1001450	2 Large
Ghana	238540	1 Small	Colombia	1138910	2 Large
Uganda	241040	1 Small	South Africa	1221040	2 Large
United Kingdom	244880	1 Small	Peru	1285220	2 Large
Ecuador	283560	1 Small	Iran	1633190	2 Large
Philippines	300000	1 Small	Indonesia	1904570	2 Large
Italy	301270	1 Small	Mexico	1958200	2 Large
Poland	323250	1 Small	Congo	2344860	2 Large
Malaysia	329750	1 Small	Algeria	2381740	2 Large
Germany	356980	1 Small	Argentina	2780400	2 Large
Japan	377800	1 Small	India	3287590	2 Large
Zimbabwe	390760	1 Small	Australia	7741220	2 Large
Morocco	446550	1 Small	Brazil	8547400	2 Large
Spain	505990	1 Small	United States	9363520	2 Large
Thailand	513120	1 Small	China	9596960	2 Large
France	551500	1 Small	Canada	9970610	2 Large
Kenya	580370	1 Small	Russia	17075400	2 Large

value (as with AREA) of 106, it would be more correct to divide the sample into two parts, with the year 1918 corresponding to the break point. Thus, a value of 1 is assigned to a country if that country's age is greater than 80 years (or independent and sovereign before 1918, or "pre–World War I" countries); a value of 2 is assigned a country if that country's age is equal to or less than 80 (or independent and sovereign after 1917, or "post–World War I" countries). Indeed, Table 3.6 confirms our assumption. We see that a large jump occurs in the values of AGE1800 between the 48 percent range, and the 52 percent range (from 80 years to 116 years). This has the effect of distorting the median a little, moving it further from 1918 than the actual weight of the frequency distribution would imply.

We will name the new variable, AGE18002, indicating a dichotomous structure. There are twenty-six countries with a value of 1 for AGE18002 (those countries achieving their independence before 1918), and twenty-four countries with a value of 2 for AGE18002 (those achieving their independence after 1917). Table 3.7 lists the

TABLE 3.6 Frequency Distribution, AGE1800

Valid	*Frequency*	*Percent*	*Valid Percent*	*Cumulative Percent*
6	1	2.0	2.0	2.0
26	1	2.0	2.0	4.0
32	1	2.0	2.0	6.0
34	1	2.0	2.0	8.0
35	3	6.0	6.0	14.0
37	3	6.0	6.0	20.0
40	2	4.0	4.0	24.0
41	2	4.0	4.0	28.0
49	1	2.0	2.0	30.0
50	2	4.0	4.0	34.0
51	1	2.0	2.0	36.0
52	2	4.0	4.0	40.0
75	2	4.0	4.0	44.0
79	1	2.0	2.0	46.0
80	1	2.0	2.0	48.0
96	1	2.0	2.0	50.0
116	1	2.0	2.0	52.0
126	1	2.0	2.0	54.0
130	1	2.0	2.0	56.0
136	1	2.0	2.0	58.0
141	1	2.0	2.0	60.0
168	1	2.0	2.0	62.0
175	2	4.0	4.0	66.0
176	1	2.0	2.0	68.0
181	1	2.0	2.0	70.0
186	1	2.0	2.0	72.0
187	3	6.0	6.0	78.0
196	1	2.0	2.0	80.0
197	10	20.0	20.0	100.0
Total	50	100.0	100.0	

respective scores for AGE1800 and AGE18002 for countries in CROSSNAT.50 (in ascending order of AGE1800).[15]

SUMMARY PRESENTATION OF UNIVARIATE STATISTICS

Finally, Table 3.8 illustrates a typical statistical presentation of a univariate analysis.[16] These ten statistics provide a basic, yet thorough, overview for the reader of the central tendencies within the sample, with respect to the variables under investigation (in this example, AREA, POPULATE, and AGE1800). Because of the sharp skewness of POPULATE suggested by this univariate analysis, CROSSNAT.50 includes a converted measure of population size: POP2.

TABLE 3.7 AGE1800 by Dichotomous Grouping

Independence Post-1917			*Independence Pre-1918*		
COUNTRY	AGE1800	AGE18002	COUNTRY	AGE1800	AGE18002
Ukraine	6	1 Post-1917	Australia	96	2 Pre-1918
Bangladesh	26	1 Post-1917	Romania	116	2 Pre-1918
Zimbabwe	32	1 Post-1917	Germany	126	2 Pre-1918
Kenya	34	1 Post-1917	Canada	130	2 Pre-1918
Algeria	35	1 Post-1917	Italy	136	2 Pre-1918
Tanzania	35	1 Post-1917	South Africa	141	2 Pre-1918
Uganda	35	1 Post-1917	Greece	168	2 Pre-1918
Madagascar	37	1 Post-1917	Brazil	175	2 Pre-1918
Nigeria	37	1 Post-1917	Ecuador	175	2 Pre-1918
Congo	37	1 Post-1917	Peru	176	2 Pre-1918
Malaysia	40	1 Post-1917	Argentina	181	2 Pre-1918
Ghana	40	1 Post-1917	Venezuela	186	2 Pre-1918
Morocco	41	1 Post-1917	Chile	187	2 Pre-1918
Tunisia	41	1 Post-1917	Mexico	187	2 Pre-1918
Sri Lanka	49	1 Post-1917	Colombia	187	2 Pre-1918
Pakistan	50	1 Post-1917	United Kingdom	196	2 Pre-1918
India	50	1 Post-1917	Spain	197	2 Pre-1918
Philippines	51	1 Post-1917	Russia	197	2 Pre-1918
Indonesia	52	1 Post-1917	Japan	197	2 Pre-1918
Korea	52	1 Post-1917	Iran	197	2 Pre-1918
Turkey	75	1 Post-1917	France	197	2 Pre-1918
Egypt	75	1 Post-1917	Netherlands	197	2 Pre-1918
Czech	79	1 Post-1917	China	197	2 Pre-1918
Poland	80	1 Post-1917	United States	197	2 Pre-1918
			Thailand	197	2 Pre-1918
			Nepal	197	2 Pre-1918

CHAPTER SUMMARY

In this chapter, we have explored the use of basic descriptive statistics for use within cross-national analysis. Frequency distributions and percentile analysis, along with the mean, median, mode, standard deviation, variance, and shape of the sample distribution (skewness and kurtosis), are critical descriptive and univariate statistics that stand at the forefront of conducting cross-national empirical analysis. While not as glamorous or "sophisticated" as some of the more advanced "basic" statistics that we will explore in later chapters, these univariate statistics provide the foundations upon which credible and reliable assessments of empirical cross-national data eventually rest. Univariate analysis allows us to *describe* accurately the empirical properties of an attribute within our sample and *identify* countries that are outliers, and *alerts* us to problems with sampling distribution that may either stem from errors on our part, or, more likely, require some treatment before we can use the variable in any subsequent hypothesis-testing techniques.

TABLE 3.8 Univariate Analysis of AREA, POPULATE, and AGE1800

Statistic	*AREA Sq. Kilometers*	*POPULATE*	*AGE1800 Years Independent Since 1800*
Mean	1,932,534	95,835,722	112.44
Standard Deviation	3,410,618.44	211,442,530.61	106
Median	583,705	38,645,000	106
Minimum Value	40,840	9,020,000	6
Maximum Value	17,075,400	1,210,005,000	197
25th Percentile	273,890	18,966,250	40.75
75th Percentile	1,701,035	70,454,500	187
Skewness	2.793	4.510	.059
Kurtosis	8.148	20.818	-1.786
N	50	50	50

Before univariate statistics can be applied, the student must understand that measurement issues explained in Chapter 2 will determine the level of accuracy and precision afforded by the statistical procedures employed. Indeed, the levels of measure (nominal, ordinal, interval/ratio) will determine the type of statistical univariate technique the student can employ in his or her cross-national analysis.

Finally, quantitative cross-national research must always be treated as one of several strategies to the development of theory and the accumulation of knowledge about the patterns of political behavior and institutional authority. Its role in the Ladder of Theory Building and the overall research strategy of the student is a necessary, but not entirely sufficient, task in the enterprise of systematic comparative political inquiry. Nonetheless, applied univariate analysis offers important information with regard to the overall validity of our measures. Both the analysis and the presentation of univariate analysis play central parts in the information imparted to the reader; both are also means of validating the underlying logic linking the concepts within your theory. In the next chapter, we elaborate our consideration of sample distributions, focusing more closely on the applications of the mean and standard deviation within cross-national research.

NOTES

1. Central tendency analysis is a general term commonly used to describe three distinct aspects of univariate analysis: (1) *central tendency statistics* proper, which reflect the typical statistical attribute within a sample (mean, median, mode); (2) *dispersion measures*, which reflect the degree to which individual scores in samples are dispersed around the mean (standard deviation, variance, standard error); and (3) *distribution measures*, which reflect the degree to which scores are distributed across the range of values between the high and low values within the sample (skewness and kurtosis). Throughout this text, when we refer to central tendency

measures, we in fact are referring more generally to the various statistical measures within these three aspects of univariate analysis. For a detailed overview of applying central tendency analysis to political data, see Herbert F. Weisberg, 1992, *Central Tendency and Variability* (Newbury Park, Calif.: Sage Publications), and Jack Levin and James Alan Fox, 2001, *Elementary Statistics in Social Research*, eighth edition (Boston: Allyn and Bacon), pp. 23–122.

2. Table 3.1 has been created using SPSS 10.0 *Frequencies* statistical task.

3. To obtain FREQUENCIES within SPSS 10, follow the following sequence from the main menu bar: ANALYZE▶DESCRIPTIVE▶FREQUENCIES. Once in the FREQUENCIES dialog box, select the variable (or variables) you wish to analyze from the variable list window. To specify the statistics you wish to use, select the STATISTICS button. Within the STATISTICS dialog box you will find the option for percentile analysis, where you may specify quartile or other percentile breakdown for the data.

4. To obtain the sum of all values in a sample for any variable, one must utilize the DESCRIPTIVES command in SPSS 10. Follow the sequence ANALYZE▶DESCRIPTIVE STATISTICS▶DESCRIPTIVES, and then select the variable from the variable list, and inside the OPTIONS dialog window, select SUM.

5. Thirty-eight is 76 percent of the fifty countries, not 75 percent. Why then do we sum the values of AREA for the first thirty-eight countries in ascending order of their values of AREA? Why not thirty-seven countries? One-quarter of fifty is technically 12.5, so that by the time you have added the first three-quarters of the sample (or, 12.5 x 3) you have accounted for 37.5 countries, or, rounded, 38. Thus, the thirty-eighth country in ascending order represents the closest value to the seventy-fifth percentile in a sample of fifty countries.

6. To obtain such an distribution list, one must first sort the sample by the variable one wishes to list (in ascending or descending order). This is accomplished in SPSS 10 by executing the sequence from the data editor menu bar, DATA▶SORT CASES. Once in the dialog window, select the variable you wish to sort by, indicating whether you wish to have the order of the cases in the data set sorted in ascending or descending order of their value for the specified variable. Then to obtain the distribution list, execute the sequence from the main menu bar, ANALYZE▶REPORTS▶CASE SUMMARIES. Once in the dialog box, specify the countries you would like to have included in the procedure. For Table 3.3, we specified COUNTRY and AREA.

7. For the 210 sovereign countries, territories, and protectorates in the world as of 1997, the mean areal size was 633,024.1 square kilometers.

8. For a clear and easily accessible introduction to the concept of the normal distribution and the more abstract Central Limit Theorem, see Marija J. Norušis, 2000, *SPSS: SPSS© 10.0 Guide to Data Analysis* (Upper Saddle River, N.J.: Prentice Hall), pp. 177–196; Joseph F. Healey, 1993, *Statistics: A Tool for Social Research*, third edition (Belmont, Calif.: Wadsworth Publishing Co.), pp. 120–154; and Jack Levin and James Alan Fox, 2001, *Elementary Statistics in Social Research*, eighth edition (Boston: Allyn and Bacon), pp. 133–157.

9. Figures 3.5, 3.6, and 3.7 were produced using ANALYZE▶DESCRIPTIVES▶FREQUENCIES sequence within SPSS 10. Once in the FREQUENCIES dialog box, select the chart option within FREQUENCIES.

10. As we shall see in Chapter 15, there are statistical procedures for adjusting interval-level measures that do not conform to a normal distribution. By fitting the distribution of

scores for a variable within a sample to a normal distribution, we are able to use the variable with statistical techniques that require the variable to assume a normal distribution (we call statistics that require the variables being analyzed to be normally distributed *parametric statistics*, to be discussed in more detail in Chapter 10). One option, therefore, that presents itself to someone using the variable AREA is to transform the variable to its natural log value, which has the effect in this case of setting the variable's distribution to normality. We shall demonstrate this transformation technique in Chapter 15 with the variable NET.

11. In addition to AGE1800, CROSSNAT.50 includes a measure of how many years a country has existed as an independent nation-state (AGE), the year in which it achieved its independence (INDEPEND), the country from which (if any) it achieved its independent status (FROM), and, as an alternative to AGE1800, the proportion of years that the country has been independent in its current form (PCT1800). In the case of AGE1800 and PCT1800, the number of years of a country's independence is computed by moving back from 1997 until it was not independent, or until 1800, whichever comes first. If a country had more than one period of independence, the earlier periods were not included in the computation of AGE1800 or PCT1800. Germany is treated as one political entity since 1871.

12. Robert W. Jackman, 1993, *Power Without Force: The Political Capacity of Nation-States* (Ann Arbor, Mich.: University of Michigan Press).

13. By collapsing the original range of scores for AREA, have we, in effect, stretched the meaning of the concept of areal size to the point where it no longer has relevant meaning to our theory? That can only be assessed within the context of the intended use of the concept, areal size. Strictly speaking, the concept of areal size is defined independently of the operationalization of the measure, AREA2. This variable is merely our empirical representation of the concept, areal size. While empirically different than the original representation, AREA, the variable AREA2 preserves the fundamental property of areal size—namely, the degree to which countries differ with respect to geographic size (measured in thousands of square kilometers). If we were to use the measure of AREA2 to represent the concept of economic power, or political ideology, we would be certainly be stretching the meaning of areal size. However, collapsing the measures for sound empirical reasons (in this case, because of severe violations of assumptions concerning normal distribution) does not, ipso facto, stretch a concept beyond its original and intended meaning. It does, however, limit the use of AREA2 (as it is now no longer a truly interval-level measure), and therefore, it restricts the range of credible and valid conclusions we can draw with respect to the relationship between areal size and other political phenomena. This, however, is a matter of measurement, not concept stretching.

14. To convert data from one level of measurement to another (for example, interval/ratio to ordinal) within SPSS 10, select the TRANSFORM option from the main menu bar. The RECODE VARIABLE option will allow the student to define a new variable from an old variable (the old variable being the newly created converted variable). For further details about using this procedure within SPSS, see Marija J. Norušis, 1998, *SPSS: SPSS® 8.0 Guide to Data Analysis* (Englewood Cliffs, N.J.: Prentice Hall), pp. 528–531.

15. The risk of concept stretching is more apparent and real in the case of recoding AGE1800 into AGE18002. In the case of the recoded variable, we have refined the intended use and meaning of the original concept. The original concept was defined as the continual survival of a country as a sovereign political entity, measured in years. AGE18002, however,

clearly points to a slightly different conceptual meaning, and its use as substitute for AGE1800 must be more carefully considered. AGE18002, while created to avoid severe violations of normal distribution (as with AREA2), has been empirically constructed in such a way as to allow one to use the variable as a representation of a different concept. In this case, it captures the epochal period within which a country achieved its national sovereignty. AGE1800 cannot be used as easily and effectively as a quantitative representation of this concept.Yet, AGE18002 not only reflects this conceptual representation, but it also retains the conceptual utility as a representation of a country's degree of sovereign longevity. If we chose to represent AGE18002 as a conceptual representation of colonialism, for instance, we would be in violation of concept stretching. After all, not all countries that achieved their uninterrupted sovereignty since 1917 were once colonies of empires (for example, Germany). However, if we attach conceptual significance to the epochal time period within which a country was created, AGE18002 can be an effective operational representation. Thus, we must exercise care and caution when using variables that have been transformed from their original measures. We must be careful to ask what these new measures actually represent in their transformed state, and whether they can serve as a substitute for other conceptual representations.

16. In SPSS 10, there are three basic ways by which the student can obtain basic measures of central tendency analysis: the FREQUENCIES tool, the EXPLORE tool, and the DESCRIPTIVE tool. These tools can be brought to bear on your data by following the path: ANALYZE▶DESCRIPTIVE STATISTICS▶, followed by either FREQUENCIES, DESCRIPTIVES, or EXPLORE. The former tool allows the student to produce a histogram from the CHART options, as does EXPLORE. The statistics option in FREQUENCIES allows the student to produce percentile analysis, as well as obtain all of the other basic statistics of univariate statistics listed in Table 3.1. See Marija J. Norušis,1998, *SPSS: SPSS® 8.0 Guide to Data Analysis* (Englewood Cliffs, N.J.: Prentice Hall), pp. 91–106 for more details. In addition to SPSS 10.0, many major spreadsheet packages (such as Excel®, Quattro Pro®, or Lotus 1,2,3®), can be used to convert data into SPSS data files.

4

The Role of the Normal Distribution in Cross-National Research

Terms: *Areas Under the Normal Curve, Direct Measures, Z-Scores, Standard Error, Tests for Normality*
Concept: Electoral Democracy
Demonstrations: Applying the Standard Deviation, Mean, and the Logic of the Normal Curve Within Cross-National Analysis, 4.1; Computing the Z-Score, 4.2; Assessing Degree of Normality in Sample Distributions, 4.3

In this chapter, we extend our discussion of univariate analysis by considering how we can practically apply the logic of the normal distribution to cross-national analysis. We require students to suspend their natural inclination to work exclusively from the statistical output of their sample and to consider something more abstract: the implied population estimates that follow from these sample statistics. It is very common to rely on the univariate statistics derived from our sample and from these to describe and compare countries. However, whenever you apply statistical tools of analysis in cross-national analysis or any other field of empirical inquiry, you are in effect using your sample to infer to something more interesting: the target population.

Generalizations about political behavior and institutional authority can only stand up to challenges of credibility and validity if we are able to present our findings in the context of the target population, and not merely the particular sample we have drawn. Unfortunately, as any student of cross-national analysis is all too painfully aware, data availability and the sheer limitation of the number of countries within the world make samples that perfectly conform to assumptions of the normal distribution a rarity (if not an impossibility). This, however, should not preclude students from becoming familiar with the uncomfortable, and often challenging, task of thinking beyond the properties of the literal sample to considering the more abstract, and practical, implications that are inherent within the statistical analysis of their samples.

In this chapter we will introduce you to a more detailed discussion of the logic of the normal distribution, with particular reference to the standard areas under the normal curve. Once you have grasped the logic of the normal distribution, we can then show how to use the statistical output from univariate analysis to formulate assessments of the population's general properties and to go from there to a consideration of country-specific comparisons. The workhorse statistics in this chapter are once again the mean and standard deviation.

Our goal, in this chapter and the next, is to *apply* the mean and standard deviation, not merely *interpret* their meaning. In applying these two statistics we often rely upon the construction of a critical statistic called the *z-score*. We will show how one computes and interprets a z-score, and how it plays an indispensable role in cross-national analysis.

While the beginning student often dismisses discussions of the normal distribution as boring and overly detailed, the truth is that the logic of the normal distribution offers the student of cross-national analysis important insight that is invaluable in the broader enterprise of comparison. Without a minimal appreciation of the basic language and logic of the normal curve and areas under the normal curve, the student faces the daunting task of trying to make sense out of the most basic tools of hypothesis testing within cross-national analysis.

THE LOGICAL PLACE OF THE NORMAL DISTRIBUTION WITHIN CROSS-NATIONAL ANALYSIS

At the center of hypothesis testing is the statistical concept of the normal curve, first introduced to you in Chapter 3 (Figure 3.2). In this chapter, we turn our attention to two questions. First, how does the concept of the normal curve fit meaningfully into cross-national analysis? Second, how are the mean and standard deviation crucial to the application of the normal distribution?

In this section, we summarize the five basic steps by which we apply our sample and the logic of the normal curve to quantitative cross-national analysis. This five-step process is characteristic of all quantitative research. Figure 4.1 graphically illustrates the five logical steps by which we incorporate the logic of the normal sampling distribution into cross-national analysis, and subsequently apply it to the refinement of our generalized understanding of political behavior and institutional authority.

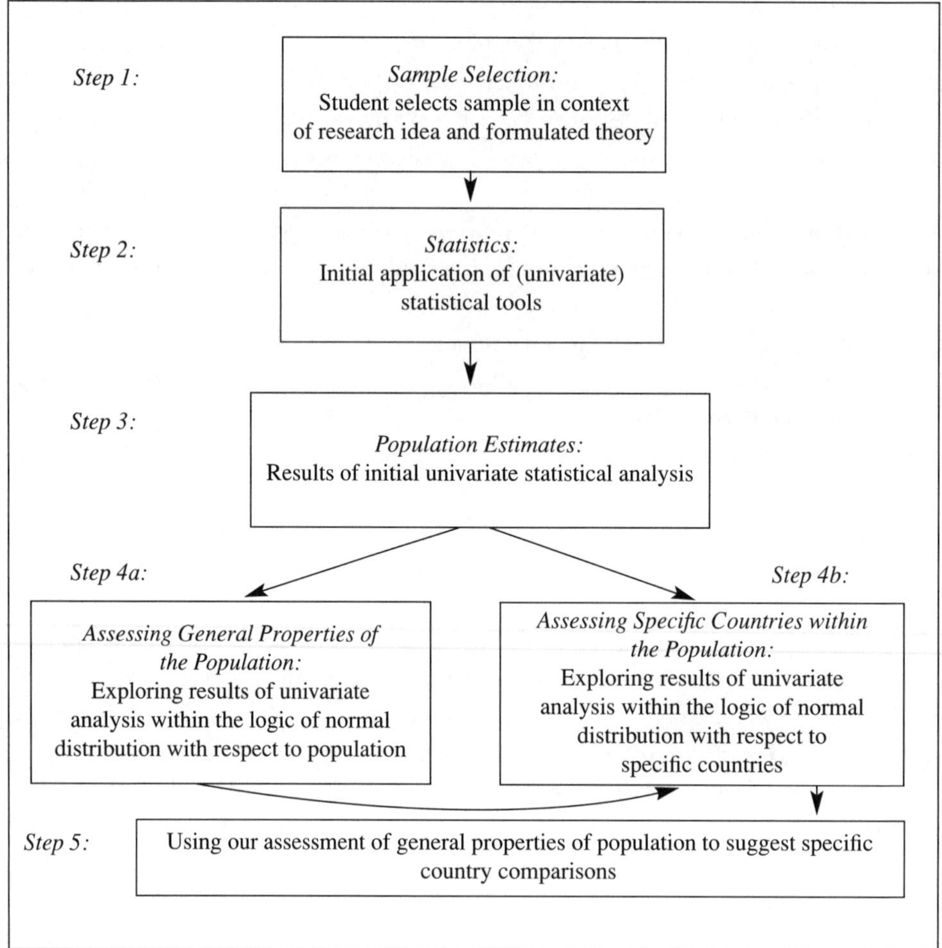

FIGURE 4.1 Steps Involved in Applying Logic of Normal Distribution to the Study of Cross-National Analysis

Sample Selection

The first step requires drawing a sample. In the case of this text, we have drawn a systematic sample of the populous countries of the world, and have done so by selecting the most populous countries of the world that have complete data for all variables in our text and that reasonably reflect the geopolitical distribution of countries around the world. The key to a "reasonable" sample is to approximate as faithfully as possible the logic of a random sample. Recall from Chapter 1 that a random sample is defined as a collection of cases (or countries) where each case (or country) has an equal probability of being selected for inclusion in the sample. However, in most instances, we can only hope to approximate a true random sample. There are only about 181 or so countries of the world we can hope to "sample" (if we are working with a true cross-national sample). By the time you factor in the realistic amount of missing data that one can expect in such a truly "random" cross-national sample, as well as the geopolitical/regional distributional issues, you are left with a much smaller effective sample. Therefore, it is often the case that students of cross-national research cannot get or do not want a purely random sample. Thus, it is important to remember that, as with normal curves, true random samples in cross-national analysis are approximations; we often deviate from the random sample in the hope that we approximate random samples with respect to particular groups or families of countries. In doing so, however, we want to remain clear as to the attributes and criteria that govern our selection.

In Chapter 1, we noted that the purpose behind using the particular sample employed in CROSSNAT.50 was to capture those countries that are the most likely to influence political behavior and institutional authority patterns globally. Population size was used as the primary criteria by which we could systematically draw a sample that would adequately approximate the target population. From this general population, we singled out our target population as being the "largest" of the most politically influential countries of the world. Constrained further by practical considerations of missing data and geopolitical/regional distribution concerns, the decision was made to draw a sample large enough to ensure reasonable approximation of the target population, but small enough to ensure complete data availability. Within these guidelines, CROSSNAT.50 represents the fifty most populous countries of the world's seventy-eight most populous countries that have complete data and do not seriously distort the geopolitical/regional distribution requirements of our sample. This strategy complies with the logic of random sampling in that each of the fifty countries within the set of the most populous countries has an equal probability of being included in the final sample, with systematic qualifications designed to insure effective representation of data and geopolitical/regional distribution.

Above all, the process of sampling for CROSSNAT.50 followed a specified logic; it was not, in other words, an ad hoc selection whereby a subsequent researcher would not be able to repeat the same procedure. Of course, in most instances, students and professionals alike will draw their data from existing databases that reflect the sampling process of another team of researchers. (You are doing this right now in relying upon CROSSNAT.50.) In almost all instances, however, those who have collected the sample of cross-national data will explain what criteria and objectives guided their sampling process. From this, you can judge whether the sample meets your needs, as governed by the theoretical question you are exploring and the concepts you are applying.

Statistics

In Step 2 of Figure 4.1, we apply univariate statistical analysis to the sample, exploring the central tendencies of the attributes in the sample that are of immediate relevance to your particular research idea and theory. The basic statistics required in this step have been explained and demonstrated in Chapter 3.

Population Estimates

In Step 3 of Figure 4.1, we consider population estimates—not merely sample descriptions. The univariate tools and statistics (frequency distributions, percentiles, mean, median, mode, and histograms, with skewness and kurtosis statistics, if desired) reveal a picture of our target population of "populous" countries, based on our sample.

Going beyond this step to Step 4a, Step 4b, and Step 5 requires students to suspend their natural inclination to avoid going beyond the literal sample characteristics and to think in terms of population estimates revealed by their sample and univariate statistics. Two options—Step 4a and Step 4b in Figure 4.1—can be used by students of cross-national analysis once the population estimates have been formulated. We may go to Step 4a and describe general properties of the implied population. Alternatively, we may opt for Step 4b and go beyond simple population properties per se and explore cross-national patterns across specific countries with respect to the target population properties.

These final two steps (identified by the bottom three boxes in Figure 4.1) require that we combine the mean, standard deviation, and the logic of the normal curve in executing various steps that can draw out the relevant information for possible use in cross-national analysis. In the next section we will review in more detail the logic of the normal curve and explain the critical role of the mean and standard deviation within this logic.

DEMONSTRATION 4.1: APPLYING THE STANDARD DEVIATION, MEAN, AND THE LOGIC OF THE NORMAL CURVE WITHIN CROSS-NATIONAL ANALYSIS

The normal distribution is an abstraction. In a sense, the normal distribution is like a compass—it points the researcher towards the true target population. Just as knowing how far off you are from true north is critical to knowing where you are and where you are going, so too it is important to know where your sample falls with reference to the true target population and to drawing meaningful generalizations from the sample. The critical difference between a compass and the normal distribution is that the navigator is reasonably certain the compass has found the true north (through magnetic force). This can be verified by coordinating compass readings with the stars. The student of statistics can never really know for sure what cases—or countries—constitute the complete target population; the target population cannot be verified by something as reliable as the galactic star system. Therefore, we can only estimate the membership of the true target population. Repeated samples of the target population only provide additional estimations—we never find the "true" target population. The target population remains, in effect, an abstraction that we approximate. This requires the student of cross-national analysis to use prudent judgment and experience gained through practice in drawing conclusions from the sample based on the "unknown" membership of the true target population.

Areas Under the Normal Curve (Steps 1 to 3 in Figure 4.1)

We have seen in Chapter 3 that within a normal curve, certain regions under the curve capture a specified proportion of scores within the sample. These regions are analogous to the latitude and longitude lines on a globe. By using a compass, navigators can pinpoint their exact location on the globe by locating true north. We noted in Chapter 3, for instance, that a normal distribution assumes that 68.26 percent of all the scores fall within a certain range of the mean. This range covers a specified area under the normal curve (the distance between points c and d in Figure 3.2). What practical significance is associated with these standard areas and the proportion of scores they represent? From an applied perspective, these regions under a normal curve allow us to evaluate the relative size of a particular score within a sample and, from this, to draw some conclusion as to how rare such a score might be, assuming we are confident that we have a reasonable approximation of the target population.

Let us consider the variable VAP, which reflects the degree of electoral democracy in a country, as of the 1990s. It measures the average proportion of eligible voters (as opposed to registered voters) who turned out to vote in national elections for each country.[1] Electoral democracy is, as Larry Diamond has argued, the minimal condition for democratic governance. In later chapters we will explore the broader requirements of liberal democracy.[2] Electoral democracy—voting participation—is not a sufficient condition of democracy. It is, however, a crucial necessary component of democracy, and for many countries, it is the critical first step on the path toward much deeper and broader political and civil freedoms. The more public participation in elections there is, the more propensity there may be within society for the eventual emergence of the more difficult and fundamental aspects of liberal democracy (true civil and political freedoms).

Table 4.1 presents the univariate analysis of VAP. Figure 4.2 reports the histogram for VAP. With a mean of 59.7 and a median of 62.2, it is clear even without examining the histogram, that the sample distribution is free of severe skewness. Indeed, the skewness statistic is -1.2, indicating the presence of a tail towards the low end (or, a negative skewness). However, with the mean and median so close in

TABLE 4.1 Univariate Analysis of VAP

Statistic	*VAP Voters, as a Proportion of Eligible Population*
Mean	59.7
Standard Deviation	21.3
Median	62.2
Minimum Value	0
Maximum Value	90.2
25th Percentile	48.85
75th Percentile	62.15
Skewness	-1.2
Kurtosis	1.7
N	50

size, we can expect these trailing outliers to be a small proportion of the total sample. Figure 4.2 confirms this: Three countries in this sample lie far to the left of most countries—meaning that these three countries held no elections. Table 4.2 reports the case summary for the sample, confirming that China, the Republic of Congo, and Nigeria had no elections between 1990 and 1997. Aside from these three "outliers," the shape of the distribution confirms relatively nicely to a bell curve, with a slight trail to the left (countries with a smaller number of voters as a proportion of voting age population) and a slight concentration to the high end (to the right).

Recall from Chapter 3 that if we know nothing else of a country, we would predict its average voting turnout as a proportion of the voting age population during the 1990s to be 59.7—the sample mean. As an example, Bangladesh's VAP value is actually 63, indicating a residual deviation from the mean of 3.3 (that is, 63 - 59.7 = 3.3). What we want to know, then, is how close any one country's VAP value is to the typical residual deviation in the target population. *In other words, assuming our sample accurately reflects the target population (meaning that we can apply the logic of the normal distribution in our analysis), how can we evaluate and compare the proximity of any given country's residual deviation of VAP from the mean with other samples and other variables?* Is this a large residual deviation, or a small deviation and thereby fairly "typical"? To answer this, we must standardize the unit of measurement (do not confuse this with the measurement level—nominal, ordinal, or interval/ratio) of the data. Only then can we accurately assess the relative degree of each country's deviation.

Standard Areas Under the Normal Curve

The method by which we convert any original value to a standardized score is by transforming scores to standard deviation units. To make such a conversion, our first task is

TABLE 4.2 Distribution List, VAP

COUNTRY	*VAP*
Indonesia	90.2
Italy	90.2
South Africa	85.5
Greece	84.7
Czech	82.8
Australia	82.7
Argentina	81.3
Turkey	79.4
Spain	79.0
Chile	78.0
Romania	77.2
Brazil	76.7
Netherlands	75.2
Sri Lanka	74.1
Philippines	73.8
Germany	72.7
United Kingdom	72.4
Nepal	71.2
Korea	70.0
Iran	67.6
Ukraine	66.1
Algeria	64.2
Malaysia	63.4
Bangladesh	63.0
Thailand	62.5
Ecuador	61.8
France	60.6
Tunisia	60.3
Canada	60.1
India	60.1
Peru	57.3
Japan	57.0
Mexico	56.8
Russia	55.0
Morocco	51.0
Uganda	50.9
Venezuela	49.9
Ghana	49.0
Poland	48.4
Tanzania	47.9
Madagascar	47.3
United States	44.9
Kenya	43.8
Pakistan	39.8
Zimbabwe	37.3
Colombia	33.8
Egypt	27.7
China	0.0
Congo	0.0
Nigeria	0.0

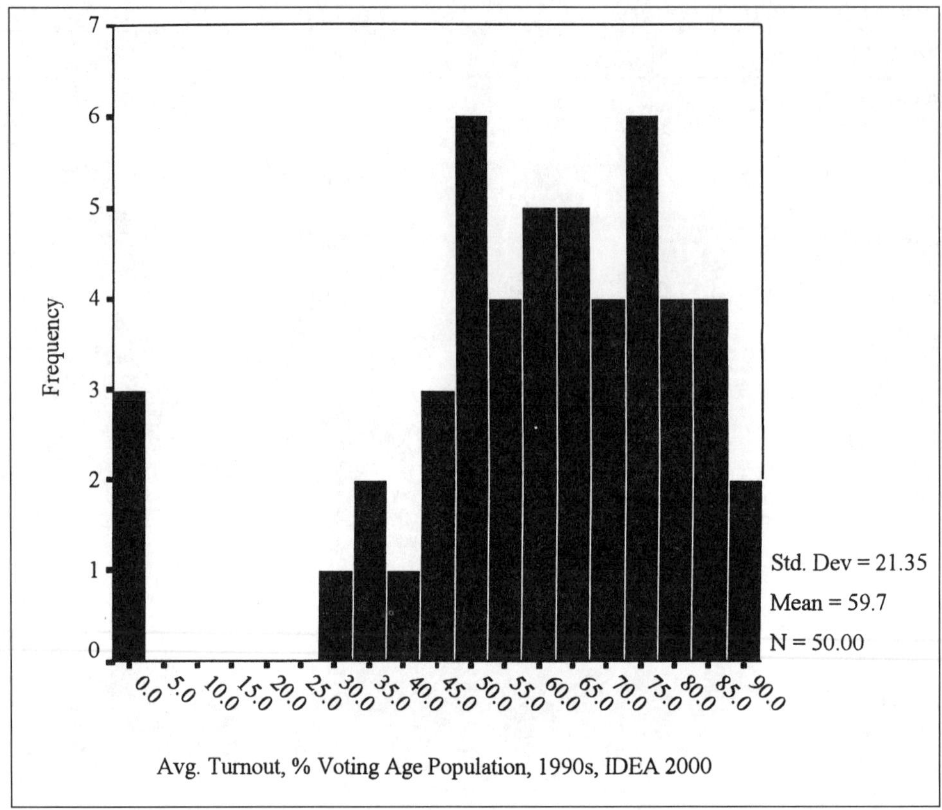

FIGURE 4.2 VAP Histogram, SPSS 10

to locate the specific ordinate under the normal curve that corresponds precisely to the original, unstandardized score. In the case of Bangladesh and VAP, for instance, we must ascertain what ordinate along the normal curve corresponds to that precise location within the standard range with respect to Bangladesh's average voter turnout of 63 percent.

Figure 4.3 maps out in detail the first three "standard" areas under a curve. This figure is virtually identical to Figure 3.2. However, Figure 4.3 partitions the curve into standardized areas on either side of the mean. Each dotted line in Figure 4.3 demarcates the boundary between standard areas under the normal curve. In Figure 3.2, point c is equivalent to the -1 standard deviation threshold in Figure 4.3, while point d in Figure 3.2 is equivalent to the +1 standard deviation threshold in Figure 4.3, and point x in Figure 3.2 represents the value 0 (the mean) in Figure 4.3. The middle solid line divides the distribution of values in half: To the right of this middle line all values in the sample are larger than the mean value, and to the left, all values are smaller than the mean of the sample. If a country had a value equal to the mean, that country's standard deviation would be zero (0), and it would be located squarely on the center line. Finally, the normal distribution

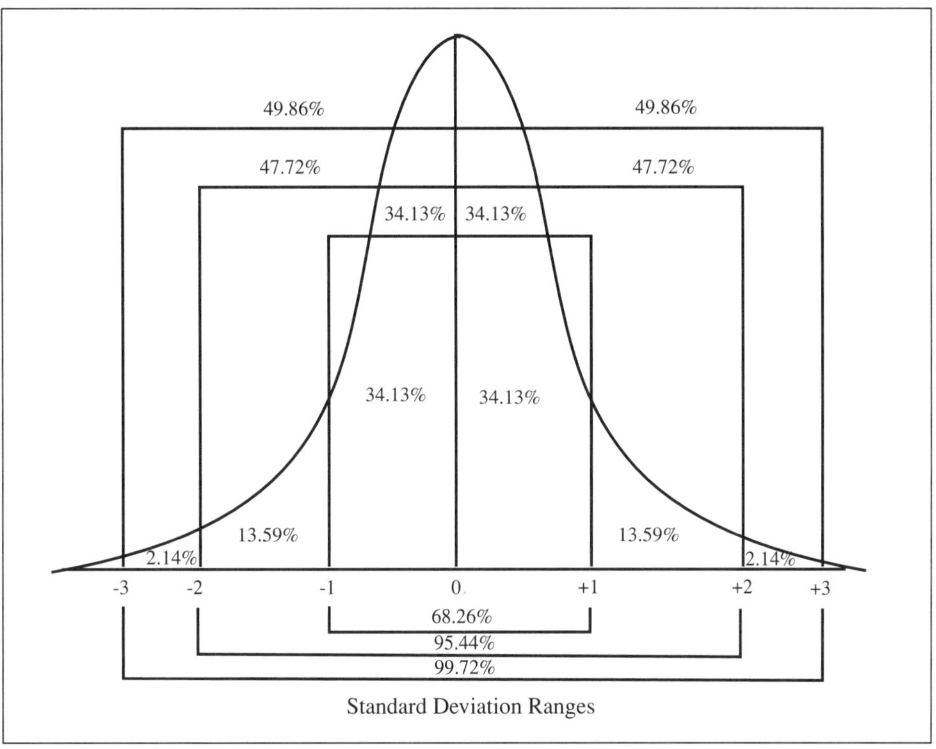

FIGURE 4.3 Standard Areas Under a "Normal" Curve Distribution and Respective Proportion of Scores Falling Within Specified Ranges

curve is, in theory, perfectly symmetrical. The standard areas to the left of the middle solid line are exactly equal to the shape (and size) of the standard areas to the right of the solid middle line. Recall, however, the normal distribution is an abstraction, per se, used as a reference point for interpretation and, ultimately, generalizations. It is important not to confuse the normal distribution with your sample distribution, which, as we have noted in Chapter 3, rarely conforms to the image of a perfect normal distribution. Indeed, a sample distribution assumes the properties of normality without having the perfect symmetry representing a perfect normal distribution. It can be somewhat flat (platykurtic), or peaked (leptokurtic), or can be somewhat skewed. What is more important when we work with sample distributions is to have some idea of how far our sample may depart from a normal distribution. As such departures increase, it becomes more difficult to assume, all things being equal, that estimates based on our sample are valid with respect to the target population. Without this validity, one cannot offer meaningful and credible general conclusions from which theory is built and hypotheses appropriately subjected to tests of falsification.

If all scores in a sample were identical, they would all fall along the line originating at point 0 in Figure 4.3. There would be no deviations from the mean. A country with this score would be equal to the mean value for the sample and would consequently have no deviation from the mean; thus, its standard value of 0. Assuming, however, that many—if not all—scores for an attribute in a sample are different (that is, the sample has variance with respect to an attribute you are analyzing), there will be a degree of deviation from the mean; each score will deviate somewhat from the mean. The degree of aggregate deviation within the sample, as we have seen, is the variance, and the standard variance is the standard deviation.

Locating a Score Along a Normal Curve

Adding the standard deviation of a sample to the mean of a sample allows one to calculate the score that is equivalent to +1 standard deviation for a particular variable. All scores that are *equal to or larger than* the mean, but *equal to or smaller than* the value for the +1 standard deviation, fall *within* the +1 standard deviation range under the normal curve. This is the area *between* 0 and +1 in Figure 4.3. Based on the logic of the normal distribution, we estimate that precisely 34.13 percent of countries in the target population of countries will have a score between the mean value computed for a variable within our sample (standard area 0 in Figure 4.3) and the +1 standard deviation range (+1 in Figure 4.3).

Subtracting the sample standard deviation from the mean allows you to compute the exact score for our variable that falls precisely at the -1 standard deviation point in a population. Any score that is *equal to or less than* the mean for the variable, and *equal to or larger than* the value of the -1 standard deviation, falls *within* the -1 standard deviation range under the normal curve. *Between* the standard area of 0—the mean—and the standard deviation range of -1, the percentage of scores in a normal distribution will be 34.13 percent, as is the percentage of scores falling between 0 and +1. Consequently, in a population, we estimate that 68.26 percent (34.13 + 34.13) of countries will have a score on a variable that *is within* $\pm$ *1 standard deviation* of the mean.

Adding the mean to *twice the value of the standard deviation* computes the precise value in the population for those countries that fall at the +2 standard deviation range. Any country that has a score on the variable *equal to or larger than* the +1 standard deviation score, and *equal to but smaller than* the +2 standard deviation, will fall within the +2 standard deviation range under the normal curve. The estimated proportion of the scores in the population lying between the +1 and the +2 standard deviation range is 13.59 percent; the estimated proportion of the scores in the population lying between the mean value (standard deviation 0) and the +2 standard deviation point in Figure 4.3 constitutes 47.72 percent of the sample (34.13 + 13.59) of the population.

Subtracting the sample mean from *twice the value of the standard deviation* pinpoints the score of a variable in the population that would fall at precisely the -2 standard deviation range. Any country that has a score on the variable *equal to or smaller than* the -1 standard deviation score, and *equal to but larger than* the -2 standard deviation, will fall within the -2 standard deviation range under the normal curve. The estimated proportion of the scores in the population lying *between* the -1 and the -2 standard deviation range is 13.59 percent; the estimated proportion of the scores in the population lying *between* the mean value (standard deviation 0) and the -2 standard deviation point in Figure 4.3 constitutes 47.72 percent of the sample (34.13 + 13.59) of the population.

Finally, *adding* the mean to *three times the standard deviation* reveals the exact value in the population of scores for a variable that falls at the +3 standard deviation point in Figure 4.3. Any country that has a score on the variable *equal to or larger than* the +2 standard deviation score, and *equal to but smaller than* the +3 standard deviation, will fall within the +3 standard deviation range under the normal curve. The estimated proportion of the scores in the population lying *between* the +2 and the +3 standard deviation range is 2.14 percent; the estimated proportion of the scores in the population lying *between* the mean value (standard deviation 0) and the +3 standard deviation point in Figure 4.3 constitutes 49.86 percent (34.13 +13.59 +2.14) of the population of scores for the variable.

Subtracting the mean from *three times the standard deviation* reveals the value for our variable that is equal to the -3 standard deviation point in Figure 4.3. Any country that has a score on the variable *equal to or smaller than* the -2 standard deviation score, and *equal to but larger than* the -3 standard deviation, will fall within the -3 standard deviation range under the normal curve. The estimated proportion of the scores in the population lying *between* the -2 and the -3 standard deviation range is 2.14 percent; the estimated proportion of the scores in the population lying *between* the mean value (standard deviation 0) and the -3 standard deviation point in Figure 4.3 constitutes 49.86 percent of the population, as indicated in Figure 4.2. Fully 99. 72 percent of the population of scores for a particular attribute will fall between -3 and +3 standard deviations—assuming a normal distribution (34.13 + 34.13 + 13.59 + 13.59 + 2.14 + 2.14).

Table 4.3 summarizes the simple formulas for computing the values associated with a particular standard deviation point in a normal distribution of scores.

Our sample of VAP scores conforms relatively well to the shape of a normal distribution, as shown in Figure 4.2 What if this were not the case? Suppose our variable in question were AREA—a variable we know from Chapter 3 to be severely skewed? Can we still employ the logic of the normal distribution in analyzing univariate output? The answer is yes—with caution. If you have not biased your selection of the sample (which we have not) by deviating too much from the assumptions of a random sample model (that is, if you have selected an attribute or criteria to sample on, such as population size, and then chosen countries by a method that allows an equal probability of most countries within that criteria framework to be selected), then you are on safe grounds in assuming that the target population itself is skewed. In univariate analysis, we must be cautious that we are reasonably confident that our skewed sample matches a target population that is skewed. The real problem with skewed (and especially bi-

TABLE 4.3 Upper and Lower Boundaries for Standard Deviation Ranges in a Sample

Formula for Upper Boundary of Range	*Formula for Lower Boundary of Range*
The ±1 Standard Deviation Range	
-1 Standard Deviation: (Mean) - (Standard Deviation) 34.13% of population	+1 Standard Deviation: (Mean) + (Standard Deviation) 34.13% of population
The ±2 Standard Deviation Range	
-2 Standard Deviation: (Mean) - (Standard Deviation x 2) 13.59% of population	+2 Standard Deviation: (Mean) + (Standard Deviation x 2) 13.59% of population
The ±3 Standard Deviation Range	
-3 Standard Deviation: (Mean) - (Standard Deviation x 3) 2.14% of population	+3 Standard Deviation: (Mean) + (Standard Deviation x 3) 2.14% of population

modal) distributions is when we try to employ more powerful statistical tools for hypothesis testing. Then, as we will see, one must make some very important decisions as to whether to transform data according to conventional practices, or to simply drop "outliers" from the sample, or to avoid using statistics very sensitive to such outliers.[3]

Applying Areas Under the Normal Curve to Cross-National Analysis: Assessing General Properties of the Population

Our next step in the process of incorporating the logic of the normal distribution to our cross-national analysis is Step 4a in Figure 4.1. This step summarizes population properties with respect to a particular variable. We could alternatively move directly to Step 4b and explore country-specific properties with respect to the attribute. We will first proceed to Step 4a. If we take as our attribute electoral democracy (VAP) from our sample, CROSSNAT.50, what can we say with respect to population properties based on the mean, standard deviation, and the logic of the normal distribution? We summarize the relevant population properties deduced so far through our statistical analysis of our sample (CROSSNAT.50):

- The mean of VAP within the sample is 59.7 percent.
- The standard deviation of VAP within the sample is 21.3 percent.
- The median value for VAP within the sample is 62.2 percent.
- Even without a histogram analysis (Figure 4.2), we can confirm that the sample is slightly skewed to the "left" (that is, a slight negative skew, with the tail of the dis-

tribution curve trailing off toward the low end of the values of VAP) because the mean is slightly smaller than the median. (We know, however, that sk = -1.2.)

With these univariate statistics in hand, we can proceed to Step 4a and note that:

- 68.26 percent of the *target population* of "populous" countries lie between ±1 standard deviation of 59.7 percent (the sample mean). Thus, 68.26 percent of the target population had between 81 percent and 38.4 percent of their voting age population actually voting in parliamentary elections during the years 1990–1997.
- 95.44 percent of the *target population* lie between ±2 standard deviations of 59.7 percent (VAP). Thus, 95.44 percent of the target population have had between 17.1 percent and 102.3 percent of their population voting in national parliamentary elections during the years 1990–1997. Of course, there cannot be a turnout rate of 102.3 percent. These numbers confirm a slight negative skewness to the sample. Indeed, we see from Figure 4.2 that the right end of the histogram has no tail at all.
- 99.72 percent of the *target population* lie between ±3 standard deviations of 59.7 percent. Thus, 99.72 percent of the target population are between -4.2 percent and 123.6 percent turnout rates.

What of Step 4b in our univariate analysis—assessing properties of specific countries in the population? Does this step reveal anything to us about relevant country-specific properties? Yes; from Table 4.2 you will find that:

- Indonesia and Italy have the highest turnout rates (90.2 percent).
- The turnout rates in the United States for the decade of the 1990s fall in the bottom quartile of the sample of populous countries.

From our population properties based upon our sample analysis and the logic of the normal distribution, we can determine that:

- Indonesia and Italy lie beyond the +1 standard deviation range (90.2 > 81); thus both the Indonesian and Italian turnout rates are larger than at least 84.13 percent of the target population. How do we know this? We know that the VAP scores for Indonesia and Italy are larger than the 50 percent of the population of countries that are equal to or smaller than the mean turnout for the sample (59.7 percent). They are also larger than the 34.13 percent of the target population we estimate to be between 0 and 1 standard deviation range. They are not, however, so large as to reach into the +2 standard deviation range—Indonesia and Italy do not have turnout rates equal to or exceeding 102 percent. Thus, 50 percent +

34.13 percent = 84.13 percent. Neither country is truly an "outlier" in the strictest sense of the term. To be an "outlier" would require (for most people) that they have a value for VAP equal to or in excess of the ±2.0 standard deviations from the mean. Neither has a VAP this large.

- China, Nigeria, and Congo each lie well beyond the -2 standard deviation range. They each have VAP scores that exceed 17.1 percent. Thus, their turnout rates for the period 1990–1997 are estimated to be smaller than 99.72 percent of the population of populous countries. They are smaller than the 50 percent of the target population that might have rates equal to or larger than the sample mean rate of 59.7. However, they do not have turnout rates that are smaller than 0. Thus, they do not reach the -3.0 standard deviation range. So, from these simple statistics, we can determine that these three countries are indeed outliers: they lie well beyond the -2.0 standard deviation range of the estimated target population. With respect to the concept of electoral democracy, we may conclude that these three countries exhibit attributes that are very much different from what we would expect in the vast majority of populous countries during the period 1990–1997.

In summary, any case in a sample that is inside the ± 1 standard deviation range is, *relatively speaking*, a *typical* country with respect to the target population. If, however, you find a country that is outside, or *beyond*, the ± 1 standard deviation range, but *within* the ± 2 standard deviation range, you know you have a country that is, *relatively speaking*, far away from the mean and therefore more different from other countries in the population with regards to the attribute captured by the variable. We label such a case within a sample distribution an "outlier."

Finally, of course, if you have a country that has a value on a variable that is *beyond* the ± 3 standard deviation range, you know you have a country that is even further from the mean and therefore *very* different, *relatively speaking*, from the population of countries with respect to a particular attribute. We label such a case within a sample distribution an "extreme outlier." As useful as these general properties are in assessing the population and specific countries, they are still just that, general. The student of cross-national analysis often requires even more specific information about particular countries (or even groups of countries). For this more specific information, we turn to the *z-score*. First, however, we must understand the place of variance within cross-national analysis.

VARIANCE IN THE CONTEXT OF COMPARISON AND APPLIED CROSS-NATIONAL ANALYSIS

As we saw in Chapter 3, the two most important statistics for cross-national comparison are the mean and standard deviation (assuming our data are measured at the interval/ratio level). Providing we have reasonably approximated a random sample and have not biased the selection of countries in our sample, the mean reflects our best estimate of the *target population's* typical score and the standard deviation reflects our best estimate of the deviation of a typical country from the population mean. The mean and the standard deviation are the crucial statistics not merely for univariate analysis, but, as we shall see beginning in Chapter 9, for hypothesis testing.

It is easy to become lulled by the simplicity of the most common univariate statistics, such as the mean and standard deviation. All too frequently, these statistics are not put to use by the student of cross-national analysis. The mean and standard deviation are reported, but without careful consideration of how they might be used within the comparative context. It is important to remember that within univariate analysis of cross-national data, the mean and standard deviation are truly useful to the student only when the statistics can facilitate actual comparison. Effective comparison in cross-national data analysis involves something so basic that many students overlook it from the beginning.

Effective and meaningful comparison requires the use of *variance*. Before you can compare anything—countries, computers, universities, professors, or automobiles–you must have variance; otherwise you are, in a sense, describing clones. The comparative enterprise is meaningless if you are never able to identify important differences across countries or cultures. Even when using a comparable cases strategy of comparative political inquiry we require variance (either in the dependent or independent variables; see Chapter 2) to test our hypotheses and more informal assumptions. Cross-national differences facilitate discovery, and eventually, explanation. Of course, good theory and sound measurement will usually deliver such variance. Therefore, before we can effectively use the mean and standard deviation in cross-national analysis, there must be some variance of scores with respect to an attribute within our sample. This is not to suggest that a discovery of no variance with respect to an attribute in a cross-national sample is without relevance. Such a discovery can be useful information.

The importance of variance is, of course, not restricted to cross-national data analysis. It is essential for any type of comparison. As we saw in Chapter 2, even in case studies, there is an implicit assumption that you have at least an image of another country in your mind from which you compare the features of the single country you are describing. This "benchmark country" may be an ideal type: a model or hypothetical construct that serves as a reference by which to compare attributes in your single country. By contrast, in cross-national analysis we rely on a sample of several country observations (for example, $N = 50$) over one or more attributes from which our comparisons are constructed. In this way, we maximize variance across many countries in a cross-national analysis (we approximate the "most-different" systems design, as explained in Chapter 2). In a case study, as we saw, we minimize variance across cultures and countries.

The important point is to understand that before we can appreciate the degree of similarity between several countries, we must first appreciate the possibilities for diversity between two countries. In order to truly measure differences concerning some empirical attribute, we must be sure that alternatives to that attribute are, in fact, possible. It would make little sense, for instance, to compare the degree of dictatorship governing European democracies (unless we were, of course, employing a more limited comparable cases strategy). No European democracy is governed by a dictator. The topic of dictatorship might be important, but not as applied to the sample we have chosen. The lack of variance in the cross-national sample would render such a question meaningless. The greater the *cross-national variance* in a sample with respect to the attribute we are exploring, the more credible and accurate our comparisons, all things being equal. Without variance in a cross-national sample, statistics are of little use in building general theory.

Residuals and Variance

In technical terms, variance, as we saw in Formula 3.2, is simply the accumulation of residual deviations of the attribute across our sample (relative to the sample size). *The residual deviation is the individual variation between a particular score in a sample (for example, the score for a country on an attribute) and the sample mean for that attribute.* Sample variance is a function of residuals. Therefore, if we have an absence of residual values in a cross-national sample with respect to an attribute, we cannot have variance in the sample with respect to a particular attribute. A country's residual deviation, in combination with variance, is what we must capture and utilize when applying the statistical method to a cross-national strategy of comparative political inquiry.

A residual, however, is of little value to us unless we have a benchmark from which we can assess the relative size of the residual. To do this, we must first determine a method of establishing the benchmark, and second, fit a measure to the benchmark that allows us to compare a residual deviation from one sample to another, regardless of the attribute or its unit of measure. This entails that we standardize each residual. By standardizing a residual, we convert its value to a universal scale. It becomes, in effect, a ratio of that universal scale.

Actually, we routinely standardize measures central to our daily activities and lives. Whenever we compute in our minds the proportion of something, we are converting a score into a standard value that affords a sense of comparison. Knowing, for instance, that the United States has an economy worth approximately 8 trillion dollars is interesting. Knowing, however, that the U.S. economy constitutes approximately 25 percent of the total value of the global economy places the value into a comparative perspective from which we can better appreciate the importance of America's aggregate wealth. We have, in effect, placed the American economy into context with reference to the world. By doing so, we have also gained a perspective on the size of the world economy. In this sense, an effective comparison between the United States and the world has been made possible because of our use of the mean in combination with a residual (that is, the deviation of American wealth from global wealth).

STANDARDIZED RESIDUALS: THE Z-SCORE

We turn our attention here to Steps 4a, 4b, and 5 in Figure 4.1. Just as we standardize the aggregate variance in a sample by comparing the sum of squared residuals to the sample size (Formula 3.2 and Formula 3.3), so too we must standardize the residual of an individual country with respect to an appropriate benchmark. That base becomes the reference for our assessment of the magnitude of difference between a score for an individual country and the population's estimated mean with respect to that attribute. The sample deviation is the estimate of the variation of values around the mean in a population. It is therefore the standard deviation that serves as the appropriate base from which we determine the relative size of an individual country's residual with respect to a particular attribute.

The proportion of the individual country's residual to the standard deviation converts the *nominal residual* of a score (the difference between the mean and the country value of an attribute) into a *standardized residual* for that country (the residual of one country relative to the typical residual across the *target population*). We call this standardized residual the *z-score. The z-score is the exact number of standard deviations from the mean of a specific country's value on a particular attribute.* The larger the z-score, the greater the difference of a country's value on a particular attribute from the estimated population mean; the smaller the z-score, the smaller the difference of a country's value on a particular attribute from the estimated population mean for that attribute. A z-score of zero indicates the country's residual is identical to the estimated population mean (reflected, of course, by the computed sample mean). Therefore, regardless of the typical deviation in the population, there is no deviation between the country that assumes a value equal to the sample mean and the population mean.

The utility of the z-score is its universal application and interpretation. Because it is calculated relative to the standard deviation of a sample, the z-score assumes a value according to the same scale used to measure areas under the normal curve. This allows us to effectively apply z-scores in cross-national analysis as a means of identifying outliers within a sample. In the next section, we explore applications of the z-score in cross-national analysis.

Demonstration 4.2: Computing the Z-Score

To begin with, you should keep in mind that a z-score is a standardized value for a score in a sample. It is the deviation of a score from the mean, relative to the sample standard deviation. It is, in fact, the precise standard deviation for a particular score. Knowing the precise standard deviation of a score allows us to estimate and appreciate better the degree to which a country is similar to or different from other countries. Z-scores also allow us to estimate more accurately the proportion of countries in the population that will fall between two specific values of a particular attribute.

Formula 4.1 depicts how one calculates the z-score:

$$\textit{Z-score} = \frac{\textit{Individual Country's Score–Sample Mean}}{\textit{Standard Deviation}} \qquad \text{Formula 4.1}$$

Employing Formula 4.1, we can compute the z-score for Ecuador's voter turnout rate (VAP):

$$\textit{Ecuador} = \frac{(61.8–59.7)}{21.3} = .099 \qquad \text{Formula 4.2}$$

For comparison, let us compute the z-score for Poland's turnout rate:

$$\textit{Poland} = \frac{(48.4–59.7)}{21.3} = –.529 \qquad \text{Formula 4.3}$$

Ecuador's turnout rate lies precisely at the .099 standard deviation range under the normal curve. Poland's turnout rate falls precisely at the -.529 standard deviation range under the normal curve. Both of these z-scores are merely "compass points" with reference to the areas under the normal curve. Two things are important about a z-score: its *size* and its *direction* (whether it is negative or positive). Remember, areas under the normal curve extend out from 0 (the standardized value of the sample mean) to ±1, ±2, ±3, and so on (see Figure 4.2; z-scores can go much higher than ±3, though this is very rare). A z-score of .099 is small (that is, it is close to 0, the sample mean), and it is in the positive direction (it is slightly larger than 0, the sample mean). It reflects Ecuador's turnout rate relative to a common scale, namely, the standard areas under the normal curve.

Looking at Figure 4.3, we may conclude that the standard value of VAP for Ecuador falls just to the right of the center line (0 standard deviation). In other words, it is slightly larger than the estimated population mean of VAP (thus, a positive direction, +). On the other hand, Poland's z-score is further from the mean than is Ecuador's and is in the negative direction. Poland's z-score for VAP is, accordingly, to the left of the center line in Figure 4.3.

Interpreting the Z-Score

With the areas under the normal curve as a reference, we have a universal reference point for comparing the relative values of voting rates (VAP) for countries in our sample. The inquisitive student is still probably asking, "What do -.529 and .099 mean?" "What is the utility of this information?" "How do these z-scores improve our ability to compare, predict, explain?"

To begin, it is important to understand that a z-score is, in effect, an estimation. It estimates for us what we should expect with respect to the relative size of a value when we move from a sample to an abstraction we call the target population. In other words, the z-score moves us to another level in our interpretation of statistics. Instead of focusing on proper names (Poland, Ecuador, the United States, and so on), we are now focusing on magnitudes—comparative, relative magnitudes. In the case of Ecuador, we know its actual turnout rate is 61.8 percent. However, converting that to a z-score allows us to conclude that any country with a turnout rate of 61.8 percent will be a country very near the mean of all populous countries for the attribute of voter turnout in elections (or, electoral democracy). This provides us with a useful base, or compass point, from which to gauge the importance and significance of this one bit of empirical information.

The inquiring student would still, no doubt, want to know what a z-score of .099 means. The answer to this question requires that we understand how we literally interpret z-scores of .099 and -.529. Each of these values represents a precise point under the normal curve that pinpoints the distance each score lies from the population mean of the target population of populous countries. Because the target population is an abstraction, for all intents and purposes a z-score reflects a standard, yet abstract, representation of a score's exact location relative to a common scale. If we located ourselves at the exact center of a distribution range, that is, at the 0 standard deviation point in Figure 4.3, we would be at the exact point that corresponds to the mean value of the variable (for example, VAP) in the population. This, of course, is based on our sample estimate. Thus the mean of the population (or, 0) represents the value of the sample mean. To our right, 50 percent of all countries in the target population would be arrayed at various locations, to our left would be the other 50 percent of the countries. The countries to the right would have larger values than the sample mean (with positive z-scores), the countries to the left would have smaller values than the sample mean (with negative z-scores).

In the case of Ecuador, we can use the z-score to estimate precisely how many countries in the target population will have a turnout rate larger than 61.8 percent. To do so, we follow these simple steps:

Step 1. Convert Ecuador's nominal value for VAP (61.8) to a standard value ([61.8-59.7]/21.3], or .099.

Step 2. Determine what proportion of the population lies between 0 and .099 in a normal distribution (that is, in a target population). To do this, you must turn to a standard statistics text where you will ordinarily find at the back of the book a standard table referred to as *Areas Under the Normal Curve*, or Z table. These are arranged in slightly different ways by each author. Ordinarily, the text will provide at least two, sometimes three, columns of figures. The first column is ordinarily the actual z-score value, the second column is the "one-tail" probability, and, if there is a third column, it reports the "two-tail" probability. Ecuador's z-score is .099. Because the normal distribution curve is symmetrical, you need not pay attention to the directional sign of the z-score when using the table. You will need the directional sign later when computing distances and proportions, as will be clear below.

Step 3. Go down the column of z-score values until you come to a value as close as possible to .099 (usually these values are rounded to .1, so it is probably .1). Note the corresponding value for either the one-tail or (if possible) the two-tail probability scores in the respective columns.[4]

Step 4. If you have only a column for one-tail probability, subtract the one-tail probability value that corresponds to your z-score from 50 (or .5, if the areas are listed in fractions). The one-tail probability value for this z-score value of .099 (rounded to .1) is approximately .460. Thus, .50 - .460 = .04. The value of .04 is equivalent to the area of the normal curve lying between .099 and 0; or, 4 percent of the target population. We know that because Ecuador is larger than the estimated population mean (59.7), the 4 percent (.04) we have computed must be added to the 50 percent (or, .5) of the population that is *smaller* than Ecuador by virtue of the fact that this 50 percent lies at or below the mean (0 standard deviation in Figure 3.3).

Step 5. Thus, .5 + .04 = .54, or, removing the fractions, 50% + 4% = 54% of the target population has a voter turnout rate *smaller* than Ecuador's. We estimate, therefore, that 46 percent of the target population has a turnout *larger* than Ecuador's 61.8 percent (or, 100 - 54 = 46).

Turning our attention for a moment to China, we note in Table 4.1 that China lies at the *bottom* of our sample in CROSSNAT.50. Its zero turnout rate for the period 1990–1997 falls below the target population mean (z-score = -2.80). Applying the steps outlined above, we estimate that China's turnout is smaller than 99.7 percent of the target population; it is larger than only .3 percent of the target population. A z-score of 2.8 has a one-tail significance value .0026. Thus, .5 - .0026 = .4974. We must travel nearly all the way to the abstract end of the tail on the left to find that point where a country whose turnout rate equals zero will be found. This distance traversed covers nearly the entire distance from 0 to the lowest score possible—an abstraction, of course. When you add the 50 percent of the population whose turnout rate is larger than China's (all those whose values of VAP would be greater than the mean) to the 49.74 percent of the countries that have turnout rates smaller than the mean, *but still larger than China's*, you derive the sum of .9974, or 99.74 percent. Thus, 99.74 percent of all countries in the target population of populous countries will be expected to have a turnout rate larger than 0 for the years 1990–1997.

At this point, it is important not to lose sight of what we meant by sample and population. Recall that our sample, CROSSNAT.50, contains the fifty largest countries in the world that also have complete data for our database and whose geopolitical-regional distribution conforms closely to that reflected in the "real" world of global politics. Thus, in a technical sense, CROSSNAT.50 is just our representation of the world's most populous countries. Another student may draw a different systematic sample, utilizing other rules of selection. Conceivably, therefore, one could repeat the sampling procedure, and for a variety of reasons come up with a slightly different set of "populous" countries in each new sample. If we were somehow able to repeat the sampling procedure 100 different times, for example, each time selecting a few different "populous" countries for our sample, we would expect that the value of 0 for turnout rate would be a very rare occurrence. Indeed, we would expect it to occur only about one time in one hundred, or about 1 percent of the time. This is another implication of the z-score. It tells us how rare or common a score might be within the abstraction we call a target population.

We expect that all (or certainly most) of the different samples of populous countries will be slightly skewed in a negative direction (assuming each sample reasonably approximates a random sample—just as does our sample of CROSSNAT.50). However, we also expect there to be some variation with respect to the mean and standard deviation of each new sample (because each sample will have a slight mix of countries), and as such, some variation with respect to the minimum and maximum values for each new sample. Therefore, we expect that there will be in each sample a clustering of countries at the high end of the value range of VAP, with no more than one or two at the very low end.

Finally, and most importantly, it should be noted that the z-score *does not* alter the shape of the sample distribution of the variable. A skewed sample will remain so after converting the sample of original scores to z-scores. These standardized measures merely provide a score by which we may readily assess an attribute's magnitude of difference across a sample, and from this, assess its relationship to the target population.[5]

Further Interpretations of the Z-Score

Z-scores also allow us to estimate the proportion of the population that falls between two values of an attribute. However, to do so we must, again, consult a standard *Area Under the Normal Curve* table. For example, what proportion of the population lies between 61.8 percent turnout rate and 48.4 percent turnout rate? To assist us in this procedure, consider Figure 4.4. In Figure 4.4, the area between Poland and Ecuador is represented by coordinate C. Following the same logic as we used to determine the area between the mean (0 standard deviation) and China's z-score of -2.8, we must first determine the distance between the 0 and .1 standard deviations (the distance between the estimated population mean and the z-score value of Ecuador), and the distance between 0 and -.53 (the distance between the estimated population mean and Poland's z-score value for turnout rate).

Consulting a table for *Areas Under the Normal Curve* will reveal that approximately .19 (.50 - .31), or 19 percent of the area under the normal curve is covered between .53 and 0; approximately .04 (.50 - .46), or 46 percent of the area under the normal curve is covered between .1 and 0. These respective regions under the normal curve are marked in Figure 4.4. The total area between -.53 and .1 is approximately 23 percent (19 + 4). In practical terms, this piece of information implies that there is a 23 percent *probability* that a given country in the population of populous countries would have a turnout rate between 68.1 percent and 48.4 percent.

We may summarize the basic information derived from Figure 4.3 and the information derived in Steps 4a, 4b, and 5:

- The estimated proportion of population less than Poland (z-score = -.53) = 31% (coordinate A in Figure 4.4; 50% - 19%). 50% = estimated proportion of countries in population equal to or greater than mean, or 0, for VAP; 19% = estimated proportion of countries in population of populous countries lying between, and including, 0 and -.53.
- The estimated proportion of population greater than Ecuador (z-score = .1) = 46% (coordinate B in Figure 4.4; 50% - 4%). 50% = estimated proportion of countries in population equal to or less than mean, or 0, for VAP; 4% = estimated proportion of countries in population lying between, and including, 0 and .1.
- The estimated proportion of population between Poland (z-score = -.53) and Ecuador (z-score = .1) = 23% (coordinate C in Figure 4.4; 19% + 4%). 19% = estimated proportion of countries in population lying between (and including) 0 and -.53 for VAP; 4% = estimated proportion of countries in population lying between mean, or 0, and .1.
- The estimated proportion of population greater than Poland (z-score = -.53) = 69% (50% +19%); 50% = estimated proportion of countries in population equal to or greater than mean, or 0, for VAP; 19% = estimated proportion of countries in population lying between, and including, 0 and -.53.
- The estimated proportion of population less than Ecuador (z-score = .1) = 54% (50% + 4%). 50% = estimated proportion of countries in population equal to or less than mean, or 0, for VAP; 4% = estimated proportion of countries in population lying between, and including, 0 and .1.

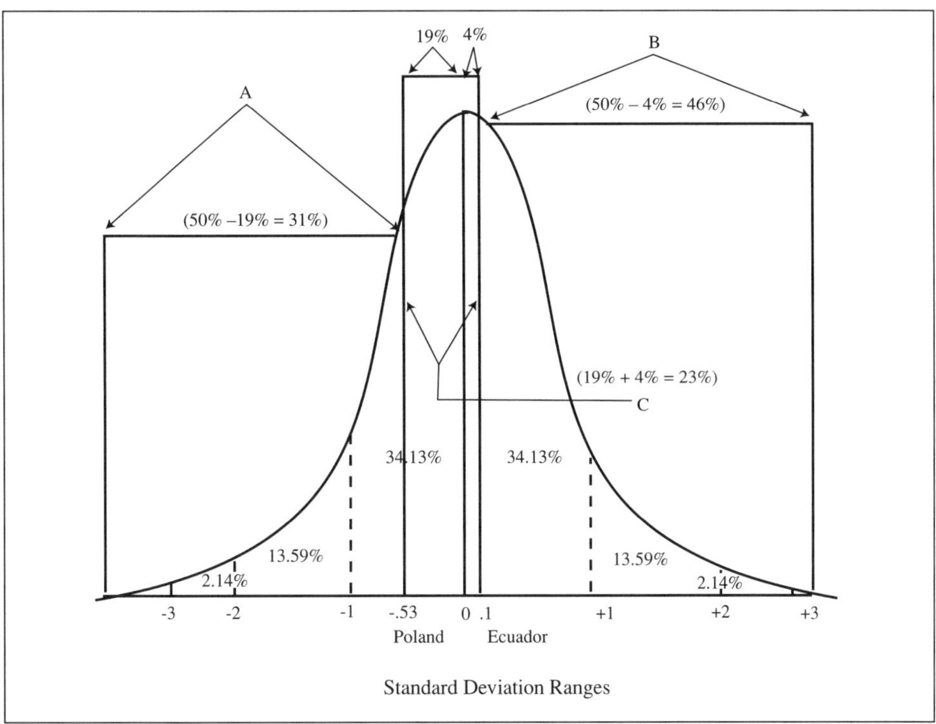

FIGURE 4.4 Interpreting a Z-Score of .1 (Ecuador, VAP) and -.53 (Poland, VAP)

Table 4.4 reports the z-scores for the fifty countries in CROSSNAT.50. The z-score values are listed under the variable name, ZVAP.

AN ALTERNATIVE TEST FOR NORMALITY WHEN USING INTERVAL/RATIO-LEVEL DATA

Exploring the distribution of values in a sample plays a crucial part in the analysis of comparative data, though the issue is somewhat hidden from view by the student who reads statistical reports and analyses in the literature. As we shall see in Chapter 5, there are a number of statistics one should become familiar with in order to assess the "shape" of a distribution and to spot extreme values in a sample that may dramatically affect even very simple univariate analysis of comparative data. When using interval/ratio-level data, there are some basic but more involved statistics that can help the student identify a "normal" distribution. One of the most common simple techniques is the Q-Q plot, or the *normal probability* plot. Two other useful statistics are the Kolmogorov-Smirnov Test and the Shapiro-Wilk's Test. We shall consider each and their role in quantitative cross-national analysis below. We begin with Q-Q Plots.

TABLE 4.4 VAP Z-Scores

	VAP Measures	
COUNTRY	*VAP*	*ZVAP*
Indonesia	90.2	1.429
Italy	90.2	1.429
South Africa	85.5	1.209
Greece	84.7	1.171
Czech	82.8	1.082
Australia	82.7	1.078
Argentina	81.3	1.012
Turkey	79.4	0.923
Spain	79.0	0.904
Chile	78.0	0.858
Romania	77.2	0.820
Brazil	76.7	0.797
Netherlands	75.2	0.726
Sri Lanka	74.1	0.675
Philippines	73.8	0.661
Germany	72.7	0.609
United Kingdom	72.4	0.595
Nepal	71.2	0.539
Korea	70.0	0.483
Iran	67.6	0.370
Ukraine	66.1	0.300
Algeria	64.2	0.211
Malaysia	63.4	0.174
Bangladesh	63.0	0.155
Thailand	62.5	0.132
Ecuador	61.8	0.099
France	60.6	0.043
Tunisia	60.3	0.028
Canada	60.1	0.019
India	60.1	0.019
Peru	57.3	-0.112
Japan	57.0	-0.126
Mexico	56.8	-0.135
Russia	55.0	-0.220
Morocco	51.0	-0.407
Uganda	50.9	-0.412
Venezuela	49.9	-0.459
Ghana	49.0	-0.501
Poland	48.4	-0.529
Tanzania	47.9	-0.552
Madagascar	47.3	-0.580
United States	44.9	-0.693
Kenya	43.8	-0.744
Pakistan	39.8	-0.932
Zimbabwe	37.3	-1.049
Colombia	33.8	-1.213
Egypt	27.7	-1.499
China	0	-2.796
Congo	0	-2.796
Nigeria	0	-2.796

Q-Q Plots

Q-Q Plots allow the student to plot the observed values in a sample against the expected normalized, or z-score, value of the case. As the z-score represents an area under the curve, we would expect that in a "normal" distribution, as one moves along the observed values in the sample, from the low scores to the high scores, the corresponding point at which a case will fall along the expected z-score would also move at a corresponding rate.

Figure 4.5 illustrates the typical Q-Q plot. These are simple hypothetical data. In this plot, the horizontal axis is the observed value of cases for a hypothetical variable in a sample. The scores range from -3 to 3. The vertical axis is the "expected" normal, or z-score, values of each case for the hypothetical variable. It also ranges from -3 to 3. The lowest value observed among the sample of fifty cases is -1.8, the highest observed value is 2.0. Based on the mean and standard deviation for the variable in the sample, as well as the number of cases in the sample, a value of -1.95 should fall at approximately -2.2 range along the "expected" axis (the vertical axis). The point of this intersection between observed and expected is represented by a point plotted on the graph in the lower left-hand corner of the graph. In the upper right-hand portion of the graph you will see the highest observed value in the sample. For an observed value of 2, we should expect a z-score of 2.4. As we advance, one case at a time, from left to right across the horizontal axis (that is, from the lowest case to the highest case in the sample), we should see the observed values change and, as well, we should see the z-score values change as the observed values reflect new locations under the curve of a distribution. This is precisely what we see in Figure 4.5. The line of points plotted in the graph extends at roughly a 45-degree angle from left to right across the graph. Furthermore, we see a straight line in the graph. This is the line presenting the "perfect" normal curve—the line on which all points would fall, if indeed we had the "perfect" normal curve. In Figure 4.5, we see that most of the points, with a few exceptions at the extreme end points of the line, are indeed on or very near the line. This is a reflection of a "normal" curve.

Kolmogorov-Smirnov (K-S) and the Shapiro-Wilk's (S-W) Statistics

In addition to the Q-Q plot, students may utilize two common statistical tests for the normality of a distribution. These two statistics—the Kolmogorov-Smirnov (K-S) statistic and the Shapiro-Wilk's (S-W) statistics—allow one to assess the normality of a distribution. These two statistics, in their own slightly different ways, test the assumption that the curves are, in fact, normal. Simply put, these two statistics compute the size of the difference between the expected values and the observed values. If the significance level of the statistics is small (customarily assumed to be a value equal to, or

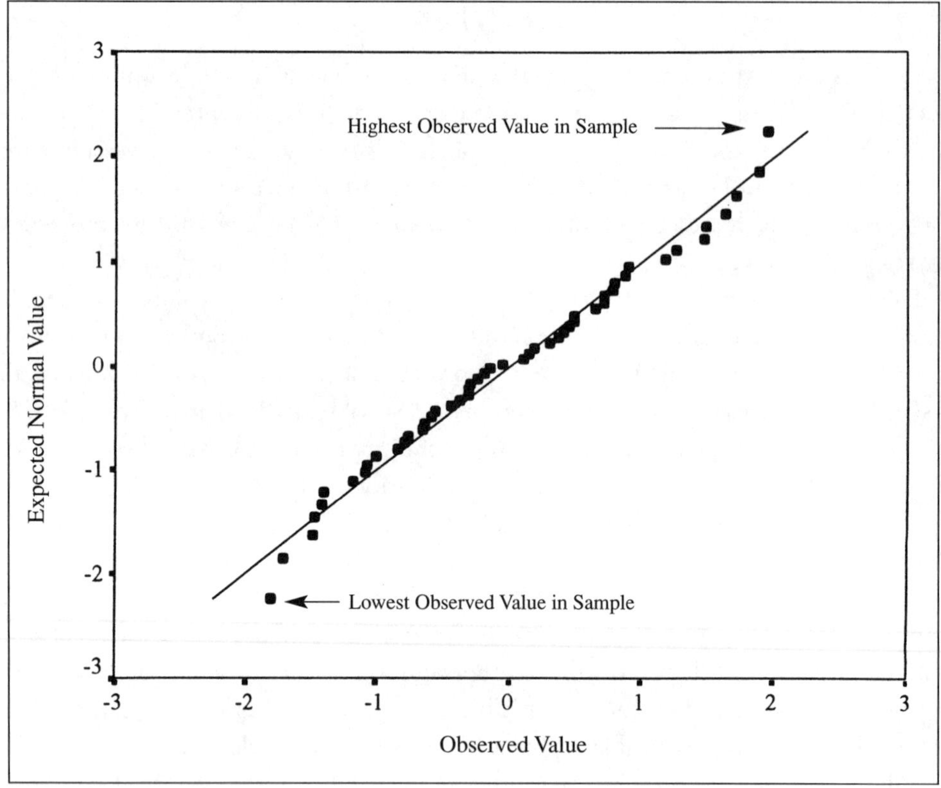

FIGURE 4.5 Normal Q-Q Plot of a (Hypothetical) Variable

less than .05), the researcher may be reasonably certain that the distribution is *not* normal. If the significance level reported for either of the two statistics is greater than .05, one may be reasonably assured that the sample safely approximates a normal distribution. The reported K-S statistic for the hypothetical data presented in Figure 3.4 is .010, with a statistical significance of .200; the S-W statistic is .965 with a reported statistical significance of .304. Each of these two statistics have significance levels much larger than .05. Thus, they confirm what we already suspect based on the Q-Q plot: The variable is normally distributed in this sample.[6]

Demonstration 4.3: Assessing Degree of Normality in Sample Distributions

We consider here in more detail the variable VAP from CROSSNAT.50. To begin, students of cross-national analysis who rely on ecological nation-state level data are frequently confronted with a simple reality: They work with small samples. A sample of fifty is relatively small; yet, it is a reasonably sufficient sample given the size of the population (approximately 190). We already know that within CROSS-NAT.50, VAP violates true normality: the scores for China, Congo, and Nigeria make the distribution somewhat different from what we would expect in a true normal distribution. A histogram confirms this (Figure 4.2), supported by the fact that there is some slight skewness and kurtosis. So too does the Q-Q normality plot, as reported in Figure 4.6: The distribution is sharply affected by the outliers at the "low" end of the Q-Q plot.

The Kolmogorov-Smirnov statistic for this Q-Q test is .108, with a statistical significance of .200; the Shapiro-Wilk's statistic is .897, with a statistical significance of .01. Both statistics are small, though the S-W statistic is larger than .05. Given the small size of the sample, the mixed statistics are not unusual. They do not indicate a severe deviation from normality, but underscore what the histogram and the univariate statistics have shown elsewhere: VAP is slightly skewed and therefore slightly askew of a perfect normal distribution, yet not a sharp departure.[7]

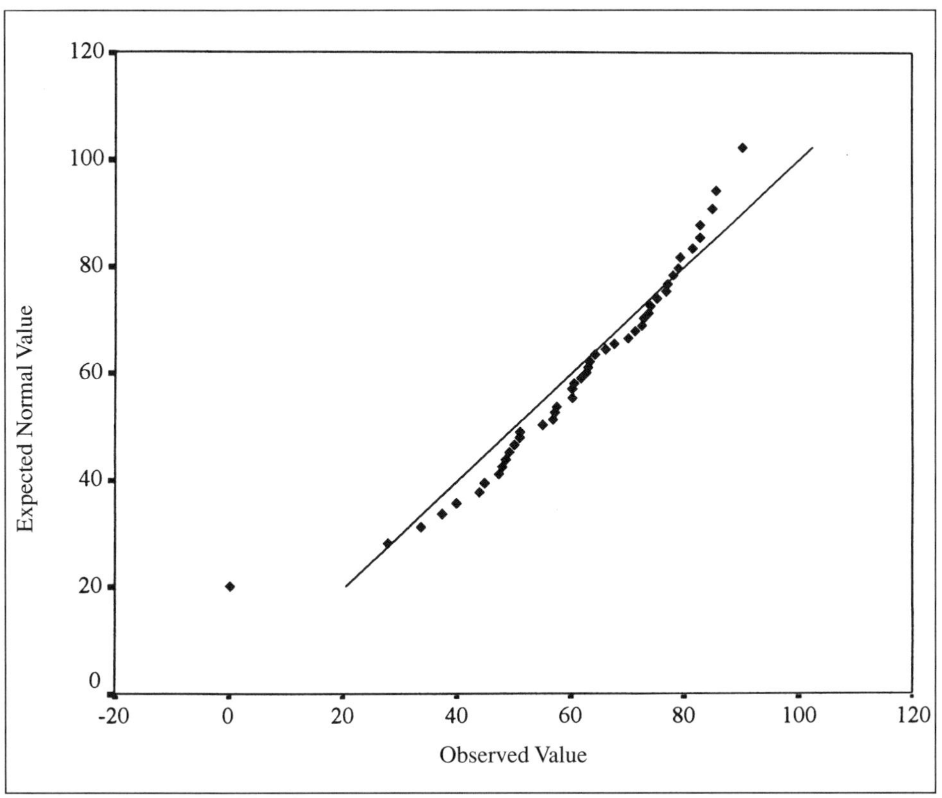

FIGURE 4.6 Normal Q-Q Plot, VAP, SPSS 10

Z-Scores, Q-Q Plots, and Normality Tests in Perspective

At this point it is natural to ask if such information is necessary in cross-national research. The answer depends entirely upon what information you are in search of, the purpose of your research, and how far you want to go in discussing properties of the population based upon your sample. Most students of cross-national analysis do not go this far. This is unfortunate. One of the principal reasons students do not go this far in their univariate analysis is because our samples are often not consistent with a perfect normal distribution. Therefore, students may often shy away from discussions of population properties and from specific country comparisons based on the logic of the normal distribution. In published literature, we do not often see an extended discussion of the residuals, z-scores, and normality plots. This is also an unfortunate, but necessary, compromise with limited space and publishing costs. It is more likely that "between the lines" of the published cross-national research a student and researcher might run across, the author has undertaken these steps in the preliminary analysis to better appreciate the sample, evaluate it in the context of population properties, and explore the patterns of interesting and potentially significant country-specific similarities and differences. These steps should become a normal habit for any student of cross-national analysis.

NOTES

1. The data are taken from The Institute for Democracy and Electoral Assistance, "Voter Turnout from 1945 to 1997: A Global Report on Political Participation", second edition. A summary of the report and some of the data included in the study may be obtained at http://www.idea.int/voter_turnout/index.html. All figures are for elections to the principal chamber of the national legislature (in the United States, for example, the House of Representatives).

2. Larry Diamond, 1996, "Is The Third Wave Over," *Journal of Democracy* 7 (July):20-37.

3. SPSS 10 allows you to actually plot the normal curve in a histogram. The normal curve is a statistical estimate—a perfect normal curve reflects a perfect bell-shaped curve. However, if, as suggested, the population itself is not a perfect bell curve, neither will be the sample. From the sample, we can determine statistically what the population curve—or the normal curve—would look like knowing the mean and standard deviation of the sample, as well as the distributions of values within the sample. This would be the "expected" normal curve—that is, the curve of the population given the statistical features of the sample. Within SPSS 10 the student can easily examine the "expected" normal curve and from this compare the departure between it and the sample curve. From this normal curve, you can also determine what scores tend to be over-represented in the sample (that is, which scores are more numerous than would be expected if the sample curve conformed exactly to the parameters of a normal curve). We can also ascertain which scores are under-represented with respect to the expected

normal curve. To obtain this normal curve, select ANALYZE▶DESCRIPTIVE▶FREQUENCIES from the SPSS 10 menu options. Once inside the FREQUENCIES procedure, select CHARTS option button, and then select HISTOGRAMS, and "with normal curve" option. This will produce a histogram graph on the chart carousel within SPSS, with the normal curve plotted over the histogram. All remaining histograms reported in the text will also provide the normal curve estimates computed by SPSS 10. See Marija J. Norušis, 2000, *SPSS: SPSS© 10.0 Guide to Data Analysis* (Upper Saddle River, N. J.: Prentice Hall), pp. 177-189 for more details.

4. One-tail probability means simply that one is considering the area on one-half of the curve—to the right or left of the center line only. A more detailed explanation of one- and two-tailed probabilities and their relevance and utility to cross-national analysis is presented in Chapter 10.

5. For an illustration of the use of dispersion measures, such as z-scores, in the literature of comparative politics, see William Mishler and Richard Rose, 1996, "Trajectories of Fear and Hope: Support for Democracy in Post-Communist Europe," *Comparative Political Studies* 28 (January): 553–581.

6. Statistical significance will be explained in detail in Chapter 9. For now, it is enough to know that by statistical significance, we mean that the statistical score reported is not likely to have happened by some random fluke, that is, it did not happen by chance alone. The score represents the true condition in a population—a population which is estimated by the sample.

7. To obtain a Q-Q plot in SPSS 10, select GRAPHS>Q-Q, then insert the variable you wish plotted. To obtain the Kolmogorov-Smirnov and Shapiro-Wilk's statistics, select ANALYZE▶DESCRIPTIVE STATISTICS▶EXPLORE sequence of options from the menu bar. Once inside the EXPLORE box, select PLOTS as your display for output. Then, still in the EXPLORE box, press the menu button for PLOTS, and select NORMALITY PLOTS WITH TESTS. This will produce the desired statistics. For further details, consult See Marija J. Norušis, 2000, *SPSS® 10.0 Guide to Data Analysis* (Upper Saddle River, N. J.: Prentice Hall), pp. 325–345.

5

The Role of Inferential Measures and Confidence Intervals in Cross-National Research

Terms: *Inferential Measures, Multidimensional (Inferential) Index Variables, Mean-Ranks, Mean-Percentages, Mean Standardized Percentages, Standard Error, Confidence Intervals*
Concept: Power
Demonstrations: Constructing an Inferential Index Measure of National Potential Power, 5.1; Confidence Intervals and Their Utility in Cross-National Research, 5.2; The Mann-Whitney Test and Comparing Sample Distribution, 5.3

It is important to begin this chapter by reiterating that z-scores should be used in conjunction with other central tendency measures derived from univariate analysis. Such an approach allows us to combine all three comparative strategies: (1) case studies, by allowing us to isolate individual countries within a sample according to specific attributes of interest, (2) comparative cases, by allowing us to isolate groups of individual countries within a sample according to specific attributes of interest, and (3) statistical analysis, by allowing us to generalize about the nature of specific attributes of interest.

In this chapter, we elaborate on our discussion concerning univariate analysis. In particular, we will illustrate how inferential measures derived from univariate analysis can be helpfully applied to cross-national analysis. We explore also in this chapter the often overlooked, but practical, use of confidence intervals.

MEASURING NATIONAL POTENTIAL POWER: APPLYING Z-SCORES TO THE CONSTRUCTION OF INFERENTIAL INDEX MEASURES IN CROSS-NATIONAL ANALYSIS

One of the most important concepts in political science—if not the most important—is power. It is also a concept entirely lacking a direct measure. While we explore this concept in later chapters, we will consider a basic indirect measure of this concept here as a means of illustrating the use of z-scores in building inferential index measures in cross-national analysis. We begin by working through the logic underlying the concept of power.

Conceptualizing Power

Power, in its most fundamental form, is the capacity of something or someone to bring energy and force to bear on someone or something and thereby alter the form, direction, or general disposition of that person or thing to a degree that significantly exceeds what change we might reasonably expect over the same space of time, absent the application of force and energy.[1] Robert Jackman reminds us that power, when applied in political science, is best understood in its social context.[2] Joseph Nye draws the distinction between "hard" and "soft" power. Hard power affords a country the ability to force other countries to do what they might not want to do. Such a power is a function of traditional measures of a country's strength: economic power, people power, and resource power.[3] Soft power is one of affect: countries do what another wants because these countries want the same thing, and they value the same values as the "powerful" country.

We explore here the traditional measures of "hard" power. Power involves the interaction of two or more parties (countries) in a defined political setting where each party possesses a set of preferences, values, and interests that are directed toward some political end. In accord with the logic of "hard" power, a nation-state claims such power when it can compel "target" nation-states to act in a manner that would be judged significantly inconsistent with the values, interests, and preferences of the "target" nation-state.

This logic further suggests that we distinguish between a nation-state's *potential power* and its *actual* power. National potential power is the degree to which a nation-state possesses the primary components from which actual power can be realized. These primary components must be converted and combined in such a way as to transform them into perceived instruments of compulsion by other nation-states. Once the government and its public have chosen to convert potential power into actual power, the primary components serve to sustain and extend a nation-state's power capacity. Without this conversion, a nation-state has only the threat of coercion by which it can compel other nation-states to act, once negotiations and mutual consent fail.

An Operational Definition of National Potential Power

Power is a complex concept, having no universally recognized operational definitions. However, we may suggest here that the primary components of power include three key resources, each of which is necessary (if not sufficient) for national potential power: *population*, *area*, and *aggregate wealth*. These are direct measures that have relevance to national potential power only through the application of theory and logical reasoning.

Potential power entails the latent capacity to convert the preferences, values, and interests of a country's elites or the broader public into reality. It is also a function of a country's ability to mobilize human and natural resources and to nurture these resources over an extended time. We may therefore conclude that *population* reflects human capital, that *area* is a reflection of potential natural resources, and that *aggregate wealth* depicts a nation's capacity to nurture and secure these resources over time. Thus, we define national potential power as a multidimensional phenomenon, that is, having several individual attributes (size, population, and wealth) each of which is related to some underlying, common attribute. Not having any particular theory or empirical evidence that would suggest that one attribute would be more important than any other to the common, underlying attribute, we may therefore operationally define national potential power as the mathematical combination of AREA, POPULATE, and GDP97. In this manner, three direct measures are combined to form a new, indirect measure of national potential power. Such a combination creates a new index measure of a country's *national potential power*.

Demonstration 5.1: Constructing an Inferential Index Measure of National Potential Power

The technical problem, of course, is that these three variables are measured in different units (*kilometers* for AREA, *number of people* for POPULATE, and *dollars* for GDP97). As such, we cannot easily combine these units in a meaningful inferential sense. Before we can derive our multidimensional index, we must convert these different units to a common scale.

Table 5.1 reports the values, rank order, and z-scores of each country for the three attributes of national potential power. We see from Table 5.1 that Russia, for instance, is ranked first, sixth, and thirteenth respectively for these three attributes. The respective z-scores for these three rankings are: 4.440; .247; and .000. If we take the mean value of these three z-scores, we arrive at our computed value for Russia's national potential power: 1.562.

TABLE 5.1 Components of National Potential Power

COUNTRY	*AREA*	*ZAREA*	*Rank*	*POPULATE*	*ZPOP*	*Rank*	*GDP97*	*ZGDP97*	*Rank*
Algeria	2,381,740	0.132	9	29,183,000	-0.315	29	130,700,000,000	-0.405	31
Argentina	2,780,400	0.249	8	34,673,000	-0.289	28	367,500,000,000	-0.218	19
Australia	7,741,220	1.703	6	18,261,000	-0.367	40	374,500,000,000	-0.213	18
Bangladesh	144,000	-0.524	45	123,063,000	0.129	8	129,700,000,000	-0.405	32
Brazil	8,547,400	1.939	5	162,661,000	0.316	5	1,060,000,000,000	0.328	9
Canada	9,970,610	2.357	2	28,821,000	-0.317	31	680,900,000,000	0.029	12
Chile	756,630	-0.345	23	14,333,000	-0.385	44	186,100,000,000	-0.361	27
China	9,596,960	2.247	3	1,210,005,000	5.269	1	3,838,000,000,000	2.517	2
Colombia	1,138,910	-0.233	16	36,813,000	-0.279	27	272,800,000,000	-0.293	22
Congo	2,344,860	0.121	10	48,200,000	-0.225	22	40,880,000,000	-0.475	43
Czech	78,860	-0.544	48	10,304,100	-0.405	49	108,298,166,272	-0.422	36
Ecuador	283,560	-0.483	38	11,466,000	-0.399	46	58,980,000,000	-0.461	40
Egypt	1,001,450	-0.273	17	63,575,000	-0.153	15	184,000,000,000	-0.363	28
France	551,500	-0.405	27	58,041,000	-0.179	19	1,291,000,000,000	0.510	6
Germany	356,980	-0.462	33	83,536,000	-0.058	12	1,745,000,000,000	0.868	4
Ghana	238,540	-0.497	41	17,698,000	-0.370	41	29,490,000,000	-0.484	45
Greece	131,960	-0.528	46	10,539,000	-0.403	48	131,900,000,000	-0.404	30
India	3,287,590	0.397	7	952,108,000	4.050	2	1,610,000,000,000	0.761	5
Indonesia	1,904,570	-0.008	12	206,612,000	0.524	4	699,800,000,000	0.044	11
Iran	1,633,190	-0.088	13	66,094,000	-0.141	13	108,600,000,000	-0.422	35
Italy	301,270	-0.478	36	57,661,000	-0.181	20	1,167,000,000,000	0.412	8
Japan	377,800	-0.456	32	123,537,000	0.131	7	3,035,000,000,000	1.884	3
Kenya	580,370	-0.396	26	23,896,000	-0.340	33	33,920,000,000	-0.481	44
Korea	99,260	-0.538	47	42,869,000	-0.251	23	624,900,000,000	-0.015	15
Madagascar	587,040	-0.395	25	11,525,000	-0.399	45	13,110,000,000	-0.497	50
Malaysia	329,750	-0.470	34	17,507,000	-0.370	42	176,400,000,000	-0.369	29
Mexico	1,958,200	0.008	11	85,121,000	-0.051	11	790,000,000,000	0.115	10
Morocco	446,550	-0.436	30	26,164,000	-0.330	32	90,310,000,000	-0.437	39
Nepal	147,180	-0.523	44	19,104,000	-0.363	38	24,270,000,000	-0.489	47
Netherlands	40,840	-0.555	50	14,952,000	-0.383	43	329,500,000,000	-0.248	20

(continued)

TABLE 5.1 *(continued)*

COUNTRY	*AREA*	*ZAREA*	*Rank*	*POPULATE*	*ZPOP*	*Rank*	*GDP97*	*ZGDP97*	*Rank*
Nigeria	923,770	-0.296	19	86,488,000	-0.044	10	108,000,000,000	-0.423	37
Pakistan	796,100	-0.333	21	113,914,000	0.086	9	200,000,000,000	-0.350	26
Peru	1,285,220	-0.190	14	21,841,000	-0.350	36	114,100,000,000	-0.418	33
Philippines	300,000	-0.479	37	65,037,000	-0.146	14	258,900,000,000	-0.304	23
Poland	323,250	-0.472	35	38,109,000	-0.273	26	252,100,000,000	-0.309	24
Romania	238,390	-0.497	42	22,775,000	-0.346	34	97,100,000,000	-0.431	38
Russia	17,075,400	4.440	1	148,081,000	0.247	6	644,200,000,000	0.000	13
South Africa	1,221,040	-0.209	15	41,743,000	-0.256	24	299,600,000,000	-0.272	21
Spain	505,990	-0.418	29	39,181,000	-0.268	25	626,300,000,000	-0.014	14
Sri Lanka	65,610	-0.547	49	18,553,000	-0.366	39	46,210,000,000	-0.471	42
Tanzania	945,090	-0.290	18	29,058,000	-0.316	30	18,090,000,000	-0.493	49
Thailand	513,120	-0.416	28	58,851,000	-0.175	17	405,600,000,000	-0.188	16
Tunisia	163,610	-0.519	43	9,020,000	-0.411	50	48,860,000,000	-0.469	41
Turkey	774,820	-0.339	22	62,484,000	-0.158	16	404,500,000,000	-0.189	17
Uganda	241,040	-0.496	40	20,158,000	-0.358	37	23,620,000,000	-0.489	48
Ukraine	603,700	-0.390	24	50,864,000	-0.213	21	111,100,000,000	-0.420	34
United Kingdom	244,880	-0.495	39	58,490,000	-0.177	18	1,224,000,000,000	0.457	7
United States	9,363,520	2.179	4	265,563,000	0.803	3	7,765,000,000,000	5.612	1
Venezuela	912,050	-0.299	20	21,983,000	-0.349	35	201,800,000,000	-0.349	25
Zimbabwe	390,760	-0.452	31	11,271,000	-0.400	47	26,930,000,000	-0.486	46

Table 5.2 summarizes the final rankings, produced by taking the mean value of z-scores (that is, AREA, POPULATE, and GDP97) for each country. The variable, POWER, records this score for each country in CROSSNAT.50. In addition, we also report the values for ZPOWER, which is the standardized value of the new index variable, POWER. This measure, then, gives the reader an idea of a nation's *relative* national potential power. Note that POWER appears sharply skewed. This is more vividly apparent when examining the ZPOWER scores: the largest z-score is that of China, 4.208, while the smallest z-score—Tunisia's—is only -.586.

Note the ease by which we can compare in Table 5.2 the respective magnitudes of *area, population,* and *aggregate wealth* across the sample. For instance, it is much easier to evaluate the respective comparative magnitudes of Russia's national potential power using z-scores than by simply looking at the original values for Russia's size and wealth. It is important, of course, to know that the population size of Congo is 148,081,000; it is more meaningful from a *comparative* respective to know that this value places it at .247 standard deviation range of population size for populous countries. In this sense we can see that z-scores allow us to appreciate the *relative* dimension of attributes.

This simple illustration demonstrates the difference applying z-scores makes. Remember, however, z-scores cannot correct or compensate for poor measurement. Our definition of national power is meant to serve as a simple illustration of using a number of variables measured in different units to construct a single index measure. If the original measures were inappropriate, or the original theory guiding the logic of national potential power is too narrow, the final index measure—no matter what its unit or scale—will suffer accordingly.

Figure 5.1 reproduces a histogram chart of ZPOWER. The distribution is highly skewed (positive), with sharp leptokurtic properties. A few countries—China, the United States, India, and Russia—stand far apart from the remainder of the populous countries.

The Utility of Z-Scores Within Univariate Analysis

Z-scores, of course, cannot transform an inferential measure into a direct measure. They can, however, make the interpretation of these inferential measures easier and more meaningful. Above all, it is important to remember that z-scores should be used in conjunction with other central tendency measures derived from univariate analysis.

While univariate analysis cannot substitute for the invaluable field research that case studies and comparable cases analysis frequently rely upon, it can serve to focus one's investigative energies by locating countries that stand apart from the rest. Or, it can confirm that certain countries are quite "average" on a particular trait. This is just another way of saying that we can obtain important comparative perspectives about such things as political behavior and institutional authority by knowing something of the mean, median, mode, standard deviation, and z-scores.[4] We shall return in Chapter 13

TABLE 5.2 National Potential Power

COUNTRY	*POWER*	*ZPOWER*	*Rank*
China	3.34	4.208	1
United States	2.86	3.604	2
India	1.74	2.184	3
Russia	1.56	1.965	4
Brazil	0.86	1.083	5
Canada	0.69	0.868	6
Japan	0.52	0.654	7
Australia	0.37	0.471	8
Indonesia	0.19	0.235	9
Germany	0.12	0.146	10
Mexico	0.02	0.03	11
France	-0.02	-0.031	12
United Kingdom	-0.07	-0.09	13
Italy	-0.08	-0.103	14
Argentina	-0.09	-0.108	15
Congo	-0.19	-0.243	16
Algeria	-0.2	-0.247	17
Pakistan	-0.2	-0.251	18
Iran	-0.22	-0.273	19
Turkey	-0.23	-0.288	20
Spain	-0.23	-0.294	21
South Africa	-0.25	-0.309	22
Nigeria	-0.25	-0.32	23
Thailand	-0.26	-0.327	24
Egypt	-0.26	-0.331	25
Bangladesh	-0.27	-0.336	26
Korea	-0.27	-0.337	27
Colombia	-0.27	-0.337	28
Philippines	-0.31	-0.389	29
Peru	-0.32	-0.402	30
Venezuela	-0.33	-0.418	31
Ukraine	-0.34	-0.429	32
Poland	-0.35	-0.442	33
Chile	-0.36	-0.458	34
Tanzania	-0.37	-0.461	35
Netherlands	-0.4	-0.497	36
Morocco	-0.4	-0.504	37
Malaysia	-0.4	-0.507	38
Kenya	-0.41	-0.511	39
Romania	-0.42	-0.534	40
Madagascar	-0.43	-0.541	41
Greece	-0.45	-0.56	42
Zimbabwe	-0.45	-0.561	43
Uganda	-0.45	-0.563	44
Ecuador	-0.45	-0.563	45
Ghana	-0.45	-0.566	46
Czech	-0.46	-0.575	47
Nepal	-0.46	-0.577	48
Sri Lanka	-0.46	-0.58	49
Tunisia	-0.47	-0.586	50

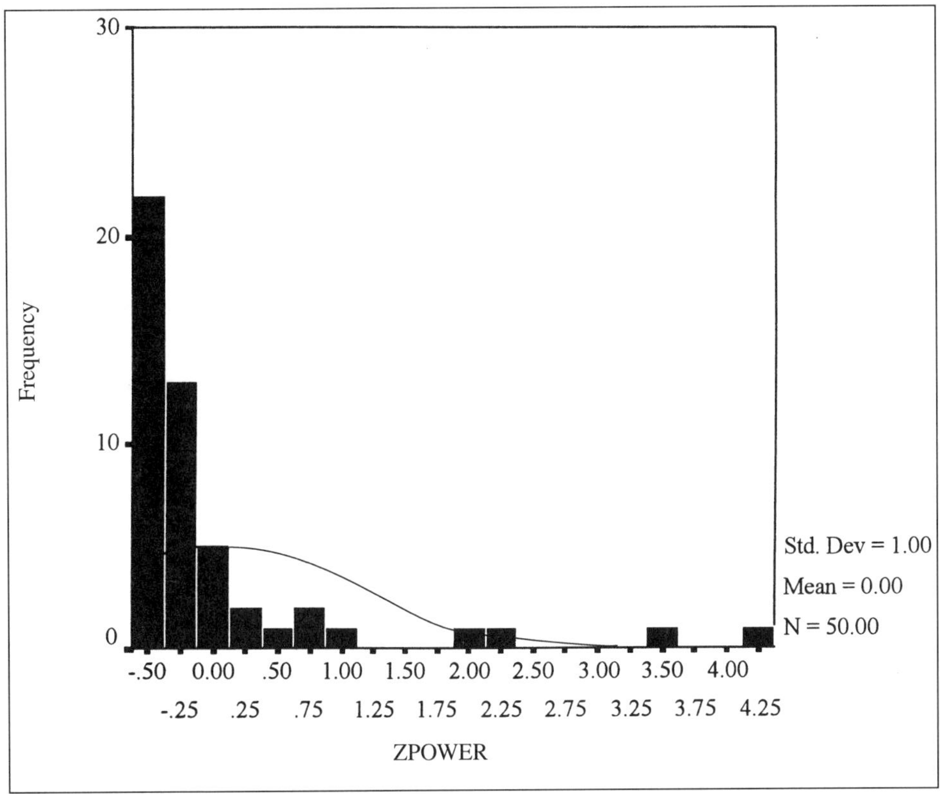

FIGURE 5.1 Histogram, ZPOWER

to index measures and demonstrate more sophisticated and involved techniques for building multidimensional measures. However, z-scores offer a convenient and useful means of constructing such measures within the cross-national research strategy.

CONFIDENCE INTERVALS

Finally, we may ask whether there is a way in which we can estimate how close our *sample mean* (that is, the mean for an attribute in CROSSNAT.50) is to the overall *target population mean* (the mean for all populous countries). After all, we use standard deviations to compute z-scores, which, in effect, measure the proximity of a score to the estimated population mean. Is there a comparable standard deviation measure of the sample mean, in effect allowing us to estimate the typical deviation we should expect from any sample drawn from the population? Indeed, statisticians rely upon two basic, but very important statistical measures for this purpose: the *standard error* and *confidence intervals*. *The standard error is the standard deviation of samples drawn from the target population; a confidence interval is the degree to which we can be sure that the true target population mean falls within a specified range of values.* Both statistics derive their importance within the context of the normal distribution.

Sampling Error

If we were to develop a predictor of a country's size, there are two things that would limit the utility of the sample mean as such a predictor: First, it is a "point estimation," and second, it is merely a statistic. A *point estimation* is a single measure from a single sample that is used to estimate the true mean of the population. And, as we have seen, a statistic (for example, a mean or a standard deviation) is merely an *estimate* of the target population. Point estimations and statistics share one thing in common—they are affected by the error that we inevitably introduce into the sampling process. In cross-national analysis, sampling error implies that we have biased our sample with countries that are too big, or too small, or too democratic, or too authoritarian, or too wealthy, or too poor, and so on. This is not to be confused with samples that may accurately reflect distorted distributions in the population (as we suspect is the case with AREA, AGE1800, and POWER). As noted above, we can reasonably assume that in the world, the population of populous countries indeed entails a skewed distribution, with a few countries being very large, and most being much smaller.

Sampling error is the unintentional exclusion of cases that might otherwise allow us a clear reflection of what the target population might look like. Returning to CROSSNAT.50, if we had unintentionally excluded all Asian countries from our sample of the fifty most populous countries, we would have had a sample that was biased; the sample would not accurately represent the population of populous countries. Note that we would not have known that we had a biased sample though. We only know that the exclusion of all Asian countries would have resulted in a biased sample because we know now that among the top fifty most populous countries in the world, as of 1997, eleven are Asian. Therefore, we can never be absolutely sure if we are unintentionally introducing sampling error at the moment we draw the sample. All we can be sure of is that as hard as we try to avoid sampling error, unintentional sampling error is inevitable. The lack of data, variability in conditions that determine the sample collection process, the unawareness that certain cases are available for inclusion into our sample, the stereotypes or personal biases we carry with us (despite our efforts to suppress these influences) all may contribute to sampling error. In cross-national analysis, when we are frequently not able to work with large samples and random samples, sampling error is a constant menace.

The effect of sampling error is to inject unwanted variability into our point estimations that we compute from a single sample. Consequently, as a result of sampling error, we must assume that if we took 100 different random samples of countries, we would find that the exact point estimation of the mean for each sample would be slightly different each time we drew a new sample. This error will cause slight deviations in the accuracy of our point estimates from sample to sample. Ordinarily, this is a matter that we must accept when working with statistics. We can, however, report the range of values that demarcate the upper and lower boundaries of our point estimations between which we believe the *true* population mean would likely fall.

The Utility of Confidence Intervals

While we can never know for sure how great the technical effect is on the accuracy of our point estimator (because we never know the *true* target population mean), we can *estimate* its effect. We do so by computing the *confidence interval. The confidence interval corrects for this error in sampling by offering a range within which we can reasonably expect the population mean to fall.* More specifically, scientists want to say they can be confident, within a degree of probability, that their sample mean falls within the range of means obtained by repeated samples. Thus, conventional practice holds that scientists must be able to say that 95 percent of repeated samples will have means between one value and another, and that the mean produced by their particular sample actually falls within that range.

In order to illustrate the abstract concept of a confidence interval, let us assume for a moment that we have a database with 181 countries (a cross-sectional database, covering only one slice in time, such as CROSSNAT.50; see CROSSNAT.181 in accompanying CD-ROM). We then assign a random number between 1 and 181 for each of the countries in the sample. We then select numbers 1 through 50 for our first sample (based on the random number assignments for each country). We repeat this procedure of assigning a new series of random numbers, 1–181 for the 181 countries, and select numbers 1 through 50 as our next sample. We execute this procedure 100 times, producing 100 different truly "random" samples of 50 countries. At the conclusion of this laborious (and completely hypothetical) exercise, we have 100 cross-national samples of 50 countries per sample. Most of the samples are slightly different from the rest—many of the same countries are in each sample, but each has just a slightly different mix. These 100 sample means are the best guess we have for estimating the *true population mean for any given variable*. So, if our variable were VAP, we could compute the mean for VAP for each sample. Keep in mind that a population is, nonetheless, an abstraction: We can never know the true target population mean (or, almost never). Thus, our sample of 100 means is on what we are basing our best guess as to what the population mean *might* be—not what it actually is. Since we do not know what the true population mean is, we can reasonably assume (as scientists do) that the true population mean falls within a range of values across distinct samples.

What determines this range of values? If we compute the mean and standard deviation of the 100 *sample means* for VAP (that is, the mean of the 100 VAP means, as well as the standard deviation of the 100 VAP means), we would be in a position to convert each of the individual sample means into a z-score. Our band (the 95 percent confidence interval) would be the range of sample means that fall within the ± 1.96 standard deviations of the 100 sample means. (A z-score value ± 1.96 is associated with 5 percent of the area under the normal curve. A z-score equal to or beyond either $+1.96$ or -1.96 indicates a score that is larger or smaller than 95 percent of the target population.) Thus, we would report that the *estimated* true population mean is somewhere between a score equivalent to a z-score that is larger than -1.96 and smaller than $+1.96$ in our sample of 100 sample means. *This range would be our 95 percent confidence interval.*

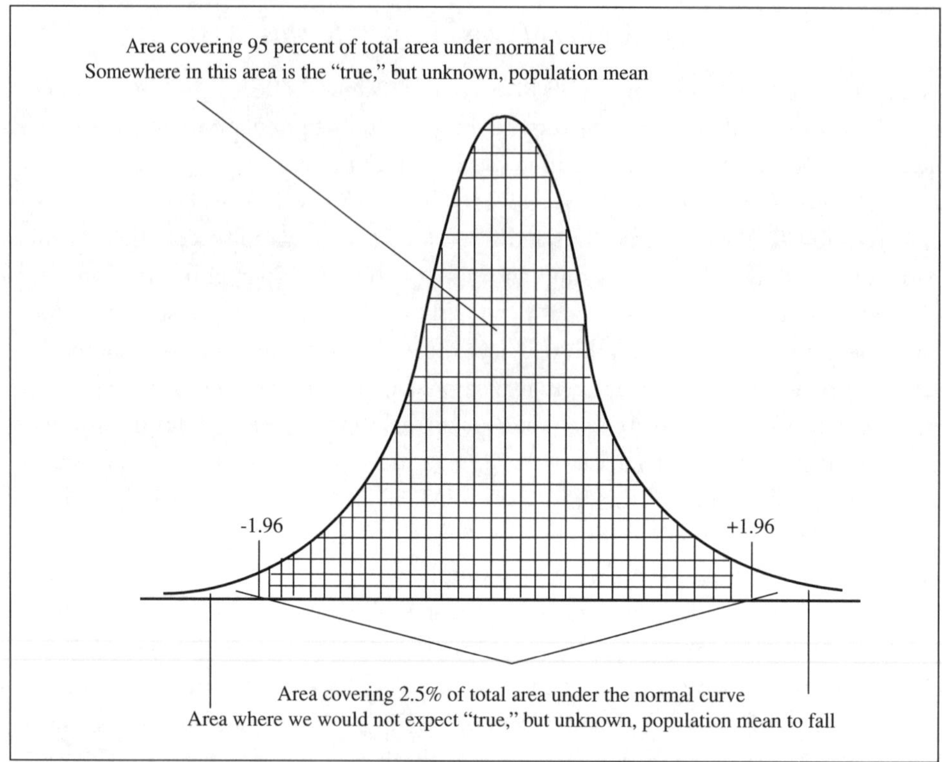

FIGURE 5.2 Graphical Depiction of the 95% Confidence Interval

Figure 5.2 depicts this concept graphically. The shaded area of the figure would be that area within which we would expect 95 percent of the sample of 100 means to fall; the non-shaded areas under the normal curve would be the areas where we would expect to find the extreme outliers—those sample means that are very large or very small compared to the sample of sample means. A sample mean that was equal to or larger than +1.96, or equal to or smaller than –1.96 would be within that extreme range under the normal curve. This would suggest that the mean (and sample) might be a fluke—an aberration of some severe sampling error on our part. Its extreme size relative to the *estimated* population would lead one to dismiss it as being beyond the acceptable threshold wherein we would be confident that it actually captures the true population mean. In other words, a mean that is equal to or larger than the score equivalent to +1.96 in our sample of 100 suggests that the measure itself is *too large to be considered a reasonable reflection of the true population mean.* Thus, the validity and credibility of such a sample would be suspect. Likewise, a sample mean that is equal to or smaller than the score equivalent to –1.96 in our sample of 100 different sample means would be *too small to be considered a reasonable reflection of the true population mean.* Again the validity and credibility of the sample itself would be suspect.

Demonstration 5.2: Confidence Intervals and Their Utility in Cross-National Research

Now, let us return to CROSSNAT.50 and a "real world" situation. We do not have 100 different sample means for VAP. We have only one point estimation (the mean value of 59.7 in CROSSNAT.50). How do we determine the range of scores that would capture the 95 percent confidence interval for the mean of a particular attribute? We begin by computing the *standard error of the distribution*. This allows us to correct for the range of variability in actual means we are likely to encounter as we collect several independent random samples (that is, if we *could* collect so many samples, which, practically, we cannot). *The standard error is technically the standard deviation of the sample means of similar sample size that we would expect to encounter if we drew repeated random samples from the target population.* Because we ordinarily do not have 100 different sample means from which to compute the standard deviation, we estimate what the standard error would be by applying Equation 5.1:

$$S_{\bar{x}} = \frac{s}{\sqrt{N}} \qquad \text{Formula 5.1}$$

where s is the sample standard deviation and N is the number of valid observations in the sample.

When we are working with very small samples (for example, less than fifty cases), it is necessary to adjust our estimate of the distribution in the population by subtracting 1 from the sample size. Why this adjustment? As we have mentioned previously, samples of small size tend to severely underestimate the true deviation of the population. They, in effect, bias our estimates. To minimize this bias, we need to slightly reduce the size of the denominator, which has the effect of allowing our estimate of the variance in the population to expand a little, thus reducing the effect of the bias in the sample. As we will see in Chapter 10, when our samples are very large (ordinarily over 200 or so cases), such adjustments make little difference. (Keep in mind here our discussion of the Central Limit Theorem.) So, for our sample (N = 50), we use the following formula to estimate the standard deviation of the sample means:

$$S_{\bar{x}} = \frac{s}{\sqrt{N - 1}} \qquad \text{Formula 5.2}$$

In our sample, the standard deviation of VAP is 21.349. Therefore, the standard error estimate for voter turnout rate of populous countries is 3.019, or $21.349/\sqrt{49}$.

The formula for the final computation of the boundaries of our confidence intervals is:

$$\bar{X} \pm [(z)(S_{\bar{x}})] \qquad \text{Formula 5.3}$$

where $\bar{X}$ is the mean, z is the standard deviation range of our confidence interval (±1.96 for 95 percent; or, if we wanted to be more strict, we could use ±2.58 for the 99 percent confidence interval), and $S_{\bar{x}}$ is the standard error (computed from Formula 3.2). Therefore, the confidence interval for voter turnout among populous countries in the world is between 65.759 percent and 53.625 percent: [59.7 + (1.96)(3.019)] for the upper limit (65.759), and [59.7 – (1.96)(3.019)] for the lower limit (53.625). These figures are those produced from SPSS 10, from the EXPLORE procedure. The degree of accuracy in the program provides a slight deviation from what one would compute working from more rounded figures. Recalling Figures 4.2 and 4.3, we can interpret the value of 65.759 as being that hypothetical score in our population of populous countries that is *larger* than 97.5 percent of the *sample means* computed from the 100 hypothetical samples drawn, and the score of 53.625 represents the score that is *smaller* than 97.5 percent of the hypothetical *sample means* drawn. This confidence interval tells us that we can be confident that 95 times out of 100 the *population mean* for voter turnout (based on the average rates for 1990–1997) of populous countries will fall between 65.759 and 53.625 percent. With reference to Figure 5.2, 65.8 percent and 53.6 percent would be the scores that would bound the shaded area; scores beyond 65.8 and those less than 53.6 would fall in the non-shaded areas.

What is the Practical Utility of a Confidence Interval?

It would be perfectly reasonable at this point to ask yourself: so what? This seems like a great deal of tedious work for something that remains rather abstract. What is the practical value of a confidence interval, and why should anyone bother with it? Computing confidence intervals is critical when you are using univariate analysis to describe and/or compare attributes of countries. They are less practical (though still useful) when you move on to bivariate or multidimensional hypothesis testing (as described in Chapter 9). At a very basic level, examining confidence intervals reinforces a habit of thinking on your part. Statistics, after all, is about measured estimates of attributes. Assuming there is always a degree of error in our estimates, we are never perfect in our measurement and sampling. We are therefore reminded by confidence intervals that we must think in terms of ranges and parameters, not exact point estimations.

Aside from this philosophical utility, confidence intervals offer a very important and immediate practical value to a student of cross-national analysis. They are guideposts by which we can judge the validity and credibility of our sample. Throughout the previous chapters, we have stressed the need in quantitative cross-national analysis to keep clear in our minds the difference between a sample and the statistical abstraction we call a population. It is obvious, however, that students of cross-national analysis have far fewer options in drawing samples from populations than do students of American politics, especially students of American political behavior and public opinion. The latter have rich sampling opportunities: 281 million people is a far larger pool from which to draw a sample than is a pool of only 180 to 190 countries. Therefore, the strategies and assumptions guiding sampling procedures have more immediate relevance for students of American political behavior than for the typical student of cross-national studies. Indeed, most discussions of sampling procedures in social science are governed by the underlying assumption that the student will be working with a diverse population from which many different samples could conceivably be drawn. When engaging in cross-national analysis, where the unit of analysis is a country or a similarly large, aggregate unit, collected across several different cultures, the population will be quite limited. This, of course, is not always the case. Rich sampling opportunities for public opinion and survey data exist in all democracies, and therefore, students of cross-national political behavior who focus on democracies—especially advanced industrial democracies such as those in Europe and North America—will also have far more options with regard to drawing samples from a given population. We will see this vividly in Chapter 10 when exploring comparative survey data drawn from newly emerging, as well as established democracies.[5]

Nonetheless, given the very real limitations of sampling within cross-national analysis, why should the student of cross-national analysis worry about statistical procedures (such as confidence intervals and normal distributions) that help us assess a sample's statistical representation of a population? After all, if there are only approximately 180 to 190 countries in the world today, and our unit of analysis is the country, the real sampling constraint facing the student is more likely not which countries are excluded from the sample because of our selection biases, but, as we noted in Chapter 1, whether enough countries have valid and reliable data on those variables we identify as central to the planned study. Questions of randomness and unbiased selection of cases therefore become secondary and must be relaxed somewhat from the stricter assumptions that generally govern more ideal circumstances.

As true as this may be, it is still important that we appreciate the fact that any two students of cross-national analysis exploring the same variables could draw very different samples of countries, as well as very different measures from the same sample of countries when working within such a restricted population. In short, applying the cross-national strategy of comparative political inquiry does not allow the student to avoid variability in sampling. And it is this variability that underlies the very real consequences of sampling error and which therefore underscores the importance of distributional issues and statistics such as confidence intervals.

Consider, for example, the sample of countries in CROSSNAT.50. Suppose we had simply selected from a "population" of 181 countries fifty countries in a strictly random manner. That is, no consideration of region, geopolitical status, or population was considered. (We will ignore for now the consideration of missing data—the one criteria that ultimately cannot be avoided.) From these 181 countries, we draw five separate samples of fifty countries. Each sample is derived by a random number assigned to each country between 1–181. Then, selecting only 1–50, we have a sample of fifty. We repeat this procedure five times for our five truly random samples. For each sample, we determine the mean, standard deviation, and standard error of mean. Each of these five samples represents, in effect, completely different samples from that of CROSSNAT.50. They have not taken population size nor geopolitical/regional distribution into effect. Thus, they are the strictest cross-national test we might have for determining how much confidence we can place in our systematic sample in CROSSNAT.50. The question we need to ask is: Can we be reasonably sure that our sample of fifty countries based on population and geopolitical/regional distribution does not greatly distort our impressions of the "real world," that is, the population of countries? Our target population of CROSSNAT.50 is not all countries, but rather *populous* countries. Yet, if we can see that we are reasonably in line with all countries, we can also be reasonably sure that we are likely to be in line with a very abstract population such as *populous* countries.

Table 5.3 reports the means for these truly random samples. Note that two of the purely random samples have means that fall beyond the lower limit estimated by CROSSNAT.50: Random Sample 3 ($\bar{X}$= 53.320), and Random Sample 5 ($\bar{X}$= 50.152). The mean of Random Sample 3 is at the 96 percent c.i. (confidence interval) based on estimates from CROSSNAT.50, while Random Sample 5 falls at the 99.75 percent c.i. based on estimates from CROSSNAT.50. The other three purely random samples fall within the 95 percent c.i. range of CROSSNAT.50.[6]

What can we conclude from this simple exercise? From the use of confidence intervals, we can gauge just how far off we may be in our estimates of population attributes when we engage in systematic random sampling. We must bear in mind the fact that CROSSNAT.50 is based on population and geopolitical/regional distribution (and therefore systematically restrictive in the selection of countries to include in the sample), as well as the fact that while an N of 50 is large enough to have enough confidence in our statistical analysis, yet small enough to ensure complete data collection, a sample of fifty is still small enough to be affected by severe outliers added in a truly random fashion to the sample. Despite this, the use of confidence intervals shows that three of the five purely random samples fall within the lower range of what we would expect 95 times out of 100, based on our estimates from CROSSNAT.50. That two random samples fall outside the lower limits estimated from CROSSNAT.50 does not mean our sample is significantly different than the "real world" population of countries, at least with respect to voter turnout. Obviously, populous countries are more likely to have, for whatever reason, slightly higher turnout rates (as evidenced by the higher mean for CROSSNAT.50 for all but one random sample). However, the differences between CROSSNAT.50 and the other random samples may not be so great as to suggest a severe distortion created by a systematic sampling procedure that renders our conclusions (with respect to voting turnout, at any rate) misleading.

TABLE 5.3 Sampling, Confidence Intervals, and Mann-Whitney Tests

Voter Turnout (VAP)					
Samples	*Mean*	*Standard Deviation*	*Standard Error of Mean*	*Mann-Whitney (significance level) Random Sample Paired with CROSSNAT.50*	*N*
Random Sample 1	59.970	28.845	3.514	.591	50
Random Sample 2	59.998	25.726	3.638	.560	50
Random Sample 3	53.320	22.345	3.160	.473	50
Random Sample 4	54.462	25.912	3.664	.436	50
Random Sample 5	50.152	27.243	3.853	.102	50
World Sample	56.432	26.517	1.999	.813	176
CROSSNAT.50	59.692	21.349	3.019	--	50

Beyond the Confidence Interval: Comparing Sample Distributions

To more directly test this and to buttress our examination of confidence intervals, we must ask a slightly different question: *Is the shape of the distribution of CROSSNAT.50 significantly different from that of the population of countries?* While we have missing data for many of the critical variables for many of the countries of the world (and therefore have limited CROSSNAT.50 to fifty countries), we do have data on voter turnout (VAP) for 176 countries as of 1997. From these data, we can directly compare the distribution of VAP in the 176-country "world" sample with that of the VAP distribution in CROSSNAT.50. This allows us to directly compare the distribution of CROSSNAT.50 to a broader population—not the target population, per se, but a practical population nonetheless. Answering this question allows us to assess whether those conclusions we may draw from an analysis of voting turnout data in CROSSNAT.50 have relevance to countries in general. It can offer further confirmation for us that our systematic sample is not so restrictive as to prevent us from drawing more general, cross-national conclusions—at least with respect to VAP. Of course, our target population is populous countries, yet we want to be reasonably confident that this systematic process of sampling does not render us a sample so distinctly different from the "population" of countries that we learn nothing of politics in general by relying on a sample of populous countries.

Confidence intervals cannot address this issue. They are sensitive to outliers. A few outliers can significantly distort the mean and therefore the confidence interval estimates. However, these outliers may not significantly affect the overall shape of the distribution of values within the two respective samples. Indeed, confidence intervals offer us some assurance that the mean of our sample approximates the mean of the population, but cannot tell us whether the *sample distribution* approximates accurately *population distribution*. Knowing that the distribution of our sample is not significantly different from that of other "random" cross-national samples affords us more information about the general utility of our sample. Therefore, how do we go beyond the confidence interval?

Demonstration 5.3: The Mann-Whitney Test and Comparing Sample Distribution

A particular statistic well suited to cross-national research and quite useful in helping us address this question is the Mann-Whitney test. This statistic compares the distribution of values for a specified variable within two *independently* drawn samples. We know that outliers may make the means and the standard error different across each sample of countries, and thus affect the confidence intervals. However, the shape of the distribution itself says something more direct than the confidence interval. The shape of the distribution tells us whether the means between the samples (no matter how far off they may be) are drawn from different populations, or whether they are in effect drawn from the same population. Notice in Table 5.3 that each of the Mann-Whitney significance levels for the five random samples is larger than .05. This value of .05 is the conventional cutoff for accepting or rejecting our hypothesis. In this case, our hypothesis is that each sample is drawn from the same population of countries. A significance score larger than .05 would indicate the two samples are the same; a value equal to or less than .05 would suggest that our hypothesis is wrong, that the samples are indeed drawn from different populations. This confirms for us that the five random samples, while having different means and standard deviations than CROSSNAT.50, are nonetheless not significantly different in the distribution of values for VAP across all five samples. Thus, while each sample may have a few different countries within it, such differences do not prevent us from drawing general conclusions from our sample.

Of greater interest is the comparison of the distribution of VAP for the world population and that of CROSSNAT.50. This comparison is reported in the bottom two rows of Table 5.3. Note that the mean of CROSSNAT.50 (59.7) clearly falls within the upper boundary of the 95 percent c.i. for the world sample (60.35), but the mean of the world sample (56.4) falls within the lower bounds of the CROSSNAT.50 95 percent c.i. (53.625). Furthermore, the Mann-Whitney test is not statistically significant (.813 > .05), confirming that the distribution of VAP for CROSSNAT.50 is *not* significantly different than that of the world sample.

While this may not be the case with every variable, it does offer one more piece of evidence to suggest that CROSSNAT.50 affords us a reasonable opportunity to draw general conclusions about the institutional nature of authority and political behavior for countries in general, though our target population remains, of course, *populous* countries. Conclusions drawn on the basis of our analysis of some of the most important political countries of the world will not prevent us from drawing conclusions about countries that extend beyond this sample range.[7] Thus, we are safe in suggesting that the patterns of VAP in CROSSNAT.50 reflect in fact the pattern of VAP in the target population of populous countries, as of 1990–1997.

The Practical Use of Comparing Sample Distributions

In terms of the usefulness of confidence intervals, students do not need to restrict their focus to scholarly or institutional reports. Every day within the popular media (especially the written media), readers are deluged with facts and figures, often reported as means of particular types of countries (for example, democracies versus autocracies, or large nations versus small, or poor nations versus wealthy). One way of checking the validity of their estimates is to compare the means reported in the media (if reported) with the confidence intervals computed from reputable sources. Remember, all one needs to check the confidence interval is the sample size, mean, and standard deviation (unfortunately, these are often conveniently overlooked by journalists hastily trying to make their point to a lay audience). In any event, you may be in a position to compare and check your point estimates with those of others, as well as compare their point estimations with your confidence intervals to draw some estimation of the validity of your findings. This practical utility afforded by the confidence interval allows us to be less reliant on the interpretations of others—an indispensable part of critical thinking on your part.

On the whole, this is an essential and basic part of science: checking and rechecking our findings in light of different findings, different samples, and the parameters estimates that follow from these procedures. This becomes especially crucial when we are working with inferential measures. Because these measures are so vulnerable to competing interpretations, we must strive to assure others about not only the measures' validity, reliability, and credibility, but also the degree of confidence we place in our statistical estimations. Only then can a general theory of political behavior and institutional authority based on careful and thorough cross-national analysis ever hope to be achieved. It all boils down to an understanding of measurement and the very rudimentary basics of sampling, the computation of a sample mean and standard deviation, as well as a basic understanding and appreciation of the areas under a normal curve. As simple as they are—and basic—they remain the core foundation of cross-national analysis.

RECAPPING BASIC MEASURES OF UNIVARIATE ANALYSIS

Let us recap briefly. The *sample mean* is the typical score of an attribute within a drawn sample. The *standard deviation* is the typical residual deviation—measured in standard units—from the mean of the sample. Based on the mean and standard deviations, we can compute the *z-score* for each case within a sample. This has the effect of standardizing the scale and unit of measurement across different variables within a sample. It converts the mean of the sample for a variable to 0 and the standard deviation to 1.

The *standard error* of the distribution is the estimated deviation—measured in standard units—of the sample of means drawn. The sample of means is hypothetical—it does not ordinarily exist in cross-national data analysis. However, we use the standard deviation to estimate the likely standard error of such a hypothetical sample of means. The *confidence intervals* are the ranges within which we can be certain, within a degree of error, that the true population falls. It is common to compute the 95 percent confidence intervals, which specify the range within which the mean for 95 out of 100 samples will fall. The larger the sample, the smaller the range of the upper and lower limits of the confidence intervals. The smaller the sample, the larger the range of the upper and lower limits of the confident intervals. Note that we cannot say that there is a 95 percent certainty that the population mean will be within the upper and lower limits of the confidence interval. Rather, we can only say that we are 95 percent certain, for instance, that the population mean falls within the upper and lower limits of the computed 95 percent confidence intervals (the shaded area in Figure 5.1). That is, if we repeated the sampling procedure 100 times, the mean for at least 95 of the samples would fall within the lower and upper ranges of the confidence intervals. We will return to confidence intervals again in Chapter 10 when we consider their role in the analysis of survey data (data based on individuals, not countries).

Finally, with our final univariate statistic in place, we are now in a position to supplement our histogram of ZPOWER (Figure 5.1) with a comprehensive univariate analysis. Table 5.4 presents a *comprehensive* univariate analysis of ZPOWER and the component measures from which it is derived. Note the sample mean of z-scores is always 0, and the standard deviation always 1.0. Even without a graphical histogram such as that reproduced in Figure 5.1, we would be able to determine from a comprehensive univariate analysis the nature of the distribution of our new variable, ZPOWER. The median (-.333) is notably smaller than the mean (0), suggesting a positive skew. In standardized samples (samples of z-scores), the 95 percent c.i. will always be -.284 –.284. The percentiles suggest a sharp clustering of scores at the low end of the range of scores; a quarter of the sample has a value equal to or less than -.509, yet by the seventy-fifth percentile, the scores of the countries in the

TABLE 5.4 Comprehensive Univariate Analysis of ZPOWER

Statistic	*Value*
Mean	0
95% c.i. (Upper)	-.284
95% c.i. (Lower)	.284
Standard Deviation	1.0
Median	-.333
Variance	1.0
Minimum	-.586
Maximum	4.208
Range	4.794
Skewness	2.938
Kurtosis	8.887
25th Percentile	-.509
75th Percentile	-.071

sample for ZPOWER are well over 3.0, the maximum score reaching 4.208 (China, see Table 5.2). Finally, of course, the skewness (2.938) and kurtosis (8.887) statistics verify sharp skewness and leptokurtic properties, consistent with the histogram in Figure 5.1.[8]

CHAPTER SUMMARY

To summarize the important points to remember about samples and univariate analysis in cross-national data analysis:

- Always be clear as to what is the population to which your analysis and conclusions apply.
- It will frequently be the case that an ideal sample will have to be pared back in the face of numerous missing data for critical variables, and in cross-national samples, to take into account important geopolitical/regional distributional considerations.
- No sample is perfect. All samples have built into them some error, either in the selection process or in the actual measures included for certain variables. Make your case as to why you have selected the sample in the context of the theory that governs your research question. Be sure to explain clearly the unavoidable limitations that restrict your sampling procedure (for example, missing data), and always be clear as to where you obtained your measures.
- In cross-national research, where the unit of analysis is the national political system, deviations from a normal distribution in your sample do not necessarily

mean you have extreme sampling error. Most likely, they simply confirm that the population from which your sample is drawn is afflicted by extreme values that make it very difficult to match precisely a normal curve. To the extent that you are clear about these deviations from a normal distribution, you are on safe grounds proceeding with your cross-national analysis (as will be demonstrated in later chapters), so long as you are further aware that when you enter the realm of hypothesis testing, you adjust your analysis to compensate for severe departures from reasonable distributions. While the most sophisticated techniques for correction are beyond the scope of this introductory text, it is also the case that venturing too far with very powerful tools of hypothesis testing in light of severe sampling restrictions should be something one undertakes only with extreme caution.

- Always execute a basic univariate analysis on the variables that are of central interest to your study, whether these variables are direct or inferential measures. Report and record these central tendency statistics for your audience, with adequate explanation as to what they mean in the context of your theory and substantive issue. The most important statistics are the mean and standard deviation, along with the minimum and maximum values of the variable. Histograms, percentiles, medians, and confidence intervals may also be appropriate, depending on your judgment as to the distribution of the values within the sample.
- Finally, remember that while performing a univariate analysis of a cross-national sample, you often gain as much by identifying those countries (or cases) which lie far from the mean and median scores within your sample as you do by being able to report the absence of outliers. Univariate analysis of samples is designed not merely to identify departures from normal distributions, but also to reveal important information about specific countries in your sample that emerges only with systematic and careful analysis. Discovery of the unexpected is as valuable to cross-national data analysis as it is to the "hard" sciences. And this potential discovery begins with careful univariate analysis of the data.

NOTES

1. See Stewart R. Clegg, 1989, *Frameworks of Power* (London: Sage Publications), especially pp. 187–240.

2. Robert W. Jackman, 1993, *Power Without Force: The Political Capacity of Nation-States* (Ann Arbor, Mich.: University of Michigan Press).

3. Joseph S. Nye Jr., 1990, "The Changing Nature of World Power," *Political Science Quarterly* 105 (Summer): 177–199.

4. Within SPSS 10, you can produce z-score values for any variable within your data base. Select ANALYZE▶DESCRIPTIVE STATISTICS▶DESCRIPTIVE. Then, select the variable (or variables) for which you would like z-score values computed. Select the option box for z-score values, and execute the program. This will produce a new variable (or variables, if you produced z-score values for more than one variable) and add it to the end of your data file. You may then select DATA▶DEFINE VARIABLE to rename this z-score variable as you wish. You may list the z-score values by selecting ANALYZE▶REPORTS▶CASE SUMMARIES sequence, indicating which variables (for each case, or country in your file) you wish to be listed and which variable (if any) you choose as your "grouping variable"—that is, the variable that distinguishes cases by some defined attribute. Within ANALYZE▶DESCRIPTIVE STATISTICS▶EXPLORE, you also have the option of requesting a list of the five highest and five lowest values for a variable in your sample. This allows an examination for possible outliers in your sample. To use this option, simply check the box marked OUTLIER in the STATISTICS window. For further detail, see Marija J. Norušis, 2000, *SPSS: SPSS© 10.0 Guide to Data Analysis* (Upper Saddle River, N. J.: Prentice Hall), pp. 67–68, and 102–104.

5. Of course, one way around the issue of small N and therefore the daunting challenges of normal distributions and proper sampling is to avoid focusing on nation-states (and national political systems) as units of analysis. Rather, by focusing on units at the sub-national level, one can address issues of national differences and achieve larger samples. For instance, rather than select as one's unit a country when comparing voter turnout, one might instead focus on a formal sub-national region (state, province, or other local units). This might limit the number of nation-states (as not all states have sub-national units), but it might possibly extend the total number of valid cases from which to draw a sample. Or, if one is interested in the stability of governments, rather than focusing on the aggregate number of formal governments a country has had during a defined period of time, the student of cross-national analysis may decide the best unit of analysis is the government (for example, cabinet or prime minister) itself. In this way, the student may have several units per nation-state, thereby improving the number of valid observations from which to sample. Finally, as we will see in Chapter 10, many questions of political behavior can be and are addressed effectively through survey research, which, in effect, samples by population within a nation-state, and thereby eliminates many of the sampling issues that face students of comparative cross-national analysis when they rely on the nation-state as the principal unit of analysis. Nonetheless, there is no escaping the basic fact of cross-national analysis: Arguably, the most potent questions are those that allow us to make distinctions between different countries and systems, and ultimately, the basic motivating reason students explore issues of comparative politics is because at some point, only by focusing on the national unit can we draw the sharp and critical distinctions between different countries that so dramatically affect politics within the world around us. Without the ability to test concepts that we suppose to be significant *within* political systems (based on our findings drawn from case or comparable case strategies of comparison) across variance of different cultural and national contexts, we cannot know if the within-system concoct has relevance beyond the system itself—that is, does it have a general, or universal, application. See Adam Przeworski and Henry Teune,

1970, *The Logic of Comparative Social Inquiry* (New York: Wiley), for the classic explanation of the logic and role of national-based variance in comparative political analysis. Also see Gisèle De Meur and Dirk Berg-Schlosser, 1994, "Comparing Political Systems: Establishing Similarities and Dissimilarities," *European Journal of Political Research* 26: 193–219, for particularly acute application and insight.

6. These data are available within CROSSNAT.181 within the text's accompanying CD-ROM.

7. Mann-Whitney tests are particularly useful for students of cross-national research because (1) so often we are drawing segments of countries from a world population, and (2) so often we are explicitly and directly comparing different groups of countries. We may, for instance, be interested in comparing turnout rates (VAP) across different regions of the world (REGION), or across different civilizations (CIVILIZ). We may want to check whether the distribution is different or the same across these groups. Indeed, in this instance, we would probably be testing the proposition that turnout rates vary across civilizations due to different cultural values (especially with respect to differing roles of men and women). Furthermore, because of the very real sampling restrictions facing students of cross-national research, and because the Mann-Whitney test is a non-parametric statistic (that is, its estimates are not as sensitive to severe deviations of normal distribution assumptions that underlie most statistics used by students of cross-national research), Mann-Whitney tests are useful as a means of running rough checks on whether we have a credible cross-national sample—as demonstrated above. Therefore, for a variety of reasons, the Mann-Whitney test statistic, while rarely seen in ordinary cross-national research, is a useful tool for students of cross-national research, regardless of their level of statistical and conceptual sophistication. To obtain Mann-Whitney tests in SPSS 10, simply execute the sequence from the main menu bar ANALYZE▶NONPARAMETRIC TESTS▶2 INDEPENDENT SAMPLES, and specify the Mann-Whitney option. See Marija J. Noruåis, 2000, *SPSS: SPSS© 10.0 Guide to Data Analysis* (Upper Saddle River, N.J.: Prentice Hall), pp. 332–334.

8. To initially explore your data within SPSS 10 and access 95% c.i. select from the main menu bar ANALYZE▶DESCRIPTIVE STATISTICS▶EXPLORE. You may then select the variable (or variables) from windows list upon which you wish to execute a univariate analysis. Pushing the STATISTICS button will allow you to choose which univariate statistics you wish to use in the analysis, including the confidence intervals (and you may select either the 95 percent or 99 percent confidence interval). Selecting the PLOTS button will allow you to choose a variety of basic or specialized plots. The HISTOGRAM and BOX PLOTS will probably be the most useful. Box plots will be discussed in more detail in Chapters 6 and 8. SPSS 10 will afford you the option of selecting a variable that will identify these cases (or countries) for you (such as the variable CODE in CROSSNAT.50). Once you have selected which statistics and plots you wish to produce in your analysis, you may then instruct the system to produce STATISTICS, PLOTS, or BOTH in the subsequent analysis. You may also select a variable by which to factor your sample. If, for instance, you wish to analyze AREA by each of the six geopolitical/regional groups separately, you may choose REGION as your FACTOR variable. This will produce univariate plots and statistics for AREA for each geopolitical/regional group, separately. The results will be written to the OUTPUT window. The graphs produced by SPSS 10 appear in a separate window, the chart carousel. Fre-

quency distributions for any variable within your sample can be obtained by ANALYZE▶DESCRIPTIVE STATISTICS▶FREQUENCIES. Within this option, you may also select histogram plots or bar charts.You may also opt to have the normal curve plotted in your histogram (as is shown in Figure 3.7). See Marija J. Norušis, 2000, *SPSS: SPSS© 10.0 Guide to Data Analysis* (Upper Saddle River, N.J.: Prentice Hall), pp. 102–107.

6

The Role of Measurement Validity in Cross-National Analysis

Terms: *Concept Stretching, Concept Traveling, Primary Properties, Secondary Concepts, Face Validity, Criterion Validity, Construct Validity, External Validity*

One of the most challenging tasks in empirical analysis is combining concepts with numbers in a meaningful fashion. Numbers without conceptual foundations are meaningless. Similarly, we cannot test the validity of our concepts without valid and reliable measures. Previously, we used the relationship between measurement and concepts (for example, in our discussion of the measures for ZPOWER and national potential power, as well as voting turnout rates, VAP) to explain how we can apply the logic of the normal sample distribution to the quantitative analysis of comparative data. Through z-scores, we effectively combined several classes of data representing direct measures (ZAREA, ZPOP, and ZGDP97) into a new, single inferential measure of national potential power (ZPOWER).

This discussion only briefly considered the fact that the rules that guide the logic of concept-building often also impose severe restrictions upon cross-national empirical research. The role of cross-national research is to expand, by use of valid and reliable statistical analysis, our general knowledge of politics. However, as our reach for broader samples of different countries and cultures extends outward, we also increase the risk that the concepts we use to simplify and expand our understanding of political phenomena may be so specific as to be appropriately applied only to a very limited set of countries and cultural contexts, thereby undermining our efforts to generalize.

Throughout the remainder of the text, we will explore the logical connections between concepts and empirical measurement in cross-national research. Specifically, we will consider what is arguably the most studied concept in comparative politics: democracy. Effective application of hypothesis-testing techniques depends ultimately on the logical integrity of our concepts and their applicability to the sample of countries employed in our analysis. We begin, therefore, with a consideration of how we may effectively combine logical concepts with empirical measures and apply these to the cross-national analysis of democracy.

MEASURING DEMOCRACY: CONCEPT STRETCHING AND CONCEPT TRAVELING

There can be little doubt that democracy, as it is usually understood, has its roots in "Western," or European, civilization. The usage of the term itself implies a set of ideals that have their origins within a particular geocultural and historical context. Ideally, the challenge before the student of the cross-national strategy of comparative political inquiry is to conceptualize democracy in such a way as to be reasonably applied to all national and cultural contexts. Concept stretching—a term attributed to Giovanni Sartori in an article first published in 1970—occurs when we extend a concept beyond the specific national and cultural context to one approximating a general context. There has been justifiable criticism that the concept of democracy was conceived and operationally defined in such a narrow way that it reflects only European and American cultural traits. This criticism underscores a major issue confronting contemporary comparativists.[1]

The Trick: To Travel, but Not Stretch

When researchers "stretch" a concept to fit a broad cross-national sample they jeopardize the credibility and validity of the final empirical results of the analysis. In contrast, when researchers add more countries to their cross-national sample, but exclude those countries that cannot be reasonably considered to be a member of the class described by the primary concept, they have appropriately "concept traveled." The trick for students of cross-national analysis is to concept travel while avoiding concept stretching. The problem is that this is often a matter of subjective judgment; no fast and simple rule exists that allows the student of cross-national analysis to know immediately if a concept has been stretched. Ultimately, the best prevention against stretching is careful and disciplined empirical analysis.[2]

Concept stretching generally applies only to complex concepts. Unfortunately, there are no standard lists in political science by which a researcher can differentiate between complex and "simple" concepts. Rather, complexity and simplicity are very much products of the picture of the political world held by the researcher. In the case of democracy, some may hold it to be a simple concept; most, however, would argue that it, like power, is clearly within the class of complex concepts.[3]

Concepts in the social sciences that are defined in terms of a single property (simple concepts) are rare. In most instances, these concepts cannot adequately capture the richness of the phenomena under investigation. As we shall see, if we define democracy in terms of free elections, we have limited the primary concept to a single, simple primary property. However, as we shall also see, democracy entails more than the simple procedure of free elections. The failure to specify and operationally define these additional critical primary properties renders the concept less useful in the cross-national analysis of our political world.

Specifically, concept stretching is a result of defining the primary concept in such explicit and refined terms—known as *primary properties*—that very few countries in a cross-national sample can reasonably be included in a class of countries described by the primary concept. We may minimize the hazards of stretching, therefore, by reducing the number of primary properties that we employ to define the meaning of the primary concept. This allows the concept to be reasonably applied to a broad cross-national sample. However, this common strategy also runs the real risk of relying upon concepts that are substantively weak, that is, they provide little useful information about our political world.

Primary Concepts and Primary Properties

One example of a common complex concept found in comparative political analysis that illustrates well the issue of concept stretching is that of social class (first discussed in Chapter 1).

Suppose we wanted to compare the proportion of people across a sample of countries according to the concept of social class. Our first task is to define the concept in such a way as to maximize cross-national and cross-cultural relevance and validity. Once we have defined the concept of social class, we must operationalize the primary components of the concept and assign numerical representations to these properties. In this manner, we may ascertain the degree to which the properties of the concept are represented within each of the countries in the sample.

To avoid concept stretching, we must ensure that we have identified the primary properties that have cross-national validity. Recall from Chapter 1 that the primary properties of social class are generally assumed to be income, education, and occupational status. We assume further that in any country included in the cross-national sample, there will be equivalent properties of education, income, and occupational classification from which operational representations can be found.

The researcher must explain logically her reasoning regarding the connection between the concept and the specified primary properties of the concept. The primary properties ideally must be necessary and sufficient to isolate the assumed effect of the phenomena in question (in this case, social class). For instance, we might, upon closer examination, discover that some countries have only two types of educational levels (that is, they have primary and secondary education, but no higher educational system), or that some countries have fewer categories of occupations than do other countries, thus reducing the range of occupations from which to estimate a hierarchy among classes. In such circumstances, should we modify our original conceptualization and redefine our primary properties? No, of course not—at least not entirely. If education (or a primary property) has equivalence across all countries in the sample, but the range of the property is greater in some circumstances than others (some have higher education, and others not), the concept has not been stretched and one need not reconstruct one's conceptualization of social class. Countries without an empirical aspect of a valid and equivalent primary property (for example, a country that has no higher educational system) are assigned a score for social class that reflects the diminished scale of the primary property within the concept as a whole. It is possible that better representation of the ranges of education that could define the primary property are available across the sample. However, as long as the principal concept has equivalent meaning across the sample (a challenge that students of cross-national analysis confront regularly), and as long as one's operationalizations of the specific primary properties are exact, concept stretching is likely to be minimized or avoided altogether.

The example of class illustrates one of the major difficulties for students of cross-national analysis. Many of the simple procedures and routines common to comparative analysis are much more daunting when the sample includes a diverse mixture of cultures and political contexts. Concept traveling is a much more realistic prospect when we deal with samples that are limited to only case studies or comparable cases strategies with quite similar cultural and historical conditions. However, for students of cross-national analysis, often the slightest attempt to concept travel meets with the risk of concept stretching, thus subjecting the results of the analysis to charges of irrelevance and inaccuracy.

There is virtually no way to fully escape this problem in cross-national analysis, despite an ongoing discussion of it. There is also virtually no way to lay out simple rules and procedures for avoiding concept stretching. As with many aspects of cross-national analysis, careful definition, disciplined syllogistic reasoning, and the tedious accumulation of knowledge about specific countries and cultures are the only real protections against the problem. However, no one is an expert on all countries, and the most careful definition and disciplined reasoning is no guarantee against the pitfalls of unintended concept stretching.

Concept Formulation, Operationalization, and Measurement

It is important here to distinguish the pitfalls of operationalization from those of concept stretching. While the two clearly are linked, concept stretching refers primarily to the assignment of primary properties of a broader phenomena which have significantly different meaning and relevance across countries in the sample. Stretching renders subsequent operationalizations of the primary properties invalid and undermines efforts to build general theory. Invalid operationalization assumes one has assigned a measurement to a primary property that does not accurately reflect the nature of the property, and therefore the principal concept.

Furthermore, the logic of concept formulation leads us back to index construction and the application of multidimensional measures. In this sense, we see that concept construction cannot be practically divorced from issues of measurement. While concept formulation always *precedes* measurement in a formal sense, in the practical enterprise of empirical research, concepts must be carefully and continually evaluated in terms of their capacity to be verified (recall Figure 1.1). Verification, as we shall see in the next chapter, requires that we go beyond simple univariate analysis to at least the application of bivariate techniques, which is central to the logic of hypothesis testing and which itself constitutes the basic activity of knowledge formation within any scientific field, including cross-national research.

The practices of concept formulation and measurement are logically connected and mutually reinforcing. Combining several primary properties may afford an opportunity to extend the reach of a concept. This, as we saw in Chapter 5, was certainly the case in the concept construction of "national potential power." Here, the construction of a valid and reliable empirical index was easily achieved by simply combining the original three primary properties of *area* (ZAREA), *population* (ZPOP), and *aggregate national wealth* (ZGDP97) in the construction of national potential power (ZPOWER).

MEASUREMENT OBJECTIVES: MUTUALLY EXCLUSIVE CLASSES AND VARIABLES

Related to the issue of concept stretching is the important matter of expressing to others, through numbers, what we think we know about our empirical political world. In other words, how do we know a country is a democracy (or autocracy, or any other form of government) and how do we express this fact to others? Does it matter if we can say with certitude that a country is a member of only one class of political authority, and not another? Alternatively, we could ask whether we even need answer these questions. After all, these questions require a degree of precision that is usually beyond the easy reach of even the most advanced sciences. Is it necessary to settle for less, and therefore severely restrict our ability to render meaningful conclusions based on our empirical analysis of complex concepts?

The Limitations of Classification

One primary tenet of comparative political research is that if we are to compare countries, we must be able to, as mentioned in the previous chapter, confidently *classify* them into mutually exclusive categories. Once we have placed countries within these mutually exclusive categories, we can then compare their similarities and differences across specified attributes and explain these differences with reference to the respective classes within which the countries reside. This standard is borrowed from the philosophy of science and widely applied throughout all domains of scientific research. Unfortunately, it has proven much more difficult to attain in cross-national political analysis than it has in studies of one culture or country (for example, the United States political system) or in other scientific fields. Using the strategy of specific classification according to mutually exclusive categories may be a counter-productive strategy in cross-national research because the majority of the most interesting political concepts are so complex as to be beyond our ability to identify both the necessary and sufficient primary properties underlying the primary concept in question. Enforcing the strictest standards of classification often compels extreme concept stretching in cross-national analysis. We expect, in other words, countries to differ with respect to the operationally defined and quantified primary properties. We need not, however, tie ourselves to the criteria that each country must be properly placed into *one* mutually exclusive class based upon an untenable assumption that an exact quantity of a particular property will include a country in a particular class, and anything short of that quantity will exclude it from that particular class.

The reason for this compromise is not that surprising. In the political world, everything is designed, managed, and modified by human beings, who are driven by a combination of passions, prejudices, fears, and anxieties, as well as values, preferences, and interests. While each human being is physiologically and anatomically constructed according to a biological pattern, our political world reflects the diversity and idiosyncracies that we celebrate as the uniqueness of the human spirit. Consequently, there are very few phenomena within the political world that are truly identical across cultures and political systems. While we can always identify some similarities that allow us to classify different countries as members of the same *general* class of political systems, it is unmistakably true that we presently lack the technological means to supplement our powers of observation with the degree of precision necessary to certify a country as being a member of a particular mutually exclusive class of countries.

In a very formal sense, the role of primary properties is to distinguish those defining necessary and sufficient features of a primary concept that allow us to classify countries according to these mutually exclusive categories. Most countries, however, cannot be placed so neatly into mutually exclusive categories. Countries are complex combinations of culture, history, institutions, and individuals. Accordingly, most countries possess some measurable degree of at least one of the primary properties that denies them membership in such tightly and mutually exclusive classes. We know, for instance, that for many of the competing conceptualizations of democracy, the death penalty is one empirical representation of a property (that is, respect for human rights) that would deny the United States membership in the class of countries classified as truly democratic. Yet, there are so many other primary properties that are believed to be either superior in their validity, or relevant in their practical effect for democracy, that this inconsistency would hardly compel most students of comparative democratic systems to dismiss any cross-national empirical study that identified the United States as a democracy.

This example illustrates the central point of this section: Across the various facets of any country's political system, one will find empirical traces of a primary property that we associate with democracy coexisting with empirical traces of primary properties that we associate with autocracy. The more specific and restrictive we become in our operational definitions of the primary properties employed to define democracy, the greater our risk of concept stretching. Ultimately, as we saw in the previous section, we either define the primary concept in such minimal terms as to render the primary concept an ineffective blunt instrument of analysis, or, we hone our definitions to the point of precision whereby we produce as many categories of democracy as there are countries in the world. Having all or most countries within the same class is as fruitless as having each country define its own unique class. Finding the middle ground between these two extremes is the objective of most efforts at comparative political research. The lack of universal agreement on those primary properties that define not only democracy but most of the primary concepts employed by students of cross-national research is the principal evidence used by critics in support of their charge that cross-national research remains a poor substitute for case study or comparable cases strategies of comparative political inquiry.

The Practical Utility of Thinking in Terms of Variables

We must begin our analysis of complex concepts, such as democracy, from a perspective that holds that our operational definitions cannot be perfectly represented by any existing measures derived from available data. On the other hand, we must be aware that our measures must come as close as possible to capturing the defining nature of the concept. We will not find the perfect measure, but this should not prevent us from avoiding measurement altogether. We should strive to appreciate the ideals that lie behind a concept, define the concept in terms of primary properties that are reasonably tied to these ideals, and then find reasonable manifestations of these properties and their related ideals within the empirical political world.

Our overall objective is, therefore, to develop a *valid* variable representation of the concept—one measured, preferably, at the interval/ratio level. However, as we shall see in Chapters 8–14, it is sometimes a practical necessity to rely upon mutually exclusive classification systems based upon numeric rankings. This necessity arises when we lack the interval/ratio level of data required to obtain the degree of precision and consequently, variance, in our measures of particular concepts. On the whole, however, we strive to supplement these ordinal rankings with data that may not allow us to easily answer the question "Is a country a democracy?" but rather, "How much of the primary properties associated with the *ideal* of democracy does a country possess?"

In sum, we need *not* unduly labor under the illusion that the goal of cross-national analysis should be to say a country is or is not a member of a class. Our goal should rather be to compare the degrees to which countries differ with respect to a baseline measure of the primary concept in question, and to subject the principal concept to careful and disciplined logical reasoning, clear operational definition, precise measurement, and appropriate data analysis.

MEASUREMENT VALIDITY AND CONCEPT VALIDATION

Before leaving our discussion of concept formulation, we must amplify the importance of measurement validity. Measurement validity, as we have seen, is simply the degree to which the variables we have operationally defined capture the intended property we wish to reflect in our empirical analysis. We have specified four types of measurement validity: face, construct, content, and criterion. Throughout our survey of basic concepts, measurement strategies, and statistical tools of cross-national analysis, we will repeatedly confront the issue of measurement validity. While defining our concepts in terms of primary properties clearly precedes operationalizations and measurement, the issues of measurement are related to the issues of concept stretching: If we cannot achieve reasonable measurement validation, statistical analysis has no credibility.

Valid to Whom?

To begin, let us consider measurement validity systematically. Remember that measurement validity assumes a degree of consensus among specialists of a given field regarding the nature and characteristics of any operationally defined concept. This consensus, found in the literature when reviewing previous findings, is informal and most certainly unspecified. Of course, like a population, the consensus can only be approximated—it can never be accurately measured. Few measures—if any—ever enjoy universal consensus expectations. The problem, of course, is that one never really knows how far off the mark of "consensus" one is until the hypothetical "consensus" has been fully tested and evaluated.

Measurement validity of operationally defined concepts varies with respect to the degree of consensus between the expected and observed patterns of the attribute across a sample. If the congruence is strong, our measure is validated; yet, if our congruence is weak, validation of our measure is jeopardized. This should not be interpreted to mean measurement innovation must be avoided. However, whenever we move from abstraction to the more practical matter of concept formulation, measurement, and data analysis in cross-national research, we live with the reality that the validity of our measures and, ultimately, the credibility of our findings will be judged by the degree of consensus between the assignment of scores in our sample and the expected pattern defined by the "consensus." Such consensus in large part depends upon whether our primary properties are sufficiently equivalent across the sample.

The process of measurement validation itself is highly informal. Rarely will the student see any open discussion of this topic in extant literature, other than in introductory texts or special studies devoted to methodological issues. However, measurement validity lies at the heart of research and in most cases is the central target in evaluating someone's research. There is no standard metric by which we gauge the degree of measurement validity. As with so many other aspects of cross-national analysis, this phase of the process is one that is governed almost exclusively by subjective judgment, based on experience, intuition, imagination, and often colored by the bias and professional preferences of the researcher.

Of the four types of measurement validity we will discuss, no one is inherently more important than the others. However, face validity is especially powerful in cross-national analysis. Why? Because almost everyone has some knowledge of most countries of the world. When a country falls into a class that is too low or too high, or when the ranking of a particular country offends those who have in their mind's eye a different ranking with respect to two or three countries, or when a country appears as an outlier in a sample, it cannot be easily hidden from the reader. There are few fields of social science research where the proper name of the case in a sample is as important and carries such impact for the validation of the research as in cross-national research.

The Logic of Measurement Validity Applied to Simple Measures

While complex concepts (that is, multidimensional index measures) are generally more fruitful in social science research and are therefore the object of most measurement strategies, all complex concepts begin with simple measures. Let us assume we have a small cross-national sample of nine countries (labeled A, B, C, D, E, F, G, H, and I). The attribute in question is signified as Var1, which we assume captures some particular property that we will label "a." Assume further that we have broken the sample of nine countries into three classes based on the distribution of Var1: Class I (high levels of "a"), Class II (moderate levels of "a"), and Class III (low levels of "a"). Finally, we assume, based on our prior theoretical reasoning, Var1 should produce a certain demonstrated effect, represented by the operationally defined Var2 (assumed to capture property "b").

To make this less abstract, let us assume that we intend to develop a measure for democracy. Thus, we define our variable Dem1 as the degree to which a country's popular will is expressed through free elections. Class I countries are "high democracies" (they have a high degree of free elections), Class II countries are "moderate democracies" (a moderate degree of free elections), and Class III are countries expressing even less democracy (free elections do not appear with regularity or salience within these countries). Finally, we assume that the intended effect of Dem1 is the degree of private enterprise within a country, reflected by our variable Entrp1, operationally defined as the proportion of private consumption within a country. In other words, countries with high degrees of democracy, we assume, have high degrees of free enterprise. With these assumptions in place, consider Table 6.1.

The table reports the "strong," "moderate," and "weak" forms of congruence between observed properties of a simple measure and the consensus expectations regarding the properties of our measure. The table is divided into the four types of validity (face, content, construct, and criterion). Each column offers an example of the conditions that would reflect a strong, moderate, or weak congruence with our hypothetical consensus expectations.

Face Validity

The far left column reports the common expectations for each of the four types of measurement validity, given the properties of the measure and sample, as described above. Each of the subsequent columns reports the properties of the measure that would approximate degrees of deviation from the consensus model. For example, by the logic of face validity commonly applied to cross-national analysis, strong congruence between our findings and prior "consensus" expectations would occur when classification of countries in the sample mirror the expected membership distribution of the "consensus" expectation. Thus, countries A, B, and C would be assigned exclusive membership in Class I, while countries D, E, and F would be assigned exclusive membership in Class II, and so on. Moderate congruence would be approximated by slight deviations in the membership of classes; weak congruence would be approximated by a greater degree of deviation. The property deviations within each model (strong, moderate, and weak) are noted in italics within Table 6.1.

Content Validity

Content validity holds that our variable actually reflects the underlying property it is intended to measure. It is in the range of content validity that concept stretching is most commonly present. For instance, assume we define "high" free elections as a proportion of the population voting in national elections within a given period of time in a country. We would be subject to the criticism that in order to define a measure of democracy that could reach as many countries in a cross-national sample as possible, we have diluted the very meaning of free elections, and consequently our measure of democracy. Elections, after all, can be free, yet because democracies grant some degree of freedom to citizens, many of the eligible citizenry will choose not to vote. Thus, attribute 1 would not accurately capture the assumed underlying property of institutionalized popular will. Other measures might be better suited to the task. This, as is obvious, is a matter of reasoning and experience. One cannot consult a table of univer-

TABLE 6.1 Strong, Moderate, and Weak Forms of Measurement Validity in Cross-National Samples, Assuming Unidimensional Primary Concept, by Face, Criterion, Construct, and Content Validity

Face Validity:
Does the measure assign class membership in accordance with common expectations?

Consensus	Measurement Congruence: Strong	Measurement Congruence: Moderate	Measurement Congruence: Weak
Class I (A, B, C)	(A, B, C)	(A, B, *D*)	(A, C, *I*)
Class II (D, E, F)	(D, E, F)	(D, E, *G*)	(*B*, *H*, F)
Class III (G, H, I)	(G, H, I)	(*F*, H, I)	(G, *E*, *D*)

Content Validity:
Does the measure align logically with the underlying property it is intended to reflect?

Consensus	Measurement Congruence: Strong	Measurement Congruence: Moderate	Measurement Congruence: Weak
Class I (Var1 = a)	Class I (Var1 = a)	Class I (Var1 ≈ a)	Class I (Var1 ≠ a)
Class II (Var1 = a)	Class II (Var1 = a)	Class II (Var1 ≈ a)	Class II (Var1 ≠ a)
Class III (Var1 = a)	Class III (Var1 = a)	Class III (Var1 ≈ a)	Class III (Var1 ≠ a)

Construct Validity:
Has the measure assigned values in accordance with the underlying property which it is intended to reflect?

Consensus	Measurement Congruence: Strong	Measurement Congruence: Moderate	Measurement Congruence: Weak
Class I (Var1 = High)	Class I (Var1 = High)	Class I (Var1 = High and Moderate)	Class I (Var1 = Low)
Class II (Var1 = Moderate)	Class II (Var1 = Moderate)	Class II (Var1 = High, Moderate, and Low)	Class II (Var1 = High, Moderate, and Low)
Class III (Var1 = Low)	Class III (Var1 = Low)	Class III (Var1 = Low and Moderate)	Class III (Var1 = High)

Criterion Validity:
Does the measure adequately account for its intended effect?

Consensus	Measurement Congruence: Strong	Measurement Congruence: Moderate	Measurement Congruence: Weak
Class I (1) = Effect I or Effect III (2)	Class I (1) = Effect I or Effect III (2)	Class I (1) = Effect I and *II*, or *Effect II* and III (2)	Class I (1) = Effect I, *II and III* (2)
Class II (1) = Effect II (2)	Class II (1) = Effect II (2)	Class II (1) = Effect II (2)	Class II (1) = Effect *I*, II, *and III* (2)
Class III (1) = Effect III, or Effect I (2)	Class III (1) = Effect III or Effect I (2)	Class III (1) = Effect III and *II*, or Effect I and *II* (2)	Class III (1) = Effect I, *II*, *and III* (2)

sally acceptable content-valid measures, as one might consult a glossary of standard technical terms.

In Table 6.1, strong congruence with respect to content validity occurs when our operational measures accurately reflect the underlying property across each of the classes of countries in our sample (that is, Var1 = property a). Moderate congruence may be approximated when the operational measure approximates the underlying property within a "reasonable" margin of error (that is, $1 \approx a$) across the classes of countries within the sample. Finally, weak congruence is reflected when operational measures entirely misrepresent an underlying property ($1 \neq a$) across the classes of countries within our cross-national sample.

Construct Validity

Construct validity in simple measures holds that our measure accurately assigns transitivity to the rank ordering of scores in the sample. Transitivity assumes that if $A > B$, and $B > C$, then $A > C$. That is, our measure of "high" free elections, for instance, must match with the consensus vision of what maximum free elections would look like. Accordingly, "low" free elections, as defined by our measure, accurately match the common picture of minimum free elections in the political world. Moderate congruence would see some deviation from consensus expectations (for example, we might operationally define free elections so broadly as to include moderately free elections within our class of high free elections). However, weak congruence will occur when our measures are in complete disagreement with consensus expectations. This would assume that our operational definition of free elections, for instance, would actually reflect minimum free elections; while our definition of "low" free elections leads to our classifying maximum free elections as low across our sample. Weak congruence would suggest major error in logic and/or measurement. Moderate congruence would reflect reasonable deviation on measurement found in most samples.

Criterion Validity

Finally, criterion validity would be strong if the measure accurately predicted the effect expected by the prior consensus. In criterion validity, we enter the hypothesis-testing phase of research. Researchers, as we shall see in Chapter 8, state their expectations (which are based on prior research, and therefore, may be assumed also to approximate the consensus) prior to actually applying the measure in a statistical test designed to gauge the efficacy of the measure in accounting for an expected effect. Thus, we may approximate a strong congruence by assuming that variable 1 accurately predicts Effect 1. If we further assign relative values to variable 1, we would also assume that Class I countries (A, B, and C) in our hypothetical example would also exhibit high degrees of attribute 2, if we expected a positive relationship. If, however, we expect an inverse relationship, strong congruence would occur if Class I countries matched with Class III countries with respect to attribute 2 (we define Class III countries with respect to attribute 2 as countries with the lowest level of attribute 2).

Moderate congruence would occur if Class I countries with respect to attribute 1 accurately matched with Class I and Class II countries, or (if we expect an inverse relationship), Class II and Class III countries with respect to attribute 2. This would reflect some deviation from our strong congruence model, but not as great as the weak congruence model, where Class I countries for attribute 1 would match with countries from all three classes with respect to attribute 2.

Relying on our example of free elections, strong congruence would find that countries with maximum free elections would match with either Class I countries according to the attribute of private enterprise, or Class III countries with private enterprise. Of course, in this example we would expect a positive relationship (Class I for attribute 1 aligns with Class I for attribute 2, and so on). Thus, we would expect Class I countries ("high" free election) pairing with Class I countries ("high" private enterprise). A weak congruence would occur if there were no pattern to the pairing across classes of countries defined by scores for the two attributes. Class I "high free elections" countries would have as great a likelihood of pairing with Class I, Class II, and Class III "private enterprise" countries.

The Logic of Measurement Validity Applied to Complex Measures

Complex measures are those that mathematically combine properties of several individual measures into a single, multidimensional measure. The purpose of a complex measure is to identify a primary concept that is believed to consist of several attributes, none of which individually can accurately capture the underlying property and quality of the primary concept. Thus, by integrating several individual primary properties of the primary concept, we are able to develop a refined and richer measure of a particular aspect of our complex political world, and, simultaneously, reduce the sheer volume of variables we must manage in subsequent research analysis. We have already explored complex measures in our discussion of national potential power in Chapter 5. Throughout this text, we will return to the issue of complex measures as we demonstrate the strategy of measurement in devising operational representation of complex aspects of the political world.

As with simple measures, the matter of measurement validity is critical to complex measures. The critical difference between the two types of measures is that with complex measures, we are working with more than one primary property. Table 6.2 summarizes the strong, moderate, and weak forms of congruence between consensus expectations and observed patterns of scores within our sample when working with complex measures in cross-national analysis.

Assessing measurement validity of complex measures shifts our attention from the properties of single measures, per se, to the properties of two or more single measures

TABLE 6.2 Strong, Moderate, and Weak Forms of Measurement Validity in Cross-National Samples, Assuming Multidimensional Primary Concept, by Face, Criterion, Construct and Content Validity

Face Validity:
Does the measure assign class membership in accordance with common expectations?

Consensus	Measurement Congruence: Strong	Measurement Congruence: Moderate	Measurement Congruence: Weak
Class I (A, B, C)	(A, B, C)	(A, B, *D*)	(A, C, *I*)
Class II (D, E, F)	(D, E, F)	(D, E, *G*)	(*B*, *H*, F)
Class III (G, H, I)	(G, H, I)	(*F*, H, I)	(G, *E*, *D*)

Content Validity:
Do the primary properties align logically with the underlying quality of the primary concept they are intended to reflect?

Consensus	Measurement Congruence: Strong	Measurement Congruence: Moderate	Measurement Congruence: Weak
Class I (1, 2, 3)	Class I (1, 2, 3)	Class I (1, 2, 4)	Class I (1, 4, 5)
Class II (1, 2, 3)	Class II (1, 2, 3)	Class II (1, 2, 4)	Class II (1, 4, 5)
Class III (1, 2, 3)	Class III (1, 2, 3)	Class III (1, 2, 4)	Class III (1, 4, 5)

Construct Validity:
Has the measure assigned values in accordance with the underlying property it is intended to reflect?

Consensus	Measurement Congruence: Strong	Measurement Congruence: Moderate	Measurement Congruence: Weak
Class I (1, 2, 3 = High)	Class I (1, 2, 3 = High)	Class I (1, 2 = High; *3 = Mod)*	Class I (*1 = Low; 2 = Mod;* 3 = High)
Class II (1, 2, 3 = Moderate)	Class II (1, 2, 3 = Moderate)	Class II (1, 3 = Mod; *2 = High*)	Class II (*1 = High; 2 = Low;* 3 = Mod)
Class III (1, 2, 3 = Low)	Class III (1, 2, 3 = Low)	Class III (1, 2 = Low; *3 = High*)	Class III (*1 = High; 2 = Mod;* 3 = Low)

Internal Criterion Validity:
Do the properties of the primary concept logically align?

Consensus	Measurement Congruence: Strong	Measurement Congruence: Moderate	Measurement Congruence: Weak
Class I (1, 2, 3)	Class I (1 = 2 = 3)	Class I (1 ≈ 2 ≈3)	Class I (1 ≠ 2 ≠ 3)
Class II (1, 2, 3)	Class II (1 = 2 = 3)	Class II (1 ≈ 2 ≈3)	Class II (1 ≠ 2 ≠ 3)
Class III (1, 2, 3)	Class III (1 = 2 = 3)	Class III (1 ≈ 2 ≈3)	Class III (1 ≠ 2 ≠ 3)

External Criterion Validity:
Does the example measure adequately account for its intended effect?

Consensus	Measurement Congruence: Strong	Measurement Congruence: Moderate	Measurement Congruence: Weak
Class I (1, 2, 3) = Effect I or Effect III (x)	Class I (1, 2, 3) = Effect I or Effect III (x)	Class I (1, 2, 3) = Effect I and *II*, or *Effect II* and III (x)	Class I (1, 2, 3) = Effect I, *II and III* (x)
Class II (1, 2, 3) = Effect II (x)	Class II (1, 2, 3) = Effect II (x)	Class II (1, 2, 3) = Effect II (x)	Class II (1, 2, 3) = *Effect I*, II, and *III* (x)
Class III (1, 2, 3) = Effect III , or Effect I (x)	Class III (1, 2, 3) = Effect III or Effect I (x)	Class III (1, 2, 3) = Effect III and *II*, or Effect I and *II* (x)	Class III (1, 2, 3) = Effect I, *II, and III* (x)

that define the primary multidimensional concept. Thus, in Table 6.2, we once again assume nine countries (A, B, C, D, E, F, G, H, I). The primary concept in this example is comprised of three single measures representing the primary properties of the multidimensional measure: 1, 2, and 3. It is also assumed that each of the individual primary properties (1, 2, and 3) reasonably meet face, content, construct, and criterion validity requirements for simple, unidimensional measures, as specified in Table 6.1. Finally, each class of countries contains degrees of all three primary properties. Class I has "high" degrees of all three primary properties; Class II is composed of moderate ranges of properties 1, 2, and 3; while Class III countries are characterized by uniformly low levels of properties 1, 2, and 3.

Let us assume once again we are working with a complex measure of democracy. Rather than representing the property of democracy with only one simple measure, free elections, we now rely on three individual primary properties: political participation, civil rights, and degree of decentralized government. We will consider each of these three variables in more detail when we explore democracy. For now, assume these represent properties 1, 2, and 3 in Table 6.2. Each primary property represents an underlying quality or property, as with the single property of free elections considered in Table 6.1.

However, when considering the measurement validity of a complex measure, it is reasonable to assume that the validity of the individual primary properties has already been evaluated. Thus, the focus of attention shifts when assessing the validity of a complex measure. Now our concern is whether these individual properties, taken together, actually allow an accurate and valid reflection of the underlying property of the primary concept, democracy.

Following the consensus expectations in the far left column of Table 6.2, we see that Class I is high democracies, Class II moderate democracies, and Class III low, weak democracies. This implies that each of the individual primary properties, 1, 2, and 3, are at high, moderate, and low levels, respectively. Countries A, B, and C define the exclusive membership of Class I; D, E, and F the membership of Class II; and so on. We also assume that the underlying primary concept, democracy, requires the full range of primary properties, 1, 2, and 3, in order to be effectively represented by empirical measures. Finally, the logic of complex measures requires that we elaborate criterion validity by considering both the *internal* and *external* predictive ability of the measure. When working with simple measures, we need focus on only the external criterion validity. However, with complex measures, we must demonstrate the relationship between the primary properties themselves (that is, internal validity), and then as a second step subsequently validate their ability to predict an effect independent of the primary concept (that is, external validity).

Face Validity. The logic of face validity for complex measures is identical to that of simple measures. Therefore, incongruence with face validity finds country membership deviating by varying degrees from the consensus expectations. If our measurement of the primary properties places countries A, C, and I into the Class I group (and consensus holds country I to actually be a "weak," or Class III, country), we may then conclude that we have a face validity issue requiring further attention to measurement.

Content Validity. Content validity for complex measures requires a slightly different logic from simple measures. Incongruence with content validity occurs when membership of primary properties deviates from the consensual expectations. Content validity assumes strong congruence between consensus expectations and the primary properties chosen to collectively capture the underlying quality of the primary concept. In Table 6.2, we see that by including properties 1, 2, and 3 we have strong congruence. However, moderate deviation occurs when property 4 is included in the definition of the primary concept. Weak congruence reflects further deviation by now including properties 4 and 5 in our definition of the primary concept.

Thus, for instance, if we substituted a measure of the GDP for civil rights (in this instance, GDP would be represented as primary property 4 in Table 6.2), or if we substituted measures of GDP, and soldiers per 1000 population, for civil rights and political participation, respectively (with soldiers per 1000 population reflecting property 5 in Table 6.2), we would seriously undermine the content validity of the primary concept of democracy. Neither GDP nor soldiers per 1000 would ordinarily be considered primary properties of democracy. They may be statistically related to democracy, but they do not reflect the inherent quality of democracy.

Construct Validity. Construct validity simply assumes that each of the countries classified as "high" with respect to the primary concept are in fact characterized by "high" levels of each of the primary properties (1, 2, 3). As the values of the primary properties deviate from high values of the primary concept (high and moderate values associated with "high" values of the primary property; or, low and moderate values of the primary properties associated with "low" values of the primary concept), the validity of the measure comes into question. Weak congruence will occur when the entire range of values for each of the primary properties are associated with each of the respective classes of countries with respect to the value of the primary concept, thus offering no clear measurement distinction between the different classes of countries.

Criterion Validity. Criterion validity logically divides into internal and external validation when working with complex measures. Internal validity holds that each of the primary properties is statistically related to each other within a reasonable margin of error (signified by the symbol $=$). Strong congruence is reflected by strong inter-correlations between the primary properties. Moderate congruence is reflected by weaker inter-correlations, but enough of a demonstrated statistical relationship to reasonably uphold the assumptions of internal validity (signified by the symbol $\approx$). Finally, weak internal criterion validity obtains when there is minimal or no correspondence between the scores of each of the primary properties in the sample (signified by the symbol $\neq$).

External Validity. External validation obtains when the primary concept, defined by primary properties 1, 2, 3, accurately discriminates the class-effect expected to follow from the primary concept. Accordingly, there must be precise correspondence between our classification of the sample with respect to the primary properties and the classification of the sample with respect to the expected effect of the primary concept. Thus, as shown in Table 6.2, when each class predicts its counterpart effect (represented by Effect x in Table 6.2, x indicating it does not matter whether that effect is operationally defined as a multidimensional or unidimensional), or its exact opposite counterpart effect, we have strong congruence, thus suggesting strong external criterion validity. Deviations from this strong congruence model are reflected in moderate and weak congruence examples approximated in Table 6.2. Moderate congruence might find high levels of the primary concept accounting for moderate as well as high levels of the effect-concept. Weak congruence would find the primary concept unable to discriminate at all. Thus, countries in our sample that have high levels of the primary concept would be just as likely to have high levels of the effect concept (x) as moderate levels and low levels of the effect concept.

Measurement Validity in Perspective

The preceding paragraphs suggest a distinct step-process in the progression from simple, unidimensional measures of primary concepts to more complex, multidimensional measures. These steps proceed from property specification, to property elaboration, and conclude with property integration and data reduction. Figure 6.1 summarizes this three-stage process.

In the stage of property elaboration, we move beyond a single primary property to multiple primary properties in order to capture the quality and underlying property characteristics of the primary concept. At this stage, each of the primary properties must be evaluated according to the logic of simple measurement validity. Following this, the multiple single measures are integrated into a single, multidimensional measure. At this stage, the logic of measurement validity appropriate for complex measures comes into play.

In assessing the overall validity of your measures, whether simple or complex, you should avoid being too conservative. Deviations from strong congruence are inevitable. Indeed, the more innovative you become, the more you are going to run the risk of appearing initially to have violated the "consensus" expectations with regard to the measures employed. In any event, since the presumed consensus expectations are a general benchmark and are not precisely specified, nor uniformly agreed upon, it makes little sense to presume that you can derive an exact estimate of the validity of particular variables employed in your analysis. An estimate of the overall validity presumes you have, however, considered the various dimensions of measurement validity and have weighed carefully the degree of congruence between your measures and the hypothetical consensus benchmark. Prudence dictates that you address thoroughly the measures you have chosen to represent a particular concept, and that you contour your

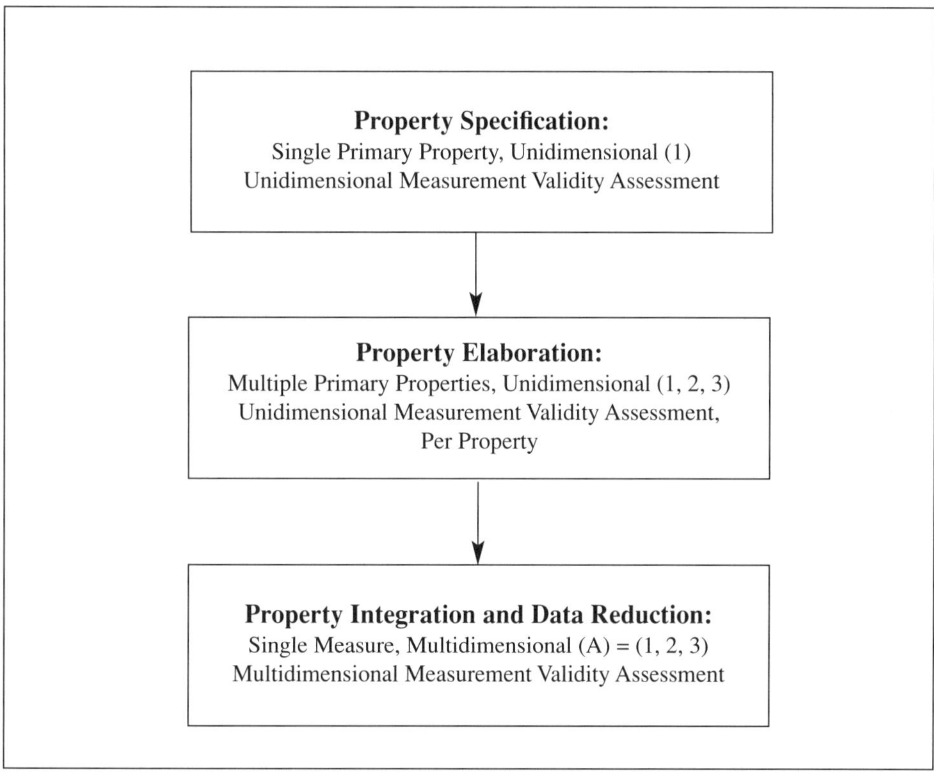

FIGURE 6.1 Progression from Simple, Unidimensional Primary Concept to Complex, Multidimensional Primary Concept

discussion of the final results of the statistical analysis with an eye to possible concerns about the underlying validity issues that always exist in the near background.

NOTES

1. Giovanni Sartori, 1970, "Concept Misinformation in Comparative Politics," *American Political Science Review* 57 (December): 1033–53.

2. See Rod Hague, Martin Harrop, and Shaun Breslin, 1998, second edition, *Political Science: A Comparative Introduction* (New York: St. Martin's), pp. 273–274.

3. David Collier and James E. Mahon Jr., 1993, "Conceptual 'Stretching' Revisited: Adapting Categories in Comparative Analysis," *American Political Science Review* 87 (September): 845–855.

7

Specifying the Primary Properties of Democracy

Concepts: *Democracy, Autocracy, Institutional Democracy, Liberal Democracy, Scope of Democracy, Scale of Democracy*
Demonstrations: BiVariate Frequency Tables, 7.1; The Bivariate Distribution of PARPEG3 by CIVIL973, 7.2

In this chapter, we further refine our understanding of democracy by logically combining the qualitative and quantitative dimensions of democracy into four subcategories: the scope and scale of institutional democracy, and the scope and scale of liberal democracy. From here, we develop measures that reflect the intrinsic nature of each of these four primary properties of democracy: *competitiveness of political participation* (reflecting the *scope* of institutional democracy); *political rights* (reflecting the *scale* of institutional democracy); *regulation of political participation* (the *scope* of liberal democracy); and *civil liberties* (reflecting the intrinsic property of the *scale* of liberal democracy).

While univariate analysis remains the central tool employed in this chapter, we will consider how we can move beyond the applications of univariate analysis to the application of bivariate frequency tables. In effect, bivariate frequency tables allow the student to systematically investigate the contingent relationship existing between two attributes across a cross-national sample. While somewhat cumbersome, bivariate frequency analysis helps summarize the data for the student by associating specific countries with specific empirical properties.

THE IDEALS AND LOGIC OF DEMOCRACY

Democracy, as an ideal, reflects the nature of political authority within a political system. Indeed, democracy is derived from the Greek language: *demos* (people) and *kratos* (rule).

On a continuum of the various known types of political authority, democratic government would likely appear towards one end, while autocratic government would appear towards the other. While many definitions of democracy differ with regard to more subtle aspects of the ideal, there is widespread agreement within the literature on the subject that democracy, as a form of governance, is a combination of two dimensions—*institutional procedures* (for example, voting, representation, and political party competition) and a set of *individual liberties* (for example, speech, press, religion) guaranteed to the citizens of a country. This intrinsic nature of democracy represents the qualitative dimension of democracy. Accordingly, to compare the degree of democratic governance across countries requires empirical measures that distinguish between these two qualitative dimensions of democracy: *institutional democracy* and *liberal democracy*.[1]

The Quality and Quantity of Democratic Governance

The institutional and liberal dimensions of democracy have been carefully developed by students of modern democracy.[2] These views, however, are not new nor limited to the twentieth century. For instance, in 1787, James Madison, writing in *Federalist* No. 51, articulated this implicit dual nature of democracy. "If men were angels," Madison reasoned in his famous treatise, "no government would be necessary. If angels were to govern men, neither external nor internal controls on government would be necessary. In framing a government which is to be administered by men over men, the great difficulty lies in this: you first enable government to control the governed; and in the next place oblige it to control itself." Madison's logic points directly to the challenge facing all democratic governments and their citizens: Both *democratic institutions* and *civil liberties* are necessary to the survival of democracy, yet neither is sufficient by itself to ensure the ideals of democratic political authority. Therefore, in working toward a specification of the primary properties of democracy, we must begin with a consideration of the role of *liberties* (protecting the people) and *institutions* (facilitating some form of accountable governance).

In addition, each of these two *qualitative* dimensions of democracy must be supplemented by their *quantitative* dimensions. This requires we specify their respective *magnitudes* of liberal and institutional democracy. Accordingly, institutional democracy and liberal democracy may be distinguished by their respective *scale* and *scope*.

In the next few sections, we will elaborate some of these basic ideals of democracy, working toward a specification of the principal properties of democracy. We begin with the necessary balance between institutional democracy and liberal democracy.

Power, Choice, and Democracy

The logic of balancing institutional democracy and liberal democracy finds its roots in the inherent conflict between the two principal pressures in any political system: the need for power and the desire for choice. W. Phillips Shively has described all political systems as a blend of *power* and *choice*. Power is often thought of as the ability to coerce another party into doing something the party would prefer not to do, and would not do, without the threat or application of power. Choice is the ability to select freely and independently from a range of options. Accordingly, in a democracy, power must be restricted and restrained, while choice must be extended in order to enhance the autonomy and freedom of individuals in society.[3]

Restraining and restricting power implies that decisionmaking in a democracy is not concentrated in the hands of a few public officials, nor is power geographically concentrated. This suggests that institutional procedures and structures of national government allow for shared power between regional and national government, as well as between a number of different actors and groups within a society. It also suggests that the incumbents of public authority are subject to regular change through a competitive political process, which has clear implications for the institutional framework governing the election of public leaders and representatives within a country.

Expanding and tolerating choice implies that the citizens are granted a degree of autonomy with regard to formulating and expressing their values and ideals within society. It further suggests that the reach and authority of government is legally constrained with respect to individuals and their private affairs. While institutions may constrain the procedural means by which power is balanced, the rights and liberties of citizens must effectively be ensured through explicit laws and constitutional provisions.

From this consideration of power and choice, we may refine our appreciation of the institutional and liberal dimensions of democracy by considering the means and opportunities by which citizens influence their interests within the political arena of a country. The *means* by which conflict over competing values in a society is reconciled is found in the institutional embodiment of accountable government within the political system; the *opportunity* that individuals and groups in society have to influence power is a function of the degree of tolerance for and commitment to reasoned compromise among free and independent citizens. Tolerance and reason are the hallmark traits of a classic liberal society. Gabriel A. Almond and Sidney Verba considered these traits to be essential to the broader concept a of a *civic culture:* a disposition within society to accept shared and restrained power, to participate in the shaping of values through political competition, and to live within the bounds of political competition, rather than passive compliance and acquiescence to central and concentrated authority.[4]

The Institutional Dimension of Democracy

Political institutions are the representation of formal political authority within a country. They are the means by which governments govern, groups and coalitions compete, and individuals participate in the ongoing process of allocating values throughout society. In effect, they channel political values and preferences. These institutions include parties, elections, the media, and organizational structures (such as the executive, the legislature, the court system, national government, regional and local government).

They reflect the collective nature of politics, that is, people and groups—formal or informal—interacting with each other according to rules and obligations enforced by an accountable government and designed to coordinate the behavior of individuals in society in order to mitigate tyranny and exploitation. *We may conclude that institutional democracy exists in a country to the extent that political institutions are responsive to a competitive, open selection process, have the capacity and right to act on behalf of the public, and are limited by rules and regulations that are open to public scrutiny and modification through political competition and participation.*

In this sense, power is restricted and restrained through institutionalized and legitimate procedural restraints on political authority. It is also diffused and dispersed throughout a political system, not concentrated and centralized. Of course, some countries are more institutionally democratic than others and some democracies are more concentrated than others. Perhaps less obvious is the fact that some countries that we might think of as democratic may in fact fall somewhat short of our expectations after we systematically analyze the empirical attributes of democracy from a comparative perspective.

The Liberal Dimension of Democracy

Yet, institutions are only half the story of political democracy. Before institutions can function in a way that we hold to be consistent with democratic political authority, there must first be, it is widely assumed, basic liberties guaranteed to the public. A liberal view of political authority holds that the legitimate authority of government grows from the primacy of individuals within society. Following the Lockean and classic political-economic underpinnings of democratic thought, the rights granted to government to act on behalf of the public through various institutions derive their legitimacy only from an explicit or implicit compact with the public. Preceding governmental authority is the public and their inherent freedoms.

Borrowing from David Held, we may conclude that *liberal democracy exists to the extent that individuals are free to determine the conditions by which they live their lives and are guaranteed equal rights and obligations in the creation and management of the laws and regulations that condition their lives.* Liberal democracy should never be equated with anarchy, that is, the absence of government. Rather, liberal democracy requires *limited* government that is controlled by individuals who have rights, and therefore by logical extension, civic obligations. These basic liberties must remain separate from the authority of any temporal government to extract or expropriate without consent.[5]

Liberal democracy should also not be confused with equality. While a sense of equality pervades liberal democracy, universal equality, as it may apply to all aspects of political behavior and authority in a country, poses a great dilemma for democracy. On the one hand it might be said that universal equality certainly restricts power, making it therefore accountable. However, equality logically threatens tolerance, the tolerance, that is, of differences and diversities within society. What must be equal, therefore, is not power, but the liberties granted people to have access to both the means and opportunities to effectively employ and apply power in the political contest over values.

Liberal democracy in its very basic, and classic, sense, is responsible democracy. Twenty-four hundred years ago, Aristotle, who is regarded by many as the founder of modern comparative analysis, argued that civic responsibility grew from the wisdom that individuals acquired only when they owned and managed property within a society. While democracy was not his preferred political system, the message of Aristotle rings true nonetheless for modern democratic governance: Without some obligations and responsibilities regarding their economic, social, and political choices, citizens have little incentive to participate in and have an impact upon the decisions and actions of government. Therefore, a defining aspect of contemporary democracy is the degree to which an individual in society enjoys some degree of freedom *from* government authority.

Scope and Scale of Democracy

While the qualitative nature of democracy is reflected in the combination of institutions and liberties, the magnitude of democratic governance within a country reflects the scope and scale of the ideal. Scope implies extent. Therefore, we may elaborate our conceptualization of democracy by distinguishing between the scope of institutional democracy and the scope of liberal democracy.

The scope of institutional democracy is the depth and extent to which competitive, pluralist political authority permeates and coordinates political behavior throughout society. The scope of liberal democracy is the extent to which liberties and their freedoms extend to the individual within society without arbitrary regulation and direction from government. Regulation is necessary—but such regulation must be constrained by open political competition and the absence of arbitrary and centralized direction. In other words, limiting the properties of liberal or institutional democracy to a few citizens and denying these properties to others significantly reduces the scope of democracy.

Scale implies range. Therefore, the scale of institutional democracy is the range of participatory and competitive political activities available to citizens in society. The scale of liberal democracy is the range of civil liberties guaranteed to citizens within society. In this instance, limiting freedoms and liberties to a few narrowly defined items severely limits the scale of democracy, in both of its broader dimensions.

In a very real sense, democratic scale, reflected in its institutional and liberal dimensions, serves to *fragment* political authority and prevent government from serving the interests of a few (for example, an oligarchy) by opening the political process up to a maximum number of participants. Democratic scope, reflected in its institutional and liberal dimensions, serves to *disperse* political authority, denying a concentration of governmental authority and political interests within society by encouraging the formation of competing centers of authority throughout society.

PRIMARY PROPERTIES OF DEMOCRACY

As stated above, the primary properties of democracy must reflect both the *quantitative* and *qualitative* dimensions of democracy. They must, in other words, capture the logic of the institutional scope of democracy, the institutional scale of democracy, the liberal scope of democracy, and the liberal scale of democracy. These primary properties are not the *only* criteria of necessary and sufficient conditions. There are, undoubtedly, other candidates for primary properties.[6] In order to minimize *concept stretching* and maximize *concept traveling*, however, these four primary properties serve as a reasonable basis upon which to measure the quality and quantity of democracy within a cross-national sample. Accordingly, for our purposes, we shall proceed from the following four primary properties of political democracy, each of which is frequently included in most definitions of democracy, specified in Table 7.1.

Measuring the Primary Properties of Democracy

Cross-national samples that extend beyond the Euro-American group of countries and employ concepts that are complex must often rely upon data that are based on the professional judgments of experts in the field. This is very much the case with the concept of democracy.[7] When direct and easily countable measures of a concept are not available, students of cross-national research improvise with judgmental data. These are data based on numbers that have been assigned with respect to a property according to the judgments of trained researchers and their staff who cull a variety of sources, often in the native language of the countries in question, to ascertain an accurate reflection of key attributes associated with a primary concept, such as democracy. Numbers are assigned to countries in the sample according to the subjective evaluations of pieces of information systematically gathered by these researchers.

Data drawn from judgments of researchers are often regarded as risky data because of the high potential for error or bias. Often, judgmental variables may appear to have a precision that unintentionally obscures the fact that a variable is distilled from judgments, that is, it was not the product of a direct count. For instance, one basic indicator of institutional democracy is the presence of strict rules that assure competitive recruitment of chief executives within countries. One cannot simply count the number of these rules. You must interpret the wording of constitutions and compare these words to actions over time within a country to see if actions comport with what one would expect if the country had competitive recruitment. Then again, you have to judge whether the competition is relatively high or low, and how these levels compare to other countries, and so on. Judgments are required. The trick is to ensure that your values and biases do not obscure objectivity when assigning numerical codes to phenomena—a difficult task under the best of circumstances.

Perhaps the only attributes of democracy that we can easily count are voting and the number of political parties in a country. Voting is not the only, nor even the ideal,

TABLE 7.1 The Primary Properties of Political Democracy

Primary Property	*Defining Attributes of the Primary Property*
The scope of institutional democracy	*Competitiveness of Political Participation:* Absence of oligarchical-factional or arbitrarily restricted political competition.
The scale of institutional democracy	*Rights Extended for Political Competition and Participation:* The *range* of opportunities guaranteed to citizens to freely and voluntarily select and sanction political leaders through regularly scheduled and enforced elections, as well as other means of citizen activity designed to ensure effective capacity of citizens to check and balance both political leadership and competing groups in society.
The scope of liberal democracy	*Institutionalized Roles for Citizen Participation:* Absence of oligarchical-factional or arbitrarily authorized political authority that denies individuals real and legitimate opportunities to participate in the distribution of political values.
The scale of liberal democracy	*Liberties Extended Citizens Independent of Political Participation:* The *range* of personal freedoms and liberties that are in some sense immune from and largely independent of the fluid nature of political contest and competition. They are the principles upon which citizens are ensured their personal liberties and that free citizens from arbitrary political coercion and persecution.

measure of institutional democracy (after all, the former Soviet Union, a totalitarian oligarchy, reported 98 percent turnout for its one-party elections). Furthermore, a country may have several parties, all controlled by the oligarchy. The former East Germany (German Democratic Republic), another totalitarian oligarchy, had three major parties, only one of which was able to control government, and all of which were controlled by the communists. So, we must rely on data that may not match our highest ideals of precision. Then again, we do not live in a perfect world, and the data we need for such measures are often beyond the physical means to obtain them. Therefore, we have an obligation to be cautious in our use and subsequent interpretation of any measure designed to capture any dimension of democracy.

For beginning students—and seasoned scholars alike—the most common means of avoiding these validity and equivalency issues is to rely on credible data sources that have already been compiled by research teams. This does not mean validity and reliability problems do not exist in these databases, but it does mean that such problems—to the extent they exist—are minimized because of the credibility given to these data by other researchers.[8]

There is a series of measures of the quality and quantity dimensions of democracy in CROSSNAT.50. These measures have been drawn from two widely regarded data sources of cross-national data. Both sources offer variables measuring democracy based on judgmental data. One set of variables comes from the Freedom House measures of political rights and civil liberties; the other set from Ted Robert Gurr and his colleagues, who have compiled one of the most extensive cross-national samples of political attributes among over 150 countries covering the years 1800–1998.[9] While the sets of measures overlap somewhat, the Freedom House measures reflect more closely the implied *scale* of institutional and liberal democracy (that is, the range of opportunities for political competition and participation, as well as civil liberties, within a country), while Gurr's data more closely approximate the implied *scope* of institutional and liberal democracy across several different countries (that is, the extension of political competition and participation throughout a society).

Freedom House affords the researcher a comparative database from which to cross-nationally compare the capacity of citizens in different societies to control the sovereignty of their political and civic values through the application and manipulation of the fundamental instruments of political representation, expression, and demonstration. Gurr's *Polity* database, on the other hand, is dedicated more to the institutional authority traits within countries. These data, therefore, afford the researcher an opportunity to cross-nationally compare the extent to which ordinary citizens in a society (what Gurr and his colleagues refer to as "subordinates" in the authority structure of society) are able to effectively neutralize, and in a sense equalize, the political and civic advantages enjoyed by the established political elites (or, super-ordinates) within a political system.[10] The two databases complement each other by their respective attention to the two fundamental dimensions of a democracy. Freedom House draws explicit attention to the more obvious aspect of democracy, namely, the *extension of citizen authority* within countries. Gurr and his collaborators, on the other hand, draw explicit attention to the other important dimension of democratic governance, the *effective dispersion of public authority*.

We have drawn and adapted four measures of democracy, two from Gurr and two from Freedom House, each representing the primary properties listed above. Each variable is technically an "extended" ordinal-level measure. By that, we mean the range of values offered for any country in the sample is fairly broad, but not technically an interval-level measure. Therefore, a country having a value of "4 " is not necessarily possessing of twice the value of democracy as a country with "2." However, it is intended to approximate that logic, and as such, we will "stretch" the technical rules and treat these data later as interval-level measures when combining them into an index measure of democracy. For now, we will work with them in the conventional manner commonly accorded ordinal data.

Scope of Institutional Democracy: PARCOMP

PARCOMP (participation competitiveness) is a variable in CROSSNAT.50 that measures the *concentration* of institutional authority via political competition within a country. It reflects both the qualitative dimension of institutional democracy and the quantitative dimension of democratic scope. It is Gurr's measure of "competitiveness of participation," as developed for his cross-national study, *Polity98*, and is defined as "the extent to which alternative preferences for policy and leadership can be in the political arena."[11] Democracy, per se, is realized when expressions of political competition are indeed reflective of genuine competition among choices (that is, "there are relatively stable and enduring political groups which regularly compete for political influence at the national level; competition among them seldom causes widespread violence or disruption").[12] Democracy is diminished greatly when, however, political competition is totally suppressed ("No significant opposition activity is permitted outside the ranks of the regime and ruling party.")[13]

The value ranges of PARCOMP (as specified within *Polity98*) are reflective of the operational logic inherent in the theory that drives the coding of Gurr's data. Namely, political participation reflects acts on the part of ordinary citizens designed to wield influence over and thereby constrain the choice and options of elites with respect to public policy and political authority. Our coding scale (1–5) is consistent with Gurr's.[14] However, we have modified the label names for simplicity and consistency with our measures of democracy. Therefore our labels for the various degrees of competitive participation range from *very low* to *very high*. The codes, labels, and descriptions of the attributes associated with PARCOMP are listed in Table 7.2.

Using univariate analysis, we find that the mean value for PARCOMP is 3.66, the standard deviation is 1.06, and the median value is 4.00. With ordinal-level data, we customarily refrain from the more comprehensive univariate analysis so useful with interval-level data and restrict our attention to the mean, standard deviation, and frequency deviations. What does a mean of 3.66 indicate with ordinal data? It should be literally interpreted to mean that the "typical" country in our sample of fifty lies somewhere between "moderate" and "high" with respect to the competitiveness of participation. Of course, no country that is measured by attributes assigned ordinal rankings can be so "precisely" divided. However, the mean clearly reports the distributional weight of the sample. The mean of 3.66 indicates the sample is distributed toward the high end of the value range, that is, toward countries with *high and very high* degrees of competitive participation (countries with numeric values of 4 and 5 for the variable PARCOMP).

This, of course, is also reflected by the median value of 4. Indeed, the median value is much more useful and appropriate to work with (though the mean is commonly reported). The median reports the midpoint, and as such can be more usefully and meaningfully interpreted than a mean when working with ordinal data. The median value of 4 confirms what the frequency distribution shows: Half the sample is either "transitional" or "competitive." This is shown in Table 7.3, which reports the frequency distribution for PARCOMP. Note the distribution is negatively skewed (both the Kolmogorov-Smirnov and Shapiro-Wilk's test are extremely low—.000 for both statistics—indicating a non-normal curve to the distribution.

The variable PARCOMP3 represents a collapsed, or recoded, version of PARCOMP. For descriptive purposes, we have reduced the number of categories in PARCOMP from five to three by collapsing into one category those countries with values of 1 and 2 in PARCOMP, collapsing into a second category those countries with values 3 and 4 in PARCOMP, and finally, contained within a third and separate category, those countries with a value of 5 for PARCOMP in CROSSNAT.50. Those countries with value of 1 and 2 for PARCOMP are now labeled as countries with "very low/low" degrees of competi-

TABLE 7.2 PARCOMP

Code	*Label*	*Description:* ***PARCOMP***
1	*Very Low*	Indicative of a country where there is suppressed political competition. That is, there is "no significant opposition activity outside the ranks of the regime and ruling party [and] the regime's institutional structure [is] matched by its demonstrated ability to suppress opposition competition."[1] These are typically totalitarian societies, authoritarian military dictatorships, or autocratic monarchies. Political authority is virtually free from pressures of dispersion and remains concentrated and monopolized. China is the only such country in CROSSNAT.50.
2	*Low*	Representing a country where there is "some organized, political competition [which] occurs outside government, without serious factionalism, but the regime sharply limits its form, extent, or both in ways that exclude substantial groups from participation."[2] These are persistant and enduring restrictions. "Large cases of people, groups, or types of peaceful political competition are continuously excluded from the political process."[3] Examples may be the lack of national political parties (only regionally and local parties), systematic exclusion of demographic groups from political participation (e.g., ethnic or racial minorities), prohibiting certain types of political expression (e.g., communist parties), systematic harassment of political opinion leaders, including assassinations, imprisonments, exile, etc. Political authority is very minimally dispersed, remaining largely concentrated and open to very limited forms of pressure from political participation and competition. Examples within CROSSNAT.50 include Congo, Indonesia, and Nigeria.
3	*Moderate*	Representing a country characterized by oligarchical-factional polities. Factions threaten democracy because they are inherently unstable and largely incoherent. They are unstable in that they represent political passions of not only a mathematical minority but are indicative of opportunistic expressions of fear or anxiety that may be used to mobilize a public for short-term and ephemeral causes. They therefore lack coherence over extended periods of time because they require new causes and fears to sustain the passions from which the factions are able to suppress political participation and neutralize effective political competition. These are less threatening overall to democracy in that they are less entrenched and enduring restrictions on political competition that one finds in restricted systems, or restricted systems that are in transition. Yet, they remain serious impediments to full democratic governance and expression. Political authority is in effect incoherent but increasingly dispersed and vulnerable to the pressures of competitive participation. Examples within CROSSNAT.50 include Bangladesh, Egypt, and Turkey.
4	*High*	Representing a country characterized by transitional political competition, that is, a country in transition from restricted or oligarchical-factional patterns to fully competitive patterns, or vice versa. These are countries that have less intense and repressive forms of factional and oligarchical restrictions of political participation, but that have yet to fully allow free and openly competitive political participation. These systems are competitive, yet enough concentrated political authority remains to block certain forms of competitive political participation, or to render it less than effective in expressing the interests of the "sub-ordinates" within society's power structure. Examples within CROSSNAT.50 include Russia, South Africa, and Brazil.
5	*Very High*	Representing a country characterized by competitive political participation, which entails a "relatively stable and enduring political groups which regularly compete for political influence at the national level [and where] competition among them seldom causes widespread violence or disruption."[4] Political authority is subject to widespread dispersal through political competition. Examples within CROSSNAT.50 include the United States, Australia, and Japan.

1. Gurr, 1997, p. 13.
2. Gurr, 1997, p.13.
3. Gurr, 1997, p. 13.
4. Gurr, 1997, p. 14.

TABLE 7.3 Frequency Distribution, PARCOMP

Characteristic of Country's Competitiveness of Political Participation (with value code)	*Frequency*	*Percent*	*Valid Percent*	*Cumulative Percent*
1: Very Low	1	2	2	2
2: Low	6	12	12	14
3: Moderate	15	30	30	44
4: High	15	30	30	74
5: Very High	13	26	26	100
Total	50	100	100	

K-S = .186, df = 50, p = .001
S-W = .882, df = 50, p = .01

tive political participation, and assume a value of 1 in the new three-category variable, named PARCOMP3. Those countries with values of 3 in PARCOMP have now been assigned a value of 2 and are labeled as countries with "moderate" degrees of competitive political participation. Finally, those countries that have values of 4 or 5 in PARCOMP now have a value of 3 in PARCOMP3, and are labeled as countries with "high/very high" degrees of competitive political participation. In the new variable of PARCOMP3, seven countries are characterized by severely restricted political competition, fifteen countries are characterized by moderately restricted political competition, and twenty-eight have open and free political competition.

Note that in recoding the data, we have not changed any value of any countries—merely combined categories. Therefore, the variable PARCOMP3 is still an ordinal variable, with less variance (because we have collapsed the number and range of categories from five to three), yet with a curve that approximates a normal curve more closely than the original variable, PARCOMP. Forcing our sample of scores into three categories smooths over important variance, but it facilitates easier interpretation in simpler techniques used to sort out cross-national patterns. It must be noted, however, that we have adjusted the range of values in the variable and have therefore reduced the degree of refinement in the measure. Nonetheless, the validity of the measure's original format is transferred to the adjusted variable. The collapsed variable does not stretch the meaning of democracy, rather it abbreviates the range of the variable by which we distinguish between the various levels of democracy across the countries in our sample, and thereby ensures a more meaningful cross-national analysis.

The Scale of Institutional Democracy: POLIT97

POLIT97 measures the scale of institutional democracy and represents the primary property of political participation and competition. It is adapted from Freedom House and is based upon its measure of the political rights granted to citizens in a country to participate meaningfully in the political process. Freedom House employs an eight-point checklist for political participation.[15] Most of the items used to codify a country's score on the variable are based on the degree to which the country has open, free, and competitive institutions for political participation and representation. Freedom House assigns each country a score ranging from 1 (total freedom with respect to political rights) to 7 (total lack of political rights). POLIT97 is derived from the original Freedom House measure (1 = maximum political rights, 7 = absence of political rights). However, to convert the measure to a scale consistent with the other measures of democracy, we have inverted the scale in POLIT97. This variable ranges from 0 (absence of political rights) to 6 (maximum political rights). We have assigned labels for each value range of POLIT97 to be consistent with our other measures of democracy. These labels range from *very low* (value = 0, or virtual absence of political rights) through *moderate* (value = 3, or moderate degrees of political rights), to *very high* (value = 5, or deeply entrenched and established political rights), with intervals in between labeled accordingly (see Table 7.5 for a full listing). Australia, Greece, and Spain are examples of countries with *very high* degrees of political rights within CROSSNAT.50, while China, Congo, and Indonesia are examples of countries coded as having *very low* degrees of political rights within CROSSNAT.50.

While there is some similarity between POLIT97 and PARCOMP, POLIT97 does not pertain to the formal dispersion of authority within a society, but rather to the amount and volume of possible, if not actual, political competition and participation within a country. Both PARCOMP and POLIT97 represent the *means* or *instruments* of institutional democracy. They reflect the capacity of citizens within a country to sanction government and in effect, to fragment political authority in order to prevent dangerous concentrations of authority immune from accountability.

Employing univariate analysis, we see that the mean value for POLIT97 is 3.86 and the standard deviation is 1.99, with a median value of 4.00. Table 7.4 reports the frequency distribution for POLIT97. Clearly the distribution is skewed in the negative direction (a clustering of scores at the maximum end of the scale).

POLIT973 is POLIT97 collapsed into a three-category variable, useful for descriptive analysis. Those countries with values of 0 or 1 in POLIT97 (those countries with *very low/low* degrees of political rights), are assigned a value of 1 in POLIT973. Those countries with values 2–4 in POLIT97 are coded as a value of 2 in POLIT973 and are those countries with *moderate* degrees of political freedoms. Finally, those countries with a value of 5 or 6 in POLIT97 are coded as 3 in POLIT973, and are those countries with *high/very high* degrees of political rights. In the new variable of POLIT973, nine countries are characterized by minimal political rights, eighteen countries are characterized by moderate political rights, and twenty-three have extensive political rights (countries with scores of 5 or 6 in POLIT97).

The Scope of Liberal Democracy: PARREG

An essential aspect of liberty is the capacity of citizens to effectively exercise their options of political participation. When political competition is unregulated—entirely unregulated—there is a lack of an organizational infrastructure for politics at the na-

TABLE 7.4 Frequency Distribution, POLIT97

Degree of Political Freedoms Extended to the Population (with value code)	*Frequency*	*Percent*	*Valid Percent*	*Cumulative Percent*
0 Minimum	4	8	8	8
1	5	10	10	18
2	4	8	8	26
3	5	10	10	36
4	9	18	18	54
5	9	18	18	72
6 Maximum	14	28	28	100
Total	50	100	100	

K-S = .177, df = 50, p= .0001; S-W = .862, df = 50, p = .01

tional level, and as such, there is a sharp restriction on the capacity of the citizens to engage in political competition in order to effectively preserve their freedoms and realize their values. Citizens lack enduring groups and associations through which their interests and values may be pursued through the process of political competition. In those situations, ever-changing interests and political violence are potential consequences that all too often emerge within countries and come to characterize the nature of political competition.[16] The individual is thus vulnerable to arbitrary and shifting alignments of power.

In order to ensure that this choice is available to a citizen, and that this choice is protected from arbitrary expropriation by government, many societies have written laws and constitutions that explicitly define the boundaries between the rights and responsibilities of the individual, and the rights and responsibilities of the government. A democracy requires that the individual within a society have some degree of autonomy relative to government in order to preserve the freedom and choices of the individual. With such liberty, government is more likely to serve the interests of the public, and not the interests of a few or the one, as liberal philosophers of the Enlightenment, such as Locke and Montesquieu, warned.

Institutionalized roles for citizen participation serve to guarantee and protect access to the arena of politics within a society and therefore ensure an avenue for political association and involvement. However, to be meaningful and effective, classic notions of liberal democracy hold that stable organizational structure and procedural guidelines define the boundaries within which arbitrary authority and tyranny cannot easily encroach. This describes the scope of liberal democracy—the sovereign space, so to speak, between citizens and their government. Absent such space, individuals may be consumed by public authority, and are, in effect, without the capacity to define the terms and/or timing of when they would choose, of their own volition, to engage in the debate and activities that shape the course of government in society. Yet, such space must be reinforced and defined through the capacities of citizens to hold that space apart from public authority. It must be a right of participation exercised, or lost through neglect.

The variable measuring the institutionalized roles for citizen participation within society is PARREG and is adapted from Gurr's data base, *Polity98*. This variable ranges from *restricted participation*, where "some organized political participation is permitted without intense factionalism but significant groups, issues, and/or types of conventional participation are regularly excluded from the political process," to " institutionalized participation" characterized by "relatively stable and enduring political groups [that] regularly compete for political influence and positions with little use of coercion . . . [and where] no significant groups, issues, or types of political action are regularly excluded from the political process."[17] This variable differs from PARCOMP in a very significant way. PARCOMP focuses on the degree of competitiveness of political participation, while PARREG focuses on the degree to which the opportunities for such competition are assured through institutionalized guidelines and rules, rather than arbitrary dictatorship or tyranny and unregulated authority patterns (violence).

The value ranges of PARREG (as specified within *Polity98*) are reflective of the operational logic inherent in the theory that drives the coding of Gurr's data. Namely, institutionalized participation reflects the commitment of political authority within a country to legitimize and protect the right and capacity of ordinary citizens to wield influence over and thereby constrain the choice and options of elites with respect to public policy and political authority. Our coding scale (1–5) is largely consistent with Gurr's.[18] However, we have modified the label names for simplicity and consistency with our measures of democracy. Therefore, our labels for the various degrees of competitive participation range from *very low* to *very high*. The codes, labels, and description of the attributes associated with PARREG are listed in Table 7.5.

Table 7.6 reports the frequency distributions for PARREG. The mean for the sample is 3.7, with a standard deviation of 1.27, and a median value of 4. As with PARCOMP and POLIT97, PARREG is not normally distributed (as can be seen from the frequency distribution, as well as the K-S and S-W statistics).

For descriptive purposes, we have reduced the number of categories in PARREG from five to three by collapsing into one category those countries with values of 1 and 2 in PARREG, collapsing into a second category those countries with values 3 and 4 in PARREG and into a third category those countries with a value of 5 for PARREG in CROSS-NAT.50. Those countries with values of 1 and 2 for PARREG are now labeled as countries with *very low/low* degrees of institutionalized competitive political participation and assume a value of 1 in the new three-category variable, named PARREG3. Those countries with a value of 3 in PARREG have now been assigned a value of 2 and are labeled as countries with *moderate* degrees of institutionalized competitive political participation within PARREG3. Finally, those countries that have a value of 4 or 5 in PARREG now have a value of 3 in PARREG3 and are labeled as countries with *high/very high* degrees of institutionalized competitive political participation. In the new variable of PARREG3, seven countries have severely restricted political competition (very low/low degrees of institutionalized competitive political participation), seven countries have moderately regulated and institutionalized participation, and thirty-six countries have high/very high degrees of regulated and institutionalized political participation.

TABLE 7.5 PARREG

Code	Label	Description: PARREG
1	Very Low	Characterized by countries where some organized political participation is permitted without intense factionalism (e.g., localized and informal forms of political expression) but significant groups, issues, and/or types of conventional participation are regularly excluded from the political process. China, Congo, and Indonesia are examples of "restricted" political systems within CROSSNAT.50.
2	Low	Characterized by countries where political participation is fluid; there are no enduring national political organizations and no systematic regime controls on political activity. What political groupings and organizations exist tend to be built around charismatic leaders, regional interests and factions, religious, ethnic, or racial clans and groups, with little consistency and endurance over time.[1] There are no "unregulated" countries within CROSSNAT.50.
3	Moderate	Characterized by countries that oscillate more or less regularly between intense factionalism and restriction, often leading to a situation where one group secures power and restricts its opponents' political activities until it is displaced in turn. These may be countries where factions rule (that is, competitive groupings struggling for power through some form of regulated political activity), but where genocide or mass killings are often carried out against traditional political and demographic minorities within the country. Examples of such countries within CROSSNAT.50 include Algeria, Egypt, and Kenya.
4	High	Characterized by countries where institutionalized political participation is established, and where there are relatively stable and enduring political groups that compete for political influence at the national level. These organizations are not necessarily elected, but "competition among them may be intense, hostile, and frequently violent." Often, extreme forms of factionalism manifest rival governments and civil wars.[2] Examples of such countries in CROSSNAT.50 are Argentina, Ghana, and South Africa.
5	Very High	Characterized by countries where political participation is fully institutionalized. There are relatively stable and enduring political groups that regularly compete for political influence and positions with little use of coercion, and no significant groups, issues, or types of political action are regularly excluded from the political process.[3] Examples of such countries in CROSSNAT.50 are Italy, Netherlands, and the United Kingdom.

1 Gurr, 1997, p. 12; 2 Gurr, 1997, p. 12; 3 Gurr, 1997, p. 12.

The Scale of Liberal Democracy: CIVIL97

Civil liberties represent the means by which individuals within society preserve and protect the space of their civic autonomy. Without civil liberties, any civic autonomy granted to a citizenship may be both fleeting and arbitrary. Civil liberties serve to institutionalize the authority of citizens within a democracy.[19]

CIV97 is the range of personal and civil liberties granted individuals in society and protected through explicit legal sanctions. The variable represents the scale of liberal democracy within a country and is adapted from Freedom House's coding on a scale identical to that of POL97. Freedom House measures a country's civil liberties along four dimensions: (1) *freedom of expression and belief*, (2) *association and organizational rights*, (3) *rule of law and human rights*, and (4) *personal autonomy and economic rights*.[20]

To convert CIV97 to a scale consistent with the other measures of democracy, we have

TABLE 7.6 Frequency Distribution, PARREG

Degree of Regulation of Political Participation (with value codes)	*Frequency*	*Percent*	*Valid Percent*	*Cumulative Percent*
1 Very Low	7	14	14	14
2 Low	0	0	0	14
3 Moderate	7	14	14	28
4 High	23	46	46	74
5 Very High	13	26	26	100
Total	50	100	100	

K-S = .314, df = 50, p = .0001
S-W = .770, df = 50, p = .01

inverted the scale and have created the new variable CIVIL97. This variable ranges from 0 (absence of civil liberties) to 6 (maximum civil liberties). We have assigned labels for each value range of CIVIL97 to be consistent with our other measures of democracy. These labels range from *very low* (value = 0, or virtual absence of civil liberties) through *moderate* (value = 3, or moderate degrees of liberties), to *very high* (value = 5, or extensive civil liberties), with intervals in between labeled accordingly (see Table 7.8 for a full listing).

The mean value for CIVIL97 is 3.38, the standard deviation is 1.63, and the median is 3.0. The Kolmogorov-Smirnov statistic and the Shapiro-Wilk's statistic are both .000. Table 7.7 reports the frequency distribution of CIVIL97.

CIVIL973 is CIVIL97 collapsed into a three-category variable, to be used for descriptive analysis. Those countries with values of 0 or 1 in CIVIL97 (those countries with *very low/low* degrees of civil liberties), are assigned a value of 1 in CIVIL973. Those countries with values 2–4 in CIVIL97 are coded as a value of 2 in CIVIL973, and are those countries with *moderate* degrees of civil liberties. Finally, those countries with values of 5 or 6 in CIVIL97 are coded as 3 in CIVIL973 and are those countries with *high/very high* degrees of civil liberties. In the new variable of CIVIL973, seven countries are characterized by *very low* or *low* degrees of civil liberties, twenty-seven countries are characterized by *moderate* degrees of civil liberties, and sixteen have *high* or *very high* degrees of civil liberties.

Finally, Table 7.8 reports the values and labels for each of the four primary elements of democracy for each country in CROSSNAT.50: *Competitiveness of Political Participation* (PARCOMP), *Political Rights* (POLIT97), *Regulation (Institutional) of Political Participation* (PARREG), and *Civil Liberties* (CIVIL97). The table reports the values and labels for each of the four measures across the countries in the sample, listed in alphabetical order.

Summary

As the above discussion of democracy illustrates, the development and formulation of complex concepts, such as democracy, is an exercise in logic. Democracy, as we have suggested, is part of the language of political science, with its roots firmly planted in the cul-

TABLE 7.7 Frequency Distribution, CIVIL97

Degree of Civil Liberties Accorded the Population (with value codes)	*Frequency*	*Percent*	*Valid Percent*	*Cumulative Percent*
0 Minimum	2	4	4	4
1	5	10	10	14
2	8	16	16	30
3	12	24	24	54
4	7	14	14	68
5	12	24	24	92
6 Maximum	4	8	8	100
Total	50	100	100	

K-S = .860, df = 50, p = .0001
S-W = .929, df = 50, p = .01

tural and historical traditions of the "Western" world. Through the process described above, we have derived the primary properties that constitute the intrinsic nature of democracy. Each of these four primary properties is inferential. We *infer* from the inherent meaning of democracy—at least as that ideal is generally understood in the literature of political science—that each of these attributes is *related* to an underlying common primary concept: democracy. Following the syllogistic reasoning as articulated above, we expect countries with higher levels of one property to exhibit higher levels of most, if not all, of the other primary properties. Likewise, we expect that lower values of one property within a country will occur with lower levels of most, if not all, of the other primary properties. The logic supporting this inferential linkage connects the scope and scale of each of the qualitative dimensions of democracy through their respective complementary roles within the intrinsic nature of democracy.

Figures 7.1 and 7.2 graphically summarize this inferential relationship between the qualitative and quantitative dimensions of democracy, respectively. Figure 7.1 plots the relationships between the *scope of institutional democracy*, arrayed along the vertical axis, and the *scale of institutional democracy*, arrayed along the horizontal axis of the graph. Institutional democracy is maximized when the competitiveness of political participation among groups, parties, and political candidates is maximized, when political rights accorded citizens are maximized, and when a concentration of factional, oligarchic, or tyrannical power is absent.

Figure 7.2 plots the relationship between *the scope of liberal democracy*, arrayed along the vertical axis of the plot, and *the scale of liberal democracy*, arrayed along the horizontal axis of the plot. Liberal democracy is maximized when institutionally regulated political participation and civil liberties are maximized. When political participation and competition are unregulated and open to the fluid and unpredictable dynamics of factions, tyrants, and oligarchies, and when civil liberties are nonexistent, liberal democracy is unable to flourish.

Finally, the logical connections between the qualitative and quantitative dimensions of democracy and the corresponding primary properties and their respective variables

TABLE 7.8: Primary Components of Democracy

COUNTRY	PARCOMP *Degree of Competitiveness of Political Participation*	PARREG *Degree of Regulated/Institutionalized Political Participation*	CIVIL97 *Extent of Civil Liberties*	POLIT97 *Extent of Political Rights*
	Values and Labels			
Algeria	3 Moderate	3 Moderate	1 Low	1 Low
Argentina	4 High	4 High	4 Moderately High	4 Very High
Australia	5 Very High	5 Very High	6 Very High	6 Very High
Bangladesh	3 Moderate	4 High	3 Moderate	4 Very High
Brazil	4 High	4 High	3 Moderate	4 Moderately High
Canada	5 Very High	5 Very High	6 Very High	6 Very High
Chile	4 High	4 High	4 Very High	4 Very High
China	1 Very Low	1 Very Low	0 Very Low	0 Very Low
Colombia	3 Moderate	4 High	3 Moderate	3 Moderate
Congo	2 Low	1 Very Low	1 Low	0 Very Low
Czech	5 Very High	5 Very High	4 Very High	6 Very High
Ecuador	4 High	4 High	4 Moderately High	4 Moderately High
Egypt	3 Moderate	3 Moderate	1 Low	1 Low
France	5 Very High	5 Very High	4 Very High	6 Very High
Germany	5 Very High	5 Very High	4 Very High	6 Very High
Ghana	3 Moderate	4 High	4 Moderately High	4 Moderately High
Greece	5 Very High	5 Very High	4 Moderately High	6 Very High
India	3 Moderate	4 High	3 Moderate	4 Very High
Indonesia	2 Low	1 Very Low	2 Moderately Low	0 Very Low
Iran	2 Low	1 Very Low	0 Very Low	1 Low
Italy	5 Very High	5 Very High	4 Very High	6 Very High
Japan	5 Very High	5 Very High	4 Very High	6 Very High
Kenya	3 Moderate	3 Moderate	1 Low	1 Low
Korea	5 Very High	5 Very High	4 Very High	4 Very High
Madagascar	4 High	4 High	3 Moderate	4 Very High
Malaysia	3 Moderate	4 High	2 Moderately Low	3 Moderate
Mexico	4 High	4 High	3 Moderate	4 Moderately High

TABLE 7.8 *(continued)*

COUNTRY	*PARCOMP* *Degree of Competitiveness of Political Participation*	*PARREG* *Degree of Regulated/Institutionalized Political Participation*	*CIVIL97* *Extent of Civil Liberties*	*POLIT97* *Extent of Political Rights*
Morocco	3 Moderate	3 Moderate	2 Moderately Low	2 Moderately Low
Nepal	4 High	4 High	3 Moderate	4 Moderately High
Netherlands	5 Very High	5 Very High	6 Very High	6 Very High
Nigeria	2 Low	1 Very Low	1 Low	0 Very Low
Pakistan	3 Moderate	4 High	2 Moderately Low	3 Moderate
Peru	3 Moderate	4 High	3 Moderate	2 Moderately Low
Philippines	4 High	4 High	4 Moderately High	4 Very High
Poland	4 High	4 High	4 Very High	6 Very High
Romania	4 High	4 High	4 Very High	4 Very High
Russia	4 High	4 High	3 Moderate	4 Moderately High
South Africa	4 High	4 High	4 Very High	6 Very High
Spain	5 Very High	5 Very High	4 Very High	6 Very High
Sri Lanka	3 Moderate	3 Moderate	3 Moderate	4 Moderately High
Tanzania	3 Moderate	3 Moderate	2 Moderately Low	2 Moderately Low
Thailand	4 High	4 High	4 Moderately High	4 Moderately High
Tunisia	3 Moderate	3 Moderate	2 Moderately Low	1 Low
Turkey	3 Moderate	4 High	2 Moderately Low	3 Moderate
Uganda	2 Low	1 Very Low	3 Moderate	3 Moderate
Ukraine	4 High	4 High	3 Moderate	4 Moderately High
United Kingdom	5 Very High	5 Very High	4 Very High	6 Very High
United States	5 Very High	5 Very High	6 Very High	6 Very High
Venezuela	4 High	4 High	4 Moderately High	4 Very High
Zimbabwe	2 Low	1 Very Low	2 Moderately Low	2 Moderately Low

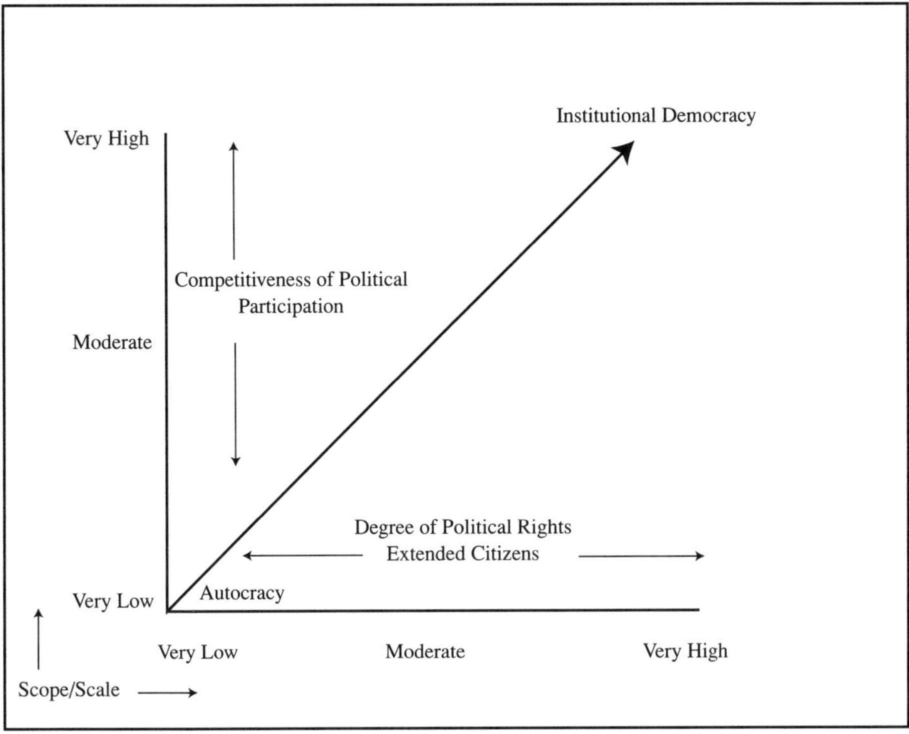

FIGURE 7.1 Scope (Dispersion of Political Authority) and Scale (Extension of Citizen Authority) of Institutional Democracy

in CROSSNAT.50 are summarized in Table 7.9. Scope implies a space within which citizens in a society have unimpeded opportunities to compete for political authority, to hold government accountable, and to sanction public authority, all within the bounds of regulated and institutionalized authority structures legitimized by tradition and constitutional provisions. Scale implies weight and displacement. How much weight and displacement citizens can bring to the political arena are effectively determined by their political rights and civil liberties. Both scale and scope are essentially quantitative properties—they can be manipulated through "social engineering" and political reform. Of course, they are not independent of the qualitative properties of democracy. The quality of democracy refers to its intrinsic nature. The distinguishing attributes of democracy require specific means of political power by which citizens may hold government accountable to the public interest and unique opportunities for citizens to access political power and thereby sanction public authority. Implicitly, intrinsic properties cannot be so easily modified, or indeed, created. Of necessity is some commitment to establish and sustain the quantitative properties whereby authority will be dispersed and effective authority extended to a country's citizens vis-à-vis their political elite (or, super-ordinates). The variables we have chosen to represent the intrinsic attributes of democracy's primary properties are, in effect, our gauge of how entrenched democracy is within a country during a specific period of time, 1997.

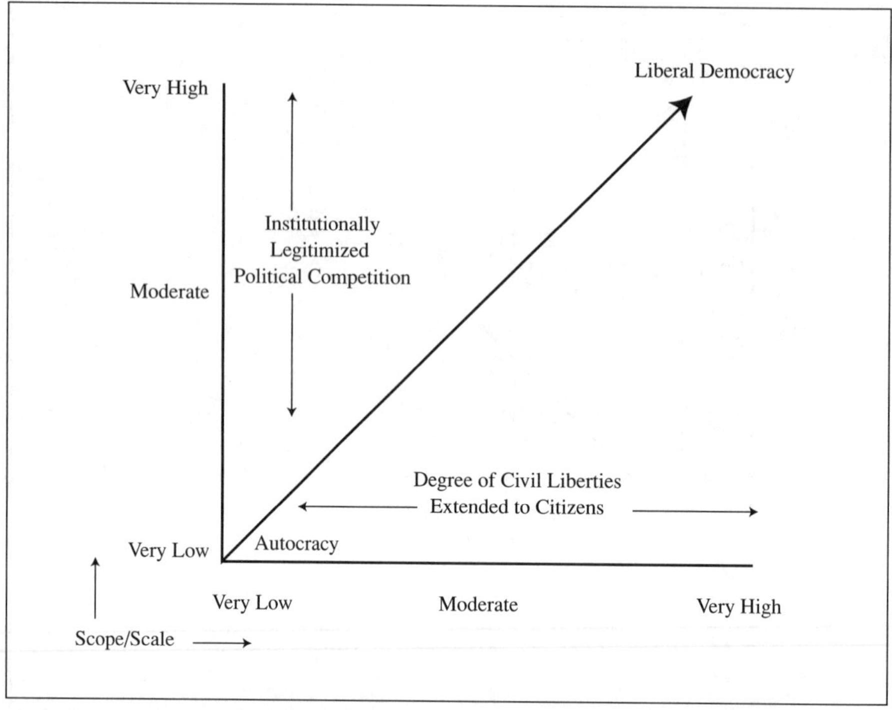

FIGURE 7.2 Scope (Dispersion of Political Authority) and Scale (Extension of Citizen Authority) of Liberal Democracy

DEMONSTRATION 7.1: BIVARIATE FREQUENCY TABLES

At the outset of this chapter, concept stretching was identified as one of the critical challenges to students of cross-national data analysis. While we can never fully escape the pitfalls of concept stretching, we can provide evidence that will assist us in assessing its likelihood. As we will see in more detail beginning in the next chapter, hypothesis testing is a powerful means of confirming the validity of our inferences, and, accordingly, assessing the degree to which we might have "stretched" our concepts.

A univariate analysis can neither confirm nor deny the validity of our logical inferences that connect primary properties together into a complex primary concept. Nor, therefore, can it provide a credible gauge for concept stretching. Univariate analysis, as we know, is designed to assess and summarize the central tendencies and distributional patterns of individual attributes across a sample. If our needs lie beyond these summary tasks, as they most often do, we must advance from univariate analysis (or, the analysis of one variable or attribute) to the correlation of two variables, referred to as *bivariate analysis*. Figures 7.1 and 7.2 suggest as much, showing that logically, the quantity dimensions of democracy should be related to the quality dimensions of democracy.

In the remainder of this chapter, we will consider the most basic form of bivariate analysis: bivariate frequency tables. From this technique, we may begin to assess the

TABLE 7.9 Primary Properties of Democracy

		Quantitative Dimensions of Democracy	
		Democratic Scope (The Dispersion of Public Authority)	*Democratic Scale (The Extension of Citizen Authority)*
Qualitative Dimensions of Democracy	Institutional Democracy: The Means of Political Power and Accountable Government	PARCOMP (Gurr, 1998) The Scope of Institutional Democracy	POLIT97 (Freedom House, 2000) The Scale of Institutional Democracy
	Liberal Democracy: The Opportunities to Access Political Power and Restrict Public Authority	PARREG (Gurr, 1998) The Scope of Liberal Democracy	CIVIL97 (Freedom House, 2000) The Scale of Liberal Democracy

strength and direction of a relationship between two attributes, and from this, evaluate the validity and accuracy of our inferences that logically connect the properties of complex concepts, such as democracy, and, as we shall see from Chapter 8 on, related concepts that are connected through theory.

The Role of Bivariate Frequency Tables

We begin by considering the assumed relationship between the *scope of institutional democracy* (PARCOMP3) and the *scale of institutional democracy* (POLIT973). As a preliminary analysis, we want to explore not only the pattern of alignment of scores for these measures across our sample, but we wish to attach the names of countries to the cases that fall within specified ranges of each attribute. In this way, we are in a better position to observe which specific countries might be labeled "high" or "low" with respect to the two attributes. Also, we can assess the face validity of the inferential measures. That is, we can determine if the pattern of country distributions across the defined range of values for the two attributes aligns with our expectations based on our general substantive knowledge of the countries. In this way, we can provide an initial assessment of the likelihood of concept stretching. It is for such purposes that the original values of PARCOMP and POLIT97 have been collapsed to three values in PARCOMP3 and POLIT973: It is simply easier and more convenient to interpret patterns in bivariate frequency tables when we have no more than three categories per variable (if possible).

Constructing a Bivariate Frequency Table

Table 7.10 reports the bivariate frequency analysis of *political rights* (POLIT973) and *competitiveness of political participation* (PARCOMP3). Our theory of democracy, especially our reasoning on the nature of institutionalized democracy summarized graphically in Figure 7.1, would clearly suggest that those countries that exhibit "high" degrees of scope of institutionalized democracy, as represented by competitiveness of political participation (PARCOMP3), will also exhibit "high" degrees in the scale of institutional democracy, as represented by political rights (POLIT973).

Table 7.10 is a *bivariate frequency table*. It illustrates how values of one variable align relative to the values of another variable, and it specifies the location of an actual case—or country—according to that country's value for the two variables, PARCOMP3 and POLIT973. A simple presentation of cross-national data in this manner provides essential information not only for the researcher using the statistical strategy of comparative analysis (as we are), but also for those who rely upon the case study and/or comparative cases strategies of comparative political analysis. Bivariate frequency tables are most often used by scholars when they are working with ordinal-level data (as we are), though such tables may also be employed as an initial step in cross-national analysis even though interval/ratio-level measures of the attributes are available to the scholar. In addition to avoiding problems we may have when we work with non-normally distributed interval/ratio- level data (as discussed in Chapter 4), there are at least two important reasons this tradeoff is a worthwhile exercise in cross-national analysis.

First, "stepping down" from interval/ratio-level data (if we had variables measured at the interval/ratio level) to ordinal-level data (by recoding the original interval/ratio level- data such as we did with respect to AREA), may require that we sacrifice some precision in our data, but it affords us in return a clearer overview of the distribution of countries along values of the two variables. We are therefore able to connect a proper name of a country (for example, Australia) with a particular value of each of the two attributes (for example, PARCOMP3 and POLIT973). This allows comparison across countries. We can therefore more easily compare Australian values to Brazilian values and in so doing, add a more concrete (and less abstract) interpretation to our analysis.

Second, by allowing us to connect the proper names of countries in our sample to particular values of the attributes under investigation, we improve our ability to identify trends and anomalies (that is, deviations in the data from our expectations) in the patterns. Indeed, this is precisely the type of information we require in order to check the *face validity* of our measures. For instance, if a variable has been measured incorrectly (if, for example, we have incorrectly coded or scored a country with respect to a particular variable), or if the actual value a country's score has been mistakenly entered into the database itself (such as a simple typing error), you will usually see it immediately in a bivariate frequency table. In Table 7.10, if the United States had been placed in the same cell as China, alarm bells should have sounded in your mind: Knowing anything about the recent history of these two countries should prompt one to ask immediately, "How can China and the United States have roughly similar patterns of institutional democracy?" The respective scores of these two countries should be quite different, as is shown in Table 7.10 (and Table 7.8). This, then, is an example of using face validity as a simple method of assessing the credibility of our measures and avoiding egregious concept stretching.

In sum, the bivariate frequency table provides simple validity checks on our data, as

TABLE 7.10 Cross-National Patterns to the Scope and Scale of Institutional Democracy: Countries Arrayed by Values of PARCOMP3 nd POLIT973

Scale/ Scope:	*PARCOMP3 = 1* *N = 7*	*PARCOMP3 = 2* *N = 15*	*PARCOMP3 = 3* *N = 28*	
POLIT973 = 1	China	Algeria		
N = 9	Congo	Egypt		
	Indonesia	Kenya		
	Iran	Tunisia		
	Nigeria			
	N = 5	N = 4	N = 0	
POLIT973 = 2	Uganda	Colombia	Brazil	
N = 18	Zimbabwe	Ghana	Ecuador	
		Malaysia	Mexico	
		Morocco	Nepal	
		Pakistan	Russia	
		Peru	Thailand	
		Sri Lanka	Ukraine	
		Tanzania		
		Turkey		
	N = 2	N = 9	N =7	
POLIT973 = 3		Bangladesh	Argentina	Madagascar
N = 23		India	Australia	Netherlands
			Canada	Philippines
			Chile	Poland
			Czech Republic	Romania
			France	South Africa
			Germany	Spain
			Greece	U Kingdom
			Italy	U States
			Japan	Venezuela
			Korea	
	N = 0	N = 2	N = 21	

well as useful comparative information. Such tables should not necessarily constitute the only tool employed in the analysis of your data, especially if you have your variables measured at the interval/ratio level. But without question, this step helps to locate possible relationships between variables, presents interesting and useful comparative information, and helps check for possible mistakes or miscalculations.

Interpreting a Bivariate Frequency Table

In a bivariate frequency table, our principal objective is to explore the pattern of matches across scores within a sample. If scores of one variable match those of another variable, we have evidence of a contingent relationship. Namely, we have evidence that one variable may be used to predict another variable. Typically, you read a bivariate frequency table from left to right, examining the distributional pattern of countries falling within specified cells in the table. Each cell represents a particular match of scores; they are the intersection of the value of one variable with a particular value of a second variable.

Let us turn directly to Table 7.10. Each cell within the table contains the names of the countries that have values within the range for the respective category of PARCOMP3 and POLIT973. The modal cell (that is, the cell with the largest number of countries within it) in Table 7.10 is that which connects "high/very high" degrees of PARCOMP3 with "high/very high" degrees of POLIT973. Twenty-one countries are characterized by high or very high degrees of institutionalized scope and institutionalized scale in their democracies.

Table 7.10 suggests that a contingent correspondence generally exists between high levels of PARCOMP and high levels of POLIT973. Namely, the value of PARCOMP3 appears to be roughly contingent upon a country's value for POLIT973. In Chapter 9, we will see how, using a contingency table analysis technique, we can actually see whether the association between the two variables is statistically significant. For now, we simply want to observe the bivariate frequency distribution and identify the countries that fall within each cell in Table 7.10. A perfectly contingent relationship would see all countries falling along a diagonal line running from the top left of the table to the bottom right, given our measurement scale. That is, countries that are very low/low in terms of the degree of their political competitiveness should also be very low/low with respect to the degree of political rights within the country. Or, put differently, countries that afford very little tolerance for the citizenry to access political power and hold government accountable should also be countries that have very few means available to the citizens for competing within the political arena. This is the case for five countries in our sample: China, Congo, Indonesia, Iran, and Nigeria. However, six countries fall off this "diagonal." For instance, Algeria, Egypt, Kenya, and Tunisia have achieved (as of 1997) moderate degrees of competitiveness within their political arena, yet they lag in terms of the rights they extend to their citizens in utilizing various instruments of representation and democratic struggle. Their value for PARCOMP3 is moderate, yet for POLIT973 is very low/low. By contrast, Uganda and Zimbabwe both have very low/low degrees of competitiveness in their political arena. Yet, (according to Freedom House) their citizens are accorded only a modicum of political rights.

Nine countries are "correctly" placed on the diagonal within the moderate range of both institutionalized scope and institutionalized scale of democracy. These nine countries have moderate levels of competitive participation (PARCOMP3 = 2) and political rights (POLIT973 = 2). Yet, as we have seen above, six countries (Algeria, Egypt, Kenya, Tunisia, Uganda, and Zimbabwe) also share at least a moderate degree of one of those two attributes. In addition, seven countries (Brazil, Ecuador, Mexico, Nepal, Russia, Thailand, and Ukraine) each have moderate degrees of political rights (POLIT973 = 2), yet enjoy high/very high degrees of competitive participation within their countries. As well, Bangladesh and India both have very high/high degrees of political rights, but only moderate degrees of competitiveness of political participation. Thus, fifteen countries (or, 30 percent) of the sample fall into cells that are "off" the diagonal in a literal sense. These are the countries in our sample that appear (as of

1997) to be under some stress with respect to developing the institutionalized properties of their democracies. They have moved "forward" on one front (scale or scope), but lag behind on the other. Thirty-five countries in our sample fall right along the diagonal; that is, they would appear to exhibit a greater degree of coherency with respect to the institutionalized nature of their democracies—both the scale and scope of their institutionalized democratic properties are evenly developed. On the whole, however, we may conclude that a contingent relationship does exist (as we would expect) between the scope and scale of institutionalized democracy among populous countries.[21]

Setting up a bivariate frequency table such as that presented in Table 7.10 helps to identify countries that stand apart from others in terms of particular attributes and also offers an opportunity to observe patterns that may not conform with our previous expectations. It should be clear that because such exercises may focus attention on a particular country, they may facilitate future case study analysis. For instance, we can see in that same table that Russia and Mexico are aligned with respect to their scale and scope of institutionalized democracy. Yet, to the casual observer, there are more than a few stark differences between these two political systems. What, then, could account for this similarity? What aspects of their political systems bring them together under one roof (by our adopted coding scheme), so to speak? Knowing this helps us to understand and appreciate the institutional differences that distinguish these two political systems, and thereby helps us refine and enlarge our understanding of not only particular countries, but also of the role and significance of certain attributes seemingly unique to both countries. And, in the process, the student may devise an alternative coding scheme by which to measure important attributes of political behavior and institutional authority within a cross-national research design.

DEMONSTRATION 7.2: THE BIVARIATE DISTRIBUTION OF PARREG3 BY CIVIL973

Finally, in order to gain a clearer picture of the comparative patterns of liberal democracy, Table 7.11 presents a bivariate frequency table of PARREG3 and CIVIL973. The logic of this bivariate relationship is summarized in Figure 7.2. The pattern of alignment of countries to cells in Table 7.11 is similar to that of Table 7.10, with some noticeable differences. The first difference is the large number of countries that fall "off" the diagonal by aligning with moderate degrees of civil liberties (value = 2) and high/very high levels of institutionalized participation. This pattern suggests that for 40 percent of our sample, the regulations for effective and legitimate political participation have been routinized in advance of the country's full extension of liberties to citizens. Thus, while the scale of liberal democracy may be well advanced, the opportunities and tolerance for political participation are limited.

The second difference in Table 7.11 from Table 7.10 is the fewer number of countries that have high/very high degrees of institutionalized participation and high/very high degrees of civil liberties (sixteen and twenty-one, respectively). Underscoring this is the fact that for seven countries in the sample (Argentina, Bangladesh, Greece, India, Madagascar, Philippines, and Venezuela) political rights have exceeded civil liberties. This is not so unusual because civil liberties are clearly closely aligned with the intrinsic nature of democracy. These are inherent freedoms in large part (or, institutional reflections of these inherent freedoms) and are generally noted as being more difficult both to create through simple reform, and to sustain once in place. These seven countries are in large measure characterized by active mechanisms of political participation and competition, yet they still retain high degrees of arbitrary judgment and authority within the government—ostensibly as a bulwark against unruly and factional politics.

Therefore, twenty-six countries (or 52 percent) of the sample are "off" the diagonal. While we might, therefore, be inclined to suspect concept stretching as a result of these contradictory relationships shown in Table 7.11, on closer examination we see that such findings are logically consistent with the intrinsic nature of and tensions within democracy.

CONCEPT FORMULATION AND MEASUREMENT IN PERSPECTIVE

The greatest challenge to students of political analysis, including cross-national analysis, is not the mastering of statistics, nor the memorizing of facts and details of particular countries or regions. It is, rather, overcoming the intimidation that stems from the natural fear that your perception of the political world around you, represented by the concepts you have either developed or refined from the inventory of concepts in the literature (such as democracy), and the measures you have chosen to empirically reflect this world (such as PARCOMP, POLIT97, PARREG, and CIVIL97) will be rejected by others as simply wrong. Andrew Hacker has written, "Each student of politics must describe the world as he sees it, holding onto the faith that his perceptions and evaluations are valid. There must be a certain arrogance here, a sense that everyone is out of step except one's self."[22] This runs, of course, somewhat counter to the common wisdom, which asserts that science is very conservative, forcing students to conform to conventional wisdom, staying within the parameters of the tried and tested.

Concept formulation and measurement are the two areas in cross-national research where the advice of Hacker may be more wise than the traditional caution and prudence. You must remember that concepts reflect *your* picture of the world. Obviously, there are those interpretations of the political world that may be grossly inaccurate and just plain wrong. But, with regard to the most important questions concerning political behavior and institutional authority, there are surprisingly few interpretations that are, in fact, absolutely right or wrong. These are perceptions, and, as with the human spirit, there will be divergence in the perceptions. Science can only advance and grow if one has the courage to formulate these perceptions, specify these perceptions as clearly as possible, connect them to the relevant literature in the field so as to demonstrate the role they might play in extending our extant theories and concepts, and offer

TABLE 7.11 Cross-National Patterns to the Scope and Scale of Liberal Democracy: Countries Arrayed by Values of PARREG3 and CIVIL973

Scale/ Scope:	*PARREG3 = 1* N = 7	*PARREG3 = 2* N = 7	*PARREG3 = 3* N = 36	
CIVIL973 = 1	China	Algeria		
N = 7	Congo	Egypt		
	Iran	Kenya		
	Nigeria			
	N = 4	N = 3	N = 0	
CIVIL973 = 2	Indonesia	Morocco	Argentina	Mexico
N = 27	Uganda	Sri Lanka	Bangladesh	Nepal
	Zimbabwe	Tanzania	Brazil	Pakistan
		Tunisia	Colombia	Peru
			Ecuador	Philippines
			Ghana	Russia
			Greece	Thailand
			India	Turkey
			Madagascar	Ukraine
			Malaysia	Venezuela
	N = 3	N = 4	N =20	
CIVIL973 = 3			Australia	Netherlands
N = 16			Canada	Poland
			Chile	Romania
			Czech Republic	South Africa
			France	Spain
			Germany	U Kingdom
			Italy	U States
			Japan	
			Korea	
	N = 0	N = 0	N = 16	

disciplined operational definitions of the concepts, followed by sensible and clear statistical analysis of the empirical evidence.

Clearly, the picture of democracy portrayed in the preceding pages should not be thought of as the only perception allowable. It is the perception that guides *our* analysis of democracy. Others may offer a slightly different perception, positing a slightly different argument, leading them to formulate an altogether different list of primary properties. The student of cross-national politics, following Hacker's advice, must balance arrogance with discipline and acquire a habit of mind that is not afraid to modify existing measures and formulations of complex concepts, yet exercises sensible prudence before setting out to reinvent the wheel. Erring on the side of caution, and therefore avoiding the risk of scorn and rejection, derision and embarrassment, does not, in the long run, advance our knowledge of the political world.

Imagination and systematic observation must be the two most important tools within the repertory of students of cross-national research. They supercede the technical tools of the craft of cross-national research and are at least as important as most of the substantive knowledge we hold about our subject matter. Without the imagination and powers of observation merged and honed through the practice of applied research, the tools are meaningless and the substantive knowledge of little use. Science has advanced because at the stage of conceptualization and measurement, students are willing to run the risk of error. History, Hacker reminds us, is replete, from Plato to Freud, with those who have had the "audacity" to focus on those aspects of their world they believed to be critical to the mastery of our environment and an appreciation of humanity. They were hardly without criticism or free of error. "Their wrongheadedness," writes Hacker, "has aided our political understanding more than the levelheaded models of those who manage to avoid criticism by confining their generalizations to the unobjectionable."[23] These are words to remember as you learn to apply the various skills and tools of cross-national data analysis.

CHAPTER SUMMARY

In this chapter, we have explored the logical foundations of democracy, with an eye to how we can convert abstract ideas into specific measures of the primary concept without "stretching." We have also surveyed the logic of measurement validity, so critical to the successful cross-national analysis of political behavior and institutional authority. With concept stretching and measurement validity as backdrops, we explored the logic and measurement of democracy in the contemporary world.

Democracy basically entails a blend of power and choice, with the means of achieving political ends concentrated within the institutional dimension of democracy, and the opportunities for influencing the outcome of political struggle governed by the liberal dimension of democracy. Further discriminating between the scope and scale of political authority, we have identified four distinct primary properties of democracy: *the scope of institutional democracy*, reflected by the competitiveness of political participation (PARCOMP), *the scale of institutional democracy*, reflected by political rights that offer the necessary tools for extending the role of the citizen within the political arena of a society (POLIT97), *the scope of liberal democracy*, reflected by institutionalized and regulated political participation within society (PARREG), and *the scale of liberal democracy*, reflected by civil liberties that accord citizens the legitimate protection against the state and provide the necessary tools for preserving their participatory role within the political arena of society (CIVIL97). Together, these four properties constitute the fundamental properties of democracy—the primary concept explored in this chapter. While these four variables, like most employed in cross-national research, are not perfect, they do closely approximate the inferred primary properties of democracy.

We have also seen in this chapter how we can prepare and apply a bivariate frequency table from which we can discern distribution patterns in the relationship between the measures of the institutional dimension of democracy and the liberal dimension of democracy, respectively. This simple technique (reported in Tables 7.10 and 7.11) has verified that for several countries, sharp "imbalances" between the primary properties of liberal democracy exist. Civil liberties lag behind the regulations provided for effective political participation. Indeed, we have seen that extending participatory rights and the attendant tools of political participation may be something more easily achieved than extending to citizens basic liberties that preserve their sovereignty and autonomy in the face of state authority. We shall return to the primary concept of democracy in the next chapter and further explore the logical and empirical means by which this crucial concept for students of cross-national research may be usefully employed.

NOTES

1. There is no single definition nor single list of concepts that universally define the notion of democracy. Indeed, as Katherine Fierlbeck has noted, the recent attention to the concept in the wake of the dramatic political changes in the world during the past twelve years has only served to undermine the clarity of our definitions of the concept. She and others distinguish between the normative and the empirical problems inherent in measuring democracy. The normative challenge grows from the widespread agreement among many that democracy is the "currency of legitimacy" for countries. "But as agreement decreases regarding what, precisely, democracy is, the less we are able to evaluate how it is working, or indeed whether it is working at all," Fierlbeck said. The empirical problem is deeply imbedded in our own beliefs about what democracy should look like. Thus, she asked, "To what extent do our beliefs and expectations of how political relations ought to be governed distort our understanding of how putatively democratic societies do in fact emerge; and, conversely, to what extent does our understanding of how democracy manifests itself temper our connection of what it ought to be." Katherine Fierlbeck, 1998, *Globalizing Democracy: Power, Legitimacy, and the Interpretation of Democratic Ideas* (Manchester, UK: Manchester University Press), pp. 1–2. There are, as we shall see, several aspects of the concept that are widely shared among students of comparative democracy. For an excellent overview of the range of definitions and conceptual thinking about democracy, see Philippe Schmitter and Terry Lynn Karl, 1991, "What Democracy Is. . . and Is Not" *Journal of Democracy* 1 (Summer): 75–88; and, Larry Diamond, 1991, "Is the Third Wave Over?", *Journal of Democracy* 1 (Summer): 20–37. See also Robert Elgie, 1998, "The Classification of Democratic Regime Types: Conceptual Ambiguity and Contestable Assumptions," *European Journal of Political Research* 33 (March): 219–230.

2. Georg Sørensen, 1993, *Democracy and Democratization: Processes and Prospects in a Changing World* (Boulder: Westview Press); Sanford Lakoff, 1996, *Democracy: History, Theory and Practice*, (Boulder: Westview Press); Kenneth A. Bohlen, 1980, "Issues in the Comparative Measurement of Political Democracy," *American Sociological Review* 57 (August): 370–390; Kenneth A. Bohlen and Robert W. Jackman, 1985, "Democracy, Stability, and Dichotomies," *American Sociological Review* 54 (August): 612–621; Kenneth A. Bohlen, 1993, "Liberal Democracy: Validity and Method Factors in Cross-national Measures," *American Journal of Political Science* 37 (November): 1207–1230; and David Held, 1996, *Models of Democracy*, second edition (Stanford: Stanford University Press).

3. W. Phillips Shively, 2001, *Power and Choice: An Introduction to Political Science,* seventh edition (New York: McGraw-Hill).

4. Gabriel A. Almond and Sidney Verba, eds., 1989, *The Civic Culture Revisited* (Newbury Park, Calif.: Sage Publications).

5. David Held, 1995, *Democracy and the Global Order: From the Modern State to Cosmopolitan Governance* (Stanford: Stanford University Press).

6. Schmitter and Karl suggest eleven different primary properties of democracy, some of which are conventional; others (such as federalism) are rarely included in comparative studies of democracy. The eleven primary properties they suggest are: political consensus, political participation, political access, responsiveness of authority, majority rule, parliamentary sovereignty, pluralism, federalism, presidentialism, and checks and balances. Diamond notes the importance of two broad dimensions of democracy: the minimalist notion of electoral democracy (reflected in part by free election and voter participation), as well as liberal democracy, which to Diamond is the minimal degree of civil freedom required to allow political competition to legitimately include more than merely electoral democracy.

7. For an example of the construction and measurement of a concept based in part upon the consensual advice of outside experts, see Markus M. L. Crepaz and Arend Lijphart, 1991, "Corporatism and Consensus Democracy in Eighteen Countries: Conceptual and Empirical Linkages," *British Journal of Political Science* 21 (July): 235–256.

8. For examples of cross-national coding efforts, see Arthur S. Banks, 1971, *Cross-Polity Time-Series Data* (Cambridge, Mass.: MIT Press); Charles L. Taylor, 1983, *World Handbook of Political and Social Indicators*, third edition (New Haven:Yale University Press); Ted Robert Gurr, Keith Jaggers, and Will H. Moore, "The Transformation of the Western State: The Growth of Democracy, Autocracy, and State Power Since 1800," *Studies in Comparative International Development* 25 (Spring 1990): 73–108; Robert Harmel and John D. Robertson, "The Formation and Success of New Parties: A Cross-National Analysis," *International Political Science Review* (October 1985): 501–523; Kenneth Janda, 1980, *Political Parties: A Cross-national Survey* (New York: Free Press and London: Collier Macmillan); and Mark Gasiorowski, 1993, *The Political Regime Change Data Project* (Baton Rouge, La: Louisiana Population Data Center, Louisiana State University). For an example of the coding process itself, see Robert Harmel and Alexander Tan, *Dominant Faction* (unpublished manuscript), produced in conjunction with the Dominant Party Project, Robert Harmel and Kenneth Janda, principal investigators, NSF Grant SES–9112491 and SES–9112357.

9. Freedom House ratings for each country's degree of democracy (political rights and civil liberties) may be found on the web at http://www.freedomhouse.org/ratings/. Ted Robert Gurr's database may be accessed through the web at http://www.bsos.umd.edu/cidcm/polity/. The codebook for his data may be obtained on the web at the same address. All references to Gurr's variables are drawn from his codebook ("Polity II: Political Structures and Regime Change, 1800–1986"), updated in 1997 and cited as Gurr, 1997. All data used in this text are drawn from Gurr's data for 1997, taken from his updated Polity98 Project. This database is a rich and comprehensive trove of data on aspects of democracy and governmental structure within over 150 countries, between 1800–1998.

10. The Polity Time Series has gone through several annual updates since 1986. The version *Polity98*, with data up to and including 1998, may be referenced on the web at http://www.bsos.umd.edu/cidcm/polity/. All references to Gurr 1997 refer to the codebook for the basic Polity Time Series database, available through the Inter-University Consortium for Political and Social Research (http://www.icpsr.umich.edu/).

11. Gurr, 1997, p. 13.
12. Gurr, 1997, p. 14.
13. Gurr, 1997, p. 14.
14. Gurr, 1997, pp. 13–14.
15. The eight key questions governing the coding of a country's degree of political rights are: (1) Is the head of state and/or head of government or other chief authority elected through free and fair elections? (2) Are the legislative representatives elected through free and fair elections? (3) Are there fair electoral laws, equal campaigning opportunities, fair polling, and honest tabulation of ballots? (4) Are the voters able to endow their freely elected representatives with real power? (5) Do the people have the right to organize in different political parties or other competitive political groupings of their choice, and is the system open to the rise and fall of these competing parties or groupings? (6) Is there a significant opposition vote, de facto opposition power, and a realistic possibility for the opposition to increase its support or gain power through elections? (7) Are the people free from domination by the military, foreign powers, totalitarian parties, religious hierarchies, economic oligarchies, or any other powerful group? (8) Do cultural, ethnic, religious, and other minority groups have reasonable self-determination, self-government, autonomy, or participation through informal consensus in the decisionmaking process? See the Freedom House methodology at http://www.freedomhouse.org/survey99/method/. For comparison and contrast, see Kenneth A. Bollen and Pamela Paxton, 2000, "Subjective Measures of Liberal Democracy," *Comparative Political Studies* 33 (February): 58–81.
16. Gurr, 1997, p. 12.
17. Gurr, 1997, p. 13.
18. Gurr, 1997, pp. 12–13. We have modified the scale somewhat of Gurr's original coding for our purposes. Gurr (1997) codes countries with "very low" or, "restricted" competitive systems as a value of "4 " in his scale. This is completely consistent with the objectives of the *Polity* project. However, these systems (for example, China) may well have some form of institutionalized political participation (that is, the government does not allow localized and largely unregulated political participation, largely a moot point, since the government allows virtually no competitive participation of any sort). This arbitrary authority and highly suppressed process may be regulated, but for our purposes, it is more consistent with minimally dispersed authority structures and sharply deprives the citizenry of opportunities to access political power and restrict public authority. Therefore, it is coded as "1" and labeled as "very low" in our scale.
19. Recently, considerable attention has been directed toward the special role of civil liberties as the primary means by which citizens achieve autonomy via the individual's role and involvement in the collective discussion and debate about policy and power within society—deliberations that must be free from coercion and institutionalized intimidation. See Jürgen Habermas, *The Inclusion of the Other: Studies in Political Theory*, edited by Ciaran Cronin and Pablo De Grieff (Cambridge, Mass.: MIT Press). For more recent analyses of the crucial role of deliberation as a means of preserving citizen autonomy, see John S. Dryzek, 2000, *Deliberative Democracy and Beyond: Liberals, Critics and Contestations* (Oxford, UK: Oxford University Press).
20. Specifically, with respect to freedom of expression and belief, the coders rate a country according to two criteria: (1) the extent of "free and independent media and other forms of cultural expression" and (2) the extent of "free religious institutions and free private and public religious expression." With respect to association and organizational rights, countries are rated ac-

cording to these criteria: (1) the extent of "freedom of assembly, demonstration, and open public discussion," (2) the extent of "freedom of political or quasi-political organization," (3) the extent of "free trade unions and peasant organizations or equivalents," and (4) the extent of "effective collective bargaining and free professional and other private organizations." With respect to rule of law and human rights, the coders rate a country according to four criteria: (1) the extent of an "independent judiciary," (2) the extent of "rule of law in civil and criminal matters," (3) the extent of the "public's protection from political terror, unjustified imprisonment, exile, or torture, whether by groups that support or oppose the system," and (4) the extent of "citizens' freedom from extreme government indifference and corruption." Finally, with respect to personal autonomy and economic rights, the coders rate a country according to five criteria: (1) the extent of "open and free private discussion," (2) the extent of "personal autonomy" within society, (3) the extent of "secure property rights," as well as "the right to establish private businesses," (4) the extent of "personal social freedoms, including gender equality, choice of marriage partners, and size of family," and (5) the extent of "equality of opportunity, including freedom from exploitation by or dependency on landlords, employers, union leaders, bureaucrats, or other types of obstacles to a share of legitimate economic gains." See the Freedom House methodology on the web at http://www.freedomhouse.org/survey99/method/.

21. Within SPSS 10, the necessary information for a bivariate frequency table can be obtained easily within the REPORTS window, accessed from the main menu bar via the ANALYZE button. In this case, execute the following sequence: ANALYZE►REPORTS►CASE SUMMARIES. Once inside the LIST THE CASES window, specify in the box which varibles you want to list. In order to construct a simple bivariate table as reported in Table 7.10, choose the variable COUNTRY to place in the VARIABLES section of the window. Our goal is to list cases by the value of their country, *according to the values of POLIT973 and PARCOMP3.* To accomplish this, place the variable names for POLIT973 and PARCOMP3 from the variable list into the GROUPING VARIABLE WINDOW (below the VARIABLES window). This will produce a table that will list countries according to every combination of values for POLIT973 and PARCOMP3. See Marija J. Norušis, 2000, *SPSS: SPSS© 10.0 Guide to Data Analysis* (Upper Saddle River, N.J.: Prentice Hall), pp. 541–544 for more details.

22. Andrew Hacker, 1967, "The Utility of Quantitative Methods in Political Science," in James C. Charlesworth Jr., ed., *Contemporary Political Analysis* (New York: The Free Press), p. 148.

23. Ibid.

8

The Role of Hypothesis Testing in Cross-National Analysis

Terms: *Explanation, Prediction, Description, Variance, Research Hypotheses, Null Hypothesis, Type I Error, Type II Error, Explicit Causality, Implicit Causality, Test Statistic, Probability Level*

In the previous chapters, we explored the logical relationship between theory, concept formulation, measurement strategies, validity, and the objectives of cross-national analysis. We explored also two principal concepts of politics: power and political authority; more specifically, *national potential power* and *democracy*. In this and the remaining chapters, we build upon this foundation to examine hypothesis testing within cross-national analysis.

Much of the political history of the twentieth century was shaped by the enduring tension between new nations created from the ashes of empire and older nations. Many countries, such as France, Great Britain, and Russia, were former empires themselves, while others, such as China, were longtime players in the game of world politics. Still others, such as Argentina and Brazil, while not being former colonies per se, had experienced the emerging class system within the world that had been building since the sixteenth century. Tensions between the older and newer nations, between the established wealthy and militarily powerful nations, and the newer and less powerful nations mounted throughout the years between 1918 and the late 1960s and early 1970s. While this tension has varied with conditions of the global environment, one constant source of tension seems to be that older nations are wealthier and are more likely to favor democratic decisionmaking, while newer nations have not, for the most part, enjoyed similar levels of economic prosperity of the older nations and are more prone to authoritarian governance. This suggests a basic question: Is age of the nation-state itself a factor that can account for differences in political orientation among countries of the world?

Hypothesis Testing in Perspective

In this chapter, we will explore this question by introducing you to the most important activity of science: *hypothesis testing*. This activity is what drives the accumulation of knowledge in all science, not just political science. It is what distinguishes (ordinarily) the case studies, as well as comparable cases, strategy of comparative political inquiry from the statistical analysis of comparative political data. Hypothesis testing requires a scientific analysis of data. Before one can reasonably evaluate the legitimacy of his or her research hypothesis, one must have a large enough sample of data to allow inference from the sample to a population. While the case study and comparable cases designs may afford us great insight into particular countries and regions, these designs, as we have seen, restrict the ability of the student of comparative politics to generalize about political behavior and institutional authority. At the core of empirical social science research is the assumption that knowledge has been based not merely on carefully crafted case studies or comparable cases, but on the further extension of the findings to something of a "generalized" test—a test that can show the range and limitations of the findings. Hypothesis testing is the means of proceeding with such an extension of our knowledge base, and empirical cross-national analysis is the first step toward building more generalized theories of political behavior and institutional authority.

While hypothesis testing may sound imposing to the beginning student, it is a basic and entirely commonsensical exercise. Indeed, whenever we believe two or more concepts, phenomena, or observable attributes are related to each other, and we wish to confirm the relationship with some degree of confidence and credibility, we have entered the domain of hypothesis testing. In Table 7.10 we examined the scope of institutional democracy, PARCOMP (as measured by its collapsed version, PARCOMP3) relative to the scale of institutional democracy, POLIT97 (POLIT973); in Table 7.11 we explored the frequency distribution of the scope of liberal democracy, PARREG (PARREG3) and the scale of liberal democracy, CIVIL97 (CIVIL973). The logic behind the use of a bivariate frequency table (Demonstrations 7.1 and 7.2) is the same that lies behind that of hypothesis testing. In effect, when we correlate the values of one variable (measured at the ordinal level) with the values of a second variable (also measured at the ordinal level), we are trying to sort out the patterns in the sample from which we can generalize to the target population. The bivariate frequency table, however, is an initial tool; it lacks the precision and power to estimate accurately the error we might expect when we predict a country's value on one attribute from its value on a second attribute. Therefore, such a table cannot allow us to credibly test hypotheses. More importantly, it cannot allow us to reject interpretations of our political world with any specified degree of confidence. Nonetheless, it is a powerful and useful start that often, as we saw, reveals information that remains hidden by the more sophisticated tools of hypothesis testing. We will explain in detail the tabulation and statistical interpretation of frequency tables in the next chapter. First, let us turn to the basics of hypothesis testing.

EXPLANATION, PREDICTION, AND CAUSALITY

Before we proceed to a step-by-step example of testing a hypothesis, we must put this all-important activity into its proper context within the cross-national study of political behavior and institutional authority. The greatest challenge to many students (and professionals) who are first introduced to the process of hypothesis testing is the abrupt and distinct shift in the tools employed. Prior to hypothesis testing, according to the logic depicted in the Ladder of Theory Building introduced in Chapter 2, the only statistics the student must confront are those which are generally referred to as descriptive statistics, namely, univariate statistics (for example, mean, median, mode). These, as their name implies, describe the tendencies of only one variable. For most students, once they move beyond the basic tools of univariate analysis or simple two-way analysis tables to explore political phenomena, the use of statistics often seems unduly technical and obtuse—especially when tied to the testing of hypotheses. The effort frequently takes on an untidy appearance. Adding more variables and countries to our analysis only renders things less neat and orderly—at first glance. We are forced to confront exceptions to the rule we are trying to establish, and there are those inevitable qualifications that we must attach to our conclusions, blurring simplicity and confounding simple "black and white" examples that we have come to rely upon in basic texts.

What might seem complicated and technical initially can be revealed as simple and driven by common sense. We begin by considering the logical relationship between explanation, prediction, and variance. If, as we have asserted in Chapter 2, the goal of the comparativist is to establish sound generalizations, then he or she must have a nominal appreciation of the role of variance and variation in the process of explanation and prediction. Taken together, explanation, prediction, and the role of variance constitute the core ingredients of hypothesis testing, which stands atop the Ladder of Theory Building, as explained in Chapter 2. Understanding how and why we move from simple description, to prediction, and ultimately to explanation is as central to the knowledge repertoire of comparative students as is knowing the difference between democracy and autocracy.

Explanation, Causality, and Statistical Analysis

Explanation is the process of logically relating two or more attributes through a cause-and-effect sequence. Through explanation, we account for something by specifying the sequence of events that gives rise to the phenomenon we are interested in explaining.

This requires that we develop theory to specify the concepts that represent the factors influencing the final outcome in question.

No matter how explicit the causal assumption, when we want to explain something, we must always address the question: *Why did something happen (or not happen), and to what can we assign responsibility for the effect?* General explanation allows one to do that regardless of culture or nation. It holds that changes in Concept A will lead to changes in Concept B in a wide variety of national or cultural settings. More specifically, it assumes that in adjusting the value of X for Concept A, regardless of cultural or national context, we can expect the value of Concept B to change by a proportionate degree relative to the change in value X within Concept A.

In contrast, description does not assume any causality; nor is it free from the specific cultural or national context. Description merely takes account of particular characteristics or specific traits of attributes within a country. As an intellectual activity, description does not explicitly or implicitly connect changes in one attribute to changes within another attribute, either within a specific cultural or national context, or across national and cultural contexts. Therefore, description cannot explain an attribute; it can, however, distinguish one attribute from another. Furthermore, description cannot directly build general explanation. However, it can lead one toward the specified connection that logically links concepts that hold the promise of building general theory. Explanation requires inference, as well as inferential measures that allow systematic assessment of our causal inferences. The logic lying behind the inference is specified in the theory connecting two or more concepts and the syllogistic reasoning that explains why the concepts are connected.

Explicit Causality. Technically, causality takes two forms in comparative analysis: the *explicit* form and the *implicit* form. *Explicit causality* may be further divided into two forms: (1) experimental or direct tests for causality, and (2) statistical controls, or indirect tests for causality. Experimental analysis allows the researcher to manually manipulate all the variables in a test, controlling the time sequence between the cause and the effect. Statistical manipulation, by contrast, assumes the student indirectly tests for the possibility of a causal relationship between two variables within a sample by use of very specific statistical tools.[1]

Explicit causality requires that we connect three or more concepts in a "cause-effect" sequence, and manipulate statistical procedures to calibrate the effects of one variable upon a second variable, controlling for the effect of the third variable on both the first variable and the second. A classic but simple example is trying to explain aggregate wealth (GDP). One hypothesis holds it is related to population size (that is, the more workers in a country, the more aggregate wealth). We would certainly find a strong relationship between aggregate wealth and the population size of a country. Yet both of these variables would be logically related to the a third variable, size of country. Areal size, in other words, determines the size of a population (up to a point), as well as the aggregate wealth of a country (both as a factor limiting population size and as a determinant of the natural resources necessary to generate wealth). In this case, the third variable in the model is, in fact, an exogenous variable. We call these techniques, *multivariate* (more than two variables), and we label such models (with three or more variables), *multivariate models*. They are much more explicit about the role of the exogenous variables than are bivariate models.[2]

Exogenous variables are the variables in a model (bivariate or multivariate) that we have not fully specified in the model itself, but that may influence the relationship we have specified in the model. The exogenous variable in our simple example above is areal size—at least it lies outside the first model tested (aggregate wealth as a function of population size). Experimental methods seek to isolate all exogenous variables by manipulating the experimental conditions and observing the post-effect properties against the pre-effect properties, attributing the change to the exogenous variables that were added following the original relationship between the two variables. Statistical methods manipulate variables and variance, not the physical settings within which experiments occur. Furthermore, the statistical method in cross-national strategies of comparison does not have as its primary mission the isolation of exogenous variables. This becomes an impossibility in statistical models—there are always many more variables than we have countries in a cross-national analysis. Rather, the student of cross-national strategies of comparison employs the statistical method to incrementally remove possible explanations through an iterative process of hypothesis testing and falsification, moving from hypothesis to hypothesis, all the while seeking to eliminate possible alternative explanations to the original hypothesis by falsifying the claims of competing hypotheses.[3] Keep in mind that indirect, statistical tests of causality can never equal direct experimental tests of causality for credibility and precision.

Implicit Causality. *Implicit causality* assumes some degree of causality to exist between two variables, but does not *directly* test for its presence. Rather, the causal implications help order our initial thinking about two variables, from which we begin the process of sorting out important information in the hope of moving on later with more direct tests of explicit causality.

Standing between a univariate analysis (that is, the process of analyzing only one variable), and a multivariate analysis (analyzing three or more variables simultaneously), is *bivariate* analysis. Hypothesis testing requires, at a minimum, bivariate analysis. Implicit causality guides bivariate analysis; only multivariate analysis can claim to (indirectly) measure explicit causality. In effect, with implicit causality, you measure the *association* between two variables. An association is simply a statistical correspondence between the variances of two variables within a sample. From our theory, we infer this correspondence to be attributed to a cause-and-effect mechanism, though we cannot directly measure the mechanism itself.

A second example (outside of the study of cross-national analysis) may illustrate the difference between causality and association. For decades, medical researchers assumed that the chemical components consumed by smokers inhaling cigarettes lead to a greater probability of contracting cancer, especially lung cancer. There were a number of theories that explained this relationship logically, and there were statistical tests that demonstrated conclusively the theory. However, medical researchers could not isolate the specific causal mechanism; they could not isolate the process that could directly explain the explicit causal connection between tobacco and cancer. However, new technologies allowed researchers to isolate the mechanism linking smoking to cancer. By manipulating tobacco residues in rats and specific chemicals within the DNA of the animals, medical researchers now know that a key protein designed to destroy cells that are cancerous, and thereby preserve the integrity of human tissue, is itself destroyed by tobacco residues, thus exposing the cell to the rages of cancer. While tobacco may not be the only factor destroying the protein, medical researchers now have a greater degree of "explicitness" than before, one that supports their original theories and goes beyond mere indirect statistical and logical association between tobacco and cancer.

In studying human affairs, especially from a cross-national sample, such direct explicit control and isolation of the explicit causal links connecting two attributes are rare. We must rely on association and the power of theory (especially careful concept formulation and measurement specification) to build our knowledge base.

The Logic and Structure of Bivariate Models

Bivariate analysis entails the measurement of the degree of association between two variables, commonly denoted as *X* and *Y*. *Y* is the variable that we wish to explain—the variable of our primary interest. *X* is the variable we use to support our theory—the variable that we think "causes" or "explains" variation in the *Y* variable. Whenever we logically connect two or more variables through an implied causal structure, we have defined a statistical model. Remember, however, in a bivariate model you can never test directly for causality. You must—at best—merely imply a *weak form* of causality. Theory, in conjunction with bivariate analysis, is the starting point for explanation.

If we wish to approximate "explicit" causality between *X* and *Y* when employing statistical analysis, we must statistically control for the possibility that a third variable (*Z*) is not itself "causing" Y, or possibly, *both X* and *Y*. If such were the case, then the relationship between *X* and *Y* is spurious. For example, suppose that you note an association between the number of firefighters responding to various fires (variable *X*), and the amount of damage occurring at those same fires (variable *Y*). Such an association might lead you to conclude that firefighters cause damage. Common logic would dictate that such is not the case. It is most likely that a third variable—size of fire—explains the association between the *X* and *Y* variables. With some notable exceptions (China), wealthy countries (if measured by their gross domestic product per person within the country) tend to be democratic, while poor countries tend to be authoritarian. Does democracy "cause" wealth? Does wealth "cause" democracy? Or, does a third variable (such as culture) "explain" both?

Prediction

Prediction follows logically from explanation. If an explanation is empirically valid, that is, if we can demonstrate the *implied* cause and effect through measurement, we can also predict the change in one attribute that will occur as a result of the change in the first attribute. As explained above, the only true cause-and-effect proof that exists is in the form of pure experimentation, where one can directly manipulate the attributes and can thereby control the chronological sequence of cause and effect. Most students have probably undertaken simple experiments in high school chemistry courses. These entail direct manipulation and observation of change within controlled time sequences. You can easily see the effect of one chemical added to a solution and compare the "before" and "after" condition of the solution.

In political science, we rarely have an opportunity to use experiments. Rather, we must work with indirect statistical designs. The required statistical tools rely upon *variance* in order to confirm or reject our hypotheses. Through the analysis of variance, we estimate the accuracy of our predictions and from these assessments, work backward to determine the credibility and validity of our assumed explanation for the relationship between X and Y. Variance, therefore, lies at the very heart of hypothesis testing, which itself is the core process required for *both* explanation and prediction. As you will see, the logic behind these common statistical tools is simple, and once explained, the output of the statistical programs found in such packages as SPSS is easily understood and readily applied to the study of comparative politics.

THE PROCESS OF TESTING HYPOTHESES

We may draw from the example of Joseph Healey and summarize the hypothesis-testing process as consisting of six sequential steps:[4]

The Six Steps in Hypothesis Testing

Step 1. Specify a theory from which you deduce some specific model linking at least two concepts.

Step 2. Prepare a succinct, formal statement of the research hypothesis *and* its null.

Step 3. Obtain a reliable sample (one that has not been biased in its selection of cases from the target population and that contains properly measured and operational data).

Step 4. Establish the threshold (probability level) within which you will accept or reject the null.

Step 5. Analyze the data with the proper statistical tool.

Step 6. Evaluate the test statistic and make a decision (accept or reject) with regard to your null.

To understand and appreciate these six steps, we will work through an example of testing a basic hypothesis relevant to comparative politics.

Step 1: Your Theory

Democracy, as we have seen in Chapter 7, entails such concepts as competitiveness of political participation, regulated and institutionalized political participation, political rights, and, of course, civil liberties. From existing theories of human behavior in general, and political behavior in particular, students of comparative politics have come to understand that the costs of democracy are quite expensive. Fundamentally, democracy requires great tolerance and patience. Things cannot and must not happen overnight; otherwise, minority rights might be trampled and the very process of consensus building will be shattered. Of course, democracy also carries with it the baggage of uncertainty and unpredictability: The fact that citizens are granted certain freedoms and civil liberties means that no one can know for sure how political power will be manifest and who will hold that power in the foreseeable future. During tumultuous periods of revolution and rebellion that often accompany the formation of new nation-states—especially when they are formed from the ashes and ruins of collapsed empires—it is often easier and more natural to institute a system of authority that values immediate effectiveness and response over the more difficult, messy, and tenuous process of compromise that characterizes democracy. In short, autocracy is often the easiest short-term solution to governance.

Thus, it is logical to expect that, *all things being equal*, more recent nation-states should be characterized by weaker democratic attributes than those nation-states that have had a longer period to evolve. Of course, there are certainly a host of other factors (that is, exogenous factors) that condition the evolution of democracy—some of which we will consider in subsequent chapters. But for now, let us work from the theory that age is a necessary ingredient in the successful maturation and formation of democracy.

Step 2: Your Research Hypothesis and the Null Hypothesis

The theory outlined in Step 1 may have described an old problem, but it also suggests the following hypothesis:

> *Hypothesis 8.1: The degree of political rights extended a population in a country varies directly with the number of years a country has been a sovereign nation-state.*

This hypothesis restates in a formal manner the theory as outlined above: In newer countries, we expect political rights to be less established than in older, more established countries. If the scale of institutional democracy is one of the primary properties of democracy, and POLIT97 is our empirical representation of the primary property, and we predict older nations to be more democratic than more recent nation-states, then we should expect POLIT97 to be *less* prominent in newer nation-states (those countries where AGE18002 = 2) than in older nation-states (those countries where AGE18002 = 1).

The Null Hypothesis. Hypothesis 8.1 is what we call the *research* hypothesis. It is distinct from the null hypothesis. *In science, you do not test the research hypothesis; you test the null hypothesis.* What is a *null hypothesis*? It is the backdrop to all research hypotheses. It states the presumed "state-of-nature," so to speak. *The null hypothesis simply holds that there is no relationship between the two variables specified in the research hypothesis.* Statistical tools are designed to test whether or not we can *reject* the null, and therefore, *accept* our research hypothesis. In essence, all hypothesis testing involves applying the appropriate tools of analysis to quantitative data for the purpose of evaluating the *null* hypothesis. Thus, our null holds that there is no association (relationship) between POLIT97 and AGE18002. In scientific literature, the null hypothesis is denoted as H_0.

The null hypothesis, in effect, depicts what is believed to be the true condition within the *target population*. The research hypothesis, on the other hand, suggests an alternative condition within the target population and relies on the sample to estimate this "true" condition. We will return to this critical distinction below in Step 4.[5]

Step 3: The Sample

As explained in Chapters 1, 2, and 3, our sample, CROSSNAT.50, is intended to target the population of *populous countries*. From the data in this sample, we can offer evidence that will support or reject the null based upon data drawn from a sample of populous countries. Other sample selections may be drawn to apply our hypothesis to repeated tests. This is the nature of science: Researchers are always involved in testing and retesting hypotheses in an attempt to refine and clarify our knowledge through the subsequent and incremental confirmation or rejection of previously rejected or sustained null hypotheses. Frequently these involve the use of particular subsets of countries drawn from the original samples (focusing, for instance, only on European countries, or African countries, or developing countries).

In the process of normal science, the ultimate objective is to identify laws. Laws in science are hypotheses that have been proven to have universal validity. That is, they are always sustained by data, regardless of the sample used. In the social sciences we have very few laws. Therefore, it is always important to be aware of the sample you are using (or samples that others have used) when testing hypotheses (or evaluating the hypothesis-testing procedure of others).

Step 4: Your Probability Threshold

Recall from Step 2 that hypothesis testing entails judgment based on empirical evidence. The decision involves whether we accept the vision of the real world, as expressed in the null hypothesis, or whether we reject that vision in favor of an alternative vision, one reflected in the sample and formalized in the research hypothesis. Fundamentally, this requires that we obtain a *probability measure of the error* we are likely to make if we proceed with the rejection of the vision expressed in the null in favor of the vision expressed in the research hypothesis.

The Logic of the Test Statistic. Whenever you test a null hypothesis, therefore, you produce a test statistic that measures three things:

- The *presence* of a statistically significant association (relationship) between two variables.
- The *strength* of this statistically significant association (relationship) between two variables.
- The *direction* of this statistically significant association (relationship) between two variables.

The principal role of the test statistic is to establish the presence of a statistically significant relationship as stated in the research hypothesis. A statistically significant relationship exists when we can be reasonably certain that the *null hypothesis* is wrong. This test statistic is measured against a probability threshold. *The probability we are interested in is whether or not the test statistic reflects a relationship within our sample, but not the target population.* The test statistic allows you to consider the possibility that because of some unique set of countries you may have selected in your sampling procedure, you may have simply come across a statistical relationship peculiar to your sample that does not hold true for the target population (recall our discussion of repeated samples and confidence intervals in Chapter 5). Someone could argue that by changing a few countries (or shifting the time frame a few years), the test statistic could slip away, and the relationship you previously thought to be present would in fact be shown to be absent in the target population. If the probability of this happening is too high, the vision of the "real" world as expressed by the null hypothesis cannot and should not be rejected.

Since we can never know for sure if a relationship exists in the true target population (because, as explained in Chapter 5, we rarely, if ever, have the opportunity to measure the true target population), we must rely on a statistical calculation of the probability that our test statistic might be simply a manifestation of the particular sample, but not reflective of the target population. In other words, our test statistic helps us in formulating our final judgment as to whether there is a probability that we might be making a mistake in accepting our research hypothesis and rejecting the null hypothesis. *Our threshold is the maximum probability of error that we can accept.*

TABLE 8.1 Rejecting or Accepting the Null Hypothesis

	Condition	
Decision	Null Hypothesis Is True ($\alpha > .05$)	Null Hypothesis Is False ($\alpha \leq .05$)
	Consequence of Decision Given Specified Condition	
Reject Null Hypothesis	Type I Error (Rejecting the null hypothesis when not warranted)	Proper Decision
Accept Null Hypothesis	Proper Decision	Type II Error (Rejecting the research hypothesis when not warranted)

Type I and Type II Errors in Assessing Thresholds. To better appreciate this crucial aspect of hypothesis testing, students are ordinarily instructed as to the nature of *Type I* and *Type II* errors. Specifically, there are two basic types of errors in hypothesis testing that must be carefully avoided. One—and the most important one to avoid—is what we call a *Type I Error*. It occurs when we *reject the null hypothesis when it should not be rejected.* The second type of error is a *Type II Error*. This occurs when *we accept the null hypothesis when it should not be accepted.* Table 8.1 presents this logic in graphical form.

In scientific research, one always begins from the premise that the null reflects the real world (even if you truly think the research hypothesis is a better approximation of the real world). The null always holds that there is no relationship between two specified variables in the population; the null always assumes that your research hypothesis is wrong. Consequently, the mathematical odds are *always* presumed to be overwhelmingly stacked in favor of the null, not your research hypothesis.

The logic behind these assumptions is quite commonly applied in "everyday" life. For instance, in the American criminal justice system, we assume that a person is innocent until proven guilty. The object of the prosecutor in felony trials is to prove "beyond all reasonable doubt" the guilt of the accused person. In hypothetical terms, H_1 would be that the accused person is guilty; the null hypothesis, H_0, would be that the accused is innocent. The jury, in its decision concerning the accused, can make one of two mistakes: It can convict a truly innocent person, or it can acquit a truly guilty person. Which of the two mistakes is more grievous? Most (though not all) would say that convicting an innocent person is far worse than acquitting a guilty person; thus, legal safeguards are put in place to prevent convicting innocent persons. The more safeguards in place to prevent convicting innocent persons, however, the more likely it is that truly guilty persons will be set free.

Similarly, in our scientific research, we can, as mentioned above, commit one of two errors: rejecting a null hypothesis that was true, or failing to reject a null hypothesis that was false. In scientific research we generally assume that committing a Type I error is more grievous than committing a Type II error. We must set a threshold that reduces the probability of committing a Type I error without overly increasing the probability of committing a Type II error. Conventionally, this threshold is the .05 level (5 percent). *That is, we can only reject the null when we are certain that there is, at maximum, a 5 percent probability that the null is actually right and that we would be making a mistake in rejecting the null in favor of the research hypothesis.* As long as we are 95 percent certain that we are not making a *Type I Error*, we can proceed to reject the null and accept the research hypothesis.

Steps 5 and 6: Analyze the Data with the Proper Statistical Tool and Obtain the Test Statistic

Statistical analysis of data within the context of hypothesis testing is directed principally toward obtaining a probability estimate of a Type I Error (the probability of rejecting the null hypothesis when the null is correct). There are two basic questions you ask before beginning the statistical test of your hypothesis. The answers to these two questions will determine the proper statistical tool to employ in testing your hypothesis.

- At what level are your variables in your model measured (nominal, ordinal, interval/ratio, or a mixed combination)?
- If at least one of the variables is measured at the interval/ratio level, does the sample distribution severely violate the assumption of having a normal distribution?

There are more specialized conditions that must be considered when employing some of the most sophisticated and powerful tools of hypothesis testing, especially when we are working with interval/ratio-level data. The two questions above, however, are the basic questions that determine the statistical application to apply in initial hypothesis testing. Table 8.2 summarizes the appropriate tools of hypothesis testing, and the conditions under which they are commonly employed.

If we are using interval/ratio-level variables, and the distributions of the variables are *not* reasonably congruent with a normal distribution (for example, bimodal distribution, as with AGE1800 in Chapter 3), then we must move down the level of measurement to the ordinal level (for example, AGE18002) and non-parametric statistics. Our principal dependent variables are all technically ordinal. Later, we will treat them as if they were interval, but for the moment, let us stay with the statistical applications that are appropriate for ordinal measures. Therefore, with both variables measured at the ordinal level of analysis, we are ready to move to the next stage, tabular analysis, or crosstabs—explained in the next chapter.

CHAPTER SUMMARY

In this chapter, we have introduced you to the fundamental aspects of hypothesis testing. Central to hypothesis testing is producing a test statistic and obtaining an estimate

TABLE 8.2 Basic Statistical Applications for Hypothesis Testing

Nonparametric Statistics		
Level at Which Variables in Hypothesis are Measured	*Statistical Procedure*	*Test Statistic Obtained by the Statistical Procedure*
Nominal-Nominal	Tabular Analysis	Chi-Square
Nominal-Ordinal	Tabular Analysis	Chi-Square
Ordinal-Ordinal	Tabular Analysis	Chi-Square
	Parametric Statistics	
Ordinal-Interval/Ratio (if ordinal variable is dichotomous)	One-Way Analysis of Variance (t-test)	T-Statistic
Ordinal-Interval/Ratio (if ordinal variable is multi-category)	One-Way Analysis of Variance (ANOVA)	F-statistic
Interval/Ratio-Interval/Ratio	Correlation; Scatterplots; Curve Fitting; Compare Mapping; Simple Regression; Multiple Regression	F-statistic (and t-statistics for individual parameter estimates in multivariate models)

of its statistical significance. In this regard, the researcher must distinguish between the null and the research hypotheses, as well as Type I and Type II errors. This decision—to accept or reject the null hypothesis—depends on the statistical calculation of expected and observed patterns to our data across the sample. As we will explain in detail in subsequent chapters, what we seek to minimize is the *error* in our model's ability to explain or predict the variance in one variable (dependent variable) from knowing the variance of a second variable (independent variable).

NOTES

1. For an excellent introduction to the difference between the statistical method and the experimental method of hypothesis testing, see Neil McK. Agnew and Sandra W. Pyke, 1994, *The Science Game: An Introduction to Research in the Social Sciences*, sixth edition (Englewood Cliffs, N.J.: Prentice Hall), pp. 70–109.

2. For a brief but clear and precise overview of the role of statistical hypothesis testing and the differences between bivariate and multivariate logic, see Richard J. Harris, 1975, *A Primer for Multi-Variate Statistics* (New York: Academic Press), pp. 1–5.

3. See Lawrence Mayer, 1996, *Redefining Comparative Politics: Promise Versus Performance* (Newbury Park, Calif.: Sage Publications), pp. 38–42.

4. Joseph F. Healey, 1993, *Statistics: A Tool for Social Research* (Belmont, Calif.: Wadsworth Publishing Company), pp. 182–185.

5. For a formal and detailed discussion of the logic surrounding the falsification process in science, and the logical differences between the research and null hypotheses, see Karl Popper, 1968, *The Logic of Scientific Discovery* (New York: Harper Torchbooks), pp. 78–92.

9

The Role of Tabular Analysis in Cross-National Analysis

Terms: *Crosstabs (Contingency Table Analysis), PRE Statistics, Measures of Association, Probability Levels (Significance Levels), Chi-Square, Kendall's Tau b and Tau c, Gamma, Somer's d*
Concepts: Age of Political System, Type of Political System, Democracy
Demonstrations: Simple Tabular Analysis, 9.1; Crosstab Analysis in Perspective, 9.2

In this chapter, we will demonstrate one of the most basic—and important—tools of statistical analysis: *crosstabs*. Tabular analysis involves presenting your ordinal/nominal-level data in a *contingency table*. This table groups data in matrix form and serves to calculate the critical test statistic in tabular analysis, the *chi-square statistic*. A contingency table is much like a bivariate frequency table as constructed in Tables 7.10 and 7.11. Rather than simply reporting the number of countries that are contained within each cell of these two tables, we have, of course, listed in Tables 7.10 and 7.11 the actual names of the countries that fall into each cell.

Tabular analysis is a technique that sorts cases in a sample according to values on the independent and dependent variable. The technique is not as common for comparativists who utilize ecological data measured at the ordinal or nominal level. It is quite common when reporting the results of hypothesis tests employing nonempirical data, namely, survey data. These data measure the attitudes or attributes of individuals (thus, they derive from surveys, or questionnaires). When working with ecological data (such as in CROSSNAT.50), the N is usually so small as to render crosstab analysis less interesting to students of cross-national research. However, this technique is a valuable tool in order to complement and confirm hypothesis tests that are based upon data that do not readily conform to normal distributions. By running a crosstabs to supplement (though not necessarily replace) a more sophisticated statistical analysis employing a technique that assumes the researcher is using data that severely depart from a normal distribution, we offer corroborating evidence to support the more sophisticated analysis. Often, of course, a cross-tabular analysis simply affords important information in its own right. Indeed, within cross-national analysis it can confirm that a bivariate descriptive table reveals a pattern of country distributions that would not occur by chance alone in the real world. Thus, it can offer powerful statistical information to supplement a simple descriptive bivariate table.

THE LOGIC OF TABULAR ANALYSIS AS APPLIED TO CROSS-NATIONAL ANALYSIS

Tabular analysis works just like a bivariate frequency table—indeed, a bivariate frequency table *is* a contingency table. Tabular analysis employs a matrix of *rows* (the values of the dependent variable) and *columns* (independent variables). The values of a dependent variable per independent variable are the intersection points within the matrix. *Cell frequencies indicate how many countries have a particular value of the dependent variable given a particular value of the independent variable.*

Marginals are the respective row and column totals. By summing these marginals we can calculate the grand total, or the total number of *valid* responses in the sample. For instance, referring back to Table 7.10, the row marginal for countries with "Very Low/Low" degrees of political rights (POLIT973 = 1) is nine. The column marginal for countries with "Very Low/Low" degrees of competitive political participation (PARCOMP3 = 1) is seven. The sum of all three column marginals for the three categories of PARCOMP3 is fifty, as is the sum of the row marginals for the three categories of POLIT973.

Before considering a particular hypothesis, it is important to keep the basic rules in mind when using tabular analysis for the study of comparative political data; namely, you should *compute within columns and compare across columns*. In other words:

- Always convert the cell frequencies into percentages *within categories of the independent variable*. That is, within SPSS 10, always specify the *column percentages* within the CROSSTABS window. Another way to remember this very important rule: Make sure your columns always sum to 100 percent (and always make sure you have specified your independent variable, X, as the column variable).
- To read a contingency table in a bivariate tabular analysis, *always compare percentages across categories of the independent variable (read right to left, or left to right, not vertically or diagonally)*.

Setting Up a Tabular Analysis

When testing for a relationship between two variables (X and Y) measured at the ordinal and/or nominal level, we assume that the values (or categories) of one variable are contingent upon the values (or categories) of another variable. Let us reconsider Hypothesis 8.1. With this hypothesis, we assume that the degree of political rights accorded a citizenry within a country will be contingent upon the number of years that country has existed as a sovereign political entity. To test this hypothesis, we must determine the chi-square of the implied pattern of country distributions across the two attributes of age and political rights.

The Chi-Square Statistic

In order to achieve a high degree of precision and confidence in our quest for explanation and, ultimately, prediction, we must employ more specific tools of research: *parametric statistics*. The use of these statistics requires that we meet (within reason) specific assumptions about the distribution of scores in a sample before we may appropriately and effectively proceed with our hypothesis tests. Basically, when we are working with interval/ratio-level data, we can meet (within reason) the assumptions of parametric statistics. When, however, we are working exclusively with ordinal- and/or nominal-level data and we wish to test hypotheses systematically, we must (at least initially) "step down" from parametric statistics to *nonparametric statistics*. Nonparametric statistics (such as the Mann-Whitney test introduced in Chapter 5) relax the more strict assumptions regarding the normality of our sample distribution essential for parametric statistics, thereby allowing us to estimate the statistical significance of our findings under different criteria than we would use if we were working with interval/ratio-level data.

One of the most widely reported nonparametric statistics used in hypothesis testing is the chi-square statistic. This statistic relaxes assumptions of normal distributions and simply tests the hypothesis that the observed number of cases within a category in a contingency table reflects the "expected" number of cases within that category. Thus, a chi-square could have been computed for Table 7.10. It would have told us whether the actual number of countries (observed) in any given cell in the table deviated in a significant degree from what would be expected if there was no relationship between the scale of institutionalized democracy and the scope of institutionalized democracy.

The chi-square statistic measures the difference between the *expected* cell frequencies in a contingency table and the *observed* cell frequencies in a contingency table. The null hypothesis holds, of course, that there is no relationship between two variables (such as POLIT97 and AGE18002). Thus, the null predicts that the cell frequencies observed in a contingency table will be randomly distributed, with no contingent structure to the distribution of cell frequencies. On the other hand, if there is a relationship (if the null is false), then the pattern of cell frequencies of POLIT97 will be contingent upon the pattern of cell frequencies shown to exist for AGE18002.

Turning to Table 7.10, we may note that a "perfect" contingent relationship would be represented by having about sixteen or seventeen countries within each of the three cells running in a diagonal from top left to bottom right of the matrix in the table. Of course, if the latter relationship had held, we would have reason for concern about the measurement validity of our data. This pattern would have reflected something entirely inconsistent with experience and theory for it would have shown that countries with significant *high* scale of institutionalized democracy would also have significantly *low* scope to institutionalized democracy. A random distribution in a 3 x 3 matrix such as Table 7.10 would have been reflected by an equal number of countries in each of the nine cells in the table (or, approximately five or six countries per cell). This would have made it impossible to discern any alignment in the distribution of the countries according to the scale of the two variables.

The chi-square measures, in effect, the aggregate difference between what the null predicts (which, of course, is randomness) and what the sample shows, as revealed by the contingency table. If the distribution of cell frequencies produced by the contingency table aligns with what the null expected (that is, no contingency shown, revealing a random pattern to the distribution of cell frequencies), the chi-square will be correspondingly small. We will have to reject the research hypothesis. On the other hand, if the distribution of cell frequencies is such that it deviates markedly from what a random pattern would predict (and what the null expects), the chi-square would be larger and we would be in a better position to reject the null and accept our research hypothesis. Note the operational logic of the contingent relationship. The student, in testing his or her hypothesis, is basically computing the differences between an expected pattern and the observed pattern. This logic is common to all techniques of hypothesis testing. It is, in effect, the measure of *model variance*, a concept we will explore in greater detail in Chapter 10. For now, let us consider the specific logic of chi-square and examine how variance across our variables in a crosstabs analysis is measured and evaluated.

The actual formula for computing the chi-square is:

$$X^2 = \sum \frac{(O-E)^2}{E} \qquad \text{Formula 9.1}$$

The chi-square is based upon the difference between observed (O) and expected (E) cell frequencies, as shown in Equation 9.1. We will explore this statistic and its formula in more detail below. For now, note that the size of the chi-square itself will also depend upon:

- The number of observations (for example, countries) in the sample
- The degrees of freedom allowed by the contingency table

Degrees of Freedom and Tabular Analysis

For comparativists working with grouped ecological data, which often entails working with samples of limited size (fewer than fifty countries), it is imperative that the two variables be collapsed to consist of no more than two categories each (that is, that the sample be bimodal). Why? Because the more categories defining an ordinal or nominal variable in tabular analysis, the larger will be the degrees of freedom in a tabular analysis.

We will consider degrees of freedom in more detail in Chapters 10 and 15. However, the concept is critical for students employing basic tools of hypothesis testing in cross-national analysis. Degrees of freedom in general refers to the number of scores in a sample that are free to vary within the constraints imposed by the properties of the model (the model being the proposed relationship between X and Y variables). Consider this simple example. You have a sample of three countries: A, B, and C. You know the sample mean for the population of the three countries is 100. You also know that country A has 50 people, and you know country B has 30 people. Once you know the values of countries A and B, and you know the sample mean is 100, you now know that country C's population cannot vary freely—it is fixed by the parameters of the model. It must be 220. Because we know that 100 x 3 = 300, and we know that country A has only 50 people, and country B has only 30. There is no freedom to vary, so to speak, for country C. Its total must be equal to that number that will accommodate the sample mean of 100.

Now, supposing you are working with ordinal-level data, not interval-level data. You have three countries and have assigned ordinal-ranked scores for areal size to each. A country is either "large" or "small." You know from your frequency distribution that there are two "large" countries and one "small" country in your sample. You also know country A is "large" and country B is "small". The size of C is not "free to vary". It must be a "large" country, because of the parameters of the model. In order to meet the requirement of two "large" countries in the sample (confirmed by the frequency distribution), country C must be "large." In this sense, the degrees of freedom are equal to the number of countries in the small sample. With three countries, only two are technically free to vary: The values of the third are determined by the parameters of the model. Thus, the degrees of freedom are known to be the number of countries (3) minus the one that is not free to vary (1), or n–1, or in this case 3–1 = 2. This is the logic of what we call degrees of freedom. Let us consider it in a little more detail with respect to computing the statistical significance of chi-square tests in crosstabs.

In parametric statistics, the constraints (or, the degrees of freedom) are the number of cases in the sample and the number of variables within the model. In a chi-square test (or, tabular analysis), we focus *primarily* upon the number of categories that exist in our two variables (X and Y). You will recall from Chapter 7 that POLIT97 contains seven categories (the scores range between 0 and 6) and PARCOMP contains five categories (1 through 5). In tabular analysis, it is the distributions of scores for categories across the variables in the model that are critical to estimating the degrees of freedom for a chi-square test.

Computing Degrees of Freedom in Crosstabs

There are two components to the final degrees of freedom for chi-square statistics within crosstabs. One component is the distribution of scores for each category of the dependent variable across the categories of the independent variable (this is the pattern of country distributions one observes as one reads a contingency table left to right, one row at a time). The first component of the degrees of freedom for a chi-square is equivalent to the distribution of outcomes across the row (dependent) variable. Therefore, the degrees of freedom for the row variable is equal to n –1, where n is the number of categories for the row variable. The second component of the degrees of freedom for a chi-square is equivalent to the distribution of outcomes across the column (dependent) variable. Therefore, the degrees of freedom for the column variable is equal to n – 1, where n is the number of categories for the column variable.

The degrees of freedom for the chi-square is equal to the *product* of (1) *the column variable's degrees of freedom*, multiplied by (2) *the degrees of freedom for the row variable*. In a 2 x 2 table (where both the independent variable, the column variable, and the dependent variable, the row variable, have two independent categories, such as "High" and "Low"), the degrees of freedom will be equal to (2 – 1) x (2 – 1) = 1 x 1 = 1.

Implications of Sample Size When Using Tabular Analysis

The implications of the degrees of freedom for a tabular analysis are important in cross-national research when using ecological data. If you have only a few countries in the sample (for example, n < 50), many of the resulting matrix cells will have no matches (the cells will be empty, as is the case in several of the cells in Tables 7.10 and 7.11). A critical limitation to effectively using crosstabs when testing hypotheses employing aggregate data (such as in CROSSNAT.50) is that when you have too many cells with too few observations, you cannot accurately estimate the difference between observed and expected frequencies. This condition produces unreliable chi-square estimates. (Indeed, with fewer than five *expected* scores per cell, chi-square estimates are often considered unreliable.) Thus, if both variables are simply dichotomous, the contingency table will be a 2 x 2 table, or a four-cell table, two rows and two columns (note that in Tables 7.10 and 7.11, we have constructed 3 x 3 matrices). In 2 x 2 tables, you have fewer restrictions on the variance of your variable (there are only four possible matches in a 2 x 2 table, compared to nine possible matches in a 3 x 3 table, or sixteen in a 4 x 4 table), and you have improved the probability that all cells will have sufficiently large observed frequencies (that is, each cell will have enough countries in it), thus allowing a more accurate estimate of the chi-square.

These complications are less problematic when you have large survey databases, where the unit of analysis is the individual and the sample size is often much larger than 500. When you have 500 people in a sample and a 3 x 3 matrix, you are reasonably assured that each cell will have enough people in it to allow an accurate computation of the chi-square. Nonetheless, whether your data are individual-based and large samples, or small samples based on ecological data, you will still want to be able to interpret your contingency table. We will have more to say about this below, but for reasons of ease in interpretation, and because our sample size in CROSSNAT.50 is 50 (n = 50), we have opted to introduce you to tabular analysis using the simplest format possible—2 x 2 contingency tables.

Sample Distribution Assumptions and Chi-Square

Recall that the chi-square statistic is a nonparametric measure. The distribution of a chi-square is not shaped as a normal (or even a t distribution) as with interval/ratio-level data. Indeed, it is assumed to be a skewed distribution, with a long trail. What is the chi-square distribution? A chi-square distribution assumes that in a sample of 100 computed chi-squares (drawn from 100 different samples), the vast majority will be relatively small. This is consistent with the logic of the null hypothesis. It is assumed (all things being equal) that most research hypotheses will fail. This is not because they are poor hypotheses. Rather, the "real world" is not easily refuted by hypotheses. Therefore, the statistical probabilities that a research hypothesis will be supported by a large chi-square is itself thought to be a rarity. Most chi-squares in the population of samples will not be large enough to refute the null hypothesis.

Another assumption of chi-square that results from its nonparametric nature is that chi-square does not assume directionality. That is, it simply measures the difference between observed and expected observations, per cell. The researcher has to interpret whether the direction of these deviations matches his or her hypothesis (measures of association used with crosstabs may help, but because of the nature of ordinal data, these too may be misleading, as we will see below). Therefore, the shape of the curve to a chi-square distribution has only one tail—stretching to the high end of the value range.

In our hypothetical sample of 100 chi-squares, most chi-square scores will be small, and only a very few will have such a large size as to be considered worthy of supporting your research hypothesis, and therefore challenging the null hypothesis. In order to reject the null, the computed chi-square for any given sample must be so large that it is placed far out to the left of the standard chi-square distribution. That is, it must be larger than at least 95 percent of all chi-squares that we would expect to be computed in a sample of different chi-squares. The minimum size of a chi-square required for rejecting the null will depend upon the degrees of freedom in the model. The smaller the degrees of freedom in a continency table analysis, the smaller the size of the chi-square required.

Why? Logically, with a small matrix (2 x 2), and therefore with only one degree of freedom, you cannot expect to have as many "errors" (number of observations per cell minus the expected number of observations per cell) as you would if your matrix were 5 x 5 (or, twenty-five cells). In a 5 x 5 matrix, there are over six times as many cells within which error will be observed, and as such, the sum total of errors in a matrix will grow accordingly. Statisticians control for this by factoring in the degrees of freedom when estimating the minimum size of a chi-square required before one may assume its size is so large as to be a "rare" event, and therefore supportive of the research hypothesis. Once obtaining a chi-square, therefore, we must assess the probability that a chi-square of an observed size would be likely to occur five times or less in a hypothetical sample of 100 chi-squares, *if the null were in fact true.*

Statistical Significance and the Chi-Square

The exact degrees of freedom are calculated by using the number of rows and columns in a contingency table (which is why the number of categories we use to define a variable becomes important in the computation of chi-square statistics). To recap, the degrees of freedom are computed according to the simple formula:

DF = (number of rows – 1) (number of columns – 1)

The number of rows in a table is equal to the number of categories in the *dependent variable* (for example, POLIT973), and the number of columns is equal to the number of categories in the *independent variable* (for example, AGE1800). Therefore, in Hypothesis 8.1, if we were to use POLIT97 and AGE18002, we would have a table with 7 x 2 cells, or fourteen cells. With only fifty cases in our sample, that is not only too few cases for obtaining a reliable chi-square, one is also unlikely to discern meaningful patterns to country distributions across the cells. If we employed POLIT973, our matrix would be reduced to 3 x 2, or six cells. This is much more reasonable, but still troublesome for a safe computation of chi-square. Therefore, we will recode POLIT97 once again. This time, we will collapse POLIT97 into two categories and will use the median value of POLIT97 as our guide. The median value of POLIT97 (see Table 7.4) is 4. Thus, we will assign all countries in the sample whose value for POLIT97 is less than 4 the value of 1 ("Low/Moderate") for our new variable, POLIT972. Those countries in CROSSNAT.50 that have a value of 4, 5, or 6 for POLIT97 will now have a value of 2 ("High") for the new variable, POLIT972. This now affords us a tabular model of 2 x 2 matrix size. Our degrees of freedom will, therefore, equal 1: [(2–1)(2–1) = (1)(1) = 1].

The significance level of a chi-square (or any statistical test) is the estimated probability that such a chi-square score would be found in a sample, *if we also assume the null hypothesis is correct*. Returning to our hypothetical sample again of chi-square statistics, if the null is assumed to be correct, we would expect most chi-squares to be small (small, that is, relative to the degrees of freedom in the model). There would, of course, be some that would be larger than the rest. These would be located toward the high end of the distribution's tail (thus, the chi-square, as noted above, is positively skewed, with a tail stretching to the right of the main "hump" in the distribution, which lies far to the left, or at the low end of the range of chi-square values). The significance value is, therefore, a *probability*. It informs you of the probability of discovering a chi-square of the size you have in your sample (with its degrees of freedom), *assuming the null is correct.* Most chi-squares will be too small to be interpreted as being a rare "event." A rare chi-square is one that is very large, given the degrees of freedom in the model.

Conventionally, in social science, the minimum significance level we must obtain before we can say we have a truly unusual, and rare, chi-square is referred to as the *alpha level* (α). The minimum alpha level required before we can reasonably assume our chi-square is so large that the null must be wrong is .05. That is, there must be no more than a 5 percent probability that we could have reasonably expected to have found a chi-square of the size we have, *if the null were correct*. If our alpha level (α) is equal to or larger than .05, we may conclude that this chi square is too rare to have occurred if the null were correct. Therefore, we must conclude that the null is an incorrect depiction of the real world. (Keep in mind here our discussion of Type I and Type II errors in Chapter 8.) In this circumstance, we may reject the null and accept the research hypothesis, and we may do so being reasonably assured that we will not commit a Type I error (that is, we will not incorrectly reject the null).[1]

In any 2 X 2 contingency table *with our threshold (or, alpha) level set to .05*, the chi-square must be at least 3.841. This can be confirmed by consulting any basic statistics textbook for a chi-square table, usually found at the back of the text.[2] If our contingency table is 2 X 2, in order to reject the null, *regardless of the number of countries in our sample*, we must obtain at least a chi-square value of 3.841. The fewer the countries in our sample, of course, the more difficult it is to obtain a chi-square of 3.841 in a 2 X 2 table. Furthermore, if we have variables that have more than two categories, our degrees of freedom will increase, and so will the minimum size of the chi-square required to meet a .05 threshold. For instance, a 3 X 3 table would have four degrees of freedom, in turn requiring a chi-square of 9.49 before we could reject the null at the .05 probability threshold.

DEMONSTRATION 9.1: SIMPLE TABULAR ANALYSIS

Remember, while we are not technically arguing that a causal relationship exists between POLIT972 and AGE18002, we are structuring our analysis of this relationship *as if* we were. We are therefore implying a causal relationship, but we cannot test for this *directly* and we must be cautious not to state our findings as if we have confirmed or rejected such a causal relationship. We simply cannot adequately demonstrate causality on a bivariate model. Our theory, presented above, clearly suggests that it is logical for a country's degree of political rights allowed a citizenry to be contingent upon the country's time as a sovereign, independent country.

TABLE 9.1 Crosstabs, POLIT972 by AGE18002, SPSS 10

			AGE18002		
			1 Post–1917	*2 Pre–1918*	*Total*
POLIT972	1 Low/Moderate	Count	14	4	8
		Expected Count	8.6	9.4	18.0
		% within AGE18002	58.3%	15.4%	36.0%
	2 High	Count	10	22	32
		Expected Count	15.4	16.6	32.0
		% within AGE18002	41.7%	84.6%	64.0%
Total		Count	24	26	50
		Expected Count	24.0	26.0	50.0
		% within AGE18002	100.0%	100.0%	100.0%

The Structure of a Contingency Table

Our first task is to sort out the relationship. Table 9.1 reports the contingency table for our crosstab analysis of POLIT972 by AGE18002—a test of Hypothesis 8.1.[3] Within each cell, there are three pieces of information: the count of countries, the expected count of countries, and the percentage of the column total (in Table 9.1, labeled as "% within AGE18002"). At the far right lower corner of the table is the total number of valid observations: 50. The *marginal frequencies* are merely the sum of the frequencies across each row and down each column, and are found at the far right (row marginals) and at the bottom of the table (column marginals). Thus, there are a total of 24 total "Post–1917" countries within AGE18002, and 26 "Pre–1918" countries within AGE18002. Summing the row marginals always equals the total number of valid observations (24 + 26 = 50); summing each of the column marginals always equals the total number of valid observations (18 + 32 = 50).

The count refers to the actual number of cases in the sample (in the case of our CROSSNAT.50 sample, the cases are individual countries) that share the attributes represented by the intersection of the categories across the two variables. We see that fourteen countries in the sample achieved their independence after 1917 and have "low/moderate" degrees of political rights. On the other hand, twenty-two countries in the sample achieved their sovereign independence before 1918 and have "high" degrees of political rights. Based on the distribution of marginals and the number of cases in the sample, if the null were completely true, we would have expected only 8.6 countries created after 1917 with "low/moderate" degrees of political rights, and only 16.6 countries formed before 1918 with "high" degrees of political rights. Clearly, there are more countries in the latter cell and fewer in the former than expected. This pattern holds for the remaining two cells in the matrix. The difference between the expected and the observed counts constitute the "residuals" in our model. The larger the squared values of these residuals, the more likely the assumption of the real world (with respect to the relationship between sovereignty and political rights) as represented by the null hypothesis must be viewed with skepticism.

The cell percentages, which are reported beneath each cell frequency, refer to the cell frequency as a proportion of the total column frequency reported for that particular column. These are the most important statistics in the table with respect to providing a clear substantive interpretation of the table. Therefore, the fourteen countries that were formed after 1917 and that have "low/moderate" degrees of political rights constitute 58.3 percent of the twenty-four countries formed after 1917. The twenty-two countries that were formed before 1918 and that have "high" degrees of political rights constitute 84.6 percent of those countries formed before 1918. Each of the marginal frequencies has its equivalent column percentage as well. Therefore, the eighteen countries that value "low/moderate" degrees of political rights constitute 36 percent of the fifty countries in the sample. Note also that the labels of each variable category are placed according to how we have specified the variables: The row variable (POLIT972) labels are placed before each row, and the column variable (AGE18002) labels are placed atop each column.

Interpreting a Contingency Table

To interpret the meaning of a contingency table, and assuming you have specified your independent variable as your column variable, and you have specified column percentages to be reported in the table, *always read the column percentages moving left to right across each row*. If there is a contingent relationship, the column percentages should change significantly as we move across each row. In Table 9.1, we see that there is a sizeable difference between the percentage of countries with "low/moderate" degrees of political rights (POLIT972) that achieved their independence after 1917, and the proportion of those countries with "low/moderate" degrees of political rights formed before 1918 (58.3 percent and 15.4 percent, respectively). As you move across the column of AGE18002, in other words, the percentages of countries that fall into each category of AGE18002 decline *sharply,* falling from 58.3 percent to 15. 4 percent. Moving down one row, we see that 41.7 percent of those countries that were formed after 1917 have "high" political rights, while 84.6 percent of those countries formed before 1918 have "high" degrees of political rights.

Clearly, there appears to be a strong association between the age of a country's independence and its degree of political rights. Those countries that have been more recently formed have a 71.4 percent greater probability of having "low/moderate" degrees of political rights than those countries formed prior to 1918 (fourteen versus four). As you move from the post–1917 category to the pre–1918 category, the percentage of countries that are characterized by "low/moderate" degrees of political rights drops off sharply, while, on the other hand, the proportion of countries that are characterized by "high" degrees of political rights increases sharply, by more than 100 percent (ten versus twenty-two).

TABLE 9.2 Chi-Square Results from Crosstabs, POLIT972 by AGE18002, SPSS 10

	Value	df	Asymp. Sig. (2-sided)	Exact Sig. (2-sided)	Exact Sig (1-sided)
Pearson Chi-Square	9.992[b]	1	.002		
Continuity Correction[a]	8.214	1	.004		
Likelihood Ratio	10.416	1	.001		
Fisher's Exact Test				.003	.002
Linear-by-Linear Association	9.792	1	.002		
N of Valid Cases	50				

a. Computed only for a 2 X 2 table.
b. O cells (.0%) have expected count less than 5. The minimum expected count is 8.64.

The Role of Chi-Square Within Tabular Analysis

Table 9.2 reports the chi-square statistical output from SPSS 10. Note there are several versions of a chi-square statistic reported in Table 9.2. The Pearson chi-square is the standard chi-square statistic.[4] Its size, 9.992, is much larger than the minimum required 3.841. The significance level of a chi-square of 9.992 with 1 degree of freedom is .002 (reported technically as the two-sided asymptotic significance). Thus, we may assume that the probability of a chi-square of this size occurring in a sample, if the null were correct, is 2 in 1000. This is well below the minimum threshold set for our alpha level (.05), so we may *reject* the null and *accept* the research hypothesis. Based on our crosstabular analysis presented in Table 9.1, it is clear that older countries (those formed prior to 1918) have a significantly higher degree of political rights than those countries formed more recently (those whose independence has been gained after 1917).

Measures of Association in Tabular Analysis

To this point, we have provided two important pieces of information in our contingency analysis: (1) We know from Table 9.1 that there is a clear pattern to the relationship between the age of a country and its degree of political rights, and (2) we know from Table 9.2 that this relationship is statistically significant—it cannot be dismissed as a random fluke. Often, we may want to supplement our analysis by examining closely the *levels of association* that we commonly derive from contingency analysis. Measures of association allow us to consider how strong is the relationship between two variables. Ideally, we would like a measure that tells us precisely how much of a change in one variable results in a specified degree of change in the other variable. However, when working solely with ordinal-level data, this is not entirely possible, so we often must settle (at least initially) for an equivalent logic. When working with nominal-level data, no meaningful measure of association is really possible, nor logical, since, of course, nominal-level data do not allow us to make assumptions about "more or less" of specific attributes. Consequently, we are denied an opportunity to offer credible measures of association that have any meaningful interpretation when working solely with strictly nominal-level data in crosstabs.

Nonetheless, when our variables are measured at either the ordinal level or the nominal level, there are measures of association that are available to the student of cross-national analysis, and when working with relatively small samples, these can be quite useful supplements to our interpretation of the hypothesis test.

Table 9.3 reports the most commonly reported and utilized measures of association derived from crosstabs.[5] These measures of association are broken into two categories:[6]

- Those used when at least one of your variables is measured at the nominal level
- Those measures of association used when both variables are measured at the ordinal level

These statistics are further divided into those measures of association that are:

- PRE statistics (proportional reduction in error measures)
- Chi-square based

What is a PRE statistic? PRE measures of association measure the *proportional reduction in errors* (or PRE) when we "predict" the value of the dependent variable for a case in our sample knowing the value of that country's independent variable, over the error we would *expect* if we were to predict the value of that country's dependent variable *without knowing* the particular value of that country's independent variable. If we were forced to guess the value of a country's dependent variable knowing nothing about the value of the independent variable for the country, our best means of prediction would be the sample mean of the dependent variable. What if, however, we know the value of the independent variable for the country? This new information would provide us with more useful information (assuming our theory could logically link the two variables) from which to refine and improve our predictive power. If we used merely the mean value to predict the value of a country's dependent variable, we would obviously be right sometimes, and wrong sometimes. If we were to use the additional information provided by the independent variable to predict the value of the dependent variable, we would be right sometimes, and wrong sometimes as we moved through our sample of countries. By comparing the errors (the number of times we're wrong) across the two strategies, we can compute how much of a reduction in errors in our predictions we would find when using the information provided by the independent variable over the errors we obtained when using only the mean of the sample to predict the dependent variable. The more successfully we can predict the value of the dependent variable from values of the independent variable, the stronger the relationship between X and Y. If knowing X adds nothing to our predictive capacity over that which we could obtain from predicting the value of Y from the mean of Y, we may conclude that X has no independent relationship to Y.

In Hypothesis 8.1, we have two strategies available to us. We may predict the value of a country's POLIT972 from the mean of POLIT972 within the sample, or, alternatively, we may try to predict the value of POLIT972 from the value of a country's AGE18002 vari-

TABLE 9.3 Measures of Association in Contingency Table Analysis (Crosstabs)

	Type of Measures of Association Derived from Contingency Table Analysis	
Level at which Variables in Model are Measured	*Chi-Square Based*	*Proportional Reduction of Error Based*
Nominal	Phi-Coefficient Coefficient of Contingency Cramer's V	Lambda
Ordinal	Kendall's Tau b Kendall's Tau c	Gamma Pearson Coefficient Spearman's Coefficient

able—the independent variable in our model. When using ordinal-level data, we substitute the mode of the dependent variable for the mean of the dependent variable in the sample. Thus, in POLIT972, the mode is "High" degrees of political rights. We would be right if we predicted every country in the sample to have a "High" degree of political rights 64 percent of the time, and wrong 36 percent of the time (eighteen countries, or 36 percent of the sample, have "Low/Moderate" degrees of political rights). However, if we knew the value of each country's period of independence (before or after 1917/1918), and there was a reasonable relationship between a country's period of independence and its degree of political rights, we would reduce our errors in prediction. This difference between the two sets of errors is the proportional reduction of error, or the PRE. The larger the PRE, the stronger the association between the two variables in the model.

Lambda and Cramer's V

The most widely used measure of association in tabular analysis when one of the variables is measured at the nominal level and the other at the ordinal level is the *lambda* (λ). This is a PRE statistic. The formula for lambda is:

$$\Lambda\ (\lambda) = \frac{(E_{-IV})-(E_{+IV})}{(E_{-IV})}$$ Formula 9.2

The term (E_{-IV}) represents the number of errors we would make in predicting the score of any country in our sample if we did not know any values of the independent variable for the country in the sample. The term (E_{+IV}) represents the error we would make in predicting the scores of countries in our sample on the value of the dependent variable if we knew each country's score on the independent variable. Lambda estimates the proportional reduction in errors we would make if we knew the values of the independent variables when predicting the scores of countries on the dependent variable over the errors we would make if we did not know the scores of the countries on the independent variable in the sample.

Ordinarily, lambda is computed assuming the row variable is the dependent variable. It can also be computed assuming the column variable is dependent (though this is not recommended). The value of lambda varies between 0 and 1.00. If the sample is extremely skewed in the distribution of scores within a contingency table (if some cells have significantly smaller scores in them than other cells within the same row), lambda can be highly distorted and provide misleading estimates of the actual relationship between two variables.

In this case, most scholars compare the lambda with the *Cramer's V* (V) score. Cramer's V is a non-PRE statistic. Basically, it relies on the chi-square statistic (X^2) to compute the degree to which two variables are associated with each other. It controls for the number of rows and columns in the contingency table, and therefore assumes an upper limit of 1.00 (perfect association between two variables) and 0 (no association between two variables). The measure is asymmetric, meaning that it does not matter which variable is nominal and which is ordinal, or, which is independent and which is dependent. If the V is much larger than the λ, the V may be preferred by the student.

Additional measures of nominal-based variables in tabular analysis include the *Pearson's coefficient of contingency* (C), and the *phi* (ø). Neither is a PRE statistic; both are measures of association, as with V. Neither of these statistics has any relevance for the findings reported in Table 9.1. Both variables tested in Hypothesis 8.1 are measured at the ordinal level. For this, we need to consider Kendall's Tau, gamma, and the correlation statistics for contingency tables.

Kendall's Tau b, Gamma, and Somer's d

When both variables in a tabular analysis are measured at the ordinal level and the matrix is square (that is, the number of rows equals the number of columns, such as a 2 X 2 contingency table), the most commonly used measure of association is Kendall's Tau b (τ_b). This is perhaps the most popular and widely cited measure of association for contingency table analysis when employing ordinal level measures. Because of the computation of the Tau b, some statisticians place less weight on the statistic's role as a true PRE measure.

The Tau b is based on comparing pairs of cases in a sample. The measure is based on a comparison of concordant, discordant, and tied pairs. Consider Table 9.4. This table reports the values for POLIT972 and AGE18002 from ten countries taken in sequence from CROSSNAT.50. There are nine consecutive pairs of cases (countries) in the table. A concordant pairing is when the values of both variables (in this case, AGE18002 and POLIT972) increase as you move from the first case in the pair to the second case in the pair. In Table 9.4, pair 9a, 10 (Tanzania and Thailand) represents a concordant pair. The values of AGE18002 and POLIT972 increase as you move from Tanzania to Thailand (from 1 to 2 in values). A discordant pair is when both variables move in opposite directions from the first case in the pair to the second case in the pair.

TABLE 9.4 Examples of Pairing Cases

Case	*COUNTRY*	*AGE18002*	*POLIT972*	*Pair of Cases*	*Condition*
1	Peru	2 Pre-1918	1 Low/Moderate	-- --	-- --
2	Philippines	1 Post-1917	2 High	1,2	Discordant
3	Poland	1 Post-1917	2 High	2,3	Tied
4	Romania	2 Pre-1918	2 High	3,4	Tied, POLIT972
5	Russia	2 Pre-1918	2 High	4,5	Tied
6	South Africa	2 Pre-1918	2 High	5,6	Tied
7	Spain	2 Pre-1918	2 High	6,7	Tied
8	Sri Lanka	1 Post-1917	2 High	7,8	Tied, POLIT972
9	Tanzania	1 Post-1917	1 Low/Moderate	8,9	Tied, AGE18002
10	Thailand	2 Pre-1918	2 High	9,10	Concordant

This is the condition for pair 1,2 (Peru and Philippines) in Table 9.4. Peru's value for AGE18002 is 2 (pre–1918) while that of the Philippines is 1 (post–1917); Peru's value for POLIT972 is 1 ("Low/Moderate" political rights) while the value of POLIT972 for the Philippines is 2 ("High" political rights). There may also be exact pairs, where the values of *both* variables are identical (as in pair 2,3, for instance, in Table 9.4). Finally, there may be a tie on one variable, but not on the other. This is the case in pair 3,4 in Table 9.4, as well as in pairs 7,8 and 8,9.

In measures of association based on pairing cases, a relationship is positive if most pairs are concordant. That is, countries that have a high value on one variable will also have a correspondingly high value on the second variable; or, if they have a low value on one variable, they will have a low value on the second variable. If most of the pairs are discordant, the relationship is negative (that is, if countries have a high value on one variable, they are likely to have a low value on the second variable). If concordant and discordant pairs occur in equal numbers throughout the sample, there is no association between the two variables. Ties present computational challenges, and for this reason, Tau b is often the preferred measure of association for students.

Tau b ranges in value between +1 and –1. A positive sign suggests that as the value of the independent variable increases, so does the value of the dependent variable within a country. This is indicative of a preponderance of concordant pairs within the sample. A negative sign indicates that as the value of the independent variable increases, the value of the dependent variable decreases. This is a negative relationship, indicating a preponderance of discordant pairs in the sample. Therefore, it is important to keep in mind the scaling of your respective variables in your bivariate model. In Table 9.1, we have set the value of 1 to mean a respondent has *less* of the measured attribute, and 2 to mean the respondent has *more* of the measured attribute for each of the two variables. Thus, a positive value for the Tau b would mean that there is a general tendency within the sample for respondents with larger values on the independent variable to also have larger values on the dependent variable. This would be different if a value of "1" for the dependent variable did not refer to "less" of something than a corresponding "1" in the independent variable. This is why, if at all possible, you always set your scaling to a similar pattern for all variables (for example, "low" scores correspond to "less" of an attribute, and "high" scores correspond to "more" of an attribute). This also means that there is the corresponding tendency to have respondents showing lower scores on the independent variable with lower scores on the dependent variable.

Therefore, in Table 9.1, there is the overall tendency to have countries with more recent independence (score = "1") to also have "low/moderate" degrees of political rights (score = "1"). The size of the Tau b reported in Table 9.5 (.447) is often simply interpreted as a PRE measure: It would be common to conclude that we have very substantially improved our ability to accurately predict a country's score on POLIT972 with knowledge of its corresponding score on AGE18002. This is not exactly the case, however.

Tau b is not strictly a PRE measure. The value of .447 indicates a strong positive relationship, but it cannot be interpreted to mean that we have reduced our errors by 44.7 percent in our predictions by knowing the value of the independent variable (as a true PRE measure would). The computation of Tau b and the nature of its denominator (the details of which need not concern us here) make a simple PRE interpretation impossible. How, then, should we interpret a Tau b of .447? It means, basically, that for each increase in the unit value of the independent variable (for example, AGE18002 in our model), the value of the dependent variable (POLIT973 in our model) changes by .447 units. Whether this is a "positive" relationship or a "negative" relationship depends on how we have coded the values of the ordinal variables. Since our two variables have low scores for low values of each variable, we know that as we move from a score of 1 to a score of 2 in AGE18002, the value of POLIT973 increases by .447 units, or, for instance, from 1 to 1.447. Obviously, there can be no value of 1.447 for POLIT973 (the actual scores are either 1, 2, or 3). However, it does reflect the size of the proportional impact we estimate the age of a country's independence to have on the country's degree of democracy. The standard error (.124) reported in the statistics output from SPSS 10 in Table 9.5 indicates that we can be 95 percent confident that the true Tau b in the population is between .695 and .199.

The reported statistical significance of the chi-square statistic can tell us also the probability that the Tau b (as with all bivariate measures of association in tabular analysis) will be statistically significant. In this case, the Tau b is significant at the .000 level, allowing us to reject the null hypothesis. From Kendall's Tau b we conclude that a relatively strong relationship exists between the age of a country and its degree of political rights, and that this relationship is certainly a strong one.

If we do not have a square matrix (let's say we have a 2 x 3, or a 3 x 2 contingency table matrix), we must rely on the Tau c (τ_c) statistic. This makes the necessary corrections for the calculations required when the matrix is not square.

Additional measures of association for ordinal measures are Somer's d, and Goodman and Kruskal's gamma (γ). The value of a gamma ranges from +1 to –1. The gamma statistic also relies on an analysis of concordant and discordant pairs. It does

TABLE 9.5 Measures of Association (Ordinal Data), POLIT972 by AGE18002 (SPSS 10)

Symmetric Measures

		Value	*Asymp. Std. Error*[a]	*Approx. T*[b]	*Approx. Sig.*
Ordinal by Ordinal	Kendall's Tau b	.447	.124	3.488	.000
	Gamma	.770	.139	3.488	.000
	Spearman's Correlation	.447	.124	3.462	.001[c]
Interval by Interval	Pearson R	.447	.124	3.462	.001[c]
N of Valid Cases		50			

a Not assuming the null hypothesis.
b Using the asymptotic stadard error assuming the null hypothesis.
c Based on normal approximation.

not handle ties as efficiently as do the Tau b and c measures, however. The value of a gamma in Table 9.5 is .770. This value indicates that we have many more concordant pairs than discordant. A negative gamma would indicate we had many more discordant pairs. A gamma of 0 in a 2 X 2 table indicates no relationship. A gamma is far less popular among social scientists and statisticians than the Kendall's Tau. Its properties make the measure unreliable in certain circumstances. Therefore, it is wise to use the gamma only in conjunction with the Tau measures. If the measures are quite different, it is wise to opt for the Kendall's Tau.[7]

The Somer's d statistic is a gamma statistic with a slight modification: It is asymmetric. Kendall's Tau b and c, as well as gamma, are asymmetric. Asymmetric means the computation of the statistic requires one to specify one of the variables as the dependent variable, and the other as an independent variable. However, in Somer's d, we must specify which of the two variables (based on our theory) is independent and which is dependent. Thus, it is an asymmetric measure of association. In Table 9.6 we see that the Somer's d statistic (assuming AGE18002 is the dependent variable), is .465 (standard error = .128), and has a statistical probability of .000.

For Kendall's Tau b, gamma, and Somer's d, virtually no relationship exists between two variables if the Tau b is smaller than .1. This would indicate the number of concordant pairs virtually equals the number of discordant pairs. If the measure of association for ordinal data is between .1 and .2, it is considered to be in the "weak" range. If the measure of association for ordinal data is between .2 and .3, the relationship is considered "moderately strong". If the measure of association for ordinal data is between .3 and .4 (as is our model reported in Tables 9.5 and 9.6), it is considered "strong," and anything greater than .4 is generally considered "very strong."

Pearson Correlations and Spearman's Correlation

Finally, if our ordinal variables are ordered in a meaningful manner—namely, a value of "1" indicates an attribute that has less of something than a case with an attribute

TABLE 9.6 Somer's d Measure of Association (Ordinal Data), POLIT972 by AGE18002 (SPSS 10)

Directional Measures

			Value	*Asymp. Std. Error*[a]	*Approx. T*[b]	*Approx. Sig.*
Ordinal by Ordinal	Somer's d	Symmetric	.447	.124	3.488	.000
		POLIT972 Dependent	.429	.123	3.488	.000
		AGE18002 Dependent	.465	.128	3.488	.000

a Not assuming the null hypothesis.
b Using the asymptotic stadard error assuming the null hypothesis.

score of "2," and so on—one may use correlation measures. There are two basic correlation measures. The Pearson Correlation statistic is technically used with interval/ratio-level data, but, in a sample of fifty cases may be used as a measure of the relationship between two variables. We will discuss this measure in detail in Chapter 13. For now, it is enough to know that the Pearson Correlation statistic simply uses the actual values of each case in the sample to determine whether the value of one variable varies with the value of the other variable across the sample. The value of a Pearson Correlation statistic ranges from –1 to +1. As with Tau b, Somer's d, and gamma, these are not PRE measures—they are measures of pure association. In Table 9.5, the Pearson Correlation statistic is .447 (standard error = .124). We interpret this the same way as we did the Tau b of .447. Thus, a change in one unit in the independent variable (AGE18002) produces a corresponding .447-unit change in the dependent variable (POLIT972). This, however, has little meaning in a 2 X 2 contingency table, thus confirming a strong association between AGE18002 and POLIT972.

More meaningful is the Spearman's Correlation coefficient. It does not base its correlation on the actual values of the variables in the sample. Rather, Spearman's ranks the values of the attribute across cases. The value of Spearman's ranges between –1 and +1. However, note that in a 2 X 2 table, the value of the Pearson Correlation statistic and the Spearman's are virtually identical (.447, standard error = .124). It is more proper to report the Spearman's than the Pearson, unless you have more than two rows and columns, which requires a larger sample than fifty.

Measures of Association in Ordinal-Level Models

What statistic should you report? Depending upon the level at which your variables in the model are measured, you should report the measure of association that seems to you to make more sense. Reporting more than one (for instance, reporting the gamma and the Kendall's Tau b in a 2 X 2 table with ordinal data) is a common practice. However, avoid jumping around from statistic to statistic and reporting only the largest statistics. And, remember, the measures of the association do not constitute a test of the statistical significance. That is solely the domain of the chi-square. If a chi-square is statistically significant, so too will be the measure of association. However, it is often the case that a statistically significant relationship will be shown to exist, but the strength of the relationship between the two variables will be weak, at best. We will explore this in more detail beginning in Chapter 10. Measures of association are no substitute for (1) knowing how your data are measured and coded (or recoded) and (2) being able to offer a clear and meaningful substantive interpretation of the contingency table itself. Never rely solely on the chi-square, and never, ever, rely solely on a measure of association for contingency tables to tell anyone the story you are trying to portray with your crosstab analysis.

DEMONSTRATION 9.2: CROSSTAB ANALYSIS IN PERSPECTIVE

It would be misleading, however, if the student were to conclude that the primary use of crosstab analysis is to produce a chi-square statistic for the purpose of testing hypotheses. Indeed, while this technique, as simple and straightforward as it is, has been a staple in the repertoire of hypothesis testing for social scientists for decades, it is nonetheless also a fact that contingency table analysis plays a far more important role in the simple discovery and sorting out of complex information. As with bivariate descriptive tables discussed in the previous chapter, crosstabs has its greatest role to play in helping the researcher discern important patterns among countries (or other units of analysis central to cross-national analysis). The flexibility and utility of crosstabs make it one of the most important tools in cross-national analysis.

Properties of Governance and Political Rights

To demonstrate, let us consider the relationship between political rights and the age of a country's current independence. Hypothesis 8.1 suggests, and Table 9.1 clearly confirms, that the degree of political rights, or the scale of institutionalized democracy, is higher and more extensive in countries that achieved their current sovereign status prior to 1918. For those that achieved their current sovereign status since 1917, the degrees of political rights are of a distinctly lesser quantity. This suggests a refinement to Hypothesis 8.1 may be in order. Our theory linking age to democracy asserted that countries that had more recently attained their current sovereign status are lacking in deeply entrenched instincts and habits of democratic governance. Institutional aspects, as well as intrinsic components of democracy, have yet to become firmly entrenched in countries that have more recently achieved their independence. As such, we should expect the degree to which newer countries extend political rights to their citizens to be lower and more restricted than in those nations that have dealt with the emergence of democratic pressures and reform over a longer period.

In 1999, senior researchers at Freedom House produced an analysis of what they term the "century of democracy." Their basic argument is simple: Throughout the twentieth century, two struggles occurred simultaneously. One was the struggle for national sovereignty, the other was the struggle for individual autonomy—democracy. While their study does link the success of democracy to economic prosperity, and while they briefly consider the linkage between the government heritage of a country earlier in the century and its current degree of democracy, the study does not ask the specific question: Does age offer an advantage to countries in terms of attaining democratic governance, and, is this advantage a direct result of the burden of newer countries' more recent past?[8] Crosstab analysis is an ideal tool to help us sort out the necessary initial information and to help us refine and eventually test the refinement to Hypothesis 8.1.[9]

The researchers at Freedom House classified the properties of governance that characterized a country at three points in the twentieth century, 1900, 1950, and 2000. These properties divide all countries into nine types of political systems: democracies, restricted democracies, constitutional monarchies, absolute monarchies, traditional monarchies, authoritarian regimes, totalitarian regimes, colonial dependencies, and protectorates.[10] This is a *nominal*-level variable. From this logic, it seems clear that if the age of a country's current sovereignty does have a role in shaping a country's recent degree of political rights, it is probably related to the type of regime the country had in its recent past. Specifically, older countries, by definition, should be less likely to have a recent colonial or protectorate past, and as such, less likely to have had to overcome the hurdles of both sovereignty and democratic development during recent decades. The struggle for both national sovereignty and individual autonomy, if conducted more recently, was likely to be associated with lower degrees of political rights and institutionalized democracy by 1997.[11] This struggle often pits indigenous elites who have prospered under the colonial rule or protectorate against previously excluded segments of the population who demand more inclusion in the political process. Often, this conflict is reinforced along ethnic, linguistic, racial, and regional lines.[12] We expect, in other words, a "civic deficit" to be more likely to prevail among those countries only recently removed chronologically from the ties of colonialism and protectorate status, relative to either democracies as of 1950 or authoritarian countries as of 1950.[13] Therefore, this suggests the following simple hypothesis:

> Hypothesis 9.1: Countries attaining their current sovereign status before 1918 are more likely to have been democracies by 1950 than countries that obtained their current sovereign status after 1917.

Combined with Hypothesis 8.1, we may therefore offer a third hypothesis, which logically follows from Hypotheses 8.1 and 9.1:

> Hypothesis 9.2: Countries that were colonial possessions or under protectorate status in 1950 are less likely to have achieved "high" degrees of political rights by 1997 than those countries that were not colonial possessions or under protectorate status in 1950.

To begin, consider Table 9.7. This table reproduces the crosstabs in output from SPSS 10. It demonstrates how the technique can be an effective means of sorting relationships that involve nominal and ordinal data—and doing so in a meaningful way for students of cross-national research. Note Table 9.7 reports both the column percentages and the row percentages (in addition to the cell counts). Thus, we see that in our sample, 82 percent of all countries that were democratic in 1950 were also formed before 1918 (nine of eleven countries), and, that of the twenty-six countries in our sample that were formed before 1918, nine (or 35 percent) were countries that were democratic in 1950. Thus, in 1950 the most common type of political system among those in our sample that were formed prior to 1918 was democracy.

The second most common type of political system in 1950 to be found among those countries in our sample that were formed prior to 1918 was authoritarian. All five of the authoritarian political systems in our sample were formed before 1918, constituting 19 percent of the twenty-six countries in CROSSNAT.50 formed prior to the end of World War I. Yet, one third of the twenty-four countries that achieved their current sovereign status after 1917 were colonial possessions in 1950 (eight of twenty-four countries). Indeed, all of those countries that were colonial possessions in 1950 were formed after 1918. One in five of the twenty-four countries formed after 1917 were restricted democracies in 1950 (five of twenty-four), and five (or 21 percent) were protectorates. On the whole, the chi-square for the table was statistically significant (21.194, p = .003).

However, a contingency table with a large number of cells and only fifty cases means that several cells are bound to have expected frequencies less than five. Indeed, thirteen cells had expected frequencies less than five, making any statistical inference from the table based on chi-square computations risky. Nonetheless, the pattern seems unmistakable: There is a sharp distinction between democracies and colonial possessions and protectorates with respect to their pattern of formation. In our sample of populous countries, countries that were democracies as of 1950 were much more likely to have formed prior to 1918 than were those countries that, as of 1950, were not democracies. This, of course, is going to be the case for colonial possessions and protectorates. But it is also the case for restricted democracies. Half of the sample's six totalitarian systems as of 1950 had formed prior to 1918, half after 1917. Being democratic by 1950 apparently may well have depended upon whether the country had achieved independence prior to the end of World War I. However, does being a colony or protectorate in 1950 restrict a country's probabilities of achieving high degrees of political rights by 1997?

In this case, the crosstab analysis is not very useful as a tool for hypothesis testing—the large number of expected cell frequencies less than five in Table 9.7 renders any chi-square estimates far too unreliable. However, it does expose some interesting and potentially important patterns. For instance, what are the two countries that were democracies in 1950 yet had formed *after* 1917? Or, what countries are the two which as of 1950 were protectorates, yet were formed prior to 1918?

TABLE 9.7 Crosstabs, SYS1950 by AGE18002, SPSS 10

			Age of Country		
			1 Post–1917	*2 Pre–1918*	*Total*
Type of Political System	1 Democracy	Count	2	9	11
		% within SYS1950	18.2%	81.8%	100.0%
		% within AGE18002	8.3%	34.6%	22.0%
	2 Restricted Democracy	Count	5	3	8
		% within SYS1950	62.5	37.5	100.0
		% within AGE18002	20.8	11.5	16.0
	3 Constitutional Monarchy	Count	1	3	4
		% within SYS1950	25.0	75.0	100.0
		% within AGE18002	4.2	11.5	8.0
	5 Absolute Monarchy	Count		1	1
		% within SYS1950		100.0	100.0
		% within AGE18002		3.8	2.0
	6 Authoritarian Regime	Count		5	5
		% within SYS1950		100.0	100.0
		% within AGE18002		19.2	10.0
	7 Totalitarian Regime	Count	3	3	6
		% within SYS1950	50.0	50.0	100.0
		% within AGE18002	12.5	11.5	12.0
	8 Colonial Dependency	Count	8		8
		% within SYS1950	100.0		100.0
		% within AGE18002	33.3		16.0
	9 Protectorate	Count	5	2	7
		% within SYS1950	71.4	28.6	100.0
		% within AGE18002	20.8	7.7	14.0
Total		Count	24	26	50
		% within SYS1950	48.0	52.0	100.0
		% within AGE18002	100.0	100.0	100.0

Table 9.8 supplements Table 9.7. It reports the actual values for the current age of a country as well as its regime status-type as of 1950 (as well as some other variables we will explain shortly). We note from Table 9.8 that Turkey and India were the two nations that achieved their current sovereign status after 1918 and were also democracies as of 1950. Germany and Japan are the two countries that achieved their current sovereign status prior to 1918, and yet were protectorates as of 1950.

To achieve a more reliable test of Hypothesis 9.1, we have collapsed SYS1950 into three categories, according to their propensity toward democratic governance by 1950 as well as their independent sovereignty. The first category are those countries that had laid the foundations for democratic evolution in 1950. These are those regimes that, as of 1950, were democracies, restricted democracies, or constitutional monarchies. They may, as with restricted democracies and constitutional monarchies, have been deficient in many of the primary properties of democracy as of 1950, but the foundations were there (including nation-state sovereignty) and the road to democracy would seem to be, all things being equal, relatively easier for these countries than for others in the sample. These countries are coded as "3" and are labeled "democracies" in the new variable SYS19503. The second category are those countries substantially deficient in primary democratic principles, yet sovereign nation-states by 1950. This group of countries includes those that by 1950 were authoritarian regimes, absolute monarchies, traditional democracies, or totalitarian regimes. They are coded as "2" in CROSSNAT.50 and are labeled as "authoritarian" in SYS19503. Finally, those countries that were lacking in the foundations of democratic governance as of 1950 and had not yet achieved nation-state sovereignty were labeled as "colonial/protectorates." These are assigned a value of "1" in SYS19503.

Table 9.9 reports the second tabular analysis of Hypothesis 9.1. The chi-square (13.138) is not only statistically significant ($p = .001$) but is also reliable, as there are no cells with expected frequencies less than five. Further, the Eta statistic suggests a relatively strong association between the nominal category (type of political system) and the ordinal attribute (age of a country's current sovereign status). The Eta is a standard PRE statistic and is designed to allow us to interpret the strength of association between a nominal-level variable and an ordinal-level variable in a contingency table analysis, such as is presented in Tables 9.7 and 9.9. It can range between 0 and 1. Table 9.9 confirms what we have already established from an examination of the patterns in Table 9.7: Democratic and authoritarian countries (as of 1950) were much more likely to have formed prior to 1918 than is the case for those countries that as of 1950 were colonial/protectorate countries.

What of Hypothesis 9.2? We already know that the age of a country's current independent status is related to the degree of the country's political rights and institutional scale of democratic development. Hypothesis 9.2 suggests this link may be additionally related to the actual nature of the country's sovereign status as of 1950. In other words, we expect those countries that were colonial possessions and protectorates as late as 1950 to have relatively few political rights as of 1997. These countries have had a shorter period of time to manage both the pressures of national development and democratic evolution and have evolved from a history of political suppression.[14]

Table 9.10 reports tabular analysis of type of political system (SYS1950) by degree of political rights (POLIT972). As with Table 9.7 we have reported both the column and the row percentages (in addition to the customary counts, per cell). However, note that we have reversed rows and columns: The implied dependent variable, POLIT972, is assigned the column variable, while the implied independent variable, SYS1950, has been assigned the row variable. *This was done merely for the convenience of presentation.* The chi-square will not be affected, nor the Eta computation, as these are symmetric measures. Yet, it requires you be careful as to how you interpret the corresponding row percentages and column percentages reported in each cell.

There is some immediate evidence to support Hypothesis 9.2. Those countries that were colonial possessions in 1950 are much more likely to have "low/moderate" de-

TABLE 9.8 Countries by Age (Current Sovereignty), Type of Political System, 1950 (SYS1950), Type of Political System, 1950 Recoded (SYS19503), and Degree of Political Rights, 1997 (POLIT972)

COUNTRY	*AGE18002*	*SYS1950*	*SYS19503*	*POLIT972*
Algeria	1 Post-1917	8 Colonial Dependency	1 Colonial/Protectorate	1 Low/Moderate
Argentina	2 Pre-1918	6 Authoritarian Regime	2 Authoritarian	2 High
Australia	2 Pre-1918	1 Democracy	3 Democratic	2 High
Bangladesh	1 Post-1917	2 Restricted Democracy	3 Democratic	2 High
Brazil	2 Pre-1918	6 Authoritarian Regime	2 Authoritarian	2 High
Canada	2 Pre-1918	1 Democracy	3 Democratic	2 High
Chile	2 Pre-1918	1 Democracy	3 Democratic	2 High
China	2 Pre-1918	7 Totalitarian Regime	2 Authoritarian	1 Low/Moderate
Colombia	2 Pre-1918	2 Restricted Democracy	3 Democratic	1 Low/Moderate
Congo	1 Post-1917	8 Colonial Dependency	1 Colonial/Protectorate	1 Low/Moderate
Czech	1 Post-1917	7 Totalitarian Regime	2 Authoritarian	2 High
Ecuador	2 Pre-1918	1 Democracy	3 Democratic	2 High
Egypt	1 Post-1917	3 Constitutional Monarchy	3 Democratic	1 Low/Moderate
France	2 Pre-1918	1 Democracy	3 Democratic	2 High
Germany	2 Pre-1918	9 Protectorate	1 Colonial/Protectorate	2 High
Ghana	1 Post-1917	8 Colonial Dependency	1 Colonial/Protectorate	2 High
Greece	2 Pre-1918	3 Constitutional Monarchy	3 Democratic	2 High
India	1 Post-1917	1 Democracy	3 Democratic	2 High
Indonesia	1 Post-1917	2 Restricted Democracy	3 Democratic	1 Low/Moderate
Iran	2 Pre-1918	3 Constitutional Monarchy	3 Democratic	1 Low/Moderate
Italy	2 Pre-1918	1 Democracy	3 Democratic	2 High
Japan	2 Pre-1918	9 Protectorate	1 Colonial/Protectorate	2 High
Kenya	1 Post-1917	8 Colonial Dependency	1 Colonial/Protectorate	1 Low/Moderate
Korea	1 Post-1917	9 Protectorate	1 Colonial/Protectorate	2 High
Madagascar	1 Post-1917	8 Colonial Dependency	1 Colonial/Protectorate	2 High
Malaysia	1 Post-1917	8 Colonial Dependency	1 Colonial/Protectorate	1 Low/Moderate
Mexico	2 Pre-1918	2 Restricted Democracy	3 Democratic	2 High
Morocco	1 Post-1917	9 Protectorate	1 Colonial/Protectorate	1 Low/Moderate
Nepal	2 Pre-1918	5 Absolute Monarchy	2 Authoritarian	2 High

Netherlands	2 Pre-1918	1 Democracy	3 Democratic	2 High
Nigeria	1 Post-1917	8 Colonial Dependency	1 Colonial/Protectorate	1 Low/Moderate
Pakistan	1 Post-1917	2 Restricted Democracy	3 Democratic	1 Low/Moderate
Peru	2 Pre-1918	6 Authoritarian Regime	2 Authoritarian	1 Low/Moderate
Philippines	1 Post-1917	2 Restricted Democracy	3 Democratic	2 High
Poland	1 Post-1917	7 Totalitarian Regime	2 Authoritarian	2 High
Romania	2 Pre-1918	7 Totalitarian Regime	2 Authoritarian	2 High
Russia	2 Pre-1918	7 Totalitarian Regime	2 Authoritarian	2 High
South Africa	2 Pre-1918	2 Restricted Democracy	3 Democratic	2 High
Spain	2 Pre-1918	6 Authoritarian Regime	2 Authoritarian	2 High
Sri Lanka	1 Post-1917	2 Restricted Democracy	3 Democratic	2 High
Tanzania	1 Post-1917	9 Protectorate	1 Colonial/Protectorate	1 Low/Moderate
Thailand	2 Pre-1918	3 Constitutional Monarchy	3 Democratic	2 High
Tunisia	1 Post-1917	9 Protectorate	1 Colonial/Protectorate	1 Low/Moderate
Turkey	1 Post-1917	1 Democracy	3 Democratic	1 Low/Moderate
Uganda	1 Post-1917	9 Protectorate	1 Colonial/Protectorate	1 Low/Moderate
Ukraine	1 Post-1917	7 Totalitarian Regime	2 Authoritarian	2 High
United Kingdom	2 Pre-1918	1 Democracy	3 Democratic	2 High
United States	2 Pre-1918	1 Democracy	3 Democratic	2 High
Venezuela	2 Pre-1918	6 Authoritarian Regime	2 Authoritarian	2 High
Zimbabwe	1 Post-1917	8 Colonial Dependency	1 Colonial/Protectorate	1 Low/Moderate

TABLE 9.9 Crosstabs, SYS19503 by AGE18002, SPSS 10

			Age of Country		
			1 Post–1917	*2 Pre–1918*	*Total*
SYS19503	1 Colonial/ Protecorate	Count	13	2	15
		% within SYS19503	86.7%	13.3%	100.0%
		% within AGE18002	54.2%	7.7%	30.0%
	2 Authoritarian	Count	3	9	12
		% within SYS19503	25.0	75.0	100.0
		% within AGE18002	12.5	34.6	24.0
	3 Democratic	Count	8	15	23
		% within SYS19503	34.8	65.2	100.0
		% within AGE18002	33.3	57.7	46.0
Total		Count	24	26	50
		% within SYS19503	48.0	52.0	100.0
		% within AGE18002	100.0	100.0	100.0

$x^2 = 13.138$, df = 2, p = .001

grees of political rights as of 1997 than are the other types of political systems. This pattern is also present for those countries that were protectorates as of 1950, though the pattern is not as strong as with colonial possessions. Six of the eight countries in CROSSNAT.50 that were colonial possessions as of 1950 had "low/moderate" degrees of political rights in 1997. The corresponding proportion was four of seven for those countries that were protectorates as of 1950. Over half the countries in our sample that have "low/moderate" degrees of political rights and institutionalized democratic scale as of 1997 were colonial possessions or protectorates in 1950 (55.5 percent, or ten of eighteen countries).

From Table 9.8 we can see that the two former colonial possessions as of 1950 (Ghana and Madagascar) had achieved high degrees of political rights by 1997. The three protectorates of 1950 that had achieved high degrees of political rights by 1997 were the three principal zones of American and Anglo-American political-military protection during the cold war: Japan, Germany, and Korea.

Table 9.11 confirms Hypothesis 9.2. Specifically, those countries that were late leaving colonial status are also much less likely to have achieved "high" degrees of political rights by 1997. Authoritarian systems (as of 1950) in our sample were more successful, on the whole, than former colonial possessions and protectorates (as of 1950) in achieving one of the primary properties of democratic governance—institutionalized scale. While the chi-square (9.050) is statistically significant (p = .001), there was one cell with an expected frequency of less than five (the expected value was computed as 4.32). Given the size of the chi-square, and the fact that only one cell had an expected frequency less than five, we have reasonable confidence in the estimated chi-square and may proceed to reject the null.

TABLE 9.10 Crosstabs, SYS1950 by POLIT972, SPSS 10

			Degree of Political Rights		
			1 Low/Moderate	*2 High*	*Total*
Type of Political System, 1950	*1 Democracy*	Count	1	10	11
		% within SYS1950	9.1%	90.9%	100.0%
		% within POLIT972	5.6%	31.3%	22.0%
	2 Restricted Democracy	Count	3	5	8
		% within SYS1950	37.5	62.5	100.0
		% within POLIT972	16.7	15.6	16.0
	3 Constitutional Monarchy	Count	2	2	4
		% within SYS1950	50.0	50.0	100.0
		% within POLIT972	11.1	6.3	8.0
	5 Absolute Monarchy	Count		1	1
		% within SYS1950		100.0	100.0
		% within POLIT972		3.1	2.0
	6 Authoritarian Regime	Count	1	4	5
		% within SYS1950	20.0	80.0	100.0
		% within POLIT972	5.6	12.5	10.0
	7 Totalitarian Regime	Count	1	5	6
		% within SYS1950	16.7	83.3	100.0
		% within POLIT972	5.6	15.6	12.0
	8 Colonial Dependency	Count	6	2	8
		% within SYS1950	75.5	25.0	100.0
		% within POLIT972	33.3	6.3	16.0
	9 Protectorate	Count	4	3	7
		% within SYS1950	57.1	42.9	100.0
		% within POLIT972	22.2	9.4	14.0
Total		Count	18	32	50
		% within SYS1950	36.0	64.0	100.0
		% within POLIT972	100.0	100.0	100.0

$X^2 = 12.536$, df = 7, p = .084

The use of crosstab analysis (in conjunction with a listing of cases, as shown in Table 9.8) to discern key cross-national patterns, as well as to offer initial tests of basic hypotheses, underscores the utility of contingency tables. From tabular analysis, we have not only established a link between the age of a country's current sovereignty and its degree of political rights, but we have refined our understanding by showing that the relative lateness of a country's leaving colonial or protectorate status had also slowed the progress of institutionalized democratic scale by the close of the century.

Beyond these conclusions, we have seen that particular countries fall outside the patterns for their group. For instance, Table 9.10 draws attention to the one democracy in 1950 within our sample that by 1997 had achieved only "low/moderate" degrees of political rights. Table 9.8 confirms this country to be Turkey. Or, we see from Table

TABLE 9.11 Crosstabs, POLIT972 by SYS19503, SPSS 10

			Type of Political System, 1950			
			1 Colonial/ Protectorate	*2 Authoritarian*	*3 Democratic*	*Total*
Degree of Political Rights, 1997	*1 Low/Moderate*	Count	10	2	6	18
		% within POLIT972	55.6%	11.1%	33.3	100.0
	2 High	Count	5	10	17	32
		% within POLIT972	15.6	31.3	53.1	100.0
Total		Count	15	12	23	50
		% within POLIT972	100.0	100.0	100.0	100.0

$X^2 = 9.050$, df = 2, p = .011

9.10 that only one authoritarian country in 1950 within our sample had failed to achieve "high" degrees of political rights by 1997. Table 9.8 confirms this country to be Peru. China's unique status is underscored as well in Tables 9.8 and 9.10: It is the only totalitarian state as of 1950 that had not achieved "high" degrees of political rights among its citizenry by 1997. These tables also highlight the special status of Algeria, Congo, Kenya, Malaysia, Nigeria, and Zimbabwe within our sample. These former colonial possessions as of 1950 remained at the "low/moderate" range of political rights in 1997, as did Morocco, Tanzania, Tunisia, and Uganda—all former protectorates as of 1950. Finally, the political systems of Colombia, Indonesia, and Pakistan are brought into relief by the use of crosstab analysis and the listing of case values in Table 9.8. These are the three countries in our sample that were restricted democracies in 1950 and by 1997 had not yet achieved "high" degrees of political rights, as had the other five restricted democracies in 1950 in our sample: Bangladesh, Mexico, Philippines, South Africa, and Sri Lanka. Thus, through the application of crosstabs, we may effectively move up and down the ladder of theory building, offering important information for not merely the student of the cross-national design, but to those of the case study and comparable cases design, as well.

CHAPTER SUMMARY

In the previous chapter we introduced you to the fundamental aspects of hypothesis testing. In this chapter, we found that central to hypothesis testing is producing a test statistic and obtaining an estimate of its statistical significance. Our initial exploration of this process focused on the basics of one of the most venerable of tools within the repertoire of the student, crosstab analysis. As shown in Demonstrations 9.1 and 9.2, it remains one of the most practical and useful statistical tools for students of comparative politics. We have also introduced you to the technical concept of *variance* and the central place it occupies within the hypothesis-testing procedures. We shall return to this crucial technical aspect of hypothesis testing in later chapters with explicit attention being given to the difference between *sample variance* and *model variance* and the role of statistical error in testing hypotheses within the social sciences. Indeed, variance (and error) is the central component of hypothesis testing and its role and logic must be appreciated within the context of each of the core statistical tools of analysis commonly employed at the basic level by the student of comparative politics.

Finally, from our analysis in Demonstrations 9.1 and 9.2, we determined that the scale of institutional democracy is significantly greater for those countries formed before 1918 than for those countries formed after then, and that this may be further refined to specify the impact of "late" colonial/protectorate status. Countries that were under colonial possession and protectorate status as late as 1950 were, by the close of the century, much less likely to have achieved "high" degrees of political rights among their citizenry.

NOTES

1. Often, however, in the literature of empirical social science, the significance level will simply be referenced as the p value, or *p* (meaning, probability level). Thus, conventionally, to reject the null, the condition p £ .05 must be met. If p > .05, the null cannot be rejected. Alternatively, these conditions may be stated: α£ .05, or α > .05, respectively.

2. An excellent source for such tables, for the student who wishes a little more detail, is M. G. Blumer, 1979, *Principles of Statistics* (New York: Dover Publications, Inc.), p. 234. The formal principles that lie behind chi-square ($\div^2$) distributions may be found in Blumer's classic text, pp. 124–132, with a detailed discussion of the principles that lie behind significance levels for chi-square statistics, pp. 154–161. Also see Jack Levin and James Alan Fox, 2001, *Elementary Statistics in Social Research*, eighth edition (Boston: Allyn and Bacon), pp. 265–308.

3. This table has been produced in SPSS 10, by executing the sequence from the main menu bar, ANALYZE►DESCRIPTIVE STATISTICS►CROSSTABS. In the CROSSTABS window, specify the row variable (dependent variable) and the column variable (independent variable). In the STATISTICS window select Chi-Square, and in CELLS window select Column percent. Note that we have also selected Expected frequency count as well in the STATISTICS window for illustration. Ordinarily, expected counts would not be reported. See Marija J. Norušis, 2000, *SPSS: SPSS© 10.0 Guide to Data Analysis* (Upper Saddle River, N.J.: Prentice Hall), pp. 122–125.

4. In smaller samples (N < 100), one may want to report the likelihood ratio chi-square. This corrects for small sample size in the computation of the chi-square. However, in large samples the two statistics are virtually identical. Note in Table 9.2, the likelihood ratio is slightly larger (10.416) than the standard Pearson chi-square. For the vast majority of cases common in cross-national analysis, the Pearson chi-square or its sample-size adjusted statistics, the likelihood ratio, are the only two chi-square statistics required. See Marija J. Norušis, 2000, *SPSS: SPSS© 10.0 Guide to Data Analysis* (Upper Saddle River, N.J.: Prentice Hall), pp. 309–321.

5. To obtain measures of association from crosstabs within SPSS 10, open the STATISTICS window option from the crosstabs box, and select those measures you wish, based on the conditions of your model (the type of data in the model, and the kinds of conclusions you prefer—PRE or not).

6. For more detail on these and the other statistics presented in Tables 9.2 and 9.3, consult Marijia Norušis, 2000, *SPSS© 10.0: Guide to Data Analysis* (Upper Saddle River, N.J.: Prentice Hall), pp. 351–368.

7. The "Approx. T" in Table 9.5 reflects the relative size of the Tau b statistic within a population of Tau b scores. This distribution is similar to that of a chi-square distribution. A t-score larger than 1.96 will be statistically significant at the .05 threshold. As shown in Table 9.5, the statistical significance of the Tau b computed from the tabular analysis reported in Table 9.1 is .000. This means that if we assume the null hypothesis to be correct (namely, that there is no relationship between AGE18002 and POLIT972), the probability of obtaining a Tau b of .447 in our model is likely in less than 1 in 1000 cases. Thus, we may accept our research hypothesis: POLIT972 clearly increases relative to AGE18002 across nations.

8. Freedom House, "Democracy's Century: A Survey of Global Political Change in the 20th Century," available on the web at http://www.freedomhouse.org/reports/century.html.

9. For an example of how crosstab analysis has been applied as a first step in cross-national analysis, where the unit of analysis is the country itself, see Robert L. Perry and John D. Robertson, 1997, "Political Markets, Bond Markets, and the Effects of Uncertainty," *International Studies Quarterly* 42: 131–160.

10. *Democracies* "are political systems whose leaders are elected in competitive multi-party and multi-candidate processes in which opposition parties have a legitimate chance of attaining power or participating in power"; *restricted democracies* "are primarily regimes in which a dominant ruling party controls the levers of power, including access to the media, and the electoral process in ways that preclude a meaningful challenge to its political hegemony. In the first half of the century, states with restricted democratic practices included countries that denied universal franchise to women, racial minorities, the poor, and landless"; *monarchies* "are divided into three groups: constitutional monarchies, in which a constitution delineates the powers of the monarch and in which some power may have devolved to elected legislatures and other bodies; traditional monarchies; and absolute monarchies, in which monarchic power was exercised in despotic fashion"; *authoritarian regimes* "are typically one-party states and military dictatorships in which there are significant human rights violations"; *totalitarian regimes* "are the one-party systems that establish effective control over most aspects of information, engage in propaganda, control civic life, and intrude into private life. Typically, these have been the Marxist-Leninist and national socialist regimes"; *colonial* (and imperial) *dependencies* "are the territories that were under the domination of the large imperial systems that predominated in the first half of the century"; and *protectorates* "are countries that have by their own initiative sought the protection of a more powerful neighboring state or are under the temporary protection and jurisdiction of the international community." See http://www.freedomhouse.org/reports/century.html for a detailed report on the methodology and coding for the Freedom House study.

11. See Kenneth A. Bollen, 1983, "World System Positions of Dependency and Democracy: The Cross-National Evidence," *American Sociological Review* 48: 468–479.

12. See especially Seymour Martin Lipset, Kyoung-Ryung Seong, and John Charles Torres, 1993, "A Comparative Analysis of the Social Requisites of Democracy," *International Social Science Journal*, 136: 155–175; Samuel Huntington, 1996, *The Clash of Civilizations and the Remaking of the World Order* (New York: Touchstone Books), pp. 63, 209–212; Kristian S. Gleditsch and Michael D. Ward, 2000, "War and Peace in Time and Space: The Role of Democratization," *International Studies Quarterly* 44 (March): 1–29; Robert Jackman, 1993, *Power Without Force. The Political Capacity of Nation-States* (Ann Arbor, Mich.: University of Michigan Press); and Lars Rudebeck, Olle Törnquist, and Virgilio Rojas, eds., 1998, *Democratization in the Third World: Concrete Cases in Comparative and Theoretical Perspective* (New York: St. Martin's Press).

13. See Larry Diamond, 1994, "Rethinking Civil Society: Toward Democratic Consolidation," *Journal of Democracy* 5 (July): 5–17.

14. See Stuart Corbridge, 1993, "Colonialism, Post-Colonialism and the Political Geography of the Third World," in Peter J. Taylor, ed., *Political Geography of the Twentieth Century: A Global Analysis* (London: Bellhaven Press), pp. 171–205.

10

The Utility of the Difference of Means Test and the Study of Civic Culture

Terms: *Survey Data, Difference of Means (t-test), Within-Group Variance, Between-Group Variance, Proportional Representation, First-Past-the-Post*
Concepts: Political Environment, Political Culture, Civic Culture, Political Efficacy (Internal/External), Political Trust, Satisfaction with Democracy, Electoral System
Demonstrations: Mann-Whitney U Test, 10.1; Difference of Means Test, 10.2; Box-Plots, 10.3; Voting Turnout and Electoral Systems, 10.4

In this chapter, we continue with our examination and application of variance in the analysis of data, the consideration of the logic of measurement, and the systematic testing of hypotheses in bivariate models. We move on to the foundations of hypothesis testing in cross-national analysis with *parametric statistics*. As we noted in Chapter 8, the use of these statistics requires that we meet (within reason) specific assumptions about the distribution of scores in a sample before we can appropriately and effectively proceed with our hypothesis tests. Students of cross-national analysis are not always afforded the luxury of having data that are truly interval/ratio, nor are they able to work with sizable samples that minimize the variance differences between ordinal- and interval/ratio-level data. However, through careful combination of both parametric and nonparametric statistics (nonparametric statistics relax assumptions of normal distribution), the student of cross-national analysis can advance our understanding of institutional authority and political behavior through the effective application of hypothesis testing to cross-national data. In this chapter we explore one technique that has, like crosstabs, been a statistical staple for decades and offers important analytical and descriptive firepower for the student of comparative politics: the difference of means test. To understand and appreciate this analytical tool, we consider one of the central concepts of cross-national analysis: political culture.

Institutions and actors central to political authority are essentially influenced by the *political environment* within which they reside. The political environment may be broadly thought of as those pressures that ultimately define how institutions of political authority operate, regardless of whether those institutions are democratic or autocratic in nature. Thus, if we wish to know why some countries are more politically democratic than others, or why, for example, some political democracies exhibit lesser degrees of competitive political participation than others, we must consider the specific characteristics of the political environment that condition the evolution and formation of political authority in countries. The environmental influences of key interest to students of comparative politics typically include: (1) the complexity of the population, (2) the diversity of the population, (3) the degree of human suffering, (4) wealth and resource inequities, (5) the level of society's development, (6) national economic capacities, and (7) political values and cultural influences. In this chapter we focus more narrowly upon a specific set of values and cultural influences. We consider how political efficacy and democracy affect the political environment of countries. Our initial comparison is between a small sample of countries that were democratic prior to the end of the cold war (or were part of the Western democratic tradition throughout the duration of the cold war era, extending from 1948–1991) and those countries that were either part of the former Soviet Union or were under the direct influence of Soviet political and military influence during the cold war (Central and East European countries).

Because political culture consists of values, attitudes, and beliefs of individuals in society, we must rely upon different data than we have to this point. Therefore, we introduce the student to survey data, specifically, cross-national survey data. Cross-national survey data, however, are not as readily available for a large number of countries as are ecological/aggregate data, which we have explored in the context of CROSSNAT.50. Nonetheless, despite this sample restriction, we can still gain important insight into the patterns of beliefs and attitudes that must be factored into our broader cross-national conceptualization of political behavior and patterns of institutional authority.

The chapter is organized into three parts. The first portion of the chapter consists of two sections that consider the general concept of political culture: a section concerning political efficacy and another concerning political affect. In this portion we will consider citizens' perceptions of their influence on politics within their countries, their perceptions of the utility of elections, the reliability of politics within their country, and finally, their overall assessments of how democracy works within their society. The second portion of the chapter consists of several sections that systematically introduce the student to the particular procedures and practices involved in recoding survey data. This entails the careful modification of original survey data in order to convert the data into a more readily interpretable format that can be later applied to hypothesis testing. The final portion of the chapter explores the application of difference of means tests with applications to measurement of political culture within the political environment and institutional aspects of political systems.

THE CHALLENGE OF POLITICAL CULTURE

To this point our unit of analysis has been the country. One reason for this is that data concerning governments and institutions are typically collected on a national basis. Another reason is because nation-state institutions remain in the mind of many comparativists the principal focus of comparative study. The primary role of nation-states is one of context. The nation-state encompasses what Adam Przeworski and Henry Teune refer to as "system-level" variance. Indeed, as we have noted before, the primary role of cross-national analysis is that of exploring the system-level variance as a complement to "within-system" (or variance within a single country).[1] As Lawrence Mayer notes, "When a relationship between within-system concepts differs in structure or significantly in magnitude from one system to another, the reasonable inference is that some system level variable has a causal impact on the original [variable]."[2] Without the system-level variance operationalized, it is more difficult to achieve hypotheses within comparative politics that can contribute meaningfully to general theory.

Within any country, the institutional structure and its functional logic exist within a cultural environment that plays a significant role in shaping the structure and functions of institutional politics within countries. This culture, in turn, is to some degree conditioned by the very pattern of policies and consequences that follow from the formal political authority within that country. Of particular interest to students of politics is that aspect of the culture that shapes the attitudes and beliefs directed toward political authority and power. We call this system-level concept the *political culture* of a country.

Political culture is the aggregate of beliefs and attitudes of a populace concerning their political institutions and the authority underlying these institutions. The political culture is crucial in coordinating the patterns of exchange and interaction between citizens and their rulers within a political system. Political culture ultimately provides the basic foundation for the legitimacy upon which government depends and upon which political authority assumes validity and authority.[3]

The aggregate political behavior of citizens in a country (such as strikes, revolts, voting, protest, acts of violence, or simply abstaining from the political process) is thought to be at least indirectly related to the attitudes and beliefs of a citizenry with respect to key political and economic resources. Political culture, as Gabriel Almond has noted, is an empirical concept, not a theory per se; it is a tool in the construction of theories.[4]

One problem in the study of political culture as an empirical concept is that it is very difficult to measure and accurately compare across different countries. Much of how we conceptualize comparative political culture is based on a survey analysis conducted almost forty years ago by Gabriel Almond and Sidney Verba.[5] This painstaking field research effort laid the foundations for most subsequent analyses of political culture.

THE COMPARATIVE ANALYSIS OF POLITICAL CULTURE

In this chapter, we will explore ways in which one can empirically study political culture and effectively treat data based on individuals' attitudes and beliefs. We begin by focusing on some of the primary components of political culture. The data required for this task are *survey data*. Until recently few cross-national studies relied on survey analysis. This has changed somewhat.[6] Ronald Inglehart has pioneered such studies with the Eurobarometer surveys exploring various aspects of political culture and public opinion in the countries that compose the European Union.[7] Though survey data are more difficult to obtain, some of the most important research in cross-national research is based on survey data. While such data present new challenges to the beginning student (as well as seasoned professionals), they constitute a major component of the research repertoire of cross-national researchers. As Mayer reminds us, "The unique role of the comparative method in building explanatory theory arises from the fact that one may identify two distinct types of objects for analysis: the attributes of individuals and attributes of the whole systems [i.e., nation-state political systems]."[8] The bridge between these different levels, especially with respect to political culture, is survey data.

What Are Survey Data?

When working with survey data, our attention is drawn to the distinction between *qualitative data* and *quantitative data*. Data derived from survey analysis are much more qualitative than those we ordinarily obtain in aggregated, ecological databases. What is the difference between qualitative and quantitative data? Neil K. Agnew and Sandra W. Pyke explain that qualitative data are collected with the intention of allowing the researcher to assess the reality of the individual as perceived by that individual within a specific contextual setting. The individual's view of reality comes only after interaction with his political environment. Thus, it is the subjective reality of the person (or persons) under study that is measured by qualitative data. With quantitative data, the objective reality of the event or experience is measured by a researcher who is not part of the interactive process. A researcher using qualitative data assumes that he can place meaning to the data because he can understand what the actors themselves see as reality within a contextual setting. A researcher using quantitative data, on the other hand, makes no assumptions about the perceived reality of the person under observation. The data have nearly universal meaning to any outside observer. No assumptions are made about the subjective meaning of a measured event or response. Aggregated, ecological data, such as the GDP of a nation, or the areal size of a country, are quantitative data.

By these criteria, not all aggregated, ecological data are purely quantitative. As we have seen in Chapters 2–7, some measures that are aggregated in ecological databases are themselves based on judgments, which, of course, reflect a degree of subjective assessment and inference by the researcher. They are not truly qualitative data, however, because there are no assumptions about how an actor (or actors) within a contextual setting perceives reality as a function of the interaction with the environment. Survey data, on the other hand, have a distinctly subjective content to them. And, quite explicitly, behind these data lies the assumption that the individual's perception of reality we are measuring is very much a function of that person's interaction with his political environment. For example, behind our measure of an individual's attitude toward abortion lies the assumption that the respondent's evaluation of the object (abortion) is a function of that person's interaction with an environment in which abortion has some meaning and forms a part of that person's reality.[9]

Survey data are drawn from a specific process. A researcher asks another person (the respondent) to respond to a specific question. The question is usually put forward on a questionnaire, though it is probably more common in many polls to have the question put forward either in person or over a phone. The researcher who builds the survey questionnaire is interested in obtaining information from the individual that will allow the researcher to both compare attitudes and beliefs across different segments of a population, as well as to test a number of hypotheses the researcher has about the relation of attitudes, beliefs, and background traits.

Responses to survey questions are closed. That is, the questionnaire requires the respondent to select (usually) one response from a set of two or more choices. The researcher selects the wording of the question and the respondents match their response to the item that most closely approximates their perception of reality. This is how it works, at least in principle.

Herein lies the rub with survey data. Because the researcher wants to maximize criterion validity, content and construct validity are often jeopardized in conducting survey polls. The construct and content validity of survey data reflect the extent to which the questions themselves were technically correct, scaled appropriately, and asked in a manner that would not bias or influence the response. Criterion validity, on the other hand, reflects the degree to which the results of the responses can be generalized from the sample to the population within a reasonable degree of accuracy and confidence. In other words, criterion validity asks whether the survey is measuring what it is supposed to be measuring. Correlations and matches supporting criterion validity, however, cannot overcome construct and content validity problems that are incorporated into the original measures.

Concept stretching is always a problem in cross-national research, as we have seen. When employing survey data in cross-national research, concept stretching becomes an even greater threat to the validity and credibility of the research findings. The nature of survey research forces the researcher to impose a subjective judgment on both the questions asked and responses received.

In order to obtain this external validity, closed responses are most frequently used by the researcher, making it easier for the researcher to simplify and summarize the response patterns across the sample. Closed responses, however, may not allow us to gauge accurately the true attitude and belief of the respondent. To achieve responses that allow empirical analysis, the survey itself may be contoured to reduce the accuracy of the response itself. The resulting neat and tidy responses may well mask the unrealistic assumptions that lie behind the actual method of eliciting the response.

The Difference Between Survey-Based Cultural Studies and Pooled Cross-National Samples

The necessary survey data that allow researchers to measure and compare political culture are derived most commonly from surveys of citizens within individual countries. This presents an immediate distinction between most studies of political culture and institutional analysis. Because it is assumed that most institutional analyses (such as those presented in Chapters 4–9) are based on quantitative data, samples of aggregated, ecological (and therefore, quantitative) data more readily accommodate cross-national statistical analysis. As explained in Chapter 2 (Table 2.1 and Figure 2.2), cross-national quantitative data based on aggregated, ecological data combine data drawn from several different countries. Inferences are then drawn on the basis of the analysis of this "pooled" cross-national sample to the population of countries as a whole (or at least, with regards to that attribute most similar to the sample, such as most populous countries, as in CROSSNAT.50).

To "pool" means to combine data from all the different countries into one single sample. We can do this because there are no subjective, contextual qualifications thought to significantly affect the meaning of the data from country to country. (Obviously, this is not always the case.) Refinements to our cross-national theory are then based on the results of this cross-national analysis.

By contrast, surveys work from samples of citizens within individual countries. These are qualitative data, as we have seen. Therefore, if you remain at the original level of analysis—the individual—you cannot easily eliminate the specific contextual setting affecting the perceived realities of the respondents. However, data analysis and hypothesis testing can be and are performed on these individual country samples when the unit of analysis remains the individual. These individual country samples are pooled, but generally not across countries. *They are generally pooled across citizens of the single country.* Inferences are then extended to the population of citizens within the country—but not within the population of all citizens across the globe. Refinements to our general theory come by comparing results across countries—not by analyzing a truly cross-national sample.

Figure 10.1 summarizes the logic of cross-national studies that rely on aggregated ecological data. Our theory refinement would be based on different samples comprising slightly different time periods or countries within the sample.

Figure 10.2 summarizes the logic of comparative analysis using survey data, when we keep the unit of analysis at the level of the individual. This, of course, is the comparable cases strategy of comparison, explained in detail in Chapter 2. This approach would dictate decisions when comparing cultures across different countries based on qualitative survey data. Our theory refinement would be based on *repeated* analyses of different country surveys, as well as different specific country samples.

Why this difference between cross-national samples based on aggregated, ecological data and samples based on survey data? Survey data drawn from one country (and therefore one political culture) have a unique cast to them. *Survey data are language- and therefore culture-specific*. These data are based on explicit written or verbal communication between the person asking the question (surveyor) and the respondent. Because all languages have idiomatic expressions associated with particular words and symbols of the language, one cannot easily move across cultures (or countries) and be sure that the meaning of the response of one language would be identical to that of another language. Therefore, there is reluctance among researchers to pool survey data when those data are pooled at the original individual unit of measure.

Great efforts at language standardization have been made by specialists, but these efforts have not entirely eliminated the concern of many that cross-national survey data represent greater obstacles to cross-national comparison than do ecological data. Therefore, when relying upon survey data, students of comparative cultures are advised to focus their analyses on one country (and one culture) at a time, and not pool the sample, as in studies relying on aggregated ecological data.

As we will see, should we proceed to *aggregate* (or summarize population characteristics) the individual data and thereby convert the data from the original unit of measure (the individual person, or survey respondent) to an ecological, or aggregate unit (the country within which the respondent resides), we may then be better placed to proceed with traditional cross-national pooled studies, as depicted in Figure 10.1. For instance, rather than pooling survey data drawn from the United States and Great Britain into one survey, we might first simply execute a frequency analysis or a crosstabs (Chapter 9) on the data for the United States and Great Britain and obtain what are in effect the marginals. We may now have a figure that shows 20 percent of the British favor more taxes for the rich, while 10 percent of Americans favor higher taxes for the rich. This allows us to include both the British percentage and the American percentage into a pooled cross-national sample that might be applied to comparing the degrees of support for taxing the rich in democracies. We cannot answer any question about what factors influence an individual to hold an opinion (as we could have, had we remained at the original level of analysis—the individual respondent). However, we are able to perform a more standard cross-national analysis on a different

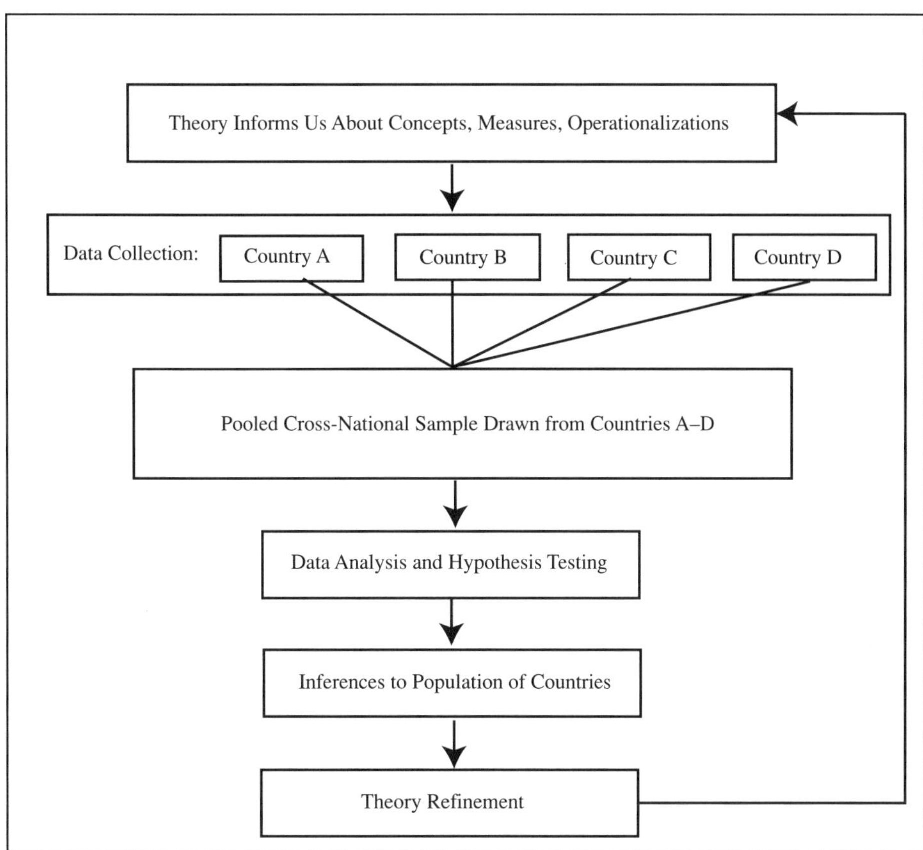

FIGURE 10.1 Logic of Traditional Cross-National Analysis Design (Employing Aggregated Ecological Data with Country as Unit of Analysis)

question (the comparative support across democracies for taxing the rich). We shall draw on this procedure later in this chapter.

TECHNICAL CONSIDERATIONS WHEN USING SURVEY DATA

The ISSP Database

How does one obtain survey databases? Unless a researcher conducts the survey himself (or contracts for this labor-intensive and expensive process from experts), the researcher is left with the option of obtaining the data from existing surveys. The Inter-University Consortium for Political and Social Research (ICPSR) at the University of

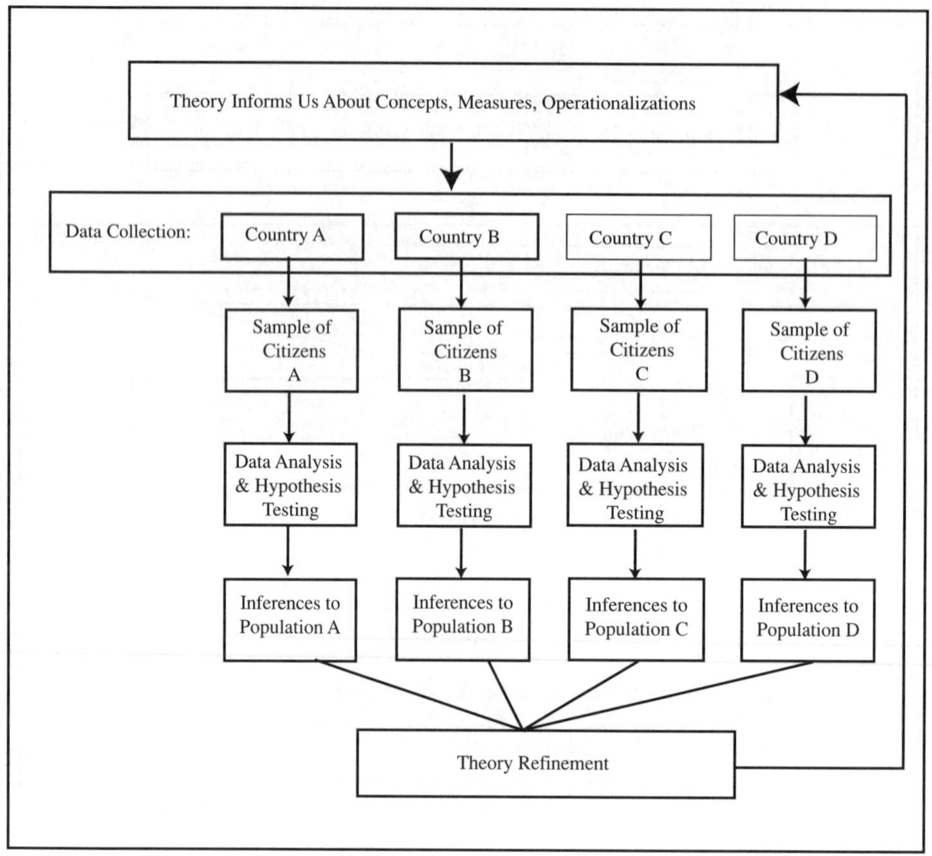

FIGURE 10.2 Logic of Cross-National Analysis When Employing Survey Data with Individual as Unit of Analysis

Michigan is the principal repository of major survey databases (as well as databases not containing surveys). Members of the consortium have access to the vast collection of various databases, and they may select from the main ICPSR catalog those studies that most closely fit the research question at hand.

Another outlet for comparative social survey data is the Central Archive for Empirical Social Research of the University of Cologne, Germany (Zentral Archive für Empirische Sozial Forschung an der Universität Köln-or, the ZA), which is part of GESIS consortium of social science research with headquarters in Berlin.[10] The ZA has coordinated the International Social Survey Programe (ISSP). This ongoing annual project entails surveying the public of twenty-nine nations. The topics of each survey vary, but one continuing theme is the Role of Government. The first Role of Government ISSP study was published in 1985 (ZA Study #1490). The most recent available survey is Role of Government III (ZA #2900), produced in 1996. This survey covers twenty-five countries (with two separate surveys each for Great Britain,

Israel, and Germany). The survey contains 190 variables. We will draw on this survey to consider political efficacy and political trust—two critical aspects of the broader political culture in a democracy. The objectives of the survey were to obtain insight into what citizens in the various countries thought of their government and what they thought the government should and should not do with respect to particular policy areas. Each variable reports the results of a specific question asked of the respondent (all questions are closed questions). All variables are either ordinal or nominal (with the exception of the respondent's age, which is interval). Within each country, there are missing data, which reflect the failure of the respondent to provide a valid response from the questionnaire. In several instances, certain questions were not asked of citizens in particular countries.

Recoding Survey Data

We saw in previous chapters that it is often the case that the researcher must find a way to refashion the original structure of the variable in order to match the meaning of the principal concept under examination (or to accommodate levels of measurement issues). This is also the case with survey data. For instance, suppose someone begins from the initial proposition that one's overall satisfaction with the way democracy works in his or her country is shaped in part by the extent of one's education. To explore this proposition, the researcher will want to see if people who have more years of formal education are more satisfied with the way democracy works in their country than are those people with fewer years of formal education.

In the data set titled ROG3 (that is, Role of Government III), SATDEMO contains the responses from individuals who were asked this question: "All in all, how well or badly do you think the system of democracy in [respondent's country] works these days?" The respondent had four choices for an answer:

1. "It works well and needs no changes"
2. "It works well but needs some changes"
3. "It does not work well and needs a lot of changes", or
4. "It does not work well and needs to be completely changed"

Four categories offer many more opportunities for variance than just two categories, and may well be ideal. In other circumstances, it may be that the researcher merely wishes to compare patterns of responses between those who think their democracy works well in general, and those who do not think it works well in general. This is especially true if, as we have seen in Chapter 9, the researcher intends to employ a crosstabular analysis and wishes to run a simple 2 X 2 table and reduce the prospects on cells with expected frequencies less than five. In this circumstance, the researcher may wish to simply collapse the categories logically into two combined response patterns:

1. "Works Well" (categories 1 and 2 of the original variable) and
2. "Does Not Work Well" (categories three and four of the original variable)

This has the effect of converting the original variable into a new dichotomous (or two-category) variable (SATDEMO2).

POLITICAL EFFICACY AND POLITICAL TRUST

One of the most important roles of political culture is to orient one to the norms and values of the political system—that is, the collection of institutions and rules that coordinate and stabilize a country. This type of "diffuse support," as it is commonly known (diffuse because it is not directed toward any particular institution or rule), comes about when the citizens within a culture have a sense of what Almond and Verba referred to as "civic culture." This entails a delicate balance between the willingness to hold government and public authority accountable to the public for its actions and the positions that politicians may take, while on the other hand, exacting enough restraint to allow public authority a space within which to operate. This balance between restraint and action requires, many argue, a healthy blend of political efficacy and political trust.

Political efficacy was originally defined in the literature of voting behavior as being "the feeling that individual political action does have, or can have, an impact upon the political process, i.e., that it is worthwhile to perform one's civic duties."[11] Oscar Gabriel has further drawn out the distinction in the literature between one's external efficacy and internal efficacy. External political efficacy is the perception by individuals that their government and its institutional structure are responsive and open to their needs and demands. Internal political efficacy is the sense that one is competent and important enough to make a difference within the political environment in which one operates.[12] Traditionally, internal political efficacy is assigned the standard label as simply efficacy, while external political efficacy is more closely identified with a sense of political trust. The two attributes are crucial to founding the political culture in a sense of civic culture. The civic culture is described by Almond as "a substantial consensus on the legitimacy of political institutions and the direction and content of public policy, a widespread tolerance of a plurality of interests and belief in their irreconcilability, and a widely distributed sense of political confidence."[13]

Table 10.1 reports the four basic measures drawn from the ISSP Role of Government III (ZA #2900). The four variables reflect approximations of political efficacy and political trust. They each capture an aspect of the political culture that together undergird the health and stability of the civic culture within a country. The four basic variables (AVGCIT, ELECTS, PROMISES, and SATDEMO) have each been recoded into simpler variables (AVGCIT3, ELECTS3, PROM3, and SATDEMO2, respectively). In the third column, the question asked of the respondents and the choices they were given (in the original variable) are noted. In each case of the recoded variables

TABLE 10.1 Measures of Political Efficacy, Trust, and the Satisfaction with Democracy

Attribute	*Variable in ROG3*	*Question/Responses*
Internal Political Efficacy	AVGCIT	"The average citizen has considerable influence in politics": 1. Strongly Agree 2. Agree 3. Neither Agree nor Disagree 4. Disagree 5. Strongly Disagree
Internal Political Efficacy	AVGCIT3 (AVGCIT recoded)	"The average citizen has considerable influence in politics": 1. Agree (1, 2) 2. Neither (3) 3. Disagree (4, 5)
Internal/External Efficacy	ELECTS	"Elections are a good way of making governments pay attention to important political issues facing our country": 1. Strongly Agree 2. Agree 3. Neither Agree nor Disagree 4. Disagree 5. Strongly Disagree
Internal/External Efficacy	ELECTS3 (ELECTS recoded)	"Elections are a good way of making governments pay attention to important political issues facing our country": 1. Agree (1, 2) 2. Neither (3) 3. Disagree (4, 5)
External Efficacy	PROMISES	"People we elect as (MPs) try to keep the promises they have made during the election": 1. Strongly Agree 2. Agree 3. Neither Agree nor Disagree 4. Disagree 5. Strongly Disagree
External Efficacy	PROM3 (PROMISES recoded)	"People we elect as (MPs) try to keep the promises they have made during the election": 1. Agree (1, 2) 2. Neither (3) 3. Disagree (4, 5)
Overall Confidence in Democracy	SATDEMO	"All in all, how well or badly do you think the system of democracy in [respondent's country] works these days?": 1. It works well and needs no changes 2. It works well but needs some changes

(continues)

TABLE 10.1 *(continued)*

Attribute	*Variable in ROG3*	*Question/Responses*
		3. It does not work well and needs a lot of changes 4. It does not work well and needs to be completely changed
General Health of Civic Culture	SATDEMO2 (SATDEMO recoded)	"All in all, how well or badly do you think the system of democracy in [respondent's country] works these days?": 1. Works Well 2. Does Not Work Well

AVGCIT3, ELECTS3, and PROM3, value 1 represents values 1 and 2 from the original variable, 2 is the value of 3 from the original variable, and 3 represents values 4 and 5 from the original variable. In the case of SATDEMO2, the value of 1 represents the values 1 and 2 from the original variable, and 2 reflects the combined values 3 and 4 from the original variable.[14]

Descriptive Analysis of Survey Data: Central Tendencies

When working with a cross-national sample of survey data, the student must confront two critical questions: (1) How can we summarize the data in a meaningful way? and (2) Can we move from a comparable cases approach to a cross-national strategy and achieve a meaningful hypothesis test? To begin, consider Table 10.2. The table reports the sample mean, standard deviation, and 95 percent confidence intervals for each of the four variables across each of the twenty-one country-samples. We must ask, then, "What does a mean indicate when working with survey data?"

Technically, as noted above, the mean often cannot be properly evaluated in a sample where the attribute being summarized is measured at the ordinal level. Ordinal data do not conform to the assumptions of normal distribution patterns from which we may infer from a sample to a target population. As a mean is the basic parametric statistic, it is technically inappropriate to rely on a mean when summarizing a sample of ordinal data. However, given the usually very large size of survey samples (almost always in excess of 500), researchers frequently "bend" the rules a little. This can be justified somewhat because the Central Limit Theorem (see Chapter 2) holds that if the sample is large enough, the distribution will assume a normal curve. With this as a backdrop, it is common to find researchers reporting the mean and standard deviation of the response values for a survey question. From these two statistics we can then compute the confidence interval for variables based on survey data.

Consider Australia as an example. The mean response for AVGCIT in this sample is 3.51. Of course, there are five discrete values for AVGCIT (see Table 10.1). There

TABLE 10.2 Basic Central Tendency Statistics for Measures of Political Efficacy, Trust, and Satisfaction with Democracy (ROG3)

	AVGCIT			*ELECTS*			*PROMISES*			*SATDEMO*		
Country	*Mean*	*Std*	*95% c.i.*	*Mean*	*Std*	*95% c.i.*	*Mean*	*Std*	*95% c.i.*	*Mean*	*Std*	*95%c.i.*
Established Democracies												
Australia	3.51	0.99	3.47–3.56	2.16	0.96	2.12–2.20	3.26	1.03	3.21–3.30	2.11	0.52	2.08–2.13
West Germany	3.53	1.03	3.48–3.57	2.27	1.03	2.22–2.31	3.47	1.05	3.42–3.51	2.06	0.56	2.04–2.09
Great Britain	3.67	0.94	3.61–3.74	2.25	0.97	2.18–2.31	3.29	1.01	3.22–3.36	2.25	0.64	2.21–2.03
United States	3.22	1.09	3.16–3.28	2.17	0.93	2.12–2.22	3.38	1.07	3.32–2.45	2.30	0.62	2.26–2.33
Italy	3.54	1.18	3.47–3.62	2.59	1.22	2.52–2.67	4.17	1.04	4.11–4.23	2.91	0.74	2.86–2.95
Ireland	3.47	1.13	3.40–3.54	2.09	0.99	2.02–2.15	3.39	1.11	3.32–3.46	2.13	0.61	2.09–2.17
Norway	3.49	0.96	3.43–3.54	1.99	0.80	1.94–2.03	3.14	0.98	3.08–3.19	2.03	0.52	2.00–2.06
Sweden	3.69	1.00	3.63–3.75	2.22	0.96	2.16–2.28	3.54	0.99	3.48–3.60	2.40	0.69	2.36–2.44
Canada	3.41	1.08	3.34–3.47	2.50	1.07	2.44–2.57	3.30	1.03	3.24–3.36	2.25	0.62	2.21–2.28
Philippines	2.76	0.96	2.71–2.82	2.25	0.81	2.21–2.30	2.91	0.99	2.86–2.97	2.46	0.89	2.41–2.52
Japan	2.80	1.46	2.71–2.89	2.45	1.33	2.37–2.53	3.96	1.20	3.88–4.03	2.18	0.65	2.14–2.22
Spain	3.36	1.06	3.31–3.40	2.31	1.02	2.27–2.36	3.73	1.03	3.68–3.77	2.41	0.80	2.37–2.44
France	3.37	1.29	3.29–3.44	2.62	1.35	2.54–2.70	3.63	1.10	3.56–3.69	2.36	0.67	2.32–2.40
Recent Democracies of East Europe and the Former Soviet Union												
East Germany	3.82	1.04	3.75–3.88	2.33	1.17	2.46–2.61	3.69	1.02	3.63–3.76	2.43	0.61	2.39–2.47
Hungary	4.04	0.99	3.99–4.10	2.95	1.13	2.89–3.01	3.88	0.96	3.82–3.93	2.99	0.69	2.96–3.03
Czech Republic	3.92	0.93	3.86–3.98	2.46	1.12	2.39–2.53	3.56	0.99	3.50–3.62	2.62	0.73	2.57–2.67
Slovenia	3.98	0.97	3.92–4.02	2.82	1.23	2.74–2.90	3.64	1.13	3.57–3.72	2.58	0.69	2.53–2.62
Poland	3.65	1.07	3.58–3.72	2.22	1.00	2.16–2.29	3.57	1.08	3.50–3.64	2.47	0.67	2.43–2.31
Bulgaria	3.59	1.09	3.51–3.67	2.23	0.99	2.16–2.31	2.86	1.05	2.78–2.94	2.66	0.74	2.60–2.71
Russia	3.91	1.10	3.85–3.97	2.46	1.21	2.39–2.52	3.99	1.01	3.93–4.05	3.11	0.74	3.07–3.15
Latvia	3.41	1.03	3.35–3.48	2.70	1.09	2.64–2.77	3.93	0.94	3.88–3.96	2.68	0.70	2.64–2.72

TABLE 10.3 Computing the Mean from Ordinal Data in Survey Database AVGCIT (ROG3)

Values Within Variable (AVGCIT)	*Relative Frequency of Value (f)*	*Weighted Value (Value x Relative Frequency) (I)*
1	29	29
2	431	862
3	324	972
4	1066	4,264
5	241	1,205
	Σ_f = 2,091 (Valid Responses)	Σ_I = 7,332
		Σ_I/Σ_f = 3.51 (Mean)

could not be a "typical" value of 3.51. But, we could say, hypothetically, that with the Australian target population, the "typical" Australian response was to indicate the respondents' tendency to disagree with the idea that "the average citizen has considerable influence on politics." Literally, as we know from Chapter 3, the mean is a point estimation: 3.51 is the best "estimate" for any given respondent randomly selected from the Australian sample (without, of course, any further information known of that respondent).

How is this mean derived? The logic of computing the mean when using ordinal data is the same as when we employ ecological data. However, the steps are altered because of the nature of the ordinal data. Table 10.3 specifies the steps involved in computing the mean from ordinal data in a survey database. To compute the mean, we first multiply the value of an item by the number of respondents (that is, relative frequency) for that value. In AVGCIT, the value of 1 has 29 respondents; the value of 2 has 431 respondents, and so on. Therefore, we obtain weighted values (I) for the variable of AVGCIT: 29 (1 x 29), 862 (2 x 431), and so on. We then sum the five relative frequencies, thereby obtaining the number of valid responses in the sample (N = 2,091), as well as the weight (I) for each value (7,332). We then divide the sum of the weights (Σ_I) by the valid responses in the sample (Σ_f). The resulting quotient is the mean response for the sample, 3.51. Of course, no one can select a value of 3.51—the respondent's choice was simply a discrete 1, 2 3, 4, or 5. In theory, however, we estimate the "typical" Australian respondent to fall at the 3.51 point: generally leaning toward the "disagree" range.

To compute the standard deviation of ordinal data in a survey database, we follow the same logic that we employ when working with ecological data. Table 10.4 illustrates the steps involved in the process. We begin by deriving the deviation of each value in the response by subtracting the value of each response from the sample mean (3.51). For the first value, the resulting value is –2.51 (or, 1 – 3.51 = –2.51); for the second value in AVGCIT the resulting value is –1.51 (or, 2 – 3.51 = –1.51). We then eliminate the directional sign of the value's deviation by squaring the derived variation

TABLE 10.4 Steps in Computing Standard Deviation from Ordinal Data in Survey Database AVGCIT (ROG3)

Values Within Variable (OBEY) (x)	*Relative Frequency of Value (f)*	*Sample Mean*	*Variation (x – Sample Mean) (v)*	*Variation² (v^2)*	*Weighted Variation (v^2 x f)*
1	29	3.51	-2.51	6.3001	182.7029
2	431	3.51	-1.51	2.2801	982.7231
3	324	3.51	-.51	.2601	84.2724
4	1066	3.51	.49	.2401	255.9466
5	241	3.51	1.49	2.2201	535.0441
	$\Sigma_{f-1} = 2091$				$\Sigma_v{}^2 = 2040.6891$
					$\Sigma_v{}^2/\Sigma_f = .975939$
					$\sqrt{\Sigma_v{}^2/\Sigma_f} = .99$

($-2.51^2 = 6.3001$; $-1.51^2 = 2.2801$). We then determine the total variation for each response value by multiplying the squared variation by the relative frequency for the value (6.3001 X 29 = 182.7029, and so on). We then sum these total variations (2,040.6891), divide by 2,091 (2,040.6891 ÷ 2,091 = .975939), and take the quotient's square root in order to place the deviations back into a standard base ($\sqrt{.975939}$ = .99). The typical deviation for a response from the mean response in the Australian sample is .99. Hypothetically, a "typical" Australian respondent deviates by .99 values from the choices offered in the survey.

Table 10.2 also reports the 95 percent confidence intervals. These, as you will recall from Chapter 5, are the range of values within which we are 95 percent confident the true population mean falls. The computation for a confidence interval in survey data is identical to that of ecological/aggregate data, once the mean and standard deviation have been reported for the survey data. For Australia, we can be confident that the true population mean is found in the range between 3.47 and 3.56. Compare this to that of the United States. The American sample has a mean (AVGCIT) of 3.22, indicating a stronger American willingness to suggest agreement with the notion that average citizens can make a difference (as the value declines, the typical respondent is moving toward "agree" as the answer). However, there is much more variation to these answers than in the Australian sample, as evidenced by the relatively large standard deviation in the American sample (1.09). This is further underscored by the broad range within the American confidence intervals. The American 95% c.i. range is from 3.16 – 3.28, or a range of .12 units, in contrast to the Australian sample, which has a unit range of only .9. France and Japan have even larger standard deviations (1.29 and 1.46, respectively) and therefore, broader 95% c.i. ranges (3.29 – 3.44 and 2.71 – 2.89, respectively).

As useful as these univariate statistics are, they are nonetheless one-dimensional. That is, they provide only a summary of the typical score within the country-sample for each of the variables. In this sense, they offer a comparison across countries for one score—the mean. They do not offer a second dimension—an assessment of the distribution patterns, which would allow one to see the variance patterns within a country. Indeed, the mean, while powerful, does not have the same meaningful interpretation to it as does a simple frequency distribution. Consider Table 10.5. This table reports the frequency distributions (percentages of valid respondents) for the recoded variables: AVGCIT3, ELECTS3, PROM3, and SATDEMO2. We have chosen to use the recoded variables because they offer more clarity and smooth out the uneven variance across the categories of the original variables without seriously distorting information.

Two conclusions emerge from the univariate analysis presented in Table 10.5. First, one gets a slightly different picture from distributions than from means alone. And second, sharp differences exist between the established Western-based democracies and those of the recently established democracies of East and Central Europe (as of 1996).[15] For instance, whereas from Table 10.2 we can say that the typical established democracy tended to have its "typical" citizen somewhere near the midrange of scores on the scale for each of the four variables, we can say something much more meaningful from Table 10.5. For instance, while we know from Table 10.2 that the United States has a mean score of 3.22 for AVGCIT, we see from Table 10.5 that approximately two of three respondents (67.8 percent) said they were either "uncertain" about whether the average citizen could make a difference (19.6 percent) or expressed some degree of disagreement with this position (48.2 percent). On average, the established democracies had just over one-quarter of their citizens expressing an affirmative sense of political efficacy (27 percent), while the typical established democracy as of 1996 found approximately three-quarters of its citizens expressing ambivalence about a citizen's political efficacy (19 + 54 percent). For recently formed democracies of East and Central Europe, the respective figures are 14.6 percent and 85.4 per cent (13.8 percent + 71.6 percent). Perhaps more telling is the fact that while the average percentage of citizens across the established democracies expressing a positive evaluation of democracy is 69.4 percent, the corresponding percentage for newer democracies of East and Central Europe is 42.9 percent.[16]

Table 10.5 clearly suggests that the degree of political efficacy, political trust, and satisfaction with democracy in democracies varies by the status of a country's democratic system. More specifically, we see that within those countries that had established their democracy prior to 1991 and within the democratic West, there is a much stronger sense of political efficacy, trust, and satisfaction with democracy among respective populations than is the case for those democracies that have acquired democratic governance out of the ashes of communist collapse in East and Central Europe. The size of percentages across the two groups appears on the surface to be somewhat large. Furthermore, there are clearly differences within each group of democracies. Italy, for instance, as of 1996, hardly appears satisfied with elections, or the general state of Italian democracy. Among the more recent democracies included in Table 10.5, the Latvians are more efficacious than other recent East and Central European

TABLE 10.5 Frequency Distributions, Recoded Variables, Measures of Political Efficacy, Trust, and Satisfaction with Democracy (ROG3)

	AVGCIT3				*ELECTS3*				*PROM3*				*SATDEMO2*		
Country	*Agree*	*Uncertain*	*Disagree*	*N*	*Agree*	*Uncertain*	*Disagree*	*N*	*Agree*	*Uncertain*	*Disagree*	*N*	*Well*	*Not Well*	*N*
						Established Democracies									
Australia	22.0	15.5	62.5	2091	76.7	11.0	12.4	2099	29.2	24.7	46.1	2090	83.7	16.3	2043
West Germany	19.1	23.6	57.4	2266	70.6	14.9	14.5	2250	21.4	24.9	53.7	2176	83.2	16.8	2258
Great Britain	13.7	18.0	68.3	937	72.0	14.6	13.4	952	23.5	28.2	48.4	941	70.8	29.2	876
United States	32.2	19.6	48.2	1265	75.6	12.1	12.3	1277	25.3	21.3	53.4	1273	71.3	28.7	1246
Italy	24.9	17.1	58.0	1077	59.2	15.1	25.6	1084	10.5	10.7	78.7	1091	28.6	71.4	1064
Ireland	29.7	10.2	60.1	980	79.1	6.9	14.0	984	29.7	14.3	56.0	979	80.8	19.2	943
Norway	18.0	23.7	58.3	1292	84.2	9.3	6.5	1308	28.7	35.9	35.3	1291	88.1	11.9	1279
Sweden	12.1	25.9	62.1	1144	70.5	19.4	10.1	1160	14.9	34.6	50.5	1158	59.8	40.2	1170
Canada	25.0	19.3	55.7	1151	61.6	17.3	21.1	1152	25.7	29.3	45.0	1146	74.9	25.1	1126
Philippines	46.7	25.6	27.7	1160	73.2	17.0	9.8	1182	40.9	26.1	33.0	1174	57.4	42.6	1108
Japan	49.9	15.1	35.0	1165	58.7	18.7	22.5	1153	14.1	19.4	66.6	1145	73.5	26.5	1092
Spain	26.6	18.1	55.3	2237	70.3	13.7	16.0	2291	16.4	17.2	66.4	2257	62.5	37.5	2312
France	31.0	15.1	53.9	1249	58.9	10.1	31.0	1273	20.2	19.9	59.9	1267	67.1	32.9	1272
Mean	27.0	19.0	54.0	—	70.0	13.9	16.1	—	23.1	23.6	53.3	--	69.4	30.6	–
				Recent Democracies of East Europe and the Former Soviet Union											
East Germany	13.1	18.0	68.9	1066	58.9	17.7	23.5	1053	15.4	21.3	63.3	1034	60.8	39.2	1040
Hungary	9.7	8.7	81.5	1452	42.0	23.5	34.5	1355	10.8	18.6	70.7	1422	22.5	77.5	1403
Czech Republic	9.4	14.0	76.6	1064	59.7	18.3	21.9	1048	15.7	27.9	56.4	1028	48.3	51.7	1043
Slovenia	10.3	11.6	78.1	949	48.3	19.7	32.0	932	19.4	21.2	59.4	957	49.4	50.6	926
Poland	16.7	14.0	69.2	1075	71.9	16.1	11.9	1022	17.4	20.3	62.3	1029	57.2	42.8	1034
Bulgaria	18.1	15.6	66.3	956	68.7	18.1	13.2	936	41.5	29.3	29.2	815	44.7	55.3	865
Russia	12.7	12.4	74.9	1566	60.7	16.6	22.7	1515	11.5	15.4	73.1	1535	18.1	81.9	1360
Latvia	26.6	15.8	57.6	1367	53.7	16.7	29.5	1338	9.6	16.2	74.1	1373	41.9	58.1	1319
Mean	14.6	13.8	71.6	—	58.0	18.3	23.7	—	17.6	21.3	61.1	—	42.9	57.1	–
Mean (All)	22.3	17.0	60.7	—	65.5	15.6	19.0	—	21.0	22.7	56.3	—	59.3	40.7	–

democracies; the Poles are more confident about the role of elections; Bulgarians trust their politicians to keep their promises; and East Germans (now part of the democratic and wealthy German Federal Republic) seem nearly as satisfied with democracy as their more established democratic partners in the West. It seems reasonable that the foundations of civic culture would be slower to take hold in countries that for three generations or more have been governed by authoritarian governments, where citizens have been socialized in a political culture devoid of competitive and meaningful elections, and where autonomous associations have been either banned outright or subordinated to the social collective and sharply regulated by state authority.[17]

Table 10.5 suggests, in effect, that the *variance patterns* within each group as well as across each group of democracies seem to challenge the primary assumption that the sample of twenty-one democracies (as of 1996) consists of a *single* sample. Thus we cannot assume a *single* mean represents the best predictor of the "typical" degree of political efficacy, trust, and satisfaction among the citizens within the sample. Nor can we assume there is one single population of democracies within our political world.

Rather, the data in Table 10.5 suggest we might modify our thinking and ask whether in fact there are not *two separate* samples in the broader group of twenty-one democracies (and therefore within the target population). Each sample has a *different* mean, the *size* of each mean is significantly different, and the *variance* of scores around each separate mean produces more error (the difference between the score and the mean of the sample) than we would find if we computed the comparable error in the larger sample of twenty-one democracies as a whole. If this was shown to be the case, we would, in effect, conclude that the means and variance patterns of the two separate samples were a product of some independent attribute that is crucial to political culture in general—something that was of different character and value in each separate group of countries that might account for the difference in the mean. In our case, we hypothesize that the independent factor that sharply distinguishes one group of democracies from the other is the extent of the broader democratic socialization. Citizens within established democracies of the West have been socialized into the nature and role of democratic governance and behavior (that is, their citizens have been exposed to the norms and values of democracy) for much longer and in much more intense circumstances than have their counterparts in the recent democracies of East and Central Europe. Thus, one group of democracies will see their citizenry holding a different level of political efficacy, political trust, and satisfaction with democracy than will be the case for the other group of democracies. At least, that is the "working" (or, not yet formalized) hypothesis that emerges from Table 10.5. How could we test this hypothesis?

Comparative Analysis and the Logic of Grouping

Actually, thinking in terms of broader "group" patterns is something quite common to students of cross-national analysis. Classification schemes are something that are common to students of science, and they are often effectively used to simplify and order a complex political world. By trying to specify the primary components of a broader concept, we often try to organize countries or units of our analysis into groups of countries according to how much of certain primary attributes the countries possess or do not possess. Efforts to achieve classification often lead students of comparative politics to suggest "types" of political systems.

Generally, a typology does not specify all the *necessary and sufficient* primary components that may distinguish different political systems, or countries, or other units of analysis of interest to the student of cross-national analysis (such as different types of political parties). Rather, they have a more general, less-specified core of critical attributes that seem to distinguish types of countries. For instance, Arend Lijphart's pioneering cross-national analysis focused on two types of democracies, which he labeled *consociational* and *non-consociational* democracies. This research was further refined into a typology of democracies that built on existing literature and utilized commonly known characteristics of democratic governance. His new typology distinguishes democracies according to whether they were *majoritarian* or *consensual*.[18]

We have already seen in Chapter 2 another strategy of comparativists, which involves grouping countries according to broad civilization attributes.[19] Other students of comparative political systems have distinguished, or grouped, countries according to the nature of the executives.[20] Still other scholars have contributed to our understanding of the political world by distinguishing countries according to the nature of interest-group involvement in government decisionmaking. This typology draws the distinction between *corporatist* and *non-corporatist* political systems.[21] Of course, students also attribute broader geo-cultural influences when they draw distinctions between countries according to the geographical location (Asian, Latin American, African, and so forth). And indeed, as we shall see in the next chapter, broader patterns of political and economic organization have long offered widely utilized classification schemes, such as those that distinguish countries according to whether their political economies are socialist, capitalist, developed, developing, industrial, post-industrial, agricultural.

The nature of grouping countries and national-level political systems often entails assessing attributes across countries that are merely measured at either the nominal or ordinal level. The measurement of these attributes is not so refined as to provide variables that have continuous values. Rather, scholars often broadly assign membership of countries to groups based on coding schemes that rank these countries along scales that attribute "more" or "less" of some broader empirical characteristic (for example, "more" democratic socialization or "less" democratic socialization). We have seen this in Chapter 7 with respect to the measurement of the primary components of democracy. Often, this grouping is merely dichotomous, the attribute assuming two broad values ("more," "less"). Other classifying variables may have several levels ("none," "some," or "many"). The important point is that students of comparative politics, often faced with daunting measurement challenges, commonly rely upon grouping strategies in order to discern relationships between key attributes that help in sorting out the pattern of governance and institutional authority across different countries in our political world, and from this they refine their conclusions for more precise and reliable general theory.

If both variables within a bivariate model are measured at either the ordinal or nominal level, we may rely on *nonparametric* statistics and employ cross-tabular analysis or other measures based on chi-square (for example, Mann-Whitney U). If, as is commonly the case, we have one variable that has continuous values and is therefore consistent with interval- or ratio-level measures, while the second variable is either ordinal or nominal, we may want to move to parametric statistics. This has the advantage of offering more precision and providing more confidence in our hypothesis test. However, parametric statistics also assume a reasonable approximation of a normal distribution. With small samples, the student may want to employ initially both nonparametric and parametric statistics in order to provide complementary confirmation. While some students of cross-national analysis prefer to avoid nonparametric analysis at any cost, prudence would dictate that sometimes it will be necessary to rely on a nonparametric application.

In our case, we have the advantage of having our original data (individual-based survey data) converted to interval-level data by computing the frequencies per category of the recoded original variables of political efficacy, trust, and satisfaction with democracy. The percentages reported in Table 10.5 are interval-level data. The unit of analysis has shifted with the aggregation of the ordinal data, from the person to the country. We cannot test hypotheses directed to individual behavior, yet we can explore patterns across countries to answer questions central our understanding of comparative institutional authority and behavior and to assert differences in political beliefs and attitudes across countries based on differing national experiences with democracy. The working hypotheses we wish to explore may now be specified:

Hypothesis 10.1a: The mean of the respective percentages of those citizens within established Western democracies who "agree" that "citizens have considerable influence on politics" will be significantly *larger* than the mean of the respective percentages of those citizens in recent democracies of East and Central Europe who "agree" that "citizens have considerable influence on politics."

Hypothesis 10.1b: The mean of the respective percentages of those citizens within established Western democracies who "neither agree nor disagree" that "citizens have considerable influence on politics" will be significantly *smaller* than the mean of the respective percentages of those citizens in recent democracies of East and Central Europe who "neither agree nor disagree" that "citizens have considerable influence on politics."

Hypothesis 10.1c: The mean of the respective percentages of those citizens within established Western democracies who "disagree" that "citizens have considerable influence on politics" will be significantly *smaller* than the mean of the respective percentages of those citizens in recent democracies of East and

Central Europe who "disagree" that "citizens have considerable influence on politics."

Hypothesis 10.2a: The mean of the respective percentages of those citizens within established Western democracies who "agree" that "elections are a good way of making governments pay attention to the important political issues facing our country" will be significantly *larger* than the mean of the respective percentages of those citizens in recent democracies of East and Central Europe who "agree" that "elections are a good way of making governments pay attention to the important political issues facing our country."

Hypothesis 10.2b: The mean of the respective percentages of those citizens within established Western democracies who "neither agree nor disagree" that "elections are a good way of making governments pay attention to the important political issues facing our country" will be significantly *smaller* than the mean of the respective percentages of those citizens in recent democracies of East and Central Europe who "neither agree nor disagree" that "elections are a good way of making governments pay attention to the important political issues facing our country."

Hypothesis 10.2c: The mean of the respective percentages of those citizens within established Western democracies who "disagree" that "elections are a good way of making governments pay attention to the important political issues facing our country" will be significantly *smaller* than the mean of the respective percentages of those citizens in recent democracies of East and Central Europe who "disagree" that "elections are a good way of making governments pay attention to the important political issues facing our country."

Hypothesis 10.3a: The mean of the respective percentages of those citizens within established Western democracies who "agree" that "people we elect as MPs try to keep the promises they have made during the election" will be significantly *larger* than the mean of the respective percentages of those citizens in recent democracies of East and Central Europe who "agree" that "people we elect as MPs try to keep the promises they have made during the election."

Hypothesis 10.3b: The mean of the respective percentages of those citizens within established Western democracies who "neither agree nor disagree" that "people we elect as MPs try to keep the promises they have made during the election" will be significantly *smaller* than the mean of the respective percentages of those citizens in recent democracies of East and Central Europe who "neither agree nor disagree" that "people we elect as MPs try to keep the promises they have made during the election."

Hypothesis 10.3c: The mean of the respective percentages of those citizens within established Western democracies who "disagree" that "people we elect as MPs try to keep the promises they have made during the election" will be significantly *smaller* than the mean of the respective percentages of those citizens in recent democracies of East and Central Europe who "disagree" that "people we elect as MPs try to keep the promises they have made during the election."

Hypothesis 10.4a: The mean of the respective percentages of those citizens within established Western democracies who say that "all in all, the system of democracy *works well* in our country these days" will be significantly *larger* than the mean of the respective percentages of those citizens in recent democracies of East and Central Europe who say that "all in all, the system of democracy *works well* in our country these days."

Hypothesis 10.4b: The mean of the respective percentages of those citizens within established Western democracies who say that "all in all, the system of democracy *does not work well* in our country these days" will be significantly *smaller* than the mean of the respective percentages of those citizens in recent democracies of East and Central Europe who say that "all in all, the system of democracy *does not work well* in our country these days."

These eleven hypotheses may be summarized as such:

Hypotheses 10.1a, 10.2a, 10.3a, and 10.4a: $\bar{X}_{ED} > \bar{X}_{RD}$
Hypotheses 10.1b, 10.1c, 10.2b, 10.2c, 10.3b, 10.3c, and 10.4b: $\bar{X}_{ED} < \bar{X}_{RD}$
The Null for each hypothesis: $\bar{X}_{ED} = \bar{X}_{RD}$
Where: $\bar{X}$ is the mean for the respective response pattern (agree, neither agree nor disagree, or disagree)
$_{ED}$ represents established, Western democracies
$_{RD}$ represents recent democracies of East and Central Europe

Note that each hypothesis (10.1a–10.4b) specifies not only an expected difference in the mean of the respective percentages for the two groups, but also specifies the direction of that difference. That is, we expect the typical proportion of citizens in established democracies to reflect more political efficaciousness, both internally and externally, more confidence and trust in the politicians to keep their promises, and more satisfaction with the state of democracy in their country than we do the typical proportion of citizens in more recent democracies of East and Central Europe (Hypotheses 10.1a, 10.2a, 10.3a, and 10.4a, respectively). However, we expect larger proportions of the public across more recent democracies to indicate less political efficaciousness, less trust, and less satisfaction with the way democracy works in their country (Hypotheses 10.1c, 10.2c, 10.3c, and 10.4b) and that the more recent democracies will have typically larger portions of their citizenry indicating an ambivalent orientation (neither agree nor disagree) to their civic culture (Hypotheses 10.1b, 10.2b, and 10.3b, respectively). The null hypothesis simply holds that there should be no statistically significant difference in the means across the two groups of democracies for any of the respective proportions (that is, variables).

DEMONSTRATION 10.1: THE MANN-WHITNEY U TEST

The results reported in Table 10.5 have been preserved in the data set EFFICACY.21. With such a small sample size (N = 21), it would be prudent to begin by testing the hypotheses with a nonparametric tool, as this will relax strict assumptions about the normal distribution of the sample. Furthermore, with such a small sample size, a parametric test that computes variance measures could be sharply influenced by just one country—an outlier. For instance, we have already noted that with respect to the "agree" proportion in AVGCIT3, Latvia is an "outlier" for the more recent democracies of East and Central Europe in the sample (Latvian % "agree" = 26.6), while Sweden is such an "outlier" for the more established democracies (Swedish % "agree" = 12.1). Therefore, as the sample size declines, it is more likely that one may have a severely skewed distribution in our continuous variable. The reason: The possibility of just one or two "outliers" distorting the sample increases as the sample size declines.

The Mann-Whitney U Test

The Mann-Whitney U test is ideally suited as a first step if it is suspected that such outliers may distort a distribution. You will recall from Chapter 5 that the Mann-Whitney U test relaxes the assumptions of strict normality in our sample distribution (in this case, the sample of scores measuring the respective proportions). The Mann-Whitney U statistic cannot technically be used to directly test differences of the means (which is strictly what the hypotheses call for). Rather, it can test for differences in the overall size of the values of a variable across two samples. It relies upon ranks of scores within a sample, rather than actual values of a score within a sample. If the Mann-Whitney U test shows some statistical significance, it offers further support for more sophisticated parametric tests.[22]

To grasp the simple logic of the Mann-Whitney U test, consider Table 10.6. This table lists the twenty-one countries in the sample EFFICACY.21 in ascending order according to the value of the variable AVGCIT31 (the proportion of those in each country who said they "agree" with the statement "the average citizen has considerable influence on politics"). Remember, these percentages have been computed from the original data reported in the survey data set, ROG3. The first column reports the country name, the second column reports the democracy (established Western democracies are coded as 1, more recent democracies East and Central Europe are coded as 2), the third column reports the overall rank of the country's score for AVGCIT3, from 1–21, and the fourth column reports the actual value of AVGCIT31 for the country (the proportion of citizens in their country-sample who said they agree that citizens make a difference in politics). Seven of the first ten countries (in ascending order of AVGCIT31) are recent democracies, nine of ten countries ranked 11–20 are established Western democracies. The respective ranks for the eight recent East

TABLE 10.6 Country Ranks, AVGCIT3, by Democracy (EFFICACY.21)

Country	*Democracy*	*Rank*	*AVGCIT1*
Czech Republic	2	1	9.4
Hungary	2	2	9.7
Slovenia	2	3	10.3
Sweden	1	4	12.1
Russia	2	5	12.7
East Germany	2	6	13.1
Great Britain	1	7	13.7
Poland	2	8	16.7
Norway	1	9	18.0
Bulgaria	2	10	18.1
West Germany	1	11	19.1
Australia	1	12	22.0
Italy	1	13	24.9
Canada	1	14	25.0
Spain	1	15	26.6
Latvia	2	16	26.6
Ireland	1	17	29.7
France	1	18	31.0
United States	1	19	32.2
Philippines	1	20	46.7
Japan	1	21	49.9

and Central European democracies are 1, 2, 3, 5, 6, 8, 10, and 16. Those of the thirteen established Western democracies are 4, 7, 9, 11, 12, 13, 14, 15, 17, 18, 19, 20, and 21. The *mean rank* for recent democracies of East and Central Europe is 6.38, and that of the established Western democracies is 13.85. The mean ranks for all the variables used to test Hypotheses 10.1a–10.4b are reported in Table 10.7.[23]

The specific statistical equation used to compute the Mann-Whitney U statistic, which is based on the two mean ranks, is exceedingly cumbersome and of little value in this context.[24] However, we can say that the smaller the Mann-Whitney U statistic, the more perfectly aligned are the ranks, and therefore, the larger are the differences between the mean ranks across the two groups. In the case of AVGCIT31, the Mann-Whitney U score computes to 15. Is this enough to reject the null? In other words, what is the probability of obtaining a Mann-Whitney U score of 15 *if we assume the null to be correct?*

The answer is reported in Table 10.8 along with all the Mann-Whitney U scores for all the hypotheses. The probability of obtaining a Mann-Whitney U score of 15 if the null is correct is .007. However this is a two-tail test of statistical significance, which assumes you have not predicted direction in your hypothesis. That is, it assumes you have not predicted which group of democracies will have a larger or smaller mean rank. In fact, we have.

TABLE 10.7 Mean Ranks, by DEMOCRAC (EFFICACY.21) SPSS 10

	Democracy	*N*	*Mean Rank*	*Sum of Ranks*
AVGCIT31: Agree	1 Established/West	13	13.85	180.00
	2 Recent/E-EC Europe	8	6.38	51.00
	Total	21		
AVGCIT32: Neither Agree/Disagree	1 Established/West	13	13.69	178.00
	2 Recent/E-EC Europe	8	6.63	53.00
	Total	21		
AVGCIT33: Disagree	1 Established/West	13	7.54	98.00
	2 Recent/E-EC Europe	8	16.63	133.00
	Total	21		
ELECT31: Agree	1 Established/West	13	13.62	177.00
	2 Recent/E-EC Europe	8	6.75	54.00
	Total	21		
ELECT32: Neither Agree/Disagree	1 Established/West	13	8.83	109.00
	2 Recent/E-EC Europe	8	15.25	122.00
	Total	21		
ELECT33: Disagree	1 Established/West	13	9.00	117.00
	2 Recent/E-EC Europe	8	14.25	114.00
	Total	21		
PROM31: Agree	1 Established/West	13	12.77	166.00
	2 Recent/E-EC Europe	8	8.13	65.00
	Total	21		
PROM32: Neither Agree/Disagree	1 Established/West	13	11.77	153.00
	2 Recent/E-EC Europe	8	9.75	78.00
	Total	21		
PROM33: Disagree	1 Established/West	13	9.31	121.00
	2 Recent/E-EC Europe	8	13.75	110.00
	Total	21		
SATDEM21: Works Well	1 Established/West	13	14.38	187.00
	2 Recent/E-EC Europe	8	5.50	44.00
	Total	21		
SATDEM22: Does Not Work Well	1 Established/West	13	7.62	99.00
	2 Recent/E-EC Europe	8	16.50	132.00
	Total	21		

One- and Two-Tail Significance Levels

What is a two-tail test, and how does it differ from a one-tail test? The logic of hypothesis testing is simple. If we assume the null to be the correct assessment of reality, we would expect that in a population of (for instance) 100 separate difference of means tests, we would find a distribution of resulting t-scores. Some would be large, some would be small, some would be positive, some would be negative, and some would be zero. If we could collect these 100 different t-statistics and plot them, we would see a

TABLE 10.8 Mann-Whitney U Values and Respective Statistical Significance Values Computed from Mean Ranks (EFFICACY.21)

Hypothesis and Relevant Variable	*Mann-Whitney U*	*p (2-tail)*	*p (1-tail)*	*Decision on Null*
Hyp. 10.1a: AVGCIT31 (Agree)	15	0.007	.004	May Reject
Hyp. 10.1b: AVGCIT32 (Neither)	17	0.011	.006	May Not Reject*
Hyp. 10.1c: AVGCIT33 (Disagree)	7	0.001	.000	May Reject
Hyp. 10.2a: ELECT31 (Agree)	18	0.014	.007	May Reject
Hyp. 10.2b: ELECT32 (Neither)	18	0.014	.007	May Reject
Hyp. 10.2c: ELECT33 (Disagree)	26	0.06	.03	May Reject
Hyp. 10.3a: PROM31 (Agree)	29	0.096	.05	May Reject
Hyp. 10.3b: PROM32 (Neither)	42	0.469	.235	May Not Reject
Hyp. 10.3c: PROM33 (Disagree)	30	0.111	.06	May Not Reject
Hyp. 10.4a: SATDEM21 (Works Well)	8	0.001	.000	May Reject
Hyp. 10.4b: SATDEM22 (Does Not Work Well)	8	0.001	.000	May Reject

* reject on basis of direction

normal distribution to the t-statistics. The null does not predict that every t-statistic will be 0. Rather, it simply says that we should not expect a t-statistic to be so different from 0 that we may reject the null. The logic of the null makes room for the assumption that error and variation in the real world are going to see some diversity—some variation in t-statistic across different samples. However, the variation should not be so great—if the null is correct—that we should find a t-statistic that is significantly different from 0. What would be significantly different from 0? A t-statistic that is so different from the zero that we would expect to find it five or fewer times in 100, if the null were true.

Look back at Figure 5.2. Each of the tails (the unshaded areas under the curve) represents 2.5 percent of the total area under the curve. If we do not specify direction in a hypothesis, we are in effect saying that we expect the t-statistic to be significantly different than 0. However, we are not saying we expect it to be larger or smaller. Therefore, we will accept a t-statistic that is larger than 0 or smaller than 0, but in order to reject the null it must be significantly larger or smaller than 0. For the threshold requirements, the t-statistic must be at least ±1.96 standard deviations from the mean (which the null assumes to be zero). Anything less would be different, but not different enough, so to speak. It would, in effect, simply be within the reasonable range of expected variation, but not so rare as to constitute a serious threat to the validity of the null. Why the threshold of ±1.96? Because as shown in Figure 5.2, this is the area under the normal curve where 5 percent of the cases can be expected to fall. Together, the tails of the curve (the $+1.96$ and the -1.96 ranges) sum to 5 percent of the total area under the curve.

If, however, we specify direction within the hypothesis, it affects the location, but not the total size of the critical region. A predicted *negative* sign would imply that the size of the resulting test statistic would be in an absolute sense large, but in a relative sense, it would be in a particular direction—negative. Thus, if we require a .05 probability level in our test statistic, as is customary, our critical region is 5 percent of the area under the normal curve. However, because we expect a negative direction to the relationship, we do not have a critical region to the right of the center line in Figure 5.2. This region would be in the positive range of the areas under the normal curve—the area where we would not expect to find our test statistic in a normally distributed range of test statistics.

To correct for this modification, we simply move the critical region on the right tail of the curve in Figure 5.2—the unshaded area under the normal curve—to the left side of the curve and "attach" it to the critical area on the left side of the curve. This produces an area under the curve that is still 5 percent of the total area under the curve, but that is located exclusively to the left side of the curve, consistent with the predicted negative direction to the test statistic. This is graphically illustrated in Figure 10.3. The effect of direction is to reduce the size of the t-statistic, from –1.96 to –1.67. However, adding direction to our hypothesis also means that we *must* obtain a test statistic that conforms to the direction we have predicted. No matter how large the test statistic, if its direction is opposite that predicted, we cannot reject the null hypothesis.

The same logic would apply when we predict a positive relationship. However, in the case of a predicted positive relationship, we would move the shaded area on the left tail in Figure 5.2 to the *right* and attach it to the unshaded area already on the far right tail. This would be the critical region under the normal curve where we would expect to find a test statistic falling if the relationship was positive and we were to reject the null. This is graphically illustrated in Figure 10.4.

Therefore, when we have predicted direction, we assess "one-tail" probability estimates of the test statistic. The "one-tail" refers to the fact that with direction, we now have only one side of the curve comprising the critical region under the normal curve where we must find our test statistic if it is to be large enough and in the predicted direction.

So, in order to reject the null, we must first determine whether the relative size of the mean ranks is in fact in the *direction* we have predicted. In the case of AVGCIT31, the relative size of the respective mean ranks is in our predicted direction: The established democracies have a larger mean rank for scores on AVGCIT31, indicating they have on the whole not only different proportions of people indicating they believe average citizens do make a difference in politics, but that in fact within these democracies the proportions of people saying they agree that citizens matter in politics is higher than in more recent democracies of East and Central Europe. When we have predicted direction in our hypothesis and the difference in the respective mean ranks is as predicted, we may divide the two-tail statistical significance estimate in half. Thus, our statistical significance for the Mann-Whitney U score of 15 is actually .004 (.007/2), meaning, the probability of obtaining a Mann-Whitney U score of 15 and having the relative size of the respective mean ranks directionally consistent with our hypothesis, *if we assume the null to be correct*, is actually 3.5 in 1000.

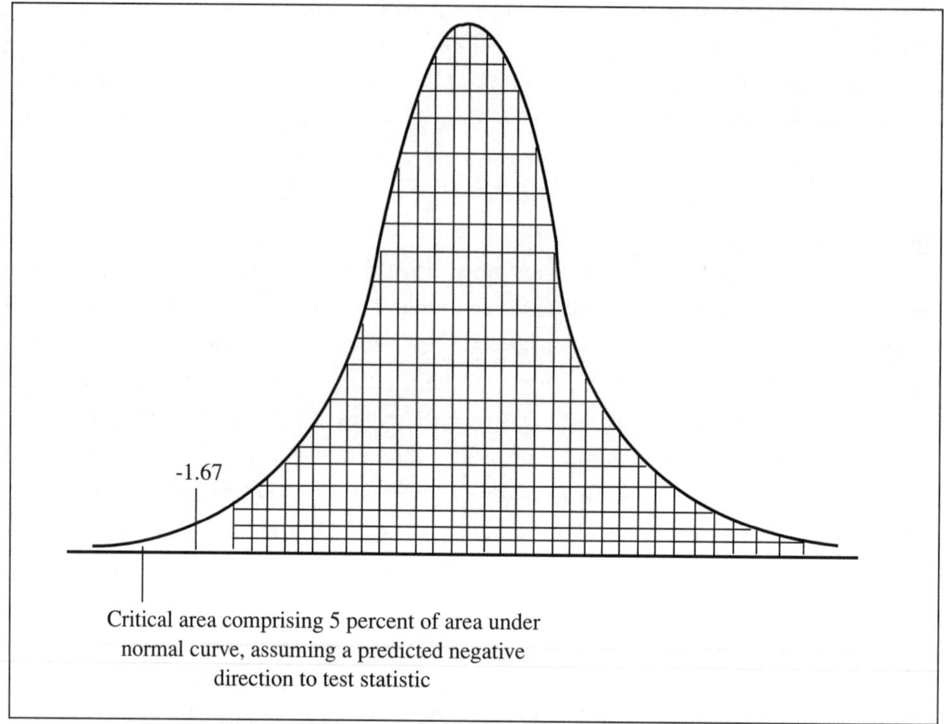

FIGURE 10.3 Graphical Depiction of Critical Region Under Normal Curve Assuming a Negative Relationship

Nonparametric Results

From Table 10.8 we see that we may reject all but three of the null hypotheses. The established democracies have higher mean ranks for AVGCIT32—the variable that reflects the proportion of citizens who express ambivalence about whether the average citizen has a considerable influence on politics within their country. The mean rank for the established democracies is 13.69 (indicating a higher proportion of citizens indicating they neither agree nor disagree with the statement that the average citizen makes a difference in politics), while the mean rank for the recent democracies of East and Central Europe is only 6.63. This underscores the picture portrayed in Table 10.5: More of the citizens in the recent democracies of East and Central Europe are willing to express clear disagreement with the idea that citizens play a considerable role in politics, than is the case with citizens in the more established democracies. In the established democracies, the modal category is clearly "disagree": They have weak political efficaciousness. However, this proportion among these democracies is typically much smaller than for the recent democracies of East and Central Europe.

In the case of the citizens trusting their politicians to keep their electoral promises, it is clear that with respect to the "agree" and "disagree" categories (PROM31 and

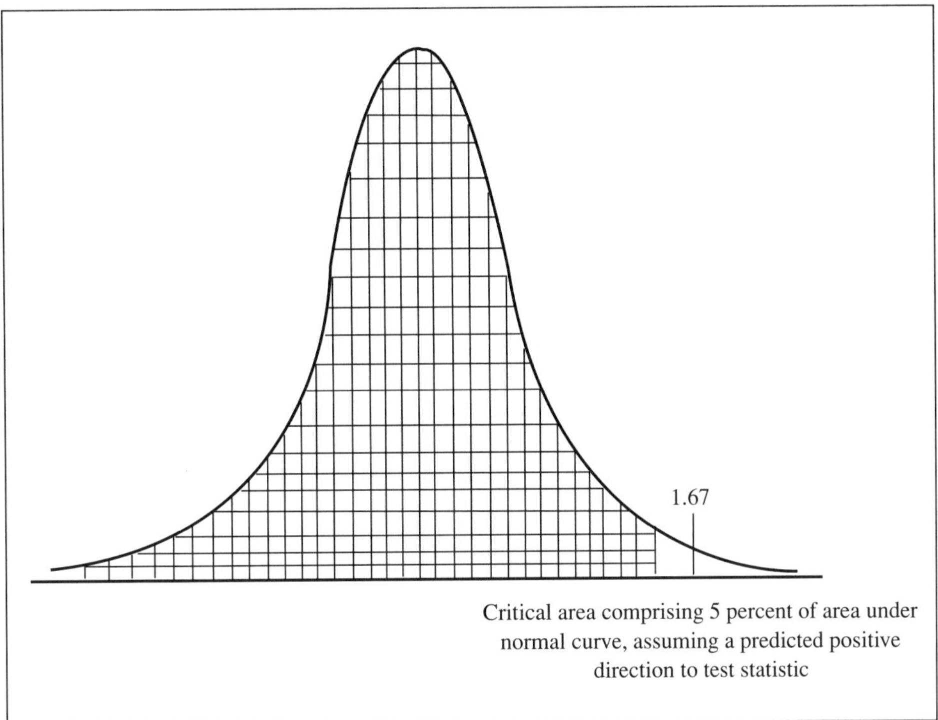

FIGURE 10.4 Graphical Depiction of Critical Region Under Normal Curve Assuming a Positive Relationship

PROM32), the direction is as predicted: Citizens in established democracies are slightly more likely to agree that politicians try to keep their electoral promises (mean rank, PROM31 = 11.77) than are the citizens of East and Central European democracies (mean rank PROM31 = 9.75). Citizens of established democracies are also less likely to disagree with the notion that politicians are likely to keep their electoral promises (mean rank = 9.31) than are the citizens of East and Central Europe (mean rank = 13.75). However, the sizes of the differences are on the borderline of the acceptable threshold for rejecting the null, p = .05 and .06, respectively. Thus, one must concede that the difference between the two groups of democracies with respect to trust of politicians is weak. Democratic socialization would seem to have only a marginal influence, at best, in shaping one's trust in politicians to keep their campaign promises. In other words, skepticism about the trustworthiness of politicians to keep their campaign promises is something of a general attribute across democracies—at least as reflected in our sample as of 1996.

One final cautionary note. Keep in mind that we are not working with a true "random" sample. Rather, our sample of twenty-one countries is a "fixed" sample. That is, we have taken a given array of countries, all within a more general set that we might classify as "democracies," and tested a hypothesis that applies only to that set of countries. The target population—all democracies—has not been randomly sampled in deriving our sample of twenty-one democracies. We used, rather, an existing set of countries from the set and have provided initial findings to suggest a conclusion that has no bearing beyond this set of countries. This is a common practice within the literature. This caveat, however, does not render our conclusion false. It simply limits our range of generalization from the findings. We may reject the null, but must be sure we explain to the relevant audience that we cannot generalize beyond that small set of countries, and even within this set (democracies), we must remain cautious because we have not established a sampling procedure. We have simply taken a fixed set of similar countries (and therefore avoided concept stretching).

DIFFERENCE OF MEANS

The Mann-Whitney U statistic clearly points the way to the general conclusion that established democracies of the West are more likely to have a civic culture that approximates the ideal bases of democratic politics than are the more recent democracies of East and Central Europe. However, if the student of comparative politics seeks more precision, as well as findings that may offer more exact conclusions regarding the different patterns across the two groups of democracies, the student may move to a difference of means test (often referred to as the t-test). The Mann-Whitney U test is based on ranks. It makes no assumption about variance in the sample. Indeed, there is no accounting for how much larger Japan's value for AVGCIT31 is than Sweden's. It is larger and is ranked accordingly (in ascending order, Japan's value for AVGCIT31 is ranked 21, and Sweden is ranked 4). But no variance is computed.

Figure 10.5 reports the histogram for AVGCIT31. While the distribution does not conform perfectly to a normal distribution (the curve represents what should be a normal distribution for this variable), country scores are not concentrated at one end or the other of the scale, and, it is not poly-modal (more than one hump to its curve). Having already explored the nonparametric test, we may proceed to parametric analysis knowing the potential limitations such an analysis holds.

What is a difference of means test? As its name implies, it tests the null hypothesis that there is no difference in the means between one group and another with respect to an attribute that is measured as a continuous variable—a variable approximating at least an interval-level measure. In essence, the difference of means test allows us to validate or refute our assumption that the mean in one group (or sample) of countries is statistically different than the mean in the second group (or sample) of democracies. The null holds that there is no difference in such variance, implying the population of democracies with respect to the attribute in question (AVGCIT31) does not consist of two different groups, but only one. If we believe the attribute of political socialization varies across our two groups of democracies, this will show up in the size of the mean for the two groups.

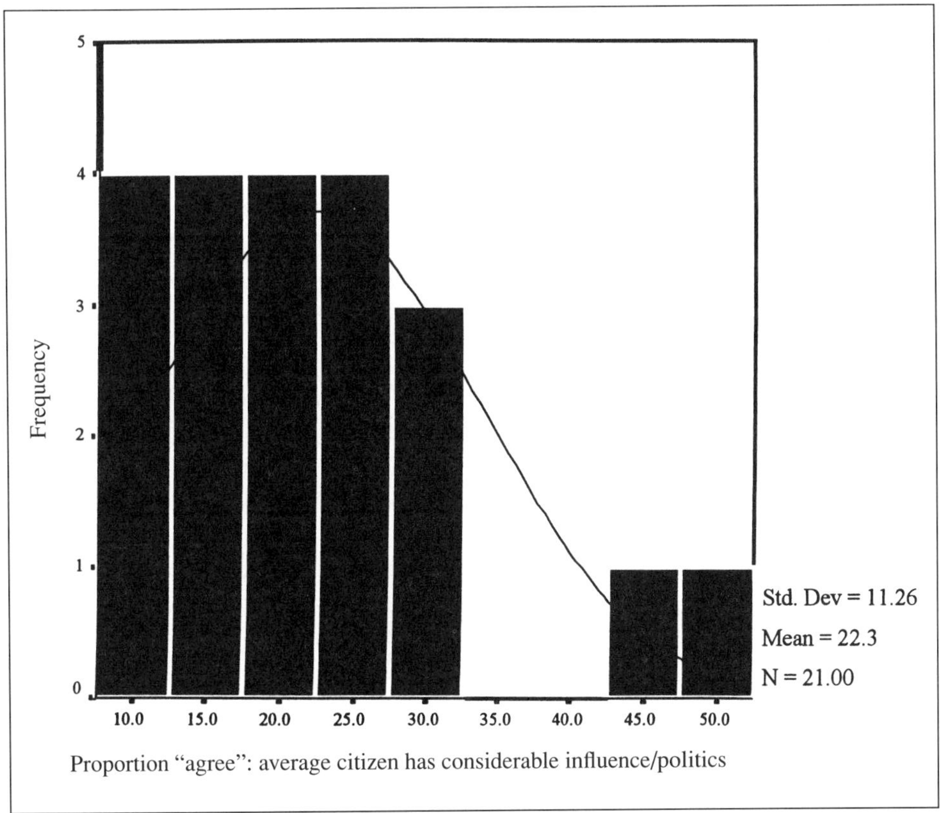

FIGURE 10.5 Histogram, Proportion who Agree that Citizens Influence Politics (AVGCIT31)

The Logic of the Difference of Means (t-test)

A t-test is a member of the family of statistical procedures called "analysis of variance" techniques. As the name implies, these statistics measure the variance patterns of the dependent variable relative to the variance patterns of the independent variable. Specifically, a t-test procedure determines whether there is a significant difference between mean values of a dependent variable (for example, AVGCIT31) across the two categories of the independent variable (for example, DEMOCRACY) in a bivariate model. You have, no doubt, seen many examples where someone will compare a mean of one group with the mean of another group (such as comparing voting turnout rates among the wealthy and the poor or comparing the grade point average of freshmen and sophomores in a university).

All too often, unfortunately, the reader is presented with comparisons across groups without supporting evidence to confirm that the differences can be properly explained by the attribute of the group variable. If we observe that the "wealthy" vote more than the "poor," we cannot conclude that this confirms the relationship between wealth and voting turnout; in other words, we cannot be certain that this fact is not simply a fluke of the particular sample we have chosen. We cannot generalize to a population of circumstances. Our findings are based only on a particular sample and setting. And, for the sake of illustration, if we find that sophomores have a higher GPA than freshmen in college, we cannot conclude that one more year of collegiate experience is the explanation for this difference. We need more evidence. We need the proper statistical tools to go beyond casual speculation.

To even suggest such an association (and implied causality), we must first be able to show that the difference of the observed means is larger than we would have expected if we had simply randomly assigned GPAs or voting rates to people in both groups. This is at the heart of t-tests and analysis of variance techniques. It is what we imply when we hypothesize that citizens within more recent democracies will exhibit weaker democratic attributes than citizens within established democracies. We need more than the means between the two groups of countries. We also need specialized measures of *variance.*

As we have suggested, the t-test and other analysis of variance statistics require some basic assumptions be met to appropriately test our hypothesis. First, the individual groups themselves within the whole sample cannot be biased in the selection of countries to the sample, meaning that the inclusion of a country in one group cannot determine the selection of a second country into a second group. The two samples (groups) must be independent. Second, the distributions of the dependent variable (for example, AVGCIT31) within each of the categories of the independent variable (DEMOCRACY) should have variances that are not greatly different. This second condition means that the scores of the dependent variable are spread somewhat evenly above and below the mean of each of the respective groups. Substantial violations of either of these two conditions reduces the "robustness" of the test. A robust test is one where there is sufficient variance in the dependent variable to be compared with the variance in the values of the independent variable. T-tests are able to tolerate some violations of these stricter assumptions. Indeed, as we shall see, when we employ a statistical test within the t-test procedure to test for the equality of variance, and when such equality cannot be assumed, adjustments to the estimate of the difference of means can be made that still allow a reliable estimate. However, we should try to avoid severe violations of this assumption.

Z-Scores and a Cursory Examination of the Difference of Means

The t-statistic reflects the degree to which the variance of the dependent variable (AVGCIT31) across the whole sample deviates from the respective variances of the dependent variable across each of the two groups (or, subgroups) separately. This can often be seen very simply by converting our measures to standard scores (z-scores). Recall from Chapter 4 that a z-score is merely a different way of expressing the value of a score in a sample. It reflects the relative proportion of the score to the sample mean, in standard units. A sample of z-scores (that is, a sample of raw scores converted to z-scores) has a mean of 0 and a standard deviation of 1. The z-score is computed by subtracting the value of the raw sore from the mean, and dividing this quotient by the sample standard deviation (see Formula 4.1, Chapter 4). If we compute the z-score for AVGCIT31 across the sample of twenty-one democracies, we can more easily discern sharp deviations among country-scores from the sample mean. The larger a z-score (±), the greater the difference between a score and the sample mean.

Consider Table 10.9. This reports the z-score values for each of the variables in the dataset EFFICACY.21. Japan's z-score for AVGCIT31 is 2.451. This means that Japan's degree of political efficaciousness is nearly 2.5 standard deviations from the sample mean, or, alternatively, that the degree of Japanese political efficaciousness is *greater* than 99.29 percent of the target population (see Chapter 4). The z-score for the citizens of the Czech Republic is –1.142, indicating that the citizenry of the Czech Republic has a sense of political efficaciousness that is *weaker* than 92.22 percent of the target population. Of more immediate relevance for our purposes is the respective mean of the z-scores for the two separate groups of democracies in Table 10.9. The sample mean for all twenty-one z-scores of AVGCIT31 is 0. However, the separate mean z-score for the thirteen established democracies is .419, and that of the eight East and Central European democracies is -.681. Immediately, this suggests that the variance of the sample of twenty-one democracies does not accurately reflect the respective variance of the two groups of democracies. If the sample variance were identical to the respective group variance, the mean z-score for each group would be closer to 0 than is the case here. Indeed, for many of the variables in Table 10.9, the standard deviation of the z-scores within each group sharply differs, as well. The standard deviation of the z-sores for AVGCIT31 among the established democracies is .931, while the corresponding standard deviation for recent democracies of East and Central Europe is only .455.[25] Again, this underscores the evidence we already have that the two groups are distinct with respect to the primary attribute of political efficacy. The question, again, is whether this difference in means and the variance upon which the means are based are statistically significant, or only reflective of the normal range of differences one would expect across samples, *even if the null were true*.

Variance and the Logic of a Difference of Means Test

To determine the statistical significance of differences of means and variance across groups within a population, we partition the variance within the population into its three logical and separate components. The technical names we give to these three separate components of variance in a standard difference of means test are:

- *Total Sum of Squares* (equivalent to the overall sample variance)
- *Within-Group Sum of Squares* (equivalent to variance within each defined group)
- *Between-Group Sum of Squares* (which is the difference between the *total sum of squares* and the *within-group sum of squares*)

TABLE 10.9 Standard Scores (Z -Scores) for Measures of Political Efficacy, Political Trust, Satisfaction with Democracy (EFFICACY.21)

Country	*AVGCIT31*	*AVGCIT32*	*AVGCIT33*	*ELECTS31*	*ELECTS32*	*ELECTS33*	*PROM31*	*PROM32*	*PROM32*	*SATDEM21*	*SATDEM22*
					Established Western Democracies						
Australia	-0.023	-0.316	0.134	1.064	-1.164	-0.805	0.890	0.307	-0.750	1.220	-1.220
West Germany	-0.284	1.383	-0.256	0.491	-0.171	-0.548	0.037	0.333	-0.187	1.198	-1.198
Great Britain	-0.764	0.219	0.575	0.618	-0.244	-0.676	0.268	0.826	-0.582	0.576	-0.576
United States	0.880	0.549	-0.951	0.961	-0.866	-0.816	0.465	-0.216	-0.209	0.605	-0.605
Italy	0.233	0.018	-0.206	-0.591	-0.110	0.812	-1.143	-1.818	1.655	-1.536	1.536
Ireland	0.660	-1.430	-0.048	1.293	-2.187	-0.605	0.948	-1.276	-0.021	1.078	-1.078
Norway	-0.375	1.408	-0.187	1.779	-1.577	-1.523	0.841	2.006	-1.542	1.444	-1.444
Sweden	-0.906	1.869	0.101	0.481	0.969	-1.085	-0.673	1.807	-0.423	0.028	-0.028
Canada	0.245	0.482	-0.384	-0.363	0.432	0.257	0.505	1.002	-0.827	0.781	-0.781
Philippines	2.172	1.812	-2.512	0.734	0.364	-1.118	2.165	0.521	-1.716	-0.093	0.093
Japan	2.451	-0.398	-1.954	-0.640	0.801	0.435	-0.760	-0.504	0.758	0.714	-0.714
Spain	0.385	0.233	-0.413	0.462	-0.481	-0.362	-0.505	-0.831	0.745	0.160	-0.160
France	0.774	-0.393	-0.521	-0.621	-1.393	1.468	-0.090	-0.428	0.268	0.390	-0.390
Mean	0.419	0.418	-0.509	0.436	-0.433	-0.351	0.227	0.133	-0.218	0.505	-0.505
Standard Deviation	0.931	0.906	0.791	0.722	0.891	0.792	0.826	1.047	0.866	0.718	0.718
					Recent Democracies of East Europe and the Former Soviet Union						
East Germany	-0.811	0.213	0.617	-0.624	0.531	0.545	-0.616	-0.218	0.522	0.075	-0.075
Hungary	-1.115	-1.737	1.580	-2.228	1.998	1.896	-1.120	-0.629	1.062	-1.838	1.838
Czech Republic	-1.142	-0.630	1.205	-0.543	0.697	0.361	-0.585	0.790	0.012	-0.547	0.547
Slovenia	-1.060	-1.138	1.318	-1.631	1.056	1.584	-0.174	-0.228	0.228	-0.496	0.496
Poland	-0.490	-0.621	0.643	0.614	0.147	-0.859	-0.396	-0.364	0.444	-0.105	0.105
Bulgaria	-0.370	-0.297	0.424	0.308	0.630	-0.700	2.229	1.003	-1.993	-0.727	0.727
Russia	-0.848	-0.971	1.076	-0.455	0.270	0.454	-1.043	-1.103	1.240	-2.060	2.060
Latvia	0.388	-0.252	-0.241	-1.113	0.298	1.285	-1.245	-0.981	1.317	-0.867	0.867
Mean	-0.681	-0.679	0.828	-0.709	0.703	0.571	-0.369	-0.216	0.354	-0.821	0.821
Standard Deviation	0.455	0.532	0.516	0.830	0.527	0.883	0.982	0.672	0.936	0.673	0.673

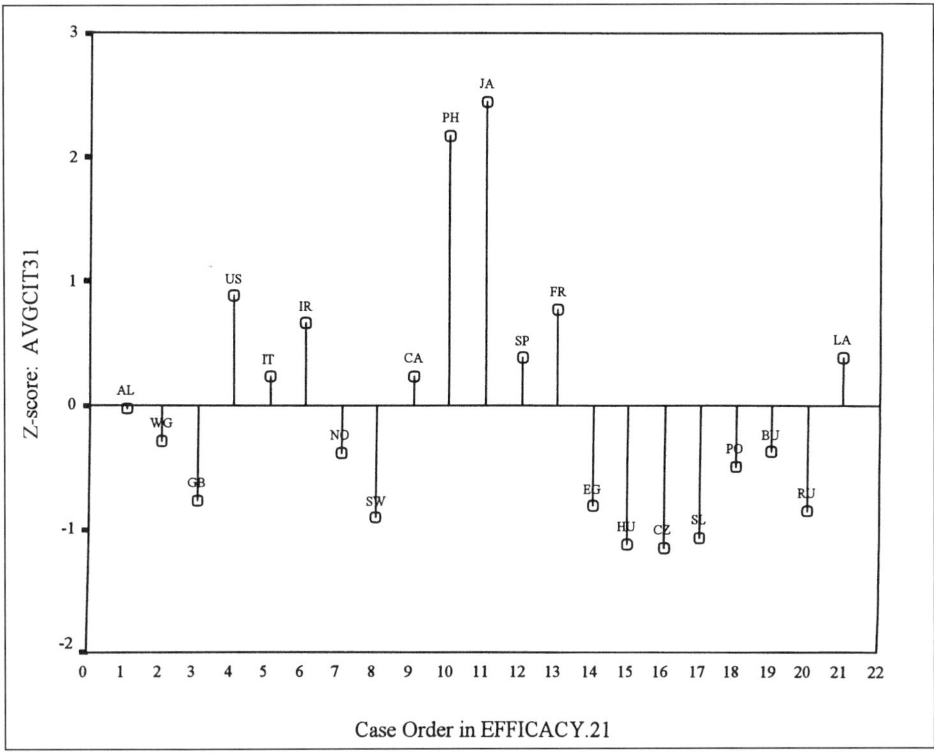

FIGURE 10.6 Z-Scores by Country

Consider Figure 10.6. The horizontal axis in this table reflects each of the twenty-one countries in the sample, EFFICACY.21, ordered by their appearance within the dataset. The vertical axis measures the respective z-score value for AVGCIT31 (in EFFICACY.21, this is presented by variable ZAVGCT31). Each country's z-score for AVGCIT31 is plotted with the country's abbreviated code adjacent the marker indicating the value of the z-score. The sample mean is represented by the horizontal line intersecting the vertical axis at 0. The mean for any sample of z-scores (based on a sample of the entire set of twenty-one democracies) is 0. The spikes extending from the line representing the mean to the individual score for each country reflect the error for that point estimate. In other words, the best predictor for any individual score is the mean. The further an actual score is from the mean, the greater the error. If we measured the distance of each spike and squared its value (to correct for lines that fall above or below the line representing the mean), we would have the Total Sum of Squares for the sample—the variance of the sample of z-scores for AVGCIT31. The shorter the spikes, the smaller will be the error, and the smaller will be the sum of squares for the sample. This, of course, holds whether the data are z-scores or raw data. A z-score simply makes comparison easier to visualize—it does nothing to the variance in the sample. It simply places the variance, and individual error, on a standard scale.

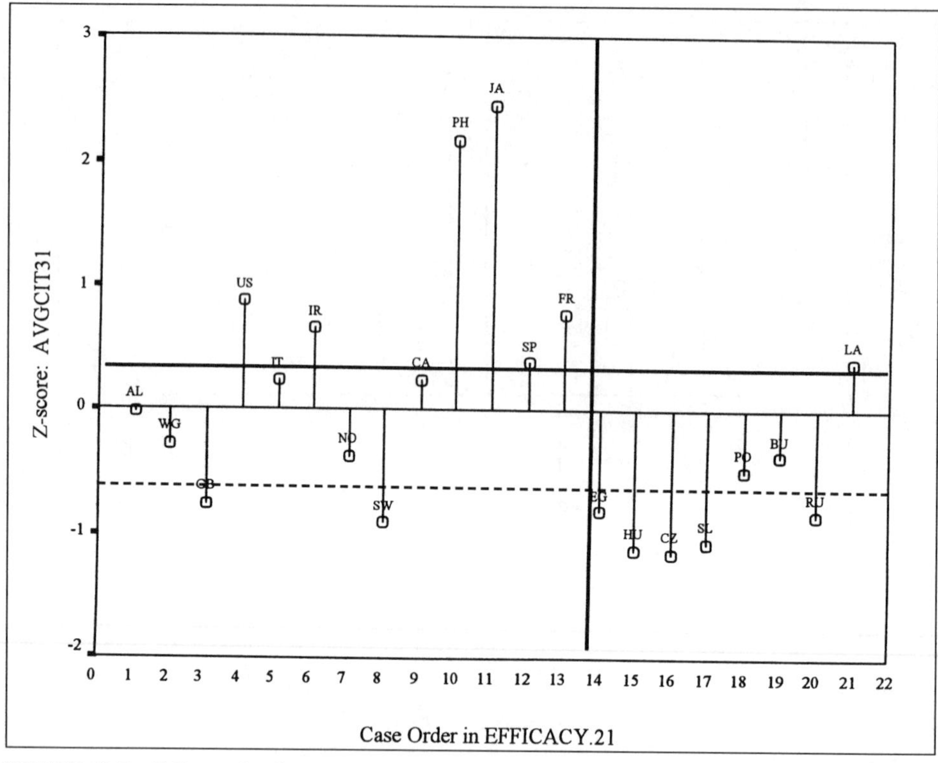

FIGURE 10.7 Z-Scores by Country and Democracy

Now consider Figure 10.7. This has three critical differences from Figure 10.6. First, the means for each group separately have been represented by the horizontal lines above and below the sample mean line. Second, the horizontal axis has been divided in two, thus identifying those countries that are the established democracies of the West from those that are recent democracies of East and Central Europe. The dividing line is the thick vertical line between France (FR) and East Germany (EG). This reflects the partition of the within-group variance required for difference of means tests. To the left of the thick vertical horizontal line are all the established democracies, and to the right are the recent democracies of East and Central Europe. The third distinguishing feature of Figure 10.7 is the spikes running from each country's z-score for AVGCIT31 to the respective group mean line. The lengths of the spikes, for the most part, are shorter than they are in Figure 10.6. Why? Because the mean of the particular group is a better predictor of each country's z-score than is the mean of the sample as a whole. There are, of course, some exceptions. For example, all those established democracies whose z-scores for AVGCIT31 are smaller than the sample mean—Germany (WG), Great Britain (GB), Norway (NO), and SWEDEN (SW)—were closer to the sample mean than the mean of the group of established Western democracies. Thus, their spikes in Table 10.7 are longer than they are in Figure 10.6. This is also the case for Latvia: Its z-score value of AVGCIT31 is closer to the sample mean as a whole than to the group mean for recent democracies of East and Central Europe.

Overall, however, if we square the length of the distance between each spike and the respective point within the separate groups of democracies, we should find (if our hypotheses have any basis in truth) that the sum of these squared values for each separate group is smaller than would be the case if we worked from the sample mean and not the individual group mean. This is reflected in the following simple equation:

(Total Sample Sum of Squares – Within-Group Sum of Squares) >
(TotalWithin-Group Sum of Squares), or
(Betweeen-Group Sum of Squares) > (Within-Group Sum of Squares)

The null hypothesis predicts that the mean value of AVGCIT31 for established Western democracies will be the *same* (or nearly the same) as the mean value of AVGCIT31 for more recent democracies of East and Central Europe. Our research hypotheses are specified in hypotheses 10.1a–10.4b, except now we are predicting differences in means across the two groups, not differences in ranks. If there is an association between political efficacy (AVGCIT31) and the democratic socialization of a country (DEMOCRAC), then we should find that the *within-group variance* for each group of AVGCIT31 is much *smaller* than the *sample total variance* of AVGCIT31.

If the *Total Sum of Squares* equals the *Within-Group Sum of Squares* (which is the sum of each group's separate sum of squares), there is no difference in variance between the sample and the respective groups. Thus, the means will be the same. This has the logic of the PRE—the proportional reduction in errors explained in Chapter 9. That is, if we find the *Total Sum of Squares* equals the *Within-Group Sum of Squares*, there is no improvement in our ability to predict the values of AVGCIT31 for any country by knowing the group to which that country belongs (DEMOCRAC) over what we would expect if we were to guess the value of AVGCIT31 for the country to be the sample mean of AVGCIT31. This is precisely what the null predicts: no proportional reduction in any errors in predicting the value of X (AVGCIT31) from Y (DEMOCRAC) over that we would find if we simply argued that the value of a country's AVGCIT31 equals the sample mean of AVGCIT31.

Equation 10.1 defines a t-test statistic:

$$t = \frac{\bar{X}_1 - \bar{X}_2}{\sqrt{\left[\frac{\sum x_1^2 + \sum x_2^2}{N_1 + N_2 - 2}\right]\left[\frac{N_1 + N_1}{N_1 N_2}\right]}} \qquad \text{Formula 10.1}$$

where $\bar{X}_1$ is the mean of variable X for Group 1, and $\bar{X}_2$ is the mean of variable X for Group 2; x_1^2 is the sum of the squared nominal deviations for Group 1 (nominal deviation $= \bar{X}_1 - X_i$ in Group 1), x_2^2 is the sum of the squared nominal deviations for

Group 2 (nominal deviation = $\bar{X}_2 - X_i$ in Group 2). The denominator of Formula 10.1 is the standard error estimate of the mean. This formula may also be stated in terms of the variance components entailed in analysis of variance techniques. Thus:

$$t\text{-test} = \sqrt{\frac{\left[\frac{BGV}{k-1}\right]}{\left[\frac{TWGV}{N-k}\right]}} \qquad \text{Formula 10.2}$$

Where BGV is *between-group variance* (the difference between the total sample sum of squares and the total within-group sum of squares), TWGV is *total within-group variance*, k is the number of groups in the independent variable (in a t-test, k = 2), and N is the number of cases in the sample. The N and k terms establish the degrees of freedom within the model. The difference of means may vary by the number of groups in the independent variable (in a t-test, the independent has only two groups, as in our model, Western democracy or East/Central European democracy), as well as by the total number of cases in the model (as in our case, twenty-one). However, once you know the mean of one group, you will know the mean of the second group (thus, k – 1), and as all cases are assigned to one group or another in the model, all cases in the model are free to vary except the last case in each group, which must assume a size necessary to equal the group's mean value. So, the second component of the degrees of freedom in a standard t-test model is N –2 (in our case, nineteen).

This may seem unduly cumbersome and complex, but its logic is simple and central to understanding the basis upon which we utilize variance to test hypotheses. The difference of means and its variance measures reduces to this simple point: *If we have no improvement in our ability to accurately estimate the value of a score for a country from the group mean to which that country belongs, over the accuracy we could expect if we were to predict the value of a country from the sample mean itself, we have no basis to our claim that we have two independent samples.*[26]

DEMONSTRATION 10.2: DIFFERENCE OF MEANS TEST

Tables 10.10 and 10.11 report the core statistical results of a difference of means test executed in SPSS 10.[27] The output consists of two parts: an analysis of the means (Table 10.10) and an analysis of the variance across the specific groups of countries in the respective models (Table 10.11). The output reported in Tables 10.10 and 10.11 represents the key diagnostic statistics for difference of means. It is not common to report all these statistics in a t-test (ordinarily, only the mean, standard deviation, N, t-statistic and p value are reported). However, the output offers additional information for the student should additional questions arise. Let's turn directly to the analysis of

TABLE 10.10 Summary of Means, AVGCIT31 (EFFICACY.21) SPSS 10

	Democrac	*N*	*Mean*	*Std. Deviation*	*Std. Error Mean*
AVGCIT31	1 Established/West	13	26.983	11.328	3.142
	2 Recent/E-EC Europe	8	14.593	5.812	2.055
AVGCIT32	1 Established/West	13	18.983	4.648	1.289
	2 Recent/E-EC Europe	8	13.772	2.864	1.013
AVGCIT33	1 Established/West	13	54.034	11.241	3.118
	2 Recent/E-EC Europe	8	71.635	7.697	2.721
ELECT31	1 Established/West	13	70.042	8.213	2.278
	2 Recent/E-EC Europe	8	57.987	9.912	3.505
ELECT32	1 Established/West	13	13.852	3.807	1.056
	2 Recent/E-EC Europe	8	18.346	2.363	.836
ELECT33	1 Established/West	13	16.106	7.016	1.946
	2 Recent/E-EC Europe	8	23.666	8.208	2.902
PROM31	1 Established/West	13	23.107	8.187	2.271
	2 Recent/E-EC Europe	8	17.648	10.213	3.611
PROM32	1 Established/West	13	23.590	7.453	2.067
	2 Recent/E-EC Europe	8	21.286	5.023	1.776
PROM33	1 Established/West	13	53.303	12.695	3.521
	2 Recent/E-EC Europe	8	61.066	14.415	5.097
SATDEM21	1 Established/West	13	69.356	15.501	4.299
	2 Recent/E-EC Europe	8	42.860	15.254	5.393
SATDEM22	1 Established/West	13	30.644	15.501	4.299
	2 Recent/E-EC Europe	8	57.140	15.254	5.393

variance, as the means and standard deviations reported in Table 10.10 (as well as their respective confidence intervals) are straightforward.

Levene's Test for Equality

The Levene's test for equality (the details of which are not important here) tests the hypothesis that the variances of the two respective groups are equal. The F statistic for the Levene's test is the measure of its equality, and the corresponding significance value indicates whether we may reject the null of equality (based on the size of the F score, which itself is conditioned by the number of countries in our sample, and the number of variables in the model). If p is equal to or less than .05, we may reject the null and assume the variances of the two respective groups are *not* equal. In this case, the computation for the degrees of freedom is adjusted accordingly and one must rely on the

TABLE 10.11 ANOVA Statistics, AVGCIT31 (EFFICACY.21) SPSS 10

		Levene's Test for Equality of Variances		T-Test for Equality of Means						
									95% Confidence Interval of the Difference	
		F	*Sig.*	*t*	*df*	*Sig. (2-tailed)*	*Mean Difference*	*Std. Error Difference*	*Lower*	*Upper*
AVGCIT31	Equal variances assumed	2.102	.163	2.851	19	.010	12.389	4.345	3.295	21.484
	Equal variances not assumed			3.300	18.621	.004	12.389	3.754	4.521	20.258
AVGCIT32	Equal variances assumed	1.989	.175	2.841	19	.010	5.212	1.835	1.372	9.051
	Equal variances not assumed			3.179	18.986	.005	5.212	1.639	1.780	8.643
AVGCIT33	Equal variances assumed	.353	.559	-3.885	19	.001	-17.601	4.530	-27.083	-8.119
	Equal variances not assumed			-4.253	18.671	.000	-17.601	4.138	-26.273	-8.929
ELECT31	Equal variances assumed	.212	.651	3.022	19	.007	12.054	3.989	3.706	20.403
	Equal variances not assumed			2.884	12.828	.013	12.054	4.180	3.012	21.097
ELECT32	Equal variances assumed	2.941	.103	-2.987	19	.008	-4.494	1.505	-7.643	-1.345
	Equal variances not assumed			-3.338	18.977	.003	-4.494	1.346	-7.313	-1.676
ELECT33	Equal variances assumed	.145	.708	-2.250	19	.036	-7.560	3.360	-14.593	-.528
	Equal variances not assumed			-2.164	13.158	.049	-7.560	3.494	-15.099	-2.164E-02
PROM31	Equal variances assumed	.001	.982	1.352	19	.192	5.459	4.038	-2.993	13.912
	Equal variances not assumed			1.280	12.491	.224	5.459	4.266	-3.794	14.713
PROM32	Equal variances assumed	1.796	.196	.770	19	.451	2.304	2.993	-3.962	8.569
	Equal variances not assumed			.845	18.745	.409	2.304	2.725	-3.405	8.013
PROM33	Equal variances assumed	.000	.983	-1.294	19	.211	-7.763	6.001	-20.323	4.797
	Equal variances not assumed			-1.253	13.485	.231	-7.763	6.194	-21.097	5.570
SATDEM21	Equal variances assumed	.013	.909	3.826	19	.001	26.497	6.925	12.003	40.990
	Equal variances not assumed			3.842	15.154	.002	26.497	6.897	11.809	41.184
SATDEM22	Equal variances assumed	.013	.909	-3.826	19	.001	-26.497	6.925	-40.990	-12.003
	Equal variances not assumed			-3.842	15.154	.002	-26.497	6.897	-41.184	-11.809

estimates that are specified for the "equal variance not assumed" row within the output. If $p > .05$, we may accept the null and work from the output that estimates the degrees of freedom (and therefore the analysis of variance computation of the t-test, as shown in Equation 10.2) based on the assumption that the variances of the two groups are equal. In each of the eleven models reported in Table 10.11, the Levene's test confirms equality of variance.

The T-Statistic

In the case of AVGCIT31, we note the t-statistic to be 2.851 (assuming equal variance across the two groups of countries). While not reported in the output shown in Table 10.11, the total sum of squares in the model is 2536.636, the total within-group sum of squares is 1776.433, and the resulting total between-group sum of squares is 760.203 (2536.636 – 1776.433).[28] Controlling for the respective degrees of freedom as specified in Equation 10.2, the t-statistic computes to 2.851. From this t-statistic, we know that the variance in the whole sample is far greater than the variance in the separate samples. Indeed, the t-statistic tells us that the variance within the groups is tighter and less prone to error, and is therefore more accurate in predicting the value of a country's political efficacy within the group, than is the case for the sample as a whole. In other words, using the whole sample would result in greater error overall and less accuracy in estimating the degree of political efficaciousness among citizens of a democracy.

If a t-statistic is at least ±1.96, the score will be statistically significant ($p \leq .05$), whether we have or have not predicted direction. If we have predicted direction (as we have), we need a t-statistic of at least ±1.65, depending on the direction of our prediction. Generally, if the t-statistic is negative (-), the mean score for the set of countries (or cases) specified as Group 2 in the model will be *larger* than the mean score for those countries specified as Group 1. If the t-statistic is positive (+), the mean score for the set of countries (or cases) specified as Group 1 in the model will be *larger* than the mean score for those countries specified as Group 2. In our model, Group 1 contains the Western democracies, and Group 2 the East and Central European democracies (see Table 10.10). Note the t-statistic for AVGCIT31 is 2.851. The mean for established democracies (Group 1) is 26.983 while that of East and Central Europe is 14.593. Thus, Group 1 > Group 2, resulting in a positive (+) t-statistic. On the other hand, we note the t-statistic for AVGCIT33 (those who disagree that citizens have a considerable influence on politics) to be –3.885. The mean for established democracies in this model is 16.106, while that of East and Central Europe is 23.666. Thus, as Group 1 < Group 2, the direction of the t-statistic is negative (-). In summary, in order to reject the null, we must make sure the direction of the t-statistic conforms to our prediction.

Table 10.11 confirms that the t-statistic for two models are in a direction *contrary* to our specified hypothesis: AVGCIT32 and PROM32. In the case of the former model, the t-statistic is statistically significant ($p = .01$). However, the direction is wrong for our hypothesis (as already suggested in the Mann-Whitney U test). In the case of PROM32 and PROM33, neither t-statistic is statistically significant ($p = .225$ and .105, respective one-tail values), results consistent with those of our Mann-Whitney U test. Indeed, the t-statistic for PROM31 also fails to meet the threshold requirement for rejecting the null hypothesis ($p = .096$, one-tail). This is slightly different than the Mann-Whitney U test, which showed this model to be on the border of statistical significance ($p = .05$). In this case, with a contradiction between the parametric and non-parametric tests, one would be prudent in not rejecting the null. Note finally that the reported p values in Table 10.11 are based on two tails. Recall from our discussion of the Mann-Whitney U test that if we predict direction, we simply divide the two-tail p by 2 to derive the relevant p. However, as noted above, with direction predicted (and depending upon the direction predicted) a t-statistic of ± 1.65 will always meet the minimum threshold requirement for rejecting the null ($p \leq .05$)—so long as the direction conforms to our prediction. If no direction is predicted (if your hypothesis merely predicts a significant offense in the respective group means), a t-statistic of ± 1.96 will be required to meet the minimal threshold for rejecting the null.

Thus, we may conclude that for seven of our eleven hypotheses (10.1a, 10.1c, 10.2a, 10.2b, 10.2c, 10.4a, and 10.4b), we may reject the null and accept the research hypothesis. There is no statistically significant difference across the two groups of democracies in the degree to which citizens perceive their politicians as trustworthy—at least when it comes to keeping campaign promises. Democratic socialization seems not to be an independent factor in modifying this form of political trust.

Mean Difference

This difference of means statistic simply reports how greatly the two means differ. In the case of the model for AVGCIT31, the two means differ by 12.389, or, because AVGCIT31 is measured as a percent, we note the two means differ by 12.389 percent. The final two columns in Table 10.11 report the 95% c.i. for the mean difference. In the case of AVGCIT31, we see that we can be 95 percent confident that the mean difference in group-means may fall between 3.295 percent and 21.484 percent. However, because the t-statistic is statistically significant, we also know that the 95% c.i. range will not contain the value of 0—the value we would find if there was no difference between the means of the two groups.

Thus, between the Mann-Whitney U tests and the difference of means analysis, we may conclude that there appears to be a pattern separating established democracies of the West from the more recent democracies in East and Central Europe. East and Central European citizenry tend to have a less developed sense of political efficacy, have greater doubts about the role of elections as instruments of holding government accountable, and are significantly less satisfied with the overall way democracy works within their countries (as least based on comparative social survey data from 1996).

However, they share statistically equivalent degrees of distrust of politicians to abide by their electoral campaign promises, suggesting a general concern for the sincerity of public elected officials across democracies of East and West.

DEMONSTRATION 10.3: BOX-PLOTS

Finally, a useful tool for graphically portraying the variance patterns across groups is a box-plot. Box-plots are a form of a histogram. However, they are ideally suited to comparing the different shape of the distribution across groups. Of course, one may rely on histograms as well. Box-plots, however, offer a convenient means of summarizing several important aspects of variance across two groups that are not easily achieved in a standard histogram.

Figure 10.8 presents a box-plot of AVGCIT31 for the twenty-one countries in EFFICACY.21. This is produced in SPSS 10. Box-plots are read only in a vertical direction—the horizontal scale has no meaning. The box itself measures the range of values in a sample between the second quartile and the third quartile, or the twenty-fifth percentile and the seventy-fifth percentile. Thus, 50 percent of all cases in a sample fall within the box. The shorter the box, the smaller the variance among the scores between the twenty-fifth and seventy-fifth percentiles. The taller the box, the greater range in values between the twenty-fifth percentile score and the seventy-fifth percentile score. The horizontal bar in the box presents the median value for the sample. If the bar is toward the top of the box, it suggests a *negative skew* (a few trailing cases toward lower scores). If the median line is toward the bottom of the box, it suggests a *positive skew* to the distribution (a trail of cases toward the high end of the scale). Extending out from the box are "whiskers." The distance captured from the top whisker to the bottom whisker represents 1.5 box lengths. The top whisker is the highest recorded value in the sample that is within 1.5 box lengths; the bottom whisker is the lowest value recorded in the sample within 1.5 box lengths. The longer the whiskers extend out from the box, the greater the spread in values. The more asymmetrical the length of the whiskers, the more skewed the sample distribution. If a score lies beyond the 1.5 box-length range, it is an *outlier*; if it lies beyond 3.0 box lengths, it is an extreme outlier. Outliers are denoted in SPSS 10 with the symbol °, and *extreme outliers* are denoted by the symbol *.[29]

In Figure 10.8, one immediately notices the different shapes of the two boxes. The East and Central European box is flat, while the box for the Western democracies is taller. For established democracies, 50 percent of the thirteen countries fall within the range of approximately 20 percent and 30 percent who indicate they agree with the statement that citizens can have considerable influence upon politics. Furthermore, we see the effect of Latvia upon the East and Central European sample: it "pulls" the distribution toward the positive skew. (Latvia is not identified as an outlier in Figure 10.8, but we know from Table 10.6 that Latvia has a much larger value for AVGCIT3 than the other seven countries in the East and Central European group, thus "pulling" the

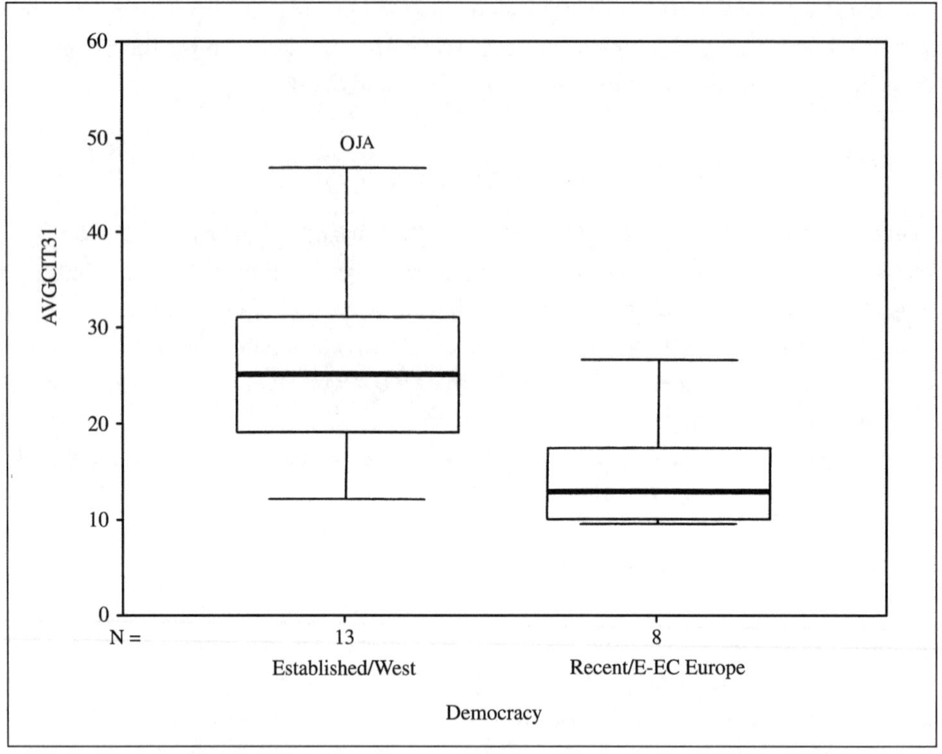

FIGURE 10.8 Box Plot, AVGCIT31, by Group (DEMOCRAC)

whisker upward from the box in Figure 10.8.) Finally, we note that Japan is an outlier—it lies beyond the upper boundary of the 1.5 box length, yet not so far as the 3.0 box length.

The box-plot underscores the effects of outliers. From Tables 10.5 and 10.6 we saw that four cases in the sample, Sweden, Philippines, Japan, and Latvia were quite removed from the mean within their respective samples. The box-plot underscores the effects of these four countries again (especially that of Philippines and Japan for the established Western democracies, and Latvia for the Central and East European sample). These scores stretch the spread in values within their respective groups and in the case of Latvia, pull the sample strongly toward a severe positive skew.

Outliers

The principal danger posed by outliers is committing Type I errors. In other words, outliers may cause us to reject the null because the outlier causes a statistically strong relationship that would not exist if that single outlier (or a few outliers) were not in the sample. This raises a question that each student of cross-national analysis must confront eventually. Should we drop the outliers? The answer is generally, no. Of course, there are times and circumstances when this would be considered appropriate within statistical analysis. For instance, if we suspect an error in the data coding, or if we believe the case should not have been included in the sample because its attributes are not consistent with the rules governing sample selection (for instance, including China in a sample of Western democracies), then dropping the case is necessary. However, in cross-national analysis, each country represents valuable variance in samples for which complete data are often very difficult to obtain. It is potentially important information to know that Japan stands so far apart from the other Western democracies in the instance of political efficacy. And it is also important information to know that Latvia, a Baltic country that was a former republic of the Soviet Union, has so much more political efficacy than the other East and Central democracies. Therefore, never equate an outlier with a "failure" in your analysis. You should not try to hide or disguise such residual errors. They can certainly cause problems. However, they are important pieces of information that help us understand the real world of politics around us. They allow us to appreciate the total dimensions of a relationship between two concepts. There are sophisticated techniques beyond the scope of this text that can treat the effect of such outliers, but for now, it is important to remember that outliers are legitimate variance (assuming no coding or case-selection error) and their elimination from the sample merely distorts reality.

Indeed, outliers are residuals that, as we have seen earlier in Chapters 4 and 5, constitute some of the most crucial pieces of information students of cross-national research rely upon in their research. They provide quantitative cross-national research with its unique contribution to comparative political inquiry. This is aptly described by Lawrence Mayer, who notes, "When a theory that had been suggested by the data in several other settings is falsified in a given system, the task at hand is to delineate in generic terms those attributes in which the deviant-case systematic differs from the systems in which the theory was supported, attributes that could logically account for the deviant-case results."[30] Outliers, therefore, provide useful information crucial to theory building (as we have seen in Chapters 7 and 9, and as we will see again throughout the remaining chapters), yet they can also be problematic for parametric statistical procedures.

One prudent course of action is always to run the analysis with the outliers in, and then repeat the analysis with the outliers out. Yet, this is not justified if the variance you are only temporarily eliminating cannot be legitimately extracted from the sample because of coding problems or section error. That is why using a nonparametric tool (such as Mann-Whitney) is so useful—indeed, preferred. Additional evidence based on less stringent variance assumptions offers some assurance that the results are credible. In our case, as both the Mann-Whitney U and t-test generally confirm the same conclusion, we are on reasonable grounds offering our conclusions with reasonable confidence the results are not the result of outliers distorting the odds of obtaining such results if the null were correct.

DEMONSTRATION 10.4: VOTING TURNOUT AND ELECTORAL SYSTEMS

As a final demonstration, let us consider data from CROSSNAT.50. Returning for a moment to voter turnout (Chapter 4), it has long been a working hypothesis among students of comparative politics that the choice of an electoral system may have something to do with the voting turnout of a country.[31] How does voting turnout relate to the constitutional rules governing elections?

The Relationship Between Votes, Seats, and Election Turnout

All electoral systems are distinguished by two critical features: the *magnitude of representation* within each district and the *algorithm* by which a winner in a district is determined. The district magnitude may be 1 (meaning only one winner in an electoral district, and therefore only one representative from the district to the respective chamber of the national legislature) or more than one (multi-district representation, where a district may have more than one representative in the same chamber of the national legislature). District magnitudes frequently vary across districts with democracies: Some districts may have two or three representatives, others as many as nine or ten.

The American and British systems of elections are, in this regard, relatively simple and straightforward. Both countries practice a method of elections at the national level known as *"first-past-the-post."* This method assigns electoral victory to *one* political candidate per electoral district, based on a simple plurality principle. This method is part of a broad family of election methods known as *Single-Member Plurality/Majority*. In the United States and Britain, a winner needs only a plurality of votes cast. The two basic advantages of this method are, first, it affords a closer and more accountable relationship between a district and its elected representative to the national legislature, and, second, by assigning a single representative to the district, one can claim at least a plurality of votes within the district, ensuring, in theory, a more refined and loyal commitment of the representative to the district's interests (rather than a commitment solely to the national political party).

There is a highly disproportional nature to single-member/plurality systems. They "waste" votes. Why? Within any district, a party may win a *plurality* of votes and win the district's single seat, yet never come close to receiving a *majority* of votes cast in the district. In other words, candidates who win by a plurality (and not by a majority) will have had more citizens vote against them than for them. When one adds up the total votes cast for a party across *all* the electoral districts in a country, one frequently finds the party receiving a larger proportion of seats in the legislature than the aggregate vote would normally account for across the districts. For instance, in Britain following the May 1997 general elections to the House of Commons, nearly two in three of the 659 seats in the chamber were awarded to the Labour Party based on the outcome of elections across the 659 electoral districts. Yet, Labour received only 43 percent of the total vote cast by British voters in the election. The Conservative Party managed to win only a quarter of the 659 seats to the Commons, yet it had received over 30 percent of the total British vote.

The absolute difference between the seats won and the percentage of the aggregate vote received by a political party is the measure of the *disproportional* nature of elections. Between 1945 and 1996, Britain's average degree of disproportional distribution was 10 percent, meaning on average, there was a gap of 10 percent between the number of seats in the House of Commons a party won and the proportion of votes it received across the country as whole. In France (also single-member, for the most part), the measure of inefficiency since 1945 has been approximately 21 percent. In American presidential elections (again, one winner, though the electoral college confounds the clear plurality concept—think of the 2000 presidential race), 15 percent of the vote on average has been "wasted," while the corresponding figure for elections to the House of Representatives was 12 percent.

In contrast to first-past-the-post is the *proportional representation* (PR) system of voting. There are three general types of proportional representation systems in the world today: the *party list* system, the *mixed member* system, and the "*choice*" system, consisting of the *single transferable vote* (STV) and *single non-transferable vote* (SNTV) electoral methods. List systems require the voters to select from a list of parties noted on their voting ballot. In some electoral democracies, such as Russia, this list will also include the names of individual candidates for voters to chose from. In most PR systems, however, the list is closed—no personal names appear on the ballot, only the names of political parties. The mixed-member system allows voters to distribute the allocation of seats to their national legislature via PR and single-member plurality. This method and variants of it are used in Japan, Hungary, Italy, Germany, Bolivia, and New Zealand. Finally, the STV system allows voters to indicate their preferences among candidates on their ballot, and the process cycles through the preferences assigning the highest preference to those candidates who need the vote in order to win. Ireland utilizes the STV system of elections. The SNTV system does not allow a cycling process, but does afford the voter the opportunity to list preferences for candidates, assigning in effect seats to parties and candidates based on their respective preference rankings by the voter. Taken together, the three types of PR systems are covered under the broader umbrella of *multi-member proportional* electoral systems, the main alternative to the single-member plurality/majority family of electoral systems.

In *multi-member PR* systems, seats to the national legislature are not allocated for a district by plurality or majority algorithms. Rather, each party is awarded a number of seats from the district according to the proportion of votes received by the party in the district. Votes are more closely matched with subsequent seat allocations, thus minimizing the degree to which a democracy must violate principles of "one-person-one-vote."

Because of the more proportional distribution of votes, we expect that proportionally based electoral systems will generate a greater incentive for eligible citizens to turn out and vote. On the other hand, because of their disproportional allocation of seats to votes, we expect plurality and majoritarian-based electoral systems to discourage electoral turnout. Our hypothesis is summarized below:

> Hypothesis 10.12 Countries with majority/plurality electoral systems will have a significantly smaller voter turnout (of eligible voters) than those countries with proportional-based electoral systems.

Difference of Means Test: Electoral Systems (ELECT2) and Voter Turnout(VAP)

Table 10.12 presents the list of countries in CROSSNAT.50, grouped by their type of electoral system. These data are taken from The World Policy Institute.[32] Table 10.13 reports the results of a difference of means test. From Table 10.13, we see confirmation of our hypothesis. The mean voter turnout (VAP) for those countries with proportionally-based electoral systems had a mean of 68.8 during the 1990s, while those with plurality- and majority-based electoral systems had a mean VAP value of 52.7 percent. The t-statistic of –3.080 is statistically significant ($p = .001$). We may conclude that proportionality tends to be associated with higher electoral turnout of electoral voters than majority and plurality systems. While further research would of course be required to more thoroughly "tease out" the reasons for the relationship, there can be little doubt that a real pattern exists across the two types of electoral systems with respect to voter turnout.

CHAPTER SUMMARY

This chapter has explored political culture, and more specifically, the foundations of civic culture. We have shown how we may work from comparative survey-based data to explore important cross-national questions and to move from nominal- and ordinal-based data to interval/ratio-level measures.

The study of political culture introduces the student to the first of several concepts that we group under the label of "the political environment." Comprised of the aggregate of political attitudes and beliefs within a specified population, political culture plays a major role in establishing the foundations for legitimate government and in contributing to the political motivations and behavior of individuals within society. It is also one of the most difficult concepts to study. To study empirically the political culture, students of comparative politics rely on survey data, with individuals in society as the unit of analysis. This presents unique challenges for the researcher. Measuring concepts empirically across different languages and historical traditions makes survey research and cross-cultural analysis particularly susceptible to concept stretching.

Central to hypothesis testing is the task of producing a test statistic and obtaining an estimate of its statistical significance. In this chapter we have focused on the basics of the difference of means test (or, the t-test), a practical and useful statistical tool for stu-

TABLE 10.12 Electoral Systems, Grouped (CROSSNAT.50)

Majority/Plurality Systems	*Semi-Proportional/Proportional Systems*
Australia	Algeria
Bangladesh	Argentina
Canada	Brazil
Congo	Chile
Egypt	Colombia
France	Czech Republic
Ghana	Ecuador
India	Germany
Iran	Greece
Kenya	Indonesia
Korea (South)	Italy
Malaysia	Japan
Morocco	Madagascar
Nepal	Mexico
Nigeria	Netherlands
Pakistan	Peru
Philippines	Poland
Tanzania	Romania
Thailand	Russia
Uganda	South Africa
Ukraine	Spain
United Kingdom	Sri Lanka
United States	Tunisia
Zimbabwe	Turkey
	Venezuela

Note: China has no formal national election system.

TABLE 10.13 Difference of Means, Voter Turnout (VAP), by Electoral System (ELECT2) (CROSSNAT.50)

Statistics/Groups	*Majority/Plurality Electoral Systems*	*Proportionality Electoral Systems*
Mean	52.742	68.752
Standard Deviation	20.884	15.175
Standard Error of Mean	4.263	3.035
N	24	25
t-statistic	-3.080	
p	0.001	

Levene's Test for Equality of Variances: F = .671, p= .417.

dents of comparative politics. We have also discussed at length the role of variance and the central place it occupies within the hypothesis-testing procedures. In this context, we have drawn attention to the difference between the different components of variance computed within a difference of means test and the different form of statistical error that is computed within each component. We will return again and again to the variance (and error) aspect of hypothesis testing as we explore additional statistical tools of analysis useful to the student of comparative politics.

Finally, from our analysis of the difference of means test (supported by the Mann-Whitney U test) we have demonstrated that political efficaciousness, confidence in elections, and degree of satisfaction with democracy vary across democracies. We attribute this in part to the degree of democratic socialization. A second demonstration confirmed that electoral turnout varies with electoral system rules.

NOTES

1. Adam Przeworski and Henry Teune, 1970, *The Logic of Comparative Social Inquiry* (New York: Wiley).

2. Lawrence Mayer, 1996, *Redefining Comparative Politics: Promise Versus Performance* (Newbury Park, Calif.: Sage Publications), p. 43.

3. How may we distinguish a "civilization" from a "culture?" While some scholars, such as Samuel Huntington, have spoken of civilizations with eloquence and insight (see Chapter 3), there can be no doubt that the term civilization has been one that is difficult to clearly define and is often not very clearly distinguished from culture. Perhaps the most useful distinction is that offered by Ferdinand Braudel. He observes that during the last two centuries, civilization has come to refer to "characteristics common to the collective life of a period or a group." Culture, on the other hand, refers to those values we commonly associate with a specific single group or nation, usually based on language and race/ethnicity issues, and therefore limiting the range of the concept to a more restricted and narrow spatial and temporal context. Culture is a component of civilization; civilization, to the extent it retains some of its earlier legitimacy as a concept, is something more encompassing. As Braudel notes, "To discuss civilization is to discuss space, land and its contours, climate, vegetation, animal species and natural and other advantages. It is also to discuss what humanity has made of these basic conditions: agriculture, stock breeding, food, shelter, clothing, communications, industry, and so on." Thus, we may speak of a German political culture and mean the orientation of Germans to their political institutions, to political authority, and to other political culture and forms of political authority. When we speak of the German civilization, we speak of the broader orientations of Germans to a comprehensive style and pattern of living and survival, to a set of broader values and deeper concerns that stretch beyond the borders of the contemporary Federal Republic of Germany and exist wherever German peoples have settled throughout Europe. See Ferdinand Braudel, 1994, *A History of Civilizations*, translated by Richard Mayne (New York: Penguin Books), pp. 7 and 10. For an examination of why culture is so important as an element to understanding politics and political conflict, see Lawrence E. Harrison and Samuel P. Huntington, eds., 2000, *Culture Matters: How Values Shape Human Progress* (New York: Basic Books).

4. For a rich insight into and perspectives on the concept of political culture and its definition with the study of comparative politics, see Gabriel A. Almond, 1980, "The Civic Culture Concept," in Gabriel A. Almond and Sidney Verba, eds., 1980, *The Civic Culture Revisited* (Boston: Little Brown): pp. 1–36.

5. Gabriel Almond and Sidney Verba, 1963, *The Civic Culture: Political Attitudes and Democracy in Five Countries* (Princeton: Princeton University Press).

6. See, for instance, Ronald Inglehart, Miguel Basañez, and Alejandro Moreno, 1998, *Human Values and Beliefs: A Cross-cultural Sourcebook: Political, Religious, Sexual, and Economic Norms in 43 Societies: Findings from the 1990–1993 World Values Survey* (Ann Arbor, Mich.: University of Michigan Press); and Jan W. van Deth and Elinor Scarbrough, eds., 1995, *The Impact of Values: Beliefs in Government*, Vol. 4. (Oxford, UK: Oxford University Press).

7. See, for instance, Ronald Inglehart, 1990, *Culture Shift in Advanced Industrial Society* (Princeton: Princeton University Press). Eurobarometer data are available from the ICPSR, http://www.icpsr.umich.edu/. As well, the European Union maintains a web page with several Eurobarometer surveys posted for general use, at http://europa.eu.int/comm/dg10/epo/.

8. Lawrence Mayer, 1996, *Redefining Comparative Politics: Promise Versus Performance* (Newbury Park, Calif.: Sage Publications), p. 42.

9. The matter of cultural subjectivity is a critical problem whenever we work with subjectively coded data. Such cultural subjectivity biases the interpretation of the data and events one is observing. The concept of democracy is one that, to many scholars, is often laden with cultural subjectivity, riddled with biased judgments growing from the coders' cultural preferences and hidden prejudices. See Ronald H. Chilcote, 2000, *Comparative Inquiry in Politics and Political Economy: Theories and Issues* (Boulder: Westview Press), pp. 17–30.

10. The main web page for the ZA, listing its organization, newsletters, databases, and publications, can be found at http://www.za.uni-koeln.de/. The main web page for GESIS is located at http://www.social-science-gesis.de/index-e.htm. For a useful explanation of how the ISSP data may be effectively used in quantitative cross-national research, see Erwin K. Scheuch, 2000, "The Use of ISSP for Comparative Research," *Nachrichten* (Zentrum für Umfragen, Methoden und Analysen–ZUMA), 47 (November): 64–74.

11. Angus Campbell, Gerald Gurin, and Warren E. Miller, 1954, *The Voter Decides* (Evanston, Ill.: Row, Peterson), p. 187.

12. Oscar W. Gabriel, 1995, "Political Efficacy and Trust," in Jan W. van Deth and Elinor Scarbrough, eds., 1995, *The Impact of Values: Beliefs in Government,* Vol. 4. (Oxford: Oxford University Press), pp. 359–360.

13. Gabriel A. Almond and Sidney Verba, eds., 1980, *The Civic Culture Revisited* (Boston: Little Brown), p. 4.

14. Within each country-sample, there are missing data. Missing data occur when the respondent either does not answer the question or the answer falls into the range of "Can't Choose" or "No Answer." In the variable AVGCIT, for instance, 1,289 respondents (across all twenty-one country-samples) answered "Can't Choose," and another 256 respondents answers were coded as "No Answer," indicating they did not offer an answer. These 1,545 respondents were excluded from the analysis. The five categories for the original variables noted in Table 10.1(and four categories for SATDEMO) do not include the category for "Can't Choose" or "No Answer." Yet, the data set assigns a unique value for a respondent who "Can't Choose" as 8, and those who offered no answer as 9. Values 8 and 9 are simply ignored in the analysis—they are codes for missing data. In SPSS and other programs, missing data are coded separately in the database and excluded from all analysis. Once one recodes an original variable, any values not specifically noted in the recode will be treated as missing data for the new variable. For more detail, see Marija J. Norušis, 2000, *SPSS 10.0: Guide to Data Analysis* (Upper Saddle River, N.J.: Prentice Hall), p. 37.

15. For an inventory of social science survey data of East Central and former Soviet nation-states, see Gábor Tóka, 2000, *Inventory of Political Attitude and Behavioral Surveys in East Central and the Former Soviet Union* (Bergisch Gladbach: Edwin Verlag).

16. Note that we cannot say the typical citizen within established democracies, or the typical citizen within newly established democracies of East and Central Europe. This is because we have not computed the mean of the pooled sample. Rather, we have computed correctly the mean of the country-sample means. Thus, we must restrict our conclusions to the typical percentage within a country, not a typical respondent.

17. See Tina Rosenberg, 1995, *The Haunted Land: Facing Europe's Ghosts After Communism* (New York: Random House), and Mary McCauley, 1997, *Russia's Politics of Uncertainty* (Cambridge, UK: Cambridge University Press), for insight into the cultural context following the transition from communism. For a more conventional but insightful and thorough consideration of the political, economic, and social changes associated with the transition, see Graham Smith, 1999, *The Post-Soviet States: Mapping the Politics of Transition* (London: Oxford University Press), and J. William Derleth, 2000, *The Transition in Central and Eastern European Politics* (Upper Saddle River, N.J.: Prentice Hall).

18. Arend Lijphart, 1999, *Patterns of Democracy: Government Forms and Performance in Thirty-six Countries* (New Haven: Yale University Press).

19. Samuel P. Huntington, 1997, *The Clash of Civilizations and the Remaking of World Order* (New York: Touchstone Books).

20. Matthew Soberg Shugart and John M. Carey, 1992, *Presidents and Assemblies: Constitutional Design and Electoral Dynamics* (Cambridge, UK: Cambridge University Press).

21. See Gerhard Lembruch and Philippe Schmitter, eds., 1982, *Patterns of Corporatist Policy-Making* (London: Sage).

22. For more detail, see Marija J. Norušis, 2000, *SPSS: SPSS© 10.0 Guide to Data Analysis* (Upper Saddle River, N.J.: Prentice Hall), pp. 333–334.

23. Table 10.7 replicates the output from SPSS 10 (with minor editing for our purposes) obtained from executing a Mann-Whitney U procedure. Within SPSS execute the following sequence from the main menu bar: ANALYZE▶NONPARAMETRIC TESTS▶2 INDEPENDENT SAMPLES, then select the variables for analysis and the single grouping variable (in EFFICACY.21, COUNTRY), specifying the exact scores that designate each group within the grouping variable. The Mann-Whitney U statistic is the default.

24. See R. Lyman Ott, 1993, *An Introduction to Statistical Methods and Data Analysis*, fourth edition (Belmont, Calif.: Duxbury Press), pp. 283–284.

25. If we computed the mean and standard deviation of the raw scores for political efficacy (AVGCIT31) for each group of democracy separately, then, of course, the mean for the z-scores in each separate group would be 0, with a standard deviation of 1. However, the z-scores reported in Table 10.9 are not computed from the separate samples but from the entire sample of twenty-one countries. Thus, the mean reported in Table 10.9 is the average z-score for each group separately.

26. For more detail about difference of means tests, consult R. Lyman Ott, 1993, *An Introduction to Statistical Methods and Data Analysis*, fourth edition (Belmont, Calif.: Duxbury Press), pp. 260–277. For an illustration of the use of difference of means tests to test hypotheses within the literature of cross-national analysis, see Keith Jaggers, 1992, "War and the Three

Faces of Power: War Making and State Making in Europe and the Americas," *Comparative Political Studies* 25 (April): 26-62.

27. The output is obtained by executing the following sequence from the main menu of SPSS 10: ANALYZE▶COMPARE MEANS▶INDEPENDENT-SAMPLES T TEST, then select those variables you wish to specify as your dependent variable or variables—if you have more than one model to test. (In a bivariate model using the difference of means test, it does not matter from a technical perspective which of your two variables is your dependent and independent variable, as true causality cannot be tested—only assumed. We are only measuring association between the dependent and independent variables in the bivariate model. However, the dependent variable *must* be a continuous variable—interval or ratio level measure.) Then, select from the variable list the variable you wish to specify as your grouping variable, and the values that distinguish the groups. See Marijia Norušis, 2000, *SPSS© 10.0: Guide to Data Analysis* (Upper Saddle River, N.J.: Prentice Hall), pp. 233–241.

28. Should you wish to see the respective values of the portioned variances, employ the COMPARE MEANS option rather than the INDEPENDENT-SAMPLE T TEST option within the MEANS list from the main menu of SPSS 10. See Marija J. Norušis, 2000, *SPSS: SPSS© 10.0 Guide to Data Analysis* (Upper Saddle River, N.J.: Prentice Hall), pp. 85–87.

29. To obtain box-plots in SPSS 10, you may either use the EXPLORE option from the ANALYZE▶DESCRIPTIVE STATISTICS option or you may obtain them from the main bar from this sequence: GRAPHICS▶BOXPLOTS. To obtain the BOXPLOTS shown in Figure 10.8, within the BOXPLOT window, select the default (simple box-plots, summarizing groups of cases) and the define the box-plot. This requires selecting the variable whose variance you want to plot, and the variable that serves as the category axis (in our case, DEMOCRAC). You may also select the option for labeling cases. In Figure 10.8, we chose the variable CODE as the variable to label any outliers in the box-plot. Thus, Japan (code = JA) is identified as an outlier with its code adjacent the symbol. Choosing the label option allows one to identify the outliers. See Marija J. Norušis, 2000, *SPSS: SPSS© 10.0 Guide to Data Analysis* (Upper Saddle River, N.J.: Prentice Hall), pp. 100–108.

30. Lawrence Mayer, 1996, *Redefining Comparative Politics: Promise Versus Performance* (Newbury Park, Calif.: Sage Publications), p. 48.

31. G. Bingham Powell Jr., 2000, *Elections as Instruments of Democracy: Majoritarian and Proportional Visions* (New Haven: Yale University Press); Robert E. Bohrer, 2002, *Decision Costs and Democracy: Trade-Offs in Institutional Design* (Hampshire, UK: Ashgate Publishing, Ltd.); G. Bingham Powell Jr., 1989, "Constitutional Design and Citizen Electoral Control," *Journal of Theoretical Politics* 1 (April): 107–30; Robert W. Jackman, 1986, "Elections and the Democratic Class Struggle," *World Politics* 39 (April): 123–146; Arend Lijphart, 1999, *Patterns of Democracy: Government Forms and Performance in Thirty-Six Countries* (New Haven: Yale University Press); Giovanni Sartori, 1994, *Comparative Constitutional Engineering: An Inquiry Into Structures, Incentives, and Outcomes* (New York: New York University Press); Electoral Reform Society on the Internet at http://www.electoral-reform.org.uk/; The Center for Voting and Democracy, on the Internet at http://www.igc.org/cvd/. Also see Arend Lijphart's election web page, at http://dodgson.ucsd.edu/lij/index.html.

32. On the Internet at http://worldpolicy.org/americas/democracy/table-pr.html.

11

The Political-Economic System

Concepts: *Structure, Function, Political Economy, Political Sub-Systems, Economic Exchange Sub-System, International Exchange, Market Power, Market Authority, Human Development, Gender Empowerment, Gender Development, Gender Equality*

In this chapter we proceed further with our consideration of the political system and its environment. Most students of politics hold mental images of the political world that more often than not are far less refined and precise than typical hypothesis testing would tolerate. This often forces students of comparative politics to reshape their conceptual arguments in terms that accommodate these less precise images. In doing so, precision and accuracy are traded for simplicity and clarity.

In conjunction with our consideration of the political system and its environment, we will explore one of the most powerful and commonly held images of the contemporary political world: the degree of *market freedom* within nation-states. In this chapter, we see how we may empirically distinguish countries by the extent to which government authority regulates and directs the allocation of resources within a society. At one extreme are those countries where most market decisions (for example, consumers' decisions to buy, producers' decisions to manufacture and sell, the prices the producers charge and the consumers pay, and the volume and content of inventory stocks) are predominately the result of the explicit decisions made by government bureaucracy. At the other extreme are those political economies where one finds such market decisions to have minimal restrictions and guidance from government and state bureaucracy.

In this chapter we also consider one of the more obvious aspects of a global economy: the degree to which a country's political economy and its markets are exposed to *international competition and exchange*.

In the next chapter, we will explore these concepts in conjunction with a particular tool of statistical analysis that follows logically from the difference of means already introduced to you: Analysis of Variance (or ANOVA) and its nonparametric version, the Kruskal Wallis H test. Before turning to the ANOVA technique and considering its utility in cross-national analysis, we must first elaborate the concepts of the political system and political environment so we can place the comparative analysis of political behavior and institutional authority into perspective.

SYSTEMS, STRUCTURES, AND POLITICAL ENVIRONMENT

System implies a collection of mutually reinforcing *structures* that perform certain functions specifically designed to produce a basic product or output. Few systems—especially those in the social world—are ever self-contained. Most must deal with *environmental effects*, those influences and distractions that are outside the structures that perform the basic tasks of the system.

A *structure* is merely the routine interaction between any two roles within a system. A *role* is represented by that actor, or institution, within the system that is granted some responsibility and task to carry out some function within the system. A *structural relationship* is when two or more actors or institutional bodies interact regularly and in a predictable pattern with respect to their formal and legitimate functions. The combination of a professor and a student is a structural relationship (the student and professor interact in a regular manner, each within his or her respective roles within the system of higher education). All systems can be broken down into smaller and smaller fragments of a larger whole as we define the range of functions performed by various structures more narrowly. The combined set of structures make up the aggregate, macro-system. Portions of the system comprised by sets of structures that perform distinctly different functions in cooperation with various roles constitute a "sub-system," or alternatively, a "micro-system."[1]

In modern societies, we may speak of a political-economic system consisting of a political sub-system (the network of functional interactions between institutions and citizens for the purpose of allocating resources through the use of public authority and the state) and an economic sub-system (the network of market transactions whereby individuals exchange tangible resources with one another for the purpose of producing and supplying specified goods and services), both existing within a broader political culture (the network of beliefs and attitudes regarding the role of government in the affairs of citizens). The market sub-system operates with individual actions; the political sub-system is essentially collective action.[2] The political-economic system is, therefore, the coordinated (functional) actions between the collective (government) and individuals (the market transactions), within a cultural setting. Politics and the economy are the two basic forms of activities that affect a nation's resource allocation. These resources are both tangible, in that they assume specific fungible characteristics, such as money, weapons, students, teachers, and so on, as well as intangible, such as values we attach to their priority.

The Political-Economic System and Its Various Sub-Systems

To reiterate, students of comparative politics generally envision the political-economic system of a country as comprised of three basic sub-systems, as shown in Table 11.1.

One would typically think of a country's political sub-system as having further sub-systems wherein relevant actors interact in a "functional" manner, and thereby create their respective sub-system structures. Within the political sub-system these may include *party sub-systems* (with different political parties and their respective constituents and elected representatives as critical role-players), *legislative sub-systems* (with the various chambers of the legislative bodies of national government, their leadership positions, and various committees being among the central role-players), *electoral sub-systems* (with voters and candidates working within the electoral laws as the central role-players), and *executive-legislative sub-systems* (with political and state executives, legislative leaders and committees, and various constituency interests serving as the central role-players). Combined, political and economic sub-systems, within a particular political culture, constitute the *political economy* of a country.

This logic is summarized in Figure 11.1. The more the two sub-systems overlap, the less sovereignty the individual has in the market system; the less the sub-systems interact, the more authority the market commands in human affairs. In modern society, it would be impossible to imagine the two sub-systems to be completely independent. The economy requires public authority to ensure the compliance of contracts, to enforce rules, and to protect people from the moral hazards (corruption, dishonesty, graft, theft, and so forth) that threaten the integrity of any exchange system. The nature of the political economy is therefore defined by the range of shared responsibilities between the market and the state, between the individual and the collective.

Both sub-systems, however, exist within a broader cultural environment that helps hold the relationship of the two spheres in balance. (For example, think how the activities of Wall Street influence the actions of political parties in the United States.) The broader values and priorities of a country determine such things as how active government should be in addressing economic issues like unemployment or in protecting a country's domestic markets from international exchange. Who decides how much these spheres overlap is the process of cultural and social development within a country. Generally, the balance between the spheres is achieved either over a long period of evolution, whereby experiences become embedded within the culture and serve to balance the relationship between the markets and government, or it occurs through abrupt traumas experienced by a country that push the spheres either further apart or closer together.

TABLE 11.1 The Three Basic Sub-Systems of a Political Economy

Sub-System	*Description*
cultural	from which preferences ultimately emerge, comprising the collection of beliefs, attitudes, and collective experiences of a population.
political	those institutions and actors which regularly interact in the process of articulating, aggregating, and processing the demands of the public in a country.
economic	(often merely referred to as a market), consisting of the network of individuals who act on their private interests and individual priorities through transactions whereby scarce resources are exchanged for the purpose of allocating goods and services in the country.

Beyond these two sub-systems lies the international environment. It, too, plays a critical role in shaping the structural patterns within various political systems. For instance, the perceived Soviet threat very much influenced the economic and political system of all Western democracies during the cold war. Indeed, in a country such as Italy, the international system clearly shaped the structure of the political party system. The end of the cold war led almost immediately to the collapse of that party structure and its replacement with a new party system. Other countries, including Mexico, Brazil, Argentina, South Africa, and China are all to varying degrees seeing the influences of the broader international environment work to erode traditional patterns of political authority and, in turn, the nature of economic exchange within their countries. Today, perceptions of economic competition shape relations between nation-states to a degree perhaps far greater than at any time since the end of World War II. Indeed, within the last quarter of a century, nature's ecological system itself has come to play an indirect role in shaping interactions within several countries. For example, ecological parties in Europe have been instrumental in changing the political agenda of party sub-systems within various political systems, leading recently to international conferences designed to restrict the independent actions of countries with respect to air and water pollution.[3]

In a broader sense, therefore, there are a number of pressures that color the environment within which the political-economic system and its surrounding culture exist. Thus, if we wish to know why some countries are more politically democratic than others, or why, for example, some nominally democratic countries exhibit less scope of democracy than others, we must consider the specific facets of the political environment that condition the evolution and formation of political authority in those countries. Specifically, we must explore the political economy of a country.

The Environment of a Country's Political Economy

An important question is: What are some of the more important, yet broad, environmental influences that comprise the environment within which the political economy

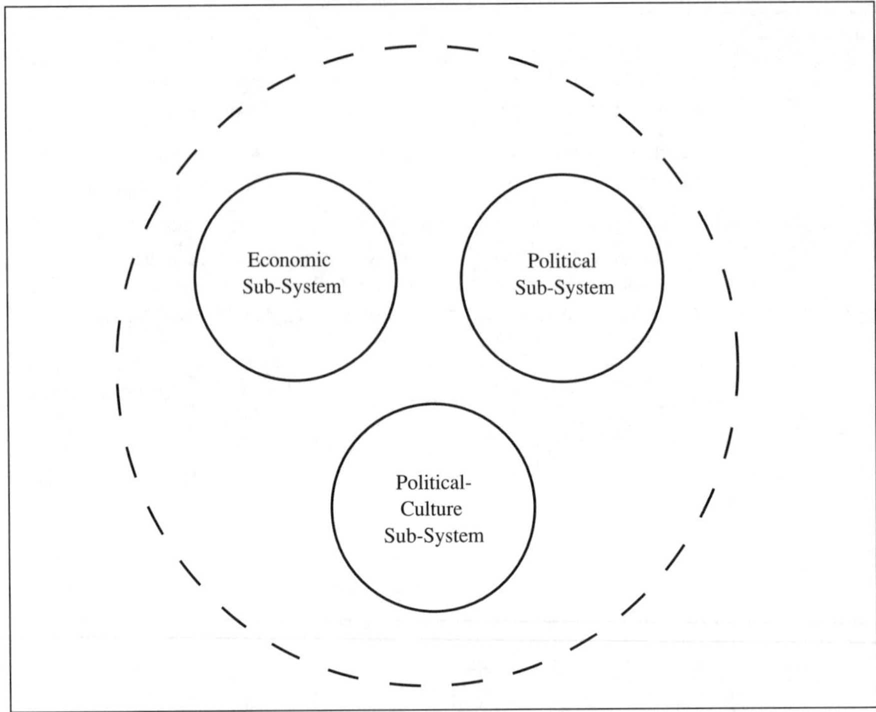

FIGURE 11.1 The Core Sub-System Components of the Political Economy of a Country

of a country operates? More important is the question of how we measure them. Figure 11.2 expands upon Figure 11.1 by depicting the environment within which a political economy operates.

Typically, the environment of a country's political economy is shaped by the effects of history and policy, reflected in such conditions as the degree of human suffering within society, gender inequality, population diversity, the persistence of the polity itself, government stability, and economic equality. These conditions may serve to limit the options and choices of actors within the political-economic sub-systems (especially the economic and political).

More distant from the social and economic environment of a country's political economy lies the international environment. Of interest to many comparativists is the particular shape and membership of the political-economic power hierarchy within the international system, and the extent to which countries enjoy a degree of influence in the international financial and commercial system. For instance, it is reasonable to expect, all else being equal, that a country that enjoys a select status with respect to the international financial and commercial markets may also be able to address such issues as prosperity, inequality, international exchange, and the forces of modernity better than a country that has a much lower place within the international political-economic hierarchy of power. The latter country may simply find the available

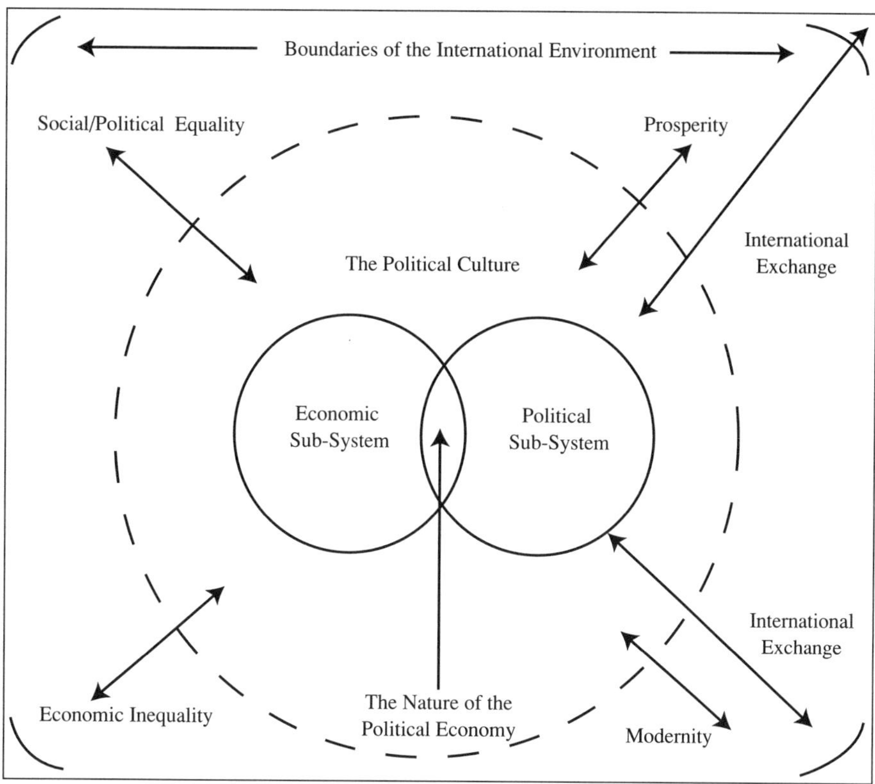

FIGURE 11.2 The Environment of a Country's Political Economy

resources (including foreign investment) more restricted and difficult to obtain, thus limiting the options and choices within the political-economy of the country, thereby limiting the government's and market's capacity to redress these problems. Indeed, it is reasonable to assume that one should be able to trace from the patterns of institutional authority, economic exchange, and (to a lesser extent) political culture, the location of a country within the international political-economic hierarchy of power and/or the extent to which that country enjoys influence within the international financial and commercial markets.

Beginning with this chapter, we will consider some of the more basic, but complex, components of the environment within which political authority operates. Of particular importance to us are those structural conditions within the environment of the political economy that have the greatest potential to divide and separate a population, and consequently generate competing, and often conflicting, preferences and demands on policymakers for resolution.

We begin by considering the extent to which the *international exchange* may affect the environment of a country's political economy. Moving closer to the domestic political economy of a nation-state, we then explore ways of distinguishing and measuring aspects of the economic sub-system of a political system. Specifically, we will introduce the concept of market ideology and employ a recent and innovative measure of the concept of economic freedom by which to capture the inherent logic of broadly defined categories of the political economy.

THE CENTRALITY OF INTERNATIONAL ECONOMIC EXCHANGE

In 1990, President George Bush proclaimed a "New World Order," suggesting that with the end of the long struggle between the "Second World" and the "First World," the "cold war" had become largely academic. Suddenly the old classification schemes based on the international system of political-economic power seemed less relevant for policy purposes, though they remained important concepts for social scientists.[4] This new world order was reflected in the attention afforded the global economy and, more specifically, the seemingly manageable effects of expanding commercial and financial international transactions. This new order had the effect of adding a new scheme to the hierarchy of the international power structure, replacing the old three-tier system, consisting of the "First World," or the wealthy democracies, the "Second World," or the communist countries, and the "Third World," or the nonaligned former colonies and protectorates. To many, it is more appropriate now to think of the international system as having a new pecking order. Countries at the top of the order have the most robust political economies, open to international exchange and able to command a presence within the new international economic order. At the bottom of such a hierarchy are those countries whose political economy is more restricted to international exchange and which therefore command at best limited authority and presence within the international economic order. Within each of these categories, however, lie very diverse and complex differences with respect to indigenous political economies.[5]

International Exchange: INTEX

How do we measure the extent to which a country is open to international exchange in the "new world order?" One of the most comprehensive studies of the international economic system is *Economic Freedom of the World, 2000,* part of a series sponsored by Fraser Institute of Vancouver, British Columbia.[6] The project identifies twenty-three separate indicators of "economic freedom," defined simply as the maximization of personal choice, protection of private property, and freedom of exchange.

The twenty-three separate indicators are grouped into seven broader categories of economic activity critical to economic freedom (size of government, economic structure and use of markets, monetary policy and price stability, freedom to use alternative currencies, legal structure and security of private ownership, freedom to trade with foreigners, and freedom of exchange in capital markets). The *freedom to trade with foreigners* is the specific category we employ to estimate a country's degree of openness to international exchange. This measure is based on an index of two subcategories of measures: (1) *A country's taxes on international trade*—the country's revenue from (a) taxes on international trade as a percent of exports plus imports, (b) the country's mean tariff rate, and (c) the country's standard deviation of tariff rates—and (2) *non-tariff regulatory trade barriers*—(a) the percent of a country's international trade covered by non-tariff trade restraints, and (b) the actual size of a country's trade sector compared to the expected size. The score is set by the authors of the study to an interval scale ranging from 1 to 10. A score of 10 would indicate maximum freedom to trade with foreigners: Revenues from trade would be high, tariff rates would be low, and their standard deviation low (constant); the percent of a country's foreign trade covered by non-tariff trade would be high and the actual size of a country's trade sector would match its expected level, given the country's total economic wealth. A score of 1 would indicate a country at the opposite end of the "freedom to trade with foreigners" scale. The measure INTEX within CROSSNAT.50 reflects this measure for our sample.[7]

Table 11.2 reports the scores of INTEX for each of the countries in CROSSNAT.50, in descending order of values. Our sample range extends from 8.7 (Czech Republic) to 3.7 (Madagascar and Zimbabwe). The key central tendency statistics are reported at the bottom the table. Note the distribution is not normal (K-S = .131, p = .03).[8]

MARKET IDEOLOGY AND THE ECONOMIC EXCHANGE SUB-SYSTEM

In Chapter 7 we explored the various components of democracy, which, in effect, allow us also to assess the comparative nature of the political sub-system across countries. To more fully appreciate the political economy of a society, we need a measure of market authority. In effect, as we noted with regard to Figure 11.2, as the economic and political sub-systems become indistinguishable from each other, the power of the state in the form of collective authority suppresses the autonomy of the markets. On the other hand, as the two spheres of authority become, in effect, separated into autonomous domains, the authority of the state and its collective logic is minimized and the authority of the market and its individualistic logic becomes dominant within society. In most societies, as shown in Figure 11.2, a balance exists between the two spheres of the market and the collective—each remains integrated with the other, and, more importantly, the authority of the market and that of the state are constrained in a web of mutual countervailing pressures, in effect balancing the impact of each other on society.[9] Let us consider the concept of market authority within a comparative perspective.

The Nature of Market Authority

The economic sub-system consists of the routine interactions in a society that explicitly coordinate retail, commercial, and financial exchanges. Collectively, these define

TABLE 11.2 Openness of Economy to International Exchange (INTEX)

COUNTRY	*INTEX*	*COUNTRY*	*INTEX*
Czech Republic	8.7	Peru	7.0
Netherlands	8.6	Malaysia	6.9
Germany	8.5	Bangladesh	6.9
France	8.5	Indonesia	6.9
Canada	8.5	Ghana	6.7
Spain	8.5	Argentina	6.6
United Kingdom	8.5	Nepal	6.6
Australia	8.4	Kenya	6.4
Italy	8.4	Tanzania	6.3
Turkey	8.3	Brazil	6.2
Greece	8.1	Uganda	5.9
Chile	8.0	Korea	5.8
Japan	7.9	Sri Lanka	5.8
Mexico	7.9	Morocco	5.3
United States	7.8	Pakistan	5.0
South Africa	7.7	Poland	5.0
Venezuela	7.4	Iran	4.8
Philippines	7.4	Algeria	4.7
Ukraine	7.3	Tunisia	4.6
China	7.2	India	4.1
Russia	7.1	Congo	4.0
Ecuador	7.1	Nigeria	3.9
Colombia	7.0	Egypt	3.8
Thailand	7.0	Madagascar	3.7
Romania	7.0	Zimbabwe	3.7

Central Tendency Statistics	
Mean	6.7
Standard Deviation	1.5
95% c.i.	6.2–7.1
Median	7.0
Skewness	-.558
Kurtosis	-.783
Kolmogorov-Smirnov	.131 (df = 50, p = .03)
Shapiro-Wilk's	.905 (df = 50, p = .01)
N	50

the major markets which, when all are combined, constitute the "economic system." Market authority may be understood to consist of six general conditions:

- The *freedom* buyers and sellers have to produce and purchase what they need according to their own preferences (that is, consumer sovereignty).
- The assurance that what producers have produced, consumers consumed, and sellers sold constitutes *private property* that cannot be expropriated from owners by the state without due process and just compensation.
- The *sanctity of money and capital* as the principal source of future growth and security within a country.

- The *availability and accuracy of information* about a market (the market is not afflicted by censorship and restrictions about what buyers and sellers want).
- The *accessibility and inclusiveness* of the market (that is, the ease by which new buyers, sellers, and producers can come into the market on their own volition).
- The distribution of *risk and reward* in market transactions within the economic system, which determines who receives the bulk of rewards for their initiative (that is, the rules that determine whether the actions of private individuals are rewarded with private capital that is the property of the individual, or whether those rewards are the property of the state).

When consumer sovereignty, the sanctity of money and capital, private property, information availability, accessibility/inclusiveness, and private risk/reward are maximized in a country, we conclude that the economic exchange sub-system is capitalist in nature, governed by a *capitalist market ideology.*

Capitalism is often associated with the highest form of market authority.[10] When these conditions are absent or minimized, we may conclude that the country's economic exchange sub-system is *state-directed,* governed by the political collective. These are generally the polar extremes of *market authority*.

Between the Polar Extremes

Between these two polar extremes of capitalism and state-directed markets, there are, of course, varying degrees of market authority. One form of market authority somewhat midway between these extreme forms of market authority is *mixed capitalism,* common to countries that are characterized by an active public sector working with private business and consumers to provide minimum securities against the unexpected failures and inequities that can occasionally accompany capitalism. The state, in other words, exists *alongside* sovereign buyers, sellers, and producers. The private market finds the state as a *partner*, not as a *dictator.* The private markets within mixed capitalist systems are still dominant, and property is still largely the sovereign domain of private buyers, sellers, and producers, but the state has a much more visible and active role than generally preferred and allowed under a capitalist market ideology. Often, it is the case in the mixed capitalist market ideologies that the state, even in its limited capacity as an actor in the economy, must assume a major share of the responsibility of providing key social services and welfare provisions to the public, creating a public market where buyers, producers, and sellers must inevitably coordinate their economic behavior with the government to a relatively larger degree than found in countries where a capitalist market ideology prevails. In this sense, consumer sovereignty, while still existent in many individual markets within the economic system, is nonetheless quite constrained in other markets within the mixed capitalist country.

Further from mixed capitalist economic exchange sub-systems are those we shall label *state capitalist* systems. These types of economic exchange sub-systems are guided by a market ideology that places more restrictions on free enterprise and the sovereign activities of the buyers, sellers, and producers. The state is not only a major actor, but *the* dominant player, having direct control over much larger portions of private property than even in a mixed capitalist state. Still, in a relative sense, *state capitalist* societies have a modicum—a glimmering—of private markets, where some freedom is allowed, where some consumer sovereignty is present, and where the accessibility and inclusiveness of the markets is at least superficially present. Economic freedoms and sovereignty in these countries are, however, precariously dependent on the guidance and support of state-concentrated resources and authority. Risk is almost always still quite diffused, and unlike *mixed capitalist* societies, the state plays the key role in determining how much freedom, sovereignty, accessibility, and inclusiveness to allow within the economic system. Another distinguishing characteristic of a state capitalist system is the substantial role played by alternative markets, otherwise known as "black markets," wherein little confidence is placed in the formal and legitimate markets, and much distrust is directed toward the state agencies that control the formal market. The problem with these markets is they reduce certainty and long-term investments, which are the hallmark of economic security and property rights within a society.[11]

Figure 11.3 graphically illustrates the comparative differences that distinguish the different types of market authority, based on the broader categories of producer/supplier sovereignty and consumer/individual sovereignty.

Economic Freedom: ECON97

How can we measure the varying degrees of market authority? The *Economic Freedom of the World* project can be effectively employed to derive an interval-level measure of market authority within a country. You will recall that the principal objective of this project is to offer a more refined and accurate measure of economic freedom—a concept that lies at the heart of market authority. The authors of the project operationalized twenty-three indicators that, when combined, provide an overall measure of the degree of economic freedom within a society. The indicators explored by the *Economic Freedom* study were grouped into seven categories of economic activity critical to market freedom, each closely resembling the six characteristics of a capitalist market noted above. These seven categories, their respective operationalizations, and the relative weight of each component within the categories (that is, the relative "contribution" or importance of a separate measure to the overall index measure of *economic freedom*) are listed in Table 11.3.

Within CROSSNAT.50, the variable ECON97 represents the value of economic freedom (as of 1997) computed for each of the fifty countries in the sample. The measure assumes a high score of 10 (maximum economic freedom, equivalent to the highest form of market authority, "capitalism") and a low score of 0 (minimum economic freedom, equivalent to the lowest form of market authority, "state-directed" market authority).

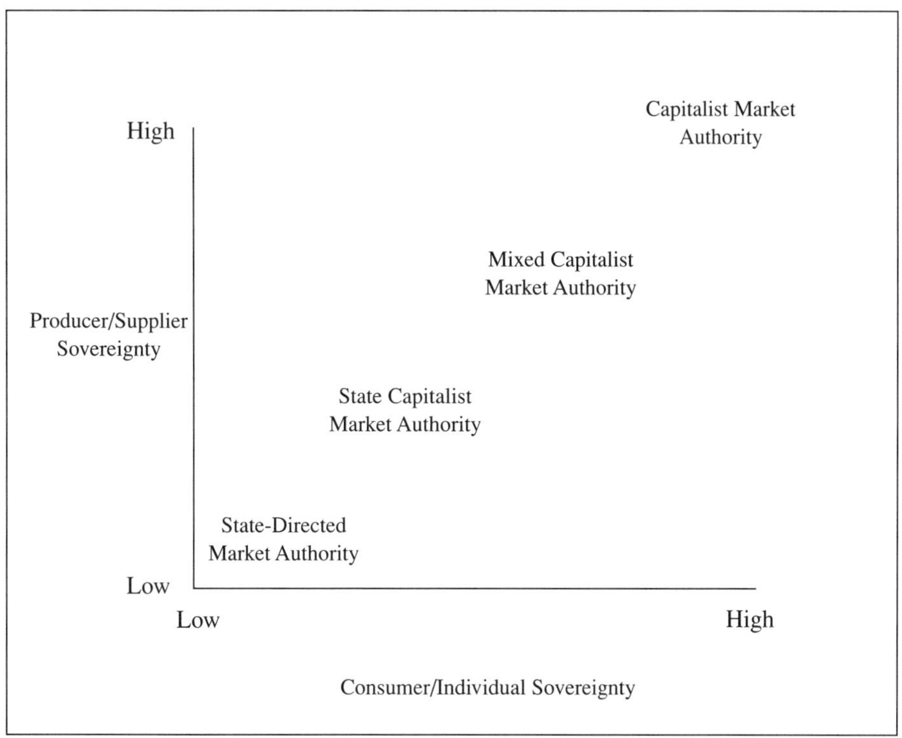

FIGURE 11.3 Comparative Market Authority

Table 11.4 reports the scores of ECON97 for each of the countries in CROSS-NAT.50, in descending order of values. Our sample range extends from 9.0 (United States) to 3.9 (Madagascar). The key central tendency statistics are reported at the bottom of the table. Note that we may not reject the null hypothesis, which holds the sample to be normally distributed (K-S = .122, p = .07).

PROSPERITY: HUMAN DEVELOPMENT: HUMDEV

Standing between the political-economic core of a political system and its international environment is the domestic environment. As shown in Figure 11.2, that environment includes a number of pressures that are the by-products of both the domestic political-economic authority and the pressures of the international economy. These by-products are wrought by the interactions of various actors within the domestic political economy in the pursuit of their interests, as well as by the effects that follow from the competitive pressures of external economic (and sometimes, political) factors emanating from beyond the borders of the nation-state. One of these by-products is social prosperity. This entails more than just economic prosperity, measured often as the per capita wealth of a citizenry, or the aggregate economic power of the citizenry

TABLE 11.3 The Major Components of Economic Freedom and Respective Weights

Category	*Operationalization*
Size of Government	General government consumption expenditures in a country as a percent of total consumption transfers (weight = 5.5%); and subsides in a country as a percent of GDP (weight = 5.5%)
Economic Structure and Use of Markets	Government enterprises and investment as a share of the country's economy (weight = 4.6%); extent to which businesses in a country are free to set their own prices (weight 4.8%); top marginal tax rate in a country and the income threshold at which it applies (weight = 3.6%); and the use of conscripts to obtain military personnel in the country (weight = 1.2%)
Monetary Policy and Price Stability	Average annual growth rate of the country's money supply during the last five years minus the growth rate of real GDP during the last ten years (weight = 3.2%); the standard deviation of the annual country's inflation rate during the last five years (weight = 3.0%); and the annual inflation rate of the country during the most recent year (weight = 3.0%)
Freedom to Use Alternative Currencies	Freedom of citizens in country to own foreign currency bank accounts domestically and abroad (weight = 7.3%); and the difference between the official exchange rate and the black market rate in a country (weight = 7.3%)
Legal Structure and Security of Private Ownership	Legal security of private ownership rights in a country, or the "risk of confiscation" principle (weight = 5.5%); the viability of contracts in a country, or the "risk of contract repudiation by the government" principle (weight = 5.7%); legal institutions supportive of the principles of rule of law and access to a nondiscriminatory judiciary, or the "rule of law" principle (weight = 5.3%)
Freedom to Trade with Foreigners	Revenue from taxes on international trade in a country as a percent of exports plus imports within the country (weight = 4.0%); mean tariff rate within a country (weight = 4.2%); standard deviation of tariff rates within a country (weight = 4.0%); percent of international trade in a country covered by non-tariff trade restraints (weight = 3.3%); and the actual size of trade sector within a country compared to the expected size (weight = 1.5%)
Freedom of Exchange in Capital Markets	Percent of deposits within a country held in privately owned banks, the "ownership of banks" principle (weight = 4.7%); percent of credit within a country extended to private sector, the "extension of credit" principle (weight = 3.6%); interest rate controls and regulations in a country that lead to negative interest rates (weight = 4.2%); and restrictions on the freedom of citizens in a country to engage in capital transactions with foreigners (weight = 4.6%)

within the nation-state. Social prosperity also entails the ability of citizens within a country to make a moral or legal claim on government. This capacity requires more than just the political and institutional opportunities afforded by institutional scale or scope, or liberal scope and scale (as discussed in Chapter 7). It takes more than political efficacy, as well (Chapter 10). It also requires some degree of capacity and choice: the capacity to actually exercise one's rights vis-à-vis the state and other groups, and the availability of choices with respect to the strategies and options a person may have in pursuing his or her interests.

David Held develops the concept of *nautonomy*, or the asymmetrical allocation and provision of life chances for citizens within a society. Key to these life chances are basic provisions of social resources, including the capacity to engage one's self in not only

TABLE 11.4 Economic Freedom as Market Authority (ECON97)

Country	*ECON97*	*Country*	*ECON97*
United States	9.0	Turkey	6.6
United Kingdom	8.9	Egypt	6.6
Australia	8.6	Sri Lanka	6.5
Canada	8.6	Ghana	6.4
Netherlands	8.5	Tunisia	6.3
Argentina	8.4	China	6.2
Japan	8.3	Uganda	6.1
Thailand	8.2	Morocco	6.0
Spain	8.2	Venezuela	6.0
Chile	8.2	Poland	6.0
Germany	8.1	Brazil	5.9
France	8.0	India	5.8
Congo	7.9	Pakistan	5.6
Italy	7.9	Colombia	5.6
Philippines	7.9	Tanzania	5.6
Peru	7.9	Russia	5.4
Mexico	7.7	Nepal	5.3
Malaysia	7.5	Bangladesh	5.3
Greece	7.4	Iran	5.0
South Africa	7.3	Zimbabwe	5.0
Korea	7.3	Nigeria	4.7
Indonesia	7.2	Romania	4.6
Czech	7.1	Ukraine	4.5
Ecuador	7.0	Algeria	4.1
Kenya	6.8	Madagascar	3.9

Central Tendency Statistics

Mean	6.7
Standard Deviation	1.4
95% c.i.	6.3–7.1
Median	6.7
Skewness	-.217
Kurtosis	-.991
Kolmogorov-Smirnov	.122 (p = .07)
N	50

the defense of one's interests through the exercise of his or her political rights (whether those rights are extensive or restricted themselves), but also the definition and creation of new opportunities, through political competition, the exercise of civil liberties, and the application of skills within the economy. Each of these life chances is conditioned by the rules and procedures, as well as the opportunities, produced through the transactions of the political economy.[12]

The United Nation's Development Program has developed a single measure built upon an index of individual variables which seeks to measure the extent to which a society has provisioned such life chances. They label this indicator the *Human Development*

Index, and define it as *the process of creating an enabling environment for citizens within a country which permits the people to enjoy long, healthy, and creative lives.*[13]

How then are people enabled? How are their broader human rights maximized and sustained in the creation and defense of their "life chances?" People are enabled partly through political participation and activity, and partly through the application of their talents, which, in effect, depend upon the person's well-being and the range of opportunities for active personal engagement in the politics and economy of a country.

The United Nations produces an annual assessment of the progress of human development. Its *Human Development Report* records for each country (that is, for those countries that have complete data) the degree of human development in the country. The composite measure for human development combines scores on life expectancy within the country, adult literacy rates, educational enrollment among the population, and the adjusted per capita income for citizens within the country. The score ranges from 0 to 1.0: 1.0 reflecting the highest possible human development, and 0 indicating the lowest possible degree of human development. Prosperity may be evaluated by the use of this general measure of human development.

Within CROSSNAT.50, the variable HUMDEV reports the development index score for each country in the sample. These data are reported in Table 11.5, in descending order. The scores range from .932 (Canada) to .404 (Uganda). The K-S statistic indicates we may not reject the null hypothesis of normality in the distribution, although the deviation appears not to be severe (K-S = .126, p = .05).

SOCIAL/POLITICAL EQUALITY: GENDER DEVELOPMENT AND EMPOWERMENT

At a fundamental level, extending and sustaining human capabilities is rarely distributed in equal proportions across countries. Different talents, opportunities, and social roles help divert the flow of resources from what might otherwise be considered a strictly equitable proportion. One of the most widespread obstacles to balanced development of human capabilities across society is gender inequality. The political economy often provides far greater rewards and opportunities to men than to women. Roles within society may, for various reasons, relegate women to a status based solely upon their gender. These roles have to do with bearing children, raising families, and, consequently, often foregoing educational and career opportunities. These social roles carry with them unique hazards for health—both physical and mental—as well as for economic and political power. We may therefore distinguish two primary properties of gender development in a broader sense: *gender equality* and *gender empowerment*.

Measures of Gender Equality

Measuring gender equality requires a certain degree of judgment mixed with more discrete empirical measures. The United Nations Development Programme has esti-

TABLE 11.5 Human Development Index as Prosperity (HUMDEV)

COUNTRY	*HUMDEV*	*COUNTRY*	*HUMDEV*
Canada	0.932	Brazil	0.739
United States	0.927	Peru	0.739
Japan	0.924	Turkey	0.728
Australia	0.922	Sri Lanka	0.721
Netherlands	0.921	Ukraine	0.721
United Kingdom	0.918	Iran	0.715
France	0.918	China	0.701
Germany	0.906	South Africa	0.695
Italy	0.900	Tunisia	0.695
Spain	0.894	Indonesia	0.681
Greece	0.867	Algeria	0.665
Korea	0.852	Egypt	0.616
Chile	0.844	Morocco	0.582
Czech Republic	0.833	Zimbabwe	0.560
Argentina	0.827	India	0.545
Poland	0.802	Ghana	0.544
Venezuela	0.792	Kenya	0.519
Mexico	0.786	Pakistan	0.508
Colombia	0.768	Congo	0.479
Malaysia	0.768	Nepal	0.463
Thailand	0.753	Nigeria	0.456
Romania	0.752	Madagascar	0.453
Russia	0.747	Bangladesh	0.440
Ecuador	0.747	Tanzania	0.421
Philippines	0.740	Uganda	0.404

Central Tendency Statistics

Mean	.717
Standard Deviation	.158
95% c.i.	.672–.762
Median	.740
Skewness	-.452
Kurtosis	-.863
Kolmogorov-Smirnov	.126 (p = .05)
N	50

mated gender equality along two broad dimensions across nations. The first dimension is the *Gender Development Index (GDI)*; it measures the degree of social development for women within society. The GDI is based on an index measure of women's respective levels for literacy, education, life expectancy, and personal income. The higher the score of the *Gender Development Index*, the greater the degree of female development within the country. The *Human Development Index* measures social development for *both* men and women in a society. The score of the Gender Development Index for each country is recorded in the variable GENDEV within CROSSNAT.50, while the respective scores for human development for each country are recorded in the variable HUMDEV.

Measures of Gender Empowerment

The second dimension of social/political inequality is identified as the capacity of women to not merely have some influence through elections, but to directly participate within institutions of political power, including serving as elected municipal councilors and national parliamentary representation and serving in national governing cabinets. Once again, the United Nations Development Programme produces an index measure of gender empowerment. The *Gender Empowerment Index* reflects the degree of gender inequality in key areas of political participation and decisionmaking (for instance, the number of female legislators and heads of state). This measure is an indicator of the opportunity, not merely the capacity, that women have within society to involve themselves in the decisions and affairs of politics and economics. Again, as with *Human Development* and *Gender Development*, the maximum score is 1.0, with 0 representing the lowest possible degree of female empowerment. The measure of *Gender Empowerment* is represented in the variable GENPOW within CROSSNAT.50.

Table 11.6 reports the values (in descending order) for both *Gender Equality* (GENDEV) and *Gender Empowerment* (GENPOW). *Gender Development* ranges in value from .928 (Canada) to .397 (Uganda). However, the variable is normally distributed (K-S = .120, $p = .07$).

Gender Empowerment scores in CROSSNAT.50 range from .742 (Canada) to .152 (Uganda). The variable is also normally distributed (K-S = .082, $p = .200$).

DEMOCRACY, MARKET AUTHORITY, AND THE ENVIRONMENT OF THE POLITICAL ECONOMY

While our discussion to this point has sorted out the basic logic and intrinsic nature of the political economy and various components of its environment within countries, we have left unexplored one of the more obvious questions: Are the choices about how to organize political authority associated with distinctive patterns of market authority and the environment of the political economy? The scope of institutional democracy, for instance, would seem to be a critical constraint on gender empowerment. Indeed, without a strong commitment to the scale of liberal democracy within a society, one could hardly imagine a high degree of market authority, as it is based on the rights of consumers and producers, through property rights, to pursue their individual interests with minimal restrictions from the collective, or state.[14] This would also likely be the case for the broader measure of human prosperity/human development. While the specific differences between male and female development would seem to logically require a high degree of commitment to expanding access to the political arena, as reflected in the scope of liberal democracy, the broader phenomenon of human development reflects a general condition of prosperity that would logically require broad citizen opportunities for participation in and access to those political resources within the political economy necessary to mobilize the physical and cultural resources re-

TABLE 11.6 Social and Political Equality as Gender Development and Gender Empowerment

Gender Development				*Gender Empowerment*			
COUNTRY	*GENDEV*	*COUNTRY*	*GENDEV*	*COUNTRY*	*GENPOW*	*COUNTRY*	*GENPOW*
Canada	0.928	Ecuador	0.728	Canada	0.742	Thailand	0.407
United States	0.926	Peru	0.726	Germany	0.740	Greece	0.404
Australia	0.921	Turkey	0.722	United States	0.708	Ukraine	0.402
Japan	0.917	Sri Lanka	0.712	Australia	0.707	Romania	0.400
Netherlands	0.916	Ukraine	0.712	Netherlands	0.702	Brazil	0.367
France	0.916	China	0.699	United Kingdom	0.614	Indonesia	0.362
United Kingdom	0.915	Iran	0.696	South Africa	0.582	Tunisia	0.353
Germany	0.904	South Africa	0.689	Spain	0.555	Korea	0.336
Italy	0.894	Tunisia	0.681	Italy	0.523	Sri Lanka	0.321
Spain	0.888	Indonesia	0.675	Czech	0.521	Nepal	0.315
Greece	0.861	Algeria	0.642	Ecuador	0.516	Ghana	0.313
Korea	0.845	Egypt	0.603	Colombia	0.515	Bangladesh	0.304
Chile	0.832	Morocco	0.565	Mexico	0.511	Morocco	0.301
Czech	0.830	Zimbabwe	0.555	Poland	0.504	Turkey	0.280
Argentina	0.814	Ghana	0.540	France	0.499	Egypt	0.275
Poland	0.800	India	0.525	Japan	0.494	Iran	0.264
Venezuela	0.786	Kenya	0.517	China	0.491	Algeria	0.245
Mexico	0.778	Pakistan	0.472	Venezuela	0.484	Kenya	0.244
Colombia	0.765	Congo	0.465	Philippines	0.480	India	0.240
Malaysia	0.763	Nigeria	0.442	Malaysia	0.451	Congo	0.206
Thailand	0.751	Nepal	0.441	Chile	0.449	Nigeria	0.198
Romania	0.750	Madagascar	0.432	Zimbabwe	0.430	Madagascar	0.190
Russia	0.745	Bangladesh	0.428	Russia	0.422	Pakistan	0.176
Philippines	0.736	Tanzania	0.418	Peru	0.421	Tanzania	0.165
Brazil	0.733	Uganda	0.397	Argentina	0.415	Uganda	0.152

Central Tendency Statistics

Mean	.723	Mean	.413
Standard Deviation	.157	Standard Deviation	.156
95% c.i.	.662–.754	95% c.i.	.369–.458
Median	.740	Median	.411
Skewness	-.582	Skewness	.344
Kurtosis	-.602	Kurtosis	-.436
Kolmogorov-Smirnov	.120 (p = .07)	Kolmogorov-Smirnov	.082 (p = .200)
N	50	N	50

quired to overcome constraints to prosperity. Allowing citizens within a domestic market to actively and freely exchange goods and services with foreign markets (INTEX) would seem to be a prospect greatly enhanced by the extension of citizen authority, or the scale of institutional democracy.

Thus, these propositions may be formalized in the following hypotheses:

Hypothesis 11.1: *Gender equality* in a country is positively associated with the *scope of liberal democracy* in the country.

Hypothesis 11.2: *Gender empowerment* in a country is positively associated with the *scope of institutional democracy* in the country.

Hypothesis 11.3: *Human development* in a country is positively associated with *scale of liberal democracy* in the country.

Hypothesis 11.4: *Market authority* in a country is positively associated with the *scale of liberal democracy* in the country.

Hypothesis 11.5: The degree of *international exchange* in domestic markets of a country is positively associated with the *scale of institutional democracy* in the country.

To test these five basic hypotheses, we will, in the next chapter, employ an extension of the t-test: the one-way ANOVA (analysis of variance) method. After introducing you to the basic logic of ANOVA, we will then test these hypotheses with the non-parametric equivalent of ANOVA, the Kruskal Wallis H test (similar to the Mann-Whitney U test).

CHAPTER SUMMARY

In this chapter we have highlighted the political-economic system and its surrounding environment. We have suggested that the core components of the political-economic system are political and economic sub-systems, shaped by the tug and pull of market and public authority. Within the environment of the political economy, prosperity, social and political equality, and international transactions are common factors that are both influenced by and act to constrain the activities of the economic sub-systems. Our examples have drawn attention to the generally close association between democracy and the various elements of the political economy, and its environment.

NOTES

1. The literature on political systems, as well as their structure and functions, is extensive. See David Easton, 1971, *The Political System: An Inquiry Into the State of Political Science* (New York: Knopf) and David Easton, *A Systems Analysis of Political Life* (New York: Wiley). For a more contemporary consideration of systems analysis and politics, see Robert Jervis, 1997, *Systems Effects: Complexity in Political and Social Life* (Princeton: Princeton University Press). See David Easton, 1990, *The Analysis of Political Structure* (New York: Routledge) for a thorough analysis of the role and utility of structural-functional analysis within political science. For one of the most widely regarded and cited explanations of the structural-functional and systems theory application to comparative political analysis, see Gabriel A. Almond and G. Bingham Powell Jr., 1966, *Comparative Politics: A Developmental Approach* (Boston: Little Brown), brought up to date with contemporary considerations in Gabriel A. Almond, G. Bingham Powell Jr., Kaare Strom, and Russel J. Dalton, 2001, *Comparative Politics: A Theoretical Framework* (New York: Long-

man), pp. 39-55. For a more heuristic approach, see Henry Teune and Zdravko Milnar, 1978, *The Developmental Logic of Social Systems* (Beverly Hills, Calif.: Sage).

2. David N. Balaam and Michael Veseth, 2000, *Introduction to International Political Economy*, second edition (Upper Saddle River, N.J.: Prentice Hall); Robert A. Isaak, 2000, *Managing World Economic Change: International Political Economy*, third edition (Upper Saddle River, N.J.: Prentice Hall); and Ronald H. Chilcote, 2000, *Comparative Inquiry in Politics and Political Economy: Theories and Issues* (Boulder: Westview Press).

3. Lars Rudebeck, Olle Törnquist, and Virgilio Rojas, eds., 1998, *Democratization in the Third World: Concrete Cases in Comparative and Theoretical Perspective* (New York: St. Martin's Press).

4. See Anton Bebler and James Seroka, eds., 1990, *Contemporary Political Systems: Classifications and Typologies* (Boulder: Lynne Rienner); and Brad Roberts, ed., 1990, *The New Democracies: Global Change and US Policy* (Cambridge, Mass.: The MIT Press).

5. The literature on globalization is vast. However, a good starting point, accessible to the beginning student and useful for the more experienced scholar, is: John Micklethwait and Adrian Wooldbridge, 2000, *A Future Perfect: The Challenge and Hidden Promise of Globalization* (New York: Crown Business). More academic studies include: Frans Buelens, ed., 1999, *Globalisation and the Nation-State* (Cheltenham, UK: Edward Edgar); Robert Gilpin (with Jean Millis Gilpin), 2000, *The Challenge of Global Capitalism: The World Economy in the 21st Century* (Princeton: Princeton University Press); Susan Strange, 1996, *The Retreat of the State: The Diffusion of Power in the World Economy* (Cambridge, Mass.: Cambridge University Press); Susan Strange, 1998, *Mad Money: When Markets Outgrow Governments* (Ann Arbor, Mich.: University of Michigan Press); David Held, 1995, *Democracy and the Global Order: From the Modern State to Cosmopolitan Government* (Stanford: Stanford University Press); Ronald Chilcote, 2000, *Theories of Comparative Political Economy* (Boulder: Westview Press); and Katherine Fierlbeck, 1998, *Globalizing Democracy: Power, Legitimacy, and the Interpretation of Democratic Ideas* (Manchester, UK: Manchester University Press).

6. James Gwartney, Robert Lawson (with Dexter Samida), 1999, *Economic Freedom of the World, 2000* (Fraser Institute), on the web at http://www.fraserinstitute.ca/publications/books/econ_free_2000/.

7. What makes the *Economic Freedom of the World* project so intriguing to the student of cross-national analysis is that the authors did not stop at merely gathering the bits and pieces of data. Following the collection of the initial data, the authors confronted an issue we have already discussed at length and will return to again, namely, the process of building an index measure—a measure based on several separate measures. With twenty-three separate variables broken up across seven subcategories comes the issue of "data reduction." That is, deriving a credible, equivalent, and valid single measure that accurately reflects the contribution of each component to an overall quantified measure of economic freedom. This, in turn, led the authors to confront the matter of weighting the variables. To weight means to assign a proportional contribution of a single measure to the broader multi-component measure. The authors of the *Economic Freedom* study relied in earlier versions of their study on a panel of experts to offer their estimates of an individual component's contribution to the overall measure of a country's economic freedom. They submitted to two different panels of experts the list of variables used to construct their various index measures (such as international exchange, and their overall index of economic freedom) and asked the experts to assign their own weight to

each of the variables based on their expert judgment of the countries and/or the economic variables. In the 2000 report, however, this process was replaced with a particular method that we will introduce you to in the next chapter: principal components factor analysis. From this data reduction technique based on variance and correlation techniques, the authors of the 2000 study derived both estimates of the weights for each of the twenty-three components in their measure of economic freedom (thus estimating how much of a contribution each component made to the overall measure of economic freedom), and they were also able to extract a single, standardized measure of economic freedom for each country on their sample, based on the weighted contributions of the various components of economic freedom.

8. While conventional measures of foreign trade are often used rather than more involved indices of international market integration as a measure of a country's degree of openness to the world economy, the variable INTEX offers us a much broader and more valid measure of the full commitment of the country's markets to international economic interaction.

9. For an interesting and insightful perspective on this, see Susan Strange, 1996, *The Retreat of the State: The Diffusion of Power in the World Economy* (Cambridge, Mass.: Cambridge University Press).

10. The classic exposition of the virtue of the market as a counter to the rising popularity of the philosophy of socialism and planned economies during the twentieth century may be found in N. G. Pierson, Ludwig von Mises, Georg Halm, and Enrico Barone, eds., 1935, *Collectivist Economic Planning; Critical Studies on the Possibilities of Socialism* (London: G. Routledge & Sons, Ltd.); Ludwig von Mises, 1944, *Omnipotent Government: the Rise of the Total State and Total War* (New Haven: Yale University Press); Ludwig von Mises, 1949, *Human Action: A Treatise on Economics* (New Haven: Yale University Press); and Friedrich A. von Hayek, 1944, *The Road to Serfdom* (Chicago: University of Chicago Press).

11. For a classic analysis of these models of political economy, see Joseph Schumpeter, 1950, *Capitalism, Socialism and Democracy* (New York: Harper). Also see John R. Freeman, 1989, *Democracy and Markets: The Politics of Mixed Economies* (Ithaca, N.Y.: Cornell University Press); David Landes, 1998, *The Wealth and Poverty of Nations* (New York: W. W. Norton); Adam Przeworski, 1985, *Capitalism and Social Democracy* (Cambridge, UK: Cambridge University Press); Robert Heilbronner, 1985, *The Nature and Logic of Capitalism* (New York: W. W. Norton). The model of mixed capitalism grew in popularity among the more advanced economies of the world as a response to the devastation wrought by World War I. Faced with shattered economies, displaced populations, declining markets, trade restrictions, inflation, and rising mercantile logic, the public and their elite alike turned to planning a vehicle to rationally overcome what appeared as chaos and pitiless Darwinian economics accompanying market failure following the decades after the war. The political consequences that followed the war seemed to many to require actions to control the disruption and restore order in an atmosphere of rising suspicions, anxiety, and nationalism. For an excellent analysis of the political-economic consequences of World War I and their role in shaping relationships between the market and the state, see Mark Mazower, 1998, *Dark Continent: Europe's Twentieth Century* (New York: Vintage), and Eric Hobsbawm, 1996, *The Age of Extremes: A History of the World, 1914–1991* (New York: Vintage Books).

12. David Held, 1995, *Democracy and the Global Order: From the Modern State to Cosmopolitan Government* (Stanford: Stanford University Press), pp. 160–188.

13. United Nations Development Programme, 1999, *Human Development Report 1999* (New York: United Nations Publications), pp. 127.

14. For a discussion of the relationship between democracy and liberal, capitalist economies, see Marc F. Plattner, 1998, "Liberalism and Democracy: Can't Have One Without the Other," *Foreign Affairs* 77:2 (March/April): 171–180; and Fareed Zakaria, 1997, "The Rise of Illiberal Democracy," *Foreign Affairs* 76:6 (November/December): 22-43. For insight into the requirements for economic freedom and the powerful and central role of property rights in the comparative success of capitalist development, see Hernando De Soto, 2000, *The Mystery of Capital: Why Capitalism Succeeds in the West and Fails Everywhere Else* (New York: Basic Books). For cultural interpretation of the comparative rates of capitalist development, see Lawrence E. Harrison and Samuel P. Huntington, eds., 2000, *Culture Matters: How Values Shape Human Progress* (New York: Basic Books); and John R. Hanson II, 1999, "Culture Shock and Direct Investment in Poor Countries," *The Journal of Economic History* 50:1 (March): 1–16.

12

The Role of One-Way Analysis of Variance and Cross-National Analysis

Terms: *Nonlinearity, Curvilinearity, Exponential Relationship*
Demonstrations: Kruskal Wallis H, 12.1; ANOVA, 12.2; Multiple Comparisons in One-Way ANOVA Models, 12.3; Directly Testing for Linearity in One-Way ANOVA Models, 12.4; The Measures of Association in One-Way ANOVA Models, 12.5; Applied Residual Analysis Drawn from ANOVA, 12.6

In this chapter we explore a particular tool of statistical analysis that follows logically from the difference of means (and Mann-Whitney U statistic) discussed in Chapter 10: Analysis of Variance (or ANOVA), and its nonparametric version, the Kruskal Wallis H test. Basically, the term ANOVA applies to any statistical technique that compares the variance of two or more variables when testing hypotheses. More technically, the specific techniques we associate with ANOVA are an extension of the t-test introduced in Chapter 10. Simple, bivariate ANOVA models, known as one-way ANOVA models, require that the independent variable have at least three categories (in contrast to only two, as in the t-test). Thus, the variance patterns assume a different characteristic with an ANOVA model. As such, the researcher can ascertain with more confidence whether the bivariate relationship in question is characterized as being linear, curvilinear, or exponential. ANOVA, therefore, is a combination of tabular analysis and correlation analysis.

ONE-WAY ANALYSIS OF VARIANCE

As with a t-test (discussed in Chapter 10), the critical components of a one-way ANOVA test are the within-group variance, the between-group variance, and the (whole) sample variance. The research hypothesis guiding the application of ANOVA assumes the within-group variance is small, the between-group variance is large, and both the within-group variance and between-group variance are distinctly different than the sample variance, as a whole. The null hypothesis holds, therefore, that within-group variance and the sample variance are identical; thus, the between-group variance is no different than the within-group variance. If, however, our theory suggests that the population is better understood as consisting of three or more distinct and independent groups, identified by their distinctively different means, we require an independent variable consisting of three or more categories, each with a unique value (1,2 3, and so on). While the logic of the statistical test is identical to a t-test, the technique we use is slightly different; we must move from a t-test to one-way ANOVA.

One-way ANOVA extends the t-test by allowing us to test for a *linear* relationship between two variables (X and Y variables) in the bivariate model. Remember, a t-test cannot specifically test for linearity because we have only two categories for the independent variable. Before we can test for a linear trend, we require at least three distinct values for the independent variable. Linearity can be tested directly because with three or more categories, you have more variance across your categories of the independent variable. Thus, ANOVA extends our use of linear analysis in hypothesis testing. It also allows us to preserve the categorical labels and grouping, and therefore serves as a first step in treating complex analysis issues on terms that are familiar and credible to students of comparative politics. It does not, however, need to be used exclusively for linear analysis. Linear analysis assumes the independent variable is measured at the ordinal level. As we shall see at the conclusion of this chapter, ANOVA is a useful tool of "discovery" as well, for it can identify differences in means across nominal groups, and in so doing, refine our understanding of the political world and direct our attention to important new hypotheses.

The specific form of ANOVA we will introduce is *one-way analysis of variance*. One-way ANOVA segregates the sample into groups based on values of only one variable in a bivariate model (technically, this is the independent variable). With relatively small samples ($N < 100$), two- or three-way ANOVA (analysis of variance models that have more than one variable attribute defining groups of countries within the sample) is more problematic. In this chapter, we will consider only one-way ANOVA.

In this section, we begin by exploring the logic of nonlinearity. We shall then offer three examples of applying ANOVA: a standard linear ANOVA model, a curvilinear ANOVA model, and an exponential ANOVA model. We shall also explore the identification and treatment of outliers identified within the ANOVA model and offer basic guidelines from which you may formulate a judgment as to what to do with the outliers if identified.

The Application Criteria for ANOVA

There are three critical criteria regarding the sample that govern the appropriateness of applying ANOVA. These criteria apply as well to the t-tests introduced in Chapter

10. First, the data must meet the criterion of *independence*. This assumes that each of the scores in the respective subsamples (groups) was derived independently of the scores in the other groups. Specifically, it is necessary that the scores for the independent variable be independent of each other within the sample. That does not mean the scores cannot be correlated with each other. It means, however, that in assigning a score of an attribute to one country, you have not defined the value of a score that will be assigned to another country in the sample. If, for instance, a country's degree of gender empowerment (GENPOW) is dependent upon another country's degree of gender empowerment, the assumption of independence has been violated.

The second criterion is the *normality of distribution* within the individual groups in an ANOVA test. It is not necessary that the groups have perfectly normal distributions (this, of course, is almost never possible). However, there should be no severe violation of a normal distribution within any of the groups. Specifically, there can be no severe skewness or bimodality within any of the groups in the ANOVA. The larger the subsample size, the less likely this is a problem. However, in cross-national analysis, with sample sizes of fifty or less, the issue of normality can become more problematic, especially as you divide the whole sample into increasing numbers of subsamples. This is another reason why, with a sample size less than 100, you should be extremely cautious in defining more than three or four subsamples within your whole sample. Examining the univariate statistics and histograms should be a regular procedure within an ANOVA test. Ordinarily, examining the standard deviation and mean of each group in the independent variable (provided by the ANOVA program in all statistical packages) is sufficient to check this assumption.

Finally, each group in an ANOVA test must have *equal variance* among its samples. Obviously, it is not necessary to have exactly equal standard deviations across the various subsamples. There should not be, however, severe differences between the respective standard deviations. Generally, if the number of cases for each group is equal, or close to equal, the criterion of equal variance across groups will not be violated. Again, a simple check of the central tendency measures provided by ANOVA can determine the degree of equality of variance across the groups in the ANOVA test.

If you discover a violation of the independence criterion, you may first examine the model using a nonparametric test. The appropriate nonparametric technique to apply is the Kruskal Wallis H test. If you find agreement between the results of the Kruskal Wallis H and the ANOVA tests, you are on firmer ground from which to offer your conclusions based on the ANOVA.

Nonlinearity as a Reality

Using analysis of variance techniques requires that we understand the difference between linear and nonlinear relationships. In the real world of politics, nonlinearity is far more common than many beginning students of cross-national analysis might realize. A nonlinear relationship exists between two variables when the values of one vari-

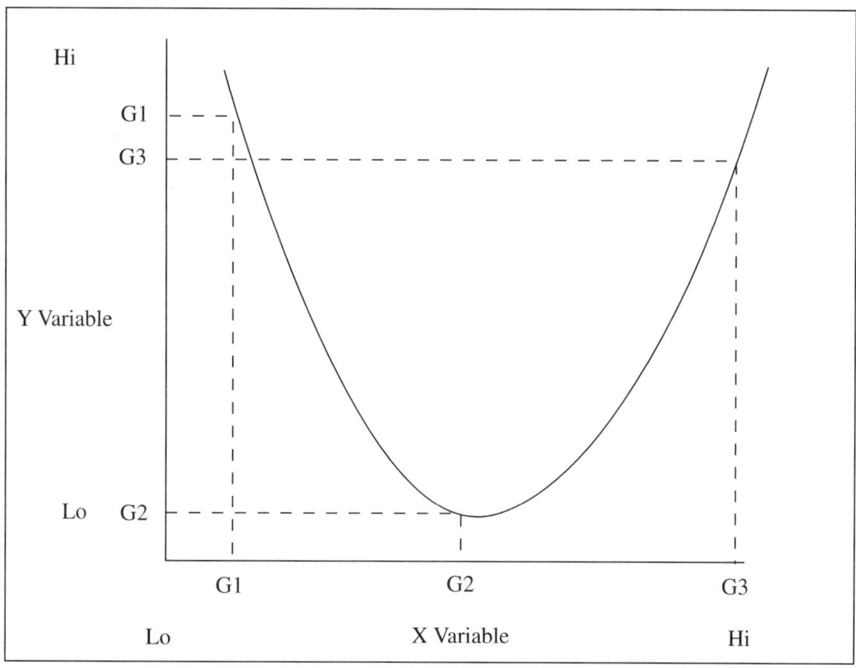

FIGURE 12.1 "Concave" Curvilinear Relationship

able do not change in direct proportion to the values of a second variable. There are two types of nonlinear relationships that are frequently encountered by students of cross-national analysis: *curvilinear relationships* and *exponential relationships*. Further, there are two types of curvilinear relationships: "concave" and "convex" curvilinear relationships. As well, there are two exponential relationships: positive and negative (or inverse), just as with standard linear relationships.

Curvilinear Relationships. Figure 12.1 depicts a typical "concave" curvilinear relationship. The distinguishing characteristics of this common type of nonlinear relationship are simple enough: as values for Group 1 (G1) and Group 2 (G2) increase along the X axis, we see that the values of G1 and G2 along the Y axis decline accordingly—a typical inverse relationship. Beyond the value of G2 along the X axis, however, additional values of the X variable are associated with *increasing* values for the Y variable, as seen by G3 along the Y axis. The original inverse direction is reversed at the G2 value on the X axis. Thus, the two extreme values for the X variable, as represented by the G1 and G3 groups, result in similar values along the Y axis.

Figure 12.2 depicts the "convex" curvilinear relationship, which is the mirror image of the "concave" curvilinear relationship. Both curvilinear relationships are occasionally found in ANOVA models.

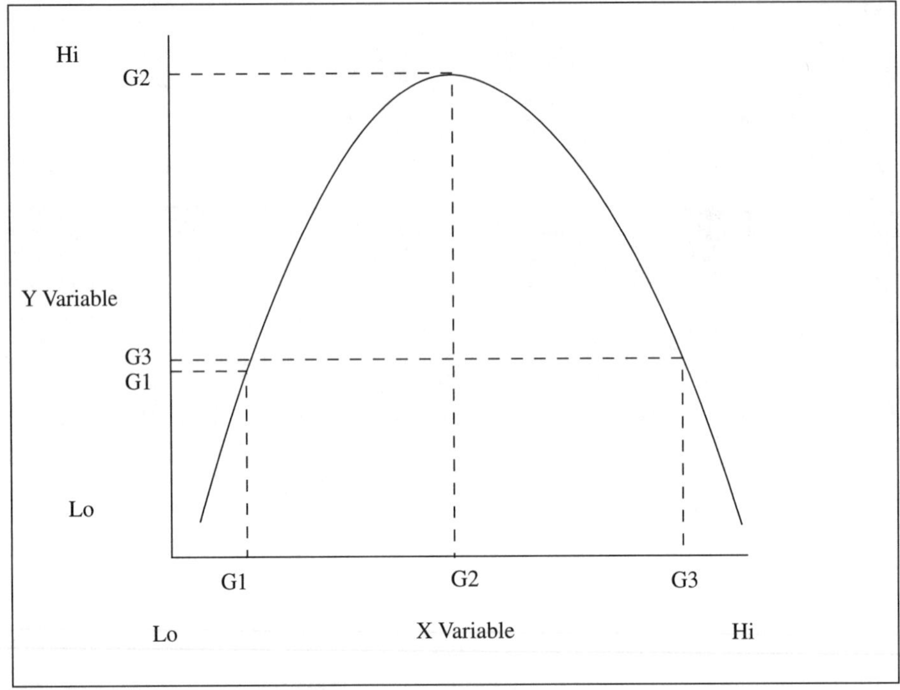

FIGURE 12.2 "Convex" Curvilinear Relationship

Exponential Relationships. The second type of nonlinear relationship is *exponential.* These relationships resemble S curves: They represent relationships between two variables that change by a constant *percentage* of the dependent variable. That is, X is associated with a change in Y multiplied by an exponential power. In a standard linear relationship, the change in values of the dependent variable relative to the independent variable are constant across the values of the dependent variable. In an exponential relationship, the associated values of the dependent variable change relative to the independent variable by a constant *percentage* of the dependent variable. Thus, as one moves along the values of the X variable, the corresponding value for the Y variable increases as a *percentage*, not a constant. This is illustrated in Figures 12.3 and 12.4 below.

In Figure 12.3, we see that as one moves along the X axis, each increasing increment in the X value for a country is associated with values of Y that reflect an exponential, percentage change. Note that the distance between G2 and G3 along the X axis is rather short, reflecting a relatively small difference in size between the values of G2 and G3. Yet, the change from G2 to G3 along the X axis corresponds to a *much larger difference* between G3 and G2 along the Y axis. This reflects the percentage (that is, exponential function) implied in the relationship. The negative exponential relationship, depicted in Figure 12.4, illustrates the same phenomenon for inverse exponential relationships.

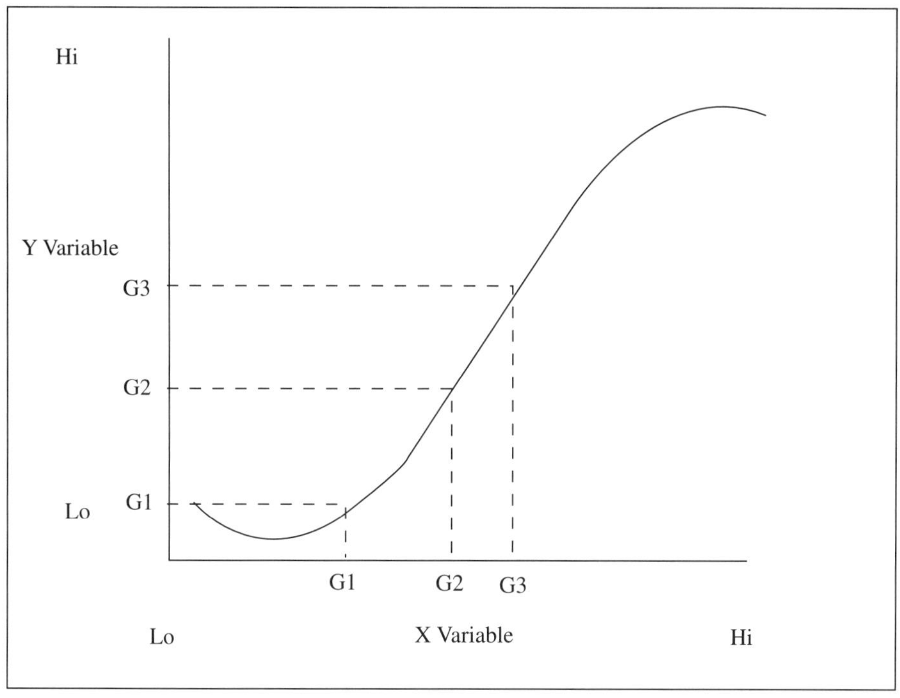

FIGURE 12.3 Positive Exponential Relationship

To summarize, an exponential nonlinear relationship means that with each increment of change in the X variable, we will find an exponential value of Y corresponding to that X value. In short, there is a dramatically greater effect of the X variable on the Y variable in an exponential relationship than in a simple linear relationship. One thing must be kept in mind: If you find an exponential relationship characterizing two variables in a bivariate model, you can be sure that the exponential trend cannot continue. Natural limitations and laws of our physical universe almost always dictate that in time, the exponential growth will flatten and slow. In the study of comparative politics, it is often quite challenging to account for these exponential relationships, as we shall soon see. Nonlinear relationships in general require a little more thinking as to why they are curved or exponential. That is why they are so important and useful: They are often counterintuitive to our normal tendency to think in linear terms.

DEMONSTRATION 12.1: KRUSKAL WALLIS H TEST

If we confront samples that severely violate assumptions of normality, or are very small ($N < 50$), and we have an ANOVA model, we are well advised to first execute the nonparametric equivalency of the analysis of variance technique. As you will recall from Chapter 10 in our discussion of the Mann-Whitney U test, the nonparametric

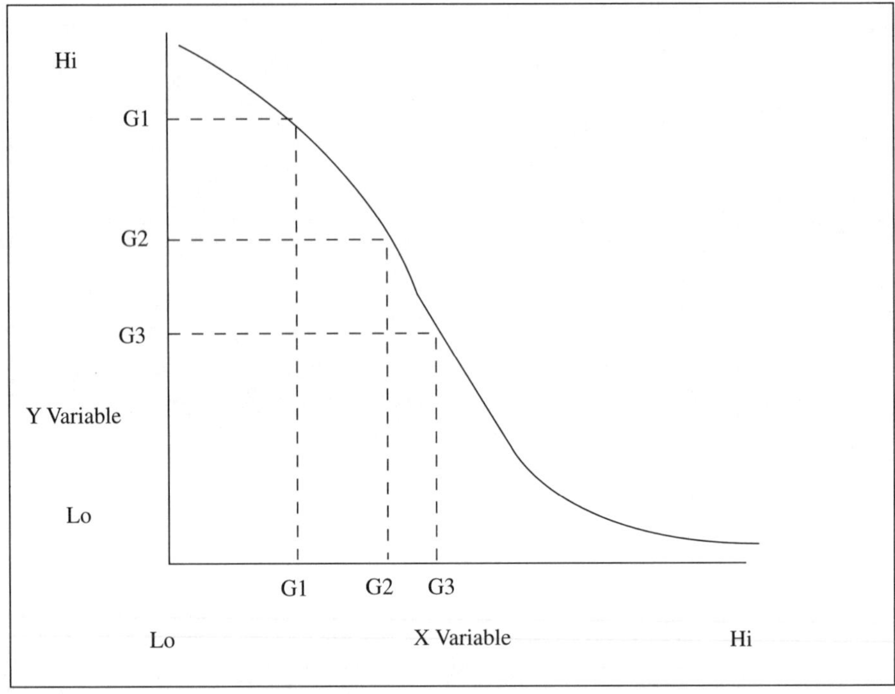

FIGURE 12.4 Negative Exponential Relationship

techniques of variance do not rely on the actual values of the dependent variable in the sample (for example, GENPOW); rather, they compare ranks along an ordinal scale. Thus, extreme violations in distribution that would otherwise undermine the model's credibility are avoided.

The Model

The Kruskal Wallis H analysis merely compares rank-orders across the three groups. As we saw in Table 11.6, if we rank-ordered all the countries in our sample of GENPOW values, we would expect in the Kruskal Wallis H test to find that the ranks for the first group (the group of countries with the least degree of gender empowerment) would be significantly smaller in number than the ranks in the second group (that group of countries with greater degrees of gender equality than the first group, but less than the third group), and we would furthermore find that by the time we reached the third group of countries in ascending order of rank with respect to GENPOW, the mean rank score would be larger than the previous two groups.

The Kruskal Wallis H test is ideal for initially testing Hypotheses 11.1–11.5. We know that one of the five implied dependent variables specified in Hypotheses 11.1–11.5 is not normally distributed (HUMDEV), though the degree of departure from normal distribution is slight. However, we still need to ensure that outliers are not severely distorting the distribution of values within our sample of scores for INTEX, HUMDEV, GENPOW, GENDEV, and ECON97. Table 12.1 reports the z-scores for GENDEV, GENPOW, HUMDEV, ECON97, and INTEX. There is only one country at or beyond the ±2.0 range (Madagascar, ECON97), though each variable reflects slight skewing in the negative direction, as the negative z-scores extend out to the –2.0 range, while the positive z-scores extend out no further than +1.4 range.

The Results

To test hypotheses 11.1–11.5, we will use the recoded variables from the four measures of democracy (PARCOMP3, PARREG3, POLIT973, and CIVIL973). Table 12.2 reports the basic statistics derived from a Kruskal Wallis H test taken from SPSS 10. The output resembles a Mann-Whitney U test.[1] However, instead of only two categories in the independent variables, we now have three ordinal categories. The relevant statistics are the same, however. The analysis reports the value and labels of each of the respective ordinal categories of the independent variable. It then reports the number of countries within each of the respective ordinal categories, followed by the final column, which reports the mean rank for each country within the respective category. In all five models, testing hypotheses 11.1–11.5, we note the mean ranks increase in size as you move from the low ordinal values (1) through the high value (3). We also note that in each model, the largest increment of increase occurs between the moderate value of the independent variable (2) and the highest value of the independent variable (3). For instance, note that with respect to GENPOW, the mean rank for the two lowest values of PARCOMP3 are 15 and 15.1, respectively. However, by the time we get to the third and highest value of PARCOMP3 (3), we see the average rank of a country climb steeply to 33.7. This suggests an *exponential* (see Figure 12.3) relationship exists between gender empowerment and the scope of institutional democracy (the competitiveness of political participation within a society). This pattern is repeated for GENDEV by PARREG3.

The findings suggest that all the hypotheses specified in Chapter 11 are supported in our initial analysis utilizing a nonparametric equivalent for the ANOVA technique. We are not, recall, suggesting that any of the components of democracy *cause* market authority, international exchange, gender empowerment, or human development. Rather, there is a clear association between the primary properties of democracy and the extent to which market authority and environmental byproducts of the political-economic system exhibit certain traits. Nonetheless, we do suggest, and our findings confirm, that the intrinsic nature of democracy is clearly associated with the structural and cultural conditions that favor market authority over state authority, international economic exchange over autarky, gender empowerment rather than gender exclusion, gender equality rather than gender inequality, and human development rather than poverty and underdevelopment.

TABLE 12.1 Standardized Scores, Gender Development (ZGENDEV), Gender Empowerment (ZGENPOW), Human Development (ZHUMDEV), Market Authority (ZECON97), and International Exchange (ZINTEX)

COUNTRY	*ZGENDEV*	*COUNTRY*	*ZGENPOW*	*COUNTRY*	*ZHUMDEV*	*COUNTRY*	*ZECON97*	*COUNTRY*	*ZINTEX*
Uganda	-1.917	Uganda	-1.917	Uganda	-1.972	Madagascar	-2.069	Zimbabwe	-1.952
Tanzania	-1.788	Tanzania	-1.788	Tanzania	-1.865	Algeria	-1.923	Madagascar	-1.929
Bangladesh	-1.726	Bangladesh	-1.726	Bangladesh	-1.745	Ukraine	-1.632	Egypt	-1.875
Madagascar	-1.702	Madagascar	-1.702	Madagascar	-1.663	Romania	-1.559	Nigeria	-1.810
Nepal	-1.646	Nepal	-1.646	Nigeria	-1.644	Nigeria	-1.486	Congo	-1.744
Nigeria	-1.640	Nigeria	-1.640	Nepal	-1.600	Zimbabwe	-1.267	India	-1.668
Congo	-1.498	Congo	-1.498	Congo	-1.499	Iran	-1.267	Tunisia	-1.354
Pakistan	-1.455	Pakistan	-1.455	Pakistan	-1.316	Nepal	-1.048	Algeria	-1.261
Kenya	-1.177	Kenya	-1.177	Kenya	-1.247	Bangladesh	-1.048	Iran	-1.208
India	-1.128	India	-1.128	Ghana	-1.089	Russia	-0.975	Pakistan	-1.121
Ghana	-1.036	Ghana	-1.036	India	-1.083	Colombia	-0.830	Poland	-1.104
Zimbabwe	-0.943	Zimbabwe	-0.943	Zimbabwe	-0.988	Pakistan	-0.830	Morocco	-0.892
Morocco	-0.881	Morocco	-0.881	Morocco	-0.849	Tanzania	-0.830	Korea	-0.592
Egypt	-0.647	Egypt	-0.647	Egypt	-0.635	India	-0.684	Sri Lanka	-0.585
Algeria	-0.407	Algeria	-0.407	Algeria	-0.326	Brazil	-0.611	Uganda	-0.499
Indonesia	-0.203	Indonesia	-0.203	Indonesia	-0.225	Morocco	-0.538	Brazil	-0.313
Tunisia	-0.166	Tunisia	-0.166	South Africa	-0.136	Venezuela	-0.538	Tanzania	-0.206
South Africa	-0.117	South Africa	-0.117	Tunisia	-0.136	Poland	-0.538	Kenya	-0.198
Iran	-0.074	Iran	-0.074	China	-0.098	Uganda	-0.465	Argentina	-0.069
China	-0.055	China	-0.055	Iran	-0.010	China	-0.392	Nepal	-0.058
Sri Lanka	0.025	Sri Lanka	0.025	Sri Lanka	0.028	Tunisia	-0.319	Ghana	0.025
Ukraine	0.025	Ukraine	0.025	Ukraine	0.028	Ghana	-0.246	Malaysia	0.129
Turkey	0.087	Turkey	0.087	Turkey	0.072	Sri Lanka	-0.174	Indonesia	0.144
Peru	0.111	Peru	0.111	Brazil	0.141	Egypt	-0.101	Bangladesh	0.156
Ecuador	0.124	Ecuador	0.124	Peru	0.141	Turkey	-0.101	Thailand	0.209
Brazil	0.155	Brazil	0.155	Philippines	0.148	Kenya	0.045	Peru	0.220
Philippines	0.173	Philippines	0.173	Ecuador	0.192	Ecuador	0.191	Colombia	0.222
Russia	0.229	Russia	0.229	Russia	0.192	Czech	0.264	Romania	0.223

Romania	0.259	Romania	0.259	Romania	0.223	Indonesia	0.337	Russia	0.270
Thailand	0.266	Thailand	0.266	Thailand	0.230	Korea	0.410	Ecuador	0.287
Malaysia	0.340	Malaysia	0.340	Malaysia	0.324	South Africa	0.410	China	0.323
Colombia	0.352	Colombia	0.352	Colombia	0.324	Greece	0.483	Ukraine	0.386
Mexico	0.432	Mexico	0.432	Mexico	0.438	Malaysia	0.556	Venezuela	0.453
Venezuela	0.481	Venezuela	0.481	Venezuela	0.476	Mexico	0.701	Philippines	0.511
Poland	0.568	Poland	0.568	Poland	0.539	Congo	0.847	South Africa	0.669
Argentina	0.654	Argentina	0.654	Argentina	0.696	Philippines	0.847	United States	0.774
Czech	0.753	Czech	0.753	Czech	0.734	Peru	0.847	Japan	0.791
Chile	0.765	Chile	0.765	Chile	0.804	Italy	0.847	Mexico	0.829
Korea	0.845	Korea	0.845	Korea	0.854	France	0.920	Chile	0.898
Greece	0.944	Greece	0.944	Greece	0.949	Germany	0.993	Greece	0.928
Spain	1.110	Spain	1.111	Spain	1.119	Spain	1.066	Turkey	1.106
Italy	1.147	Italy	1.148	Italy	1.157	Thailand	1.066	Australia	1.107
Germany	1.209	Germany	1.209	Germany	1.195	Chile	1.066	Italy	1.165
United Kingdom	1.277	United Kingdom	1.277	France	1.270	Japan	1.139	Germany	1.181
France	1.283	France	1.283	United Kingdom	1.270	Argentina	1.212	Spain	1.191
Netherlands	1.283	Netherlands	1.283	Netherlands	1.289	Netherlands	1.285	France	1.204
Japan	1.289	Japan	1.289	Australia	1.296	Canada	1.357	United Kingdom	1.220
Australia	1.314	Australia	1.314	Japan	1.308	Australia	1.357	Canada	1.223
United States	1.345	United States	1.345	United States	1.327	United Kingdom	1.576	Netherlands	1.285
Canada	1.357	Canada	1.357	Canada	1.359	United States	1.649	Czech	1.306

TABLE 12.2 Kruskal Wallis H Test

		Summary Statistics	
Independent Variable	*Ordinal Value of Dependent Variable*	*N*	*Mean Rank*
	Dependent Variable = GENPOW (Hypothesis 11.1)		
PARCOMP3	1 Very Low/Low	7	15
	2 Moderate	15	15.1
	3 High/Very High	28	33.7
	chi-square (χ^2) = 20.031 (p = .000)		
	Dependent Variable = GENDEV (Hypothesis 11.2)		
PARREG3	1 Very Low/Low	7	11.6
	2 Moderate	7	13.1
	3 High/Very High	36	30.63
	χ^2 = 15.930 (p = .000)		
	Dependent Variable = HUMDEV (Hypothesis 11.3)		
CIVIL973	1 Very Low/Low	7	12.7
	2 Moderate	27	19.8
	3 High/Very High	16	40.7
	χ^2 = 26.769 (p = .000)		
	Dependent Variable = ECON97 (Hypothesis 11.4)		
CIVIL973	1 Very Low/Low	7	17.2
	2 Moderate	27	20.8
	3 High/Very High	16	37.1
	χ^2 = 15.235 (p = .000)		
	Dependent Variable = INTEX (Hypothesis 11.5)		
POLIT973	1 Very Low/Low	9	12.0
	2 Moderate	18	22.0
	3 High/Very High	23	33.5
	χ^2= 15.721 (p = .000)		

We must note that variance is a potential problem in the distribution of scores for PARREG3. However, the chi-square for the model linking the scope of liberal democracy and gender equality is nonetheless borderline. On the whole, therefore, we may conclude there appears to be nothing that would suggest a more sophisticated ANOVA model cannot be employed for more precise estimates of the difference of means across the groups within the categories of the independent variable.

DEMONSTRATION 12.2: ANOVA

Table 12.3 presents the summary statistics from SPSS 10 of the ANOVA model testing the relationship between GENPOW and PARCOMP3.[2] These summary statistics are no different from those you have seen from the difference of means test. As with the Kruskal Wallis H test, we note an exponential relationship: The mean values of gender

TABLE 12.3 Summary of Means, Gender Empowerment (GENPOW) by Scope of Institutional Democracy (PARCOMP3), ANOVA (SPSS 10)

GENPOW					*95% Confidence Interval for Mean*			
	N	*Mean*	*Std. Deviation*	*Std. Error*	*Lower Bound*	*Upper Bound*	*Minimum*	*Maximum*
1 Very Low/Low	7	.30043	.12888	4.8713E-02	.18123	.41962	.152	.491
2 Moderate	15	.30693	9.6647E-02	2.4954E-02	.25341	.36045	.165	.515
3 High/Very High	28	.49961	.13556	2.5618E-02	.44704	.55217	.190	.742
Total	50	.41392	.15610	2.2076E-02	.36956	.45828	.152	.742

empowerment (GENPOW) for those countries with very low/low and moderate levels of competitive political participation (PARCOMP3) are virtually identical`$_1$= .300 and $\bar{X}_2$= .307, respectively). However, for those countries with high/very high levels of competitive political participation, the mean for gender empowerment ($\bar{X}_3$) rises sharply to .500.

ANOVA and the F Statistic

Table 12.4 reports the analysis of variance statistics produced from SPSS 10. The basic test statistic produced by ANOVA is the F statistic. The F statistic reflects the difference between the between-group variance and the within-group variance in the model. Specifically, the F statistic is derived by dividing the *mean square between-groups* by the *mean square within-groups* statistic and represents the statistical probability of the model being an improvement over the sample variance for predicting the value of the Y variable, GENPOW. Note that the mean square between groups is .234, while the mean square within groups is .015.

Considering the F statistic in more detail helps us place the one-way ANOVA test into proper perspective, especially with regard to the t-test introduced in Chapter 10. The one-way ANOVA test and its derived test statistic, the F statistic, assume different properties than the t-test and the derived t-statistic. In Chapter 10, we saw that in a t-test, where k = 2, the degrees of freedom within a model will be determined by the principal properties of the model: namely, the number of scores and groups within the model. The "between-group" variance is always equal to k–1 (where k is the number of groups in the independent variable). In other words, all scores in the model are free to vary with the exception of one score, which must assume whatever value is necessary to ensure that both values of the dichotomous independent variable have at least one member in each group. The "within-group" variance is the basis for determining the model variance, and is dependent upon the number of scores within the sample, relative to the number of groups within the model. Within a sample of size N, all scores of the dependent variable are free to vary with the exception of two scores. Two scores in the sample of the Y variable will have their values constrained by the sample

TABLE 12.4 ANOVA Results, Gender Empowerment (GENPOW) by Scope of Institutional Democracy (PARCOMP3) (SPSS 10)

GENPOW	*Sum of Squares*	*df*	*Mean Square*	*F*	*Sig.*
Between Groups	.467	2	.234	15.118	.000
Within Groups	.727	47	1.546E-02		
Total	1.194	49			

mean and standard deviation of the respective groups in the model. Therefore, as shown in Chapter 10, the degrees of freedom for a t-test is determined according to the simple formula, N – k, where k is values equal to 1 (or k – 1), and N denotes sample size.

A t-test with a sample size of 50 always yields 1 and 48 degrees of freedom: 2 – 1 = 1; 50 –2 = 48. In a one-way ANOVA test, the properties of the independent variable are not constant; that is, the number of groups into which the independent variable may be divided can range from three to almost any number, so long as the number of groups allows for an adequate number of cases within each group's subsample. Therefore, as with a t-test, the degrees of freedom for a one-way ANOVA model are based on the *between-group variance* and the *within-group variance* restrictions. The between-group restrictions assume k – 1 scores for the independent variable are free to vary within a sample. However, because k is not constant, as in a t-test, the restrictions of the between-group variance will vary across different one-way ANOVA models.

The within-group variance restrictions assume, as in a t-test, N – k scores are free to vary with respect to the dependent variable. In a sample of fifty scores and three groups (N = 50, k = 3), the degrees of freedom for a one-way ANOVA model will equal 2 and 47: 3 – 1 = 2; 50 – 3 = 47. However, if the independent variable defined four groups, the degrees of freedom would be 3, 46: 4 – 1 = 3; 50 – 4 = 46.

Statisticians apply a slightly different set of assumptions to the variance patterns of one-way ANOVA test statistics—the F statistics. The t-statistic is derived from a t-test where only two groups exist within the between-group variance component. The shape of the distribution curve for the population of t-statistics is shown by statisticians to be slightly flatter than a normal distribution. Therefore, the probability of t-statistics must be evaluated in terms of a student t distribution that reflects this more platykurtic property of t distribution.

F statistics derived from ANOVA models assume a slightly more peaked distribution. This is consistent with the assumption that ordinarily a one-way ANOVA mode will contain more scores in the sample than a t-test. This is a reasonable assumption in most cases because in a one-way ANOVA test you are dividing the sample into more than two groups, which would require more scores to ensure an even distribution of scores across the respective groups.

The F statistic in Table 12.4 is 15.118 [.234/.015]. The probability level of an F statistic of 15.118 with a sample of 50 (that is, N = 50) and a three-group dependent variable (k = 3) will have 47 degrees of freedom for the within-group variance estimates (N – k, 50 – 3 = 47) and 2 degrees of freedom for our estimated between-group variance (k – 1, 3 – 1 = 2). The likelihood of obtaining an F statistic this large if the null were correct, with a three-category independent variable and a sample of fifty cases, is less than 1 in 1000, or p = .000. Thus, we know we may reject the null with a great deal of confidence that we will not commit a Type I error. We may therefore confirm our research hypothesis (Hypothesis 11.2): Gender empowerment increases with institutional political competition in society (though we cannot claim an explicit causal connection between gender empowerment and liberal democracy).

Graphics

To examine the shape of the relationship, specifically, to gauge the degree of differences between the various groups within the model with respect to the dependent variable, two graphics are particularly useful in ANOVA models. The first is that which you have already seen in Chapter 10: box-plots. Figure 12.5 reports the box-plot for gender empowerment by the scope of institutional democracy. As suggested by the ANOVA test and the Kruskal Wallis H test, the relationship between gender empowerment and the competitive degree of political participation within a country varies exponentially across countries. Those countries with lower levels of an established scope for institutional democracy are much less likely to experience significant degrees of gender empowerment. The "take-off" does not seem to occur among countries until the scope of institutional democracy has proceeded further along. This, of course, would require further analysis beyond the cross-sectional analysis offered here, but the graphics and the ANOVA test suggest a heavy concentration of gender empowerment exists among nations at the high end of the scope of institutional democracy. Note, however, that even among the more democratic developed countries in the sample, the tails (whiskers) are much longer than among the countries with less democracy. This suggests that even among the most democratically developed nations, there is a fair degree of variance with respect to gender empowerment—a finding that can be verified statistically elsewhere, yet becomes vividly apparent with the use of a box-plot graphic.

The second graphic of great utility in ANOVA models is the error plot. Figure 12.6 reports such an error plot for the relationship between gender empowerment and the scope of institutional democracy (produced in SPSS 10). An error plot, like a box-plot, is aligned vertically—only the vertical scale is important. The plots map out the range of values within which the 95 percent confidence intervals fall for each group of the independent variable. Thus, we see that the 95% c.i. for gender empowerment among the very low/low democracies extends from .18 – .42. This, of course, is also reported in Table 12.3. The mean values for each group are represented by the small box midway between the upper and lower bounds of the 95% c.i. range.

What is useful about the error bar plot, however, is the ease by which one can immediately grasp the degree of difference across the means and variance within each group of the independent variable. If each group were "perfectly" different and

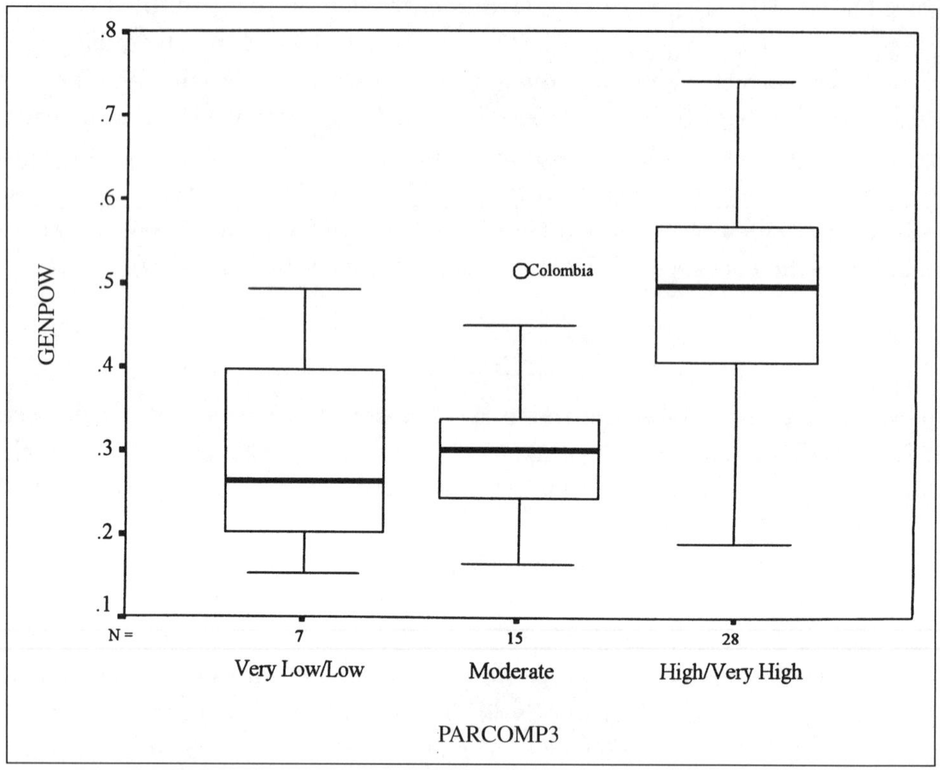

FIGURE 12.5 Gender Empowerment by Scope of Institutional Democracy

unique, the range of each error plot would not overlap at all with any of the others. Each would define a unique and separate range of scores along the scale of the dependent variable. Note in Figure 12.6, however, that the lower two groups of democracies are entirely overlapping. Indeed, the range of the 95% c.i. for the "moderate" group lies entirely within the 95% c.i. for the "very low/low" democracies. Thus, gender empowerment does not discriminate well countries with lower levels of democracy. The ranges for the lowest degree of institutional democracy are much larger than that shown for either the "moderate" or the "high/very high" democracies in Figure 12.6. Once again, this merely confirms what the Kruskal Wallis H has suggested, and the ANOVA analysis has shown statistically, and what has been also revealed in Figure 12.5 with the box-plots: There is an exponential structure to the relationship between the scope of institutional democracy and gender empowerment. This helps draw out distinct differences between what we expected (and specified in our hypotheses) and what is in fact reality within the political world around us. Analyzing what is causing gender empowerment to remain potentially "suppressed" even at moderate levels of institutional democracy is a task requiring the application of a case study, or perhaps, a comparable cases design, in order to refine our focus for further cross-national analysis.[3]

The Logic of Multiple Comparisons

What is apparent from both the Kruskal Wallis H and ANOVA analyses to this point, with respect to the relationship between GENPOW and PARCOMP3, is that the power in the model is provided by the difference between well institutionalized democracies and gender empowerment. By power, we mean the ability to explain something from the analysis of variance in our models. So far, what we can explain from our nonparametric and parametric statistical analysis is simple: The null hypothesis, which holds that all means across the categories of the dependent variable (GENPOW) are equal, must be rejected. The mean values of gender empowerment for the three groups of countries, distinguished by their scope of institutional democracy, are not equal. However, as the analysis also shows, both in terms of statistical results and graphical display, the differences seem less of a three-way distinction than a simple dichotomous distinction. That is, very highly developed democracies seem much more open to gender empowerment than countries with less scope of institutional democracy. It does not seem to matter if the country has very low scope or moderate degrees of such scope. If the country is not a highly evolved democracy, with respect to the competitive nature of political participation, it does not have very high degrees of gender empowerment. Yet, the F statistic easily achieves the minimum alpha level required for rejecting the null hypotheses. Is something wrong?

Nothing is wrong, but it is not ideal, either. This is an all too common conclusion in cross-national analysis. What is not ideal is the distribution of the number of countries across the three categories of the independent variable. Ideally, these should be more equal in number to meet the strictest requirement of ANOVA—a requirement that students of cross-national analysis rarely can easily meet. Of course, we have already run a nonparametric analysis in hopes of adding some credibility to the ANOVA findings in light of this variance issue. However, the ANOVA model does not, by itself, tell us something that we really would like to know: Is every group in the model different with respect to its mean value on the dependent variable? The F statistic does not test this assumption. It merely indicates that the means are not equal across all groups in the dependent variable. Thus, the null of assumed equality among means is rejected. That does not confirm, however, that some of the groups in the independent variable may not be similar—indeed, virtually identical. How can we know more precisely what the differences are between the specific groups in the sample? More precisely, how can we know if the mean values for the groups are indeed statistically significant?

Demonstration 12.3: Multiple Comparisons in One-Way ANOVA Models

This can be confirmed in an ANOVA test by utilizing multiple comparison procedures. One might ask: Why not simply run a series of t-tests across the groups? This, as statisticians will tell you, simply inflates artificially your chances of being able to falsely reject the null, thus running the risk of committing a Type I error. Within ANOVA, one wishes to execute a multiple comparisons test, which corrects for the number of paired comparisons you are making and reduces greatly the possibility of committing a Type I error. There are many such statistical techniques of multiple comparisons available to the student. All are divided into two groups: those that assume the variance between the groups in the independent variable is equal, and those that are designed to be used when we assume the variance across the groups is not equal. With small groups, such as in our case of three, there will not be much difference at all between the estimates based on multiple comparisons assuming equal variance among the groups and multiple comparisons among groups assuming unequal variance. Nonetheless, when running an ANOVA (such as in SPSS 10) it is always a good idea to specify a *homogeneity-of-variance test* and obtain the Levene's statistic. If this statistic is not significant ($p < .05$), equal variance must be assumed. If the Levene's statistic is significant ($p \leq .05$), we must reject the null and assume variances across the groups are not equal. This will assist you in selecting the appropriate multiple comparison test.[4]

Table 12.5 reports the output from SPSS 10 of the Bonferroni multiple comparisons test within ANOVA.[5] This output reports the results of two different multiple comparisons tests: a Bonferroni test and a Tamhane test. The former is appropriate when you assume equal variance across all three groups. The latter is appropriate when you assume unequal variance across the groups. At first glance, this seems like a terribly busy table. Indeed, it has three components that are crucial: the cross-category difference of means comparisons, the reported mean difference, and the statistical significance of the mean differences.

Note the comparison of values for the dependent variable (GENPOW) between categories of the independent variable (PARCOMP3), or what we call the *cross-category comparison of means*. The first such cross-category difference of means comparison is between those countries that have a *very low/low* scope of institutional democracy (PARCOMP3) and those countries that have a *very low/low* scope of institutional democracy (PARCOMP3). Of course, this is comparing the same group, so there is no mean difference to compute; thus the cell to its right, under the heading "Mean Difference," is empty. The second cross-category comparison is between those countries that have a *very low/low* scope of institutional democracy (PARCOMP3) and those countries that have a *moderate* scope of institutional democracy. Here, the mean difference between the countries across these two groups of the independent variable is -.007. This difference has statistical significance of 1.000—meaning, it is not at all statistically significant. So, we must conclude there is no statistically significant difference between the mean gender empowerment score between countries that have very low/low scope of institutional democracy and those with moderate scope of institutional democracy.

This confirms what we have already seen. However, we see the third comparison is between those countries with *very low/low* scope of institutional democracy (PARCOMP3) and those countries with *very high/high* scope of institutional democ-

TABLE 12.5 Bonferroni Multiple Comparisons, GENPOW by PARCOMP3, ANOVA (SPSS 10)

Dependent Variable: GENPOW

	(I) PARCOMP	(J) PARCOMP3	Main Difference (I–J)	Std. Error	Sig.	95% Confidence Interval	
						Lower Bound	Upper Bound
Bonferroni	1 Very Low/Low	1 Very Low/Low					
		2 Moderate	-6.50476E-03	5.6913E-02	1.000	-.14780	.13479
		3 High/Very High	-.19918*	5.2542E-02	.001	-.32962	-6.873E-02
	2 Moderate	1 Very Low/Low	6.5048E-03	5.6913E-02	1.000	-.13479	.14780
		2 Moderate					
		3 High/Very High	-.19267*	3.9784E-02	.000	-.29145	-9.390E-02
	3 High/Very High	1 Very Low/Low	.19918*	5.2542E-02	.001	6.8733E-02	.32962
		2 Moderate	.19267*	3.9784E-02	.000	9.3902E-02	.29145
		3 High/Very High					
Tamhane	1 Very Low/Low	1 Very Low/Low					
		2 Moderate	-6.50476E-03	5.6913E-02	.999	-.16540	.15239
		3 High/Very High	-.19918*	5.2542E-02	.015	.35783	-4.053E-02
	2 Moderate	1 Very Low/Low	6.5048E-03	5.6913E-02	.999	-.15239	.16540
		2 Moderate					
		3 High/Very High	-.19267*	3.9784E-02	.000	-.28205	-.10329
	3 High/Very High	1 Very Low/Low	.19918*	5.2542E-02	.015	4.0529E-02	.35783
		2 Moderate	.19267*	3.9784E-02	.000	.10329	.28205
		3 High/Very High					

* The mean difference is significant at the .05 level

racy. In this case, the average significance in gender empowerment scores across countries within these two groups is statistically significant (p = .001). Thus, we have confirmed that the differences generally recognized in the ANOVA model (Table 12.3, Figures 12.5 and 12.6) seem focused now—they lie at least between the highest end of institutional democracy and its lowest end. As we move down across the three separate boxes for the cross-category comparisons, we see the only statistically significant differences in gender empowerment values across the groups are between the countries with very high/high scope of institutional democracy, and those with very low/low and moderate scope. Therefore, our assumptions, based on the Kruskal Wallis H test, the ANOVA summary analysis, and both the box-plots and error bar plots are correct—the relationship is exponential; gender empowerment does not occur in a constant, linear pattern across different levels of the scope of institutional democracy. Rather, it is concentrated among those countries with the highest degrees of competitive political participation.

Demonstration 12.4: Directly Testing for Linearity in One-Way ANOVA Models

There are methods by which we can estimate the degree of linearity within an ANOVA model. These should not serve as substitutes for graphical examination, or descriptive statistical examination. However, they are two more diagnostic tools that the student of cross-national analysis may find useful and of particular help in confirming the linear nature of the model at hand. Various versions of ANOVA procedures estimate the degree of linearity in the relationship between the two variables in a model, as in our example, GENPOW and PARCOMP3. One variant of a standard ANOVA procedure produces an F statistic for linearity (separate from the F statistic produced for testing the null of equal means across groups). The larger the F statistic of linearity, the less this difference, and the *less likely* a nonlinear relationship exists between the two variables. Our implied null hypothesis for a test of linearity is *a nonlinear relationship* between our two variables in the one-way ANOVA model. However, some programs report the direct nonlinear estimates, as well.

Consider Table 12.6. This output comes from SPSS 10, and is from the procedure MEANS.[6] Note the linearity and nonlinearity F statistics. Each is technically significant (F = 25.201 and 5.035, and p = .000 and .030, respectively). The F statistics in this case reflect the amount of error one finds if one compares a linear assumption to a nonlinear assumption. In this case, while both are technically statistically significant, the linear score is far more powerful, indicating an assumption of linearity is more accurate if one wishes to "predict" values of the dependent variable, than is an assumption of nonlinearity. That both the F statistics for linearity and nonlinearity are statistically significant suggests some deviation from a perfect linear model. Indeed, our

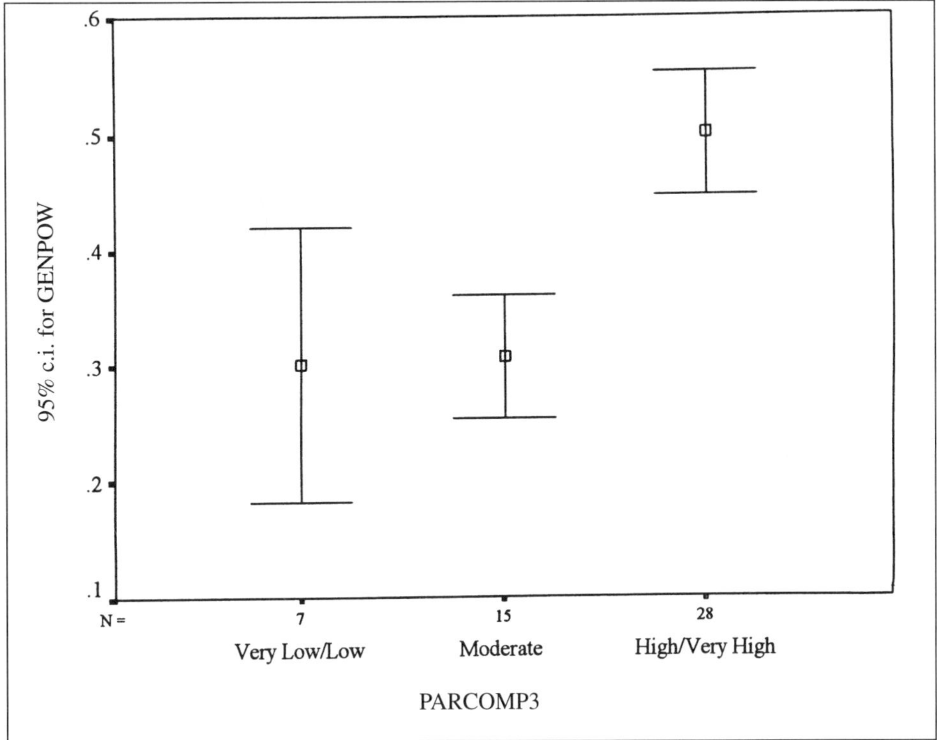

FIGURE 12.6 Error Bar, Gender Empowerment by Scope of Institutional Democracy

summary statistics and graphical analysis have shown this departure to be an exponential relationship. Nonetheless, we are safe in cautiously concluding that the true relationship between gender empowerment and the scope of institutional democracy is more linear than nonlinear.

Demonstration 12.5: The Measures of Association in One-Way ANOVA Models

Table 12.7 reports the measures of association one may wish to obtain for examination from an ANOVA test. The Eta (E^2) statistic is a PRE statistic. As such, it measures the *proportional reduction in errors* we will achieve when we "predict" a country's level of gender empowerment (GENPOW) from that country's scope of institutional democracy (PARCOMP3). It is a direct measure of the model's *power.*[7] The E^2 is computed by dividing the *between sum of squares* (in our case, .467) by the *total sum of squares* in the sample (1.194). The resulting E^2 of .391 indicates that we will reduce our errors in correctly predicting a country's value for GENPOW by 39.1 percent knowing a country's PARCOMP3 value, than if we did not know that country's PARCOMP3 value.

TABLE 12.6 Test for Linearity, ANOVA (SPSS 10)

			Sum of Squares	*df*	*Mean Square*	*F*	*Sig.*
GENPOW * PARCOMP3	Between Groups	(Combined)	.467	2	.234	15.118	.000
		Linearity	.390	1	.390	25.201	.000
		Deviation from Linearity	.078	1	.078	5.035	.030
	Within Groups		.727	47	.015		
	Total		1.194	49			

TABLE 12.7 Measures of Association, ANOVA (SPSS 10)

	R	*R Squared*	*Eta*	*Eta Squared*
GENPOW * PARCOMP3	.571	.326	.626	.391

Another way of interpreting the E^2 statistic is to say that 39.1 percent of the variance in GENPOW can be "explained" by differences in the competitiveness of political participation across countries. Recall from Chapter 9 that a PRE measure of .391 is a *moderately strong* relationship.

Table 12.8 reports the various descriptive summary statistics and ANOVA results for Hypotheses 11.1–11.5. As we have already anticipated with the Kruskal Wallis H test, all the hypotheses can be accepted with the exception of Hypothesis 11.2: There is no difference in the mean values of gender empowerment across countries with varying degrees of the scope of liberal democracy (PARREG3). Table 12.9 (Bonferroni multiple comparisons) confirms that each of the statistically significant models has an exponential nature to the relationship between the dependent and independent variables. However, the degree of international change in a country tends to change most significantly between very low/low levels of the scale of institutional democracy across countries, and those with moderate scale of liberal democracy. There is no statistically significant difference in the mean value of INTEX in countries with moderate scale of liberal democracy and those with very high/high scale of liberal democracy.

Demonstration 12.6: Applied Residual Analysis Drawn from ANOVA

Analysis of variance draws particular attention to the key activity of cross-national analysis: comparison. However, it is generally not enough merely to report the analysis of variance and summary of the data across the specified range of values in our independent variable. It is also worth the effort to examine extreme values within each of the groups of our independent variables. Table 12.10 reports an analysis of outliers drawn from the model predicting the value of human development (HUMDEV) from the scale of liberal democracy (CIVIL973)—Hypothesis 11.3.[8] Within each category of the independent variable (CIVIL973), we have listed the top three to five countries with the largest and smallest values for HUMDEV. We have also converted these values to their z-score equivalent, *within the group*. Thus, the z-score of 1.134 for Iran is its relative location within the group of seven countries who have very low/low scale of liberal democracy. It is not Iran's relative value within the whole sample of fifty countries.

TABLE 12.8 ANOVA Test

Independent Variable	Ordinal Value of Dependent Variable	N	Mean	Standard Dev.
		Summary Statistics		
	Dependent Variable = GENPOW (Hypothesis 11.1)			
PARCOMP3	1 Very Low/Low	7	.303	.129
	2 Moderate	15	.307	.097
	3 High/Very High	28	.499	.136
	F = 15.118 (p = .000, df = 2,47)			
	Dependent Variable = GENDEV (Hypothesis 11.2)			
PARREG3	1 Very Low/Low	7	98.223	1.123
	2 Moderate	7	98.164	1.128
	3 High/Very High	36	98.751	1.544
	F = .748 (p = .479, df = 2,47)			
	Dependent Variable = HUMDEV (Hypothesis 11.3)			
CIVIL973	1 Very Low/Low	7	.593	.107
	2 Moderate	27	.657	.139
	3 High/Very High	16	.871	.070
	F = 21.306 (p = .000, df = 2,47)			
	Dependent Variable = ECON97 (Hypothesis 11.4)			
CIVIL973	1 Very Low/Low	7	5.900	1.347
	2 Moderate	27	6.333	1.156
	3 High/Very High	16	7.788	1.143
	F = 9.712 (p = .000, df = 2,47)			
	Dependent Variable = INTEX (Hypothesis 11.5)			
POLIT973	1 Very Low/Low	9	5.138	1.312
	2 Moderate	18	6.497	1.095
	3 High/Very High	23	7.386	1.453
	F = 9.746 (p = .000, df = 2,47)			

The mean and standard deviation of the respective groups are noted in the middle two columns of the within-group summary statistics domain of the table.

From this table, we are able to specify some important country-specific comparisons within the context of our theory linking the political economy to its domestic and international environment. Note for instance the three countries with highest values among those seven countries that have a very low/low degree of civil liberties: Iran, China, and Algeria (.715, .701, and .665, respectively). Their scores for human development are *higher* than the lowest five countries in the moderate range of civil liberties (Uganda, Tanzania, Bangladesh, Madagascar, and Nepal). Indeed, four of these five countries with moderate degrees of civil liberties (Uganda, Tanzania, Bangladesh, and Madagascar) have achieved less human development than the three countries in the sample with the lowest values of human development within the very low/low

TABLE 12.9 Bonferroni Tests, ANOVA Models

Cross-Category Comparison of Means		*Mean Difference Between Categories*
PARCOMP3		*Dependent Variable = GENPOW*
1 Very Low/Low	1 Very Low/Low	--
1 Very Low/Low	2 Moderate	-0.007
1 Very Low/Low	3 High/Very High	-0.199*
2 Moderate	1 Very Low/Low	0.007
2 Moderate	2 Moderate	--
2 Moderate	3 High/Very High	-0.193*
3 High/Very High	1 Very Low/Low	0.199*
3 High/Very High	2 Moderate	0.193*
3 High/Very High	3 High/Very High	--
PARREG3		*Dependent Variable=GENEQ*
1 Very Low/Low	1 Very Low/Low	--
1 Very Low/Low	2 Moderate	0.05835
1 Very Low/Low	3 High/Very High	-0.528
2 Moderate	1 Very Low/Low	-0.058347
2 Moderate	2 Moderate	--
2 Moderate	3 High/Very High	-0.5864
3 High/Very High	1 Very Low/Low	0.528
3 High/Very High	2 Moderate	0.5864
3 High/Very High	3 High/Very High	
CIVIL973		*Dependent Variable=HUMDEV***
1 Very Low/Low	1 Very Low/Low	--
1 Very Low/Low	2 Moderate	-0.064
1 Very Low/Low	3 High/Very High	-0.27825*
2 Moderate	1 Very Low/Low	0.064
2 Moderate	2 Moderate	--
2 Moderate	3 High/Very High	-0.21425*
3 High/Very High	1 Very Low/Low	0.27825*
3 High/Very High	2 Moderate	0.21425*
3 High/Very High	3 High/Very High	
CIVIL973		*Dependent Variable=ECON97*
1 Very Low/Low	1 Very Low/Low	--
1 Very Low/Low	2 Moderate	-0.433
1 Very Low/Low	3 High/Very High	-1.887*
2 Moderate	1 Very Low/Low	0.433
2 Moderate	2 Moderate	--
2 Moderate	3 High/Very High	-1.454*
3 High/Very High	1 Very Low/Low	1.887*
3 High/Very High	2 Moderate	1.454*
3 High/Very High	3 High/Very High	--
POLIT973		*Dependent Variable=INTEX*
1 Very Low/Low	1 Very Low/Low	--
1 Very Low/Low	2 Moderate	-1.358
1 Very Low/Low	3 High/Very High	-2.248
2 Moderate	1 Very Low/Low	1.358
2 Moderate	2 Moderate	--
2 Moderate	3 High/Very High	-0.889
3 High/Very High	1 Very Low/Low	2.248
3 High/Very High	2 Moderate	0.889
3 High/Very High	3 High/Very High	--

*p ≤ .05

**Variance is unequal, Tamhane's test of multiple comparisons reported

TABLE 12.10 Outlier Analysis, HUMDEV by CIVIL973, ANOVA

Category/Value:			*Within-Group Summary Statistics (HUMDEV)*			
CIVIL973	*Range*	*Potential Outliers*	*Value*	*Mean*	*Stand. Dev.*	*Z-Score*
1 Very Low/Low	Highest	Iran	.715	.593	.108	1.134
N= 7		China	.701	.593	.108	1.003
		Algeria	.665	.593	.108	.669
	Lowest	Nigeria	.456	.593	.108	-1.273
		Congo	.479	.593	.108	-1.059
		Kenya	.519	.593	.108	-.688
2 Moderate	Highest	Greece	.867	.657	.139	1.511
N = 27		Argentina	.827	.657	.139	1.223
		Venezuela	.792	.657	.139	.971
		Mexico	.786	.657	.139	.928
		Colombia	.768	.657	.139	.799
	Lowest	Uganda	.404	.657	.139	-1.821
		Tanzania	.421	.657	.139	-1.698
		Bangladesh	.440	.657	.139	-1.561
		Madagascar	.453	.657	.139	-1.468
		Nepal	.463	.657	.139	-1.396
3 High/Very High	Highest	Canada	.932	.871	.070	.864
N = 16		United States	.927	.871	.070	.793
		Japan	.924	.871	.070	.750
		Australia	.922	.871	.070	.722
		Netherlands	.921	.871	.070	.707
	Lowest	South Africa	.695	.871	.070	-2.506
		Romania	.752	.871	.070	-1.695
		Poland	.802	.871	.070	-.985
		Czech	.833	.871	.070	-.544
		Chile	.844	.871	.070	-.387

range of civil liberties (Nigeria, Congo, and Kenya). These overlaps, so to speak, account for the poor discrimination of human development at low ends of the human development scale as reflected in Tables 12.8 and 12.9. Our analysis of variance has drawn attention to a couple of interesting anomalies. First, despite lower levels of civil liberties, some countries are able to do much better in providing for the basic prosperity of the citizens (Iran, China, Algeria, Nigeria, Congo, and Kenya). Other countries, with many more civil liberty protections as a foundation from which to build, remain severely constrained in their human development levels (Uganda, Tanzania, Bangladesh, Madagascar, and Nepal). All things being equal, these countries may be serious candidates for democratic retrograde, while countries such as China and Iran have clearly found a way to provide for human development at respectable levels while remaining far less committed to civil liberties. Other countries that are singled out as anomalies are South Africa (within-group z-score = –2.506) and Romania (within-group z-score = –1.695). The latter's level of civil liberties belies its esteemed status as a recent entrant to the higher ranks of countries with established civil liberties. We shall see in Chapter 17 that this is associated with a phenomenon we label "liberalizaton gap."

From this exercise we may see that the model may be able to demonstrate the trends we wish to see in order to confirm or reject our hypotheses, and from this to build systematically our understanding of politics and its relationship to the broader political-economic environment. However, the analysis of the outliers allows us to pinpoint those cases (countries) that stand apart from the others because their expected degree of human development does not align with the actual values for human development, given their degree of civil liberties. In order to understand why these outliers are so far from their expected values, we must consider additional theory refinement and further hypothesis testing—the grist of social science, and a fundamental contribution of cross-national analysis. We shall do so in Chapter 17.

Using ANOVA to Analyze Nominal-Level Data

Finally, ANOVA can be a useful tool in summarizing nominal-level data. While we cannot test hypotheses based on the logic of ordered data using nominal-level data, we can use the logic of ANOVA to test the null hypothesis that the means of an attribute are identical across nominal categories. Table 12.11 reports the summary statistics for market authority (ECON97) across the six major geo-political regions of the world (REGION6). Note the F statistic is reported below the table, with the appropriate degrees of freedom. The null may be rejected: The means across the six groups are not identical. Figure 12.7 reports the error plots for this analysis. Table 12.11 and Figure 12.7 underscore the differences in market authority that exist across the global community and confirm its concentration in the most industrially advanced nations of the West and Western Europe.

CHAPTER SUMMARY

In this chapter we have considered why and how the Kruskal Wallis H test and ANOVA technique can be useful tools in applied cross-national analysis. The use of one-way ANOVA (and multiple comparisons) within the cross-national analysis of empirical data is a useful tool when we are forced to work with variables measured at the ordinal/nominal level of measurement. The tool offers a powerful means of exposing critical patterns across groups of nation-states and, in conjunction with box-plots and error bar plots, is an effective strategy to isolate and discover critical differences (as well as similarities) across individual countries. It remains one of the most basic tools within the repertoire of the comparativist.

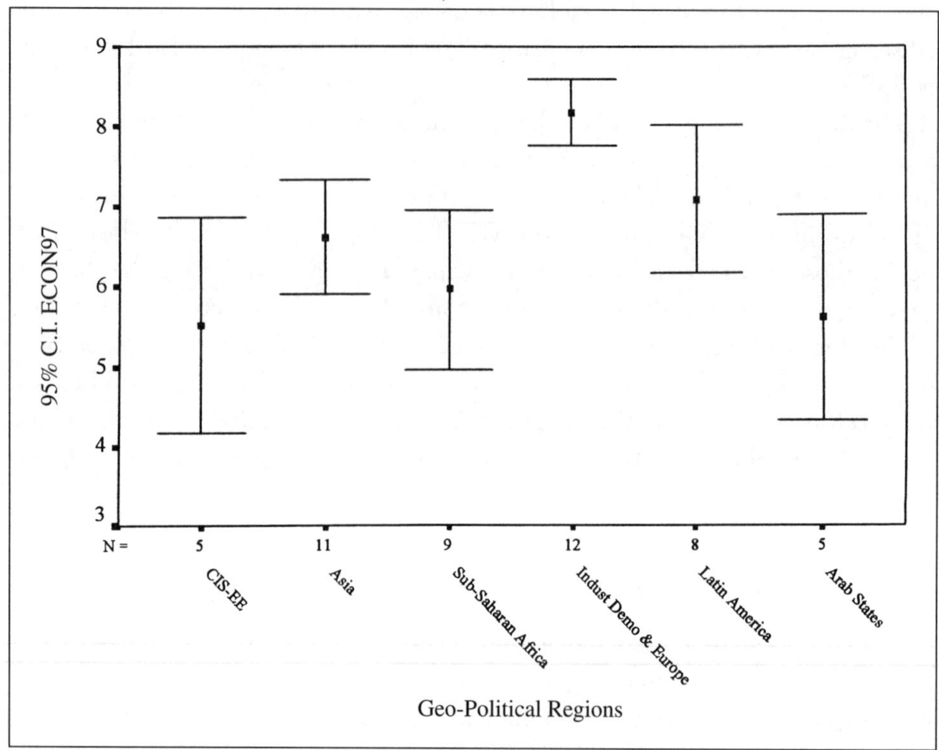

FIGURE 12.7 Market Authority by Geo-Political Regions

TABLE 12.11 Summary Statistics, Market Authority by Geo-Political Regions

	Summary Statistics, Market Authority (ECON97)						
Geo-Political Regions	*N*	*Mean*	*Std. Dev.*	*Std. Error*	*95% c.i.*	*Minimum*	*Maximum*
CIS-EE	5	5.52	1.076	0.481	4.184 – 6.856	4.5	7.1
Asia	11	6.618	1.053	0.318	5.911 – 7.326	5.3	8.2
Sub-Saharan Africa	9	5.967	1.292	0.431	4.973 – 6.960	3.9	7.9
Industrial Democracies	12	8.175	0.666	0.192	7.752 – 8.598	6.6	9.0
Latin America	8	7.088	1.122	0.397	6.150 – 8.025	5.6	8.4
Arab States	5	5.6	1.032	0.462	4.319 – 6.881	4.1	6.6
Total	50	6.738	1.372	0.194	6.348 – 7.128	3.9	9.0

F= 8.449 (p = .000, df= 5,44)

NOTES

1. To execute a Kruskal Wallis H test within SPSS 10, follow the sequence ANALYZE ▶NONPARAMETRIC▶K INDEPENDENT SAMPLES from main menu bar when in the K INDEPENDENT SAMPLES window. Select your variable that is measured at the interval level (such as GENPOW), or the test variable, from the index window and place it into TEST VARIABLE LIST window. Select your variable measured at ordinal level (such as PARCOMP3) from the VARIABLE LIST window and place it into the GROUPING VARIABLE window specifying the minimum value the variable assumes (for example, 1) and the maximum value it assumes (for example, 3). Select OPTIONS within the window and Kruskal Wallis H statistic. You may also choose DESCRIPTIVES option from additional descriptive statistics. For more details, see Marija J. Norušis, 2000, *SPSS: SPSS© 10.0 Guide to Data Analysis* (Upper Saddle River, N.J.: Prentice Hall), pp. 334–335. For additional detailed information on nonparametric tests, see Jack Levin and James Alan Fox, 2001, *Elementary Statistics in Social Research*, eighth edition (Boston: Allyn and Bacon), pp. 265–308.

2. To execute an ANOVA test in SPSS 10, select ONE-WAY ANOVA from the COMPARE MEANS option off the ANALYZE list from the main menu bar. Within the ONE-WAY ANOVA window, select the OPTION button and from there, select the DESCRIPTIVE button to specify the output shown in Table 12.3. See Marija J. Norušis, 2000, *SPSS: SPSS© 10.0 Guide to Data Analysis* (Upper Saddle River, N.J.: Prentice Hall), pp. 259–270 for more details. For additional detailed information on ANOVA models, see Jack Levin and James Alan Fox, 2001, *Elementary Statistics in Social Research*, eighth edition (Boston: Allyn and Bacon), pp. 240–264. For an example of the use of Kruskal Wallis H test and ANOVA within the literature of comparative politics, see Marijke Breuning, 1999, "Ethnopolitical Parties and Development Cooperation," *Comparative Political Studies* 32:6 (September): 724–751.

3. To obtain an error bar plot in SPSS 10, from the main menu bar, select GRAPHS▶ERROR BAR. In the window, assign your variable accordingly. See Marija J. Norušis, 2000, *SPSS: SPSS© 10.0 Guide to Data Analysis* (Upper Saddle River, N.J.: Prentice Hall), p. 523 for more details.

4. The test for homogeneity (the Levene Statistic) in ANOVA tests within SPSS 10 may be specified from the OPTIONS button in the ONE WAY ANOVA procedure window.

5. To obtain the Bonferroni multiple comparisons test, as well as other multiple comparison tests within ANOVA, select the POST HOC option button in the ONE WAY ANOVA window. For more details, see Marija J. Norušis, 2000, *SPSS: SPSS© 10.0 Guide to Data Analysis* (Upper Saddle River, N. J.: Prentice Hall), pp. 270–274.

6. MEANS is an alternative ANOVA method within SPSS 10 of the COMPARE MEANS option within the ANALYZE list of options from the main menu bar. To obtain the output shown in Tables 12.6 and 12.7, select the OPTIONS button in the MEANS window, and then select ANOVA and TEST FOR LINEARITY.

7. To obtain an Eta statistic, select the option ANOVA TABLE and ETA in the OPTIONS window of the MEANS procedure (ANALYZE▶MEANS▶OPTIONS).

8. To obtain these extreme cases within defined groups, use the EXPLORE procedure off the DESCRIPTIVE STATISTICS option from the ANALYZE list on the main menu bar of SPSS 10. Select the variables you wish to analyze (such as HUMDEV) by the category you wish to have it examined within (for example, CIVIL973). From CROSSNAT.50, we selected the

variable COUNTRY by which to label individual outliers in the analysis—this allows one to recognize the particular country-case that has been identified as a potential outlier. To obtain the list of outliers in your output, within the EXPLORE window select the STATISTICS option, and within this window, select OUTLIERS. The program lists the top three to five cases within each group. It will not produce the z-scores as reported in Table 12.10—these have been computed from the mean and standard deviations reported in the EXPLORE output.

13

The Role of Linear Analysis and the Conceptualization of Political Empowerment

Terms: *Multivariate (Multidimensional) Index Measures, Spearman Correlation, Pearson Product Moment Correlation, Linear Analysis, Scatterplots, Nonlinearity*
Concepts: Political Empowerment, Citizen Autonomy
Demonstration: Spearman Correlation, 13.1; Pearson Correlation, 13.2

In Chapter 7, we introduced the student to perhaps the most daunting challenge in cross-national analysis: the need to devise a single valid and reliable empirical measure of a complex and multifaceted concept that captures the full range and richness of the concept's primary properties, without stretching the operational definition of the concept beyond reasonable limits. In this and the next chapter, we explore the logic and mechanics of devising index measures. More specifically, we shall use linear analysis to help us construct a complex measure, or index, of *political empowerment* from our four primary properties of democracy (CIVIL97, POLIT97, PARCOMP, and PARREG) introduced in Chapter 4 and briefly considered in Chapter 7. From this, we shall then explore the various assumptions that lie behind *citizen autonomy*. The concept is adapted from David Held's analysis of modern democracy. *Citizen autonomy* depends upon the political, economic, and social empowerment of citizens within a nation-state. ECON97 and HUMDEV already reflect (through complex indexes) economic and social empowerment, respectively. We must devise a single measure for the third component of *citizen autonomy*, *political empowerment*.

To do so, we continue our consideration of "linear" analysis. Essentially, linear analysis consists of those tools of statistical inquiry that allow us to predict (and thereby explain) the values of the Y variable from the values of the X variable. This, of course, is identical to the logic underlying crosstabs, t-tests (difference of means), and analysis of variance techniques. Indeed, linear analysis and hypothesis testing constitute the core activities involved in the systematic analysis of comparative political data. Specifically, in this chapter, we will consider *Pearson Product Moment Correlation* analysis, which is the basic measure of association between interval/ratio-level variables. It requires interval-level data, or data that can assume the properties of interval measures within reason.

In the next chapter, we will consider a particular technique often relied upon by students of cross-national analysis to reduce complex data into a single measure. The tool, factor analysis, is generally beyond the basic repertoire of statistical tools for the beginning students of cross-national analysis. However, by demonstrating its fundamentals and applying it in a simple fashion, we can see how we may utilize more efficiently and effectively the shared variance between primary properties of a complex concept to construct a single, multidimensional measure of the primary concept.

Before we can appreciate factor analysis and the utility of multidimensional measures derived through its application, we must first consider the logic of the Pearson Product Moment Correlation. This technique measures the shared variance between two interval/ratio-level variables in a bivariate model. As such, it is part of the family of statistical tools that analyzes variance. As we will see, many complex techniques, such as factor analysis, apply the mechanics and logic of the Pearson Product Moment Correlation analysis. Few tools are as versatile and are so widely relied upon as the Pearson Product Moment Correlation. We will also consider the correlation's nonparametric version, the Spearman correlation.

We begin by extending our discussion of multidimensional index measures, first introduced in Chapter 5. We will then consider strategies for linking the primary properties of democracy identified in Chapter 7 into a single multidimensional measure. It is at this point that we will introduce the Pearson Product Moment Correlation and later, in the next chapter, the basics of factor analysis.

BEYOND THE MEAN Z-SCORE METHOD IN BUILDING A MULTIVARIATE INDEX MEASURE

A *multidimensional measure* is a single variable that is derived from the combination of two or more related, but separate, variables. Therefore, all multidimensional index measures have one thing in common: they all require at least two variables used in combination to fashion a broader, more meaningful measure of a fundamental concept that is not accurately represented by any one of the variables alone. It is important to remember the three basic rules of multidimensional index construction, as outlined by Louise White:[1]

- *Accurateness* (the index must be valid in that it measures what you want it to measure)
- *Simplicity* (it must be understood by the reader and user of the index)
- *Significance* (each variable must theoretically and empirically contribute something to the index)

We have already explored the idea of multivariate index measures in Chapter 5 in our brief discussion of *national potential power* based on measures of a country's areal size, its economic wealth, and its population (see Tables 5.1 and 5.2). Using z-scores for the three primary properties, we constructed a single index measure of national potential power (ZPOWER). In building a multivariate index measure of a country's national potential power, we in effect reduced the volume of separate variables used to explore a primary concept—power. This has the distinct advantage of allowing us to manage data more efficiently, and to more efficiently gauge the underlying concept of interests.

Tenuous Assumptions

When moving, however, from single measures to multivariate index measures, we run the risk that we might stretch the meaning of a concept beyond reasonable limits to force cross-national data into a specific definition. Combining several measures may force us to include variables in our analysis that cannot be appropriately applied to a few or many countries within our cross-national sample. As discussed in Chapter 6, the best way to avoid concept stretching is to be clear about the logic that underlies the intrinsic nature of the primary concept and to reduce primary properties to those that seem to be the most likely to capture the intrinsic nature of the primary concept.

We also noted in Chapter 6 that it is better to work within a statistical variance framework when developing multivariate index measures. That is, rather than assuming the largely untenable position that a primary concept such as democracy consists exclusively and wholly of four primary properties, we assume instead that in reality, most countries possess varying degrees of the primary properties comprising democracy. Some countries have more of these attributes than others. *The goal, therefore, of statistical analysis, in conjunction with concept formulation, is to measure how much of any given primary property a country possesses.* We may thereby evaluate the degree to which a country exhibits the attributes associated with the concept. However, with respect to the primary properties of democracy, we do not assume that all countries will all be equally democratic. Isolating the primary properties of democracy allows us to estimate the degree to which the primary concept characterizes the political environment of a country.

In this regard, we know from Chapter 5 that the simplest way to reduce data and devise a multivariate index measure is the mean z-score method of converting data to their standardized values and combining them into a single, additive measure. You will recall that the advantage of the mean z-score method is its efficient use of variance in constructing a multivariate index measure. *However, this method treats each component of the measure as an equal factor in the computation of the multidimensional variable.* This has the effect of implying that each of the primary properties combined to measure a complex primary concept contributes equally to the final effect captured by the multivariate measure. In our measure of ZPOWER we once again assumed implicitly that each of the component measures used in the computation of the final multivariate measure had an equal contribution toward the final effect: national potential power. This is a tenuous assumption. How, then, can we redress this effectively and yet not violate issues of validity?

The Logic of the Factor Method

We shall demonstrate in the next chapter another method of operationally defining an index measure. This method will be referred to as the *factor method*, a technique that allows us to *statistically weight* individual variables used in the construction of the multivariate index. You will recall from Chapter 11 that a statistical weight is merely a value we attach to a property to accurately reflect that property's proportional contribution to the overall effect we are measuring. The variable of ECON97 is in fact a factor-weighted variable which was derived using the factor method by the authors of the study, *Economic Freedom of the World, 2000*. Weighting has the effect of estimating the relative contribution of each property included in the construction of a multidimensional index measure. The weight itself is determined by the degree to which the variance of one variable matches that of another variable within the multidimensional index.

The factor method of constructing a multivariate index measure is a logical extension of the advantages offered by the mean z-score method, with an additional advantage. The factor method employs the logic of model variance to determine how closely matched the variance of the individual variables are in the multivariate index measure. In effect, the factor method assigns weights to each of the primary properties included in the construction of a multivariate index measure. These weights indicate the relative importance of the primary property to the definition of the final multivariate index measure representing the primary concept. We thereby avoid the often tenuous assumption that each of the constituent primary properties contributes *equally* to the definition of the final multidimensional measure.

The Rationale for Multidimensional Index Measures

Why would we want to construct multidimensional indexes in cross-national research? Because in drawing comparisons among countries, and in trying to understand the nature of something very broad, but very fundamental, it is useful to continually refine and enlarge our formulation of the concept. Compound measures merely represent the operational form that is assumed by these enlarged and refined concepts. Such compound measures provide the basis for cross-national generalizations.[2]

Students of cross-national data analysis are often faced with concepts that are best measured by combining several reliable and valid measures. All index measures, though broad in nature, offer a degree of succinctness to your analysis that is simply impossible when working with many separate, but logically related, operational variables. Construction of such index measures is governed first and foremost by your theory and the logical relationships implied by the theory. We are also, however, guided by statistical analysis, which gauges the empirical validity of such constructions.

REFINING THE MEASURE OF DEMOCRACY: POLITICAL EMPOWERMENT

In Chapter 7 we reasoned that democracy can be logically broken down into two qualitative dimensions, the *institutional* and the *liberal*. These dimensions serve to illustrate different ways by which political authority might be legitimized. *Institutional democracy* legitimizes political authority through the granting of open political competition and participation and by diffusing governmental authority across and throughout a country. *Liberal democracy* legitimizes political authority by counterbalancing government's power and authority with individual autonomy and civil liberties. The institutional dimension of democracy measures the capacity of citizens to act on their freedoms (through the ballot and other forms of institutionalized political choice), while liberal democracy reflects the capacity of individuals to preserve their sovereignty in relation to government. In this sense, the *scale* of *both* institutional and liberal democracy (POLIT97 and CIVIL97) underscores citizens' opportunities to act on their interests, while the *scope* of *both* institutional and liberal democracy (PARCOMP and PARREG) captures the range and extent to which citizens' interests can be legitimately pursued through institutionalized and competitive processes.

Implicit within our reasoning is the assumption that some of these primary properties may in fact be strongly related to each other. That is, it would be logical to expect that some of these attributes may reinforce other attributes. Our initial examination of the bivariate frequency tables (Tables 7.10 and 7.11) certainly suggested some degree of contingent relationships between the components of democracy. It would not, however, be surprising to find that one (or more) of these primary properties of democracy is independent of the other properties.

Toward a Single, Multidimensional Measure of Political Empowerment

To sort this out, we must measure the extent to which these attributes of democracy are related to each other. Our immediate objective is to determine which of the four primary properties seem independent of the others and which are strongly related to others within the set. Eventually, through this analysis, a clearer picture of the intrinsic nature and extent of democracy within our sample (and by extension, the target population) will emerge. This picture requires we specify statistically how much and in what way each of the individual attributes—POLIT97, CIVIL97, PARCOMP, and PARREG—contributes to the formation of a broader and more fundamental underlying concept.

Such a concept would subsume all the individual properties of democracy, yet transcend the contributions of each individual property. In this sense, we may think of these four properties as not merely capturing the relevant components of democracy, but, if taken together, as reflecting empirically the broader *political empowerment* of citizens within a society. Indeed, each primary property is presented as a slightly different variant on a singular theme: the capacity of citizens to be self-determining with respect to their associations and activities within the collective pursuit of values. Nonetheless, political empowerment also recognizes the limits imposed by the demands of a society. Pure populist democracy cannot exist without the rights of individuals being trampled by the activities of others. Therefore, empowerment requires the capacity to act as well as the recognized and legitimate limits imposed on individual sovereignty by carefully proscribed and defined constitutional rules of governance. Empowerment is minimized when state regulation supercedes the citizen's role in defining the limits of political participation and competition, and when there is no effective regulation offered by the state to ensure the freedom of individuals within society.[3]

To statistically construct such an index measure from our four properties of democracy, we will turn to one of the most widely used tools of social science, the *Pearson Product Moment Correlation,* and its nonparametric alternative, the *Spearman correlation*. We will employ these techniques in order to initially assess the strength and direction of the relationships existing between our four foundation attributes, POLIT97, CIVIL97, PARCOMP, and PARREG. From there, it is a natural step toward understanding factor analysis, the tool we will use to statistically derive a single multidimensional index measure of *political empowerment*.

THE LOGIC OF CORRELATION ANALYSIS

To begin, recall from Chapter 8 that in stating a hypothesis, we are in fact asserting our belief that we can better explain the attribute represented by the Y variable by taking account of a second attribute, represented by the X variable, than if we rely solely on the sample mean of the Y variable. The logic guiding the construction of a multidimensional index measure of democracy starts from the assumption that there is enough shared variance among the four individual measures of democracy to support the conclusion that together, these primary properties define a single underlying primary concept—*political empowerment*. How do we measure this shared variance?

Whenever we think that a group of attributes can be combined to form a single, broader measure, we must measure the extent to which there is robust variance among the primary properties of the complex concept. In this sense, our initial task is one of *exploration*, rather than explicit hypothesis testing. We assume initially that most (if not all) of the pairs of bivariate correlations should be *positive* and *statistically significant*. Because we have four variables (POLIT97, CIVIL97, PARCOMP, and PARREG), we will have six separate bivariate correlations to consider. (These bivariate correlations are: (1) POLIT97 with CIVIL97; (2) POLIT97 with PARCOMP; (3) POLIT97 with PARREG; (4) CIVIL97 with PARCOMP; (5) CIVIL97 with PARREG; and (6) PARCOMP with PARREG). Therefore, to initially explore the relationships between each of these pairs of relationships, we require a statistical tool that is appropriate for the given task.

Initial Considerations

Our choice of statistical tool is governed in this case by two fundamental considerations: the *level of measurement* of the variables and our assumption about the *nature of the relationship* between the variables. First, the four primary variables are technically measured at the ordinal level. This presents us with a choice: Do we treat these variables as interval (though they are technically not), or should we choose to find some way to change them into an interval measure (as, for instance, we did with the survey data in Chapter 10). Two of the variables have a fair degree of variance, with seven categories (CIVIL97 and POLIT97). Nonetheless, as we can see from Table 13.1, none of the four variables is normally distributed. Indeed, from Tables 7.1–7.7, we know each is somewhat skewed. Yet, none is bimodal. Therefore, before deciding to treat these four variables as interval—or, to subject them to an analysis with a tool that assumes a reasonable approximation of interval properties (such as a Pearson correlation)—we shall examine each first using a nonparametric tool and compare these findings to those findings we obtain from using a parametric tool of correlation.

A second issue is *linearity*. In order to employ the tools of correlation, we must assume some degree of linearity to their relationship. We will have much more to say about linearity later in this chapter. For now, it is enough to recall from Chapter 12 that linearity holds that changes in the value of one attribute correspond to a proportionate change to the value of a second attribute, and that this relationship of direct proportionality is *unidirectional*, that is, continuous over a range of values within a sample. A positive linear relationship reflects a condition existing between two variables where higher values of one variable always correspond to higher values of a second variable over a sample. (By the same token, corresponding lower values across two variables would also show a positive relationship.) A negative linear relationship reflects a condition existing between two variables where higher values of one variable generally correspond to lower values of a second variable across a sample. For example, our assumption of a *positive* relationship leads us to expect that countries exhibiting "high" levels of civil liberties (CIVIL97) should also exhibit generally "high" levels of political rights (POLIT97). Again, by using either the Spearman's Rho or the

TABLE 13.1 Tests of Normality, Primary Properties, Democracy

Variable	*Kolmogorov-Smirnov*	*df*	*Sig.*	*Shapiro-Wilk's*	*df*	*Sig.*
CIVIL97	0.202	50	0.003	0.929	50	0.010
PARREG	0.314	50	0.000	0.770	50	0.010
PARCOMP	0.186	50	0.000	0.882	50	0.010
POLIT97	0.177	50	0.000	0.862	50	0.010

Pearson correlation, we may ascertain the extent to which there is linearity in the relationships.

DEMONSTRATION 13.1: THE SPEARMAN CORRELATION

As with Mann-Whitney U and the Kruskal Wallis H tests already introduced, the Spearman correlation (r_s) relies on ranks, rather than actual values. The Spearman correlation ranges in value between –1.0 and +1.0. As such, the consequences of having sharp departures from normal distributions—as we face with at least some of the variables that represent the primary properties of democracy—can be avoided while ascertaining the extent to which a relationship exists between two variables. A ±1.0 r_s coefficient implies a perfect match between ranks (as the rank of one variable increases, or decreases, so too does the rank of the second variable in the model—by equal and exact degrees of change). A value of 0 implies a totally random alignment of ranks across the variables within the sample.

The Elements of Bivariate Correlation

The computational detail of the Spearman correlation, and that of the Pearson correlation, are rather involved. To derive a correlation coefficient for a bivariate model, it helps to once again think in terms of three components. Together, these three components compose the structure of variance within a standard bivariate correlation model. One component compares the value of each country's Y variable to the sample as a whole. The second component does the same for each country's X value with respect to the sample of X scores. These two components constitute the variance for the Y and X variables, respectively. The third component compares directly the score of Y for each country in the sample to each country's score for X in the sample. The total variance would be, in effect, the variance we find when we try to explain X values from knowledge of the sample of X scores, as well as when we try to explain, or predict, the value of Y variables from the sample of Y values. If the direct comparison of X to Y values (the third component of the variance structure) matches the total variance we find when working separately from the X and Y variables, we can be assured that a relationship of some sort exists between Y and X. Why? Because the variance of Y is matched by the variance patterns of X. The extent of that match is verified by simply comparing it against the total variances we find across the X and Y variables alone (the first and second components of the variance structure).

This may seem intimidating, but it is a matter of simply summing and squaring the values of the X and Y variables in the sample, executing a very simple and straightforward equation, and one has a correlation coefficient—or, an estimate of shared variance between Y and X. This logic applies to both the parametric and nonparametric correlation coefficients. The only difference is that the Spearman correlation (r_s) works from rankings of the X and Y variables across a sample, and the Pearson Product Moment Correlation works from the actual values of X and Y for each country within the sample. Thus, the Spearman correlation is much less sensitive to extreme skewness in values.

Applying the Spearman Correlation

This can be illustrated briefly by turning to Table 13.2. We depart momentarily from our four primary measures of democracy in CROSSNAT.50 and return for simplicity of illustration to our data in EFFICACY.21. In Table 13.2 we present the detailed breakdown of the components of variance for a Spearman correlation of two variables: the degree of satisfaction with the way democracy works within a country (SATDEM21) and the degree of perceived corruption of public officials within a country (CPI). We have already discussed SATDEM21 in Chapter 10. What is CPI? The corruption perception index—or, CPI—is a measure of public belief that public officials use their public office for personal and private gain at the expense of the public interest. This variable is produced by Transparency International, an organization dedicated to monitoring and measuring aspects of public and private corruption among major countries of the world. The index is based on seventeen public opinion polls across ninety-nine major exporting countries. As the value of the CPI increases, the degree of perceived corruption *declines*. Thus, in Table 13.2, the Russian public perceives their public officials to be more "corrupt" than the Norwegian public perceives Norwegian public officials. It is important to note, however, that we cannot say from these data that Russian officials are in fact more corrupt than Norwegian public officials. All we can do is estimate the public's perception of corruption within the ranks of their bureaucrats and politicians, at a particular moment in time (1997–1998).[4] The scale of CPI runs from 0 to 10. A score of 10 reflects a country with approximately half as many people within society believing public officials are corrupt as a country with a score of 5, and so on. Table 13.2 underscores the working hypothesis that as the public's *perception of corruption* rises within a country, so too does the overall level of *dissatisfaction* with democracy.

The Spearman coefficient for this model is reported in the far right-hand corner, r_s = .775. Thus, in effect, our third component of variance structure discussed briefly

TABLE 13.2 Spearman Correlation, Variance Structure, SATDEM21 by CPI (EFFICACY.21)

	Values		*Rankings*		*Variance Measures*		
Country	*SATDEM21(Y)*	*CPI(X)*	*X*	*Y*	X^2	Y^2	*XY*
Russia	18.1	2.4	1	1	1	1	1
Hungary	22.5	5.2	8	2	64	4	16
Italy	28.6	4.7	7	3	49	9	21
Latvia	41.9	3.4	3	4	9	16	12
Bulgaria	44.7	3.3	2	5	4	25	10
Czech Republic	48.3	4.6	6	6	36	36	36
Slovenia	49.4	6.0	9.5	7	90.25	49	66.50
Poland	57.2	4.2	5	8	25	64	40
Philippines	57.4	3.6	4	9	16	81	36
Sweden	59.8	9.4	21	10	441	100	210
East Germany	60.8	8.0	15.5	11	240.25	121	170.50
Spain	62.5	6.6	11.5	12	132.25	144	138
France	67.1	6.6	11.5	13	132.25	169	149.50
Great Britain	70.8	8.6	17	14	289	196	238
United States	71.3	7.5	13	15	169	225	195
Japan	73.5	6.0	9.5	16	90.25	256	152
Canada	74.9	9.2	20	17	400	289	340
Ireland	80.8	7.7	14	18	196	324	252
West Germany	83.2	8.0	15.5	19	240.25	361	294.50
Australia	83.7	8.7	18	20	324	400	360
Norway	88.1	8.9	19	21	361	441	399

Summary Statistics for Computing Variance Components and Spearman Correlation

Sums:	$\Sigma X = 231$	$\Sigma Y = 231$	$\Sigma X^2 = 3309.5$	$\Sigma Y^2 = 3311$	$\Sigma XY = 3137$
Variance Components:	$N = 21$	$S_{yy} = 770$	$S_{xx} = 768.5$	$S_{xy} = 596$	$r_s = .775$

above (the XY variance component) captures about 75 percent of the total variance in the X and Y samples combined. If we were to square the value of the Spearman coefficient, we would obtain an estimate of how much variance in X actually captures variance in Y, specifically. Thus, $.775^2 = .601$; or, 60 percent of the variance in Y is accounted for, or "determined" by variance in X. A squared correlation coefficient is referred to technically as the *coefficient of determination*. In the case of the Spearman coefficient, it has less precise meaning than in the case of its parametric counterpart—the Pearson coefficient. Nonetheless, the intuitive meaning is identical: About 60 percent of the variance in ranks across the Y variable in the sample (SATDEM21) is matched by the variance in the ranks of the X variable in the sample (CPI).

The specific computation is less important than the actual appreciation of what a correlation coefficient implies. However, to help you appreciate the logic of the correlation, Formula 13.1 provides the simplified version of the statistic's computational logic. This formula is the same for both the Spearman (r_s) and the Pearson coefficient (r). Equation 13.1 presents the formula for computing a Spearman coefficient, based on the three components with the variance structure of the bivariate correlation model.[5]

$$r_s = \frac{S_{xy}}{\sqrt{S_{xx}\ S_{xy}}} \qquad \text{Formula 13.1}$$

Let us consider the formula in the context of Table 13.2. The sums ($\sum$) beneath each column are used for the final computation for the Spearman coefficient. Note there are a number of ties—countries with similar raw scores; therefore their respective ranks are tied. For instance, Slovenia and Japan tie for the tenth rank in the CPI measure (6.0). Of course, as the Spearman correlation coefficient works only with ranks, and not values, the sum of X and Y will always be identical. (In our case, $\sum X = 231$, and $\sum Y = 231$.) The three variance components of the correlation are represented by S_{yy} (the variance within the Y sample, or 770), S_{xx} (the variance within the X sample, or 768.5), and S_{xy} (the variance between the X and Y sample, or 596). The computation of the correlation coefficient follows the logic of comparing the components of variance in the model. The numerator in Formula 13.1 is the variance component comparing the values of Y directly with those of X (the computation for this component need not concern us here, however, it is derived by comparing the product of the X ranks and the Y ranks with the sums of the X ranks and the Y ranks, standardized by the sample size, or N—in our case, 21). The value of the numerator is 596.[6] The denominator indicates that the separate variance components of the sample of Y values and those of the X values must be reset to their original scale. Thus, the product of these two variance components represents the total variance in the model for the X and Y variables, and the square root places that product back to the scale that will allow direct comparison to the scale on which the numerator is measured. The ratio of the XY component of variance to the total variance is thus computed to be .7747, or r_s = .775. The statistical probability of obtaining an r_s this large *if the null was true*, would be less than 1 in 1000. We may therefore reject the null and conclude that there is initial evidence to support the argument that public perceptions of how well democracy works (within democratic countries) declines as the general public perceives public officials as corrupt. Of course, it is much easier (and more error-free) if we simply execute a correlation analysis within SPSS 10.[7]

Table 13.2 clearly reveals where some error occurs in our ability to estimate the value of Y from the variance in X. For instance, Sweden's rank for CPI is the lowest (meaning, that in this sample of twenty-one countries, it ranks twenty-first on CPI values and has the smallest perceived corruption among the twenty-one countries). Yet, Sweden is in the middle of the sample with respect to its rank for satisfaction with democracy (rank = 10). Hungary (8, 2), East Germany (16, 11), and Japan (10, 16) are examples of other democracies in the sample whose respective ranks are far apart. These countries run up the error—the rank of the independent variable (CPI) is not

TABLE 13.3 Spearman Correlation Coefficients, Primary Properties of Democracy (SPSS 10)

			CIVIL97	*PARCOMP*	*PARREG*	*POLIT97*
Spearman's Rho	CIVIL97	Correlation coefficient	1.000	.875**	.854**	.927**
		Sig. (2-tailed)		.000	.000	.000
		N	50	50	50	50
	PARCOMP	Correlation coefficient	.875**	1.000	.930**	.894**
		Sig. (2-tailed)	.000		.000	.000
		N	50	50	50	50
	PARREG	Correlation coefficient	.854**	.930**	1.000	.889**
		Sig. (2-tailed)	.000	.000		.000
		N	50	50	50	50
	POLIT97	Correlation coefficient	.927**	.894**	.889**	1.000
		Sig. (2-tailed)	.000	.000	.000	
		N	50	50	50	50

** Correlation is significant at the .01 level (2-tailed).

well matched with the rank of the dependent variable (SATDEM21) in these countries.[8] Thus, this error will reduce the overall value of r_s.

Table 13.3 presents the Spearman coefficient output from SPSS 10 for the correlations among the four primary properties of democracy we have specified. The table presents a "redundant" matrix of coefficients. That is, each bivariate relationship is reported, with the correlation coefficients repeated as we move across the respective variables in the rows and columns within the matrix. For instance, the Spearman correlation for PARCOMP and CIVIL97 is given twice, once for the column under PARCOMP, and once across the row for PARCOMP. This has no bearing at all on the computation—it is merely a stylistic issue. We note that each of the four primary properties is strongly correlated. With the smallest Spearman coefficient at .854 (CIVIL97 with PARREG), we may be well assured that there is robust covariance within these relationships, suggesting a common and singular fundamental concept, such as *political empowerment*.[9]

Below are the basic rules of thumb we use in evaluating the meaning of correlation coefficients for Spearman and Pearson coefficients:

To be of real value in hypothesis testing, the coefficient's size is:

Too small if:
r or r_s is less than .10, (though it may be statistically significant in large samples)
Weak if:
r or r_s is between .11 and .20
Moderately Strong if:
r or r_s is between .21 and .50
Strong if:
r or r_s is between .51 and .70

Very Strong if:
r or r_s is greater than .70

DEMONSTRATION 13.2: PEARSON CORRELATION

With the results of our nonparametric analysis in place as a basis for comparison, we now turn our attention to one of the most important and widely used parametric statistical measures in the social sciences: the *Pearson Product Moment Correlation*. Known as the correlation coefficient, and represented by the letter *r*, this is one of the two most widely reported statistics in hypothesis testing within the social sciences (the other being the chi-square statistic).

As with the Spearman coefficient, the correlation coefficient (r) ranges in value between –1 and +1. When two variables (for example, X and Y) within a sample are perfectly correlated in a *positive direction*, the correlation coefficient will be +1.000 (that is, rXY = 1.000). When two variables are perfectly *inversely* (that is, *negatively*) *related*, the correlation coefficient will be –1.000 (that is, rXY = –1.000). In the context of our discussion of variance presented in Chapter 10, we would conclude that when two variables are perfectly correlated (either negatively or positively), their variance would be identical: There would be 100 percent shared variance between the two variables (X and Y).

The Logic of Pearson Correlation

Let us briefly recap what we mean by shared variance. This implies that as the variance of one variable (X) matches that of the other (Y), we are better off relying on the model to predict any value of Y within the sample, rather than relying merely on the sample mean of Y. The sample mean of Y, remember, is the best estimate we have of a score within a sample of scores for Y. However, it is not perfect—there is variance in the model. When working with standard linear correlation, we rely on a second variable (X) in our bivariate model to tell us how much variance in Y is matched, case by case, in the variance of scores for X. A coefficient of ±1.0 indicates the variance in X is perfectly aligned with that of Y: The degree to which a score in Y deviates from its sample mean of Y is matched perfectly by the same degree of variance from the sample mean of X. Thus, X is a better predictor of Y than the sample mean of Y (and, in a bivariate model, the contrary holds as well—Y is a perfect predictor of X). As a coefficient approaches 0, we know that the variance of X and Y are completely independent. That is, each time a case in Y deviates from the sample mean of Y, the same case records a variance in its X value from the sample mean of X that is not proportional to that of the variance from the case in Y from the mean of Y. As this is repeated case by case over the entire sample, we have no way of improving our ability to predict Y from X that can reliably improve upon our use of the respective sample means to predict scores.

TABLE 13.4 Pearson Correlation, Variance Structure, SATDEM21 by CPI (EFFICACY.21)

	Variable Values		*Variance Measures*		
Country	*SATDEM21 (Y)*	*CPI (X)*	X^2	Y^2	*XY*
Russia	18.1	2.4	5.76	327.18	43.41
Hungary	22.5	5.2	27.04	507.29	117.12
Italy	28.6	4.7	22.09	816.33	134.29
Latvia	41.9	3.4	11.56	1757.76	142.55
Bulgaria	44.7	3.3	10.89	2001.66	147.64
Czech Republic	48.3	4.6	21.16	2335.03	222.28
Slovenia	49.4	6.0	36.00	2435.63	296.11
Poland	57.2	4.2	17.64	3266.89	240.06
Philippines	57.4	3.6	12.96	3294.84	206.64
Sweden	59.8	9.4	88.36	3579.52	562.39
East Germany	60.8	8.0	64.00	3692.90	486.15
Spain	62.5	6.6	43.56	3900.85	412.21
France	67.1	6.6	43.56	4497.01	442.59
Great Britain	70.8	8.6	73.96	5009.28	608.68
United States	71.3	7.5	56.25	5090.58	535.11
Japan	73.5	6.0	36.00	5407.37	441.21
Canada	74.9	9.2	84.64	5605.04	688.77
Ireland	80.8	7.7	59.29	6529.60	622.21
West Germany	83.2	8.0	64.00	6924.78	665.72
Australia	83.7	8.7	75.69	6997.57	727.77
Norway	88.1	8.9	79.21	7764.38	784.23

Summary Statistics for Computing Variance Components and Pearson Correlation

$\Sigma X = 132.6$	$\Sigma Y = 1244.5$	$\Sigma X^2 = 933.2$	$\Sigma Y^2 = 81741.47$	$\Sigma XY = 8527.15$
$N = 21$	$S_{yy} = 7990.03$	$S_{xx} = 96.35$	$S_{xy} = 669.02$	$r = .763$

To see why this is the case, consider first the data presented in Table 13.4. As with the Spearman correlation, the Pearson correlation coefficient can be understood as a function of three components of variance. These are noted at the bottom of Table 13.4. Note how the computation is identical to the Spearman, with the obvious difference that in the Pearson correlation, you work from the actual values of X (CPI) and Y (SATDEM21). The resulting correlation coefficient (r) is .763, quite similar to that of the Spearman r_s. Thus, both statistical estimates offer up quite similar results.

THE LINEARITY ASSUMPTION

Before leaving our introduction to the logic and mechanics of correlation analysis, we must turn to an elaboration of our earlier initial discussion of linearity and stress a point often taken for granted by students and professionals, and frequently to the detriment of their analyses and appropriate interpretation of the data. Correlation coefficients are technically a measure of a *linear* relationship. Because our initial exploration assumes linearity between our four foundation measures (CIVIL97, POLIT97,

PARCOMP, PARREG), we are correct in employing the correlation coefficient (r). However, as we saw in Chapter 12, the assumption of linearity is all too often in the real world of comparative political analysis a dangerous assumption to make without further exploration. Indeed many, if not most, bivariate relationships include a *nonlinear* component in addition to a linear component. This may sound abstract and technical, but it is very basic and common to our experiences from everyday life (recall Chapter 12). For now, we need to be sure we are clear on what a linear relationship assumes.

As with correlations, most students can easily and intuitively grasp the essentials of a linear relationship. Let us begin with a positive linear relationship. In a positive *linear* relationship the variance in one variable (X) is *directly proportional* to that of a second variable (Y). Since this is exactly what an r coefficient means, we see immediately that the correlation coefficient (r) and the degree of linearity in a relationship are the same. Figure 13.1 illustrates graphically a *perfect positive linear relationship*.

The Slope in Scatterplots

The respective variance for each country is expressed as XY1, XY2, and XY3. The dotted lines connecting Y1, Y2, and Y3 with X1, X2, and X3 intersect at the exact points of the respective scores for the X and Y variables for each country. A *perfect* positive correlation means that the distance between X1 and X2 is *exactly* equal to the distance between Y1 and Y2; as is the distance between X2 and X3, and Y2 and Y3, and so on. The size of the variance in size between one country's X value and a second country's X value is exactly proportionate to the size difference between the first country's Y value and the second country's Y value. Thus, knowing one country's X value allows us to predict exactly the value of that country's Y value—if, of course, r = 1.000!

Connecting these intersection points for each country creates a straight line—referred to as the *slope*. The *slope* represents the direction and strength of the relationship. The angle, moving upward from left to right, represents a positive relationship: Values (or variations) of Y increase in step with values (or variations) of X. The correlation coefficient for this relationship would be rXY = 1.000. We will discuss slopes (also known as *least squares* lines) in more detail in Chapter 15 and will see some examples of them later in this chapter. *For now it is enough to know that a strong, linear and positive relationship would be graphically depicted by a line like the one shown in Figure 13.1.*

In Figure 13.1, we observe a *perfect* correlation between the Y variable and the X variable (r = +1.000). This, of course, means that the value of the Y variable is exactly proportional to the value of the X variable for each case. Therefore, each dot, representing the intersection of the respective X and Y values, falls exactly along the slope. It is essential that you remember for now that the slope *does not* connect the dots. Rather, the slope represents the *expected* value of the Y variable, given a corresponding value of the X variable. This is, as you will recall from Chapter 8, the basis of prediction within hypothesis testing. Because in our simple illustration in Figure 13.1 there is a perfect

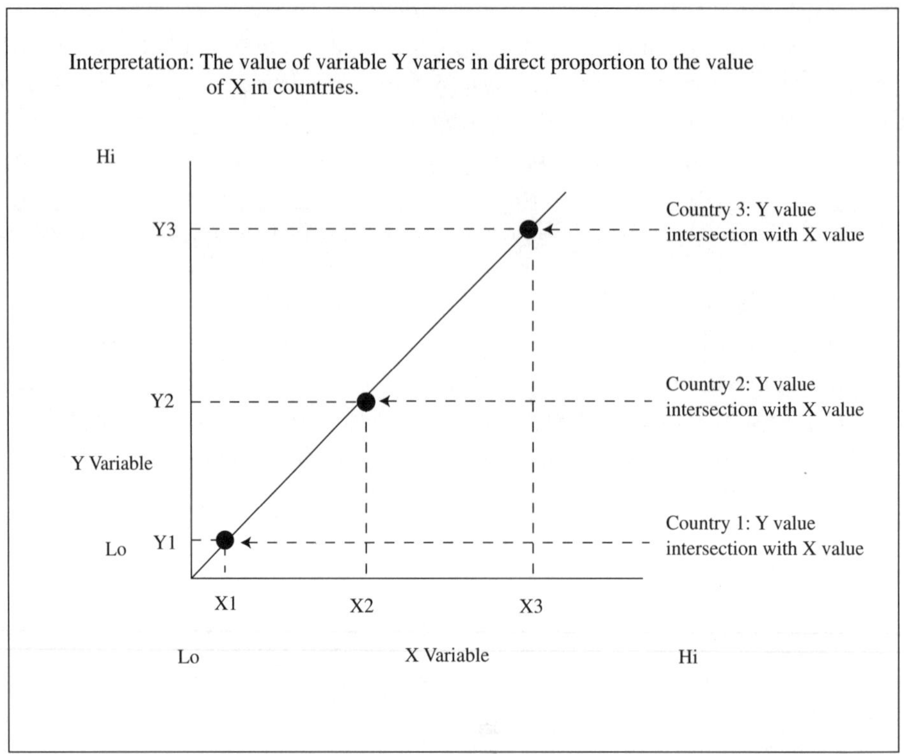

FIGURE 13.1 A Positive Linear Relationship

correlation between Y and X, each dot will fall precisely on the slope. In the real world, however, you rarely have a perfect correlation. As such, you rarely find a circumstance where the intersection points will fall precisely on the slope. Rather, they will be scattered about the slope (thus, we call a plot that aligns values of an X variable with values of a Y variable, a scatterplot). This will be discussed in detail in Chapter 15.

For now, we can illustrate this point and a positive linear relationship by plotting the scores for SATDEM21 by CPI using our data from EFFICACY.21. Figure 13.2 is a scatterplot produced from SPSS 10. We will see much more of scatterplots and discuss them in more detail in Chapter 15. However, at this point, it is useful not only to help illustrate the concept of linearity and the correlation coefficient, but also to visualize the logic of the error components (or, variance components) with the bivariate correlation model.

Visualizing the Components of Variance in Scatterplots

Note in Figure 13.2 we have produced two lines. The horizontal line represents the mean of SATDEM21, while the diagonal line represents the actual slope. Keep in mind that the slope represents the expected value of Y when we predict the value of Y from X,

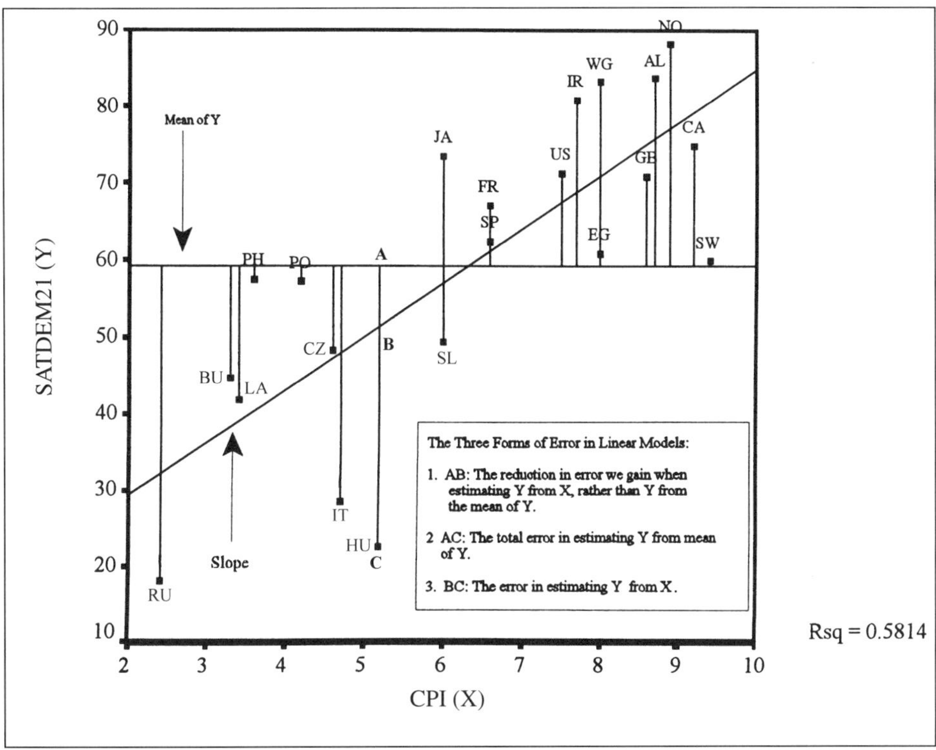

FIGURE 13.2 Scatterplot, SATDEM21 by CPI (EFFICACY .21) SPSS 10

rather than predicting the value of Y from the mean of Y. Note finally that each line has a spike that extends from the mean to the dot (with the code for each country adjacent to the dot). The spike is the length of what we call the residual. The residual, as we saw in Chapter 5, is the variance of each score from the mean. The longer the spikes, the greater the error we can expect in trying to predict a value of Y from the mean of Y.

These aspects of the graph allow us to better visualize the three components of error that in effect correspond to the three components of variance in bivariate linear models. Notice we have assigned the letters A, B, and C at specific points along the spike of Hungary (HU). Point A corresponds to the mean value of the sample, which also corresponds to the expected value of Hungary's degree of satisfaction with democracy (A). Point B is the intersection of the slope (the expected value of Hungary's degree of satisfaction with democracy) and spike. In effect, this represents the reduction in error that we gain when we try to estimate the value of Y in Hungary from the sample of X values, rather than from the sample of Y values (or, the mean of Y). Point C represents the observed value of Y, or Hungary's actual degree of satisfaction with democracy. Note it is actually much lower than both the mean for the sample and the expected value (B). If the segment of AB is identical to segment AC along the spike, there is no error in our ability to accurately estimate with our model the value of Y for a country in the sample. If this was generally the case for all twenty-one countries in our sample, we would know just from the graphical display of the relationship between X and Y that the value of the S_{xy} component in the variance structure would equal the $\sqrt{S_{xx}S_{yy}}$ component with the sample (see Formula 13.1). This would be approximately the case if all countries in our sample were as close to the slope as is the case with Spain (SP). It is virtually on the slope itself. The greater the distances in a spike covered by segment AB, the less "power" our model has in predicting the value of Y from the sample of X values. So, in the case of Hungary, knowing the value of CPI within our example will not help us very much in accurately estimating the value of Hungary's satisfaction with democracy. Thus, the numerator in Formula 13.1 would be much smaller than the denominator. *The closer the spikes in the sample are to the slope, the less the error we encounter when we estimate values of Y from the value of X for a country within our sample.*

What happens when a residual does not reach the slope, as in the case of Latvia (LA), Bulgaria (BU), and the Czech Republic (CZ)? This simply means the value of Y (SATDEM21) was in fact closer to the mean of Y in the sample than what was expected given the country's value of X. Or, in this case, because of the way we measure SATDEM21, we know that Latvia and Bulgaria (and to a much lesser extent, the Czech Republic) have more satisfaction with democracy than we would have expected given the degree to which their respective publics perceive the corruption among their politicians and public officials. That gap between the residual and the slope is error—error in predicting the value of Y from X. In essence, Latvia works to expand the size of the denominator in Formula 13.1, not increase the size of the numerator. This is also the case (on the other side of the mean in Figure 13.2) with Canada (CA), Great Britain (GB), and especially Sweden (SW).

Finally, note the RSQ figure in the lower right area of Figure 13.2 (RSQ = .5814). This is the Pearson r^2 ($.763^2$), and, as with the square of r_s (Spearman correlation coefficient), represents the total variance in Y that can be matched and "determined" by the variance in X. As each dot draws closer to the slope, the value of the r^2 increases, as does, of course, r, and, in terms of Formula 13.1, the numerator reaches parity with the denominator. In essence, there would be no dots off the slope if $r = \pm 1.00$ (and segment AB would be identical to segment AC). The slope would be a perfect 45 degree angle (running upward or downward, depending on whether the relationship was positive or negative). It does not matter if the slope is up or down, that is, if the relationship is positive or, as in Figure 13.3, negative. The closer the dots are to the slope, the greater the variance in Y is matched by that in X, thus confirming a strong statistical relationship between X and Y.

One last point. Because the slope is the estimate of Y based on the variable of X, and because the bivariate Pearson correlation model measures linearity, the closer the slope of the line (positive or negative) comes to a seventy-five degree angle, the stronger the relationship between X and Y. On the other hand, if there is no statistical relationship between Y and X—if the dots are randomly scattered all about the mean

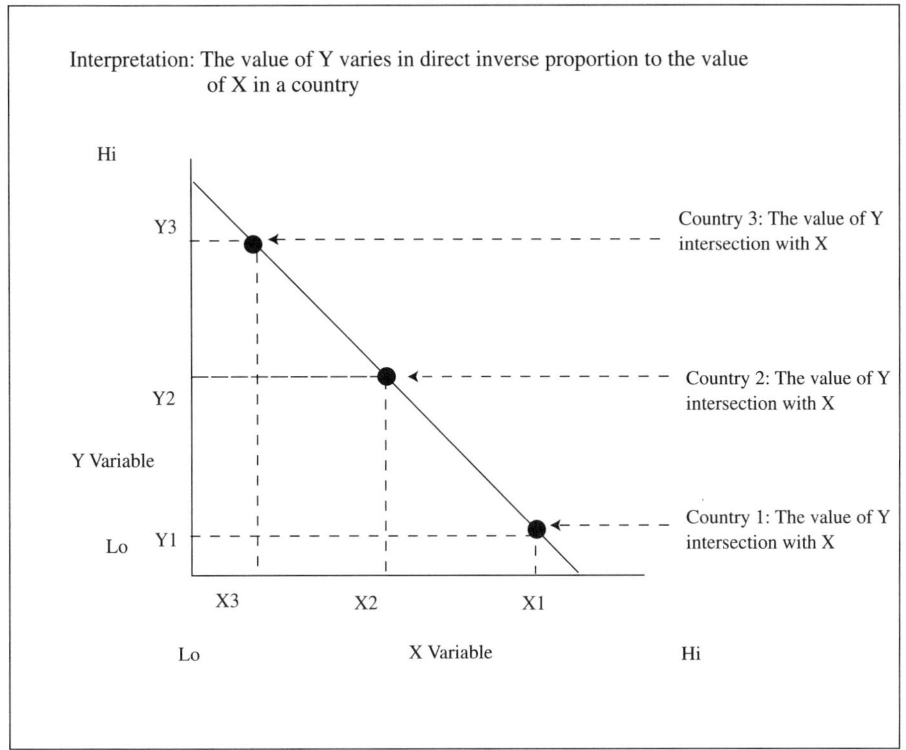

FIGURE 13.3 A Inverse Linear Relationship

of Y, the slope will approach a perfect horizontal line equal to the mean of Y. Why? Because in that situation, the mean of Y is as good an estimate of Y as is the value of X. Thus, the two lines converge; knowing the value of X makes no difference in predicting the value of Y.

Figure 13.4 illustrates this basic point. This graph plots the linear relationship between perceptions of public corruption (CPI) and the proportion of people within democracy who agree that citizens can make a difference in politics (AVGCIT31). The data are from EFFICACY.21. Note the mean and the slope nearly converge, the residuals are lengthy and on both sides of the slope (and mean), and in the end, the r^2 falls to a minimal .001. The model has no power. If you wish to estimate the value of AVGCIT31, you would be nearly as well off using the mean value of AVGCIT31 as to estimate its value from the country's value of CPI. And, of course, if you hypothesized a relationship between AVGCIT31 and CPI, you cannot reject the null.

Correlation Analysis and Skewed Samples

In cross-national analysis, skewed samples are common. A few countries, because of their population and/or areal size, or their economic power, will usually stand apart

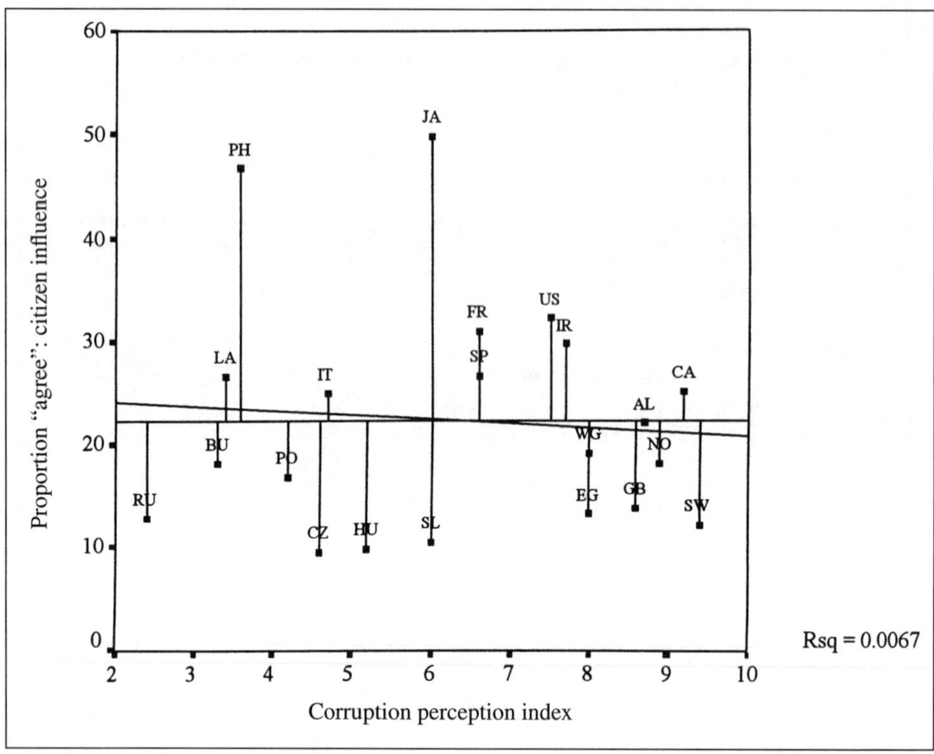

FIGURE 13.4 AVGCIT31 by CPI (EFFICACY.21)

from the rest (for example, China and the United States). It should be clear as well that such sharp skewness in the sample of either the independent variable and/or dependent variable will make it virtually impossible to obtain a reliable estimate of the values for the Y variable from the X variable. When the scores of one of the variables in a bivariate model are sharply skewed, the mean and standard deviation for that variable will be sharply distorted. Because the variance of the sample will be very much influenced by the mean, the standardized sample variations will deviate sharply across the two samples, thus reducing the capacity of the model to accurately predict the values of one variable from that of the other. Therefore, when the sample of one or both of the variables is severely skewed, assumptions of linear analysis are severely violated, making any statistical tool based on linear analysis inappropriate for hypothesis testing. This is another reason it is important to execute a simple univariate analysis (and a histogram, if possible) before proceeding to hypothesis testing.

Consider Figure 13.5. This plots the relationship between military personnel (as a percentage of the total population) in a country and the country's size (in thousands of square kilometers). Both variables have been converted to z-scores for ease of interpretation and both are drawn from the CROSSNAT.50 sample. Note the effect of skewness in

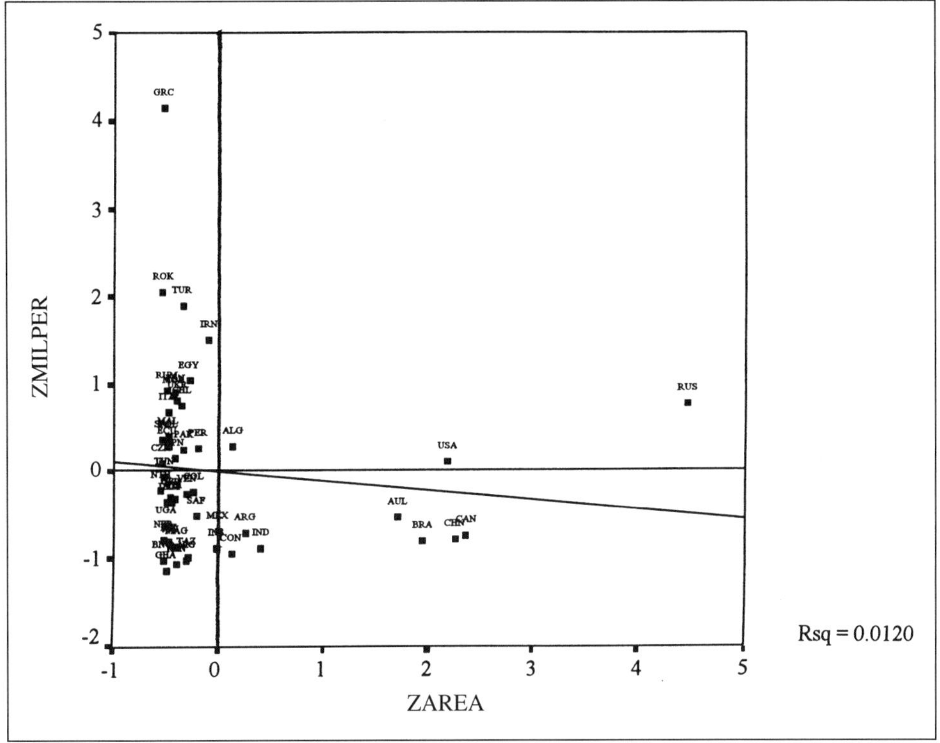

FIGURE 13.5 Scatterplot, ZMILPER by ZAREA (CROSSNAT .50)

both variables. From a simple univariate analysis, we can confirm that the skewness of ZAREA is 2.793 while that of ZMILPER is 1.745. However, the skewness of both variables is clearly revealed by simply marking the means of both variables in the graph. The horizontal line is the mean for ZMILPER (in z-scores, recall, the mean for any sample of values is 0), while the straight vertical line is the mean for ZAREA. Note that these two lines intersect at the far lower left of the plot. This simply confirms graphically what we already know—both variables are affected by trailers at the high end of their value range that, in effect, skew the distribution sharply. In other words, a few outliers in the sample of both variables sharply distort the linearity assumption.[10]

This, once again, raises the issue of outliers. Certainly, the plot itself is meaningful—without it, we might not appreciate the relative differences between a few countries and the bulk of countries within the world. Yet, it also means that without a plot, we might incorrectly assume there is no relationship at all between the number of military personnel and the size of country. Indeed, the proper conclusion would be that there appears two worlds: the world of the large and not-so-militarily-dense countries (Russia, United States, Australia, Brazil, China, and Canada), and the world of the small, but militarily dense countries (Greece, Korea, and Turkey). The lesson to be drawn from this discussion: Because skewness is common within cross-national analysis, plotting the bivariate models is often both useful and prudent (and, within SPSS 10, easy, as we shall see).

NONLINEAR MODELS AND CURVE-FITTING DIAGNOSTICS

The above discussion draws attention to a basic fact when working with cross-national data: The assumption that all relationships are linear is risky—and foolish. While one may actually hypothesize a nonlinear relationship, more often than not students may discover nonlinearity in models when they examine scatterplots. We will examine nonlinear models in more detail in Chapter 15. However, within bivariate correlation analysis, it is important to be aware of nonlinearity when assessing the correlations coefficients without first examining scatterplots. This is particularly critical when the correlation coefficient falls in the range $.1 < r < .5$: For instance, as we saw earlier in our discussion of Spearman correlation coefficients, we assess a relationship as weak or strong, depending upon the size of the correlation coefficient. However, the Pearson correlation coefficient measures strictly linear association. If there is a nonlinear aspect to the shape of the relationship—that is, if the values of the dependent variable do not change in a unidirectional fashion relative X, or, if they change in an exponential, rather than a proportional scale, relative to Y, a standard Pearson correlation coefficient will miss this departure from linearity. Indeed, the nonlinear aspect of the relationship will be registered as error. Thus, when examining a coefficient alone, we may observe a weak coefficient ($r < .3$). However, upon examination of the scatterplot, we may discern a nonlinear aspect to the shape of the curve. Adjusting the equation we use to compute the slope can help us capture the nonlinear distribution, and minimize the error. This will not concern us here (it will in Chapter 17). However, by employing an equation that adjusts the computation to take account of the possibility of a nonlinear relationship between X and Y, we may refine our description of how two variables are related and thereby lay the foundation for further theory building.

The size of the correlation coefficient does matter, however. Where $r \geq .7$, one is relatively certain the relationship is linear. Indeed, there may be a slight "bend" to the shape of the plots, but we will know from the size of the correlation coefficient that this nonlinear characteristic is not enough to produce sufficient error to render the linear assessment inaccurate. With correlation coefficients at or above .7, the nonlinear effect is, therefore, minimal.

Examples of Nonlinear Relationships

Let's consider some simple examples for illustrations. We have already seen in Figure 13.4 and Figure 13.5 nonlinear relationships. However, neither model has enough shared variance—linear or not—to warrant substantial further analysis. Figure 13.6,

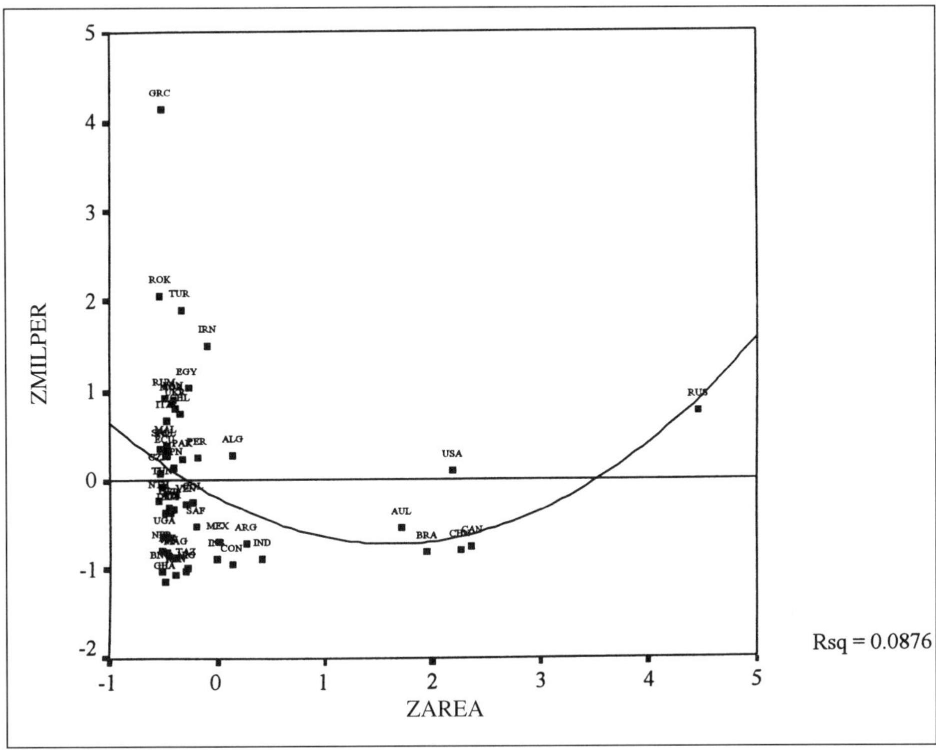

FIGURE 13.6 Scatterplot, ZMILPER by ZAREA (Curvilinear)

for example, reports the scatterplot of ZMILPER by ZAREA, the same plot produced in Figure 13.5. However, in Figure 13.6, we have statistically *fitted* the curve to a shape that better reflects the contour of the scatterplots. This curve is nonlinear, and indeed, the r^2 increases from .01 in a linear estimate of the shared variance to .09 in a nonlinear estimate. The value of linear diagnostics is very simple: to see if there is in fact a different way to understand the relationship between two variables.

How did we do this? How do we get a nonlinear plot? We will discuss the actual equation in Chapter 15. The simple answer is we computed the bends in the slope that would best fit the shape of scattered plots arrayed in the graph around the mean of Y. The calculus can be complicated and intimidating. However, linear diagnostics are quite intuitive; they allow us to imagine ways in which phenomena may operate in the world differently from how we might causally assume.

Let's walk through the logic of curvilinear analysis, trying to stay away from complicated calculus and focusing instead on the application and utility in cross-national analysis of nonlinear diagnostics. Think of a line, or slope, as the estimate of Y based on values of X. Formula 13.1 allows us to compute the estimate of linear variance. There is, as we see in Figure 13.4, Figure 13.5, and explicitly in Figure 13.6, a nonlinear aspect in some models. If we think so, we may adjust our estimate of Y based on X values by adding a second component to Formula 13.1. This has the effect of simply adjusting our estimate of Y by slightly changing the way X relates to Y. As Formula 13.1 assumes a linear relationship, the value of X is not modified. If, however, we assume a significant nonlinear component in the relationship between X and Y, we may statistically modify the computational value of X to reflect this. The calculus need not concern us here. Suffice it to say for illustration that if we assume the slope is actually curvilinear, that is, if we think the slope crosses the mean of Y *twice*, either once on the way up and again on the way down (as illustrated hypothetically in Figure 12.1, as in a *concave* curvilinear model), or once on the way down and a second time on the way up again (as suggested in Figure 12.2 and shown to be the case in Figure 13.6—a convex curvilinear model), we simply add a component to Formula 13.1 that factors in the expected effect of a curve, or bend, in the data.

Figure 13.6 had such a second element added to the formula used to compute the curved (convex) slope in the relationship between ZAREA and ZMILPER. It did not make much difference though—the relationship between ZAREA and ZMILPER is driven by a few outliers and adjusting the estimate of Y by modifying X to reflect a curvilinear approximation of Y did not significantly alter the model's overall power. It is still highly statistically insignificant.[11]

Most nonlinear models fall within a very narrow range of types—as we have already said, they are either *exponential* (when Y seems to grow exponentially, or geometrically in size, as the value of X increases, rather than proportionally), or *curvilinear*, when as in Figure 13.6, the slope has a clear bend to it, indicating that at some point the direction of the relationship between Y and X is actually reversed. In most instances, simple exploratory diagnostics will suffice to ascertain whether a significant nonlinear aspect to the relationship exists between two variables. These exploratory diagnostics are available in the scatterplot option within SPSS 10 and do not require manual formulaic transformations of X by the student. However, for more sophisticated modeling, which takes us beyond the scope of this text, students would be required to utilize the TRANSFORMATIONS option in SPSS and compute the value transformation of X and, as we shall see in Chapter 15, run a new model to estimate the curve.[12] We will consider the equation adjustment later in Chapter 15. For now, let us examine two more simple examples of nonlinear bivariate models before turning directly to the correlation coefficients of our primary properties of democracy.

Let us consider a different nonlinear pattern commonly found in cross-national samples. Figure 13.7 tests the simple hypothesis that voting turnout in a country is conditioned by the number of political parties within a country. This suggests that turnout in a country rises as the availability of political options within a country rises: the more political parties, the greater the overall turnout in the population. The variable PARTIES represents the number of political parties in the lower chamber of a bicameral (two-chamber) legislature/parliament, or, if there is only one chamber in the legislature/parliament (unicameral), it represents the number of parties in the single chamber of the parliament/legislature.[13] The data in Figure 13.7 are taken from CROSSNAT.50. The graph presents once again two slopes: a linear slope and a curvilinear slope. Each slope was

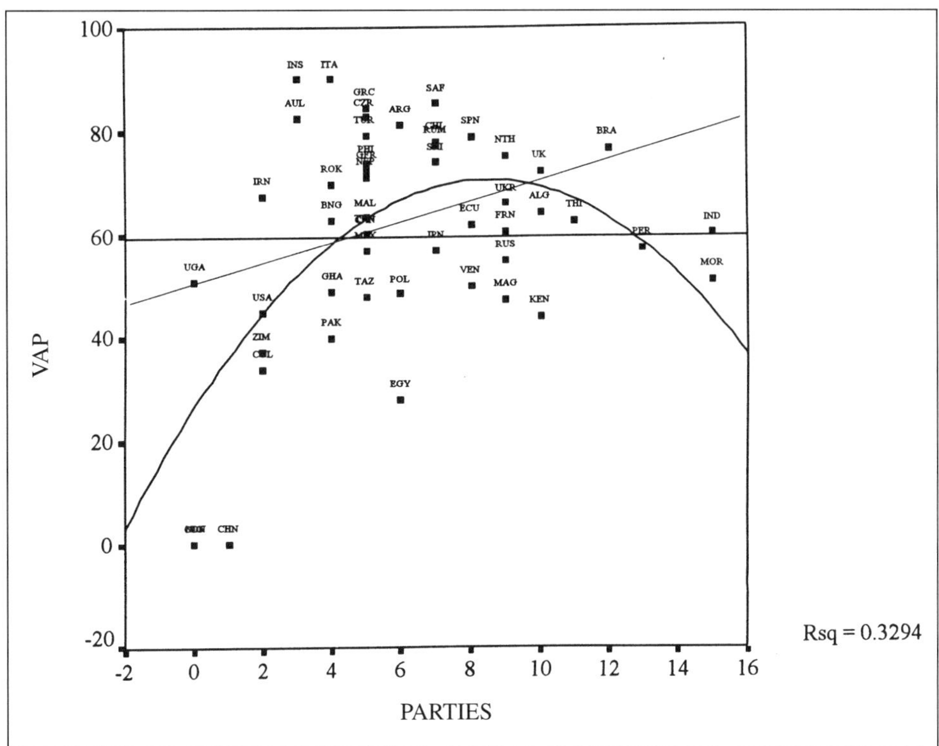

FIGURE 13.7 Scatterplot, VAP by PARTIES (Curvilinear)

plotted within SPSS, one using the linear option and the other using the curvilinear (or, technically, the QUADRATIC) option. However, the plot allows only one line to be produced at a time. We have edited the curvilinear output to reflect the linear slope. The r^2 for the linear model is .094, that of the curvilinear model is .329. By fitting a curve to the line, we have sharply reduced errors in our estimate of Y from X. While a large amount of error still exists (we are accounting for only 33 percent of the variance in VAP with the curvilinear mode), we have more than doubled our ability to accurately estimate the value of VAP from PARTIES by fitting the slope to a curve.

This is an example of where a small linear estimate, reflected in the small r coefficient, is in fact curvilinear, and statistically significant. This is a concave slope—note the curve actually crosses the mean value of the dependent variable (VAP) twice. What does this tell us? The curvilinear plot suggests that additional political parties within a country are associated with more voter turnout, *up to a point*. Beyond that point, additional parties within a country are associated with a sharp drop in voter turnout. The possible reasons for this are the grist for further analysis (either case study or comparable cases, or, more refined cross-national hypothesis testing). However, the curve clearly opens the door to the conclusion that voters may indeed "tune out" when their political environment becomes cluttered with so many competing voices. Indeed, especially in countries with limited degrees of democracy, additional political parties may be seen by the public as the "same old song"—simply offering nothing new to the choices before the voters. In any event, without further analysis, we can only speculate. Nonetheless, the curve-fitting diagnostics allow us to refine our thinking. Without the additional step of plotting what was otherwise a weak linear correlation coefficient, we might have correctly assumed the lack of a linear relationship and left it at that. The plot allows us to confirm that a substantial nonlinear variance pattern exists and indeed a relationship between voting turnout and parties exists—it is just not a simple linear model.

Figure 13.8 presents yet another common nonlinear pattern found in cross-national samples. This plot approximates an exponential form of nonlinearity. It has one bend in it, yet it is not as sharp as that shown in Figure 13.7. The model plots the values of a country's *gross domestic product* (per capita, that is, per person, measured in dollars), or GDPPC97, by the degree of *gender empowerment*, or GENPOW (see Chapter 12). The theory guiding this analysis holds that in countries where the economy is highly productive, women are not only likely to be integrated within the economy, but will also have political and commercial responsibility to greater degrees than where the economy is poorer and where women must remain within traditional roles outside the mainstream of the economy and the political system.[14] This hypothesis is in fact supported by the linear estimate ($r^2 = .626$). Note the linear slope is not that different from the curved slope. Indeed, the curvilinear slope improves the r^2 only minimally, to .651. If we had not checked for curvilinearity, we would have still been safe in our conclusion that the relationship between a country's wealth (GDPPC97) and gender empowerment is linear, and strong. This underscores the point that with large r coefficients, you will not find a nonlinear component that threatens the linearity assumptions of the model.

Finally, Figure 13.9 demonstrates a more complicated and statistically more involved model, but one that is not at all uncommon in cross-national analysis and that can be easily examined with use of linear diagnostics within SPSS 10. Often, the relationship between our X and Y variables assumes a particularly dynamic character. In cross-national analysis, if we have distinct groups of countries that tend to co-vary in the Y attribute in distinctly different ways from each other, the curve can be "fitted" to reflect this trend. Figure 13.9 reveals such a condition. It shows the plot of the gross domestic product of a country (ZGDP97) by the country's areal size (ZAREA). The data are from CROSSNAT.50. There are three slopes computed for this bivariate relationship (all three produced one at a time from SPSS 10): the linear slope ($r^2 = .192$), the curvilinear slope ($r^2 = .270$), and the cubic slope ($r^3 = .353$).

The difference between a cubic slope and a standard curvilinear slope (technically referred to as a quadratic slope) is the number of "bends" in the curve of the slope. The cubic slope has three bends, while the quadratic slope has only two. The quadratic slope crosses the mean of the dependent variable twice, while the cubic slope crosses it three times. The computation of the cubic slope requires a slightly different transformation of the X variable than the quadratic model. This transformation is added to the equation along with both the standard formula for estimating the correlation between

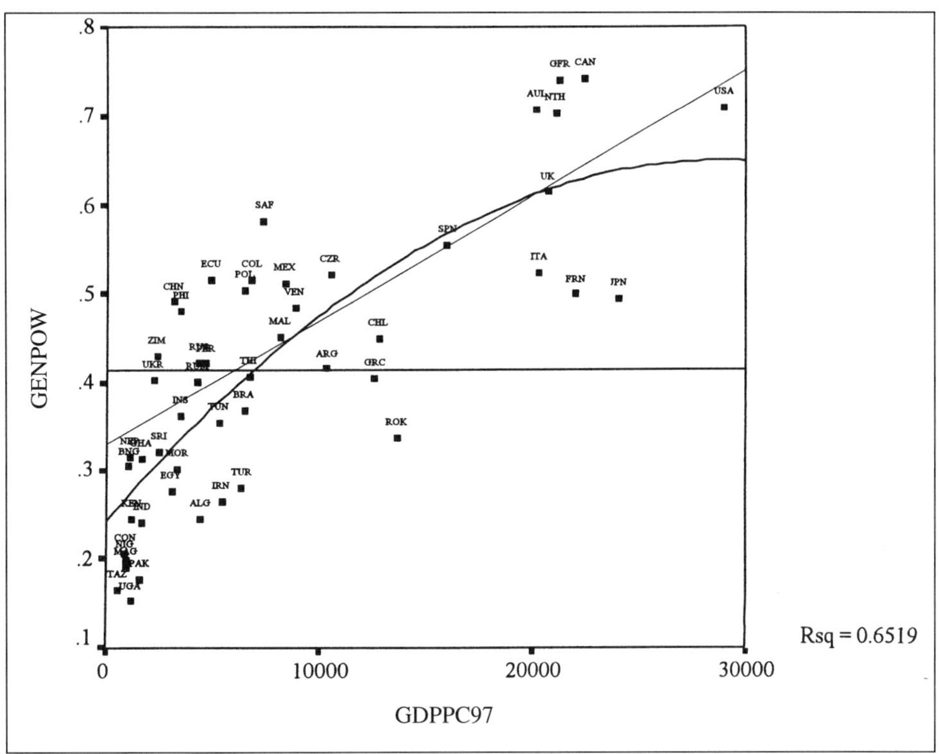

FIGURE 13.8 Scatterplot, GENPOW by GDPPC97

X and Y (reflected in Formula 13.1) and the transformation required for the quadratic estimate.[15] In Figure 13.9, we see that as we progress from the linear estimate to the cubic estimate, the power of the model increases accordingly, until we have gone from less than 20 percent of the variance in Y determined by X to 35 percent of the variance in Y determined by X. Again, this will not often be the case in linear models. Indeed, it is rather uncommon to find a cubic relationship. Yet, if our theory suggests the possibility, or our examination of the scatterplot reveals such a pattern, the cubic plot can be useful in sorting out the implications and in confirming our suspicions.

A cubic estimate, besides being somewhat complicated mathematically, also runs the risk of stretching the reliability of the model. In other words, you need a large N in order to have a reliable cubic model. With fifty cases, as in CROSSNAT.50, the bends in the curve are often the result of a single case. This has the effect of rendering the model somewhat unreliable. This implies that a slight change in the sample will eliminate the power of the cubic estimate, because it could alter that one country's relative proximity to the mean Y and the slope. Remember, a scatterplot takes its shape as a result of the relative displacement of all cases in the sample. Adding or dropping cases will not change the values of any cases (they will still have the same X and Y values), but the variance in the model will change, and as the variance changes, so does the estimate of Y from X, and thus the slope.

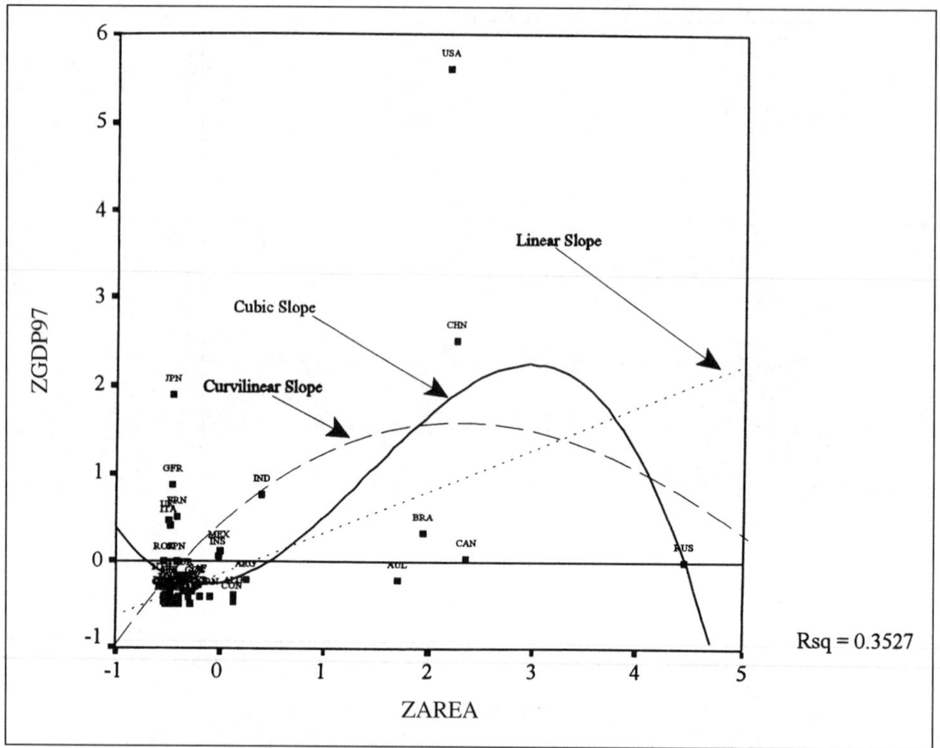

FIGURE 13.9 Scatterplot, ZGDP97 by ZAREA

So, an unreliable model is one where there are not enough cases anchoring a particular shape to the slope. If a cubic model relies merely on one case—an outlier—to pull that third bend, it is in effect a relatively unreliable estimate. Put differently, it may mean the cubic model is based on a fluke, a random incidence of an outlier driving the entire model.

This seems to be what is at work in Figure 13.9. We see that Russia (RUS) is driving the second bend. Indeed, the middle "hump" in the cubic slope is determined primarily by two cases: the United States (USA) and China (CHN). So, what might we conclude from Figure 13.9? While it opens a doorway to new questions, it cannot be seen as definitive. It clearly draws attention to the fact that something sets Russia, the United States, and China apart from even very large countries such as Canada, Brazil, and Australia. And, it also helps identify four groups of countries within our sample: those that are generally small and relatively poor (located in the cluster at the lower left of the plot); those that are large and exceptionally wealthy (China and the United States), and those that are large but not as "exceptionally" wealthy (Australia, Brazil, and Canada). Lastly, it also singles out the unique situation of Russia at the turn of the century: large, but relatively poor. It also highlights the power of the Japanese economy: a small country, but an exceptionally wealthy one. In effect, cubic models help us refine our standard theory, but they should be approached with prudent caution and a healthy dose of skepticism. In most cases, the cubic slope offers no improvement in the power of either a standard linear or at best a quadratic (curvilinear) slope. When it does, make sure it has a reliable foundation to the pattern it suggests.

Correlation and Scatterplots in Perspective

At this point, we need to be reminded of an important caveat in using correlation analysis. Strictly speaking, it is not a very useful hypothesis testing tool, *if used independently of scatterplots.* We have introduced you to correlation analysis because it plays a central role in initial exploratory analysis and in building a multidimensional measure, which we will explain in more detail. It is also the basic element of all linear statistical analyses relying on interval/ratio-level data. Nonetheless, this statistical tool is rarely sufficient by itself. Always try to supplement the Pearson coefficient (r) with scatterplots, especially when exploring your hypotheses for the first time. Correlations are good for measuring bivariate relationships that are *linear*.

Keep in mind that linearity is not always a reasonable assumption to make about bivariate relationships in the real world of politics. We have seen that in cross-national analysis, few models are perfectly linear. Yet, most have *more* linearity than nonlinearity. The *stronger* the correlation coefficient, the *less* nonlinearity within the model. A weak correlation may be reflective of a random distribution of X values around the mean of Y (as in Figure 13.5). Or, as in Figures 13.7 and 13.9, it may mask a strong nonlinear relationship. *If r approaches 0, it does not necessarily mean there is no relationship; it simply means there is no linear relationship*. The scatterplots help us determine if there is a nonlinear relationship. The correlation technique, when used alone, helps us sort out relationships initially; it should not be the final step in any hypothesis testing procedure.

THE CORRELATION COEFFICIENTS FOR THE FOUR PRIMARY PROPERTIES OF DEMOCRACY

What then of the bivariate relationship between our four primary properties of democracy: CIVIL97, POLIT97, PARCOMP, and PARREG? Table 13.5 presents the redundant matrix for the Pearson correlation coefficients for the four variables. Note its appearance is identical to that of Table 13.3 and the Spearman correlation coefficients. Furthermore, the size of the r coefficients match closely the respective r_s coefficients. Each of the coefficients in Table 13.5 is very strong (all being larger than .7), and each is in a positive direction. Thus, we may conclude that (1) as with the Spearman correlation coefficients in Table 13.3, there is a strong, positive, and linear association between each of the four primary properties of democracy, and (2) the coefficients match closely those of the Spearman correlations, indicating no significant impact or steep skewness in our model that might seriously distort linear estimates among the variables.[16]

It is important we appreciate here that our goal with the correlation analysis of the four primary properties of democracy up to this point in this chapter has not been to

TABLE 13.5 Pearson Correlations, Primary Properties of Democracy

		CIVIL97	*PARCOMP*	*PARREG*	*POLIT97*
CIVIL97	Pearson correlation	1.000	.868**	.790**	.912**
	Sig. (2-tailed)		.000	.000	.000
	N	50	50	50	50
PARCOMP	Pearson correlation	.868**	1.000	.910**	.875**
	Sig. (2-tailed)	.000		.000	.000
	N	50	50	50	50
PARREG	Pearson correlation	.790**	.910**	1.000	.850**
	Sig. (2-tailed)	.000	.000		.000
	N	50	50	50	50
POLIT97	Pearson correlation	.912**	.875**	.850**	1.000
	Sig. (2-tailed)	.000	.000	.000	
	N	50	50	50	50

** Correlation is significant at the .01 level (2-tailed).

verify an *implied* "causal" relationship between any of the four variables. That is, our analysis is not driven by the theoretical assumption that PARCOMP causes PARREG, or CIVIL97 causes POLIT97. Rather, we are using the correlation coefficients to simply *verify* the presence of high levels of shared variance among the four primary properties. Of course, correlation coefficients are more often used explicitly in different settings to test "assumed" causality, though, as you recall, a bivariate model can never directly test explicit causality. Rather, it can only verify an associated, or implicit causal relationship; that is, bivariate models allow one to assess the veracity of one's "suggested" causal relationship between two or more attributes. That is not the case here. We are using correlation analysis for what might be described as merely a *neutral* purpose—a practice commonly employed in cross-national analysis. We wish only to ascertain the extent of shared variance among the four properties. Our principal goal is to capture this shared variance, and from this, devise a single, efficient measure that can represent the fundamental concept that binds all four of these properties—something that transcends the meaning of any one of the four primary properties of democracy. As we have suggested at the outset of this chapter, that common underlying concept is, we believe, *political empowerment*. Having verified the extent to which our four primary properties share common variance, we may now proceed to the next step, discussed in Chapter 14: reducing our volume of variables by constructing a simple yet compound variable from these four that can measure *political empowerment* in a valid and reliable manner.

CHAPTER SUMMARY

In this chapter we have explored in some detail linear analysis, specifically, the Spearman correlation and the Pearson correlation methods as essential tools for multidimensional index constructions. As these measures are based on linear assumptions, we also drew attention through examples to the fact that students in cross-national analysis often must confront the issue of nonlinear relationships, as well as sharply skewed samples. We demonstrated how, through the use of SPSS 10, we can explore the shape of bivariate relationships. We shall build upon the fundamentals of linear analysis presented in this chapter in more detail in subsequent chapters.

NOTES

1. Louise G. White, 1999, *Political Analysis: Technique and Practice,* fourth edition (Belmont, Calif.: Wadsworth Publishing Company), pp. 255–257.

2. Andrew Bebler and James Seroka, eds., 1990, *Contemporary Political Systems: Classifications and Typologies* (Boulder: Lynne Rienner).

3. David Held, 1995, *Democracy and the Global Order: From the Modern State to Cosmopolitan Governance* (Stanford: Stanford University Press), pp. 145–147.

4. See Kimberly Ann Elliott, 1997, *Corruption and the Global Economy* (Washington, D.C.: Institute for International Economics); Paul Heywood, 1997, ed., *Political Corruption* (Malden, Mass.: Blackwell); and Ashok K. Jain, 2001, "Corruption: A Review," *Journal of Economic Surveys* 15 (February): 71–121. For an in-depth cross-national analysis of the relationship between culture and corruption, see Martin P. Paldam, 2001, "The Big Pattern of Corruption: Economics, Culture and the Seesaw Dynamics," forthcoming, *European Journal of Political Economy,* and Martin P. Paldam, 2001, "Corruption and Religion: Adding to the economic model," *Kyklos* 54 (May): 383–414. Data for our analysis were obtained from Transparency International, on the web at http://www.gwdg.de/~uwvw/icr.htm.

5. For greater detail presented in a clear yet precise fashion, see R. Lymann Ott, 1993, *An Introduction to Statistical Methods and Data Analysis,* fourth edition (Belmont, Calif.: Duxbury Press), pp. 460–468.

6. The $\sum XY$ (or, the sum of the product of X and Y for each country in the sample) is 3137, shown in the far right column of Table 13.2. The $\sum X$ is 231, as of course will be the $\sum Y$, as we are working with ranks (1–21) in a Spearman, and the sum of rank for the X and Y variables will be identical. The S_{xy} value is derived simply by computing the product of $\sum X$ and $\sum Y$, or (231 x 231), and dividing this by the number of cases in the sample, N, or 21. This computes to [(53,361)/(21)], or, 2,541. This value is then subtracted from the $\sum XY$ to obtain a standardized measure of the net variance in Y ranks accounted for by X ranks. Thus, 3,137 – 2,541 = 596. The number itself has no readily intuitive meaning, other than a statistical representation of how much net variance in Y can be matched by X. However, to determine how close our model approaches the total variance in X and Y, we must compute S_{yy} and S_{xx}. These are the estimates of variance in each variable. To eliminate directions, we must obtain two squared values, one for the sum of Y and X ranks (or, $(\sum Y)^2 = 231^2 = 53{,}361$, and $(\sum X^2) = 231^2 = 53{,}361$), as well as the square of the sums of each X and Y values, or $\sum X^2$ (3,309.5) and $\sum Y^2$ (3,311). To compute S_{yy} we first estimate the average variation in the ranks of the Y variable by dividing the $(\sum Y)^2$ by the number of countries in the sample (21); or, 53,361/21 = 2541. We then subtract this value from $\sum X^2$, or 3,309.5 – 2,541 = 768.5. We repeat this process on the Y ranks (3,311 – 2541 = 770). The product of these two terms is computed (768.5 x 770 = 591,745). This product is reset to its scale within the sample, or $\sqrt{591{,}745} = 769.250$. The final comparison of the vari-

ance components is thus computed by deriving the ratio of the XY variance (596) to the total variance (769.250), or 560/769.250 = .775.

7. To obtain a Spearman correlation, as well as Pearson correlation, within SPSS 10, choose the CORRELATE program from the ANALYZE list off the main menu bar. Select the bivariate option in the CORRELATE list, and once in the BIVARIATE CORRELATION box, specify Spearman's and/or Pearson's.You may also specify a Kendall Tau b, should you desire.You may specify the type of significance test you prefer—a one-tail or two-tail. Within the OPTIONS box, you may also request descriptive statistics be produced for each variable you have selected from the VARIABLE LIST window in the CORRELATE window.You must select at least two variables for a bivariate correlation. The output will correlate each variable with every other variable listed in the window. See Marija J. Norušis, 2000, *SPSS: SPSS© 10.0 Guide to Data Analysis* (Upper Saddle River, N.J.: Prentice Hall), pp. 419–421, for more details.

8. East Germany's CPI value is that of West Germany's: There is no separate estimate of eastern Germany. This presents somewhat of a problem, as value of SATDEM21 is based on a separate sample of German citizens living within the former East German states of the German Federal Republic. Deleting East Germany from the sample has little effect on the overall value of the Spearman coefficient and does not alter the final decision with respect to the null.

9. Note that our working concept of *political empowerment* is not statistically derived, but it emerges from our theory. That is, it is a logical construction following from the theory that links the concepts of civil liberties, political rights, competitive participation, and regulated and institutionalized participation within countries. Another scholar may have a different theory as to what underlies the common, shared variance across these four primary properties. However, our working theory suggests political empowerment. Correlation does not tell us the theory—it confirms the veracity and validity of our theoretical assumptions. For a brief yet excellent discussion of the role of theory and where it comes from, see W. Phillips Shively, 2002, *The Craft of Political Research*, fifth edition (Upper Saddle River, N.J.: Prentice Hall), pp. 13–29 and 150–153. For an example of the use of index construction and correlation analysis within the literature of cross-national analysis, see Frank S.Cohen, 1997, "Proportional Versus Majoritarian Ethnic Conflict Management in Democracies," *Comparative Political Studies* 30:5 (October): 607–630; and John D. Robertson, 1990, "Transaction-Cost Economics and Cross-Natonal Patterns of Industrial Conflict: A Comparative Institutional Analysis," *American Journal of Political Science* 34 (February): 153–189.

10. Actually, one has the option of considering a power transformation of variables such as AREA, if, and only if, the transformation does not alter the fundamental substantive interpretation of the variable itself. In the case of AREA, we might consider a log (base 10) power transformation. However, as our goal here is merely illustration, we will not transform the highly skewed variable AREA. See Chapter 15 and our discussion of LGNET.

11. The Pearson correlation coefficient (r) for the relationship between ZMILPER and ZAREA is -.110 (p = .448, 2-tail). However, the Spearman r_s = -.188 (p = .192, 2-tail). While still statistically not significant, the Spearman s smoothed some of the extreme effects of serious skewness in the two samples with its use of ranks, rather than values.

12. Within SPSS 10, one may select from the GRAPHS option on the main menu bar, SCATTER as the tool. Once in the scatterplot window, you have a choice of the type of scatterplot to choose. The basic, or *simple*, SCATTERPLOT is the default. Once in the SIMPLE

SCATTERPLOT window, assign your independent variable, dependent variable, and, if you wish to have the plots identified, select the variable that will assign an identifying label adjacent each dot (as we have in Figures 13.2 and 13.4–13.6). Once you have selected your options, press OK. Once the graph is produced (in the special graphics window called the CHART CAROUSEL), you may edit the graph by double-clicking it with the right mouse button. This opens the CHART EDITOR window. To edit the graph, and to check for the effect of curvilinearity on your model, select from the CHART EDITOR menu the sequence CHART▶OPTIONS. Once in the OPTIONS window, select FIT OPTIONS, and from here you may select the QUADRATIC REGRESSION option—the option to fit a simple curvilinear or exponential model that we assume has, in effect, only one bend—sharp or slight. Also within the CHART/OPTIONS window, you may select the r-square statistic and the regression line. Note that if you have selected a variable by which to label the dots, you must select the LABELS ON option in the OPTIONS window. All graphs can be copied from the EDIT button, selecting COPY CHART, within the CHART EDITOR menu bar. Then, once in either WordPerfect or Word, you may select the PASTE SPECIAL option from the EDIT command, and the graph will be imported as a "picture" file into your word document, from where you may edit it with the graphics editor of the word processor. See Marija J. Norušis, 2000, *SPSS: SPSS© 10.0 Guide to Data Analysis* (Upper Saddle River, N.J.: Prentice Hall), pp. 133–162, for more details. For a more detailed discussion of advanced diagnostics for curve-fitting statistics, see R. Lymann Ott, 1993, *An Introduction to Statistical Methods and Data Analysis*, fourth edition (Belmont, Calif.: Duxbury Press), pp. 545–560, or Lawrence C. Hamilton, 1992, *Regression with Graphics: A Second Course in Applied Statistics* (Pacific Cove, Calif.: Brooks/Cole Publishing Company), pp. 57–58 and 145–182. An excellent discussion of the logic of nonlinear models can be found in William D. Berry and Mitchell S. Sanders, 2000, *Understanding Multivariate Research: A Primer for Beginning Social Scientists* (Boulder: Westview), pp. 63–72. For an example of the use of scatterplots—both linear and nonlinear—in the literature of cross-national analysis, see Rein Taagepera, 1999, "The Number of Parties as a Function of Heterogeneity and Electoral System," *Comparative Political Studies* 32:5 (August): 531–548.

13. Data are taken from the Interparliamentary Union, as of 1997. See http://www.ipu.org/. The linkages between parties, elections, and democracy are extensively explored through quantitative cross-national analysis in G. Bingham Powell Jr., 2000, *Elections as Instruments of Democracy: Majoritarian and Proportional Visions* (New Haven: Yale University Press); Robert E. Bohrer, 2002, *Decision Costs and Democracy: Trade-Offs in Institutional Design* (Hampshire, UK: Ashgate Publishing, Ltd.); and Arend Lijphart, 1999, *Patterns of Democracy: Government Forms and Performance in Thirty-six Countries* (New Haven: Yale University Press).

14. Susan J. Carroll and Linda M. G. Zerelli, 1999, "Feminist Challenges to Political Science," in Stella Z. Theodoulou and Rory O'Brien, eds., *Methods for Political Inquiry: Discipline, Philosophy, and Analysis of Politics* (Upper Saddle River, N.J.: Prentice Hall), pp. 37–76; and Susan J. Carroll, 1989, "The Personal is Political: The Intersection of Private Lives and Public Roles Among Women and Men in Elective and Appointive Office," *Women and Politics* 9 (April): 51–67. For a detailed cross-national analysis of women in the political and economic markets, see United Nations Development Programme, 1995, *Human Development Report 1995* (New York: Oxford University Press).

15. To obtain a cubic slope within SPSS 10, select CUBIC REGRESSION from the CHART▶OPTIONS▶FIT OPTIONS window within the SCATTER procedure.

16. Within SPSS 10, a correlation matrix can be obtained by executing the same sequence as for Spearman correlation. See Marija J. Norušis, 2000, *SPSS: SPSS© 10.0 Guide to Data Analysis* (Upper Saddle River, N.J.: Prentice Hall), pp. 419–421, for more details.

14

Factor Analysis as a Tool of Data Reduction Within Cross-National Analysis

Terms: *Factor Analysis, Eigenvalues, Factor Scores, KMO Statistic, Bartlett's Sphericity Test*
Concepts: Political Empowerment, Citizen Autonomy
Demonstration: Factor Analysis, 14.1

With the discussion of correlation analysis now in mind, we are ready to turn to the principal important concept of this chapter: *political empowerment*. Recall that our principal objective concerning democracy is to devise a single multidimensional measure that reflects the extent to which citizens within a society are politically empowered to pursue their interests and to protect their rights through free and extensive opportunities for political participation. If, as we have argued, democracy is basically a derivative of four primary properties—*the scale of institutional democracy* (POLIT97), *the scale of liberal democracy* (CIVIL97), *the scope of institutional democracy* (PARCOMP), and *the scope of liberal democracy* (PARREG)—how can we construct a single measure that incorporates these properties into an operational definition that allows us to devise a reliable and valid measure of *political empowerment*?

As we saw in Chapter 5, one method of devising a single compound measure of a complex concept is to convert the values of the variables in the index to z-scores, and sum these z-scores. This was our method in devising the variable, POWER. However, the drawback to the method is that it treats each variable as if it makes an *equal* contribution to the final measure of national potential power. Summing values does not take into account the variance within the sample and, therefore, cannot allow us to draw on the shared variance to estimate each variable's contribution to an underlying concept, such as *political empowerment*.

While we know from Table 13.5 that each of the four primary properties of democracy is strongly correlated, the differing variance of each (even though there are technically ordinal data) provides a slightly different contribution to whatever underlying measure we might devise that draws on the shared variance of all four variables. Thus, by treating each variable as having an *equal* contribution, as we do when we sum z-scores, we eliminate the *relative* contributions that each separate variable offers, and thus, we run the risk of both underestimating the importance of the contribution of some of these variables in defining the underlying concept, as well as overestimating the importance of others in defining the underlying concept. This has the further effect of misrepresenting the intrinsic nature of the underlying concept.

What we need is a method that statistically defines a new variable based on the *weighted* contribution of each variable to the underlying concept. Such a weighted measure draws on the variance patterns of the variables in the index and therefore allows us to better understand the intrinsic nature of the new underlying concept we have statistically created through conceptual logic. Factor analysis offers this possibility.[1]

ILLUSTRATING THE LOGIC OF FACTOR ANALYSIS

For students who are not familiar with matrix algebra, factor analysis is more easily understood if we keep in mind that it serves as a statistical technique to find the best linear fit, or correlation, between several variables within a proposed model of a single multidimensional concept. While the mathematics of factor analysis are very complex (and are beyond the scope of this text, and not necessary to effectively utilize the tool), the logic of the technique is simple to grasp if we compare three hypothetical examples of constructing a multidimensional index measure using the basic features of factor analysis.[2]

The Logical Connection Between Simple Correlations and Factor Analysis

To begin, consider Table 14.1. This table lists the three variables within each of three separate hypothetical models we will examine in this section solely for the purpose of illustration. The first model proposes a single concept identified by the unique properties of ZPOLIT97, ZDEATHRT, and ZLGPOP. Note that the measure of a country's population (ZLGPOP) has been power transformed to smooth its variance. Factor analysis does not require normally distributed variables; however, like all basic measures of linear analysis, it is very sensitive to variables that are severely skewed. Recall from Chapter 2 that POPULATE is a highly skewed variable. We have fit the values of this variable within our sample (CROSSNAT.50) to approximately a normal distribu-

TABLE 14.1 Three Hypothetical Models of Proposed Multidimensional Index Measures to be Constructed Using Factor Analysis (Principal Components)

Model 1:	*Model 2:*	*Model 3:*
ZPOLIT97 *(Z-scores, scale of institutional democracy)*	ZPOLIT97	ZPOLIT97
ZDEATHRT *(Z-scores, crude death rate per 1000 people, 1997)*	ZCIVIL97 *(Z-scores, scale of liberal democracy)*	ZCIVIL97
ZLGPOP *(Z-scores, population size, power transformed to smooth distribution and reduce effect of outliers)*	ZLGPOP	ZPARCOMP *(Z-scores, scope of institutional democracy)*

tion. This was done by using a standard (base 10) log transformation (see Chapter 15 for more detail on such power transformations). Then we set the transformed variable to a standardized distribution (z-scores). The second model combines ZPOLIT97 with ZCIVIL97 and ZLGPOP, while the third model proposes a combination of ZPOLIT97, ZCIVIL97, and ZPARCOMP. These models are hypothetical (that is, we have no theory that actually connects them, with the obvious exception of the third model, which has been explored in Chapter 6). However, the data are actual data drawn from CROSSNAT.50. The intent in this section is to illustrate the logic of factor analysis, not test actual hypotheses.

Table 14.2 reports the Pearson correlation coefficients for each of the five variables used across the three hypothetical models described above. Note the strong and statistically significant correlations between the measures of democracy (ZPOLIT97, ZCIVIL97, and ZPARCOMP), yet the lack of any meaningful relationship between ZDEATHRT and ZLGPOP, with each other as well as with the three measures of democracy. Factor analysis is a tool that relies upon a sophisticated application of Pearson correlations as explained in Chapter 13. With such poor shared variance among ZDEATHRT and ZLGPOP and the other three variables in the models, we can expect our factor analysis of each proposed model to confirm a lack of a single, well-defined underlying conceptual dimension whenever the model incorporates either ZDEATHRT and ZLGPOP.

The Logical Connection Between Scatterplots and Factor Analysis

The objective of the factor analysis is to find which vector, within a space whose dimensions are determined by the number of variables in the model, best captures the

TABLE 14.2 Pearson Correlation Coefficients, Variables Within Proposed Models for Factor Analysis Illustration

	Variables				
	ZPOLIT97	*ZCIVIL97*	*ZPARCOMP*	*ZDEATHRT*	*ZLGPOP*
ZPOLIT97	–	.912*	.875*	-.066	-.122
ZCIVIL97		–	.868*	-.068	-.198
ZPARCOMP			–	-.125	-.201
ZDEATHRT				–	-.049
ZLGPOP					–

* = p ≤ .05

variance of all the variables within the space. We have already seen how a slope in a simple bivariate scatterplot reports the best fit between two variables in a two-dimensional space. This best fit is based on plotting a straight line through the distribution of scores relative to two variables. A factor analysis is based on the same logic. However, it plots the slope, or straight line (implying a linear relationship), for a multivariate model in a multidimensional space. Indeed, the factor analysis computes, via an iterative algorithm, as many alternative slopes for a model as there are variables in the model. The variance computed around each slope allows us to determine whether one slope or more are needed to capture a significant proportion of the total variance of scores in the sample, across all the variables in our model. The total variance of the scores, of course, is the sum of the distances each score falls from the means of each variable in the model. If the variables in the model are strongly correlated, a single slope can capture the variance of all the variables in the model, thus confirming a common, singular identity among the variables in the model.

The advantage of this is not merely to confirm such a singularity (after all, we can surmise as much in a small model from looking at the Pearson correlation coefficients). Rather, it is, as we will see later in the discussion of factor analysis, to obtain a single summary measure of this singular dimension (or, if there is more than one such unique component across the variables, a score for each such meaningful component) that makes factor analysis such a useful tool for students of cross-national analysis. Factor analysis affords us a means by which to compute a single measure of how close each case in the sample comes to representing the defined concept represented by more than one variable. Thus, rather than three different measures representing a concept, we may discover that we have (as our theory suggests in each of the three hypothetical models above) only one—if, that is, the factor analysis confirms the singular identity of the variables. However, if the variables in our model are not strongly correlated, a single slope cannot effectively capture the variance, thus confirming the lack of a single, underlying relationship between the variables, and thus refuting our assumption that a single concept is in fact represented by the variables in the factor model. We can see, therefore, that factor analysis is a useful tool in helping assess our assumptions about the primary properties of broader concepts.

The factor analysis procedure produces as many slopes as there are variables in the factor model. In fact, there can never be more than K–1 slopes that produce enough variance to be worthy of consideration (where K is the number of variables in the model). Any slope, of course, will accurately reflect the variance of two variables in a bivariate relationship, as we have seen in our discussion of scatterplots. Let us consider this comparison more closely.

Recall that in a bivariate model, the slope's axis is defined by the relationship between two variables, one of which serves as the Y axis, or the variable that is the principal variable in the analysis upon which the slope is anchored (in Figure 13.2 it is SATDEM21). In a factor analysis, with more than just two variables in the model, each slope represents the best fit based upon a different variable serving as the principal axis upon which the slope was anchored. In effect, if one has a model with three variables, there will be three slopes computed, each with a different variable in the model serving as the principal, or anchor, variable from which the slope's axis is computed in the multidimensional space. The first slope is the strongest, or "best" slope—the one that is determined to capture the most of the total variance of all scores within the space. The second slope in factor analysis is designed to account for the remaining variance not captured by the first slope, using a different variable as its anchor. The process proceeds in an iterative fashion accordingly. If the first slope captures so much of the total variance in the model that there remains only a fraction of the total variance left unexplained for subsequent iterations to capture, one can conclude that the variance of all the variables in the model is best represented by the first slope, and from this, we may conclude a single identity to the variables in the model.

A Graphical Depiction

It is very helpful for students not familiar with factor analysis to visualize the process of aligning the variance within the space defined by the variables in a factor model. Most factor analyses, of course, use more than three variables. Indeed, three variables is essentially too few for the model. To use factor analysis on three variables is probably unnecessary. However, for purposes of easier illustration, we will rely on the three models above and their respective three variables.

Each of the three models above defines a three-dimensional space—a cubic space. Why? Because there are three variables in each model. When one uses many variables, the space conforms increasingly to the shape of a sphere. With three variables, the vectors are still arrayed in right angles to each other and the model's dimensionality takes on the shape of a cube.

We have presented a series of graphic illustrations for each of the three models specified in Table 14.1 to compare and contrast the role of shared variance in factor analysis. Figures 14.1a–c report three different visual perspectives of the spatial array of cases within the first model above (ZPOLIT97, ZDEATHRT, and ZLGPOP), while Figures 14.2a–c report three different visual perspectives of the spatial array of cases within the second model above (ZPOLIT97, ZCIVIL97, and ZLGPOP), and Figures 14.3a–c report three different visual perspectives of the spatial array of cases within the third model above (ZPOLIT97, ZCIVIL97, and ZPARCOMP). Each perspective is designed to highlight the array of the distribution of scores in the sample we see when we shift the orientation of the Y axis.

Note there are three axes in the three-dimensional space: a Y axis, an X axis, and a Z axis. In Figure 14.1a, the Y axis is represented by ZPOLIT97, the X axis by ZDEATHRT, and the Z axis by ZLGPOP. The Y axis is bounded by Points AB, the X axis by Points AC, and the Z axis by Points CD. To orient you to the cube in each figure, imagine you had a clear cube in front of you, with one side (plane) facing you squarely. Twist the cube a quarter turn clockwise, while you tilt the cube toward you a little. This is the position of the cube reflected in each of the figures. This position helps us examine the three-dimensional aspect to the pattern of the dots (or, observations in the sample). To further help with orientation, we have included spikes that run from the floor of the cube to each observation. Unlike spikes in scatterplots shown in the previous chapter, these spikes do not reflect residual error. *The longer the spike, the further the observation is from the floor, and therefore the greater the country's value of each of the three variables defining the space.* Each dot, of course, reflects the score for a country corresponding to each of the three variables in the model.

Figure 14.1b shifts the perspective by rotating the cube to highlight the relationship between ZLGPOP and ZDEATHRT, in effect rotating the Y axis from ZPOLIT97 to ZLGPOP, with ZDEATHRT as the X axis, and ZPOLIT97 as the Z axis. In turn, Figure 14.1c rotates the cube to highlight the last of the three bivariate relationships in the model's defined space, ZPOLIT97 as the Y axis, ZLGPOP as the X axis, and ZDEATHRT as the Z axis. These three rotations exhaust the possible combinations of X, Y, and Z axis alignments for our examples. We have provided these three perspectives for each of the three models reported in Table 14.1.

What would a "perfect fit" look like in the Figure 14.1a? Assuming the scaling of the values for each of the variables is in the same direction (in other words, a value of 1 in ZPOLIT97 is equivalent to less of a property, as is the case in each of the other two variables), we would see a tightly aligned cluster of scores spread narrowly along the vector defined by Points AE in Figure 14.1a. If there were a positive correlation between each of the variables, the spikes would be low at the A end of the vector and grow proportionally larger as we moved up the vector to Point E. If there were a negative correlation between each of the three variables, the "sausage" shaped cluster of dots representing scores for each country for each of the three variables would be tightly arrayed along the vector defined by Points BD. In this case, the spikes would be very tall at the B end of the vector, and decline in size proportionally until we reached

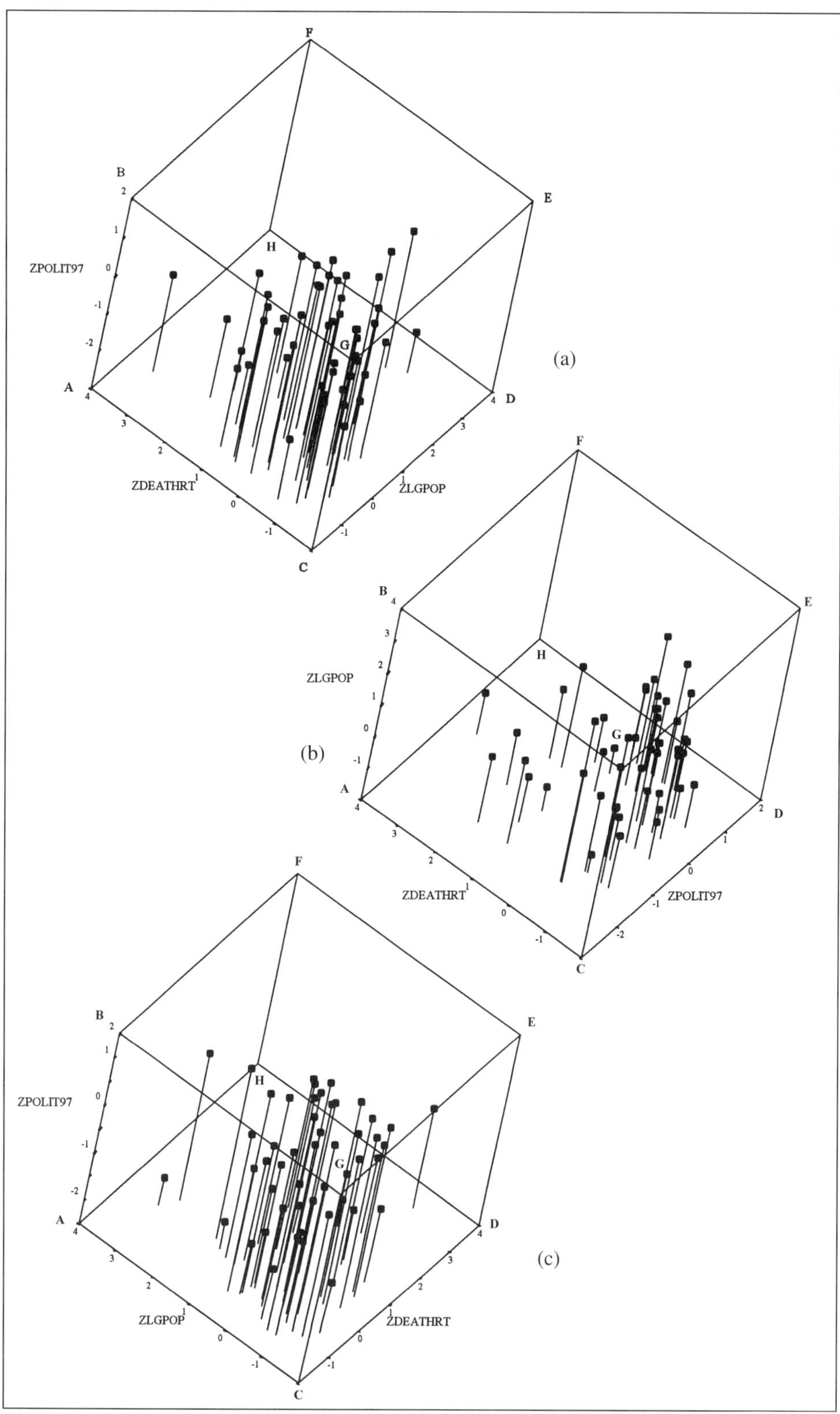

FIGURES 14.1a–c First, Second, and Third Perspectives, Spatial Representation of Multidimensional Index Based on ZPOLIT97, ZDEATHRT, and ZLGPOP.

Point D. Any tight cluster of dots running along diagonal vectors defined by Points AE, BD, CF, would represent very strong correlations, with the size of the spikes showing a distinct and definite pattern to change in size as you move from one end of the diagonal vector to the other.

Let us consider Figures 14.1a–c. We know from the previous correlation analysis reported in Table 14.1 that there is very limited shared variance between any of the three variables in Model 1. The distribution of the dots in Figures 14.1a–c, and especially, the pattern in the *length* of the spikes themselves, underscore the lack of any scaling; there is no meaningful pattern of scores with respect to any of the combinations of the three bivariate relationships in the model. If, for instance, a statistically significant linear relationship existed between ZPOLIT97 and ZDEATHRT, we would expect the size of the spikes in Figure 14.1a to gradually change (either gradually grow larger or smaller) as we followed the path of the axis linking ZPOLIT97 and ZDEATHRT within the cube. Yet, note that the spikes remain relatively constant in size across the range of values defined by points BC. Furthermore, most of the scores are bunched at the lower end (toward Point C) in Figure 14.1a. There is no scaling, thus there is no relationship between ZPOLIT97 and ZDEATHRT in Figure 14.1a—a fact already confirmed by the correlation matrix above.

This pattern is repeated with slight variations for each of the remaining two bivariate perspectives shown in Figures 14.1b and 14.1c. As there is no bivariate relationship existing among any of the pairs in the space shown in Figures 14.1a–c, it is also the case that no single slope drawn through the space of dots in the cube will offer any significant reduction in error over that error we would expect if we estimated a score from the sample mean of the variable itself. Therefore, is there anything to our previous assumption that these three variables, ZPOLIT97, ZDEATHRT, and ZLGPOP share a common underlying single dimension, reflecting a common conceptual identification? The answer, of course, is no. There are, in fact, three separate dimensions, or components (or, factors), in this model. One is for ZPOLIT97, a second unique factor is ZDEATHRT, and a third unique factor is ZLGPOP. In other words, these three variables are independent of each other and any assumption that they measure a common concept is disconfirmed by this simple graphical exercise.

Compare, for instance, Figures 14.1a–c to Figures 14.2a–c (the model of ZPOLIT97, ZCIVIL97, and ZLGPOP). This second set of figures reflects the array of observations in a three-dimensional space defined by the Model 2 specified in Table 14.1. We know already from Table 13.5 that one of the three bivariate relationships is statistically significant (ZPOLIT97 and ZCIVIL97). And, we see in Figure 14.2a that this is reflected in the pattern of observations within the cubic space. Note that as we move in Figure 14.2a along the axis defining the relationship between ZPOLIT97 and ZCIVIL97 (diagonal BC), the size of the spikes consistently and proportionally grows shorter. In other words (as we know from the correlation matrix in Table 14.2), as scores for ZPOLIT97 decline across countries, so do the corresponding values for

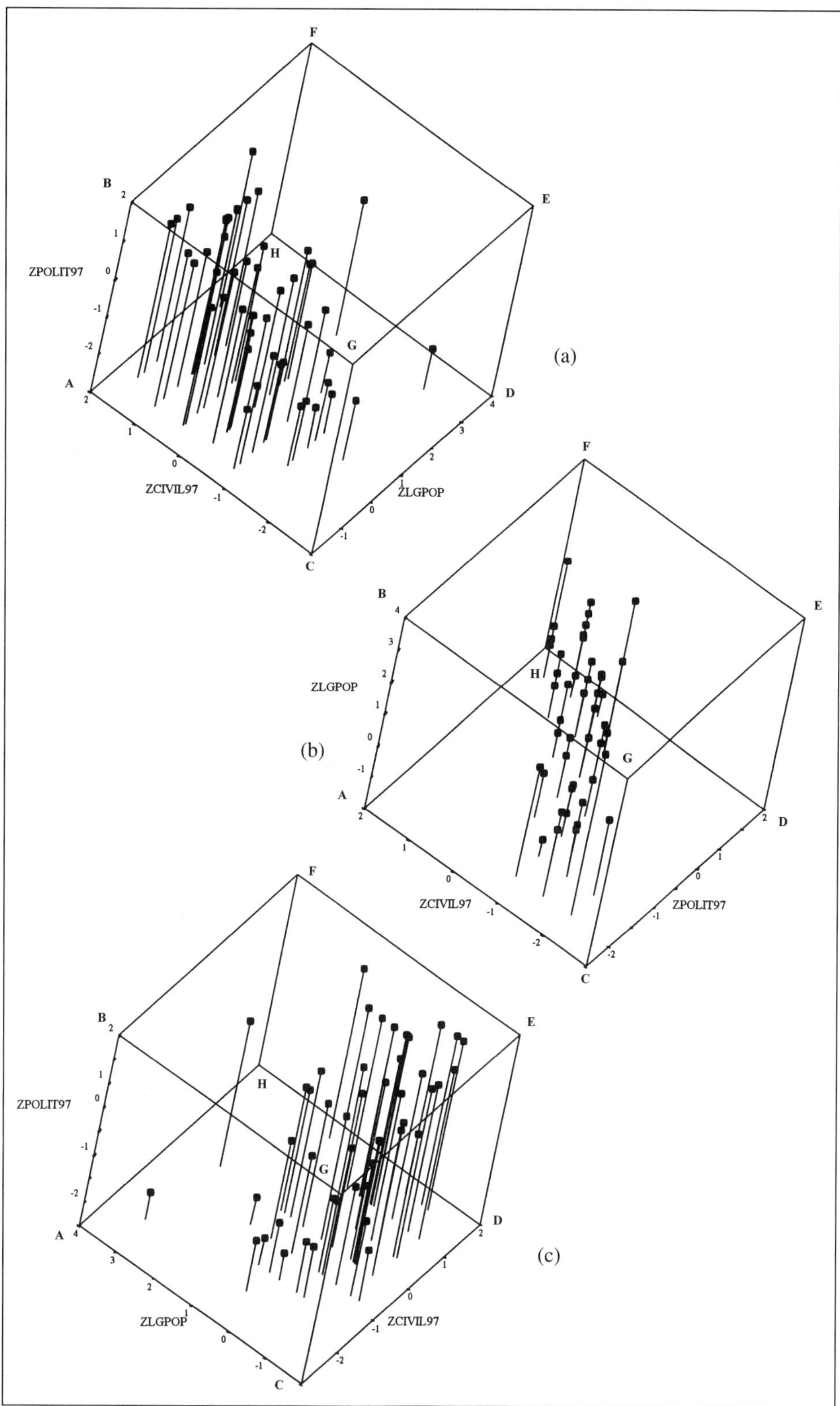

FIGURES 14.2a–c First, Second, and Third Perspectives, Spatial Representation of Multidimensional Index Based on ZPOLIT97, ZCIVIL97, and ZLGPOP.

ZCIVIL97, reflecting a positive relationship. Moving on to Figures 14.2b and 14.2c, however, we see that the proportional scaling in the size of the spikes disappears, as does the spread of values along the entire range of the axis for the relationships of ZL-GPOP and ZCIVIL97, and ZPOLIT97 and ZLGPOP.

Thus, Model 2 identifies one strong component of shared variance in the space. This component is defined by the two variables, ZPOLIT97 and ZCIVIL97. Thus, there is a slope in the space, but the slope runs only along one axis: BC. It does not run along a diagonal cutting through the middle of the cube (such as, for instance, a slope along the vector AE would do). Thus, in Model 2, the variable ZLGPOP is essentially lost. It has no clear identity with respect to either of the two other variables, and as such, is simply a residual component within the model. If we were to assert that, based on Model 2, population was indeed related in some way to democracy, and as such, postulate that these three variables collectively comprise some intrinsic common concept, we would be stretching matters considerably. Population has no significant statistical relationship to the underlying properties of democracy, and any overarching concept that purports to include population along with the scale of institutional and liberal democracy would be questionable, at best.

Turning to the last three figures (Figures 14.3a–c), reflecting Model 3 from Table 14.1, we observe a totally different picture from that reflected in the previous six figures (Figures 14.1a–c and Figures 14.2a–c). Now we see vividly that regardless of the rotated perspective, we have a well scaled and tightly distributed array of the dots within the cubic space. They all fall along the axis CF . We also note the number of dots we can see in the space has declined. This is because we are working with three measures (ZPOLIT97, ZCIVIL97, and ZPARCOMP) that are technically ordinal, and several countries share identical locations across all three variables, thus their dots fall on top of each other in Figures 14.3a–c and cannot be clearly separated in this spatial depiction. Nonetheless, there is enough variance in the model to confirm that each of the three measures lies along a common identity—a single component (defined by the diagonal, and slope, CF). Thus, all three variables tap a common underlying conceptual factor.

Each of these three sets of figures graphically depicting Models 1–3 in Table 14.1 can be statistically summarized by reporting the variance for each of the slopes computed by the factor algorithm. We call these estimates the *eigenvalues*. The total variance explained by any identified component within a space bounded by the number of variables in the model is the *eigenvalue*. The eigenvalue is essentially the total variance among all the possible combinations of components within the model. Each factor analysis will report as many eigenvalues as there are variables within the model, though only K–1 (where K is the number of variables in the model) will have any possibility of expressing enough variance to be meaningful to the researcher. Therefore, by examining the eigenvalues, or the components of variance within a factor analysis model, we may determine the extent to which there is a unique shared identity to any of the variables in the factor model.

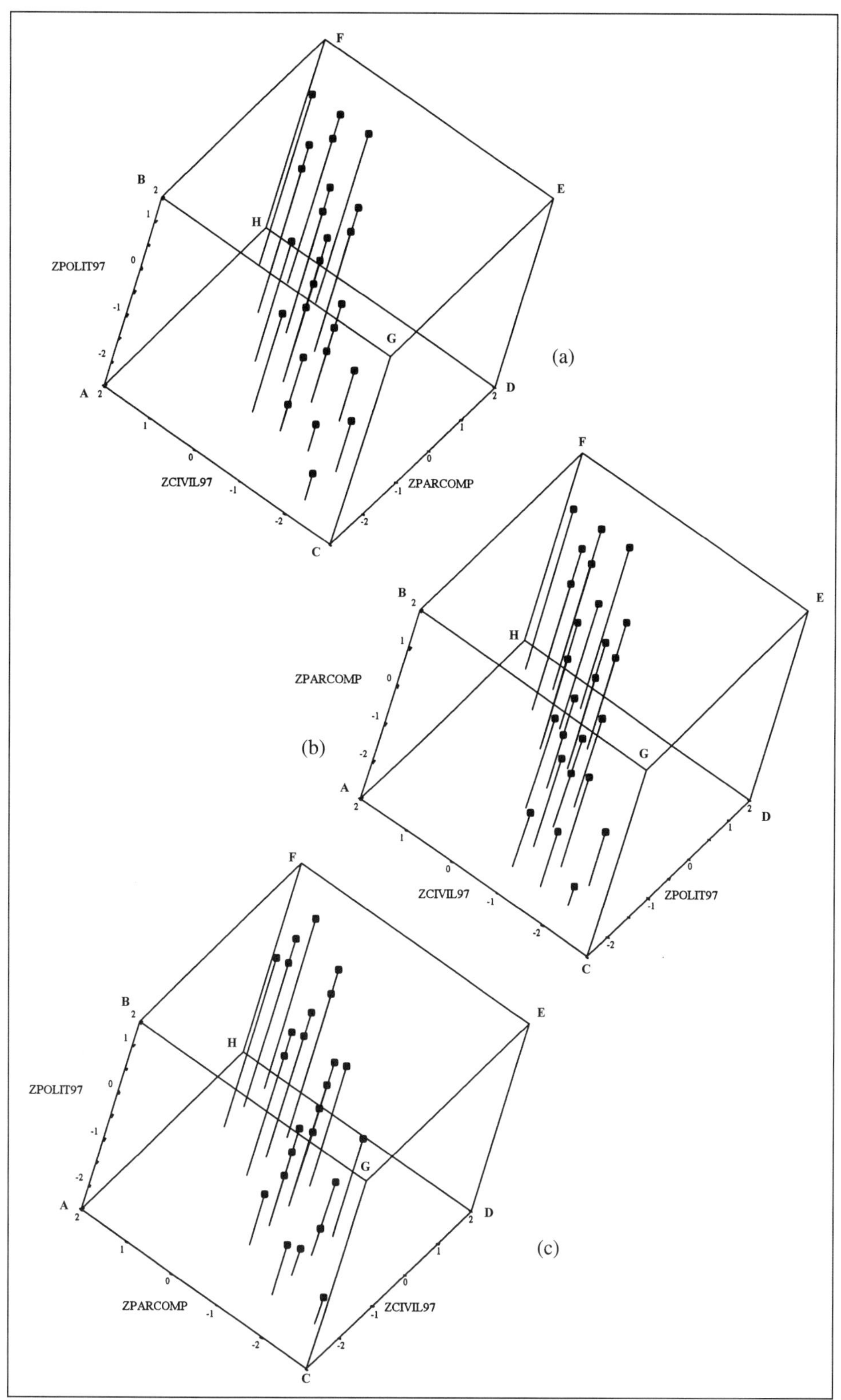

FIGURES 14.3a–c First, Second, and Third Perspectives, Spatial Representation of Multidimensional Index Based on ZPOLIT97, ZCIVIL97, and ZPARCOMP.

TABLE 14.3 Component Variance (Eigenvalues) Across the Hypothetical Models of Proposed Multidimensional Index Measures Constructed Using Factor Analysis (Principal Components)

	Components of Variance Within the Three Models		
Multidimensional Models (Table 8.6)	*First Eigenvalue*	*Second Eigenvalue*	*Third Eigenvalue*
Model 1:	1.123 (37.4%)	1.039 (34.6%)	.838 (27.9%)
Model 2:	1.965 (65.5%)	.950 (31.7%)	.008 (2.8%)
Model 3:	2.770 (92.3%)	.142 (4.7%)	.008 (2.9%)

Table 14.3 reports the actual eigenvalues computed from the common method of factor analysis (principal components) applied to each of the three illustrative models above. Note that for Model 1, the first eigenvalue (reflecting the first, and "best," linear slope plotted for the three variables in the space) is equal to 1.123, which is 37.4 percent of the total number of components within the model (3). Thus, the first defined component of Model 1 captures 37.4 percent of variance among the observations across three variables in the cubic space defined by the factor model. The second eigenvalue (the next "best" slope) accounts for an additional 34.6 percent of the total variance (an eigenvalue of 1.039), while the third eigenvalue accounts for the remaining total variance, or 27.9 percent (or, .838 of 3). As there are only three variables in the model, and each captures roughly equal proportions of the total variance in the space, we may conclude there is no data reduction possible here: No combination can produce a common identity, per se.

The eigenvalues for Model 2 reveal something slightly different. The first eigenvalue does somewhat better in terms of capturing shared variance within the spatial dimensions of the model. This is because of the strong relationship between ZPOLIT97 and ZCIVIL97. This first eigenvalue is 1.965 (or, 65.5 percent of the total variable). Because we know that ZLGPOP has no strong statistical relationship to either ZPOLIT97 or ZCIVIL97, we also know that a fair amount of variance is still left unaccounted for by the first slope. Indeed, 34.5 percent is left over. The second eigenvalue in Model 2 reports an eigenvalue of .950, or 31.7 percent of the remaining 34.5 percent. The final eigenvalue captures the little bit of variance left after this three-variable factor has accounted for the best linear combinations of ZPOLIT97, ZCIVIL97, and ZLGPOP.

Finally, Model 3 shows what we can expect when we have a well-defined singular identity across K variables within a factor model. We know that all three variables in this model are statistically significant. We therefore expect, and see in Table 14.3, that the first eigenvalue will capture this singular identity, or component, and report a slope that accounts for the vast majority of the total variance in the total spatial dimension of the model. The first eigenvalue of 2.770 accounts for 92.3 percent of the total variance in the space defined by the three variables in the factor model, ZPOLIT97,

ZCIVIL97, and ZPARCOMP. There remains only 7.7 percent of the variance in the space left to be accounted for, far too little to reflect a second unique identity across the three variables.

In larger factor models, where we have many more than three variables, it is often the case that the eigenvalues will report two or three (or, perhaps more) unique components that include several dominant, or defining, variables within each component. We know from Model 2 that the dominant, or defining, variables in the strongest component are ZCIVIL97 and ZPOLIT97. They are the only two of the three that are strongly correlated with each other. They would therefore define the underlying intrinsic nature of the reported underlying identity, or concept, captured by the factor analysis. On the other hand, Model 3 also has only one dominant identity. However, all three variables in Model 3 will have a role in significantly defining the intrinsic nature of the underlying concept, because all three are so strongly correlated with each other.

Had we proposed a model with, say, ten variables, we might well have seen two distinct components defined, with five of the variables strongly correlated with each other and reflecting the primary properties of one of these two identities, and the other five variables defining the primary properties of the second component. It must be noted, however, the larger the number of variables one includes in a factor model, the more difficulty there is in properly identifying unique components. Variance is too often shared among too many of the variables for a clear demarcation to be statistically identified. Yet, when working with a relatively simple model (as we will within this chapter, and subsequent chapters), clear and clean identification of a single common underlying component is much easier to ascertain and is much more reliable as a valid depiction of defined concepts than one might find with larger models.

DEMONSTRATION 14.1: FACTOR ANALYSIS

With the logic of factor analysis as a foundation, let us now turn our attention to devising a single multidimensional measure of *political empowerment*. To begin, let us state the basic proposition that guides our thinking with regard to *political empowerment* and that corresponds to our expectations based on the correlation matrix reported in Table 13.5:

> *The correlations (Table 13.5) among the four individual measures of the primary properties of democracy share enough variance collectively to be properly understood as representing a single, broader measure, which we term, political empowerment.*

This use of basic statistical logic is something people apply in their everyday lives. For example, college admissions officers have data on every student applying for admission to a university. These data include SAT scores, high school grades, letters of recommendation, size of the high school, the high school's average SAT over the past several years, and various demographic data on the student. All these data are assumed to be related to a common underlying concept: academic success. These measures are almost always indexed into a few variables (if not a single variable) that will allow the admissions officer to compare one student's likely academic success with other prospective students. Admissions officers also want to predict a student's likely academic success over the four years of college. Factor analysis has been frequently used in an effort to devise the right scale (a scale is essentially an index measure composed of several variables) measuring academic success. The goal of the admissions officers is the same as ours: reducing data to a single (or a few) meaningful measures of a more fundamental, and seemingly complex, concept.

Ultimately, our objective is to obtain a single measure of democracy for each country, based on that country's combination of the four individual foundation attributes of democracy. We call these single measures *factor scores*. Understanding how we obtain these scores allows us to understand the process of factor analysis itself.

The Steps Involved in Obtaining Factor Scores

Factor analysis entails three basic steps:

- The computation of a standard correlation matrix, as in Table 13.5, and assessing the shared variance among the variables in the analysis
- The extraction of the common, underlying factor from the correlation matrix itself
- Finally, the deriving of a single measure of a country's *political empowerment*

Determining the Power of the Shared Variance. The first step in obtaining factor scores is to determine whether a factor analysis is appropriate, given the *linear* relationships between the variables (CIVIL97, POLIT97, PARCOMP, and PARREG). There are two common measures to assess whether there is enough shared variance among the variables to proceed with a factor analysis: the KMO statistic and Bartlett's test. The KMO (Kaiser-Meyer-Olkin) statistic measures how close the shared variance is across all four variables shown in Table 13.5. It is, in effect, a measure of power, in this case, the power of the variables to define an underlying concept, such as *political empowerment*. The KMO statistic ranges between 0 and 1.0. A KMO of less than .5 indicates insufficient shared-power variance among the pairs of variables to proceed with a factor analysis. The Bartlett's test assesses the validity of the null hypothesis that the correlations among the variables (as shown in Table 13.5) are in fact devoid of enough variance to proceed with the factor analysis. It does not test shared variance, but rather, aggregate variance. The test statistic reported for Bartlett's is a chi-square, and if the significance level of the chi-square is small enough ($p \leq .05$), we may reject the null

TABLE 14.4 KMO and Bartlett's Test from Factor Analysis of Primary Properties of Democracy (SPSS 10)

Kaiser-Meyer-Olkin Measure of Sampling Adequacy		.788
Bartlett's Test of Sphericity	Approx. Chi-Square	245.799
	df	6
	Sig.	.000

and assume the variance in the correlation matrix is sufficient to proceed with the analysis. If this chi-square cannot be rejected, and if the KMO is not at least .5 (preferably, .6 or more), it is unwise to proceed with factor analysis. It will not produce reliable and valid findings.

Table 14.4 presents the output from SPSS 10 of the first phase of the factor analysis: the assessment of the variance in the sample. The KMO statistic is very strong (.788), well above the minimal level conventionally required for a reliable factor analysis. The Bartlett's test reports a chi-square of 245.799 ($p = .000$), indicating enough aggregate variance within the sample to proceed with the analysis.[3]

Extracting Common Factors. As we noted earlier, the initial objective of factor analysis is to identify the common underlying concept that links the variables in the analysis. Of course, factor analysis as a statistical tool does not tell you the name of this concept. Your theory does that. What factor analysis does tell you is there is a common, *linear* structure to the variables in the analysis that forms a single dimension. This is the dimension we hold to represent the single underlying concept that transcends the individual variables in the model. To determine whether there is a common underlying single concept linking these variables, we must assess the *factors*. Factor analysis technically confirms for us common underlying statistical relationships to a set of variables. The factors, therefore, represent underlying concepts that statistically connect all the variables in a linear analysis.

Table 14.5 reports the analysis of variance in the factor analysis from which we may assess the number of relevant factors produced by the analysis. Table 14.5 may seem imposing because it is loaded with technical terms.

The procedure for extracting a factor is based on a technique called *principal components*. This complex process simply defines a linear combination of the variables in such a way as to maximize the shared variance among the variables. As we saw in our graphical demonstration of the logic of factor analysis, if all the variables are so closely correlated with each other that their shared variance leaves very little error, the factor analysis will report only one component that has enough power to adequately capture the common underlying concept. This is the case in Table 14.5. Note that the first component in Table 14.5 accounts for over 90 percent of the total variance among all four variables in the analysis. Dropping any one of the variables from the model leaves so little variance left unexplained that there is no need to look for any more than one common underlying component. The analysis shows that in components 2–4 there is an aggregate of less than 10 percent of variance left to try to find a second common

TABLE 14.5 Total Variance Explained and Factor Assessment, from Factor Analysis of Primary Properties of Democracy (SPSS 10)

	Initial Eigenvalues			*Extraction Sums of Squared Loadings*		
Component	*Total*	*% of Variance*	*Cumulative %*	*Total*	*% of Variance*	*Cumulative %*
1	3.603	90.067	90.067	3.603	90.067	90.067
2	.235	5.879	95.947			
3	.100	2.506	98.453			
4	6.188E-02	1.547	100.000			

Extraction Method: Principal Component Analysis

underlying concept. This is far too little variance to support any other underlying concept. Thus, the model has extracted, or confirmed, one very dominant component, consisting of all four variables.

The total variance explained by this component, or factor, is the *eigenvalue*. The eigenvalue for the first factor in Table 14.5 is 90.1. This means that 90.1 percent of the shared variance of the four variables is captured, or determined, by this rather abstract underlying component. The first column in Table 14.5 reports the total variance. With four variables in the model, the sum total for the variance in the model will equal 4. The first component's variance, or eigenvalue, is 3.603, or, 90.1 percent of the total variance (3.603 is 90.1 percent of 4.0).

The second part of Table 14.5 (*Extraction Sums of Squared Loadings*) may be ignored—these are specialized summaries of the first half of the model used for more detailed and involved diagnostics. We may conclude from Table 14.5 that the factor analysis has extracted, or produced, one common underlying concept. This concept represents over 90 percent of the total shared variance among the four variables.

Obtaining a Country Score for Political Empowerment: Factor Scores. The third and final stage of our analysis produces individual scores for each country. These scores, or factor scores, reflect how strongly each variable is correlated with the underlying factor that has been extracted by the analysis. Alternatively, the factor score allows us to gauge how strongly the factor dimension is correlated with the variables. To do so, we examine the *factor loadings.* They reflect, in effect, how much each variable contributes to the definition of the underlying factor. In this way, we can better evaluate the relative contribution (that is, weighted contribution) of each of the underlying components of democracy. The factor loadings for our variables are reported in Table 14.6.[4]

All the variables are positively correlated with the factor, meaning, therefore, that *political empowerment*—our defined factor—is *positively associated* with *increasing* values of CIVIL97, POLIT97, PARCOMP, and PARREG. In other words, the more prevalent these variables are in a country, the more a country will be characterized by *political empowerment*—consistent with our theory. If we square each of these factor loadings, we obtain a statistic called the *communality*. This is similar to an r^2 in a Pearson correla-

TABLE 14.6 Factor Loadings (Component Matrix) from Factor Analysis of Primary Properties of Democracy (SPSS 10)

	Component
	1
CIVIL97	.940
POLIT97	.958
PARREG	.935
PARCOMP	.963

Extraction Method: Principal Component Analysis

tion analysis. The communality of each variable is simply the extent to which the variance of the variable is explained by the underlying factor. So, we can see that *political empowerment* accounts for well over 90 percent of the variance of each of our four variables. We conclude that in countries to which we ascribe large degrees of *political empowerment*, institutionalized political competition/participation, political rights, and civil liberties would be very salient within the political environment. Based on our sample, the scope and scale of institutionalized democracy have slightly more weight in the definition of our underlying concept, *political empowerment* ($PARCOMP_f$ = .963, and $POLIT97_f$ = .958). Yet, the differences are slight: All four primary properties significantly contribute to the definition of *political empowerment*.

Once a single factor has been identified, we can determine through the factor analysis technique a country's individual score for *political empowerment* (POLEMPOW). These are the *factor scores*. All factor scores are equivalent to standardized values (z-scores). Accordingly, we know that a country with a large, positive factor score will have substantial opportunities for political competition and participation (PARCOMP, PARREG), extensive civil liberties (CIVIL97), and political rights (POLIT97). These four variables may not be equally apparent within any given country. On the other hand, a large, negative factor score reflects a country that is the counterpart to a democracy—a political autocracy. This country has minimal or no opportunities for political competition and political participation, minimal or no civil liberties, and is characterized by relatively limited political rights. A country with a factor score approaching 0 will have no consistent pattern to the alignment of the primary properties. A blend of democracy and autocracy characterizes political authority within these countries. We know that not all of these variables will have the same degree of importance in defining the degree of *political empowerment* within a country, though the differences are very slight. The factor scores themselves are based on the weighted contribution of each of the four variables used to define the common factor of democracy.

Table 14.7 reports the original z-scores for each of the four primary properties and the derived factor scores (in descending order) for the countries in CROSSNAT.50. Because the data for our four primary variables are measured at the ordinal level in their original scale, the variance within *political empowerment* will be somewhat reduced. As a result, we have multiple ties across the countries. Nonetheless, the Kolmogorov-Smirnov statistic for the interval-level variable, POLEMPOW, is .115 (p = .1, df = 50), and the skewness is -.513, allowing us to reject the null that the variance is not normally distributed. The face validity of *political empowerment* (POLEMPOW) seems easily confirmed. The Netherlands, Canada, Australia, and the United States are statistically at the high end of *political empowerment* (POLEMPOW = 1.131), while China (an outlier) stands alone with a citizenry statistically estimated to have minimal degrees of *political empowerment* (POLEMPOW = –2.281), with Iran (–1.896), Nigeria, and Congo (–1.869 each) close behind. In the middle range are those countries that have inconsistent patterns of democracy, thus relegating their citizenry to what might be described as moderately weak forms of *political empowerment*. India (-.013), Bangladesh (-.013), Ghana (.014), Brazil, Mexico, Ukraine, Nepal, and Russia (.105 each) are examples of these countries.

Prudent Application of Factor Analysis

Factor analysis is a complicated, and often, somewhat controversial, technique. Models that rely on many more variables than our four-variable model often lead to definition of components to which it seems difficult to attach much valid meaning. This problem underscores the controversy surrounding the use of factor analysis as a tool often applied to "hunt" for relationships among variables without adequate consideration of the logical foundations of the primary properties involved in the analysis. Regardless of what you input into a factor analysis, the procedure will produce underlying factor dimensions that demonstrate high correlations among a group of variables. It produces statistical estimates, not theory. However, this method of "hunting" puts the cart before the horse, so to speak. Theory must always dictate what variables should be correlated with each other. Theory should also dictate the underlying factor dimension that we expect to emerge from the analysis. We should not construct the statistical estimate and then fit the theory to that estimate.

Our theory, in other words, should direct the application of factor analysis as a method of validation and data reduction. The factor analysis may validate the measures by confirming expected correlations and producing a single measure that can help in assessing the face validity, and later, the construct validity of the derived single multidimensional measure. The procedure also allows more manageable hypothesis testing subsequent to the factor analysis by reducing the number of variables required in a correlation analysis.

The procedure should not, however, be substituted for hypothesis testing techniques. The difference between employing the technique as a tool for data reduction and as a complement to theory, rather than as a tool of discovery per se, is not always easy to see. However, if you restrict your usage of factor analysis to data reduction following careful consideration of the underlying logic linking the primary components of a primary concept, you will have applied the technique in a prudent fashion.

TABLE 14.7 Primary Properties of Democracy (Z-Scores) and Political Empowerment Score (Factor Score from Factor Analysis)

Country	*ZPARCOMP*	*ZPOLIT97*	*ZPARREG*	*ZCIVIL97*	*POLEMPOW*
Netherlands	1.262	1.075	1.027	1.61	1.31
United States	1.262	1.075	1.027	1.61	1.31
Canada	1.262	1.075	1.027	1.61	1.31
Australia	1.262	1.075	1.027	1.61	1.31
Spain	1.262	1.075	1.027	.995	1.15
United Kingdom	1.262	1.075	1.027	.995	1.15
Italy	1.262	1.075	1.027	.995	1.15
Czech	1.262	1.075	1.027	.995	1.15
France	1.262	1.075	1.027	.995	1.15
Japan	1.262	1.075	1.027	.995	1.15
Germany	1.262	1.075	1.027	.995	1.15
Korea	1.262	.573	1.027	.995	1.016
Greece	1.262	1.075	1.027	.381	.989
South Africa	.320	1.075	.237	.995	.693
Poland	.320	1.075	.237	.995	.693
Chile	.320	.573	.237	.995	.559
Romania	.320	.573	.237	.995	.559
Philippines	.320	.573	.237	.381	.399
Venezuela	.320	.573	.237	.381	.399
Argentina	.320	.573	.237	.381	.399
Ecuador	.320	.070	.237	.381	.265
Thailand	.320	.070	.237	.381	.265
Madagascar	.320	.573	.237	-.233	.239
Russia	.320	.070	.237	-.233	.105
Nepal	.320	.070	.237	-.233	.105
Ukraine	.320	.070	.237	-.233	.105
Mexico	.320	.070	.237	-.233	.105
Brazil	.320	.070	.237	-.233	.105
Ghana	-.622	.070	.237	.381	.014
India	-.622	.573	.237	-.233	-.013
Bangladesh	-.622	.573	.237	-.233	-.013
Colombia	-.622	-.432	.237	-.233	-.281
Sri Lanka	-.622	.070	-.553	-.233	-.352
Peru	-.622	-.935	.237	-.233	-.414
Turkey	-.622	-.432	.237	-.848	-.441
Malaysia	-.622	-.432	.237	-.848	-.441
Pakistan	-.622	-.432	.237	-.848	-.441
Morocco	-.622	-.935	-.553	-.848	-.780
Tanzania	-.622	-.935	-.553	-.848	-.780
Tunisia	-.622	-1.437	-.553	-.848	-.913
Egypt	-.622	-1.437	-.553	-1.462	-1.074
Algeria	-.622	-1.437	-.553	-1.462	-1.074
Kenya	-.622	-1.437	-.553	-1.462	-1.074
Uganda	-1.564	-.432	-2.133	-.233	-1.147
Zimbabwe	-1.564	-.935	-2.133	-.848	-1.441
Indonesia	-1.564	-1.94	-2.133	-.848	-1.709
Congo	-1.564	-1.94	-2.133	-1.462	-1.869
Nigeria	-1.564	-1.94	-2.133	-1.462	-1.869
Iran	-1.564	-1.437	-2.133	-2.077	-1.896
China	-2.506	-1.94	-2.133	-2.077	-2.281

Choices

The preceding discussion of factor scores and the alternative measures of democracy that we have derived through factor analysis is not meant to suggest that the only useful index measure of a variable is derived from this procedure. Far from it. Furthermore, it is not meant to suggest that merely adding together z-scores (as we did to construct the measure of POWER) is an inappropriate means of devising a compound measure. Indeed, it is the preferred method by many students. It would also be a mistake to conclude that you must always construct multivariate measures of a comparative political phenomena.

Most importantly, it is a simple fact that in political science (and especially cross-national analysis) there are few measures that are universally accepted as "standard" variables by researchers. As we have noted in Chapter 6, the concept of democracy is operationally defined in a wide variety of ways by different scholars. Some of these measures are multivariate index measures, and some are not. There is no one measure that is always considered the *one* that must be used. So too with the concept of *political empowerment*. Indeed, some scholars may observe the underlying concept as something other than *political empowerment*.

The key lesson to take away from this discussion of the measurement of *political empowerment* is that it is always important to understand and appreciate the role of theory and operational procedures in the analysis of cross-national data. Theory guides the formulation of concepts, which in turn shapes the final operational definition of a variable. The results will depend heavily upon the sample and the availability of reliable and valid data. Each of these constraints varies from research context to research context. As was noted in Chapter 6, there is room for creativity in research—indeed, it is the obligation of the student to run the risk of failure when striking out to formulate concepts and explore important political phenomena. Yet, one should strive to avoid abusing the basic rules of measurement and data analysis.[5]

We hope that you gain a keen appreciation of the need for explicit clarity when defining, explaining, and justifying your measures. In comparative politics, where data often cross so many different national, cultural, and linguistic boundaries, this is even more essential than it might be if the data were drawn solely from one national or cultural setting.

Don't Confuse Current Events Analysis with Comparative Political Analysis

Something to keep in mind is the fact that cross-national analyses are designed to reveal patterns of variance across a sample; they are not necessarily designed to describe current events. These data within CROSSNAT.50 are a few years old now (more recent data for all the countries are not yet possible for all our variables), and as we know, a lot has happened to a number of individual countries during the past few years. If, however, our measures are valid and reliable, and our sample of populous countries is representative, then we can be reasonably confident that the *patterns of variation across variables in the sample* will accurately reflect general patterns of political behavior and institutional authority across countries in the target population. We can, in effect, extrapolate from these findings to the political world around us. Conditions in countries may have changed since the data were collected, but if the *concepts* the data reflect remain valid and relevant, the *findings* offer an opportunity to refine and enlarge our understanding of the political world around us—regardless of current events. *Of course, you should never ignore current events.* They help inform your theory, and they provide crucial opportunities to test your theories as changes in our political world unfold before us. Furthermore, as you move down the Ladder of Theory Building, you will need to be abreast of critical changes that have emerged within individual or specific groups of countries.

BEYOND POLITICAL EMPOWERMENT: CITIZEN AUTONOMY

David Held has drawn attention to the difference between being empowered through democratic institutions and civil liberties and possessing the capacity to "reason self-consciously, to be self-reflective and to be self-determining, and to act, in principle, as the author or maker of one's own life, in public and private realms."[6] More specifically, this requires that at least four outcomes be realized through democratic politics:

- Protection from the arbitrary use of political authority (that is, civil liberties and political rights)
- Public consent to regulative and authoritative institutions (competitive political competition and institutionalized and regulated political participation)
- The creation of those circumstances that allow citizens to develop their character and nature and to have free and open access to both expressing and realizing their diverse capacities and social interests (human development)
- Maximizing economic opportunity and the provisions of distributional resources (economic freedom and market authority)

Citizen autonomy, therefore, is not citizen autarky (individual isolation free of responsibility), but the freedom and capacity of individuals within society to share in the rewards that come from being both participants within society (with all the shared obligations and responsibilities that follow) as well as recipients of society's distributions (with implied opportunities to achieve an equal political and social status).

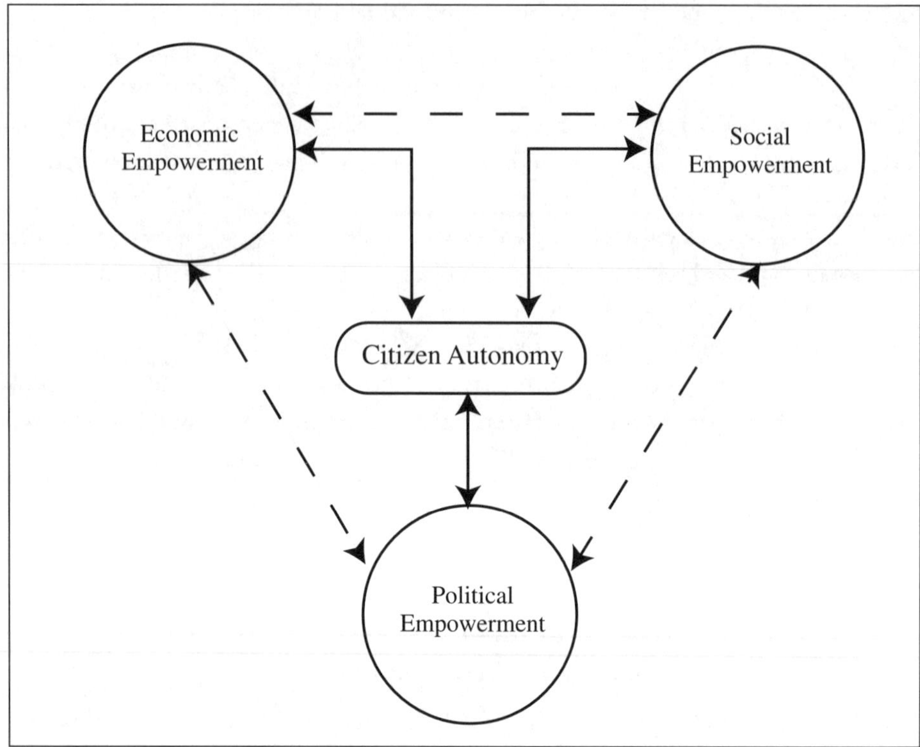

FIGURE 14.4 Citizen Autonomy and Its Form of Empowerment

Deriving an Index Measure of Citizen Autonomy

Thus, as a full measure of a political system's range of empowerment afforded its citizens, we require a measure that approximates the full range of *citizen autonomy*. This must include measures of political, economic, and social empowerment. As suggested above, the index measure of human development approximates the empirical parameters of social empowerment. Lacking education and the basic resources for survival, citizens have little opportunity to realize their full potential as human beings with equal responsibilities and obligations within society. They are simply too busy trying to survive from day to day in the worst scenarios. They can hardly be self-reflective. Economic freedom and its implications for market authority capture the essence of economic empowerment. Lacking the freedom to acquire and preserve private property, as well as being denied the rights of market reciprocity, citizens can hardly hope to achieve self-respect, let alone realize their self-consciousness. *Political empowerment* itself, drawn from the primary properties of democracy, underscores the need to ensure the democratic principles within society through which economic and political development can proceed toward effective *citizen*

TABLE 14.8 Pearson Correlation Coefficients, Primary Properties of Citizen Autonomy

Variables	*HUMDEV (Social Empowerment)*	*ECON97 (Economic Empowerment)*	POLEMPOW *(Political Empowerment)*
HUMDEV	1.000	–	–
ECON97	0.719	1.000	
	(p = .000)		–
POLEMPOW	0.817	0.601	1.000
	(p = .000)	(p = .000)	–

KMO = .685
Bartlett's Test of Sphericity = 59.469 (p = .000, df = 3)

TABLE 14.9 Factor Loadings and Analysis of Variance, from Factor Analysis of Primary Properties of Citizen Autonomy

Variables	*Factor Loadings: Citizen Autonomy*
HUMDEV (Social Empowerment)	0.913
POLEMPOW (Political Empowerment)	0.852
ECON97 (Economic Empowerment)	0.838

One factor extracted
Eigenvalue for Citizen Autonomy = 2.268 (75.346%)

autonomy. Lacking the political markets necessary to fashion the rules and regulations that restrain and constrain the arbitrary actions of the collective within their lives via access to the obligation and privileges of private property, citizens can hardly hope to be self-determining.[7] Figure 14.4 reflects this logic.

To ascertain whether there is indeed strong enough shared variance between these three components of *citizen autonomy*, and to derive a single compound measure of *citizen autonomy*, we can once again turn to a standard principal-component-based factor analysis. Table 14.8 reports the Pearson correlation coefficients, as well as the KMO statistics and Bartlett's test for sphericity. The variables each have sizeable correlations, though the relationship between *political empowerment* and economic empowerment is only within the upper reaches of moderately strong (r = .601).

Table 14.9 reports the factor loadings from the single factor extracted by the principal components analysis. The eigenvalue and percent of variance explained by the factor dimension extracted is also reported in Table 14.9. The loadings suggest a strong degree of coherence within the empirical measure of *citizen autonomy*.

Table 14.10 reports the individual factor scores for *citizen autonomy* derived from the analysis, as well as the other z-scores for the primary properties of *citizen autonomy*. Note that China scores somewhat higher on *citizen autonomy* than it had on the index

TABLE 14.10 Primary Properties of Citizen Autonomy (Z-Scores) and Citizen Autonomy Score (Factor Score)

Country	*ZHUMDEV*	*ZECON97*	*POLEMPOW*	*CITAUTON*
United States	1.327	1.649	1.310	1.641
Canada	1.359	1.357	1.310	1.545
United Kingdom	1.270	1.576	1.150	1.530
Australia	1.296	1.357	1.310	1.520
Netherlands	1.289	1.285	1.310	1.490
Japan	1.308	1.139	1.150	1.384
France	1.270	.920	1.150	1.287
Germany	1.195	.993	1.150	1.284
Spain	1.119	1.066	1.150	1.280
Italy	1.157	.847	1.150	1.214
Greece	.949	.483	.989	.935
Chile	.804	1.066	.559	.930
Argentina	.696	1.212	.399	.881
Korea	.854	.410	1.016	.880
Czech	.734	.264	1.150	.828
Thailand	.230	1.066	.265	.588
Philippines	.148	.847	.399	.524
Mexico	.438	.701	.105	.476
South Africa	-.136	.410	.693	.358
Poland	.539	-.538	.693	.279
Ecuador	.192	.191	.265	.248
Peru	.141	.847	-.414	.215
Malaysia	.324	.556	-.441	.171
Venezuela	.476	-.538	.399	.143
Brazil	.141	-.611	.105	-.130
Turkey	.072	-.101	-.441	-.174
Sri Lanka	.028	-.174	-.352	-.186
Russia	.192	-.975	.105	-.244
Romania	.223	-1.559	.559	-.277
Colombia	.324	-.830	-.281	-.282
Tunisia	-.136	-.319	-.913	-.518
Ghana	-1.089	-.246	.014	-.526
Ukraine	.028	-1.632	.105	-.554
Indonesia	-.225	.337	-1.709	-.610
India	-1.082	-.684	-.013	-.695
Egypt	-.635	-.101	-1.074	-.698
Morocco	-.849	-.538	-.780	-.836
Kenya	-1.247	.045	-1.074	-.891
Nepal	-1.600	-1.048	.105	-.995
Congo	-1.499	.847	-1.869	-.996
Pakistan	-1.316	-.830	-.441	-1.005
China	-.098	-.392	-2.281	-1.045
Bangladesh	-1.745	-1.048	-.013	-1.098
Iran	-.010	-1.267	-1.896	-1.188
Algeria	-.326	-1.923	-1.074	-1.249
Madagascar	-1.663	-2.069	.239	-1.348
Tanzania	-1.865	-.830	-.780	-1.354
Uganda	-1.972	-.465	-1.147	-1.401
Zimbabwe	-.988	-1.267	-1.441	-1.412
Nigeria	-1.644	-1.486	-1.869	-1.919

TABLE 14.11 Analysis of Variance, CITAUTON by Type of Political System as of 1950 and Geopolitical Region

Group	*N*	*Mean*	*Std. Deviation*
	Type of Political System as of 1950		
Colonial/Protectorate	15	-0.582	1.041
Authoritarian	12	0.032	0.724
Democratic	23	0.363	0.952
Total	50	-0.000	1.000
F = 4.672 (p = .014, df = 2,47)			
	Geopolitical Region		
CIS-East Europe	5	0.006	0.549
Asia	11	-0.316	0.743
Sub-Saharan Africa	9	-1.054	0.659
Industrial West & Europe	12	1.245	0.486
Latin America	8	0.310	0.435
Arab States	5	-0.898	0.314
Total	50	-0.000	1.000
F = 20.913 (p = .000, df = 5,44)			

measures of *political empowerment*. Its relatively open markets and its comparatively higher degree of social development compensate for the poor degree of *political empowerment*. However, China still ranks in the lowest quintile of CITAUTON scores. The sample distribution CITAUTON is within the range of normality: The Kolmogorov-Smirnov statistic is .098 ($p = .200$, $df = 50$), with a skewness of .086.

Citizen Autonomy in a Comparative Context

Finally, how do countries with differing types of political system traditions, as well as countries from different geo-political regions of the globe, compare with respect to *citizen autonomy*? Table 14.11 reports the standard analysis of variance (comparison of means) across countries grouped by type of political system as of 1950 (SYS19503) and geopolitical region (REGION6). While Bonferroni comparison tests (not reported in Table 14.11) reveal little in the way of significant difference across each of the three differing types of systems (as of 1950), the overall distribution of means reveals a clear pattern: Those countries that were democracies as of 1950 have achieved on the whole much larger degrees of *citizen autonomy* by 1997 ($\bar{X}$=.363) than either those countries that were authoritarian in 1950 ($\bar{X}$ =032) or, to an even greater degree, those countries that were in colonial or protectorate status as of 1950 ($\bar{X}$ =.582).

This general conclusion is underscored when comparing the respective means of *citizen autonomy* across the six different geo-political regions of the globe. Industrialized Western and European democracies ($\bar{X}$ =1.245) stand apart from each of the other regions: Only Latin American countries ($\bar{X}$ =.310) have *citizen autonomy* scores well into the positive range. Empowering citizens is an attribute within countries largely restricted to the wealthy and the relatively democratic—at least as of 1997.

CHAPTER SUMMARY

In this and the previous chapter we have considered how we can effectively utilize basic statistical tools of linear analysis to help us in the construction of multidimensional indexes. In particular, we have statistically derived a measure of *political empowerment* (POLEMPOW), based on the weighted contributions of CIVIL97, POLIT97, PARCOMP, and PARREG, following the logic of democracy as first detailed in Chapter 7. We have compared this variable to that produced by applying the mean z-score method of constructing a multivariate index measure (POWER). While the actual statistical technique (factor analysis) used to define POLEMPOW is often intimidating and seems overly complex, it is nonetheless within the grasp of beginning students once they have been exposed to the fundamentals of Pearson correlations and the logic of multidimensional index construction. Following our construction of *political empowerment*, we proceeded to consider the logical extension of empowerment, namely, *citizen autonomy,* as a major concept within cross-national politics. This index measure is constructed from HUMDEV, POLEMPOW, and ECON97. We then considered the cross-national distribution of *citizen autonomy*.

While we have not explicitly tested hypotheses within this chapter, we have seen how exploratory analysis can be effectively put to use in the process of constructing multidimensional indexes to be used in hypothesis testing later. Used by itself, correlation analysis is not an effective tool for hypothesis testing. However, it is essential for sorting out the possibilities and identifying the nuances that lie behind the relationships between two variables.

NOTES

1. For a more comprehensive overview of factor analysis as a tool for social science research, as well as for more detail as to its computational logic and the assumptions that lie behind the statistics, see Harry H. Harman, 1976, *Modern Factor Analysis*, third edition (Chicago: University of Chicago Press); Raymond B. Cattell, 1978, *The Scientific Use of Factor Analysis in Behavioral and Life Sciences* (New York: Plenum Press); Henry G. Law, ed., 1984, *Research Methods for Multimode Data Analysis* (New York: Praeger); Allen Yates, 1987, *Multivariate Exploratory Data*

Analysis: a Perspective on Exploratory Factor Analysis (Albany, N.Y.: State University of New York Press); Paul Kline, 1994, *An Easy Guide to Factor Analysis* (New York: Routledge); and Jae-on Kim and Charles W. Mueller, 1978, *Introduction to Factor Analysis: What it Is and How to Do It* (Beverly Hills, Calif: Sage Publications).

2. For a detailed introduction to the matrix algebra and mathematical algorithms of factor analysis, see Maurice M. Tatsuoka, 1971, *Multivariate Analysis: Techniques for Educational and Psychological Research* (New York: John Wiley and Sons), especially pp. 94–156; Richard J. Harris, 1975, *A Primer of Multivariate Statistics* (New York: Academic Press), especially pp. 23–27 and 205–224; or, John P. Van de Geer, 1971, *Introduction to Multivariate Analysis for the Social Sciences* (San Francisco: W. H. Freeman and Company), especially pp. 62–75 and 128–155.

3. To execute a standard factor analysis within SPSS 10, follow the sequence ANALYZE▶ DATA REDUCTION▶FACTOR. Within the FACTOR ANALYSIS window, select the variables you wish to include in the analysis. From the buttons at the bottom of the window, select the DESCRIPTIVES option to request the Bartlett's test and the KMO statistic. The EXTRACTION button allows other options than principal components to extract factors. The default is the principal components, as this is the most commonly used and appropriate for the common purposes to which factor analysis is used in cross-national analysis. Rotation should be used to verify that the analysis has identified only one statistically relevant factor. The various options for rotation and its logic are beyond the scope of this text. The final button, SCORES, allows you to specify individual scores for each country on the defined concept. The score for each country (measuring the country's degree of association with the defined underlying concept) is written to the data file as a new variable. It presents a z-score and has a mean of 0 and a standard deviation of 1 within the sample. For further detail on the components of factor analysis within SPSS, see the *SPSS Applications Guide*, available from Prentice Hall; and Chava Frankfort-Nachmias and David Nachmias, 2000, *Research Methods in the Social Sciences*, sixth edition (New York: Worth Publishers), pp. 427–430.

4. The most common use of factor analysis is to find the common underlying patterns to many variables in samples much larger than fifty. In these cases, it is common—indeed expected—that more than one factor dimension will be extracted. In such instances, the student would want to rotate the dimensions, which is a complicated way of saying he or she must use a mathematical technique to ensure that each factor dimension is statistically independent from the other. For an example of factor analysis as applied to cross-national analysis, see Arend Lijphart, 1999, *Patterns of Democracy: Government Forms and Performance in Thirty-Six Countries* (New Haven: Yale University Press), pp. 243–245; Robert L. Perry and John D. Robertson, 1997, "Compact and Compound Republicanism: The Political-Economy of Europe's Federal Vision," *Journal of Theoretical Politics* 9 (July): 317–345; and Frank S. Cohen, 1997, "Proportional Versus Majoritarian Ethnic Conflict Management in Democracies," *Comparative Political Studies* 30:5 (October): 607–630.

5. See Marcus E. Etheridge, 1999, "Scientific Principles in Political Study: Some Enduring Situations," in Stella Z. Theodoulou and Rory O'Brien, eds., *Methods for Political Inquiry: The Discipline, Philosophy, and Analysis of Politics* (Upper Saddle River, N.J.: Prentice Hall), pp. 130–141; and Ruth Lane, 1997, *The Art of Comparative Politics* (Needham Heights, Mass.: Allyn and Bacon), pp. 125–142.

6. David Held, 1995, *Democracy and the Global Order: From the Modern State to Cosmopolitan Governance* (Stanford: Stanford University Press), pp. 150–151.

7. For an intriguing cross-national analysis of the complex and precarious relationship between political freedoms and market freedoms, see John R. Hanson II, 1999, "Are We All Capitalists Now?," *The Independent Review* 3:4 (Spring):565–573.

15

The Role of Scatterplot Analysis and the Conceptualization of Modernity

Terms: *Simple Regression, Scatterplot, Regression Line (Least Squares), Regression Coefficient, Intercept, Coefficient of Determination, Coefficient of Nondetermination, Polynomial Equation*
Concepts: Development, Modernity, Urbanization
Demonstration: Elaborating Scatterplot Analysis, 15.1

In this chapter we continue our analysis of the conditional factors within the environment of a country's political system by considering one of the most controversial, yet important concepts within comparative politics: *development*. We begin by exploring a component of development, *modernity*. We also introduce you to a basic technique of hypothesis testing: scatterplot analysis based on simple regression. This technique builds on the logic of correlation analysis discussed in previous chapters.

At the core of *development* is the presumption that societies continually undergo changes brought on by population growth, the spread of information, and the constant pressure from the international economy. The mere need to survive and exist as a nation compels all countries to adapt to, and often adopt, customs and processes that alter existing authority structures within families, the society, and the broader political system. The process of adaption and adoption comprises the essence of a country's development. At any point in time the global landscape is colored by a diversity of countries at different levels of development. Thus, development must be properly understood as both a part and product of the political environment.[1]

Critics have cautioned that the concept of development smacks of a degree of Eurocentrism; that is, that the concept describes the world from the perspective of Western democracies and ignores the perspectives of non-Western cultures and countries. The problem—to the extent that it actually exists—is compounded by the evidence that shows that some scholars have moved beyond empirical analysis to normative prescriptions. In other words, rather than merely comparing countries according to operationally defined attributes associated with a carefully delimited definition of development, some scholars have been accused of advocating a set of preferred attributes that reflect the European and American cultural traditions. Worse, many such studies have labeled those countries that fall short of empirical levels of "modernized" societies as being inferior to those countries and societies that have much more of the quantitative attributes of a modern society.[2]

Despite these concerns, a long tradition of research has approached the study of development by specifying authority roles in the political and economic subsystems within countries and comparing the degree to which these roles are coordinated and influenced by traditional orientations. Therefore, in this chapter, we will focus on one aspect of the broader aspect of development: the degree to which a country's society has moved away from *traditional* patterns of social and political relationships toward what may generally be regarded in contemporary times as a *modernized* political and social system. One cannot ignore the implications and ramifications of these developmental changes for politics within countries, as well as between countries in the international system. As such, development is a critical conditional factor within the political environment of countries, and as a feature of development, modernization assumes a major part in that political environment.

Along with democracy, the concept of development in general (and the specific study of the attributes of traditionalism and modernity) has been the subject of extensive and often intense debate within the field of political science. Many of the most important changes in the twentieth century have been attributed to the complex interaction of democracy, autocracy, modernity, and traditionalism. Concepts that capture forces of such recognized consequence for the global political environment pose difficult challenges to the student of cross-national research. They test each phase of the cross-national research process: conceptualization, operationalization, specification, measurement, analysis, and evaluation. With this in mind, we will focus on measuring modernity as a pathway toward the broader concept of political development. We will begin in this chapter by placing the concept in perspective, and then move to specifying the primary attributes of modernity. Finally, we will, as with democracy and political-economic authority before, offer a single multidimensional index measure of modernity by which to proceed with hypothesis testing.

To explore this concept within the context of hypothesis testing, we will explore in more detail the scatterplot. From Chapter 13, we know this tool is an extension of the Pearson Product Moment Correlation analysis. As you will recall from Chapter 13, the correlation coefficient is only a measure of association and in itself is not a sufficient tool for testing linear models. However, the scatterplot is a more useful hypothesis-testing tool. It offers one the most efficient and effective methods for not only refining our conceptualization of the political environment, but an opportunity as well to effectively employ residual analysis for explicit comparison of countries.

THE CONTEXT OF DEVELOPMENT

The process of development can be roughly plotted along an exponential trajectory from a point where specific authority roles within society are governed by *traditional* rules, personalized interactions, and familiar customs, to some point where a large part of the social, economic, and political relations among citizens in a country are coordinated and governed by *specialized* and *diverse* roles. Concerning the latter end of this trajectory, it is often assumed that the pace of change and the pressure on authority roles grows exponentially—that is, the adaptation and adoption affecting modern patterns of authority roles often seem to grow at an ever-increasing pace over time—up to a point. At some point, the pace of change slows relative to earlier stages of development. It is also assumed that such change is teleological. That is, with the exception of revolution or invasion, the trajectory does not fall back toward traditionalism. Rather, modernity continues, yet at much slower rates.

Politics is, in part, the process whereby values pertaining to the legitimate use of public authority (that is, government) are allocated among individuals and groups in society. These values that divide society into groups are very much a function, in part, of the level of social development within a country. For instance, in very traditional (or, pre-industrial) societies, we are more likely to find fewer formal political institutions, more limited markets, and a diminished number of roles that differentiate people (for example, father, mother, professor, brother, boss, employee). Often the same person who occupies one role relative to a group occupies several other different roles relative to the same group (for example, the father is also the professor of and brother of, as well as boss of, the *same* people). In all societies, regardless of the level of development, conflict will exist among those with different interests, customs, or backgrounds. Yet, the nature of that conflict will depend largely on the environmental structures within a political system that are influenced by the country's stage of development. Modernity, as Ronald Inglehart notes, is rather the combination of rational authority in all phases of organizing daily activities of citizens, technological application to problem solving and organization, and the intense and widespread role of science in legitimating proposed authority patterns and behavioral attributes within society.[3]

MEASURING THE CONCEPT OF MODERNITY

Conventional measures of development place countries along a continuum between two polar extremes: *traditional* and *modern*. In this chapter, we will focus on developing a measure of modernity.[4] In other words, by empirically measuring modernity we obtain a measure of traditionalism, just as we measure autocracy by operationally defining political democracy.[5]

As with *political democracy* or *political empowerment*, the concept of *modernity* is best understood as a multidimensional concept. Specifically, it reflects the degree to which a country is not "traditional." Generally, traditionalism implies a society and, by extension, a political system, that remains committed to traditional rules of governing and coordinating social interactions and economic transactions in society. Traditionalism is associated with simpler and more limited markets and with fewer degrees of professional and economic specialization. As such, society is less specialized as a whole, and the demand for specialization within the work force is minimal. Whenever problems occur, customs and habits dictate solutions. Consequently, there is less interest in or demand for formal routine and legalized procedure. At traditionalism's extreme, abstract logic, critical to explanation and prediction, is minimal. Finally, social relationships are more rigid and "normative," that is, authority is inherited (not earned) according to custom, family, or personal choice—not merit and performance.

Traditionalism, according to Alex Inkeles and David H. Smith, is undergirded by a psychological orientation of the population toward their broader environment. For instance, traditional men and women resist new ideas and information, viewing them as threats. They focus only on the immediate and particular, not the universal and distant, let alone abstract. They deny the existence of differing opinions and conflicting attitudes, are deeply distrustful of those not known to the immediate clan and family. Technology is not highly valued—indeed, it is often seen as a threat to authority and order, characterized by patron-client relationships, and founded on deeply ecclesiastical philosophy. Traditional people tend to be pessimistic and fatalistic about the future, oriented to the short-term future and deeply wedded to the past as the guide to the future.

Modern men and women, by contrast, value new experiences and new information and are very much attuned to attitudes, opinions, and lifestyles beyond their own experiences. Planning, regulation, and calculation of the future and its correlation to present activities are central to modern men and women. Contractual obligations and responsibilities become central to the order modern men and women value. They place great value on higher formal and scientific education and are generally comfortable with the universal and abstract. They assume rewards and social status are based on performance and measured accomplishment within the context of meeting responsibilities and specified tasks with measurable outcomes.[6]

From these psychological and individual traits of the traditional man and woman, one can more easily appreciate the structural and functional aspects of a traditional society, the core traits of which are:

a predominance of *agricultural production*, instead of industrial or service economies where specialization is inherently required and developed a *lack of advanced education* within the population, thus minimizing the benefits (or vices) associated with both science and its relentless assault on custom, as well as economic and labor force specialization

hierarchical authority roles within society based on ascriptive priorities governed by custom, reflected by distinct forms of *gender-based inequalities*

Primary Properties of Modernity

Returning again to Ronald Inglehart, we may sharpen our contrast between traditional and modern society. Modern societies are almost universally described in structural-functional terms. There are eight structural aspects distinguishing modern societies. First, they are *urbanized*. This means most people in society live within large urban settings rather than sparsely populated rural settings.

Second, they are *post-industrialized*. This means they are predominately service-based industrial economies rather than agriculture- or manufacturing-based economies. This further implies that most of the wealth and economic activity within society is highly specialized and contoured to the unique needs of sophisticated consumers who contract for the skills of professionals to manage important service tasks for the population—including banking, finance, insurance, and other highly intellectual activity directed toward the needs of a population.

Third, modern societies are *highly specialized* with respect to occupations and skill requirements, consistent with a service economy.

Fourth, modern societies are distinguished by the predominance and legitimate application of *science and technology* to all aspects of social and political organization and management. This implies, for instance, that before proposals for public policy can be realized, the tools and logic of science must be shown to have certified the policy proposal as sound and beneficial, and that before judging the utility and relevance of any new application of authority (such as a new electoral system) the new proposed method or instrument must be shown to have technical superiority to that of the existing instrument or method.

Fifth, modern societies reflect *universal bureaucratization* within social organizations—meaning that all problems and issues of public authority are dealt with routinely by specialists within highly structured organizations that generally are hierarchically ordered.

Sixth, modern societies exhibit a *predominant reliance on legal-rational authority*, meaning, once again, that all decisions of public authority must be measured against a universal standard endorsed by science and demonstrated as technically superior to other standards of measurement and that such measurement allows one to precisely calibrate the exact and tangible gains and losses associated with any particular decision.

A seventh distinguishing aspect of modern societies is that there are very *high levels of social mobility* within the population. This implies that people move around quite frequently rather than remain within their place of birth and that they seek out new forms of employment with regularity, thereby having less knowledge of and psychic commitment to the myths and traditions of a place of employment or residence.

Finally, modern societies are noted for their preference for *ascribed social status*. The primary implication here is that the distribution of money and skill assignments is based on certified credentials and performance, not family or other solely personal and demographic criteria. It also holds that one's status in society is measured more by the skill credentials one has attained than the birthright of the individual.[7]

While researchers have experimented with a variety of measures designed to capture the meaning of political development, it is generally agreed that the basic form of *economic production*, the *educational level* of a country's population, the extent of *mobilization* of a population, the dependence on *science and technology* within society, and the structure of *gender relations* within society allow a proximate measure of the degree to which modernity characterizes a society (and distinguishes it from a "traditional" society). At the outset, it is important to remember, there is no normative priority guiding our consideration of this concept. It is not a question of whether modernity is good or bad. Rather, it is a matter of discerning (and summarizing) the key empirical attributes that distinguish the broader patterns of institutional authority and political behavior across diverse cultural settings.

Modernity Operationalized

In CROSSNAT.50, the variable MODERN measures *modern society,* and, like POLEMPOW, is derived through factor analysis. We use factor analysis to confirm our assumptions about the common, underlying properties of the broader phenomenon, modernity. Furthermore, our theory of modernity posits a linear relationship between the principal concept—modernity—and each of the primary properties of this concept. That is, we assume that as each of the specified properties of modernity increases across countries, the broader phenomenon of modernity itself will increase in linear, incremental fashion across a cross-national sample.

The variable MODERN reflects the primary concept of interest to us in this chapter: *modernity*. It is defined (in structural-functional terms) as the combined effect of the following five primary functional and structural properties of modern society, none of which is assumed to be a sufficient condition for modernity, but rather necessary to the "contemporary" modern society:

1. SERVICE—measuring the extent to which society relies upon professional service activities as a basis of wealth formation
2. EDUC3—measuring the degree of advanced learning within society
3. GENPOW—reflecting the degree to which society transcends traditional modes of exclusion-based, non-ascriptive rewards and opportunities

4. INTERNET, as well as its transformed value, LGNET, which will be explained below—reflecting the extent to which the population is able through communication to transcend the common boundaries of their society and its culture
5. URBAN—reflecting the extent to which a population reflects the more highly mobilized and organized urban setting

The respective z-scores for each variable have been recorded under the variable names, ZEDUC3, ZSERV, ZURBAN, ZNET (and its transformed value, ZLGNET), and ZGENPOW within CROSSNAT.50. Each variable and the theoretical reasoning linking it to the broader concept of modernity is considered below.

Service-Based Economies: SERVICE, ZSERV. Traditionally, economists have divided the major economic activities of a nation-state into three broad sectors based on the nature of production: the primary sector (agriculture), the secondary sector (industry), and the tertiary sector (services). While agriculture is commonly associated with traditionalism, the tertiary economy is strongly associated with much more economically advanced and modern, nontraditional economies.[8] Therefore, to provide a comparative assessment and balance of a country's economy as a means of measuring its degree of modernity (or traditionalism), we must include a measure of the third sector of the economy: the service sector.

The theory of political development suggests a modern society is characterized by a large service economy, while a traditional economy is largely agricultural. Where roles and structures are more formally defined and routinized, we should expect the extent of an agricultural economy to be sharply reduced. We measure the extent of a service economy by the total value added by service activity to the country's gross domestic product (SERVICE, ZSERV).[9]

Figure 15.1 presents the box-plot for SERVICE. We first introduced box-plots in Chapter 10 (see Figure 10.8). The box-plot produced in Figure 15.1 may be interpreted just as in Chapter 10. However, it is a univariate plot, rather than a comparative plot, as in Figure 10.8.[10] The distribution is slightly negatively skewed (skewness = -.407). The range of values runs from 20.4 percent (Nigeria, ZSERV = –2.40) to 71.7 percent (France, ZSERV = 1.54). Nonetheless, the sample is normally distributed (K-S = .093, p = .200, S-W = .954, p = .093).

Advanced Education: EDUC3, ZEDUC3. A central characteristic and resource of modern society is higher education. Along with routine and formal authority structures come specialized training and vocational skills. In traditional society, educational specialization assumes a less important role, consistent with traditional and less specialized authority roles. Educational specialization, however, is a highly valued and necessary feature of a modern, technologically and scientifically adept society. Advanced education is operationally defined as the gross enrollment ratio of third-level education within a society. This corresponds to the ratio of total enrollment of students in tertiary, or post-secondary, level of education, regardless of age, to the popu-

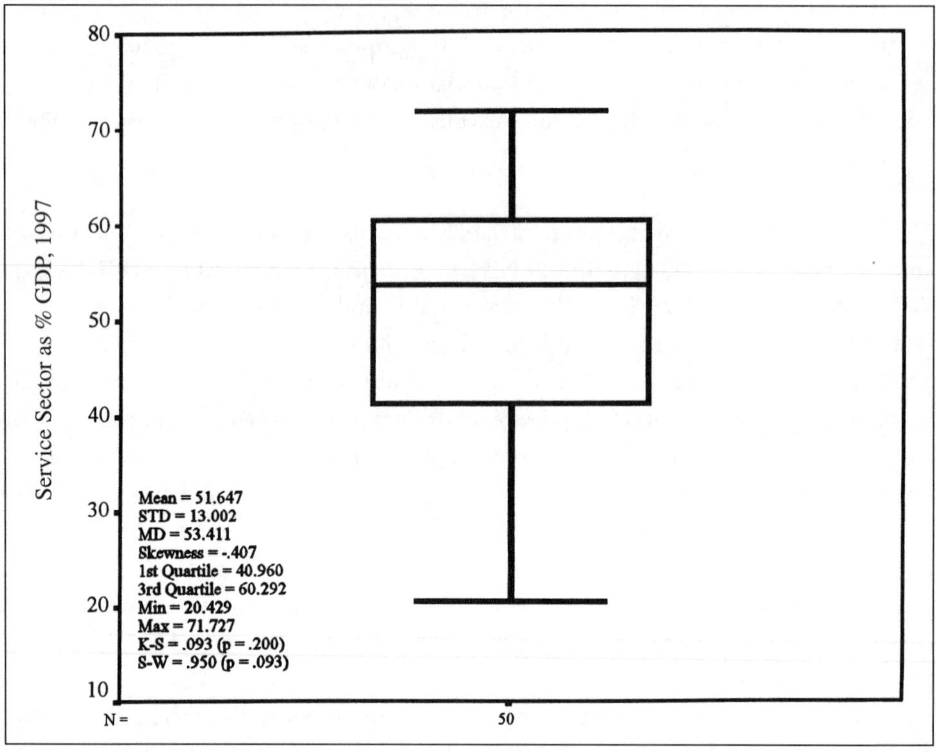

FIGURE 15.1 Box-Plot, SERVICE

lation of the age group that officially corresponds to the level of education within the country (EDUC3).[11] Third-level education is beyond the "typical" high school level and includes technical education, university training, or professional school. So, for instance, in Germany, as of 1997, the number of students enrolled in post-secondary education corresponds to 45.3 percent of those citizens in the age group within Germany that would normally be eligible for post-secondary education. In Kenya, as of 1997, however, the ratio of those enrolled in advanced education levels to the total population of the respective age group is merely 1.5 percent. It is important to note that EDUC3 cannot specify the differences in quality of education across these countries, nor does it specify the concentration of fields of speciality. However, it does reflect the overall commitment of the society to higher and professional education in general—the most reasonable cross-national comparison generally available at the moment. As well, it represents a society's exposure to formal, rational, and scientific reasoning.

Figure 15.2 presents the univariate box-plot of EDUC3. The sample is somewhat positively skewed (skewness = 1.063). The minimum value is Tanzania (.5 percent, ZEDUC3 = –1.15), the high value is Canada (90.1 percent, ZEDUC3 = 2.93). Indeed,

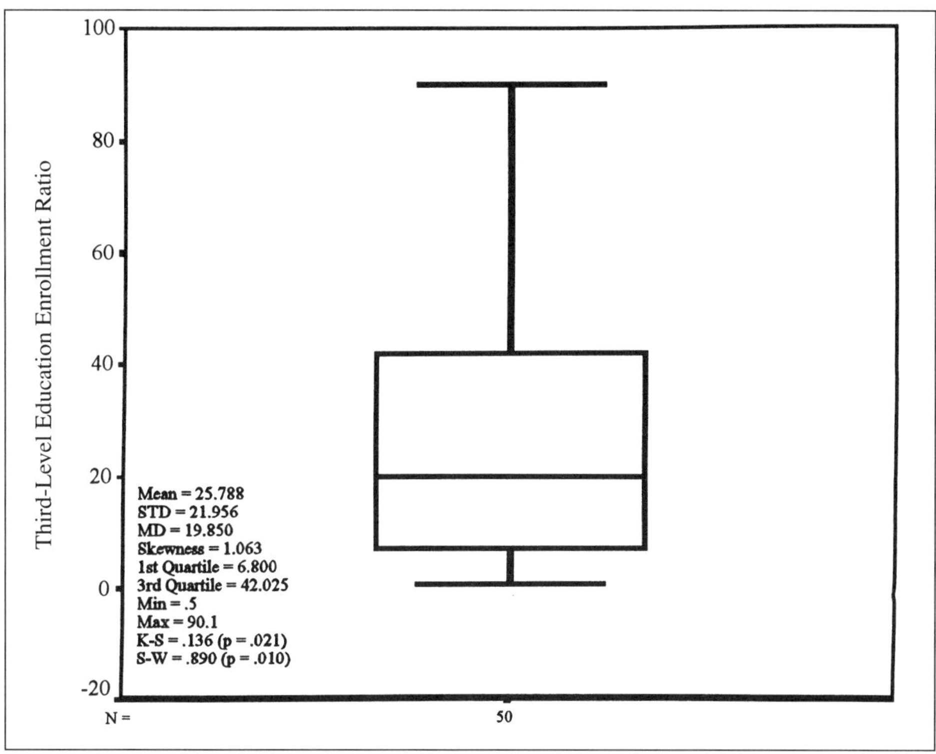

FIGURE 15.2 Box-Plot, EDUC3

normality tests indicate the sample is not normally distributed (K-S = .136, p = .01; S-W = .890, p = .02). However, there are no outliers and the deviation from normality appears minimal.

Ascriptive Social Status: GENPOW, ZGENPOW. At a fundamental level, extending and sustaining human capabilities is the advantage of achieving higher degrees of development. One of the most widespread obstacles to balanced development of human capabilities across society is gender inequality. Traditional society may, for various reasons, relegate women to a status and role within society based solely upon their gender. At a basic level, as discussed in Chapter 10, these roles have to do with bearing children, raising families, and consequently, often foregoing educational and career opportunities. These social roles carry with them unique hazards for health—both physical and mental—as well as economic and political power. However, beyond these basic roles, we may expect that modern societies extend a greater range of empowerment of women as a function of the ascriptive nature of the rational, modern society. Thus, we suggest that an accurate reflection of modernity is the ability of women to share equally political power through political participation and leadership roles.

Beyond these formal structural assumptions, Catherine Scott has argued that the very depiction of what constitutes modern itself has traditionally been laden with masculine images. Treating tradition as synonymous with household activities tied to family-/village-/clan-based economies reinforces the notion of modern as being male, while traditional is associated with activities and roles commonly associated with feminine roles. There is also the prevalent notion that modernity entails public activity—the activity in the public realm that overcomes and transforms traditional patterns of authority and social relationships. In most cases, the public realm reinforces the notion of male leadership.[12]

Recall from Chapter 11 that the United Nations (*Human Development Report*, 1999) has estimated gender empowerment (see Table 11.6). Figure 15.3 reports the box-plot for GENPOW. The accompanying central tendency measures and normality tests reiterate what we already know from Table 11.6: GENPOW is normally distributed (K-S = .082, p = .200; S-W = .954, p = .093), with minimal skewness (skewness = .344). The high value is Canada (GENPOW = .742, ZGENPOW = 2.102), while the low value is Uganda (GENPOW = .152, ZGENPOW = –1.678).

Global Communication: INTERNET, ZNET. An important element of modern society is the ability (if not willingness) of citizens to transcend traditional national and local cultural experiences. Traditional societies rely heavily on the preservation and protection of local customs and patterns of authority. These are reinforced through literature, law, and a variety of social customs. Local and national cultures across the globe today are increasingly exposed to the pressures of foreign cultural influences. Exposure to alternative authority patterns, literature, law, and patterns of social exchange confronts traditional authority with cultural competition in the form of new symbols of authority and power. Whether this new competition offers "better" and more "civilized" options is another issue. Such pressures tend, however, to force traditional societies and countries to either restrict the inflow and influence of these new symbols of power and authority, or, through political and economic competitive pressures, to adjust. How these adjustments are managed and implemented, as well as integrated with the foundations of the traditional, has become an increasingly important topic of investigation for students of the global economy. Yet, there can be little doubt that the dispersion and availability of technological means of transcending traditional culture reflect the presence of modernity within a country. The more available these technologies are to a population, the greater the opportunity for the modern to replace the traditional, all things being equal. The most prevalent and effective means of such global communication and cultural exchange is the Internet. The Internet shrinks time and space boundaries between countries and cultures, increasing geometrically the exposure of a population to new symbols and information.

Based on data from the World Bank, the variable INTERNET within CROSSNAT.50 records the Internet hosts per 10,000 people within each country (as of 1997).[13] Figure 15.4 reports the basic box-plot for INTERNET. From Figure 15.4, we

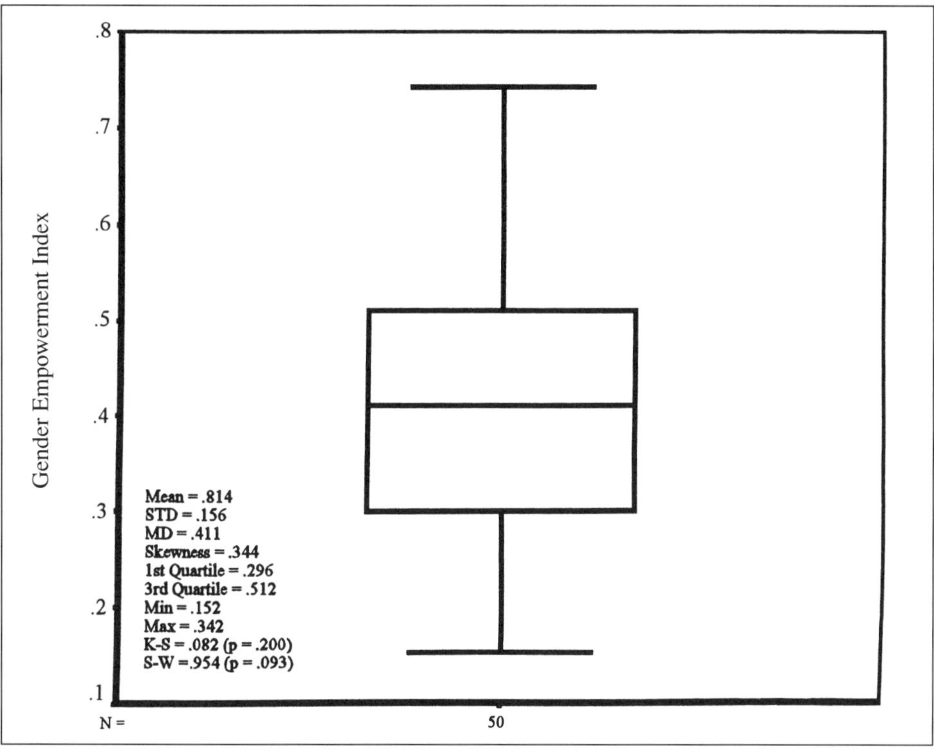

FIGURE 15.3 Box-Plot, GENPOW

discern a severely skewed (sk = 3.227) distribution—something that should not be surprising given the nature of this particular aspect of modern society (K-S = .338, df = 50, p = .000; S-W = .486, df = 50, p = .01). Five countries are "extreme" outliers (United States, Canada, Australia, Netherlands, and the United Kingdom) while two others fall within the lower "outlier" range (Germany and Japan). Given the unique nature of the Internet—its very recent invention and the natural advantage of those countries that might be very "developed" on other dimensions of the modernity complex, we should not be surprised at this very skewed distribution. Recall that with parametric statistical techniques, we assume that assumptions of normal distribution in the variable have not been *severely* violated. As we wish to eventually utilize a basic factor analysis—a technique based on parametric assumptions and one sensitive to outliers and severe skewness—to devise a single-index measure of modernity across our sample, we must find a suitable method by which we may correct the severe skewness and yet at the same time, remain faithful to the underlying structure of the distribution.

Furthermore, and equally important as any technical consideration, our theory would suggest that at the extreme ranges of INTERNET, one would not necessarily

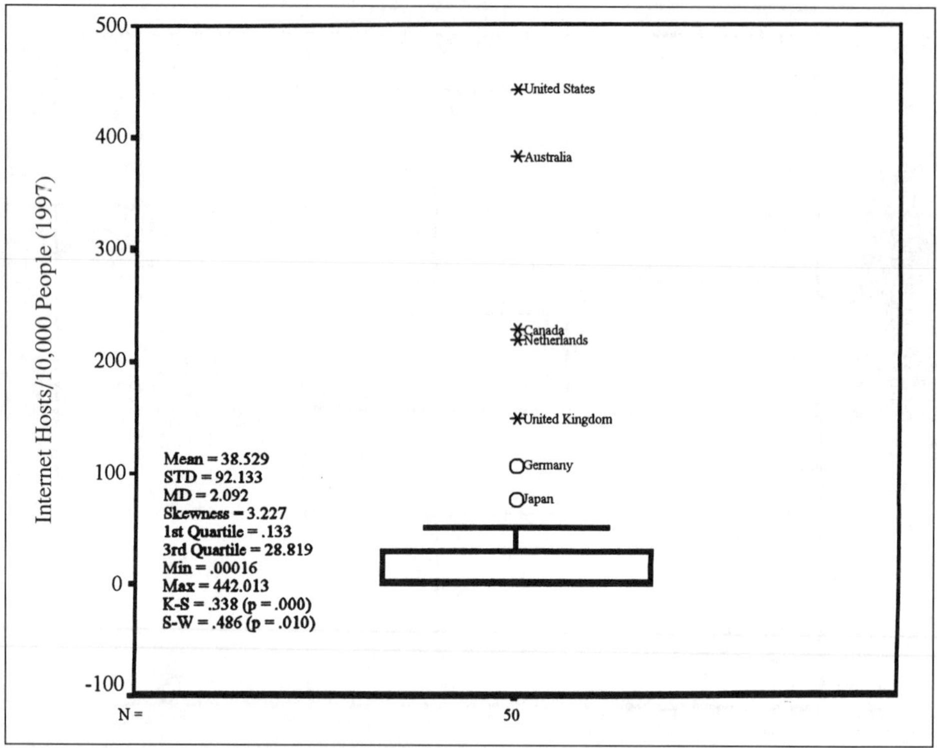

FIGURE 15.4 Box-Plot, INTERNET (1997)

have more modernity of any appreciable degree. Rather, the outliers are merely a product of the Internet's recent arrival and should not mislead us into assuming that these seven countries—especially the most extreme five—are somehow distinctly more modern solely as a result of their dense Internet connection throughout their respective populations. Our theory holds that for countries in general, as we increase Internet host access within a country, we increase the tendency of authority relationships and social relations within society to move away from patterns consistent with a traditional society and assume a nature much more consistent with modernity, as described above.

While at present, the takeoff stage of the Internet is reflected in the few very wealthy and industrially advanced societies having the means and demand for Internet connection, and while the vast majority of the rest of the world may be lagging far behind, everything about the spread of the World Wide Web suggests this severe imbalance will quickly correct itself. The correction will not mean the very wealthy countries will fall behind, but rather, they will almost certainly see their vast lead shrink relative to a group of countries that will themselves make major gains in Internet host connections. A sizeable number of countries will still lag far behind the rest. Their infrastructure is simply too little advanced to expect a short-term gain of sizeable proportions. Thus, something approximating a "normal," or at least a far less severely "non-normalized" distribution, will emerge in the world with respect to Internet host connections. Therefore, we require a transformation that will, if you like, allow us to "un-bundle" the many countries in the sample shown in Figure 15.4 that are Internet-connected to a lesser degree than our top five countries, but whose contribution to the sample variance is essential to appropriately test our assumption with the use of a parametric measure (such as factor analysis).

The transformation we require is a type of "power" transformation. Power transformations deal with severe skewness and outlier problems. The most commonly selected power transformation by students of cross-national analysis when a variable is positively skewed, such as INTERNET, is the *common logarithm*, which is based on a constant exponent used to multiply the value of the variable. In this case, the log base 10 ($\log_{10}$) value of each country's score for INTERNET has been computed. Table 15.1 reports $\log_{10}$ values for each country in CROSSNAT.50, listed in descending order of the values for INTERNET. The transformed value for the United States (442.013) is 2.65 ($\log_{10}$ 442.013 = 2.645, or $10^{2.645}$ = 442.013). That of Iran (.00016) is –3.78 ($\log_{10}$ .00016 = –3.78, or $10^{-3.78}$ = .00016). Figure 15.5 reports the box-plot of the transformed variable, LGNET ($\log_{10}$ INTERNET). The skewness is sharply reduced (-.467), while the K-S statistic is reduced to .089 (df = 50, p = .200), and the S-W statistic increases to .962 (df = 50, p = .254), indicating a normal distribution.[14]

Thus, our sample of LGNET has a normal distribution and is properly scaled with a constant value, allowing the variable's use in any further parametric-based analysis and much easier interpretation (as the congestion of the data at the low end of the scale is removed). It should be noted that unless the distortion is very severe, such log transformations (or others designed to "normalize" a distribution) will produce a set of values virtually identical to that of the original data. Such transformations should be used only in such circumstances as those described above.[15] The standardized (z-score) values for both INTERNET (ZNET) and LGNET (ZLGNET) have been computed and are included in CROSSNAT.50.

Mobilization: URBAN, ZURBAN. Urbanization is perhaps the single most commonly identified attribute of a modern, industrial society. An urban area is defined by the World Bank as a "concentration of nonagricultural workers and nonagricultural production sectors."[16] Generally, a population settlement of between 2,500–25,000 people is the minimum threshold for an urban area, though this may differ across countries. The more urbanized a society, the more integrated the labor system within a society, the more frequent and regular the interaction between specialized workers and agents of government (national and local), the more rationalized the transaction process, based as it is on more easily obtained pricing and supply information, and because of dense concentrations of people and suppliers within a limited geographic region, the more efficient the supply and distribution process. Financial and capital markets are more closely integrated with production and labor systems; thus, there is frequent and routinized interaction with other urban markets, both national and international. In short, urban

TABLE 15.1 Common Log Transformation, INTERNET (Descending Order of INTERNET Value)

COUNTRY	*INTERNET*	*LGNET*
United States	442.013	2.65
Australia	381.828	2.58
Canada	227.928	2.36
Netherlands	218.851	2.34
United Kingdom	148.834	2.17
Germany	106.692	2.03
Japan	75.794	1.88
France	49.840	1.7
Czech	47.650	1.68
Italy	36.849	1.57
Spain	30.980	1.49
South Africa	28.932	1.46
Korea	28.782	1.46
Greece	18.733	1.27
Malaysia	18.707	1.27
Chile	13.109	1.12
Poland	11.225	1.05
Russia	5.506	0.74
Argentina	5.321	0.73
Brazil	4.196	0.62
Mexico	3.735	0.57
Turkey	3.602	0.56
Peru	2.671	0.43
Romania	2.659	0.42
Thailand	2.111	0.32
Ukraine	2.074	0.32
Venezuela	2.054	0.31
Colombia	1.724	0.24
Ecuador	0.903	-0.04
Philippines	0.586	-0.23
Indonesia	0.542	-0.27
Sri Lanka	0.329	-0.48
Morocco	0.325	-0.49
Egypt	0.314	-0.5
Zimbabwe	0.237	-0.62
China	0.209	-0.68
Kenya	0.16	-0.8
Ghana	0.153	-0.82
Pakistan	0.075	-1.13
Nepal	0.074	-1.13
India	0.05	-1.3
Madagascar	0.029	-1.54
Congo	0.022	-1.65
Tanzania	0.02	-1.7
Tunisia	0.016	-1.79
Uganda	0.013	-1.89
Algeria	0.011	-1.98
Bangladesh	0.001	-3
Nigeria	0.001	-3.29
Iran	0	-3.78

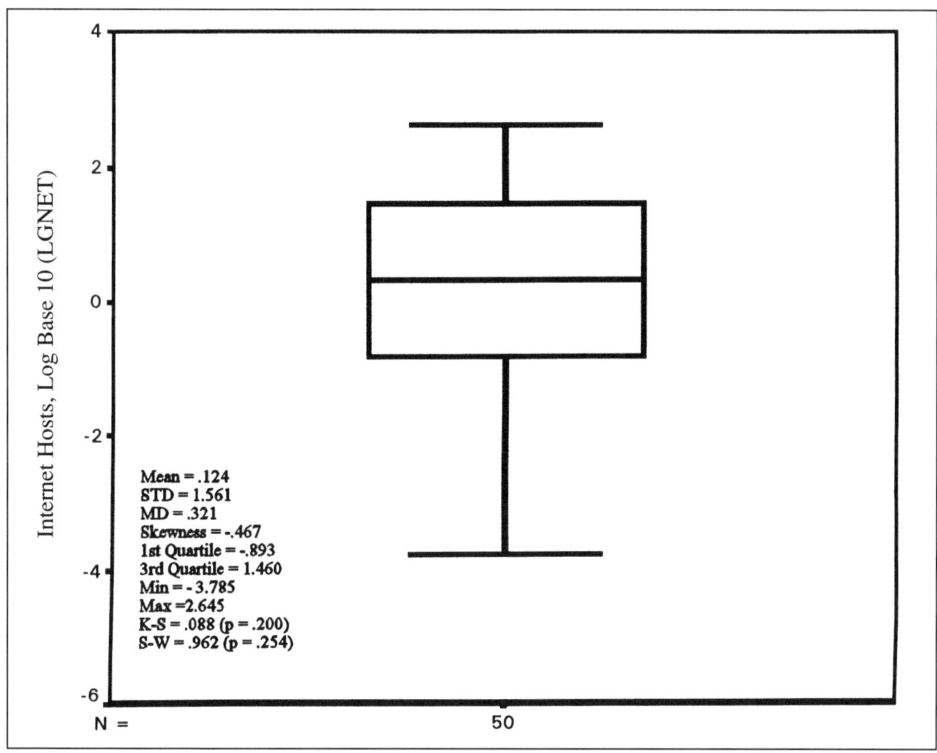

FIGURE 15.5 Box-Plot, LGNET (1997)

populations make easier communication and exchange of information among people of different social status and ethnic backgrounds, thus reducing the space and time restrictions that characterize the culture of traditional societies.[17]

Figure 15.6 reports the box-plot for URBAN within CROSSNAT.50. The sample does not severely violate assumptions of normality, though the tests of normality produce mixed results (K-S = .122, df = 50, p = .059; S-W = .922, df = 50, p = .010). There are, however, no outliers within the sample, and the skewness is very slight (skewness = -.435). The high score is the United Kingdom (URBAN = 89.320; ZURBAN = 1.385), while the low score is Nepal (URBAN = 10.940, ZURBAN = –2.041).

DERIVING A SINGLE MEASURE OF MODERNITY

In Chapters 13 and 14, we explored in some detail the logic of utilizing a sophisticated and more involved technique of index construction such as factor analysis. You will recall that before using such a technique to construct a single index measure of a concept which our theory holds to be multidimensional, we must first assess the variance of the

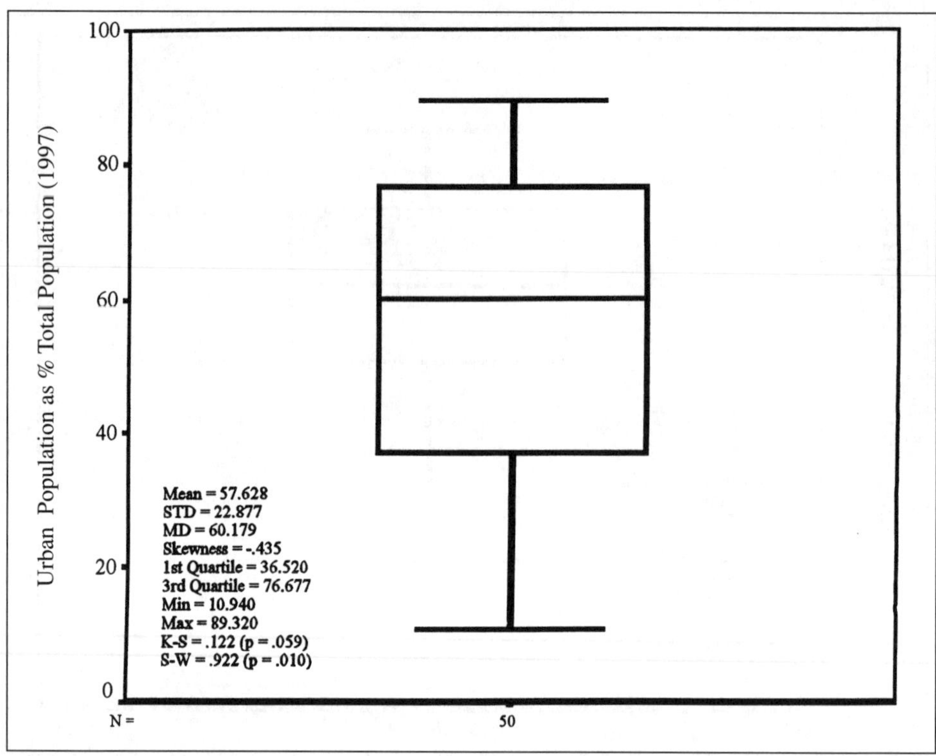

FIGURE 15.6 Box-Plot, URBAN

individual variables to be used in the analysis. Unless *each* variable is *strongly correlated* with *each* other variable in the matrix ($r^2 = .35$, at least) and in the direction predicted by the theory underlying the multidimensional concept, and, unless there is *sufficient total shared variance* among the individual variables (KMO =.6, or more), and, finally, unless the actual factor components align with our *theoretical assumptions*, we would be advised to avoid such a sophisticated linear technique. However, if such conditions are met (that is, correlations strongly align with our expectations, substantial amount of total shared variance is confirmed, and the resulting product has theoretical face validity) and so long as we are not simply throwing variables into the analysis in a "fishing expedition" to see what we can find, we are on solid grounds to proceed with the reduction of data and the construction of a single index of a complex concept through the use of factor analysis.

Recall further, the advantage of such a technique over simply summing across each country in the sample the standard scores (z-scores) of each of the variables underlying the concept and deriving an index based on the sum of each of these variables. We have seen that a distinct advantage of the factor technique, based as it is on linear analysis, is that it utilizes much more information with respect to each variable than is the case if we simply sum the z-scores for each variable across each case and derive an additive in-

TABLE 15.2 Pearson Correlation Coefficients, Primary Properties of Modernity (CROSSNAT.50) Non-Redundant Matrix

Variables	*SERVICE (N = 50)*	*EDUC3 (N = 50)*	*GENPOW (N = 50)*	*LGNET (N = 50)*	*URBAN (N = 50)*
SERVICE	1.000	0.537	0.537	0.609	0.496
(2-tail sig. level)		0.000	0.000	0.000	0.000
EDUC3		1.000	0.760	0.766	0.721
(2-tail sig. level)			0.000	0.000	0.000
GENPOW			1.000	0.822	0.642
(2-tail sig. level)				0.000	0.000
LGNET				1.000	0.676
(2-tail sig. level)					0.000
URBAN					
(2-tail sig. level)					1.000

KMO = .867
Barlett's Sphericity Test (X^2) = 160.627, p. = .0001

dex. The linear-based index produces a factor component that affords us a clearer appreciation of the degree to which each variable in the complex concept contributes to the intrinsic nature of the concept itself. An additive index treats each variable as an equally weighted component within the index. The factor analysis produces a single score that incorporates the respective weight (or relative contribution) of each variable in the analysis to the overall definition of the concept itself. This allows us a more refined appreciation of the nature of the concept, as expressed by our chosen variables.

So, we begin the process of deriving a single measure of our multidimensional index of a complex concept by examining the Pearson correlation coefficient matrix across the primary properties. Table 15.2 reports these coefficients among the five primary properties we have specified for the concept of modernity. These correlation coefficients confirm that each variable is significantly correlated with each other, and each in the expected, positive direction. In addition, the table reports two-tail significance levels (see Chapter 10 for the difference between two-tail and one-tail significance levels).

Using the factor analysis procedure described in the previous chapter, a single factor score has been produced that represents the degree of *modernity* within each country. The factor analysis confirms enough shared variance across the pairs of variables in Table 15.2 to proceed with a factor analysis (KMO = .867; Bartlett's Sphericity Test, χ^2 = 160.627, p = .0001). The procedure has produced one valid factor dimension (which we have labeled as *modernity*), accounting for 73 percent of the total variance across all the paired relationships of the five primary properties.

The underlying relationship between each of the five primary properties and *modernity*, which reflects the construct validity of our single multidimensional measure of modernity, is estimated by comparing the individual correlations of each variable with the defined factor dimension (for example, modernity). As we noted in Chapter 14,

TABLE 15.3 Factor Loadings and Analysis of Variance from Factor Analysis of Primary Properties of *Modernity* (CROSSNAT.50)

Variables	*Factor Loadings: Modernity*
EDUC3 (Third-Level Education)	.894
SERVICE (Service Economy)	.728
GENPOW (Ascription—Gender Empowerment)	.890
LGNET (Cultural Transcendence—Time and Space Reductions)	.915
URBAN (Social and Economic Mobilization)	.829

One factor extracted (principal components)
Eigenvalue for modernity = 3.646 (72.918%)

these correlations (representing the relative weight of each variable in defining the underlying concept) are the factor loadings for each variable in the analysis. These loadings are reported in Table 15.3. What these factor loadings indicate is the multidimensional nature of modernity. Our findings suggest modernity consists of a relatively Internet-connected country (LGNET = .915), with a large proportion of its respective age population enrolled in advanced education (EDUC3 = .894), and a society characterized by ascriptive merit rather than more traditional gender-role definition (GENPOW = .890). The rational and scientific/technological nature of modern societies is supported by an urban culture (URBAN = .829) and a preponderantly service-based economy (SERVICE = .728).

The factor scores derived from this analysis constitute each country's degree of modernity. The variable MODERN within CROSSNAT.50 represents each country's degree of modernity, in the form of a standardized factor score (recall from Chapter 14 that each factor score is a standardized, z-score measure of a country's degree of the defined concept). Table 15.4 rank-orders the derived measures of MODERN for the sample in CROSSNAT.50. In addition, we have recorded the standardized scores (z-scores) for each of the five primary properties from which MODERN has been computed in the factor analysis. Nigeria is the least modern country within our sample (MODERN = –1.771), while Canada is the most modern country within the sample (MODERN = 2.018). Figure 15.7 displays the box-plot for MODERN.

THE MATTER OF CULTURAL TRADITIONS, REGIONS, AND THE CONCEPT OF MODERNITY

One of the strongest criticisms leveled against the use of the concept of modernity is the assertion that the concept is based solely on attributes grounded almost entirely in Western culture and Western traditions. Modernity, in other words, reflects the West-

TABLE 15.4 Modernity and Its Primary Properties, Rank-Ordered by MODERN (CROSSNAT.50)

	Primary Properties of Modernity					
COUNTRY	*ZSERVICE*	*ZEDUC3*	*ZGENPOW*	*ZLGNET*	*ZURBAN*	*MODERN*
Canada	1.184	2.929	2.102	1.431	0.840	2.018
Australia	1.46	2.269	1.877	1.574	1.183	1.970
United States	1.52	2.496	1.884	1.615	0.827	1.969
Netherlands	1.409	1.112	1.845	1.419	1.377	1.674
United Kingdom	1.155	1.121	1.282	1.312	1.385	1.463
Germany	-0.579	0.889	2.089	1.219	1.280	1.209
France	1.544	1.203	0.545	1.008	0.762	1.163
Japan	0.660	0.770	0.513	1.124	0.909	0.935
Italy	1.132	0.770	0.699	0.924	0.400	0.908
Korea	-0.023	1.572	-0.499	0.855	1.120	0.729
Argentina	0.681	0.729	0.007	0.385	1.355	0.721
Greece	1.517	0.775	-0.064	0.736	0.084	0.681
Chile	0.745	0.206	0.225	0.636	1.161	0.678
Mexico	1.312	-0.441	0.622	0.287	0.707	0.538
Russia	0.281	0.711	0.052	0.395	0.830	0.531
Colombia	1.316	-0.327	0.648	0.072	0.695	0.517
Spain	-2.040	1.153	0.904	0.875	0.843	0.508
Czech	0.181	-0.141	0.686	0.995	0.356	0.500
Venezuela	0.273	-0.018	0.449	0.121	1.259	0.477
South Africa	0.406	-0.318	1.077	0.856	-0.345	0.402
Poland	0.222	-0.068	0.577	0.593	0.299	0.385
Peru	0.392	0.242	0.045	0.194	0.613	0.337
Ukraine	-0.307	0.716	-0.076	0.123	0.590	0.261
Ecuador	0.091	0.010	0.654	-0.108	0.117	0.180
Brazil	0.387	-0.642	-0.301	0.319	0.956	0.144
Philippines	-0.192	0.429	0.423	-0.228	-0.078	0.095
Turkey	0.392	-0.346	-0.858	0.277	0.613	-0.007
Malaysia	-0.851	-0.655	0.238	0.735	-0.111	-0.113
Romania	-1.216	-0.150	-0.089	0.193	-0.035	-0.261
Tunisia	0.514	-0.551	-0.39	-1.225	0.250	-0.378
Thailand	-0.207	-0.223	-0.044	0.128	-1.617	-0.442
Morocco	-0.012	-0.660	-0.723	-0.392	-0.194	-0.483
Zimbabwe	0.348	-0.878	0.103	-0.480	-1.068	-0.484
Egypt	-0.088	-0.145	-0.890	-0.402	-0.547	-0.496
Indonesia	-0.812	-0.660	-0.333	-0.250	-0.888	-0.670
China	-1.500	-0.915	0.494	-0.516	-1.127	-0.789
Sri Lanka	0.034	-0.938	-0.595	-0.388	-1.527	-0.813
Kenya	0.308	-1.106	-1.089	-0.590	-1.190	-0.894
Algeria	-0.959	-0.564	-1.082	-1.345	-0.021	-0.936
Ghana	-1.007	-1.111	-0.646	-0.602	-0.906	-0.988
Pakistan	-0.127	-1.020	-1.524	-0.801	-0.973	-1.070
Iran	-0.865	-0.396	-0.960	-2.504	0.106	-1.108
India	-0.544	-0.86	-1.114	-0.914	-1.320	-1.121
Madagascar	0.248	-1.088	-1.434	-1.064	-1.311	-1.133
Congo	-2.034	-0.797	-1.332	-1.139	0.105	-1.188
Nepal	-1.176	-0.960	-0.634	-0.804	-2.041	-1.291
Bangladesh	-0.220	-0.892	-0.704	-2.001	-1.668	-1.316
Tanzania	-1.571	-1.152	-1.595	-1.170	-1.398	-1.597
Uganda	-0.982	-1.093	-1.678	-1.292	-1.943	-1.640
Nigeria	-2.401	-0.988	-1.383	-2.189	-0.714	-1.771

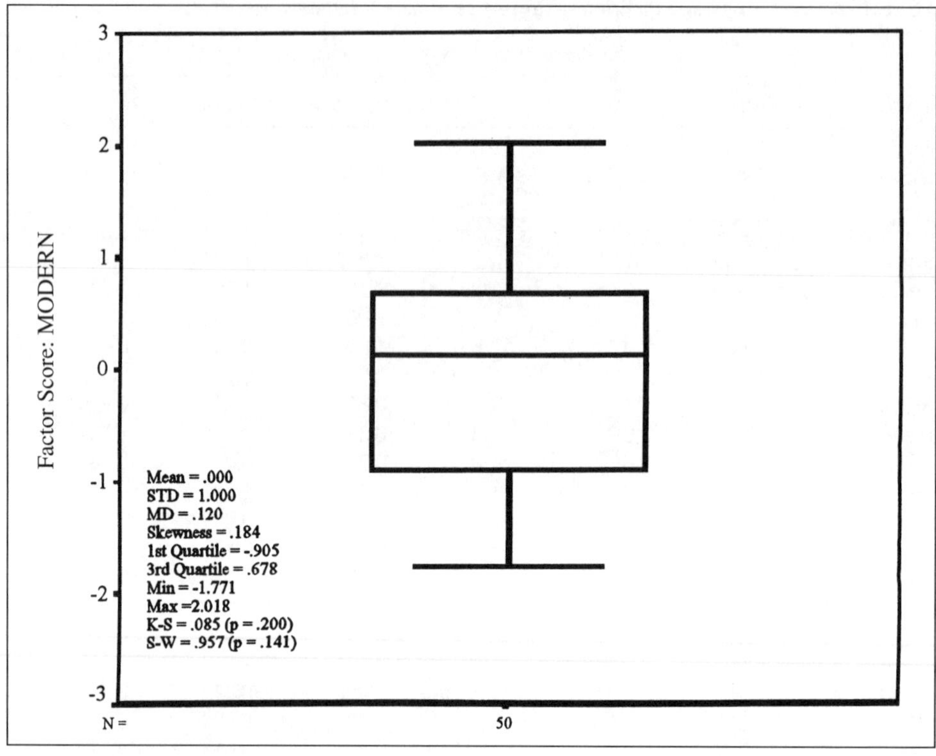

FIGURE 15.7 Box-Plot, MODERN

ern vision of what is "modern"—or, what would be seen as "modern" within American and European cultures. It does not, critics charge, capture what people in cultures outside the West might view as "modern." In an era of globalization, it is difficult to sustain the argument that certain conditions are strictly valued by the Western cultures.[18] Capital markets, for instance, seem hardly to be an instrument of growth and prosperity shunned by non-Western nation-states actively integrated within the global economy.Yet, it is difficult to dispute the obvious fact that Western countries will have certain developmental "advantages" over those countries which have suffered from colonialism, oppression, and more recently, the ill effects of stagnating human development. Clearly, nine of the ten most modern nation-states (based on MODERN scores), shown in Table 15.4, are Western, that is, European or Anglo-American. Of the twenty-five most modern countries—half the sample in CROSSNAT.50—all are either European, Anglo-American, or Latin American, with only three exceptions: South Africa (a former and recent British colony), Philippines (a former and recent American colony), and Korea. Asian, African, and the Islamic countries are absent in this group.

It is important that we not confuse the need for empirical comparison with the equally important need to temper normative evaluation. Noting sharp differences across nation-states within different cultural experiences based on empirical evidence is a far cry from labeling a culture as backward or less deserving of respect simply because of these observed differences. Quantifying the nature of differences across groups of countries is the necessary first step in appreciating the extent to which different peoples and nation-states have varying cultural and historical traditions. It is, therefore, the first and necessary step in the effort to identify and appreciate the common ground necessary for reconciliation among people who may be ignorant and suspicious of less familiar cultures and for mobilizing the public throughout the world to work toward solutions to common problems.

To see how extensive modernity differences are across the various civilizations and regions of the globe, we have first combined Huntington's classification of civilization (CIVCODES) with more general regional divisions (REGION6). Thus, we have produced a new variable within CROSSNAT.50, GEOCIV—a nominal-level variable with six values ranging from 1–6. The variable does not perfectly reflect Huntington's classification system, but it does have the advantage of allowing more direct comparison across the broader categories of major cultures of the globe and grounds these differences, where necessary, in specific geographical regions.[19]

Table 15.5 reports the six geo-civilizational groups and the countries within each respective group. Four countries in CIVCODES (Kenya, Tanzania, Nigeria, and the Philippines) are coded as "other." These four countries have no distinct civilization based on Huntington's classification scheme. However, based upon the more obvious geographical classification, these have been assigned specific groupings in GEOCIV. Kenya, Tanzania, and Nigeria have been included in the Africa group, and Philippines has been included in the Asia group. Employing a Tamhane test for multiple comparisons (see Chapter 12), we have compared the differences of MODERN across each of these separate geo-civilizations. Table 15.6 reports the abbreviated results of this simple test. The Tamhane statistic, obtained from an ANOVA test within SPSS 10, assumes unequal variance across the six groups. In fact, the Levene test statistic produced in the ANOVA procedure indicates equal variance (Levene statistic = 1.707, df = 5, p = .151). However, as each group is relatively small, we have reported the more conservative Tamhane statistic in order to assess differences across the groups.

Recall from Chapter 12 that the Tamhane statistic measures the typical degree of difference between each score in one group from that of another group. In the case of Table 15.6, the Tamhane statistics report the typical difference between a score in a group noted along the left column (a) and a country within the respective inside column (b). Note also the group means are reported in the left column. If modernity (as reflected by MODERN within CROSSNAT.50) was a strictly Western concept, we should find that typically, *all* Western countries in our sample are significantly larger than the typical country of each of the other geo-civilization groups *and* that the typical MODERN score within each of the non-Western geo-civilization groups is not significantly different from those of the other non-Western groups. This is not the case within our sample, as shown in Table 15.6.

TABLE 15.5 Countries, by GEOCIV

Geo-Civilization	*COUNTRY*	*Geo-Civilization*	*COUNTRY*
Africa (1):	Congo	Asia (2):	China
	Ghana		India
	Kenya		Korea
	Madagascar		Nepal
	Nigeria		Philippines
	South Africa		Sri Lanka
	Tanzania		Thailand
	Uganda		
	Zimbabwe		
N = 9		N = 7	
Orthodox (3):	Greece	Latin America (4):	Argentina
	Romania		Brazil
	Russia		Chile
	Ukraine		Colombia
			Ecuador
			Mexico
			Peru
			Venezuela
N = 4		N = 8	
Western (5):	Australia	Islam (6):	Algeria
	Canada		Bangladesh
	Czech		Egypt
	France		Indonesia
	Germany		Iran
	Italy		Malaysia
	Japan		Morocco
	Netherlands		Pakistan
	Poland		Tunisia
	Spain		Turkey
	United Kingdom		
	United States		
N = 12		N = 10	

Typically, each of the nation-states within the five non-Western geo-civilization groups has a modernity score *significantly lower* than the typical Western nation-state. Most notable are the typical differences in MODERN values between African and Western nation-states (–2.258) and those between Asian and Western nation-states (–1.744). Indeed, Western nation-states, primarily composed of Anglo-American and European countries, are typically significantly more modern than other countries generally included within the much broader category of Western Judeo-Christian cultures—those of Latin America (–.776) and Orthodox nation-states (–.922).

Furthermore, the typical differences across the five non-Western geo-civilization groups are not all statistically *insignificant*. The typical African country within our sample has a significantly smaller degree of modernity than Orthodox nation-states

TABLE 15.6 Mean Differences of MODERN Across GEOCIV Groups

Tamhane Cross-Group Comparisons (a - b)

Geo-Civilizations	*Africa (b)*	*Asia (b)*	*Orthodox (b)*	*Latin America (b)*	*Western (b)*	*Islam (b)*
Africa (a) (Group $\bar{X}$ = -1.033)	–	-.514	-1.336*	-1.480*	-2.258*	-.37483
Asia (a) (Group $\bar{X}$ = -.519)	–	–	-.822	-.968*	-1.744*	.139
Orthodox (a) (Group $\bar{X}$ = .303)	–	–	–	-.146	-.922*	.961
Latin America (a) (Group $\bar{X}$ = .449)	–	–	–	–	-.776*	1.101*
Western (a) (Group $\bar{X}$ = 1.225)	–	–	–	–	–	1.883*
Islam (a) (Group $\bar{X}$ = -.658)	–	–	–	–	–	–

* = ($p \leq .05$)

(–1.336), as well as Latin American nation-states (–1.480). The typical Asian nation-state also has a significantly smaller degree of modernity than Latin America (–.968), while the typical Latin American nation-state in our sample has a significantly larger degree of modernity than the typical nation-state with Islamic culture (1.101). What is clear, however, is that the typical differences in modernity scores across Islamic, African, and Asian countries within our sample are *not* significantly different. While this may support the common criticism of modernity as a Western concept, it more importantly underscores the distinct differences in experiences and traditions across Western and non-Western nation-states.[20]

Keep in mind that our underlying question here is how modernity contributes to our understanding of institutional authority and political behavior. Before we address this question, let's first consider the principal tool and its logic, which will prove useful in our empirical analysis of modernity.

THE COMPONENTS OF SIMPLE (BIVARIATE) REGRESSION AND THE USE OF SCATTERPLOTS

Since Chapter 7, we have stressed the importance of bivariate models in predicting the value of one variable (Y) from that of another variable (X). Each of the basic tools of hypothesis testing discussed so far—t-test (t-statistic), contingency table analysis (chi-square), and one-way ANOVA (F statistic)—has been presented with an eye to the one common theme that underscores the use of each tool: *The validity of a model rests upon its proven capacity to significantly reduce the error in prediction of Y (the dependent variable) from that which we would expect when working from the sample mean of Y alone.* This may be summarized as the ratio of the sample variance to the model variance, though the required computation of these respective variances is unique to the properties of the model and the specific tool required for testing the hypothesis underlying that model. How does a simple bivariate *regression model* contribute to hypothesis testing, and what is the role of variance in a regression model?

The Logic of Regression

Simple regression is nothing more than a mathematical means of predicting the value of Y (the dependent variable) from that of X (the independent variable). As with factor analysis, regression, especially more advanced applications of linear regression, is constructed on basic principles of matrix algebra. The basics of the technique can be readily grasped and the tool properly and effectively employed by understanding the fundamental properties of correlation and variance.[21] It contains only two variables (X and Y) and implies some degree of causality between the two variables. It cannot, of course, prove causality. We *regress* the values of Y on X when, in effect, we use the values of X to estimate the value of Y in a sample. Furthermore, regression ordinarily implies a model containing two interval/ratio-level variables.

We can see that the logic of regression is no different from the logic underlying other hypothesis-testing techniques. The major difference, of course, is that regression technically relies solely upon interval/ratio-level data, thus allowing a greater degree of accuracy and precision in prediction. There are advanced techniques of regression that can be appropriately used when one of the variables is not measured at the interval/ratio level, and frequently, experienced researchers will employ regression techniques on survey data measured *exclusively* at the ordinal level. These techniques require special considerations and statistical adjustments that are beyond the scope of this text (though we have used ordinal data in bivariate correlation tests in Chapter 13). Regression, as a rule, is properly reserved for use with interval/ratio-level data.

Simple regression as a tool for hypothesis testing is best employed in conjunction with a scatterplot. We have already introduced you to the scatterplot technique in Chapter 13. To review, a scatterplot simply plots the values of Y in relation to those of X on a two-dimensional graph. From a scatterplot, *which always entails the technical use of a simple regression analysis*, we can calculate a number of useful and important statistics that clarify the nature of the relationship between the two variables that are linked through an associational relationship specified by our theory. Scatterplot analysis provides three specific pieces of information critical to hypothesis testing:

- The direction of a bivariate relationship (positive or negative)
- The strength of the association between two variables in the bivariate model
- The closeness of fit and the shape of the relationship (random, linear, or nonlinear)

To understand prediction, explanation, and the corresponding significance of variance within a simple regression/scatterplot analysis, we will rely upon our discussion of correlation coefficients in Chapter 13. From our illustration sample, we will produce two simple scatterplots from which we can explore in detail the logic of simple regression and the utility of the scatterplot procedure.

Model and Sample Variance in a Simple Regression Model

Keep in mind that in all bivariate models, we have two options when predicting (and explaining) the attribute measured by our Y variable: Either we select the sample mean of Y or, find some way to draw on the variance of X (a second attribute) in order to estimate the corresponding variance in Y, and from this, compute our prediction.

The question remains: How can we actually compute a predicted value of Y from the model variance in a simple regression model? Actually, we have already done this in Chapter 13 when discussing the correlation coefficient. When we rely upon standardized values of our measures (z-scores), the correlation coefficient, as it turns out, is the principal statistical calculation involved in a simple (bivariate) regression model. In fact, from this coefficient, we compute one of the two statistical measures of a bivariate regression model—the slope, equivalent to a regression coefficient in a bivariate model. And from the slope we eventually derive our predictions of Y based on values of X, depicted by a regression line in a simple regression model. We turn first to the regression line.

The Regression Line

What is the regression line and how does it relate to the correlation coefficient? In a general sense, the regression process compares the variance of X to that of Y in a sample of countries and computes a mean difference between the two variations across scores of X and Y in the sample. This mean difference, a critical component in model variance, constitutes the regression line in a scatterplot. As you will recall from our discussion of Figure 13.2, when Y is strongly associated with X, the regression line (that is, the diagonal line in Figure 13.2) will serve as a substantially more efficient and accurate prediction of the value of Y than the sample mean of Y. When these two variables (X and Y) are weakly related, the regression line will offer little or no advantage over that of the sample mean in predicting the value of Y.

Computing the Regression Line: The Regression Coefficient

Keep in mind that the regression line—or slope—does not just appear out of the blue. The computation of the predicted values of Y (denoted as Y') can be solved with the following formula:

$$Y' = a + b(X)$$ Formula 15.1

Within this formula are the two critical statistics central to the task of accurately predicting the value of Y from X: the *regression coefficient* (symbolized by the letter b) and the *intercept* (symbolized by the letter a).

To obtain the *regression coefficient* (b) we use the same variance measures we used to derive the correlation coefficient in Table 13.4. If we were working with standardized values of X and Y (as many students of cross-national analysis prefer), the regression coefficient would be referred to as the standardized regression coefficient (or *beta coefficient),* represented by the Greek letter, β. In models using standardized measures of X and Y, the value of β is equal to the value of r which is the shared variance between two attributes in a sample.

In this instance, since we are working with unstandardized values, the formula for determining the *unstandardized regression coefficient*, b, is:

$$b = \frac{n(\sum XY) - (\sum X)(\sum Y)}{n\sum X^2 - (\sum X)^2}$$ Formula 15.2

The task of computing this is extremely cumbersome, and as you might guess, it makes things very difficult if you have many countries in your sample. Fortunately, most basic statistical packages (including basic spreadsheets) routinely calculate these coefficients, so you will never need to compute one by hand.

If we want to compute the b statistic, we may easily do so by relying on the data found in Table 13.4. Using these data for SATDEM21 and CPI (the unstandardized values for each attribute), we compute the unstandardized regression coefficient:

$$b = \frac{21(8527.92)-(132.6)(1244.6)}{21(933.62)-(17582.76)} = \frac{(179086.32)-(165033.96)}{2023.26} = \frac{14052.36}{2014.44} = 6.94$$

Formula 15.3

The computed unstandardized regression coefficient (b) tells us that we can expect the value of the dependent variable (Y), in this case SATDEM21, to increase by a rate of 6.94, relative to one unit of change in the independent variable (X), which, in this case, is CPI.

You should note immediately that this equation is very similar to that used to compute the Pearson Product Moment Correlation (r), which we examined in Chapter 13.

As we saw with correlation coefficients, the equation for the regression coefficient (as with the r statistic) is made simpler when we are working with standard scores (z-scores). The equation for the regression coefficient when working with standardized values of X and Y (z-scores) is:

$$\beta = \frac{\Sigma(Z_x)(Z_y)}{N-1}$$ Formula 15.4

This formula, of course, is identical to that of the r statistic, when using z-scores. If we were using standardized values for SATDEM21 and CPI, the value of β would be .763.

$$\beta = (\frac{15.249}{20}) = .763$$ Formula 15.5

The standardized regression coefficient (β) measures the proportional rate of change in the Y variable, given a standard unit of change in the X variable. The advantage of a standardized regression coefficient is the ease of interpretation. If our independent variable (X) and dependent variable (Y) are measured on completely different scales, the interpretation of b can be rather difficult to grasp intuitively. A standardized regression coefficient has set both variables to the same scale of measurement, allowing more intuitive understanding. Furthermore, one cannot easily compare unstandardized regression coefficients across different models and samples, as you can with standardized regression coefficients.

What if we do not have standardized values for the data and are therefore not able to simply multiply the z-score values of X by those of Y ($Z_x Z_y$)? As we have seen, it is always more convenient to work with z-scores, but it is, by no means, required. If you do not have z-scores, and for some reason, you need to compute the standardized coefficient (β), you do not apply Formula 15.2. Instead, working from the logic of variance, you simply use the standard deviations of the X and Y variables. Specifically, multiply the *unstandardized regression coefficient* by the *ratio* of the standard deviation of the Y variable to that of the standard deviation of the X variable, or:

$$\beta = b\,(\frac{S_x}{S_y})$$ Formula 15.6

Working from our sample of (unstandardized) data, we know that the standard deviation for CPI is 2.195 (that is, $S_x = 2.195$), while that of SATDEM21 is 19.986 ($S_y = 19.986$). The unstandardized regression coefficient for our bivariate model is 6.94. Even if you are using standardized values, the unstandardized regression coefficient will be the same as if you used z-score values. Therefore, you may use the b coefficient, in combination with the standard deviations of the *unstandardized* values of the X and Y variables, and from this compute by hand the *standardized* regression coefficient (known as the beta coefficient), if needed. However, most programs automatically produce the standardized (β) coefficient.

In any event, in a bivariate model, the r coefficient will always equal the standardized (β) coefficient. The r coefficient is equivalent to the correlation coefficient between X and Y in a bivariate model and is simply the square root of the coefficient of determination (or r^2), which is explained below.

Computing the Regression Line: The Intercept

Commonly in scatterplot analysis and simple regression models, we refer to the regression coefficient as the *slope*, since it reflects the degree to which values of Y adjust (or "slope" upwards or downwards) relative to the values of X. A *positive slope* indicates a positive relationship, with an upward slope to the regression line, running left to right across the graph; a *negative slope* indicates a negative association between X and Y and is reflected by a negative regression coefficient, with a downward sloping line, running left to right across the graph. (See Figures 13.1 and 13.3.)

Based on our discussion above, we are now in a position to assert that if we are using z-score values for our X and Y variables and we want to predict the value of ZSATDEM21 from ZCPI, we must multiply the value of ZCPI by the value .763, since our model calculates the value of ZCPI to be on average, about 76.3 percent of the standard value of ZSATDEM21. If the variation in X matched perfectly the variation in Y (if our model variance were 0), then we would multiply ZCPI by 1.000, because we would know that the typical variation of ZCPI was 100 percent that of the typical variation of ZSATDEM21. In other words, the sample variance of X and Y would be identical.

It should be clear now why the correlation coefficient is equivalent to the regression coefficient when we use standard values in a simple bivariate model. The correlation coefficient measures shared variation, which is precisely what is implied in the regression coefficient. Once we have set our values to a common mean and standard deviation, the amount of shared variance (the correlation coefficient) in the Y variable is equal to the proportional rate of change in Y associated with score variations in X. This holds only for simple (bivariate) regression models. If, however, we do not standardize our data, the correlation coefficient will not assume the same value as the regression coefficient, as we have seen above.

Before we can accurately *predict* values of Y from those of X, we need the *intercept*, which is in essence a starting point. The logic of a regression model holds that as you adjust your value of X in the equation, the value of Y changes. However, the actual regression line plots the expected value of Y given a value of X. The line must start at that point where X is equal to zero and then logically add this original value to each product of $Z_x Z_y$. In other words, the intercept represents the value of Y when X is zero. How do we derive an intercept? The formula for computing the intercept (a) is:

$$a = (\bar{Y} - b\bar{X}) \quad \text{Formula 15.7}$$

When your data are already standardized (z-scores), the mean and standard deviation of both the X and Y variables are identical (0 and 1, respectively). When the value of X is zero, the value of Y will also be zero. Therefore, the intercept is always 0 when working from z-score values for both X and Y.

Figure 15.8 illustrates this point. (Keep in mind that Figure 15.8 is essentially the same as Figure 13.2, except in Figure 15.8 we are using standardized values.) The slope intercepts the mean value for Y at 0.0.

For unstandardized data, our intercept would be according to the following formula:

$$a = 59.262 - (6.94)(6.314); = 59.262 - (43.81916); = 15.4 \quad \text{Formula 15.8}$$

Assuming we are working from data that are not originally standardized (that is, not z-score values for both the X and Y variables), we would estimate the predicted

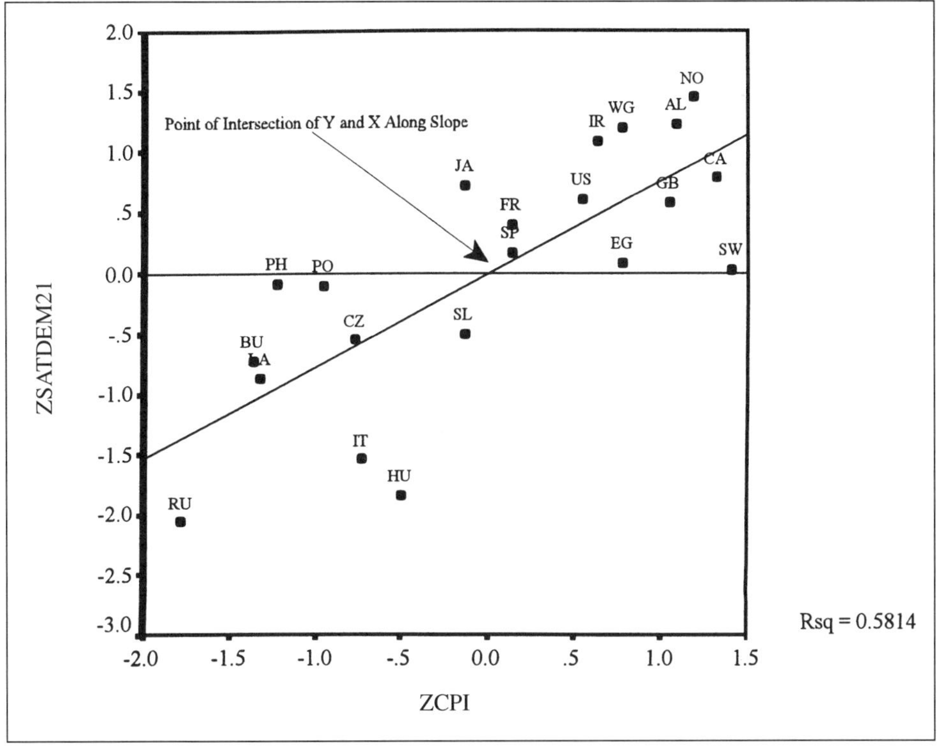

FIGURE 15.8 Scatterplot, ZDEM21 by ZCPI (EFFICACY.21)

value of any value for Y from any corresponding value of X according to the following equation:

(Unstandardized) Y' = 15.4 + (6.94) (X) Formula 15.9

If we were working from standardized values of *both* Y and X, our predicted estimates of Y for any corresponding value of X would be determined by employing the following equation:

(Standardized score) Y' = 0 + .763 (X) Formula 15.10

Estimating Y in Simple Regression

We shall focus from here upon the standardized model (in other words, we will assume our data have already been standardized—converted to z-scores—for both the X and Y variables in a bivariate model). Table 15.7 reports the z-score values for SATDEM21 (ZSATDEM21) and CPI (ZCPI). These are merely the z-scores for the values reported in columns 2 and 3 in Table 8.4. This equation tells us that in order to estimate a value of ZSATDEM21 for a country, we add the value of ZSATDEM21 that would occur independent of X (0), and then adjust (weight) our expected value of Y according to the rate by which Y, on average, varies relative to X across the sample (.763).

For instance, the value of ZCPI (X) for Great Britain is 1.041. Inserting this value into the equation for the regression line results in the following value of Y':

Great Britain Y' = 0 + .763(1.041); Great Britain Y' = .794 Formula 15.11

The point along the regression line where Great Britain's (predicted) value of ZSATDEM21 falls is precisely .794. The actual value of ZSATDEM21 for Great Britain is .576. The value .576 is 72.5 percent that of the value .794. We have, in other words, accounted for 72.5 percent of Great Britain's total variation, which, of course, confirms that our model leaves 27.5 percent of the total variation of ZSATDEM21 for Great Britain unexplained by our model.

Coefficient of Determination

Statisticians call the amount of variance explained by a model the *coefficient of determination*. This is the difference between sample (total) variance of Y values and the unexplained variance in the model. Or:

Coefficient of Determination = Explained Variance/Total Variance Formula 15.12

TABLE 15.7 Z-Score Values, SATDEM21 and CPI (EFFICACY.21)

COUNTRY	*ZSATDEM21*	*ZCPI*
Russia	-2.060	-1.783
Hungary	-1.838	-0.508
Italy	-1.536	-0.735
Latvia	-0.867	-1.328
Bulgaria	-0.727	-1.373
Czech Republic	-0.547	-0.781
Slovenia	-0.496	-0.143
Poland	-0.105	-0.963
Philippines	-0.093	-1.237
Sweden	0.028	1.406
East Germany	0.075	0.768
Spain	0.160	0.130
France	0.390	0.130
Great Britain	0.576	1.041
United States	0.605	0.540
Japan	0.714	-0.143
Canada	0.781	1.315
Ireland	1.078	0.631
West Germany	1.198	0.768
Australia	1.220	1.087
Norway	1.444	1.178

which reduces to this formula:

Coefficient of Determination $= r^2$ Formula 15.13

The Coefficient of Determination, like the E^2, is a PRE (Proportional Reduction in Error) measure: It reflects the estimated reduction in the error we can expect when predicting the value of Y from X from the error we would expect if we based our predictions of Y solely on the sample mean of Y. In our illustration sample above, we see that our coefficient of determination is .582 ($.763^2$). Thus, we have *explained* 58.1 percent of the variance of Y (ZSATDEM21) by knowing the variance of X (ZCPI), which is another way of saying that we have reduced our error in predicting Y from X by 58.1 percent over that error we would have experienced if we had simply predicted Y from the mean of Y. In Figure 15.8, the coefficient of determination is reported as the Rsq adjacent to the scatterplot.

Applying the Regression Equation

This formula for the regression line (the predicted value of Y) works for *hypothetical* values of X, as well. Suppose, for example, you wanted to estimate the *expected* value of

ZSATDEM21 for a country, knowing that country's standard value of corruption (ZCPI) is equal to .75. All you need to do is insert the hypothetical value of X (.75) into the equation for the regression line derived from our illustration sample, and run the math:

$$Y' = 0 + .763(.75); Y' = .572 \qquad \text{Formula 15.14}$$

You can see that if you moved along the X axis of Figure 15.8 until you reached the .75 point of ZCPI, and then drew a straight line up to that point in the graph that intersects with a Y value of .572, you would fall right on the regression line.

Regression models are sensitive to the variance and range of values within the sample of the independent variable. Therefore, a regression model works in a reasonably reliable manner for predicting hypothetical values only if such hypothetical values are within the high and low range of values for the independent variable in the sample. If the high score in the sample for X is 2.01, you should not use the regression equation to predict a value of Y given a value of X that is greater than 2.01. Estimation of the Y value based on values of X, when the X value lies between the high and low range of the X sample, is referred to as *interpolation*. To estimate a value of Y from an X value, when the X value is outside the high or low range of the X sample, we *extrapolate*. Extrapolation should be avoided when working with most cross-national samples when the sample size is less than 100.

The Angle of the Regression Line and the Strength of the Relationship

Finally, we can see from the equation for the regression line (Y') that as the unexplained variance in the model increases, the regression coefficient will approach zero. In other words, there would be no improvement in our ability to predict Y from X over that afforded by the sample mean of Y alone. In this instance, the product of $Z_x Z_y$ would be 0, resulting in a regression coefficient approaching zero (0). This would mean, of course, that the slope would be absolutely flat and fall along the line depicted by the mean value of Y in Figure 15.8.

As we saw in Chapter 13, the stronger the positive linear association between X and Y, the steeper will be the angle of the slope (and the closer the value of the standardized regression coefficient, β, as well as the correlation coefficient, will approach +1.000); the stronger the negative (or inverse) linear association between X and Y, the steeper will be the decline of the slope (reflected by a standardized regression coefficient, and correlation coefficient, of –1.000). As the relationship between X and Y weakens, the slope levels off to a flat horizontal line across the graph, indicative of a model that offers nothing in the way of prediction over that afforded by the sample mean of Y. Thus, one of the most important advantages to plotting a regression model with a scatterplot is to better observe the angle of the slope itself—much as the box-plot assists us in determining the strength of a relationship between two variables in a grouped data model when applying one-way ANOVA analysis.

Does a Weak Model Mean a Statistically Insignificant Model?

Once again, a reminder about the difference between the statistical strength and validity of a model and the statistical significance of the model.

The correlation coefficient (r), regression coefficient (β), and coefficient of determination (r^2) measure the *strength of relationship* between two variables. The statistical significance of the model refers to whether we can be confident, within a specified probability range, that the measured association is in fact a true and accurate reflection of the population, and not merely an artifact of a sample. *Statistical significance does not necessarily equate with strength of a relationship.*

A weak relationship can be statistically significant, as long as the sample size is large enough. Of course, the greater the strength of a relationship, the greater the likelihood of the model's statistical significance. As the size of the sample declines, the strength of the relationship must increase to compensate; as the size of the sample increases, the strength of the relationship required to achieve statistical significance is lowered accordingly.

Summarizing the Computational Logic of Simple Regression Models

Table 15.8 summarizes the step-by-step logic behind the computation of the relevant statistics in a simple regression model, assuming the values of the variables have been standardized (z-scores). Table 15.9 summarizes the key terms discussed above and central to simple regression and scatterplot analysis.[22]

DEMONSTRATION 15.1: ELABORATING SCATTERPLOT ANALYSIS

With simple regression and scatterplot analysis in perspective, it is now time to demonstrate how we combine the basics of simple regression and scatterplot analysis within the hypothesis-testing process. We return to our principal concept within this chapter: *modernity*. Specifically, we will connect *modernity* to *political authority* by exploring these three questions:

- Is there a relationship between modernity and political authority?
- Is the nature of political authority associated with (indeed, conditioned by) the level of modernity within a society?

TABLE 15.8 Computation of Simple Regression Statistics Assuming Standardized Scores in a Bivariate Model (EFFICACY.21)

COUNTRY	*ZSATDEM21*	*ZCPI*	*(ZxZy)*	*Predicted Y*	*Total Variance (Mean of Y - Y)²*	*Explained Variance (Predicted Y - Mean of Y)²*
Russia	-2.060	-1.783	3.674	-1.361	4.244	1.852
Hungary	-1.838	-0.508	0.933	-0.387	3.379	0.150
Italy	-1.536	-0.735	1.129	-0.561	2.358	0.315
Latvia	-0.867	-1.328	1.152	-1.013	0.752	1.026
Bulgaria	-0.727	-1.373	0.998	-1.048	0.528	1.098
Czech Republic	-0.547	-0.781	0.428	-0.596	0.300	0.355
Slovenia	-0.496	-0.143	0.071	-0.109	0.246	0.012
Poland	-0.105	-0.963	0.101	-0.735	0.011	0.540
Philippines	-0.093	-1.237	0.115	-0.944	0.009	0.890
Sweden	0.028	1.406	0.040	1.073	0.001	1.151
East Germany	0.075	0.768	0.058	0.586	0.006	0.343
Spain	0.160	0.130	0.021	0.099	0.026	0.010
France	0.390	0.130	0.051	0.099	0.152	0.010
Great Britain	0.576	1.041	0.600	0.795	0.332	0.631
United States	0.605	0.540	0.327	0.412	0.366	0.170
Japan	0.714	-0.143	-0.102	-0.109	0.510	0.012
Canada	0.781	1.315	1.027	1.003	0.610	1.006
Ireland	1.078	0.631	0.681	0.482	1.162	0.232
West Germany	1.198	0.768	0.920	0.586	1.436	0.343
Australia	1.220	1.087	1.326	0.829	1.489	0.688
Norway	1.444	1.178	1.701	0.899	2.084	0.808
			Σ = 15.250		Σ = 20.000	Σ = 11.643

$$ß = \frac{\Sigma(Z_x)(Z_y)}{N-1}; = \frac{15.250}{20.00}; = 763$$

$$\textit{Coefficient of Determination } (ß^2) = \frac{\Sigma(Y'-\bar{Y})}{\Sigma(Y'-\bar{Y})}; = \frac{11.643}{20.00}; = .582$$

- What is the nature of this relationship, robust or weak? Why would one expect such a relationship to exist?

The connection between modernity and political authority is widely suggested by students of comparative politics.[23] Certainly, at the core of all social order is political authority. As we have seen, political authority assumes different dimensions and degrees within and across nation-states. So does modernity. It would stand to reason that the two concepts would be associated with each other—each contributing to or constraining the extent and nature of the other within nation-states. Therefore, under-

TABLE 15.9 Standard Terms Associated with Simple Regression Analysis and Scatterplot Procedures

Term	*Definition*	*Application*
Regression (Simple)	Predicting value of Y (dependent) variable from X (independent) variable	Apply with interval/ratio-level data for testing hypotheses
Scatterplot	Plotting the value of Y with respect to the value of X	Essential to evaluating linear assumption of model, identifying residual outliers, and assessing the strength of the relationship between X and Y
Regression Line (Least Squares Line)	The line drawn through a scatterplot which minimizes the model variance and maximizes explained variance $Y' = a + b(X)$	Used in scatterplots to evaluate the strength of a linear relationship between variables in a bivariate model. Useful for identification of residual outliers and patterns of residual distribution in a bivariate model
Regression Coefficient (ß =standardized Coefficient; b = Unstandardized Coefficient)	The rate of change in Y associated with a corresponding value of X. Comparable to correlation coefficient (r) when computed from standardized data	The proportional rate of change in Y attributed to a unit of change in X. When used with standardized data, allows one to predict a standard value of Y associated with a standard value of X. Necessary in order to properly *predict* and *explain* relationship between X and Y variables
Intercept (a)	The value of variable Y when variable X is zero (0). Set to zero when computed from standardized data (z-scores)	Necessary to compute predicted value of Y from values of X
Total Variation (Total Aggregate Variance)	The difference between sample mean of Y and actual value of Y. Total variance is the sum of the squared variations across a sample	Is the baseline from which the validity and power of the model is measured
Unexplained (Model) Variation (Variance)	That portion of total variation of Y not matched, or accounted for, by the variation of X. Unexplained variance (also known as total sum of squares) is the sum of the squared unexplained variation across a sample	Represents the model variation (variance), and as such, provides a measure of the advantage one gains using a second variable (X) from which to predict values of Y in a model. Represents the residual error in a regression model
Explained Variation (Variance)	That portion of the total variation of Y that is matched, or accounted for, by the variation in X. Explained variance is the sum of the squared explained variation across a sample	Represents the remaining portion of total variation left after unexplained variation has been subtracted. It is another measure of the advantage one gains in predicting the values of Y for values of X in a model
Coefficient of Determination (r^2)	Explained variance relative to total variance in a model	Measures the power of the model, by gauging the proportionate reduction in error encountered when predicting values of Y from values of X, relative to those errors encountered when predicting values of Y from sample mean of Y. Reflects the amount of variance in Y explained by X.
Coefficient of Nondetermination ($1-r^2$)	Unexplained variance relative to total variance in model	Measures amount of variance in variable Y left unexplained by the X variable

standing something of one concept should help sharpen our understanding of the other.

Modernity and Political Authority

The assumed relationship between development and the nature of political authority can be formally stated in the following hypothesis:

Hypothesis 15.1: POLEMPOW increases with MODERN

Why might we expect *political empowerment* to be positively related to modern society? In general, democratic authority is ever-changing in nature; political authority flows from one social group or political coalition to another in a competitive, turbulent process of ongoing bargaining over and exchange for policy and votes. While the degree of change varies, of course, from country to country, this inherently unpredictable nature to policy and politics would seem to be ill suited for a traditional society. Obviously, all countries, democratic or not, are held in place by the adhesive effects of tradition and custom. Those who have traveled to other countries (or to different regions of their own) have probably observed customs and traditions that seem to make little sense in the context of the times. Yet, on a day-to-day basis, these anachronisms serve as reference points from which authority draws its legitimacy, and from which solace and stability can be gathered during periods of adversity and conflict in society. In relative terms, however, political democracies cannot long tolerate extensive traditionalism. Democracy requires, as we have seen, a high degree of accountability for the actions, obligations, and responsibilities undertaken by those in authority, as well as groups and individuals within society. Traditionalism may well blur this accountability, making it virtually impossible to hold those in authority accountable for actions not clearly and resolutely defined within the formal realm of their responsibilities.

Autocracy may well flourish in an environment where tradition easily serves to empower an exclusive group of political elite. Without the emphasis on specific formal roles of responsibility, power can be more easily concentrated, thus dampening accountability in a normal sense. Political authority is also diluted in democracies, meaning many competing groups have overlapping memberships. Autocracies are restrictive and exclusive toward groups, with power concentrated in a few people and institutions, and government and bureaucracy are intolerant of diverse and competing political viewpoints. Political empowerment would seem, therefore, to be at odds with traditionalism, all things being equal. It follows, therefore, from Hypothesis 15.1, that democratic nation-states are not likely to be "traditional," while authoritarian nation-states are not likely to be "modern."

This assumption may seem commonsensical. However, many studies have drawn attention to the importance of stability within society. Modernity implies complexity (specialization, science, and "rational" order), which in itself implies some degree of uncertainty and risk. Workers cannot always be sure that the advance of technology will not render their skills obsolete, nor can families be certain that these same technologies will not undermine the stability and personal ties found in their communities, while governments and their electorate cannot be certain cultural competition will not undermine their base of legitimacy. Samuel Huntington has drawn attention to this tension between the modern and democratic in two classic analyses of development, modernization, and traditionalism. He examined the consequences for political order in societies that were moving from the traditional to the modern.[24] His argument is simple: As societies move from traditional to modern, there is the risk of disorder, as those with newfound power either abuse this power, or fail to understand the importance of institutional stability and the need for autonomous authority in a society where all may view each other as equal. Thus, Hypothesis 15.1 must be closely examined in light of the expected tension associated with transitions from the traditional to the potentially more threatening modern.

We must be cautious here, however. Such an assumption of "causality" is at best tenuous. We are loosely assuming such a causal relationship for purposes of simplifying what is surely a complex reality. We have, of course, only a cross-sectional sample in CROSSNAT.50. We cannot test changes over time effectively with these cross-sectional data. We can, however, explore Hypothesis 15.1 as a first step toward sorting out the basic linkages and from here open the pathway toward a more systematic refinement of the nuances and peculiarities of the relationship. We expect that countries with more modernity should be more democratic, yet we also expect that relationship may well not be a perfect fit, in light of Huntington's thesis.

To test this hypothesis, we will employ scatterplot analysis. Recall that we cannot assume a true causal relationship with only a bivariate model—we can, however, *imply* one. In our case, we assume that *political authority flows from the environmental conditions that define authority roles and structures within a country*. Therefore, we will begin our analysis with POLEMPOW as the dependent variable (the Y variable, which is the primary phenomenon we are interested in understanding and explaining), and MODERN as the independent variable (the X variable used to "predict" the value of Y in a bivariate model). Note, however, that with a bivariate model, it makes little difference which is the dependent and which is the independent variable. It does makes a difference in terms of evaluating our theory, but not in terms of deriving our test statistic.[25]

Interpreting the Plot

Figure 15.9 presents this scatterplot based on data drawn from CROSSNAT.50. The dots, as you will recall from Chapter 13, represent the points where the value of the independent variable (in this case, MODERN) intersects the value of the dependent variable (POLEMPOW) for each country in our sample. The vertical line (Y axis) is

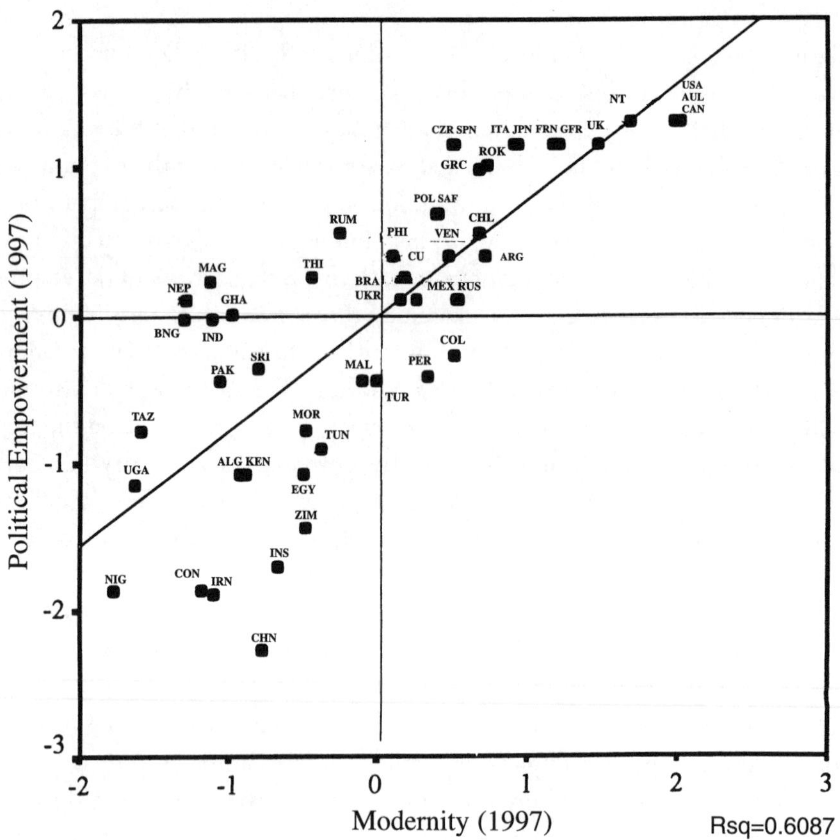

FIGURE 15.9 Scatterplot, POLEMPOW by MODERN (CROSSNAT.50)

always the dependent variable, and the horizontal line (X axis) represents the values for the independent variable.

Figure 15.9 generally confirms our Hypothesis 15.1: As the value of MODERN increases across countries, so does the value of POLEMPOW. Thus, democracy increases with modernity, supporting the theory connecting political authority to development.

What can we tell just from looking at the scatterplot and the patterns to the dots across the plot? Note there are no countries in the region of the graph that could be described as "modern authoritarian" states (lower right corner of the graph), nor are there any countries that could be see as truly non-modern democracies (upper left corner of the graph). However, the relationship is by no means "perfect." We have inserted into the graph a vertical line representing the mean value (0) for MODERN, and a horizontal line representing the mean value (0) of POLEMPOW. These two perpendicular lines help us see clearly that four countries are more "democratic" (POLEMPOW > 0) than the *typical* country, yet are less modern (MODERN < 0) than the typical country (Nepal, Madagascar, Thailand, and Romania). Additionally, two countries are slightly less democratic (POLEMPOW < 0) than the average country yet more modern (MODERN > 0) than the typical country (Peru and Colombia).

None of these observations, however, requires a regression technique in conjunction with a scatterplot. One can obtain these simply by plotting points on standard graph paper. However, the more important questions have to do with the degree to which the model (reflected by our hypothesis) is laden with *error*, and in this regard, whether we can *reject or accept the null* hypotheses (and thus, accept or reject our research hypothesis, 15.1). To obtain the necessary information needed to provide credible answers to these questions, we require a simple regression analysis in conjunction with the scatterplot. More specifically, we require that a regression line, or slope, be computed and drawn on the scatterplot to more effectively assess error and to confirm the strength of the relationship between MODERN and POLEMPOW.

The Regression Line in Scatterplot Analysis

Figure 15.9 reports the regression line as well as the residuals (the individual dots on the graph). This line represents the expected values for the *dependent variable* (POLEMPOW), given any value of the independent variable (MODERN), represented along the X axis of the graph. Recall from our discussion of scatterplots in Chapter 13 that the regression represents the *best fit of a straight line* through all the dots, or residuals, within the plot.[26]

To compute the exact regression line for a simple bivariate model such as in Figure 15.9 (which, of course, has been inserted by the SPSS 10 program itself), we need two pieces of information: (1) the intercept (a) and (2) the slope itself, or, in the case of a standard bivariate model, the correlation coefficient. Because, of course, we are using the standardized data in plotting the values of POLEMPOW against those of MODERN, the intercept is zero—remember it is always zero when working with standardized data in your regression/scatterplot model. And, once again because we are working with standardized data, we know that the correlation coefficient is the equivalent of a *standardized* correlation coefficient, or β (recall that the unstandardized correlation coefficient is signified by r).

Figure 15.9 reports the *coefficient of determination*, or $\beta^2 = .609$, which means, the standardized correlation coefficient is the square root of .609, $\beta = .780$ ($\sqrt{.609} = .780$).[27] Thus, the regression line in Figure 15.9 is presented by the equation:

$$\text{POLEMPOW} = 0 + .780(\text{MODERN}) + e. \qquad \text{Formula 15.15}$$

Inserting any value between the lowest value of MODERN in our sample (CROSSNAT.50) and the highest value in our sample, and multiplying that by the weight, .780, will produce a value that the regression line will pass through. This represents the "predicted" value of Y (or, Y').

The regression line allows one to more easily gauge the relative size of the residuals in the plot. Residuals (represented by the vertical distance of each dot from the regression line) represent the difference between the expected values of POLEMPOW and the actual values of POLEMPOW. Residuals reflect the error in our model. The degree of error in accurately "predicting" the value of POLEMPOW from that of MODERN within our model is summarized efficiently by the coefficient of determination (or, Rsq value adjacent the scatterplot). In other words, 39.1 percent (100 – 60.9 = 39.1) of the variance in the sample of POLEMPOW values has not been matched by the corresponding variance in the independent variable, MODERN. Or, MODERN cannot account for 39.1 percent of the variance recorded in POLEMPOW.

The distance between the dot (or, the actual score of the dependent variable, POLEMPOW at the actual level of MODERN for a country) and the slope allows one to more easily evaluate the degree of error in estimating values of POLEMPOW from values of MODERN for countries. The bigger the size of the residual, the greater the error. The residual is the distance between the regression line and the dot itself. If there were a perfect match, that is, if the model perfectly predicted the values of POLEMPOW, all dots would actually fall on the regression line (the slope) itself. In the real world, this does not happen often when testing meaningful and relevant hypotheses. Rather, the dots lie in proximity to the regression line. The closer to the regression line each dot lies, the more accurate the predictive power of the model (working from known values of MODERN for countries in our sample). Those dots lying farther from the regression line represent countries whose actual value of POLEMPOW is quite different from what we would *expect* given the value of MODERN. Remember, the regression line is the best fit for a straight line, given the distribution of dots in the scatterplot. That is, moving the straight line's angle in any way would increase the total error in the model. The line computed and drawn in Figure 15.9 has the least amount of error associated with it, of all the other angles that might be drawn. It is also worth noting at this point that it is often very helpful—indeed, at times essential—that you be able to actually see the name of the country associated with each dot in the plot.

Practical Value of the Regression Line

For now, however, we must consider very briefly the practical value of the regression line. What does the regression line tell us? How does it help us? To begin, we more clearly assess the role of modernity by considering the hypothetical situation of two countries, based on the results of the simple regression test. If one country has a standard value of 1 for modernity, we expect that country to have a standard value of .780 for democracy. Yet, a country with a standard value of 1.5 for modernity will have a standard value of 1.7 for democracy. In other words, a country with 50 percent more democracy than another country will have more than doubled the degree of democracy than the less modern society. Keep in mind, however, that simply because in general modern societies are more democratic does not mean that a particular country that is modern will be democratic, or a democratic country will be modern. This is a classic *ecological fallacy* (see Endnote 17 in Chapter 2). All our model allows is a generalization: Modernity tends to be strongly associated with democracy, and, from our theory, we assume the foundations of democracy are enhanced with modernity, while weakened with traditionalism.

Now, let us consider an actual case within the sample: China. Note in Figure 15.9 that China (CHN) stands apart from the rest in terms of the size of its residual. China's point in Figure 15.9 is far off the regression line, indicating the country's actual value of POLEMPOW is much lower than predicted by the model, given China's degree of modernity in 1997. Indeed, we know that the exact value of POLEMPOW for China is –2.281 (see Table 14.7). However, we also know from the regression analysis that we predicted China's value for POLEMPOW to be –1.779. The expected value is only 78 percent of the actual value of POLEMPOW for China. From this, we may ask: Why is China's level of democracy only 78 percent of what we would expect, given its level of modernity? We might further ask: Is this residual significantly larger than what we find in other countries?

Finally, the use of the regression line helps us better appreciate the pattern of residuals within the plot. Note in Figure 15.9 that the spread of residuals for those countries with *lower than average* degrees of modernity (MODERN < 0) is much greater than the spread for those countries with *higher than average* degrees of modernity (MODERN > 0). This underscores Huntington's point, summarized earlier. Countries that seem at the lower end of the modernity scale are more dispersed with respect to their democracy scores, while those countries that have achieved higher than average modernity levels are also much more alike with respect to their respective degree of democracy. These observations underscore error in our sample—especially the instance of China. These patterns, however, are much more obvious having computed and plotted the regression line than if we were to merely examine the spread of the dots. In any event, the question we may want to ask at this point is: Are there any common denominators (such as geo-civilization) that link countries that are below the mean value of MODERN and distinguish them from those countries that have scores above the mean value for MODERN? If so, what might be the linkage between democracy, modernity, and this common denominator, and how can it help us understand the comparative distribution of institutional authority and political behavior across nation-states?

Finally, what of the decision whether to reject or accept the hypothesis? The scatterplot itself does not report the significance level of the slope. We will consider the specific statistics of simple regression, including the F statistic and its corresponding significance level, in Chapter 17. For now, it is simple enough to ascertain the significance level of the correlation reported in Figure 15.9: Examine the Pearson's r between MODERN and POLEMPOW. In a simple bivariate regression, expressed graphically in

Figure 15.9, the coefficient of determination is the square of the Pearson correlation coefficient. Using SPSS 10, we see that this correlation is statistically significant ($r = .780$; $p = .000$, 2-tail test). Thus, we may reject the null and accept the research hypothesis: Democracy is positively associated with modernity.

HUMAN DEVELOPMENT AND MODERNITY, HYPOTHESIS 15.2

Before leaving scatterplots, let us consider the environment within which modernity may be realized. If modernization is a strong factor in securing democracy, what then are the environmental conditions that might nurture modernization? In Chapter 11, we introduced the reader to the United Nations' measure of human development (HUMDEV within CROSSNAT.50). If modernity entails change and the embracing of the new, then we may reason that enabling citizens within society through such basic resources as minimal education, literacy, economic opportunity, health, and minimal prosperity would be necessary before a society could undertake and realize the more demanding challenges of modernity.[28] Thus, Hypothesis 15.2 reflects this logic:

Hypothesis 15.2: MODERN increases with ZHUMDEV

Recall from Chapter 11, HUMDEV ranges in value between 0 and 1, with 1 being the highest possible degree of human development. Within CROSSNAT.50, the scores of HUMDEV range between .932 and .404; values for ZHUMDEV (the z-score values of HUMDEV) range between –1.972 and 1.359. Figure 15.10 reports the scatterplot of MODERN by the standardized values of ZHUMDEV. The scatterplot confirms our expectations. Modernity grows proportionally to human development in a very strong and very linear fashion. Increasing the standard value of human development by a factor of 1 is associated with a .912 factor increase in modernity. A country with a standard human development score of 1.5 can be expected to have a standard modernity score of 1.368.

What of residuals? At the low end of the modernity scale are two countries of interest: Iran and China. Both countries have achieved statistically average levels of human development (ZHUMDEV = -.010 and -.098, respectively). However, both have substantially lower than average modernity scores (MODERN = –1.108 and –.789, respectively). Indeed, the degree of modernity recorded for Iran is less than 1 percent of its expected degree of modernity (predicted value of MODERN = –.009), while China's actual level of modernity is only 11 percent of its expected degree of modernity (predicted value of MODERN = –.089) based on its degree of human development, as of 1997. At the high end of the modernity scale are Australia, Canada, and the United States, each with modernity scores much higher than the typical country (MODERN = 1.969, 2.018, and 1.970, respectively), as with human development

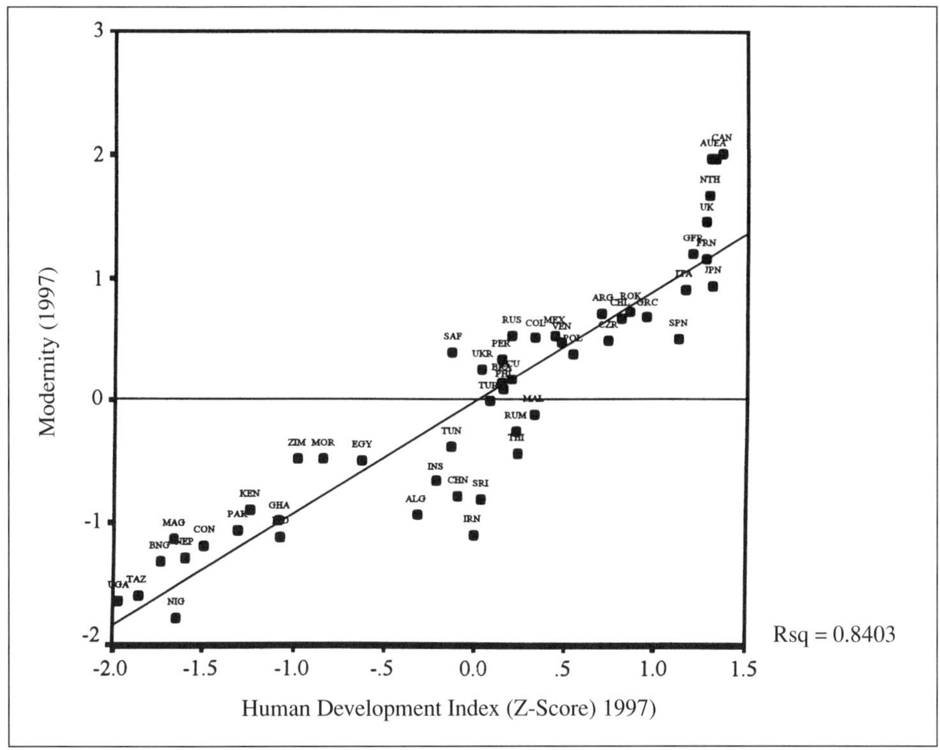

FIGURE 15.10 Scatterplot, MODERN by ZHUMDEV

scores (ZHUMDEV = 1.327, 1.359, and 1.296, respectively). Indeed, each of these respective human development scores is much larger than the model predicts; in each case the predicted level of modernity is only 60 percent of the country's actual degree of modernity as of 1997 (predicted value of MODERN = 1.210, 1.239, and 1.182, respectively).

Human Development, Modernization, and Democracy in Perspective

With 84 percent of the variance of MODERN accounted for in our simple model shown in Figure 15.10 (Rsq, or β^2 = .8403), we can be assured that these particular residuals (Iran, China, Canada, and the United States) or others are not distorting the model's predictive value. However, they draw attention once again to the use of scatterplot analysis, and its accompanying simple statistics, as a powerful tool for refining our conclusions and illuminating additional questions for future research. Specifically, examining the cases of Iran and China has directed us to a simple observation: For reasons associated either with policy or culture, or both, these two countries have traveled a different path from human development to modernity. This may be a reflection of the Eurocentric and Western bias often alleged to skew the concept of modernity and its attendant measurement, a charge we have discussed earlier. It surely, however, highlights important and real cultural and social attributes that set Iran and China apart from other Asian and Islamic nation-states and geo-civilizations. This possibility underscores the role of scatterplot analysis in the Ladder of Theory Building first proposed in Chapter 2. It draws attention to case study and comparable cases strategies for further refinement of our theories of institutional authority and political behavior.

The same logic applies to those countries at the high end of the modernity continuum. The residuals of the United States, Canada, and Australia suggest that at some point, human development seems no longer to matter much in the way of advancing modernity—at least to those countries well on their way to providing the provisions of a secure and prosperous life reflected by human development. For these three countries, as well as most of the other countries that are almost exclusively found in the Western geo-civilization group, modernity takes on a trajectory propelled by its own momentum—for better or worse.

While certainly much more refined research would be required to tease out the complexities of the link between human development and modernity, as well as the interactions among the components of modernity itself, we can, with the aid of this quantitative strategy, begin to see the evidence that leads some to conclude that a cultural gap (with its possibility of a future cultural "clash") exists across various geographic regions, reinforced by historical cultural preferences.[29] For one set of countries, a challenge to the public and their policymakers may be to contain modernity while sustaining a moderate degree of human development, while for another set of countries located within a distinctly different geo-civilization realm, the issue is how to manage the inevitable march of modernity, while remaining secure with significant human development.

Evaluating Implications

What implications does this relationship between human development and modernity hold for democracy? We know from Figure 15.9 that modernity is strongly associated with democracy. Yet, we also know several countries—especially China—seem to have distinctly lower levels of democracy than would be expected, given their achieved levels of modernity, as of 1997. We know from Figure 15.10 that despite a very strong linear relationship between human development and modernity, some countries are characterized by a suppressed level of modernity, given their achieved degree of human development.

We would expect, therefore, that (1) democracy would be strongly related to human development (as modernity is strongly related to human development, and modernity is also strongly related to democracy, it follows that democracy should be related to human development), and yet, (2) this relationship may not be *linear*. Why? Because, for a group of countries approaching moderate levels of human development, modernity is lower than expected. These less-than-modern societies should also be characterized by suppressed levels of democracy, because, as we know from Figure 15.9, democracy is significantly associated with modernity. For whatever reasons—policy, culture, or both—suppressing modernity will generally restrict the level of democracy; at least it should lower the level of achieved democratic authority given that country's level of human development. We suspect, in other words, modernity interferes with the otherwise powerful relationship between human development and democracy.

Our hypothesis, however, is based on a linear assumption—the primary assumption of any implied causal relationship. It holds:

Hypothesis 15.3: POLEMPOW increases with ZHUMDEV

Figure 15.11 presents an edited output from the SPSS 10 scatterplot procedure. It graphically reports the plot of POLEMPOW by ZHUMDEV. However, the linear and curvilinear slopes are *both* included in Figure 15.11 for comparative purposes. The basic linear relationship between democracy and human development is relatively strong ($\beta^2 = .483, p = .000$, 2-tail), yet much weaker than the relationship between modernity and democracy alone. Why? Because the relationship between human development and democracy is conditioned by the relationship between human development and modernity. It is modernity that our theory suggests acts most decisively on democracy. And, it is modernity that many countries at the moderate ranges of human development seem to either suppress or, for cultural reasons, mitigate. Because of this depressing effect of modernity, it is consequently associated with weakened democracy, as democratic authority is tied to modernity (as demonstrated in Figure 15.9).

This depressive effect on democracy through modernity means that for at least some countries at the moderate range of human development, democracy will dip sharply, as a result of modernity levels sharply dipping at this range of human development. These countries include most notably Indonesia, Iran, and China in Figure 15.11. Furthermore, and equally important, several countries at the very low end of human development will nonetheless logically have higher degrees of democracy than we might expect, given their level of human development. These countries represent the countries that for cultural and policy reasons strive to integrate democratic authority as a means to combat poverty and insecurity. Or, alternatively, democracy flourishes within these cultures and countries in spite of relatively low levels of human development (as of 1997). They are presented in Figure 15.11 by Madagascar, Nepal, and Bangladesh.

Recall from Chapter 13 that parametric tests are designed to measure linear relationships. If we observe a nonlinear pattern to our residuals (as we do in Figure 15.11),

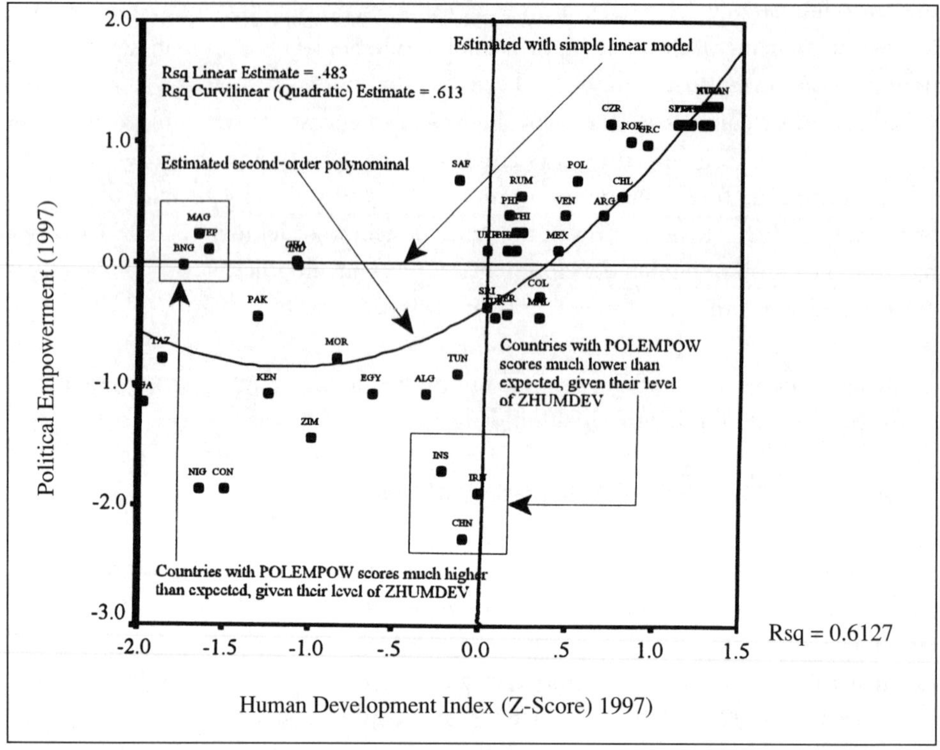

FIGURE 15.11 Scatterplot, POLEMPOW by ZHUMDEV

we must consider some rather complex and sophisticated methods to estimate the best curve. In others, a linear curve may not be the best fit. This requires we depart from standard linear regression equations. It also means we must make some very complex choices involving mathematical transformations of the equations. These go well beyond the scope of this text. However, as we noted in Chapter 13, it is far too common in cross-national research to find basic patterns that deviate from linearity for reasons that are central to theory refinement to allow us to totally ignore the steps one must consider when confronting nonlinear patterns.

The challenge is how to decide which linear transformation to use. In cross-national research, especially when working with samples of fifty or less, there are not really that many observations in the sample to adequately sustain more sophisticated transformations. For this reason, most students stay within a small range of transformations to standard regression models. As we explained in Chapter 13, these are either curvilinear, or, in some cases, exponential models.[30] In deciding to adjust your simple bivariate regression model to fit the curve, you must first look at the pattern of the residuals and determine how many "bends" are in the pattern. That is, how many times do the residuals curve around and cross the linear slope? While not always so obvious, we can see from Figure 15.11 that the residuals cross the slope twice. The bend is below the linear regression line. The bend we see occurs at approximately the mean values of human development—the point at which some countries (such as Iran and China, for instance) associated with sharply reduced modernity govern their levels of human development. This should be captured by a similar drop for the relationship between human development and democracy because of the link between modernity and democracy.

A single bend in the pattern requires a second-order polynomial transformation, or, more technically, a *quadratic* equation to adjust the simple regression model to fit more approximately the curve of the residuals. Indeed, each bend in the pattern of residuals requires a new variable be added to the simple regression equation if we are to accurately plot the curvilinear trend. If we saw that the pattern of residuals had crossed the linear slope twice, we would have required a cubic equation (see Figure 13.9 for an illustration of a cubic, or third-order, polynomial plot).

How do we obtain a slope that accurately reflects a single curve? How do we compute the slope? The mathematical computation of the residuals in quadratic, or second-order, polynomial equations need not concern us here—the precise computation is not essential to the task of diagnostic analysis. The second-order polynomial requires we insert a second term (thus the name, "second-order" polynomial) into the simple regression equation to capture the effect of the bend. This is mathematically accomplished with a term that represents the square of the value for the independent variable (X^2). This has the effect, however, of altering the simple math associated with computing the predicted values of Y.[31] Nonetheless, the standard format of the second-order polynomial is:

$$Y_i = a + \beta_1(X_i) + \beta_2(X^2_i) + e \qquad \text{Formula 15.16}$$

where β_1 is the (standardized) regression coefficient for the linear portion of variance we need to account for in a second-order polynomial, the linear estimate of variance, and β_2 is the (standardized) regression coefficient for the second portion of variance we need to account for in a second-order polynomial. The second portion of variance is the single curve, or nonlinear estimate. The intercept (a) will no longer simply be zero (as in a simple, standardized regression equation). The sum of the two terms in the equation (plus the intercept value) will total the predicted value of Y (for country i in our sample) and will take into account the single bend in the curve of the residuals. The equation below is the actual second-order polynomial equation needed to fit the curve in Figure 15.11 to a standard curvilinear model.[32]

$$POLEMPOW_i = -.374 + .860(ZHUMDEV_i) + .382(ZHUMDEV^2_i) + e \qquad \text{Formula 15.17}$$

Alternatively, of course, as noted in Chapter 13, we may simply elect to use the scatterplot analysis procedure in SPSS 10, and select the quadratic model by which the curve is plotted to the data, and the appropriate coefficient of determination (Rsq) computed for the curve estimation. That procedure, as explained in Chapter 13, is found in the FIT OPTIONS command within the simple scatterplot procedure within SPSS 10 (see Endnote 13 in Chapter 13). However, the addition of the polynomial term ($\beta_2 X^2_i$) to the simple regression model more accurately plots the slope to the pattern of the residuals, and affords us the opportunity to directly compare the linear model to the curvilinear model.

The difference between the linear model and the curvilinear model is 13 percent ($\beta^2 = .483$ v. $\beta^2 = .613$), a sizeable difference and appreciable reduction in error for the polynomial equation. The curve itself is driven by two groups of countries within the sample. These are highlighted by the boxes drawn in Figure 15.11. The first box (upper left) identifies those three countries that have notably larger values of POLEMPOW than expected, given their very low levels of human development (Bangladesh, Madagascar, and Nepal). In contrast, the second box (lower center) highlights those three countries with substantially lower than expected values of POLEMPOW, given their degree of human development (Indonesia, Iran, and China). It is important we understand one thing: There is a very strong linear relationship between human development and democracy, just as there is between modernity and democracy, as well as human development and modernity. However, we improve our reduction in error by adjusting slightly the regression equation from which we compute our slope through the addition of a simple polynomial term.

This allows us to offer some quantified evidence to support those who have asserted that democracy does not follow easily from modernity, nor, for that matter, from human development. The challenge posed by change, uncertainty, and risk associated with modernity may be a price some countries—at least their traditional leadership—may be less willing to accept. Thus, striving for human development does not necessarily lead directly to the foundations of more complex social change from which democracy flourishes. Indeed, some countries have achieved higher levels of democracy with lower levels of human development than other countries. Yet, underscoring the complex relationship between social change and development on the one hand, and democratic authority on the other, are those few countries that have managed to sustain moderate levels of democracy despite poverty and very low levels of prosperity. With the use of scatterplots and simple regression (including second-order polynomial adjustments and diagnostic plotting, as shown in Figure 15.11), we have demonstrated how these pieces within the puzzle may emerge more clearly.

Summary of Scatterplot Analysis Testing Hypotheses 15.1–15.3

Based on our scatterplot analysis of Hypotheses 15.1–15.3 above, we may conclude:

- POLEMPOW and MODERN are strongly and positively associated with each other, thus confirming Hypothesis 15.1 (Figure 15.9).

- Our test reveals that 60.9 percent of the variance in POLEMPOW is accounted for by MODERN.
- This is a highly significant relationship, with an estimated probability of committing a Type I Error of less than 1 in 1000.
- The model also suggests a relatively strong effect on POLEMPOW from MODERN, suggesting (but not explicitly confirming since we are still working only with a bivariate model) that political empowerment is difficult to develop and sustain within countries that are strongly traditional. This is reflected in the standardized regression coefficient (β), where we see that a one-standard-deviation-unit change TRADSOC is associated with a *decrease* of .780 standard deviations in POLEMPOW.
- Human development and modernity are also strongly related to each other. Indeed, the linear relationship is very robust ($\beta^2 = .840$) (Hypothesis 15.2, Figure 15.10).
- Despite such a strong, linear relationship, we note in Figure 15.10 that for some countries with relatively moderate levels of human development, modernity is much less evident than we would expect, based on our sample analysis and population estimates.
- As suspected, the association between political authority and human development is best understood as a curvilinear relationship. For several countries with moderate levels of human development, democratic authority drops far off, in opposition to our expectations (Hypothesis 15.3, Figure 15.11).
- In conclusion, we have, through scatterplot analysis and the rudiments of simple regression analysis, shown that there may be more to the assertion of those who warn that democratic order is not an automatic given for either modern or relatively well-off "developing" countries of the world. Culture and politics are more complicated in certain settings than this, and the data open the door to refining our theory to account for such differences and alternative patterns.

CHAPTER SUMMARY

In this chapter we have elaborated an index measure of the complex variable *modernity*, one of the key elements of a broader concept coloring the political environment of a country: *development*. Turning once again to basic factor analysis, we have devised a single index measure of modernity based upon the primary properties of this crucial and much examined concept. We have also introduced one of the most visually powerful tools of comparative analysis: the scatterplot and its associated simple bivariate analysis, based on simple regression analysis. We have extended our discussion of scatterplots beyond that presented in Chapters13 and 14 by more systematically considering each of the fundamental concepts of simple, bivariate regression. As with ANOVA, the scatterplot relies on variance and the measure of error to estimate the advantages of using an "independent" variable to explain and predict the values of our principal focus of attention, the "dependent" variable. From our scatterplot analysis of the relationship between democracy and modernity, modernity and human development, and ultimately, human development and democracy, we have demonstrated the strong linear relationship tying political authority to development and prosperity, but have refined this general relationship by also demonstrating that the linkage between political authority and development may not be best understood solely as a simple linear path of progress. For countries at the very low end of the development scale, democratic authority is by no means an automatic outcome to be assumed. Reforming constitutions in light of the dramatic political changes of recent years must confront the cultural traditions within which the political environment resides.

NOTES

1. Richard Peet and Elaine Hartwick, 1999, *Theories of Development* (New York: Guilford Press); Richard Grabowski, 1999, *Pathways to Economic Development* (Northampton, Mass.: Edward Elgar); and Peter Lewis, 1998, ed., *Africa: Dilemmas of Development and Change* (Boulder: Westview Press).

2. For insightful critiques of and surveys of critical perspective on modernization and development theory, see Ronald H. Chilcote, 2000, *Comparative Inquiry in Politics and Political Economy: Theories and Issues* (Boulder: Westview Press); Tony Barnett, 1989, *Social and Economic Development: An Introduction* (New York: Guilford Press); Bret Billet, 1997, *Modernization Theory and Economic Development: Discontent in the Developing World* (Westport, Conn: Praeger); and Catherine V. Scott, 1995, *Gender and Development: Rethinking Modernization and Dependency Theory* (Boulder: Lynne Rienner). Also see Joseph R. Gusfield, 1967, "Tradition and Modernity: Misplaced Polarities in the Study of Social Change," *American Journal of Sociology* 72:1 (January), pp. 351–62. For some classic and fundamental interpretations of modernization and development, see Cyril E. Black, 1966, *The Dynamics of Modernization: A Study in Comparative History* (New York: Harper and Row); and Myron Weiner and Samuel Huntington, eds., 1986, *Understanding Political Development* (Boston: Little Brown).

3. Ronald Inglehart, 1997, *Modernization and Postmodernization: Cultural, Economic and Political Change in 43 Societies* (Princeton: Princeton University Press). See also Kenneth E. Bauzon, 1992, *Development and Democratization in the Third World: Myths, Hopes, and Realities* (Washington, D.C.: Crane Russak). For classic studies, see David E. Apter, 1965, *The Politics of Modernization* (Chicago: University of Chicago Press); or Samuel P. Huntington, 1968, *Political Order in Changing Societies* (New Haven: Yale University Press).

4. Some further refine modernity into "post-modernity." Inglehart describes the contour of what he believes to be the "post-modern" society. This is characterized by the quality of life preferences, rather than the primacy of economic well-being. This distinction seems to work well for societies within the industrialized advanced democracies, but has severe limitations when applied to a cross-national sample outside this circle of similar nation-states. In any event, we make no distinction in this chapter between the common concept of modernity and

the less commonly specified concept of "post-modernity." See Ronald Inglehart, 1997, *Modernization and Postmodernization: Cultural, Economic and Political Change in 43 Societies* (Princeton: Princeton University Press).

5. For an overview and critical assessment of the various measures used by scholars to measure the concept of modernity and development, see Nancy Baster, ed., 1972, *Measuring Development: the Role and Adequacy of Development Indicators* (London: Frank Cass).

6. Alex Inkeles and David H. Smith, 1974, *Becoming Modern: Individual Change in Six Developing Countries* (Cambridge, Mass.: Harvard University Press), pp. 19–34.

7. Ronald Inglehart, 1997, *Modernization and Postmodernization: Cultural, Economic and Political Change in 43 Societies* (Princeton: Princeton University Press), p. 18.

8. Conventionally, the service economy has been seen as a post-industrial aspect of development. As industrialization is often seen as one of the central properties of a modern society, the service economy has been viewed by Daniel Bell, Ronald Inglehart, and others as being a property of the "post" phase of modernity (post-industrial, or post-modernism). Again, while certainly this distinction enjoys validity within the advanced industrialized societies, such a distinction becomes blurred when working with cross-national samples. Thus, to avoid concept stretching, we simply attribute the division of labor associated with a rising service economy as yet another attribute of development that extends from traditional society toward the modern and avoid making the more refined and abstract distinction between the modern and post-modern. See Daniel Bell, 1973, *The Coming of the Post-Industrial Society* (New York: Basic Books) and Ronald Inglehart, 1997, *Modernization and Postmodernization: Cultural, Economic and Political Change in 43 Societies* (Princeton: Princeton University Press).

9. According to the World Bank, "services" include value added in wholesale and retail trade (including hotels and restaurants), transport, and government, financial, professional, and personal services such as education, health care, and real estate services. Also included are imputed bank service charges and import duties. Value added is defined as "the *net output of a sector after adding up all outputs and subtracting intermediate inputs*." The industrial origin of value added is determined by the International Standard Industrial Classification (ISIC), revision 2. For more technical information, see World Bank's CD-ROM (*World Development Indicators, 1999*), specifically, Tables WDI 4.1 and 4.2.

10. The univariate box-plot is produced in SPSS 10 within the EXPLORE technique (ANALYZE▶DESCRIPTIVE STATISTICS), found within the PLOTS option (Box-Plots/Factor levels together). There is a distinct advantage of the box-plot over the basic histogram for students of cross-national analysis. The box-plot allows you to identify outliers. It is not as visually informative when one has a particularly bifurcated sample. Therefore, while we report the box-plot, it is always worth the student's trouble to at least examine the histogram to doublecheck the shape of the distribution.

11. Data are taken from the World Bank, *World Development Indicators, 1999* (CD-ROM). Estimates are based on the International Standard Classification of Education (ICSED). Tertiary education, whether or not committed to an advanced research qualification, normally requires, as a minimum condition of admission, the successful completion of education at the secondary level. For more information, see Table WDI 2.10 on the CD-ROM.

12. Catherine V. Scott, 1995, *Gender and Development: Rethinking Modernization and Dependency Theory* (Boulder: Lynn Rienner), pp. 23–25.

13. Internet hosts are the number of computers with active Internet Protocol (IP) addresses connected to the Internet, per 10,000 people. All hosts without a country code identification are assumed by the World Bank to be located in the United States. See Table WDI 5.11 within the World Bank's *World Development Indicators*, 1999 (CD-ROM).

14. For more detail on power transformation and the use of logarithms, see Lawrence C. Hamilton, 1992, *Regression With Graphics: a Second Course in Applied Statistics* (Pacific Grove, Calif.: Brooks/Cole), pp. 19–23.

15. For further transformation considerations, see Shelley Rasmussen, 1992, *An Introduction to Statistics With Data Analysis* (Pacific Grove, Calif.: Brooks/Cole), pp. 109–113.

16. Urban population is the midyear population of areas defined as urban in each country and reported to the United Nations. It is measured here as a percentage of the total population. For more information, see Table 3.10 in World Bank, *World Development Indicators*, 1999 (CD-ROM).

17. For an insightful explanation of how cities evolve and their implications for change, see Alberto Ades and E. Glaeser, 1995, "Trade and Circuses: Explaining Urban Giants," *Quarterly Journal of Economics* 100:1, pp. 195–258. For a full overview of the nature and role of urbanization for development and change in society, see World Bank, 2000, *Entering the Twenty-first Century: World Development Report 1999/2000* (New York: Oxford University Press), pp. 125–138.

18. See Keith E. Bauzon, 1992, "Development Studies: Contending Approaches and Research Trends," in Keith E. Bauzon, ed., *Development and Democratization in the Third World: Myths, Hopes and Realities* (Washington, D. C.: Crane Russak), pp. 35–52.

19. Samuel Huntington, 1996, *The Clash of Civilizations and the Remaking of the World Order* (New York: Touchstone Books). For an insightful analysis linking cultrue and civilization attributes to the ability of countries to adopt core aspects of modernity, see John R. Hanson II, 1999, "Culture Shock and Direct Investment in Poor Countries," *The Journal of Economic History* 50:1 (March): 1–16.

20. The sharp difference with respect to modernity between the twenty-four countries in CROSSNAT.50 that are classified as "Orthodox," "Latin American," or "Western" (or, Judeo-Christian/Western) and the twenty-six countries classified as "African," "Asian," or "Islamic" (or, non-Western) can be empirically ascertained by executing a difference of means test of MODERN. The mean for the broadly defined "Judeo-Christian/Western" group is .813, with a standard deviation of .622, while the mean score for MODERN among the "non-Western" group is –.750, with a standard deviation of .620. The ANOVA reveals an F statistic of 78.996 (t = 8.888) with 1/48 degrees of freedom, and a p value of .000. The variable WESTERN—applied in Chapter 17—does collapse GEOCIV into two broader groups: a "Western" group (containing the Latin American, Orthodox, and Western categories of GEOCIV), and a "non-Western" group (containing the African, Asian, and Islamic categories from GEOCIV).

21. For a detailed introduction to the matrix algebra and mathematical algorithms of factor analysis, see Maurice M. Tatsuoka, 1971, *Multivariate Analysis: Techniques for Educational and Psychological Research* (New York: John Wiley and Sons), especially pp. 7–38; and John P. Van de Geer, 1971, *Introduction to Multivariate Analysis for the Social Sciences* (San Francisco: W. H. Freeman and Company), especially pp. 83–111.

22. For the beginning student, Lawrence C. Hamilton, 1992, *Regression with Graphics: A Second Course in Applied Statistics* (Pacific Grove, Calif.: Brooks/Cole), pp. 29–64, is an excellent in-

troduction to simple regression and scatterplots. For more detail presented in a very comprehensible style, see R. Lymann Ott, 1993, *An Introduction to Statistical Methods and Data Analysis* (Belmont, Calif.: Duxbury), pp. 437–563. A very useful overview may be found in William D. Berry and Mitchell S. Sanders, 2000, *Understanding Multivariate Research* (Boulder: Westview), pp. 1–28.

23. There is a substantial literature on the link between development and political authority—especially the link between development and democratic political authority. See Richard Rosecrance, 1999, *The Rise of the Virtual State: Wealth and Power in the Coming Century* (New York: Basic Books); Adam Przeworski, Michael E. Alvarez, Jose Antonio Cheibub, and Fernando Limongi, 2000, *Democracy and Development: Political Institutions and Material Well-Being in the World, 1950–1990* (New York: Cambridge University Press); Bruce Bueno de Mesquita and Hilton L. Root, eds., 2000, *Governing for Prosperity* (New Haven: Yale University Press); Ronald H. Chilcote, 2000, *Comparative Inquiry in Politics and Political Economy: Theories and Issues* (Boulder: Westview Press); James F. Hollifield and Calvin Jillson, eds., 2000, *Pathways to Democracy: The Political Economy of Democratic Transitions* (New York: Routledge); Mark Robinson and Gordon White, eds., 1998, *The Democratic Developmental State: Politics and Institutional Design* (New York: Oxford University Press); Adam Przeworski, 1995, *Sustainable Democracy* (Cambridge, UK: Cambridge University Press); Larry Diamond and Marc F. Plattner, eds., 1996, *The Global Resurgence of Democracy* (Baltimore: Johns Hopkins University Press); Larry Diamond and Marc F. Plattner, eds., 1995, *Economic Reform and Democracy* (Baltimore: Johns Hopkins University Press); Shalendra D. Sharma, 1999, *Development and Democracy in India* (Boulder: Lynne Rienner Publishers); Murray J. Leaf, 1998, *Pragmatism and Development: The Prospect for Pluralist Transformation in the Third World* (Westport, Conn.: Bergin & Garvey); Claude Ake, 1996, *Democracy and Development in Africa* (Washington, D.C.: Brookings Institution); and Christopher Marsh, 2000, *Making Russian Democracy Work: Social Capital, Economic Development, and Democratization* (Lewiston, Pa.: Edwin Mellen Press).

24. Samuel P. Huntington, 1968, *Political Order in Changing Societies* (New Haven: Yale University Press); Samuel P. Huntington, 1991, *The Third Wave: Democratization in Late Twentieth Century* (Norman, Okla.: University of Oklahoma Press); and his more recent update, Samuel P. Huntington, 1997, "After Twenty-Five Years: The Future of the Third Wave," *Journal of Democracy* 8 (October): 3–12. The literature on the perils of transition from traditionalism to modernity for new democracies is rich and extensive. Two important classic studies of democratic transition are Juan J. Linz, 1978, *The Breakdown of Democratic Regimes: Crisis, Breakdown, and Reequalibration* (Baltimore: Johns Hopkins Press) and Dankwart A. Rustow, 1970, "Transitions to Democracy," *Comparative Politics* 2 (April): 337–363. For more recent research, see Adam Przeworski, 1995, *Sustainable Democracy* (Cambridge, UK: Cambridge University Press); Doh Chull Shin, 1994, "On the Third Wave of Democratization: A Synthesis and Evaluation of Recent Theory of Research," *World Politics* 47 (October): 135–170; Guillermo O'Donnell, 1992, "Transitions, Continuities, and Paradoxes," in Scott Mainwaring, Guillermo O'Donnell, and J. Samuel Valenzuela, eds., *Issues in Democratic Consolidation: The New South American Democracies in Comparative Perspective* (Notre Dame: University of Notre Dame Press), pp. 17–56; Stephan Haggard and Robert R. Kaufman, 1995, *The Political Economy of Democratic Transitions* (Princeton: Princeton University Press); T. L. Karl and Philippe C. Schmitter, 1991, "Modes of Transition in Latin America, Southern and Eastern Europe," *International Social Science Journal* 43

(May): 269–284; Stephanie Lawson, 1993, "Conceptual Issues in the Comparative Study of Regime Change and Democratization," *Comparative Politics* 25 (January): 183–205; Scott Mainwaring, 1992, "Transitions to Democracy and Democratic Consolidation: Theoretical and Comparative Issues," in Scott Mainwaring, Guillermo O'Donnell, and J. Samuel Valenzuela, eds., 1992, *Issues in Democratic Consolidation: The New South American Democracies in Comparative Perspective* (Notre Dame: University of Notre Dame Press), pp. 294–341; Gerardo L. Munck, 1994, "Democratic Transitions in Comparative Perspective," *Comparative Politics* 26 (April): 355–376; and J. Samuel Valenzuela, 1992, "Democratic Consolidation in Post-Transitional Settings: Notion, Process, and Facilitating Conditions," in Scott Mainwaring, Guillermo O'Donnell, and J. Samuel Valenzuela, eds., 1992, *Isssues in Democratic Consolidation: The New South American Democracies in Comparative Perspective* (Notre Dame: University of Notre Dame Press), pp. 57–104.

25. This is not, however, the case if we are executing a curvilinear plot. Then, because of the curve term (X^2), the r^2 will change as a result of changing the order of your dependent and independent variables.

26. Recall also from Chapter 13, and Figures 13.6, 13.7, and 13.8, that if the relationship between X and Y is not accurately reflected by a linear slope, it maybe better represented by a nonlinear slope. However, nonlinear slopes are often difficult to interpret and many times reflect merely a few outliers that severely skew the sample. Nonetheless, as we demonstrated in Chapter 13, one may easily check for nonlinear slopes, which will in fact alter the coefficient of determination to reflect a better fit of the line to the pattern of the dots, and thereby reflect a reduction in residual error. There is no appreciable decrease in error when we fit the plot in Figures 15.9 to a nonlinear slope.

27. Within SPSS 10, you may execute a scatterplot by following the sequence: GRAPHICS▶SCATTER. Select the SIMPLE solution, and enter your dependent and independent variables from the VARIABLE LIST window. You have the further option of selecting that variable (for example, CODE, as in Figure 15.9) that will label each dot on the graph for you. Once you have selected your options, press OK. Once the graph is produced (in the graphics window or CHART CAROUSEL of SPSS 10), you may select subsequent options by requesting to edit the graph. Within OPTIONS you may select the r-square statistic, regression line (which provides the coefficient of determination). Note that if you have selected a variable to label the dots, you must select the LABELS ON option in the OPTIONS window. All graphs can be copied from the EDIT button, selecting COPY CHART, within the graph editor mode. Then, once in either WordPerfect or Word, you may select the PASTE SPECIAL option from the edit command, and the graph will be imported as a "picture" file into your word processor document, from where you may edit it with the graphics editor of the word processor. See Marija J. Norušis, 2000, *SPSS: SPSS© 10.0 Guide to Data Analysis* (Upper Saddle River, N. J.: Prentice Hall), pp. 133 – 162 for more details.

28. See, for instance, Peter Askonas and Angus Stewart, eds., 2000, *Social Inclusion: Possibilities and Tensions* (New York: St. Martin's Press).

29. See Remigio E. Agpalo, 1992, "Modernization, Development, and Civilization: Reflections on the Prospects of Political Systems in the First, Second and Third Worlds," in Kenneth E. Bauzon, ed., *Development and Democratization in the Third World: Myths, Hopes and Realities* (Washington, D.C.: Crane Russak), pp. 81–97; Larry Diamond, "Is the Third Wave Over?,"

Journal of Democracy 1 (Summer 1991): 20–37; and John R. Hanson II, 1999, "Are We All Capitalists Now?," *The Independent Review* 3 (Spring): 565–573.

30. For a thorough consideration of the many different choices under appropriate circumstances to use when fitting curves to nonlinear patterns, see Lawrence C. Hamilton, 1992, *Regression with Graphics: A Second Course in Applied Statistics* (Pacific Grove, Calif.: Brooks/Cole), pp. 145–182.

31. For more detail about the quadratic, or polynomial, procedure for assessing nonlinear associations, see William D. Berry and Mitchell S. Sanders, 2000, *Understanding Multivariate Research* (Boulder: Westview Press), pp. 68–70.

32. The statistics shown in the second-order polynomial regression equation were obtained using the CURVE ESTIMATION procedure in SPSS 10. To obtain this output, select from the main menu in SPSS 10, ANALYZE▶REGRESSION▶CURVE ESTIMATION. Then, within the dialog box, select the dependent and independent variables for the model. The procedure gives you a number of useful options for residual analysis. However, ordinarily, you will select the linear model option, as well as (in this case) the quadratic model option. Note there are several curve estimation models (or regression equations) available. Quadratic and exponential are the most basic in cross-national research with a sample size of fifty or less. Others are available, as you can see. You may also save the residuals by opening the SAVE option at the lower right of the dialog box. This allows you to save the predicted values (of both the linear and curvilinear estimates), as well as the residual estimates of both the linear and curvilinear estimates. These will be inserted into your SPSS 10 data file at the end of your variable list on the data editor screen. You may use these for further residual analysis and theory refinement. The output will contain statistics for both a simple linear regression model, as well as the quadratic model (with the statistics for both terms in the second-order polynomial model). For more details of using this procedure within SPSS 10, see Marija Norušis, 1993, *SPSS for Windows: Base System User's Guide Release 6.0* (Chicago: SPSS Inc.), pp. 372–376.

16

The Role of Basic Regression in Cross-National Analysis

Terms: *Sum of Squares, Mean Sum of Squares, Standard Error of Estimate, R^2, Adjusted R^2, Standard Error of Intercept, Standard Error of b, Beta Coefficient, Confidence Interval of Regression Coefficient and Intercept, Confidence Intervals of Mean (Expected) Y*

Demonstration: Basic Regression as a Tool for Testing Hypotheses, 16.1

In this chapter, we continue our consideration of regression analysis and its application within cross-national data analysis. Our primary focus remains on simple, bivariate regression, as introduced in the previous chapter. We will, however, examine more closely important elaborations of our scatterplot and regression models. In regression analysis, we have a powerful tool not merely for hypothesis testing, but for teasing from cross-national data further insights into patterns among countries that illuminate pathways for future research.

We begin with an overview of simple regression, and then move on to a demonstration of how one derives confidence intervals and subsequently employs them in estimating values of Y from values of X (that is, the prediction process).

DEMONSTRATION 16.1: BASIC REGRESSION AS A TOOL FOR TESTING HYPOTHESES

The most imposing challenge to beginning students of regression is to sort through the flood of statistics that seem to surround the procedure. Knowing what a particular statistic is and how it can be effectively used to explore the hypothesis and research question at hand seems at first to be quite imposing. And it can be—even to professionals. Regression can be made much simpler if you realize the procedure itself consists of three separate aspects, each aspect characterized by a particular combination of substantive statistics and probability estimates. Substantive statistics allow us to describe the nature of the relationship between two variables specified within a model. Probability estimates allow us to infer from the substantive statistics emerging from the analysis of the sample to the target population. Probability estimates are the test statistics of regression analysis.

Table 16.1 summarizes the three aspects of regression and their respective statistical components.

International Economic Exchange (INTEX) and Modernity (MODERN)

To demonstrate the use of regression models, as well as the utility and practicality of confidence intervals in simple regression models, we will begin by exploring the relationship between the degree to which an economy is integrated into the global world market via international exchange of goods and services (ZINTEX) and its level of modernity (MODERN). You will recall from Chapter 11 the concept of international exchange is operationally represented by the variable INTEX (standardized, ZINTEX) and from Chapter 15, modernity (MODERN). This relationship may be formalized in the following hypothesis:

> Hypothesis 16.1: ZINTEX increases proportionately with MODERN across countries

Why should the openness to the global economy (ZINTEX) be associated with and presumably affected by the degree of modernity (MODERN) in a society? Opening markets to foreign exchange and investment, as well as to trade and commercial activity, is inconsistent with the nature and logic of a traditional society. Traditional societies, all else being equal, would surely have less to offer the international market in the way of advanced and manufactured goods and services, and the very pressure that such open economies would present to a traditional society will require a greater degree of routinization, regulation, formalization, and standardization in the face of international commerce.

The global market, so to speak, presents uncertainty and risk that run counter to the very core of a traditional society. As such, we would expect little incentive within traditional societies toward opening their economies and society in general to international influences.

On the other hand, *modernity*, with its complex social divisions of labor and specialization, as well as open communication systems (represented by Internet connections), intense service economy, and appetite for what is new, places a premium on the global, open economy. Therefore, we would expect a strong positive relationship to exist be-

TABLE 16.1 Elements of Basic Regression Analysis

Aspect	Statistical Components: Substantive Statistics	Probability Estimates (Test Statistics)
Model Summary: *Summary of overall relationship (shared variance) between XY*	R^2 *(Figure 13.2)* Adjusted R^2 (aR^2) *(Formula 16.1)*	Sum of Squares *(Regression, Residual, and Total)* F *(Regression Mean Sum Square/Residual Mean Sum Square)* prob. F Standard Error of Estimate (SSE) *(Formula 16.2)*
Hypothesis Testing (ß = 0): *Tests theory behind model (XY)*	Intercept (a) *(Formula 15.4)* Unstandardized Regression Coefficient (b) *(Formula 15.1)* Standardized Regression Coefficient (ß) *(Formula 15.2, 15.3)*	Standard Error a (SEa) (Formula 16.4) Standard Error b (SEb) *(Formula 16.3)* t value *(b/SE_b)* t_a value *(Formula 16.6)* prob. t
Substantive Refinements: *Specific comparative evidence–including case specific—which allows for refinement of theory and hypothesis testing*	Confidence Intervals of the Mean Expected Value of Y at X_i *(Formula 17.1)* Prediction Intervals of Individual Scores of Y at X_i *(Formula 17.3)* Standardized Residual Error *(Formula 17.4)*	

tween ZINTEX and MODERN. Furthermore, we would reasonably expect (again, all things being equal) that the more fundamental environmental and cultural forces that shape modernity precede any pressures for opening a market to international exchange. Consequently, we should logically expect that modernity (MODERN) itself will be the constraining factor influencing the degree of international exchange (ZINTEX). This hypothesis can be initially evaluated by using a scatterplot analysis as demonstrated in Chapter 15.[1]

As we have seen, the most important statistic is the coefficient of determination, or, the r^2, or in this case, .502. We can verify precisely that this relationship is statistically significant ($p = .0001$, 2-tail) through the use of the CORRELATION procedure in SPSS 10. To many students, and in many cases, this would be sufficient for any hypothesis test. However, there may be a much richer story to tell if we wish to take the time to analyze the model in more detail. We refer to this as diagnostic analysis. Diagnostics entails exploring the various aspects of the regression model and its component statistics to see if we can mine from this output new information that may allow us to add more important information and most importantly, discern revealing cross-national patterns in the residuals. At the core of regression diagnostics is residual analysis. In order to more thoroughly diagnose the relationship and understand the role of the residuals, and residual error within models, we need to move beyond the simple scatterplot and its basic summary statistic (as important and efficient as it is to the student) and consider the various components of the regression output itself, step by step. In this way, we are in a better position to both appreciate and understand the powerful role of residual analysis as applied in cross-national studies.

Evaluating the Model ZINTEX by MODERN

Figure 16.1 reports our initial portion of our test of Hypothesis 16.1: the scatterplot of ZINTEX by MODERN. From this scatterplot, we can see that a positive relationship exists between ZINTEX and MODERN. However, note the difference in the spread of the residuals for countries with less than average scores for international exchange ($ZINTEX < 0$), as well as modernity ($MODERN < 0$). These countries are much more dispersed around the regression line, while those countries with higher than average scores for ZINTEX and MODERN form a much tighter cluster along the regression line. Despite this spread among the less open economies, the model nonetheless accounts for over half the variance in ZINTEX ($\beta^2 = .502$). Tables 16.2–16.4 report the basic output from SPSS 10 for a standard linear regression analysis. Table 16.2 reports the summary table for the regression analysis of ZINTEX and MODERN. Table 16.3 reports the analysis of variance results of the regression test, and Table 16.4 reports the coefficient estimates from the regression analysis. While this output may appear altogether new, it contains the statistics we have presented in Formula 15.1, 15.2, 15.3, 15.4, and 15.5.

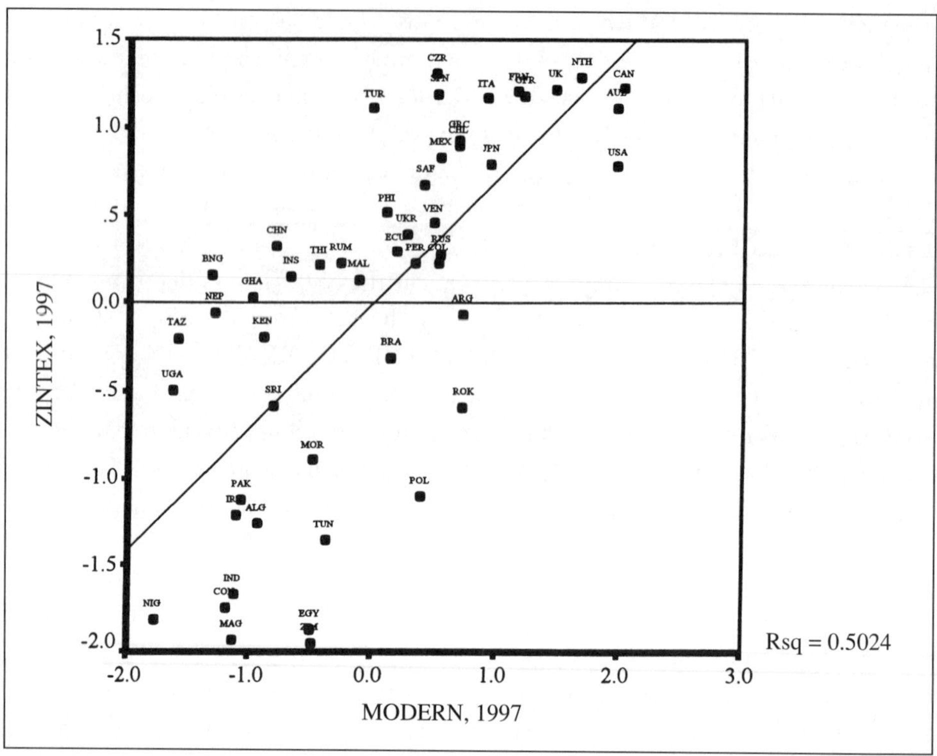

FIGURE 16.1 Scatterplot, ZINTEX by MODERN

Adjusted R Square. In the Model Summary section, you will notice the statistics for R Square and Adjusted R Square (.502 and .492, respectively). The adjusted R^2 takes account of the number of cases relative to the number of variables in the model, and allows you to extend your conclusions based on your sample to samples in general, and thereby provide a better estimate of the target population's true R^2. The R^2 is your sample estimate of the variance explained within the target population; the adjusted R^2 is an approximation of how much variance you can expect your model to explain in the population of samples. Because of error in sampling, you can always expect the adjusted R^2 to be slightly smaller—at least—than your R^2. The formula for the adjusted R^2 (aR^2) is:

$$aR^2 = R^2 - \frac{K-1}{n-K}(1-R^2) \qquad \text{Formula 16.1}$$

K refers to the number of variables in the model and N is the size of the sample. In *all* simple, bivariate regression models, K = 2 (one Y variable, and one X variable). So, the adjusted R^2 (aR^2) for our model is:

TABLE 16.2 Model Summary, Regression Analysis, ZINTEX by MODERN (SPSS 10)

Model	*R*	*R Square*	*Adjusted R Square*	*Std. Error of the Estimate*
1	.709[a]	.502	.492	.71272

[a] Predictors: (Constant), MODERN

TABLE 16.3 ANOVA Results, Regression Analysis, ZINTEX by MODERN (SPSS 10)

Model		*Sum of Squares*	*df*	*Mean Square*	*F*	*Sig.*
1	Regression	24.618	1	24.618	48.463	.000[a]
	Residual	24.382	48	.508		
	Total	49.000	49			

[a] Predictors: (Constant), MODERN

TABLE 16.4 Coefficient Estimates, Regression Analysis, ZINTEX by MODERN (SPSS 10)

		Unstandardized Coefficients		*Standardized Coefficients*		
Model		*B*	*Std. Error*	*Beta*	*t*	*Sig.*
1	(Constant)	1.94E-16	.101		.000	1.000
	MODERN	.709	.102	.709	6.962	.000

$$aR^2 = .502-\frac{2-1}{50-2}(1-.502) = .502-\frac{1}{48}(.498) = .502-((.021)(.498)) = .502-.010 = .492$$

Formula 16.2

From this, we would conclude that in general (that is, across comparable random samples of populous countries with N = 50 and K = 2), our model would account for 49.2 percent of the total variance in ZINTEX. As is clear from Formula 16.1, the more parameters in the model (that is, the more variables one enters into their regression model, extending it from a simple, bivariate regression model to a more complex multivariate regression model), the greater the variance and complexity of the model, and therefore the greater likelihood of error in the model. So, consequently, the smaller will be the aR^2. Ordinarily, it is best to report *both* the R^2 and the aR^2 in your regression table. *You never substitute, however, the adjusted R^2 for the real R^2 in formulas requiring either the R^2 or $1 - R^2$.*

The Standard Error of Estimate for Regression Models. In the last column of the Model Summary section of Table 16.2 is a useful statistic known as the *Standard Error Estimate* (often denoted as SEE). You have seen standard error estimates before, in both ANOVA analyses and with respect to both Spearman and Pearson correlation coefficient computations in Chapter 13 (see, for instance Formula 13.1). In Chapter 12, we merely introduced you to the concept of the variance components found in the correlation coefficients, which, in effect, are the same as the variance components found in simple regression. However, to fully appreciate and effectively utilize simple regression analysis in applied cross-national analysis, we must examine these standard error components here in more detail.

The standard error is the standard deviation of the residual sum of squares (discussed below). As the name implies, this statistic standardizes the residual error in one model across all similar models. It estimates the error we can expect across repeated (and different) samples of similar N and k structure (that is, size and variables) in computing the residual sum of squares—our model variance. Recall from Chapter 13 that the *model variance* in regression is the aggregate (squared) difference between the mean of Y and the predicted value of Y in each sample. As such, it is derived by the following formula:

$$SEE = \sqrt{\frac{\text{RSS}}{N-2}}$$ Formula 16.3

where RSS refers to the residual sum of squares, and N is the sample size. Table 16.3 reports the residual sum of squares (RSS) as 24.382. Employing Formula 16.2, we can compute the standard error estimate for our model in Table 10.6 as:

$$SEE = \sqrt{\frac{24.382}{48}} = \sqrt{.508} = .7127$$ Formula 16.4

As we shall see in Chapter 17, the standard error of estimate is critical in computing the confidence and prediction intervals necessary for more credible and very useful statistical diagnostics of linear relationships. The larger the SEE, the more *unstable* our estimates of error in the model, reflecting the model's overall inefficiency. When models are unstable, we have less confidence that our results can stand up to repeated replications across different samples of the same size. Thus, our findings lack credibility and elicit less confidence among those to whom we report our findings.

Analysis of Variance (ANOVA): Sums of Squares. In Table 16.3, you will notice there are three components of variance (or sum of squares) reported: the *model variance*, the *explained variance*, and the *total variance*. The *model variance* is reported as the *residual sum of squares* (RSS) in the regression output; the explained variance is reported as the *regression sum of squares*; and the total variance is reported as *total sum of squares* in regression output.

The computation of the model variance is somewhat different than we have seen with t-tests and one-way ANOVA models. This is because we are ordinarily working exclusively with interval/ratio data in regression models. However, the logic of the model variance is the same as in t-tests and one-way ANOVA models. *It is the portion of variance in Y accounted for by the addition of the X variable into our model.* Without the X variable, we would rely solely on the mean of Y to predict any given score of Y. *The explained variance is that portion of the variance in Y that is accounted for by the variance of X.* And, of course, the total variance is equivalent to the sample variance. *It is simply the total error we encounter in predicting the value of Y from the mean of Y.*

Where do these error and variance components originate? How do we place them within the mechanics of the regression procedure itself? To answer these questions, let us turn to Figure 16.2. In this figure, we have simplified a hypothetical scatterplot for purposes of illustration. The regression slope reflects the predicted value of Y, based on the variance of X. The single dot reflects the actual score of a country for the Y variable. The horizontal line represents the mean of Y ($\bar{X} = 0$ when working with z-scores). Following the logic of scatterplots, we know the closer the regression line approaches the actual value of Y, the *stronger* the regression model (that is, the more accurate is its ability to predict values of Y). The closer, however, the regression approaches the mean of Y (the horizontal line), the weaker the regression model (the less accurate is its ability to predict values of Y). The utility of Figure 16.2 is its graphical illustration of the proportional relationship of the unexplained variance (model variance) to the explained variance, and the proportion of the total variance of Y comprised by the sum of the explained and unexplained variance components.

Within Table 16.3, the respective figures for these variance components are listed under the heading *Sum of Squares*. The *regression sum of squares* is equal to the explained variance in ZINTEX, the *residual sum of squares* is the unexplained variance (equivalent to the model variance) in ZINTEX, while the total variance of ZINTEX is indicated as Total (equivalent to the sample variance of Y). Again, because we are working exclusively with z-scores, the degrees of freedom accorded the independent variable will equal the total sum of squares, which equals n–1, which in the case of our model represented in Table 16.3 is 49 (50–1).

Dividing the *residual sum of squares* (24.382) by the *total sum of squares* (49) reveals the *coefficient of nondetermination* (.498). This is that portion of the variance in Y that is *not* explained by the model. Dividing the *regression sum of squares* (the explained variance) by the *total sum of squares* (24.618/49) computes the *coefficient of determination* (.502). This is the portion of the variance in Y that is accounted for by the regression model. We will return to these statistics in a moment. First, with the variance components of a regression model specified, let us consider their significance.[2]

Degrees of Freedom in Simple Regression. Within any analysis of variance procedure, we must control for the proper degrees of freedom that affect the size of these sums of squares. There are two components of degrees of freedom in regression models, that for the *regression variance* (equivalent to the *between*-group variance in a one-way ANOVA model, see Chapter 12), and the *residual variance* (equivalent to the *within*-group variance in the ANOVA model, see Chapter 12).

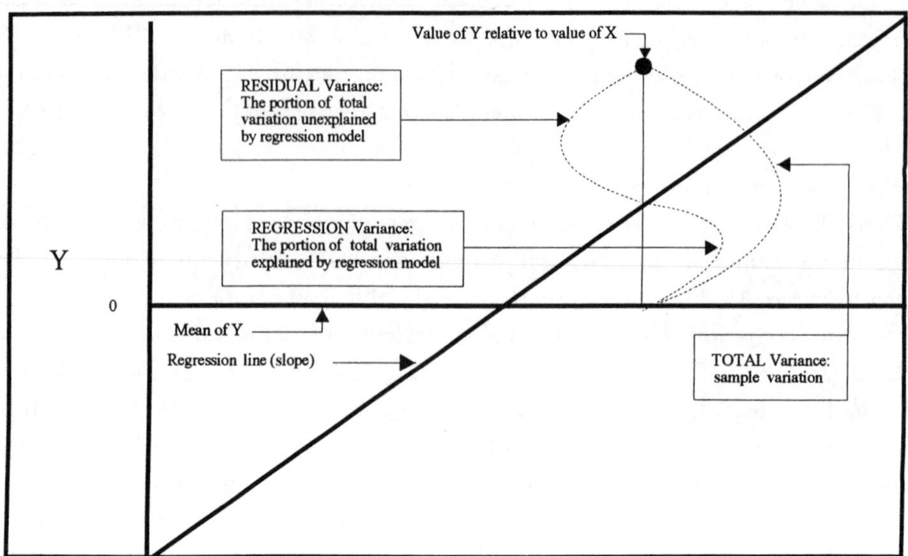

FIGURE 16.2 Sources of Variance in Simple Regression Model

In the case of the *regression sum of squares* (the explained variance) within a simple regression model, the proper degrees of freedom is 1, or k–1 (where k is the number of variables in the regression model, which is 2 in a simple regression model). By standardizing the explained variance by the degrees of freedom, we estimate the amount of the total variance that can be directly attributed to the independent variables in the model. Because a simple regression model contains only one independent variable, all of the explained variance can be directly attributed to the lone independent variable. Therefore, within the sample, the typical squared difference between the mean of Y and the predicted value of Y is 24.618; or, *mean regression sum of squares* is 24.618 (24.618/1).

As the value of the *mean regression sum of squares* increases, it reflects a growing gap between the mean of Y and the predicted value of Y. In and of itself, this statistic means nothing. However, if this value increases in relation to the unexplained variance (the model variance), it indicates a proportional improvement in our ability to predict Y from values of X over our ability to predict Y from the mean of Y.

Note we are in effect "penalized" for adding more independent variables to the model (equivalent in a one-way ANOVA model to adding more categories to the independent variable). Additional independent variables have the effect of increasing the denominator in the degrees of freedom adjustment for the explained variance factor in our regression model. This reduces the overall value of the ratio of the explained variance to the unexplained variance.

As we will see, adding more independent variables makes it more difficult, all else being equal, to achieve a large enough F statistic to reject the null hypothesis. However, if theory dictates more than one independent variable (in other words, a multivariate model), then we should proceed (though multiple regression is beyond the scope of this introductory text). Of course, eventually by adding more independent variables to a regression model, we will "over-determine" the model. In other words, eventually, the variance on Y will be totally accounted for by adding more and more independent variables. However, by adjusting for the degrees of freedom, we arrive at an accurate assessment of the model's overall efficiency. This efficiency declines, of course, as we pile on the independent variables. Succinctness in our models is rewarded not merely by way of clarity, but also by way of statistical validity.[3]

The *residual sum of squares* must also be divided by the proper degrees of freedom. In our model reported in Table 16.3, the appropriate degrees of freedom here is 48; or N-k, where N is equal to the number of valid observations in the sample, which is 50 in the case of CROSSNAT.50. Dividing these sums of squares by their proper degrees of freedom standardizes the error in the model, as measured by the respective *mean square* statistic reported in Table 16.3, .508; or 24.382/48. In this way we are able to assess more effectively the model's variability and compare these across samples of different sizes drawn from the target population.

In effect, the degrees of freedom adjustment for the residual error measures the *efficiency of the model* with respect to its size. As with the explained variance, we could easily add to the unexplained variance simply by including more cases in the sample. Each score will have a corresponding variation between it and the predicted value of Y. Therefore, the more scores in our sample, the greater the size of the residual error (or model variance). By dividing this value by the appropriate degrees of freedom, we record the magnitude of our model's efficiency in handling each new score and its corresponding error factor. As this value declines, we know the model accurately reflects the "real" world with respect to the relationship between X and Y. Furthermore, as the *mean sum of squares* for the residual error declines *relative* to the *mean square regression* variance, we achieve greater degrees of efficiency in predicting Y from values of X. This logic can be summarized in the following manner:

Efficient Regression Model = mean square of the explained variance < mean square for residual error

Inefficient Regression Model = mean square for residual error < mean square of the explained variance

Referring to Figure 16.2, we can see that an efficient regression model would see the regression line closer to each actual value of Y, and farther from the mean of Y (thus, a larger regression variance, or total variation explained by the model), while an inefficient regression model would see the regression line farther from the actual value of Y and actually approaching the mean of Y (thus, a larger residual variance, or a much larger unexplained variance in the regression model).

Error Estimates (F Statistic). As we have reminded you since Chapter 9, when *model variance* (the unexplained, residual variance in a simple regression model) declines relative to *sample variance* (the total variance in a regression model), the statistical probability that the model defeats the null hypothesis increases. Why? Because our model will provide a better estimate of the actual value of the Y attribute (through the use of our X variable) than will our reliance on the mean value of Y in the sample (without, therefore, relying on the X attribute to estimate the Y value). You will also recall that the sum of the model variance (24.618 in Table 16.3) and the regression variance (24.382 in Table 16.3) equals the total variance (49 in Table 16.3) in our analysis.

In regression, as in one-way ANOVA, we consult the F statistic to evaluate the statistical significance of the model variance. Within the context of basic regression, the F statistic is the ratio of the *mean* explained (that is, regression) variance to the *mean* model (residual) variance. In Table 16.3, the *regression mean square* is 24.618, while the *residual mean square* is .508. Therefore, the F statistic for the model reported in Table 16.3 is F = 48.463 (24.618/.508 = 48.463). An F statistic of 48.463 with 1 and 48 degrees of freedom (k–1 =1 and N–k = 48, where k is the number of variables in the model) is statistically significant at the .0001 threshold (prob. = .000).

In a simple regression model, this F statistic tests the null hypothesis, which holds the Multiple R (the correlation coefficient in a bivariate regression model) is statistically insignificant. The Multiple R is the *coefficient of determination* (or, R in Table 16.2), which, as noted above and in Chapter 15, is the ratio of the explained variance to the total variance. The F statistic (based on the technical assumptions of an F distribution curve) indicates there is less than a 1 in 1000 chance we would obtain a Multiple R as large as .492 if the null were correct. With such small odds, we are safe in assuming the null is not an accurate depiction of the relationship between ZINTEX and MODERN, and we may therefore reject it in favor of our research hypothesis (Hypothesis 16.1). We have, in effect, less than a .0001 probability of committing a Type I error in rejecting the null.

The Parameter Estimates in a Regression Model (Regression Coefficients). Under the title Coefficients in Table 16.4 are the regression model statistics, the unstandardized regression coefficient (b), the standardized regression coefficient (ß), the standard error of the regression coefficient (b), and the t statistic associated with the b statistic. These are what we commonly refer to as *parameter estimates* in a regression equation.[4] *They are the statistics upon which our estimates of the target population are based. They are the basic substantive and test statistics in a regression model.*

As we saw in Chapter 15 in our discussion of the scatterplot procedure, when we have z-score values of the X and Y variables in a simple regression model (and, when we have identical missing data for both variables, if and when the sample contains observations that have missing data) the b statistic (Formula 15.1) will equal the ß statistic. Under these conditions, both the b and the ß will equal the correlation coefficient (r), and both b^2 and $ß^2$ will be equal to the coefficient of determination (r^2), which itself will equal the Multiple R-squared, .709 in Table 16.2. *Again, these apply only to simple regression equations. In all simple (that is, bivariate) regression equations,* $ß^2 = r^2$ *will* *hold; the condition $b^2 = r^2$ will hold only when we have z-score values for X and Y and when the cases containing missing data for X and Y are identical.*

The Standard Error of b (SEb). The *standard error* is the estimate of how much the test statistic, in this case the regression coefficient (b), will vary from sample to sample (denoted in Table 16.4 as Std. Error). It is literally the estimated standard deviation of the sampling distribution of the b statistic (or, unstandardized regression coefficient). This implies that if we took 100 different random samples of (populous) countries and computed the b statistic for an identical model from each of the 100 samples, the standard deviation of the 100 b statistics produced would be .102. Consequently, we estimate that in repeated samples of simple regression models with the same variables and with N = 50, 60 percent of these models will produce regression coefficients (b) of between .607 and .811. The smaller the standard error of b (denoted commonly as SEb), the more confident we are in the accuracy of the regression coefficient as a reflection of the relationship within the target population. The larger the standard error of b, the more likely our parameter estimates will grossly distort our picture of the true target population.

The formal specification of the SEb helps us to appreciate its role in regression analysis. The standard error of the estimate is ultimately based on the overall size of the residual sum of squares. The smaller the residual sum of squares, the more stable will be the regression coefficient estimates. This is shown in the formula for computing the standard error of estimate for the regression coefficient (SEb):

$$SEb = \frac{SSE}{\sqrt{\Sigma X_i - \bar{X})^2}} \qquad \text{Formula 16.5}$$

When working with data that have been standardized (z-scores), the denominator in Formula 16.3 will always reduce to $\sqrt{n-1}$; or, with a sample of 50, $\sqrt{49}$. So, the standard error of b in Table 16.4 may be computed as:

$$SEb = \frac{.71272}{\sqrt{49}} = \frac{.71272}{7} = .102 \qquad \text{Formula 16.6}$$

The Standard Error of a (SEa). The intercept (denoted by the letter a, or when working with standardized data, β_0) has no significant substantive role within a regression model. As noted in Chapter 15, the principal purpose for reporting the intercept in a simple regression model is to estimate the value of Y when X is zero. As such, the intercept is a necessary parameter upon which we rely to estimate the value of Y from a value of X.

Formula 16.4 reports the formula needed to compute the standard error of estimate for the intercept (SEa). This is the estimated standard deviation of the sampling error of the intercept. Again, note that the stability of our intercept estimates relies ultimately on the residual sum of squares, of SSE. Its computation is quite simple and can be easily derived (especially when working with z-score data) with a hand calculator from the following formula:

$$SEa = SSE\sqrt{\frac{1}{N}+\frac{\bar{X}^2}{\Sigma(X_i-\bar{X})^2}} \quad \text{Formula 16.7}$$

When working with z-score data, the mean is always 0; so Formula 16.4 reduces to $SSE(\sqrt{1/N+0})$. For our model reported in Table 16.4, the SEa is .101:

$$SEa = [(.71272)(\sqrt{1/50})] = [(.71272)(\sqrt{.02})] = [(.71272)(.14142)] = .101 \quad \text{Formula 16.8}$$

Interpreting the Statistical Significance of the Regression Coefficient (Slope). In a simple (bivariate) regression model, the fundamental objective is to test the null hypothesis, which asserts the value of the slope (that is, the b statistic) to be zero (or, $\beta = 0$, when working with standardized values), indicating (in our model specified in Hypothesis 16.1) no relationship between ZINTEX and MODERN in the target population. To test this hypothesis, we rely on the t-statistic for the regression coefficient. Though we may specify direction within our hypothesis (as in Hypothesis 16.1), we still simply evaluate the test statistic for the regression model in terms of its deviation from 0. Furthermore, because the null specifically assumes no relationship between the X and Y variables, we employ the t statistic as the critical test statistic to evaluate the statistical significance of the regression coefficient. *However, in a simple, bivariate regression model, if the F statistic for the Multiple R is statistically significant, the t-statistic for the regression statistic will also be statistically significant.* Nonetheless, let us consider the test statistic for the regression coefficient: the t-statistic.

T-Statistic in Regression Models. The t-statistic is dependent upon the reduction of error in our estimate of the regression coefficient. The larger this error, the smaller will be the t-statistic. To calculate a t-statistic, we divide the regression coefficient by the standard error of the regression coefficient (b). Therefore, the t-statistic in our regression equation is 6.6962 (.709/.102 = 6.7).[5] This confirms that in rejecting the null, we have less than a 1/1000 chance of committing a Type I error (as reported in Table 16.4); or, there is less than a 1/1000 chance that the null itself is a true reflection of the target population.

In a simple regression (that is, bivariate model), the t-statistic for the regression coefficient will be equal to the square root of the F statistic computed for our model's variance; or, squaring the t-statistic will equal the F statistic. Thus, in a simple regression model with only one independent variable, $t^2 = F$, or, alternatively, $\sqrt{F} = t$.[6]

Interpreting the Statistical Significance of the Intercept (β_0). As with the regression coefficient, we may also estimate the statistical significance of the intercept. The t-statistic for the intercept tests the null hypothesis $\beta_0/0$. When the t-statistic is significant at or beyond the .05 range with N–2 degrees of freedom, we may reject the null and conclude that Y is close to 0 when X = 0. If $p > 0$ for t, we must reject the null and conclude that the value of Y is significantly larger than 0 when X = 0. This, however, has no substantive bearing on the decision we draw regarding the principal null hypothesis of the analysis ($\beta = 0$), nor on the substantive interpretation we apply to the relationship of Y to X based on the regression coefficient and the accompanying analysis of variance in the regression model.

Formula 16.9 reports the equation by which we may compute the t value for intercept (t_a):

$$t_a = \frac{a}{SSE\sqrt{\frac{\Sigma X^2}{N(S_{xx})}}} \qquad \text{Formula 16.9}$$

This imposing formula reduces to the simpler formula:

$$t_a = \frac{a}{SE_a} \qquad \text{Formula 16.10}$$

With respect to Table 16.4, $t_a = 0$ (or, .000/.101 = 0). The statistical significance of a t value of 0 (regardless of degrees of freedom) is 1.000. We may reject the null hypothesis and conclude that Y is not significantly different from 0 when X = 0. This, however, has little substantive utility for the researcher. Therefore, it is not common to see either SE_a or t_a reported in the results of a regression analysis. These statistics are, however, part of the routine output in advanced statistical software packages, such as SPSS 10.

Computing the Confidence Intervals for the Regression Coefficient (β) and Intercept (β_0). The reported slope in Table 16.2 ($\beta = .709$) reflects our *best estimate* of the target population's true slope, based on our sample data. Sampling error, of course, renders this estimate subject to a degree of variability. This variability would be found if we repeated our sampling of populous countries 100 different times, for instance. Each new sample would (if the sample was unbiased and random) produce slightly different estimates of the slope, given identical model properties. For this reason we calculate the standard error of b.

In addition to the standard error of b, we can estimate the range of values that will incorporate the target population's true slope 95 times of 100 in our repeated sampling. Remember from Chapter 4 that the range of values derived from a sample within which we expect to find the target population value (within a specified proportion of repeated sampling attempts) is the *confidence interval.* In regression analysis, if our slope is statistically significant (that is, if we can reject the null, $\beta \neq 0$), these confidence intervals provide an assessment of the range within which Y varies with respect to X.[7]

To compute the 95 percent confidence interval (the ordinary degree of confidence required) for the slope, we estimate the upper and lower limits of the target population's true slope:

The upper limit of the 95% c.i. for ß: ß + [(t)(SEb)]

The lower limit of the 95% c.i. for ß: ß – [(t)(SEb)]

The "t" term in the formulas above represents the value of the t-statistic that corresponds to the .05 area under the normal curve. With very large samples we may use 1.96 as the common t value to insert in the computation of confidence intervals. However, with samples that are smaller than approximately 100, variance is more restricted within the sample and therefore less likely to approximate the variance in the target population. Consequently, when computing confidence interval estimates, it is often preferred by researchers to consult a "Critical Values of t" table in a standard statistics text for more precise values of the t threshold to employ in the computation.

Based on the degrees of freedom in the model (that is, N – 2 for a simple bivariate regression model), the table will reveal the t value required for a .05 probability level. With a sample of fifty, technically, the t value is approximately 2.0 (that is, a t of 2.0 is equivalent to the .05 area under the normal curve, when we have forty-eight degrees of freedom, as we will in a bivariate model). Accordingly, we will use a t value of 2.0 for threshold level in computing the 95% c.i. for our target population slope.

With a slope (ß) of .709 and a standard error of b (SEb) of .102, we can estimate the upper limit of the 95% c.i. for the target population's slope to be .913 (.709 + [(2)(.102); or, .709 + .204). The lower limit of the 95% c.i. for the target population slope is .505 (.709 – -[(2)(.102); or, .709 – .204). From these computations we *may not* conclude that we are 95 percent confident that the true target population slope is between .505 and .913. Rather, we *may* conclude that 95 times out of 100, the computed 95% c.i. intervals will contain the true target population slope. Recall, of course, that we cannot actually ever know the true target population slope.

Notice that because our slope was statistically significant (that is, the t value for ß was 6.7, p = .0001), the confidence intervals cannot contain the value 0 (0 is not included in the range between .505 and .913). If it were included within this range, you would have to conclude that 95 times out of 100, there was a real possibility that there would be no relationship between ZINTEX and MODERN. In circumstances where we cannot reject the null hypothesis, confidence intervals have little meaning to the researcher. *This is why it makes sense only to report confidence intervals for the slope when you have a statistically significant model.*

The same logic can be applied to the intercept of the slope. An intercept simply reflects the expected value of the dependent variable (ZINTEX) when the value of the independent variable (MODERN) is 0. From the SEa (Formula 16.7) we may estimate the 95 percent confidence intervals around the intercept. These follow the same format as the confidence intervals around the slope:

The upper limit of the 95% c.i. for the intercept: $\beta_0 + [(t)(SEa)]$

The lower limit of the 95% c.i. for the intercept: $\beta_0 - [(t)(SEa)]$

Applying these equations to the data in Table 16.4 produces 95% c.i. for the intercept of between .202 and -.202 (t = 2.0, with 48 df; SEa = .101; β_0 = a = 0). We conclude that 95 times out of 100, the computed 95% c.i. intervals for the intercept (or, β_0) will contain the true target population intercept.

The confidence interval of the regression coefficient and intercept estimate the target population's "true" rate of change in Y relative to X, as well as the target population's "actual" value of Y when X is 0. *We do not work from these to predicting scores within the target population*. The respective intervals we place about our *predictions* of Y from X are the confidence intervals of the mean expected value of Y (Formula 16.7) and the *prediction intervals of the individual scores* (Formula 16.8). These will be discussed in detail later in this chapter.

USING REGRESSION STATISTICS FOR SUBSTANTIVE REFINEMENTS

It is important to distinguish between statistics relevant to the hypothesis test, and those that have more to do with substantive refinement of our knowledge of the subject matter at hand. Confidence intervals of the regression parameter (b, β) and the intercept (a, β_2), while not immediately germane to hypothesis tests, are often worth reporting (especially the confidence intervals for the slope) because they offer further refinement of our substantive knowledge of the phenomena under examination by the regression analysis.

Ordinarily, you do not turn to the confidence intervals of b (or β) to make your final determination of the hypothesis. You do turn to the confidence intervals, however, when comparing different slopes of similar model. Suppose, for instance, you estimated β=-.807, with the SEb = .17, with 95% c.i. for the slope determined to be between -.676 and -.979. And yet, another study, relying on a similar sample of equal size (N = 50) and an identical model, reports β = -.680, with SEb = .12. What relevance would that mean for you? It would mean that your initial substantive conclusions based on your analysis would be supported by the study because the second study's 95% c.i. for the slope is -.44 – -.92, a range that includes your parameter estimate of -.807. Thus, while the two sample estimates of the slope vary, both samples, in effect, confirm the relevance the other: -.807 falls within the second sample's 95% c.i. range for the slope, and -.680 falls within your model's 95% c.i. range for the slope.

While it generally takes more than one replication to effectively confirm or refute the original findings of a regression model, confidence intervals allow us to make a reasonable determination of the size of the difference among various parameter estimates. From this, we can evaluate the need to alter our substantive conclusions about the relationship between the variables in question (for example, ZINTEX and MODERN). For instance, if one study does not support another within the 95% c.i. interval, we may want to withhold any conclusions until we have had an opportunity to compare the samples and measurement procedures across the two samples.

SUMMING UP

From the results of tests of Hypothesis 16.1, reported in both Figure 16.1 and 16.3, as well as in Tables 16.2–16.4, we may reject the null hypothesis and accept our research hypothesis. *Open domestic economies increase across countries relative to the degree of modernity in the countries.* This relationship is relatively strong and positive (ZINTEX increases across countries relative to MODERN). Specifically, the analysis suggests that a 1 standard deviation increase in MODERN results in a .709 standard deviation *increase* in ZINTEX. Finally, we have computed the confidence interval for the slope (β), giving us some idea of the range within which the true slope is likely to fall.

Obviously, the model does not suggest that ZINTEX is a worthwhile goal, nor that modernity is a characteristic that should be exalted. Rather, the model reported above does allow one to appreciate better the relationship between the two phenomena and from this to gauge the degree to which one factor might be associated with the other factor. These results can only show the empirical relationship. It cannot *prove* cause and effect (though it can suggest such a relationship), and it most certainly cannot attach normative judgment to the value of either attribute.

CHAPTER SUMMARY

In this chapter we have considered in detail the major statistical components of OLS (ordinary least squares) regression (summarized in Table 16.1), as well as the utility of OLS regression in the analysis of cross-national political data. Stripped to its essentials, OLS regression rests on two key statistics: the mean and the standard deviation. As with correlation analysis, univariate analysis, and one-way ANOVA, the mean and standard deviation of the variables in the model are at the heart of the logic of hypothesis testing. They provide the measure of error variance in our data and serve as the basic statistical tools by which we gauge the distance between the "expected" and the "observed" in our samples.

At this point, it is important to remind ourselves of the place that sophisticated tools such as regression assume within cross-national research. First, regression is not an end unto itself. It is part of the Ladder of Theory Building explained in Chapter 2

(Figure 2.1). It should be employed, in this spirit, as a tool from which we may proceed with theory building. Second, in concert with our desire to use regression as a method of exposing new information, we must always remember that no matter how sophisticated or complex a tool of cross-national analysis, it is secondary in importance to earlier decisions you have made regarding (1) your theory and concept formation, (2) your sample, and (3) your measurements and their operational definitions. The statistical results of your hypothesis tests are no more credible or valid than theory, concept and measurement validity, and sampling decision will allow. Using powerful statistical tools on poorly specified theory, biased samples, and/or invalid measures of concepts with data that are not cross-nationally valid and reliable is equivalent to constructing a three-story mansion in a swamp. In the end, the weight of the mansion becomes too much for what should have been the priority from the beginning—a stable and reliable foundation. Theory, sample, and measurement are the foundations of solid cross-national data analysis; statistics are properly their loyal servants, not their masters.

NOTES

1. Robert Gilpin, 2000, *The Challenge of Global Capitalism: The World Economy in the 21st Century* (Princeton: Princeton University Press); Maarten Smeets, 1999, "Globalisation of International Trade and Investment," in Frans Buelens, ed., *Globalisation and the Nation-State* (Cheltenham, UK: Edward Elgar), pp. 7–36. See David N. Balaam and Michael Veseth, 2000, "Wealth and Power: Mercantilism and Economic Nationalism," in David N. Balaam and Michael Veseth, eds., *Introduction to International Political Economy*, second edition (Upper Saddle River, N.J.: Prentice Hall), pp. 25–44 for a basic overview of the challenges of international trade to society in an era of globalization.

2. See Lawrence C. Hamilton, 1992, *Regression with Graphics: a Second Course in Applied Statistics* (Pacific Grove, Calif.: Brooks/Cole), pp. 29–64, and R. Lyman Ott, 1993, *An Introduction to Statistical Methods and Data Analysis* (Belmont, Calif.: Duxbury), pp. 437–563, for additional detail with respect to variance components within simple regression models; Jack Levin and James Alan Fox, 2001, *Elementary Statistics in Social Research*, eighth edition (Boston: Allyn and Bacon), pp. 337–362; William D. Berry and Mitchell S. Sanders, 2000, *Understanding Multivariate Research: A Primer for Beginning Social Scientists* (Boulder: Westview).

3. In cross-national quantitative research, a distinct trade-off exists between the need to devise parsimonious models and the quest for general theory. Parsimonious models are unconstrained by numerous variables that serve to qualify our original bivariate models—to make these models more powerful and therefore more meaningful. General theory requires minimizing the unexplained, but interpretation and coherence quickly become lost as one seeks to add more and more variables to one's model to enhance its explanatory potential. This is particularly troublesome for students of cross-national research, who must always face the restriction of a limited number of cases to observe, but have many more concepts and variables to draw from in constructing their models. As we have seen in Chapter 2, we quickly find that we have more variables (more explanations) than cases by which to eliminate, or falsify, our hy-

potheses. We, in fact, "over-explain." See Lawrence Mayer, 1996, *Redefining Comparative Politics: Promise Versus Performance* (Newbury Park, Calif.: Sage Publications), pp. 47–48.

4. Within SPSS 10, you may obtain parameter estimates from regression analysis by following the sequence STATISTICS▶REGRESSION▶LINEAR. This opens the LINEAR REGRESSION window. Within this window, select from the VARIABLE LIST window the appropriate dependent and the independent variable, inserting each into its respective box within the LINEAR REGRESSION window. Accept the default option to run the regression on ENTER METHOD. You also have the option of specifying the variable that will label your cases (for example, CODE). This is appropriate for residual analysis, but not necessary for basic regression. The adjusted R^2, t values, probability levels, and standard error estimates are included as part of the default output in SPSS 10. See Marija J. Norušis, 2000, *SPSS© 10.0 Guide to Data Analysis* (Upper Saddle River, N.J.: Prentice Hall), pp. 392–399, for more details.

5. Typically, if in a regression analysis the t is significant at the .001 level, the t-statistic will be reported by the researchers in their report with double asterisks; for example, the t-statistic would be reported as 6.7**. If the statistic had been significant at only the .05–.01 range, it would be reported with a single asterisk.

6. If the t-statistic is equal to 1.96 or more, and our sample is larger than 120 cases, the regression coefficient is always statistically significant at the .05 level, at a minimum. With N = 50 (and a df therefore of 48, N – 2), we require a t of about 2.0 in order to be statistically significant at the .05 threshold. In a t distribution, the 1.96 (or 2.0 for a smaller, N = 50, sample) range is that area under a normal curve where only .05 percent of the target population will be located. Thus, if our t is equal to 2.0 *or more*, we know that the regression coefficient we have derived from the model could occur by chance or mistake alone no more than 5 times or less out of 100 different random, unbiased samples drawn from the target population. We may conclude, therefore, that if $t \geq 1.96$ (or, in our sample, $t \geq 2.0$), the regression coefficient meets our minimal threshold of .05. A simple rule of thumb universally employed by students of statistical analysis is that if a slope is *roughly twice* the size of its standard error (or, t = 2.0), it is statistically significant at the .05 level.

7. Within SPSS 10, you may obtain the 95% c.i. for both the regression coefficients (b) and slope intercept (a) by selecting the STATISTICS button at the bottom of the LINEAR REGRESSION window. This will open the LINEAR REGRESSION: STATISTICS window. Check the box marked CONFIDENCE INTERVALS. This will produce the range of values within which you can be confident that 95 times out of 100 the population slope and intercept will fall. These will be listed along with the other default output for the coefficient statistics. See Marija J. Norušis, 2000, *SPSS: SPSS© 10.0 Guide to Data Analysis* (Upper Saddle River, N.J.: Prentice Hall), pp. 393–395, for more details.

17

The Role of Residual Analysis in Cross-National Research

Terms: *Prediction Intervals of Individual Score, Parameter Estimates, Standardized Residuals, Liberalized Market, Gini Score*
Concepts: Political Empowerment,"Liberalization Gap," Inequality
Demonstration: Residual Analysis, Theory Refinement, and Subsequent Hypothesis Testing, 17.1

The main focus in this chapter will be upon the utility of regression as a tool to analyze error (that is, residuals) in our models, and from the model error, to elaborate and refine our cross-national analysis through residual analysis. As we have seen in several of the previous chapters, the use of residuals—or the examination of outliers relative to the sample distribution—is an effective way to isolate unique cases within a cross-national sample and from this to refine our theory and sharpen our conclusions. Residual analysis is more than a mundane and tedious technical exercise within quantitative analysis. Indeed, it lies at the very core of comparative political inquiry's contribution to general theory building. Residuals are the signposts guiding us to new avenues of discovery and theory refinement. They offer the possibility of conceptualizing our political world in ways we had not thought of before, because they are the empirical representation of the unexpected—the inexplicable. "Theory building," notes Lawrence Mayer, "consists of specification and analysis of factors that were part of the unexplained residuals in existing explanatory theory."[1] Thus, in regression analysis, we have a powerful tool not merely for hypothesis testing, but for teasing from cross-national data further insights into patterns among countries which illuminate pathways for future research.

With residual analysis, the researcher must be aware that, as in any model based on statistical estimates, it is the target population that is of interest to the researcher. As we already know, when working from a sample to explain an aspect of a target population or predict a likely outcome within that target population, we must always take into account the variability across different samples that will produce variability in our accuracy of explanation and prediction.

In this chapter we develop a demonstration that elaborates the relationship between modernity, democracy, and the nature of economic markets in society. From this initial analysis, we proceed to demonstrate how one can employ residual analysis to identify broader cross-national patterns among the residuals which, in turn, directs attention to new hypotheses and hypothesis tests designed to refine and broaden our initial theory.

FOCUSING ON CROSS-NATIONAL COMPARISON: EXAMINING RESIDUAL ERROR IN REGRESSION ANALYSIS

One of the crucial advantages of regression analysis is the efficiency of residual error analysis. At the core of residual error analysis is the process of prediction. To predict a value for Y from values of X confirms our confidence in the model and the theory it reflects. However, prediction draws attention to residual error—*the difference between what we expect of a given case (or country) and what we observe within our sample*. If a country is expected to be characterized by a particularly internationalized economy, for example, but our observation of that country's economy deviates sharply from that prediction (as reflected by the slope of the model), we may have reason to believe our model and overarching theory need refinement and revision with respect to that country. If a pattern emerges, as we have briefly noted in Chapter 15 with respect to Figure 15.11, the power of our theory to generalize may be in jeopardy.

Residual analysis assumes an important role, therefore, within regression analysis in particular, and cross-national analysis in general. Analyzing the variance components and parameter assessments of the regression model alone (including the confidence interval of the regression coefficient) cannot allow such a direct examination of the error terms in our model. For that we must use the parameter estimates to compute the respective residual errors and attach to each the name of the respective country. It is to this important aspect of applied regression that we will now direct our attention.

Residual Error in Regression Analysis

The residual, as we have seen, is literally the gap between our expected value of Y and the observed value of Y. We denote the predicted value of Y as Y'. As residual error increases across a sample of scores for Y, the explained variance declines and the capacity of X to accurately predict Y' is reduced accordingly. Because all scores within a regression analysis will, of course, deviate to some degree from the predicted value of the score, we are not interested in simply measuring the absolute value of the deviation.

Rather, we gauge the degree of deviation of a score relative to the sample distribution of deviations.

By exploring not merely the broad patterns of residual error in regression analysis, but also the residual error associated with specific countries within our cross-national sample, we greatly enhance our ability to refine and sharpen our comparative assessment of political behavior and/or institutional authority across countries. In this section, we will carefully consider the practical application and utility of residual analysis drawn from regression parameter estimates within a cross-national research strategy.

Interval Estimates for Predicting Y from X in Simple Regression. Sampling error reminds us that any predictions we make from estimates based on the sample will be subject to a degree of error and variability, depending upon the efficiency of the model. This is because each time we repeat a sample, we introduce new and different random and unbiased error into our sampling procedure. Therefore, just as we do with means and regression slopes, it is often recommended that we examine interval estimates associated with predictions derived from the regression coefficients.

In general, interval estimates are bands on either side of the least squares line of a regression model. The bands are drawn at a particular distance from the slope. The area between the two bands defines the upper and lower thresholds within which we may expect the value of Y to fall, given a particular value of X for a case, approximately 95 times out of 100, following repeated samples of size N and structure k (if we were able to repeat the sample 100 times). They provide a convenient means to identifying those countries in a cross-national sample that may deviate from what our model predicts with respect to the attribute defined by variable Y.

In regression analysis, there are two critical interval estimates that are commonly applied in the systematic analysis of residuals in regression analysis: *confidence intervals* of the mean *expected* Y, and *prediction intervals* of individual scores. The confidence interval of the mean *expected* Y predicts the mean *expected* value of Y at each value of X in the target population. The prediction interval of the individual score predicts an individual score of Y (denoted as Y_i) given a particular value of X. *The 95% c.i. of the mean expected Y specifies the range of values of Y_i at each corresponding value of X in the target population (based on our sample estimates) within which we would expect the typical country or case to fall within 95 times out of 100.* Or, stated differently, we cannot know the exact mean value of Y at each corresponding value of X in the target population. However, we can estimate the range within which we are confident that 95 times out of 100 the target population's mean value of Y at value X will fall.

The 95% p.i. of predicted individual scores indicates the range of values of Y for a particular case, given a value of X, which we would expect 95 times out of 100. We can never know for sure in a target population exactly what score for Y a country will assume given its value of X. Sampling and random error make this impossible. However, we can estimate the range of values of Y within which, given a specific value of X, we are confident that the country will fall within 95 times out of 100.

The best predictor of the average value of Y is the average value of X. Therefore, if the deviation (standard error) of Y scores and X scores is small (that is, if most countries in the sample have scores close to the mean of the X and Y values, and assuming the distribution of Y and X scores does not seriously violate assumptions of normality), we may expect that the band width of the 95% c.i. of the mean expected Y will be narrow and that most scores of Y for countries in our sample will fall close to or within the upper and lower thresholds of the band. As the standard error of the samples of Y and X scores becomes greater, the error we may expect in predicting the mean value of Y at any value of X will, of course, increase proportionally. This will be reflected by a much larger band width for the 95% c.i. around the slope, as well as in the pattern of residual error around the slope. Several of the scores of Y in our sample will, under these circumstances, fall outside the 95% c.i. interval.

The prediction interval of an individual score is fraught with greater error than the confidence interval of the slope. It is one thing, as we know, to estimate an average score. Our standards of exactness are relaxed. Estimating a typical score is easier than estimating a particular score. When we estimate a particular score of an attribute, we must first know the mean for the sample of scores for the attribute. Therefore, in a regression model, when we estimate Y at value X, we must have already estimated the mean value of Y at X. That is, we have already computed the confidence intervals of the mean expected value of Y. From the confidence interval of the mean expected value of Y, we then estimate what a particular score will be knowing the typical score of Y at value X.

This, of course, compounds the error. There is error included within our estimate of the typical Y score at value X, and now there is additional error in estimating a particular score relative to the mean score of Y at X. This twofold error in estimating particular scores of Y at value X is reflected in much wider band widths for the 95% p.i. We are more likely to incorrectly predict the actual value of Y for a particular country from X_i in the target population than we would in merely estimating the typical score (or the mean expected value of Y at X_i).

As with the confidence interval of the mean expected value of Y, the more efficient the regression model (that is, the smaller the residual error relative to the regression error in the model), the more accurate will be our ability to predict Y_i given a value of X. Once again, this will be reflected by narrow band widths for 95% p.i., as well as narrow band widths for 95% c.i. The less efficient our model (the smaller the explained variance relative to the unexplained variance in the regression model), the wider will be both the 95% p.i. and the 95% c.i. Our ability to accurately estimate both the particular value of Y_i at value X, as well as the *typical* value of Y at value X will, under these circumstances, decline proportionally.

An Illustration. In the context of Hypothesis 16.1, the *confidence interval* of the mean expected value of Y would allow us to estimate the typical value of ZINTEX (the average extent of economic openness) for all countries that have a particular value of MODERN. On the other hand, *prediction intervals* specify the range within which a particular country's level of ZINTEX would be, given a particular value of X. In Chapter 15 we used this logic to estimate the value of POLEMPOW to be .305 for a country with a value for MODERN of .500 (0 + .609(.500) = .305). The predicted value of .305 is a "point estimation." This was also our best "point estimate" of a particular country's value of POLEMPOW assuming the country had a value of .500 for MODERN.

We saw in Chapter 5 that a point estimation is our estimate of a score based on a sample statistic (for example, mean) which does not, however, consider the error included in our estimate. In Chapter 15, we did not specify the *prediction interval* for our point estimate of .305 for MODERN; nor did we specify the *confidence interval* for that level of MODERN. As such, we have only part of the information from which we can assess the uniqueness, or similarities, of countries with respect to our model.

Before proceeding to the computational formula of the two intervals and a consideration of their practicality, consider Figure 17.1, produced from SPSS 10.[2]

Figure 16.1 and Figure 17.1 are identical, with one critical difference: Figure 17.1 incorporates the actual upper and lower 95% c.i. bands, as well as the upper and lower 95% p.i. bands. Note that where the means of ZINTEX and MODERN intersect, the band widths are at their narrowest range. This is because *the slope will always contain that point where the mean value of Y and the mean value of Y intersect*. Note also how the 95% c.i. bands are bowed in toward the slope at this intersection and widen out as we move away from this intersection point. Finally, notice that there is virtually no curve to the 95% p.i. bands, and that the width between these bands is much wider than that between the 95% c.i. bands. Figure 17.1 is intended to provide you with a visual illustration of the relation of the *confidence* and *prediction* intervals relative to the slope. We shall return to this graphic later.

If the relationship between MODERN and ZINTEX had been statistically insignificant, the standard error of estimate in the regression model would have been much larger. Consequently, both the 95% c.i. and the 95% p.i bands would have been much wider than shown in Figure 17.1. In this sense, the band widths of the 95% c.i. and the 95% p.i. around the least squares line present evidence of how strong the relationship is between X andY in a simple bivariate model. Accordingly, when $\beta = 0$, the 95% c.i. and 95% p.i. are inaccurate; systematic residual analysis is a highly useful tool of regression analysis only if we are able to reject the null hypothesis.

Computing the Intervals for Mean Expected Value of Y. The formula for the 95 percent confidence interval of the mean expected value of Y is:

$$E(Y) = 2.0(SSE)\sqrt{\frac{1}{N}+\frac{(Xi-\bar{X})^2}{S_{xx}}} \qquad \text{Formula 17.1}$$

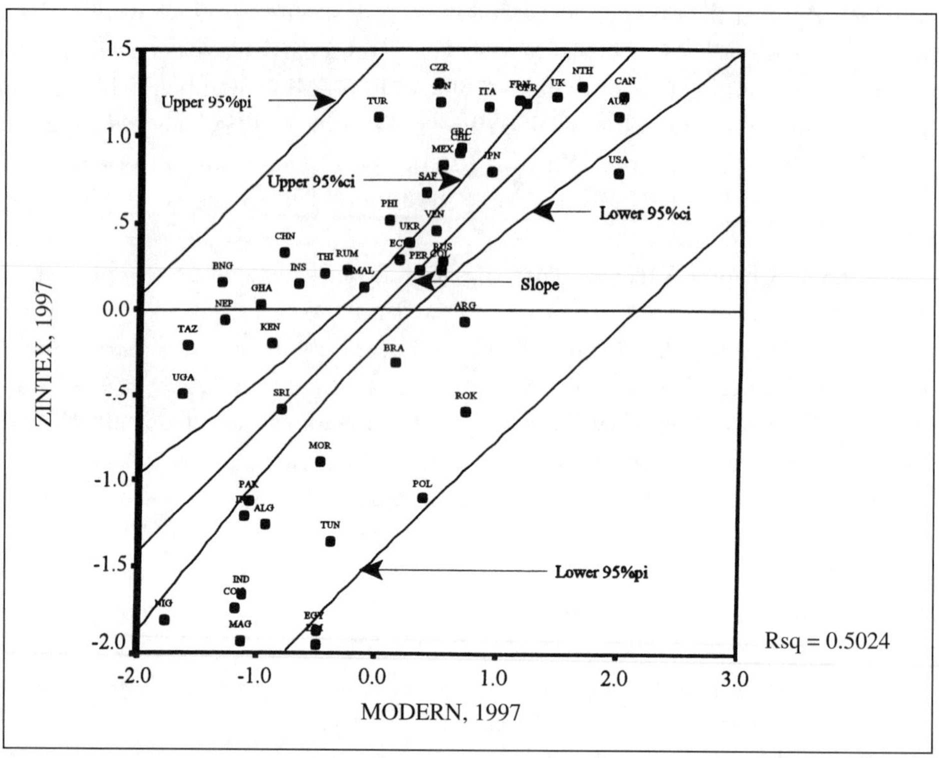

FIGURE 17.1 Scatterplot, ZINTEX by MODERN, with 95%c.i. and p.i. Bands

As we know from Chapter 16, the value 2.0 corresponds to the t value for the .05 range (or 95 percent of the area under the curve in a relatively small sample, or approximately N < 50); the SSE is the Standard Error of Estimate (for limited samples, with N < 50 or so).You will recall from our discussion of Formula 16.2 that the SSE is in effect the standard deviation of residual errors in a regression. X_i is the actual value for variable X for a country i; $\bar{X}$ is the sample mean for variable X, N is the number of cases in the sample, and S_{xx} is a measure of the total variance of X in the sample. In samples where the data have been converted to z-scores, S_{xx} will always be equal to N–1.

The components in Formula 17.1 that are to the right of the t value (2.0) represent the equation for estimating the *standard error* of the mean value of Y at X_i. When we do not have z-scores to work with, the formula for S_{xx} is:

$$S_{xx} = \sum X^2 - \frac{(\sum X)^2}{N}$$ Formula 17.2

where $\sum X^2$ is the sum of the square values of X in a sample, and the term $(\sum X)^2$ is the sum of variable X in a sample, squared. Table 17.1 reports the core components of a residual analysis of a standard linear regression produced in SPSS 10. Table 17.1 reports (1) the actual values of ZINTEX and MODERN, (2) the predicted value of ZINTEX (based on the regression equation), as well as the residual of ZINTEX and the standardized residual value, and (3) the prediction intervals—the 95 percent confidence interval (c.i.) and the 95 percent prediction interval (p.i.).

Using the value of X (MODERN) for Sri Lanka (SRI), -.813, we see that the range for the 95% c.i. based on our regression estimates reported in Table 16.2 is:

$$95\%\text{c.i.} = (2)(.713)\sqrt{\frac{1}{50}+\frac{(-.813-0)^2}{49}};= 1.43\sqrt{.02+\frac{.661}{49}};= 1.43\sqrt{(.02+.0133)};=1.43\sqrt{.033};= 1.43(.183);\approx.261$$

Formula 17.3

Thus, to determine the upper limit of the 95% c.i. for Y, we *add* the interval (.26) to the predicted value of Y (or,Y'). What is Y' (the predicted value of ZINTEX), given a value of -.813 for X (MODERN)? We estimate Y by the following linear regression model based on Table 16.2 to be:

$$Y' = \beta_0 + \beta_1(X_1), \text{ or } Y' = 0 + .709(-.813); \text{ or, } Y' = -.576$$

Formula 17.4

So, the upper limit and lower of the 95% c.i. for the mean expected value of Y at the -.813 MODERN level would be -.314 and -.839, respectively (rounding causes the slight variation between the intervals produced in SPSS 10 and reported in CROSSNAT.50, and those reported below). These are determined in the following manner:

Upper limit (95% c.i.) for the mean expected value of Y = Y' + c.i.; or, -.576 + .261 ≈ -.314

Lower limit (95% c.i.) for mean expected value of Y = Y' – c.i.; or, -.576 – .261 ≈ -.839

From these simple computations, we conclude that for countries with values of MODERN equal to -.813, 95 times out of 100 (or, in 95 percent of repeated samples of populous countries) our computed 95% c.i. intervals (-.314 – -.839) will include the target population's true mean of ZINTEX at that level of MODERN. There is a 5 percent chance that this interval range does not include the target population's true mean of ZINTEX at that level of MODERN.

If we were to repeat this computation for all possible values of X along the slope shown in Figure 17.1, we would have a continuous band of upper and lower limits relative to each possible value of X running roughly parallel to the slope. These are shown in Figure 17.1. Note that we expect much less error when we are predicting the typical

TABLE 17.1 Residual Analysis, ZINTEX by MODERN

	Scores			*Residuals*		*Prediction Intervals*			
COUNTRY	*ZINTEX*	*MODERN*	*PZINTEX*	*RZINTEX*	*ZRZINTEX*	*95% c.i. Lower*	*95% c.i. Upper*	*95% p.i. Lower*	*95% p.i. Upper*
Algeria	-1.261	-0.936	-0.664	-0.597	-0.838	-0.943	-0.385	-2.123	0.796
Argentina	-0.069	0.721	0.511	-0.580	-0.814	0.261	0.762	-0.943	1.966
Australia	1.107	1.970	1.396	-0.289	-0.405	0.945	1.848	-0.106	2.899
Bangladesh	0.156	-1.316	-0.933	1.089	1.528	-1.270	-0.596	-2.405	0.539
Brazil	-0.313	0.144	0.102	-0.415	-0.583	-0.103	0.307	-1.345	1.550
Canada	1.223	2.018	1.430	-0.207	-0.291	0.970	1.890	-0.075	2.935
Chile	0.898	0.678	0.480	0.418	0.586	0.235	0.726	-0.974	1.934
China	0.323	-0.789	-0.559	0.883	1.238	-0.818	-0.300	-2.016	0.897
Colombia	0.222	0.517	0.366	-0.144	-0.202	0.138	0.595	-1.085	1.817
Congo	-1.744	-1.188	-0.842	-0.902	-1.266	-1.159	-0.526	-2.31	0.625
Czech	1.306	0.500	0.354	0.952	1.336	0.127	0.581	-1.097	1.805
Ecuador	0.287	0.18	0.127	0.16	0.225	-0.079	0.333	-1.32	1.575
Egypt	-1.875	-0.496	-0.351	-1.524	-2.139	-0.578	-0.125	-1.802	1.100
France	1.204	1.163	0.824	0.380	0.534	0.511	1.137	-0.643	2.291
Germany	1.181	1.209	0.857	0.324	0.455	0.537	1.177	-0.611	2.325
Ghana	0.025	-0.988	-0.701	0.726	1.018	-0.987	-0.414	-2.162	0.761
Greece	0.928	0.681	0.483	0.446	0.625	0.237	0.729	-0.971	1.937
India	-1.668	-1.121	-0.795	-0.873	-1.225	-1.101	-0.488	-2.26	0.671
Indonesia	0.144	-0.670	-0.475	0.619	0.868	-0.719	-0.23	-1.929	0.979
Iran	-1.208	-1.108	-0.785	-0.423	-0.593	-1.089	-0.481	-2.25	0.680
Italy	1.165	0.908	0.644	0.521	0.731	0.369	0.919	-0.815	2.103
Japan	0.791	0.935	0.662	0.128	0.180	0.384	0.941	-0.797	2.122
Kenya	-0.198	-0.894	-0.634	0.436	0.612	-0.907	-0.361	-2.093	0.825
Korea	-0.592	0.729	0.516	-1.108	-1.555	0.265	0.768	-0.939	1.971
Madagascar	-1.929	-1.133	-0.803	-1.126	-1.580	-1.111	-0.495	-2.269	0.663
Malaysia	0.129	-0.113	-0.08	0.209	0.293	-0.284	0.124	-1.528	1.367
Mexico	0.829	0.538	0.382	0.447	0.628	0.151	0.612	-1.070	1.833
Morocco	-0.892	-0.483	-0.342	-0.55	-0.772	-0.568	-0.117	-1.7930	1.108
Nepal	-0.058	-1.291	-0.915	0.857	1.203	-1.248	-0.582	-2.386	0.556
Netherlands	1.285	1.674	1.186	0.099	0.139	0.788	1.585	-0.301	2.674
Nigeria	-1.810	-1.771	-1.255	-0.555	-0.779	-1.670	-0.840	-2.747	0.237
Pakistan	-1.121	-1.070	-0.758	-0.363	-0.509	-1.057	-0.460	-2.222	0.705
Peru	0.220	0.337	0.239	-0.018	-0.026	0.025	0.453	-1.21	1.688
Philippines	0.511	0.095	0.067	0.443	0.622	-0.136	0.271	-1.38	1.515
Poland	-1.104	0.385	0.273	-1.377	-1.932	0.056	0.491	-1.176	1.723
Romania	0.223	-0.261	-0.185	0.407	0.572	-0.395	0.025	-1.633	1.263
Russia	0.270	0.531	0.376	-0.107	-0.150	0.146	0.606	-1.075	1.828
South Africa	0.669	0.402	0.285	0.384	0.539	0.066	0.504	-1.164	1.735
Spain	1.191	0.508	0.360	0.831	1.166	0.132	0.588	-1.091	1.811
Sri Lanka	-0.585	-0.813	-0.576	-0.009	-0.012	-0.839	-0.314	-2.033	0.880
Tanzania	-0.206	-1.597	-1.132	0.926	1.300	-1.517	-0.747	-2.616	0.352
Thailand	0.209	-0.442	-0.314	0.523	0.734	-0.536	-0.092	-1.764	1.136
Tunisia	-1.354	-0.378	-0.268	-1.086	-1.524	-0.485	-0.051	-1.717	1.181
Turkey	1.106	-0.007	-0.005	1.111	1.559	-0.208	0.198	-1.452	1.442
Uganda	-0.499	-1.64	-1.162	0.663	0.930	-1.554	-0.77	-2.648	0.323
Ukraine	0.386	0.261	0.185	0.201	0.282	-0.025	0.394	-1.264	1.633
United Kingdom	1.220	1.463	1.037	0.183	0.257	0.675	1.398	-0.441	2.515
United States	0.774	1.969	1.396	-0.622	-0.872	0.944	1.847	-0.107	2.898
Venezuela	0.453	0.477	0.338	0.115	0.162	0.113	0.563	-1.113	1.788
Zimbabwe	-1.952	-0.484	-0.343	-1.608	-2.257	-0.569	-0.118	-1.794	1.107

value of Y for scores at or near the mean value of X in our sample. This is only logical: The best predictor of the mean of Y will be the mean of X. Therefore, the bands for the 95% c.i. close to their narrowest point at that point along the slope where the mean ofY and the mean of X intersect.

Computation of Prediction Intervals for Individual Scores. The formula for computing the 95 percent prediction interval for individual scores is:

$$95\%p.i. = t(SSE)\sqrt{1+\frac{1}{N}+\frac{(X_i-\bar{X})^2}{S_{xx}}}$$ Formula 17.5

where t represents the t value for the .05 threshold at n degrees of freedom, and the remaining terms are identical to those in Formula 17.1. The difference between Formula 17.5 and 17.1 is the greater range of variance specified in the square root term of the formula. This is represented by the value 1 preceding 1/N.

Returning to our example of Sri Lanka and Table 17.1, we can solve for the interval of the 95% p.i. of Y':

$$95\%c.i. = (2.0)(.713)\sqrt{1+\frac{1}{50}+\frac{(-.813-0)^2}{49}} = 1.426\sqrt{1.02+\frac{.0135}{49}} = 1.426\sqrt{(1.02+.005)} = 1.426\sqrt{1.025} = 1.426(1.034); \approx 1.450$$

Formula 17.6

With an interval of approximately 1.450 established for our 95% p.i. limits, we may then state that our lower and upper limits for the 95% p.i. of Y' for Sri Lanka (Y' = -.576; X = -.813) are (rounding causes the slight variation between the intervals produced in SPSS 10 and reported in CROSSNAT.50, and those reported below):

Upper limit for the 95% p.i. Y′ = -.576 + 1.450 ≈ .880

Lower limit for the 95% p.i. Y′ = -.576 – 1.450 ≈ –2.033

Therefore, given a value of .45 for MODERN in a particular country (for example, Sri Lanka), we conclude that 95 percent of the time we may expect the *actual* value (the target population's value) of ZINTEX to fall between the values of .880 and –2.033. This range is, as expected, much larger than the 95% c.i. range for the mean expected value of Y.

Applying Confidence Intervals of Mean Expected Value of Y. What are the practical implications of the confidence and prediction intervals for cross-national analysis? Both intervals allow us to refine our use of error in regression analysis, and from this, to provide more detailed information from which comparisons can be made between either individual or groups of countries. Yet, both provide an empirical context within which we can draw relevant comparisons across our sample of countries.

The practical utility of confidence intervals of the mean expected value of Y (Y') is as an estimate of what the *typical* score will be for Y at X_i, which is in effect estimating the *mean value* of ZINTEX for countries in the target population that have a particular level of MODERN. If, for instance, we note that a particular country, with a particular level of MODERN, has an *actual* value of ZINTEX that is *within* the lower and upper limits of the 95 percent confidence interval for that particular level of MODERN, we may conclude with reasonable confidence that this country is within the range of the typical, and therefore expected, value of ZINTEX, given its level of MODERN. This may not sound very important, but it allows us to confirm that nothing out of the ordinary seems to distinguish this country with regard to the attribute of ZINTEX *from what we would expect for the typical country with that level of MODERN*. In other words, this particular hypothetical country may have a *typical* degree of domestic economic internationalization for all countries in the target population that possess a similar degree of *modernity*.

On the other hand, suppose that another hypothetical country had an actual value of ZINTEX that was *outside* either the upper or lower limits for the 95 percent confidence intervals, at that level for MODERN. It would suggest that given its level of MODERN, that country is distinguished by an "atypical" level of ZINTEX (either higher or lower, depending upon whether it was beyond the upper or lower 95% c.i.). In other words, this particular country would be characterized by a larger (or smaller) degree of domestic economic internationalization than for the typical country at the same level of *modernism*. This might compel one to ask the obvious question of, why? This, consequently, will direct our attention toward refining our theory linking ZINTEX and MODERN—the central process of general theory building in comparative politics.

Using Interval Estimates (95% c.i.) to Cross-Nationally Compare ZINTEX with Respect to MODERN

Let us look more closely at the data from our test of Hypothesis 16.1, as graphically represented in Figure 17.1. Consider the two extreme cases in Table 17.1 and Figure 17.1: Turkey and Zimbabwe. Turkey's ZINTEX value is 1.106, its predicted value (PZINTEX in CROSSNAT.50) is -.005. The residual for Turkey is 1.111 (RZINTEX in CROSSNAT.50, with a standardized value of 1.559 ZRZINTEX in CROSSNAT.50). The standardized residual value is simply the z-score for the residual. As with all z-scores, this is simply a standardized scale and eases comparative analysis. Thus, we see that Turkey has the largest residual in the sample. The exact computation for standardized residuals is explained below (see Formula 17.7). Turkey's actual value of ZINTEX is much larger than its predicted value, given its level of modernity (MODERN = -.007). At the other extreme is Zimbabwe, with a ZINTEX value of –1.952, a MODERN value of -.484. Table 17.2 presents the prediction profiles of each of these two countries based on their respective degrees of modernity and economic openness.

We see from Table 17.1 that Turkey's upper 95% c.i. is .198, and its lower 95% c.i. is -.208. Thus, we would expect that most of the time (95 times out of 100, to be sure), the mean expected value of ZINTEX for all countries at Turkey's recorded level

TABLE 17.2 Residual Analysis, Turkey and Zimbabwe

Country	*ZINTEX* *Degree of International Exchange*	*MODERN* *Degree of Modernity*	*PZINTEX* *Predicted Value of ZINTEX*	*RZINTEX* *Residual Value of ZINTEX*	*ZRZINTEX* *Standardized Value of Residual Value of ZINTEX*
Turkey	1.106	-.007	-.005	1.111	1.554
Zimbabwe	-1.952	-.484	-.343	-1.608	-2.257

of modernity would fall between the values of .198 and -.208. Yet, Turkey's measured level of economic openness is 1.106, which is nearly five times larger than the degree of economic openness one would expect for the *typical* country at that level of modernity. A "moderately" modern society (recall a z-score near 0 signifies a mean value within the sample), Turkey nonetheless stands far apart from the "typical" moderately modern economy: It is relatively far more open to trade and international exchange. An examination of Figure 16.1 would certainly suggest that Turkey's degree of international economic exchange is much higher than expected. Yet, a more detailed residual analysis affords us a more telling and potentially significant piece of information about Turkey. The degree to which Turkey is integrated with its international environment through commercial and financial exchange is more than what one would expect. Rather, *it is far more than one would expect for the typical country at Turkey's level of modernity*. Thus, we have confirmation that Turkey is not merely different (because it has a higher degree of international economic exchange than expected). It is also significantly different from the average country at Turkey's level of modernity. Obviously, something makes Turkey stand apart from its "genre" of nation-states. Zimbabwe lies far below the lower range for the 95% c.i. interval (-.118). Indeed, it is approximately nineteen times *less* integrated with its international economic environment than would be predicted given its relatively traditional society. Obviously, these are estimates that are relative to an abstract target population. Nonetheless, they provide a powerful comparative basis from which to gauge the *relative* degree of the openness characterizing Turkey's and Zimbabwe's domestic economies.

A simple univariate analysis would not have allowed this refinement of our comparison between the two economies. Differences in political behavior or institutional authority patterns across Turkey and Zimbabwe that we might attribute to different levels of ZINTEX might, without further analysis, mislead the researcher if too much is made of the initial conclusion that the two countries have little in common with regard to the nature of their respective exposure to the international financial and economic situation. These two countries share more in common than we imagine: They both have significantly different degrees of open (or closed) economies than either of their levels of "modernism" would predict.

Let us briefly consider two different examples: Italy and Japan. Both are democratic countries, and both are among the most affluent and influential countries of the world.

Both countries, for instance, are members of the elite and powerful G-7—the seven wealthiest democracies of the world. Both countries have similar modernity levels. Yet, Italy is technically more integrated with its international economic environment—nearly a third more open to its international environment than Japan (as of 1997). Both countries have larger than expected degrees of international economic integration, yet the residual for Italy (RZINTEX = .521) is four times as large as that for Japan (RZINTEX = .128). Indeed, Italy's residual for ZINTEX is larger than approximately 76 percent of the target population, while Japan's exceeds approximately 58 percent of countries in the target population. (See Table 17.3.)

The 95% c.i. upper and lower bounds for all countries at Italy's level of modernity are .369 – .919; those for all countries at Japan's level of modernity are .384 – .941. Japan, while having a larger degree of international economic integration than would be predicted given its level of modernity is, nonetheless, not much different than the typical country with similar degrees of modernity. The degree of Japan's economic openness toward its international environment is close to what one would expect for a typical country at Japan's level of modernity. On the other hand, Italy, while very similar to Japan's level of modernity, has not only a larger degree of economic openness to its international environment than would be expected given its level of modernity, but, more important and revealing, Italy's degree of international financial and commercial exchange is much larger than would be expected for the *typical* country of Italy's degree of modernity. From the slope in Figure 17.1, we see that Japan is more open to the international economy than one would expect, based on its level of modernity. It is, however, not much different than the *typical* country at that level of modernity. While we would conclude from a standard regression and scatterplot (as in Figure 16.1) that Italy is much more open to the international economy than one would expect from a standard scatterplot, we would not be able to more fully assess Italy's degree of departure from the expected. The residual analysis demonstrates that Italy is also much more open than one would except of the *typical* country at its comparable level of modernity. *Italy is somewhat of an outlier for modern countries—its domestic economy is much more open to international trade and exchange than countries at its level of modernity.* It is more open than predicted (the size of its residual tells us this), and this degree of openness is larger than we should expect of the typical country at Italy's level of modernity.

Each of these examples offers the researcher interesting and potentially important clues as to why some countries exhibit economies more closely integrated with the international system of commercial and financial intercourse than other countries. We would know from a simple univariate analysis that they exhibit interesting differences amongst themselves with respect to the openness of their economies (that is, a univariate analysis of ZINTEX). Our analysis of their 95 % c.i. for the mean expected value of ZINTEX exposes the additional and potentially telling information that they differ as well from other countries within similar ranges of *modernity*. We have seen in Chapter

TABLE 17.3 Residual Analysis, Italy and Japan

Country	*ZINTEX* *Degree of International Exchange*	*MODERN* *Degree of Modernity*	*PZINTEX* *Predicted Value of ZINTEX*	*RZINTEX* *Residual Value of ZINTEX*	*ZRZINTEX* *Standardized Value of Residual Value of ZINTEX*
Italy	1.165	.908	.644	.521	.731
Japan	.791	.935	.662	.128	.180

12 that the application ANOVA and subsequent residual analysis within the box-plots associated with ANOVA can produce similar revelations. The critical difference is that ANOVA requires us to step down the scale of measurement, while regression preserves the greater accuracy and precision associated with interval/ratio measures.

Using Prediction Intervals in Cross-National Analysis

Just because a country, such as Italy, lies above the mean predicted level of ZINTEX for the target population of countries with Italy's level of MODERN, it does not necessarily indicate that Italy's particular value of ZINTEX is significantly far removed from what one would expect of an *individual* country at Italy's level of *modernity*. In other words, we know Italy has a domestic economy that is more open than the *typical* country at Italy's level of modernity. However, this is not the same as saying Italy is in fact significantly different than the *typical* country at that level of modernity. Remember, the mean expected value of ZINTEX is our best estimate of the true typical value of ZINTEX at a specified level of the independent variable (MODERN). As such, any given *individual* country at that level of MODERN will have a chance to fall near (above or below) the mean, but not all (or possibly, any) will necessarily fall at precisely the mean. Means do not, as we have seen, represent individual scores—they represent the best estimate of the *typical* score after taking into account the variance of all the *individual* scores in a sample. Hypothetically, as we move from one new sample of countries at a specific level of MODERN to the next, there will be differences not only in the mean of the sample (reflected by the confidence intervals for the mean expected value of Y), but accordingly there will be different variability from sample to sample with respect to individual countries' placement relative to the mean at that level of MODERN. In this sense, the prediction interval (95% p.i.) provides a different answer to the question: *If a country is not typical, just how different is it from the typical country at that level of traditionalism; is it within the normal range of scores for ZINTEX?*

As we have seen, the prediction interval incorporates two variance measures, one for the variance of the means across the hypothetical samples and the second for the variance of the countries about each mean. The practical implication of this distinction is that a country falling beyond the mean expected value of the dependent variable for that level of the independent variable may still not be significantly different from other individual scores within the target population of countries at X_i. Why? Because the variability of the individual countries about the respective means of the different samples might be so dispersed as to render an individual's score relatively "normal." And what would constitute a relatively "normal" individual score? As we have seen in Chapter 4, such a score would fall *within* two standard deviations of the mean of all the individual scores at that level of the independent variable (X_i). Of course, outlier residuals increase residual error, and as such, increase the standard error estimate (SEE). This, in turn, reduces the explained variance and weakens the model's efficiency. Therefore, the stronger the overall relationship in a simple regression model and scatterplot (that is, the larger the correlation coefficient and coefficient of determination), the less likely one will find a residual beyond the 95% p.i. upper or lower bounds.

Examining Figure 17.1, we see that only two countries—Egypt and Zimbabwe—fall below *both* the 95% c.i. and the 95% p.i. Following Formula 17.3 we know that at Egypt's level of modernity, the lower boundary for the 95% p.i. is –1.802, and Zimbabwe's is –1.794. Yet, Egypt's actual value for ZINTEX is –1.875 and Zimbabwe's is –1.952. The economies of these two countries are not only much less open than the *typical* country is expected to be at that level of *modernity,* they are also atypical for virtually *any* particular country. Thus, they may be characterized as both statistically "non-typical" (because they lie beyond the lower 95% c.i. boundary) and "non-normal" (because they also lie beyond the lower 95% p.i. boundary) with respect to the exposure of their economies to international finance and commerce for countries with their respective levels of *modernity*. These two countries are extreme outliers. Again, residual analysis helps us make a further distinction between countries and in so doing, allows us to single out those cases that require further individual attention.

The cases of Egypt and Zimbabwe are in sharp contrast with that of Italy. We saw that Italy was shown to have a slightly more open economy than the model graphically displayed in Figure 17.1 predicted and that the degree of openness in the Italian economy was in fact larger than the *typical* country at the Italian level of modernity. However, the degree of Italy's integration in the international economy cannot be characterized as beyond the normal range of scores for a country with Italy's level of modernity. The upper boundary of the 95% p.i. for Italy is 2.103, yet Italy's value for ZINTEX is 1.165, well below the range for that of an extreme outlier.

The Relation of Confidence Intervals and Prediction Intervals to Residuals

Which, then, is more important: the confidence interval of the mean expected value of Y or the prediction interval of the individual score? That depends entirely upon the question we are asking, and the answer we feel to be more pertinent within the context of our hypothesis test and our theory. It depends, in other words, on our judgment as to what is worth noting and what is worth further exploration and investigation. And that depends on the theoretical questions that drive our hypothesis in the first place.

Conventionally, the prediction interval of the individual score is used more than the confidence interval of the mean expected value of Y in social science research; the prediction interval is generally more important and pertinent to know if a country is an "outlier" (that is, both "non-typical" and "non-normal") than if a country is only "non-typical." Assuming that the residuals in a scatterplot are in fact normally distributed *at any given level of the independent variable*, the 95% p.i. is roughly equivalent to the ±2.0 standardized deviation threshold for residuals in the sample. Recall that the residual is the difference between the *expected* value of Y and the *observed* value of Y for a particular country (ignoring confidence intervals and prediction intervals). In the case of Brazil, the observed value of ZINTEX is -.313, and its predicted, and therefore expected, value of ZINTEX based on the regression equation derived from the test of Hypothesis 10.1 is .102. The difference between the observed and the predicted value of Brazil's ZINTEX value is -.415 (that is, -.313 – .102) = -.415). We cannot know, of course, if this residual is large or small relative either to those countries of similar size MODERN (the 95% p.i.), or to the forty-nine other residuals in the sample as a whole.

We can (and should), however, convert the residual to a *standardized value*. To do so, we subtract the residual from the mean value of the residuals in the sample and divide by the standard error of estimate (SSE) from the regression analysis. Because the mean of residuals is always 0, the equation reduces to the residual over the SSE, as shown in Equation 17.7:

$$ZRESID = \frac{RESID - \bar{X}}{SSE} = \frac{RESID}{SSE} \qquad \text{Formula 17.7}$$

The SSE is our best estimate of the standard deviation of the Y variable at any value of the X variable. Note here the similarity of the standardized residuals and both the confidence and prediction intervals: they all rely on the SSE for the final estimate of the standardized error in the regression model. The SSE, recall, is the standard deviation of residuals in the regression analysis. Table 17.1 contains the standardized residuals for each country in the sample.

For example, the standardized residual (ZRZINTEX) for Brazil is -.583 (–.415/.713). We already know that when we standardize a score, we are converting the value to a scale that allows us to compare the position of the score relative to a standard area under the curve. So, a standardized residual of ±1.96 (or, 2.0) would indicate a country whose residual was larger or smaller than 95 percent of the target population (assuming something approximating a normal distribution to the residuals). Assuming a normal distribution to the residuals, any residual that is ±2.0 standard deviations from the mean of the residuals will also be beyond the upper or lower 95%

p.i. interval. The prediction interval captures both the variance associated with the mean expected value of Y and the variance of individual cases about the mean estimates of Y in repeated samples. Therefore, the prediction intervals are more powerful measures of error than confidence intervals, all else being equal. To identify an *outlier* residual—that is, a country that is *both* statistically "atypical" and "non-normal"—you may either convert the residuals to standard values or you may compute the 95% p.i. and compare the value of a country's independent variable to the 95% p.i. limits.

A major residual outlier in a regression analysis will have a standardized residual that is at least ±2.0 (or, ±1.96, to be exact) in value; it will also have a value of Y that falls at or beyond the 95% p.i. interval for the sample. In this sense, the practical utility of using the prediction interval, and the standardized residual values, lies in the ease by which we can identify major residual outliers in our model. And outliers, as we know, are crucial from both a technical perspective in our analysis (they may, as we have seen in previous chapters, distort the validity and credibility of our hypothesis tests) and a substantive perspective (they allow us to spot those countries that are quite different from other countries in the sample and from what the model would expect of them relative to the attributes captured in the dependent variable).

The Respective Substantive Practicality of Confidence and Prediction Intervals

If it cannot identify a "major" residual outlier, what, then, is the practical utility of computing the confidence interval of the mean expected value of Y? The confidence interval focuses attention not on the individual case (relative to other countries), but instead concentrates attention on the difference of the individual country from the abstract "typical" country at a specific level of the independent variable. It narrows the focus to that unique "family" of countries of which the individual country is part (that is, countries that all have, in theory, identical levels of the independent variable). For instance, it is important to know that Italy and France have much higher levels of internationalized economies than other countries within their respective families (those countries with identical levels of *modernity*). They are not "major residual outliers" within their target population; neither country falls beyond the upper limit of the 95% p.i.

As such, it is incorrect to conclude that these two countries are in some way quite different from other countries in general, given our model. Nonetheless, they are distinctive within their respective "families" of countries because they have opened their economies to the pressures and uncertainties of the international economy to a notably greater extent than would be reasonably expected of other countries within their "family" (those countries in the target population at their level of "modernism"). We might ask then "What characterizes these two countries that sets them apart from their 'family'; and, why have they apparently opted for a more internationalized economy than we would reasonably expect of others within that 'family'?" If we focused only upon major outliers, we would have missed this potentially crucial evidence with respect to France and Italy because neither country is a "major residual outlier."

In sum, it is often important to know that the individual country is significantly different from what we expect of the "typical" country at that level of the independent variable (that is, why is that country different from its "family" of countries, where "family" merely defines countries of identical attributes measured by the independent variable). It is in this context that the confidence interval can be a very useful statistic to report. If, on the other hand, you are not interested in this level of comparison, and would rather limit your focus to a comparison of countries in general (not relative to any "family" of countries at a given level of the independent variable), then the confidence interval is less critical than the standardized residuals.[3]

As a rule of thumb, any country that is at least ±1.0 standard deviations from the mean will also be a country (or case) that is likely to fall outside the 95% c.i. range for the mean expected value of Y. (However, not all countries that fall outside the bands of the 95% c.i. will have standardized residuals at or beyond ±1.0.) Therefore, by computing the standardized residuals, you can effectively "flag" for closer scrutiny those countries in your sample that are not necessarily outliers, but are "non-typical." There is no rule, no right or wrong choice in your decision with respect to whether to focus on "non-typical" countries as well as "outliers." There is only your judgment, based on your theory and your knowledge of the substantive question at hand of what is most useful to your hypothesis test, and the tools of the statistical procedure that can provide you with the evidence you may need.

Interval Estimates and Measurement Validity

Finally, one of the most useful purposes of residual analysis and the application of interval estimates is confirmation of measurement validity. While content and construct validity may not be directly evaluated through residual analysis alone, it is very useful in assessing face validity of the measures. By observing the alignment of the country residuals in a scatterplot, and by going the extra step by computing the interval estimates, the student is provided with needed detail when comparing the agreement between what the consensus might expect and what the data reveal, with respect to individual countries in a bivariate model.

Table 17.4 summarizes the differences between the confidence intervals and prediction intervals used within regression analysis.

DEMONSTRATION 17.1: RESIDUAL ANALYSIS, THEORY REFINEMENT, AND SUBSEQUENT HYPOTHESIS TESTING

To help review these components of a basic regression analysis and demonstrate their utility to theory building in cross-national analysis, we will explore one more hypothe-

TABLE 17.4 Applying Interval Estimates in Systematic Examination of Residual Error in Cross-National Analysis

Respective Interval Estimate for Predictions	*Logic of Respective Interval Estimate*	*Utility of Computed Interval Estimate*
Confidence Interval (95%): (95% c.i). Compares Y_i to mean expected value of Y at X_i. Computes the estimate for the typical value of Y at X.	Estimates the interval, or range, within which the mean value of Y at corresponding value of X_i will fall. Estimates the range at value X within which you can be confident that 95 times out of 100 the typical value of Y_i will fall. Confidence band is what we expect mean expected value of Y at X to be 95 times out of 100 repeated samples. Based on standard error of estimate for mean Y, at X.	Allows assessment of degree to which Y_i (with value X) deviates from typical expected value of Y for all countries with value X. Answers this question: Does the value of Y, for Country i with value X, deviate from the typically expected value of Y at X, when "typical" is defined as the range of scores between which we can be confident that 95 times out of 100 the target population's mean value of Y will be for all countries with value X? Countries with values of Y beyond 95% c.i. band width are "atypical," for target population, with respect to Y at value X.
Prediction Interval (95%): (95% p.i.) Compares Y' to Y_i at X_i. Computes the estimates for the value of Y for a particular country with value X.	Estimates the interval, or range, of values for a particular score of Y at X within which we would expect the actual value of Y in sample to be given a specific value of X_i. Computes the expected value of Y for a *particular country* with value X. Estimates the range of values within which we can be confident that 95 times out of 100 a country with value X will have value Y. Confidence band is what we expect Y_i at X to be 95 times out of 100 repeated samples. Based on standard error of estimate for mean Y at X, *and* standard error of estimate, at X.	Allows assessment of degree to which Y_i deviates from what we expect given value of X_1. Answers this question: Does the value of Y, for Country i with value X, deviate significantly from what we would expect for a country with value X, when typical is defined as the range of scores between which we can be confident that 95 times out of 100 the target population's value of Y will be for all countries with value X? Countries with values of Y beyond 95% p.i. band width are "major" residual outliers, as well as "atypical" for target population, with respect to Y at value X.

sis that builds further upon the general phenomena of modernity within the changing nature of the political and economic environment of countries during an era of sharp "globalization." In this section, we will elaborate the use of residual analysis with simple regression to illustrate how residuals may be used not merely to identify individual countries that deviate from the cross-national pattern, but to discern broader cross-national patterns and from this, to move toward theory refinement and additional hypothesis testing. We begin by revisiting the relationship between two of the most important concepts for students of cross-national analysis, *modernity* and *democracy*. Let us return for moment to our proposed relationship between democratic political empowerment (POLEMPOW) and modernity (MODERN) specified in Chapter 15.

Modernity and Market Liberalization. In Chapter 15, we explored the relationship between modernity (MODERN) and democracy (POLEMPOW). Our theory holds that modernity opens the doorway to increased demand for democracy. Democracy, in turn, more effectively utilizes and rewards the attributes of modernity. Simply put, it would be difficult to imagine relatively higher levels of modernity within a country's culture when democratic empowerment is sharply restricted. As we will see, however, this "imbalance" does occur, and, importantly, it can occur in ways we may not have imagined without the more careful use of residual analysis and regression. As well, we will see that this imbalance carries with it consequences for society that tend to be most detrimental to the poorest nations of the world and most severe for the poorest segments among the populations of these countries.

Nonetheless, modernity, in essence, entails a degree of openness within the domestic economy, as well as mobilization of people and resources and a distinctive reliance upon and production of information-based industries. As a network of various social changes, modernity presumably responds to something very basic and, in so doing, places pressures on the barriers of political restrictions that serve to support the more traditional culture. The scatterplot analysis in Chapter 15 confirms this logic (see Figure 15.9).

Our theory, as elaborated in Chapter 15, holds that modernity was the operative force of change; it modifies the nature of political authority. In other words, *modernity* was the independent variable in our model, and *democratic political empowerment* was the dependent concept. Yet, we also know that traditionalism is associated with resistance to change; it represents a cultural preference for a stable, predictable, and secure political and economic environment. Stability, predictability, and security in traditional societies are valued more than risk, competition, innovation, and opportunity. It would seem reasonable therefore that a refinement to our theory and measurement might be in order if we wish to capture the logic of a fundamental social force working to establish the necessary foundations for modernity. It would also seem likely that the source of this social force extends beyond merely adding more political rights and civil liberties to those already available to citizens, but requires that we consider wider implications for social organization and cooperation within society.

We may begin by reviewing the core logic of the spirit of modernity. It entails transforming the way we transact with authority in society. Authority in modern societies must be increasingly demonstrated and proven; ascription and custom cannot well serve the need to innovate and mobilize society's resources. Thus, modernity requires minimal restrictions to the access and distribution of information which in turn, all things being equal, assumes an environment open and supportive for the consequent nature of social transformation—transformations that require rational and accountable authority.

While political empowerment would certainly be a necessary partner in this process, one other element is required before one can assume that the latticework of advanced education, information technology, professional and technical service-based labor markets, and urban-based social mobilization assume distinctive proportions within society. Most students of comparative political and economic development suggest that this additional necessary attribute is a liberal political economy. Liberal political economies, as we have implied in Chapter 11, are characterized by competitive and open economic *and* political markets. Liberal societies imply that *both* the political subsystem and the broader economic market subsystem are characterized by minimal restrictions to change and innovation.[4]

In liberal market systems, the authority of tradition is subject to continual testing and challenge and the rules that determine who plays within and which values can enter the respective arenas reflect an inclusive rather than an exclusive philosophy. We noted in Chapter 11 that what we now refer to as liberal economic markets are often simply referred to as free economies, where the economic markets are characterized by: (1) a reduced size of government in society, (2) open, competitive markets, (3) stable prices and monetary policy, (4) the freedom of citizens to use foreign currencies, (5) respect for property rights through strict rule of law, (6) the freedom of citizens and domestic corporations to trade with their foreign counterparts, and (7) the freedom of currency exchange markets.[5]

When liberal economic markets are combined with democratic political empowerment, the resulting effect is a powerful *liberalization* force within society. In such settings, both the political and economic subsystems are competitive and open. They open the gateway to change and innovation that, in effect, erodes traditionalism. On the other hand, when market authority is restricted and non-competitive, and political freedom reduced (thus denying the economic markets their necessary partner required in order to remove the obstacles to economic competition and freedom), the gateway to modernity is closed.

We have explored a similar concept in Chapter 14: *citizen autonomy*. However, it is not citizen autonomy, per se, that interests us here. Rather, it is a more restrictive and specialized aspect of society that concerns us. It is not the capacity of the citizen to partake in opportunities that drives modernity (though this is certainly an ally, as seen in Figure 15.10), but rather the compounding and compelling pressure of competition and pursuit of self-interest unrestricted by political or economic markets that must be isolated in our refined measure. This pressure emerges from liberalized political and economic markets.

Therefore, while Hypothesis 15.1 postulates political empowerment as a function of modernity, or a "Theory of Political Empowerment," we are positing here an alternative hypothesis. This hypothesis suggests modernity is a function of market liberalization, or a "Theory of Modernity." Figure 17.2 contrasts these two different approaches to conceptualizing the relationship between social change, democracy, and economic markets.

Devising a Measure of Liberalized Markets (LIBMARK). Following the logic of liberalized markets outlined above, we have constructed a more specialized measure of such political-economic market authority. The variable, LIBMARK, has been derived from a standard factor analysis (to review the logic and procedure of factor analysis, see Chapter 15) and captures the extended empirical attributes necessary in open, competitive, and free political and economic markets.

Using standard principal components factor analysis within SPSS 10, as in Chapter 15, we have computed the weighted index score for the degree of market liberalization within a country (as of 1997). The five variables included in the analysis are already familiar to you: (1) ZPARCOMP, (2) ZPARREG, (3) ZPOLIT97, (4) ZCIVIL97, and (5) ZECON97. The results of the data reduction procedure produced a single-factor dimension defining the degree of liberalized markets within a country LIBMARK. Table 17.5 reports the correlation coefficients and the resulting KMO statistic and Bartlett's sphericity test for the analysis: All indicate robust variance across the variables in the model. Each variable is at least moderately correlated with each other in the expected positive direction. Clearly, however, market freedom and political freedom have a fair degree of independence, as evidenced by the modest ranges of correlations between the four primary properties of democracy and ECON97.

The individual weighted contributions of each of the five variables to the index measure of LIBMARK are reported in Table 17.6. The factor coefficients indicate that the four component aspects of political empowerment play a substantial role in defining our derived measure of market liberalization (as each of these four measures is strongly correlated with the underlying concept of market liberalization). However, economic empowerment (ZECON97) is also strongly correlated (factor coefficient = .637) with the concept as well, and plays an independent and significant role in defining the measure, LIBMARK.

The values for LIBMARK are, of course, standardized scores (because they are factor scores), so the mean of the sample is 0 with a standard deviation of 1. Recall that we may interpret the factor scores in a very straightforward fashion: Countries with strong, positive scores have a much higher degree of market liberalization (LIBMARK). How do we know this? Because each variable is positively correlated with each of the other measures in the analysis (Table 17.5), and a positive factor score indi-

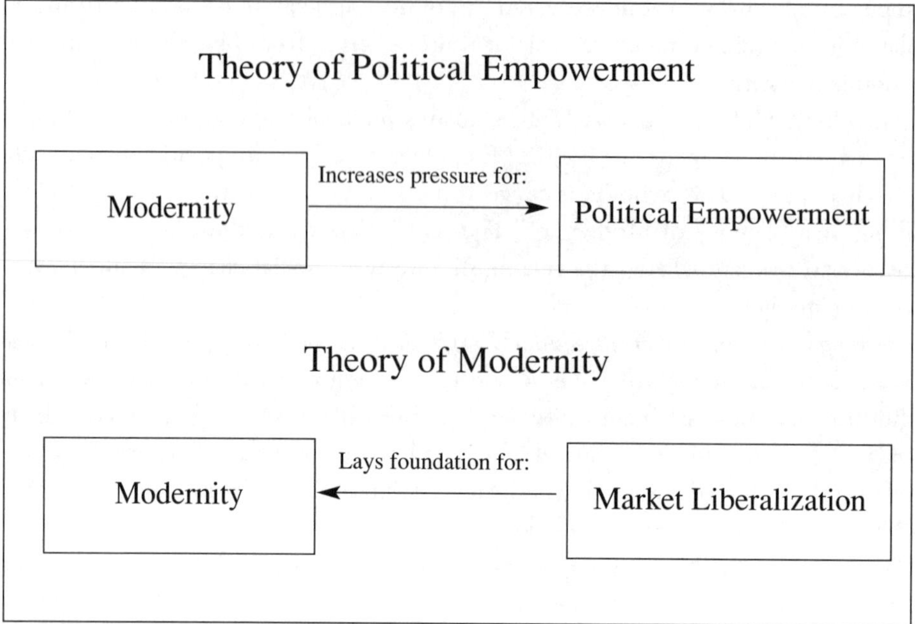

FIGURE 17.2 Alternative Conceptualization of the Bivariate Linkage Between Modernity, Democracy, and Market Liberalization

cates a strong presence of the underlying concept—LIBMARK—within the country. Thus, a strong, positive factor score reflects extensive political and economic empowerment. On the other hand, countries with strong, negative scores have authoritarian political systems and non-liberal markets. Countries that approach a value of 0 for LIBMARK have an indistinct mixture of political and economic empowerment. The maximum value is 1.455 (United States) and the minimum value is –2.130 (China). Table 17.7 reports the values for LIBMARK for each country, with the countries divided into two groups: those that have a score higher than the median value of LIBMARK (–.046), and those countries with a value above the median value for LIBMARK. A simple univariate analysis of LIBMARK confirms the variable does not severely deviate from a normal distribution, with a skewness of -.325 (Kolmogorov-Smirnov = .094, p = .200; Shapiro-Wilk's = .942, p = .030).

Are countries that are "more" liberalized (that is, with LIBMARK scores above –.046, as reported in Table 17.7), distinctively different with respect to the aspects of political and economic freedom and empowerment implied in our theory? We would, of course, assume so. However, to verify this, we have compared the mean values of each of the component aspects of the model, including a closer look at the measures for economic freedom (ECON97) used to compute our variable, LIBMARK. Table 17.8 reports the mean values of the seven individual components of economic freedom (drawn from *Economic Freedom of the World, 2000,* and included within CROSSNAT.50). In every case, except stable price and monetary policy (MON97) during the

TABLE 17.5 Pearson Correlation Coefficients, Primary Properties of Market Liberalization

Standardized Variables, Non-Redundant Matrix					
Variables	*ZCIVIL97 (N = 50)*	*ZPOLIT97 (N = 50)*	*ZPARREG (N = 50)*	*ZPARCOMP (N = 50)*	*ZECON97 (N = 50)*
ZCIVIL97		.912	.790	.868	.581
ZPOLIT97			.850	.875	.430
ZPARREG				.910	.456
ZPARCOMP					.525
ZECON97					

NOTE: All correlation coefficients are statistically significant at or beyond the .002 level ($p \leq .002$).
KMO Statistic = .782; Bartlett's Test of Sphericity, $X^2 = 269.6$, df = 10, p = .0001.

TABLE 17.6 Factor Loadings and Analysis of Variance from Factor Analysis of Primary Properties of Market Liberalization

Variables	*Factor Loadings: Market Liberalization*
CIVIL97 (The Scale of Liberal Democracy)	.946
POLIT97 (The Scale of Institutional Democracy)	.937
PARREG (The Scope of Liberal Democracy)	.920
PARCOMP (The Scope of Liberal Democracy)	.957
ECON97 (Economic Empowerment)	.637

One factor extracted (principal components)
Eigenvalue for *market liberalization* = 3.940 (78.807%)

decade of the 1990s, the market attributes of more liberalized countries were distinctly different from those of less liberalized countries, as of 1997. The variable LIBMARK2 is a dichotomous variable, with a score of 0 assigned to those countries whose LIBMARK value is less than the sample median (LIBMARK < -.046) and a score of 1 for those countries that have a value for LIBMARK greater than or equal to the sample median (LIBMARK ≥ -.046).

Table 17.9 reports the difference of means test for each of the four variables measuring the scale and scope of institutional and liberal democracy. As we would expect, each of these four components of political empowerment, which play such a strong role in market liberalization (and in the operational definition of LIBMARK), is significantly different across the two groups of countries that we have distinguished by their degree of market liberalization. The test confirms that more liberalized markets have significantly larger degrees of democracy than those countries that have less developed market liberalization.

TABLE 17.7 Market Liberalization (LIBMARK), Rank-Ordered and Grouped by Median Value (LIBMARK2)

Higher Market Liberalization (LIBMARK2 = 1; LIBMARK ≥ -.046)		*Lesser Market Liberalization (LIBMARK2 = 0; LIBMARK < -.046)*	
COUNTRY	*LIBMARK*	*COUNTRY*	*LIBMARK*
United States	1.455	Russia	-0.064
Australia	1.408	Nepal	-0.076
Canada	1.408	Madagascar	-0.121
Netherlands	1.396	India	-0.126
United Kingdom	1.296	Ukraine	-0.170
Japan	1.225	Bangladesh	-0.185
Spain	1.213	Peru	-0.237
Germany	1.202	Malaysia	-0.312
France	1.190	Sri Lanka	-0.347
Italy	1.178	Colombia	-0.389
Czech	1.084	Turkey	-0.418
Korea	0.988	Pakistan	-0.536
Greece	0.971	Morocco	-0.793
South Africa	0.694	Tanzania	-0.840
Chile	0.681	Tunisia	-0.877
Argentina	0.557	Kenya	-0.966
Poland	0.541	Egypt	-0.989
Philippines	0.498	Uganda	-1.112
Thailand	0.414	Algeria	-1.284
Venezuela	0.274	Indonesia	-1.488
Ecuador	0.272	Zimbabwe	-1.508
Romania	0.256	Congo	-1.553
Mexico	0.207	Iran	-1.923
Brazil	-0.005	Nigeria	-1.930
Ghana	-0.027	China	-2.130

K-S = .094 (p = .200)
S-W = .942 (p = .03)
sk = -.325
md = -.046

Initial Regression Analysis: Modernity by Liberalized Markets

Our refined theory is specified in Hypothesis 17.1:

Hypothesis 17.1: MODERN increases with LIBMARK across countries

Figure 17.3 reports the simple scatterplot of MODERN by LIBMARK. Table 17.10 presents the results of the simple linear regression analysis, taken from SPSS 10. The model accounts for 67 percent of the variance in MODERN (aR^2 = .665). We estimate that an increase by a factor of one standard deviation in LIBMARK from country to country will result in a corresponding increase in MODERN by a factor of .820

TABLE 17.8 Difference of Means Test, Components of Economic Freedom by Degree of Market Liberalization (LIBMARK2)

		Descriptive Statistics							
		Mean Value of Components of Economic Freedom (ECON97), as Devised by Fraser Institute By Degree of Market Liberalization (LIBMARK2)							
Countries Grouped According to Degree of Market Liberalization (LIBMARK2)	*Statistic*	*ECON97* *Economic Empowerment*	*GOVT97* *Size of Government*	*MON97* *Monetary Policy and Price Stability*	*MARK97* *Monetary Policy/ Price Stability*	*CURR97* *Freedom of Currency Exchange*	*PROP97* *Legal Structure and Security of Private Ownership*	*TRAD97* *Freedom to Trade with Foreigners*	*CAP97* *Freedom of Exchange in Capital Markets*
Lesser Market Liberalization (LIBMARK < -.046)	Mean	5.896	7.952	7.016	3.688	5.940	6.396	5.600	4.516
	N	25	25	25	25	25	25	25	25
	Std. Deviation	1.084	1.12	2.279	1.586	2.81	1.733	1.696	1.963
Greater Market Liberalization (LIBMARK > -.046)	Mean	7.580	6.936	7.640	5.74	9.040	8.652	7.608	7.240
	N	25	25	25	25	25	25	25	25
	Std. Deviation	1.09	1.402	2.779	1.695	1.693	1.378	0.979	2.02
Total Sample	Mean	6.738	7.444	7.328	4.714	7.490	7.524	6.604	5.878
	N	50	50	50	50	50	50	50	50
	Std. Deviation	1.372	1.357	2.535	1.927	2.779	1.923	1.705	2.404
		Test Statistics							
Difference of Means Test									
	t	5.476	2.830	.868	4.420	4.724	5.095	5.127	4.835
	p (1-tail, df = 1,48)	.000	.004	.195	.000	.000	.000	.000	.000

TABLE 17.9 Difference of Means Test, Components of Political Empowerment (POLEMPOW) by Degree of Market Liberalization (LIBMARK2)

		Descriptive Statistics				
		Mean Value of Components of Political Empowerment (POLEMPOW), by Degree of Market Liberalization (LIBMARK2)				
Countries Grouped According to Degree of Market Liberalization (LIBMARK2)	*Statistic*	*POLEMPOW Democratic Political Empowerment*	*CIVIL97 Scale of Liberal Democracy*	*POLIT97 Scope of Liberal Democracy*	*PARCOMP Scope of Institutional Democracy*	*PARREG Scale of Institutional Democracy*
Lesser Market Liberalization	Mean	-0.790	2.040	2.360	2.840	2.880
	N	25	25	25	25	25
	Std. Deviation	0.737	0.980	1.660	0.750	1.270
Greater Market Liberalization	Mean	0.790	4.720	5.360	4.480	4.520
	N	25	25	25	25	25
	Std. Deviation	0.445	0.840	0.810	0.590	0.510
Total Sample	Mean	0	3.380	3.860	3.660	3.700
	N	50	50	50	50	50
	Std. Deviation	1	1.630	1.990	1.060	1.270
			Test Statistics			
Difference of Means Test	t	9.170	10.380	8.139	8.644	5.996
	p	.000	.000	.000	.000	.000

TABLE 17.10 Regression Analysis, MODERN by LIBMARK, Linear Analysis

	R^2	aR^2	*Standard Error Estimate*	*N*	
Model Summary:	.820	.665	.579	50	
Source of Variance:	*Sum of Squares*	*df*	*Mean Square*	*F*	*Prob. F*
Model (Regression)	32.913	1	32.913	98.209	.000
Residual	16.087	48	.335		

Parameter Estimates:	*Coefficient (b) (Std. Err. of b)*	*β*	*95% c.i. (Lower - Upper)*	*t*	*Prob. t*
Intercept	0 (.082)		-.165 - .165	.000	1.000
LIBMARK	.820 (.083)	.820	.653 - .986	9.910	.000

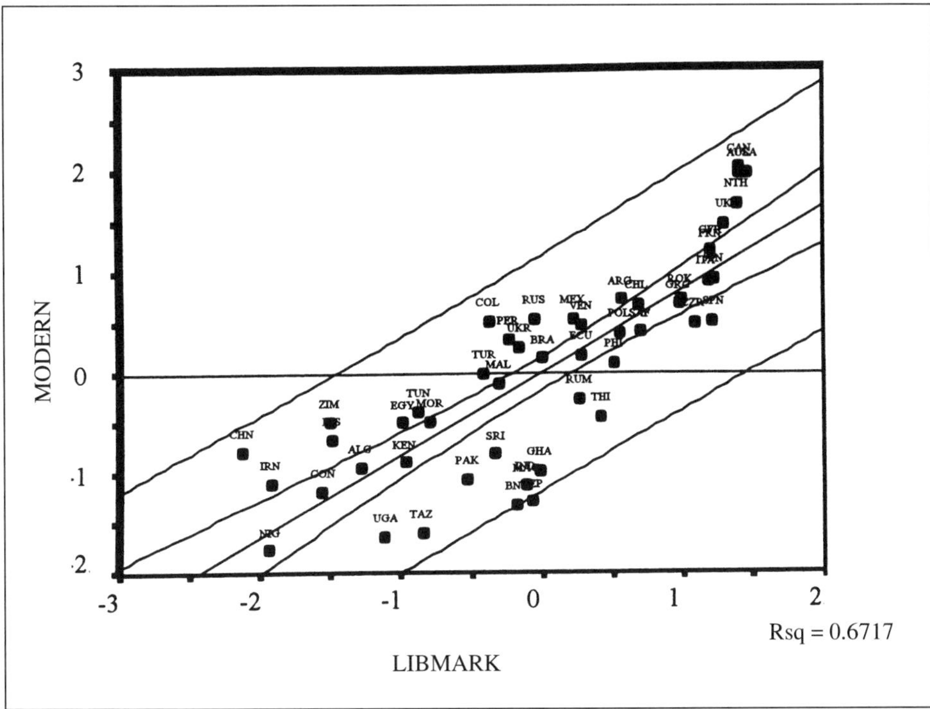

FIGURE 17.3 Scatterplot, MODERN by LIBMARK

standard deviations from country to country (β = .820, t = 9.910, p = .000). The model is statistically significant (F = 98.209, p = .000).

Note, however, that we cannot directly test the hypothesis that modernity increases *within* a country as liberalized markets grow *within* that country. We may imply this, but that particular hypothesis would require a time-series model that would connect changes in market liberalization to modernity *over time* within individual countries. Our data, and our model, are based on cross-sectional data (see Chapter 2). Thus, we can only say from our regression and scatterplot analyses that across countries, modernity is higher among countries with more liberalized markets. We draw a logical link between rising liberalization within a country and modernity, but we have not directly tested this and must be careful to avoid offering precise conclusions that are not based on the design from which the results of the analysis emerge.

Elaborating Hypothesis 17.1: A Curvilinear Model. As we know from Chapter 15, there is reason to suspect that as we move from countries that are relatively lacking in political and economic freedom to those with moderate levels of liberalized markets and pluralist societies, we are also likely to observe a drop-off in the degree of modernity, to be followed by sharply increasing degrees of modernity in those countries that have achieved much higher degrees of liberalized political and economic markets. To test for the possibility of this nonlinear relationship, we have executed a simple second-order polynomial regression (a simple curvilinear scatterplot—see Chapter 15 for a review of the logic of a simple curvilinear model).

Figure 17.4 reports the graphic results of this analysis, and Table 17.11 reports the slightly more involved results of a curvilinear regression (assuming a quadratic, or second-order polynomial structure to the relationship between modernity and political-economic market authority). There is a large improvement in the explained variance in modernity ($aR^2 = .729$). While the computations for the sources of variance are more complex for quadratic, or curvilinear, regression models, the logic remains the same. However, the way we interpret the impact of the independent variable—market liberalization—is slightly different. We do not merely assume a standard increasing linear relationship between the two variables (MODERN and LIBMARK). Rather, we parse the variance into two components: The linear effect (β_1, or LIBMARK), and the non-linear effect (β_2, or LIBMARK^2). As we see from Table 17.11, both effects are statistically significant ($\beta_1 = .898$, $t = 11.555$, $p = .000$; and $\beta_2 = .252$, $t = 3.503$, $p = .001$, respectively).

What do the findings in Tables 17.10 and 17.11, as well as Figures 17.3 and 17.4 mean? First, our findings support a positive relationship between modernity and market liberalization across countries. However, the model confirms that at some point, this relationship moves in the opposite direction, to be followed by a return to a positive relationship, as shown in Figure 17.4. The bend is fairly strong (as evidenced by a statistically significant coefficient for LIBMARK^2) and clearly articulates a distinctively curved pattern.

Second, our findings confirm for us that if we account for, or hold constant, the "bend," or curve effect, represented by LIBMARK^2, the remaining linear effect is much more powerful than a simple linear model would suggest. Note the slightly larger coefficient for LIBMARK in Table 17.11, compared to that in Table 17.10 ($\beta = .820$ and $\beta_1 = .898$, respectively). This means that once one accounts for the those countries that, for whatever reason, have experienced *much lower levels of modernity* at *higher levels of market liberalization*, there is a very sharp rise in modernity relative to increases in market liberalization among those countries that have much higher levels of market liberalization.

Exploring Broader Patterns of Residuals. As with previous scatterplots graphing the concept of modernity, Figure 17.4 reveals an interesting contrast between less modern and less liberalized countries and those that have higher levels of modernity and liberalized markets. The spread, or variance, of residuals is much greater in that region of the graph shown in Figure 17.4 that represents those countries with lower modernity and liberalization, while the spread of residuals in that region of the graph representing those countries with higher modernity and liberalization is much tighter and closer to the curve. To mine this plot further in order to draw additional information and refine our theory, we can utilize residual analysis in a slightly different manner than we did earlier in this chapter. Rather than focus merely on outliers, we can examine the resid-

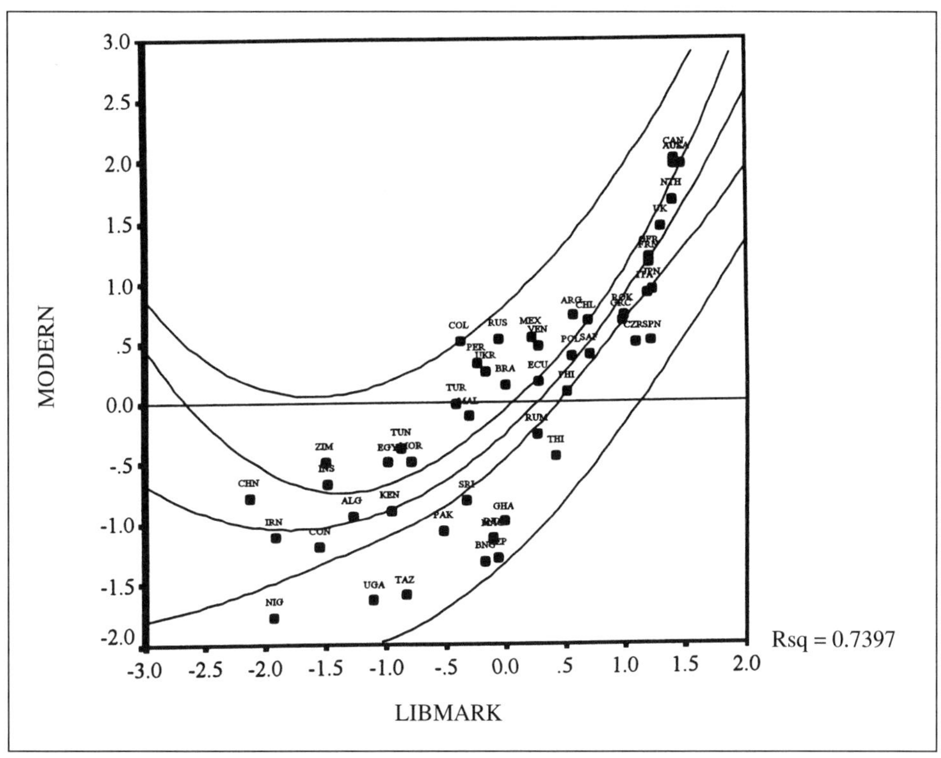

FIGURE 17.4 MODERN by LIBMARK (Curvilinear)

TABLE 17.11 Regression Analysis, MODERN by LIBMARK (Curvilinear Analysis)

	R^2	aR^2	*Standard Error Estimate*	*N*	
Model Summary:	.740	.729	.521	50	
Source of Variance:	*Sum of Squares*	*df*	*Mean Square*	*F*	*Prob. F*
Model (Regression)	36.245	1	18.122	66.775	.000
Residual	12.755	47	.271		
Parameter Estimates:	*Coefficient (b) (Std. Err. of b)*	*ß*	*95% c.i. (Lower - Upper)*	*t*	*Prob. t*
Intercept	-.247 (.102)		-.043 - -.042	-2.424	.019
LIBMARK	.898 (.077)	.898	.742 - 1.055	11.555	.000
$LIBMARK^2$	.252 (.072)	.272	.107 - .307	3.503	.001

uals across *defined groups* of countries to ascertain important patterns.

Table 17.12 groups countries according to two basic attributes: (1) the geographical and civilization tradition within which the country is classified (GEOCIV), and (2) the degree of social, political, and economic development, reflected by its degree of modernity (MODERN2) and liberalization (LIBMARK2) within the political and economic markets. We have grouped along the vertical axis of Table 17.12 at one end of the scale those geo-civilizations that are *not* Western (countries within the Africa, Asia, and Islam GEOCIV value ranges) and those groups of countries that are *more* Western on the opposite end of the scale along the vertical axis of Table 17.12 (countries in the Orthodox, Latin America, and Western GEOCIV value ranges).

Along the horizontal axis we have segregated countries according their respective values of MODERN and LIBMARK. We have used the median value of MODERN (codified in variable MODERN2 within CROSSNAT.50) and LIBMARK (codified in variable LIBMARK2 within CROSSNAT.50) to distinguish the logical type of country with respect to modernity and liberalized markets. The left half of the horizontal scale in Table 17.12 contains those countries that have authoritarian market systems. These are the countries that have non-democratic political markets and restricted, state-directed economic markets. These countries have scores for LIBMARK that are *less than* the median value for the two variables within our sample (CROSSNAT.50). In the right half of the horizontal axis in Table 17.12 are those countries that have more liberalized political and economic markets. These countries have scores for LIBMARK that are *equal to or greater than* the median value for the two variables within our sample (CROSSNAT.50). We have further divided each half into those countries that tend to be traditional, or less modern, and those that are more modern. Again, the empirical criteria for assigning countries to these groups is the countries' value of MODERN: Countries are assigned the "traditional" half of the horizontal axis if their value of MODERN is *less than* the median value for the variable in the sample (.120), and the "modern" half of the horizontal axis if their value of MODERN is *equal to or greater than* the median value of the variable. Within each cell of Table 17.12 we have included the countries that fall within the defined category and have also reported the standardized residual produced from the regression analysis in Table 17.11. The standardized residuals reported in Table 17.12 are included in the database CROSSNAT.50 as variable ZRMODCUR and have been produced from SPSS 10.[6] We have distinguished between the residuals that are within the ±95% c.i. levels, those that are beyond the ±95% c.i., yet not beyond the ±95% p.i. threshold (non-typical residuals), and those that are beyond the ±95% p.i. band (outliers).

Modernity, Market Liberalization, and Geo-Civilization Traditions. This bivariate frequency distribution reported in Table 17.12 reveals a distinct pattern to geo-civilization and broader contours of political and economic development (modernity and liberalization). African, Asian, and Islamic countries dominate the less developed end of the scale, while Western and Latin American countries dominate the more developed

TABLE 17.12 Residual Analysis, Regression Model, MODERN by LIBMARK (Curvilinear Model), Cross-National Patterns (Geo-Civilization by Modernity and Market Liberalization, 1997)

	Country Profiles Based on Modernity and Market Liberalization Countries and Standardized Residual for MODERN (ZRMODCUR)						
	Authoritarian (Non-Liberal) Markets			*Liberalized Markets*			
Geo-Civilization	*Traditional/ Authoritarian Markets (MODERN < .120; LIBMARK < -.046)*		*Modern/ Authoritarian Markets (MODERN > .120; LIBMARK < -.046)*	*Traditional/ Liberalized Markets (MODERN < .120; LIBMARK > -.046)*		*Modern/ Liberalized Markets (MODERN > .120; LIBMARK > -.046)*	
Africa	Congo	-.296		Ghana	-1.376*	South Africa	-.183
	Kenya	-.028					
	Madagascar	-1.497*					
	Nigeria	-1.400*					
	Tanzania	-1.484*					
	Uganda	-1.354*					
	Zimbabwe	1.044*					
		x̄ = -.717					
Asia	China	.436		Thailand	-1.171*	S. Korea	-.303
	India	-1.468*		Philippines	-.321		
	Nepal	-1.875*			x̄ = -.746		
	Sri Lanka	-.546*					
		x̄ = -.863					
Islam	Algeria	.093					
	Bangladesh	-1.749*					
	Egypt	.756*					
	Indonesia	.682*					
	Iran	-.127					
	Malaysia	.748*					
	Morocco	.610*					
	Pakistan	-.793*					
	Tunisia	.889*					
	Turkey	1.098*					
		x̄ = .221					

TABLE 17.12 *(continued)*

Geo-Civilization	*Traditional/ Authoritarian Markets (MODERN < .120; LIBMARK < -.046)*		*Modern/ Authoritarian Markets (MODERN > .120; LIBMARK < -.046)*		*Traditional/ Liberalized Markets (MODERN < .120; LIBMARK > -.046)*		*Modern/ Liberalized Markets (MODERN > .120; LIBMARK > -.046)*	
Orthodox			Russia	1.603*	Romania	-.500*	Greece	-.351
			Ukraine	1.255*				
				$\bar{x}$ = 1.429				
Latin America			Colombia	2.063**			Brazil	.760*
			Peru	1.503*			Argentina	.749*
				$\bar{x}$ = 1.783			Chile	.377*
							Ecuador	.314
							Mexico	1.130*
							Venezuela	.881*
								$\bar{x}$ = .702
Western							Australia	.868*
							Canada	.959*
							Czech Repub	-1.004*
							France	-.031
							Germany	.024
							Italy	-.486
							Japan	-.571*
							Netherlands	.335
							Poland	.104
							Spain	-1.357*
							USA	.719*
							UK	.234
								$\bar{x}$ = -.093

* = Non-typical residual (MODERN < 95%ci low band, or MODERN > 95%ci upper band; ** = Residual outlier (MODERN < 95%pi lower band, or MODERN > 95%pi upper band)

end of the scale. More telling are the patterns of the standardized residuals (ZRMODCUR). African and Asian countries are not only distinguished by lesser degrees of modernity and market liberalization, but have achieved *atypically lower* degrees of modernity than would be expected given their respective degrees of market liberalization.

The degree of market liberalization is very low to begin with for these countries, yet, what liberalization they have achieved (as of 1997) has produced (according to our estimates from Table 17.11) lower levels of modernity than we would expect for the *typical* countries with similar degrees of market liberalization. Indeed, except for Congo and Kenya in Africa, and China in Asia, each of the Asian and African countries with traditional social organization and state-directed authoritarian markets has modernity levels atypically lower for countries at their respective level of market liberalization. Zimbabwe is the one country that has an *atypically large* degree of modernity for a country at its level of market liberalization (ZRMODCUR = 1.044). China (ZRMODCUR = .436), Congo (ZRMODCUR = -.296), and Kenya (ZRMODCUR = -.028) have *typical levels* of modernity for their respective levels of market liberalization. The mean standardized residual for the eight African countries that are traditional and authoritarian is -.717, while it is -.863 for those four Asian countries in the same "development" range.

The pattern is somewhat different for the Islamic countries at that level of "development." All ten Islamic countries fall at the low end of the development scale (that is, they are characterized by traditional social organization and state-directed authoritarian markets). However, several, notably Egypt (.756), Indonesia (.682), Malaysia (.748), Tunisia (.898), and Turkey (1.098), have modernity levels sharply above the typical levels for countries at their level of market liberalization. Overall, the mean standardized residual for the ten Islamic countries in the sample is .221, reflecting a generally favorable modernity level, given their respective levels of openness and competition within their political-economic markets.

Western countries, which already have very high levels of modernity, in fact have modernity levels in many cases atypically *higher* than their degree of market liberalization would predict. And, of course, their level of market liberalization is already rather high by comparative standards, underscoring, perhaps, Ronald Inglehart's assertion that most of the wealthy democracies of the West have moved on to a "post-modern" phase of development.[7] This is generally true also for Latin American countries, including the two Latin American countries that are modern but generally authoritarian and characterized by restricted political and economic markets (Colombia and Peru).

Recall at the beginning of this demonstration, we noted that while modernity would not likely easily co-exist with authoritarian and non-liberalized political and economic markets, there are always exceptions. We see in Table 17.12 that indeed, four countries have societies that are characterized by relatively modernized social organization, yet have relatively authoritarian political economies: Russia, Ukraine, Colombia, and Peru. Overall, 84 percent of the sample fall along expected patterns of social organization and political-economic authority. Twenty-one countries are relatively traditional and authoritarian, and twenty-one countries are relatively modern and liberalized.

Can we draw any overall conclusion from the data in Table 17.12? To explore this, we have presented Table 17.13, which reports the difference of means tests for two groups of countries—those of the Western civilizational heritage (those within the Western, Latin American, and Orthodox categories within GEOCIV) and those with non-Western civilizational heritage (those countries within Asian, African, and Islamic categories within GEOCIV). The variable created by recoding GEOCIV into a collapsed, two-category measure is WESTERN within CROSSNAT.50. The degrees of ZRMODCUR for countries of the western civilizational heritage (WESTERN = 1) are substantially larger than those of the non-Western civilizational heritage (WESTERN = 0). Thus, we may conclude that modernity levels above those we would ordinarily expect given levels of liberalization are larger for Western nations than for non-Western countries.

Modernity, Market Liberalization, and Type of Political System as of 1950. Table 17.14 carries this analysis one step further by grouping countries according to the type of political system in the country as of 1950. Eight countries in Table 17.14 have seen their democratic status in 1950 evolve by 1997 into traditional societies with state-directed and authoritarian political economies. Most of these countries have modernity levels notably lower than one would typically expect for a country at their level of market liberalization. These countries include Bangladesh (–1.749), India (–1.468), and Pakistan (–.793). This pattern is stronger among those countries that were colonies or protectorates as of 1950 and as of 1997, are traditional, authoritarian, and state-directed political economies. These include Madagascar (–1.497), Nigeria (–1.400), Tanzania (–1.354), and Uganda (–1.354).

Among the democratic countries of 1950 that are more modern and liberalized in 1997 are the Anglo-American democracies that clearly stand apart from the other liberal democracies: Canada (.959), Australia (.868), and the United States (.719), and to a much lesser extent, the United Kingdom (.274). All have much larger degrees of modernity than we would predict given their already very high levels of market liberalization. The exceptions among those countries at the highest end of the development scale include Spain (–1.357), which was an authoritarian state from 1938 until 1975, the Czech Republic (–1.004), an authoritarian/communist society from 1948 until 1989, and Japan (–.571), an Asian authoritarian state until 1945, and essentially colonized by its military and political guardian, the United States, until the late 1950s.

However, a difference of means test reveals no statistically significant pattern to ZRMODCUR across these three groups of countries reported in Table 17.14. Table 17.15 reports the results of such a standard difference of means test.

TABLE 17.13 Difference of Means Test, ZRMODCUR by WESTERN

	Descriptive Statistics		
Countries Grouped According to Western Civilization Heritage (WESTERN)	*Mean*	*N*	*Std. Deviation*
Countries with Non-Western Civilization Heritage (WESTERN = 0)	-.370	26	0.963
Countries with Western Civilization Heritage (WESTERN = 1)	0.400	24	0.844
Total Sample	0	50	0.979
		Test Statistics	
Difference of Means Test	t	2.997	
	p (1-tail, df = 1,48)	0.002	

Moving Beyond Simple Residual Analysis: Refining and Elaborating Theory

Employing residual analysis to identify cross-national patterns is the first step toward theory refinement and modification. The next step is to explore some possible explanations that may shed further light on our proposed theory of modernity. This is classic detective work, and there are no hard and fast rules that one follows. However, an example will serve to demonstrate how residual analysis can be utilized to verify our new proportions that follow from our initial efforts.

Let us look more carefully at the pattern of residuals presented in Tables 17.12 and 17.14. The general pattern to the residuals in these two tables underscores the sharp differences that separate the broader economic and democratic development trajectories of countries in the wealthier West and those of the less affluent, and largely former colonial, Africa and Asia. For many students of comparative politics, the central issue with development—broadly defined—is not merely democracy or affluence, or even poverty. Rather, for many students of cross-national politics the more important question is what comes after affluence or poverty.[8] For many students of comparative politics, this is the degree of income inequality and concentrations of power and opportunity that afflict countries burdened by lower levels of economic and political development.[9] It is to this concept—inequality—that we turn our immediate attention as we seek to revise and broaden our conclusions and understanding of the relationship between market liberalization and modernity.

The Nature of Income Inequality. Income inequality is of particular concern to students of comparative politics for at least two reasons. First, the measure is readily obtained from various sources. The World Bank and other sources regularly report such

TABLE 17.14 Residual Analysis, Regression Model, MODERN, by LIBMARK (Curvilinear Model), Cross-National Patterns (Political System, as of 1950, by Modernity and Market Liberalization, 1997)

	Country Profiles Based on Modernity and Market Liberalization Countries and Standardized Residual for MODERN (ZRMODCUR)							
	Authoritarian (Non-Liberal) Markets				*Liberalized Markets*			
Political System	*Traditional/ Authoritarian Markets (MODERN < .120; LIBMARK < -.046)*		*Modern/ Authoritarian Markets (MODERN > .120; LIBMARK < -.046)*		*Traditional/ Liberalized Markets (MODERN < .120; LIBMARK > -.046)*		*Modern/ Liberalized Markets (MODERN > .120; LIBMARK > -.046)*	
Colonial/Protectorate	Algeria	.093			Ghana	-1.376*	Germany	.024
	Congo	-.296					Japan	-.571*
	Kenya	-.028					S. Korea	-.303
	Madagascar	-1.497*						x̄ = -..283
	Malaysia	.748*						
	Morocco	.610*						
	Nigeria	-1.400*						
	Tanzania	-1.484*						
	Tunisia	.889*						
	Uganda	-1.354*						
	Zimbabwe	1.044*						
Authoritarian	China	.436	Peru	1.503*	Romania	-.500*	Brazil	-.760*
	Nepal	-1.875*	Russia	1.603*			Argentina	.749*
		x̄ = -.720	Ukraine	1.255*			Czech Repub	-1.004*
				x̄ = 1.453			Poland	.104
							Spain	-1.357*
		s					Venezuela	.881*
								x̄ = .028

Democratic	Bangladesh	-1.749*	Colombia	2.063**	Philippines	-.321	Australia	.868*
	Egypt	.756*			Thailand	-1.171*	Canada	.959*
	India	-1.468*				x̄ = -.746	Chile	.377*
	Indonesia	.682*					Ecuador	-.314
	Iran	-.127					France	-.031
	Pakistan	-.793*					Greece	-.351
	Sri Lanka	-.546*					Italy	-.486
	Turkey	1.098*					Mexico	1.130*
		x̄= .268					Netherlands	.335
							South Africa	-.183
							UK	.234
							USA	.719*
								x̄ = -.274

* = Non-typical residual (MODERN < 95%ci low band, or MODERN > 95%ci upper band; ** = Residual outlier (MODERN < 95%pi lower band, or MODERN > 95%pi upper band)

TABLE 17.15 Difference of Means Test, ZRMODCUR by SYS19503

	Descriptive Statistics		
Countries Grouped According to Type of Political System as of 1950 (SYS19503)	*Mean*	*N*	*Std. Deviation*
Countries That Were Colonies or Protectorates as of 1950 (SYS19503 = 1)	-.327	15	0.910
Countries That Were Authoritarian as of 1950 (SYS19503 = 2)	.216	12	1.151
Countries That Were Democracies as of 1950 (SYS19503 = 3)	.100	23	.909
Total Sample	0	50	0.979
		Test Statistics	
Difference of Means Test	t	1.123	
	p (1-tail, df = 2,47)	0.293	

Bonferroni and Tamhane tests revealed no statistically significant pair-wise differences among any of the three groups of countries. (Levene's Test = .731, df = 2, p = .491)

data, though they are often several years old before they are updated by the various responsible international and national agencies. Income inequality measures are most often represented by two empirical indicators. The most common measure is the Gini index. Basically, a Gini index reflects the degree to which income within society is concentrated within a few units, such as households. A Gini of 0 indicates complete equity across all households or individuals within society. If, on the other hand, the society's total income accrues to only one person or household unit, leaving the rest with no income at all, the Gini coefficient will be equal to 1, or 100 percent inequity. A score of 50 indicates that there is proportionality in the system: namely, wealth is more concentrated in the middle income ranges of households. [10]

As an alternative to the Gini score (which can be sensitive to skewed distribution of wealth), some prefer to simply compute the ratio of the total wealth accruing to the top income categories of society to the total wealth accruing to the lower levels of society (for example, ratio of the total earnings of the top 10 percent of income earners to the total earnings of the poorest 20 percent of the population). These data are often more difficult to obtain. Therefore, the Gini is more commonly relied upon and is widely accepted as a reliable and valid measure—all things being equal—of income inequality.

Aside from the ease of obtaining relatively reliable and valid measures across different cultures and political systems, income inequality is also of interest to students of comparative politics because it offers important substantive insight into the nature of political power. Inequality underscores the foundations of political and social strife that pose challenges to various forms of institutional authority, and it highlights the central role of political conflict and resolution. Not all countries, for instance, are afflicted by ethnic and racial strife. Yet, all countries have degrees of income inequality. And, this phenomenon has been shown to be a factor in other forms of social conflict. Thus, it is a valid proxy for measuring the potential threat to the political and social stability of a nation-state and as such is frequently used in studies of cross-national analysis, especially those studies that seek to explain different patterns of development and democracy.

What might explain income inequality, and how might modernity be related to this important social phenomenon? While income inequality is complex and often a product of unique factors within given countries, we may still piece together the basic linkage between modernity and income inequality that is widely documented in the literature. Modernity, as we have noted, generally entails the introduction of technological innovation. Most important in a globally connected world are information-based technologies. Such informational-technological change skews the demand for labor skills in society. This tends to shift earnings to those at the very high end of the skill ladder. This, in turn, has the effect of also driving up unemployment of those at the lower ends, further skewing income earnings and concentrating such earnings into the hands of an increasingly smaller number of highly trained service professionals concentrated in urban centers, who also possess higher levels of education and who increasingly earn their living within the information technology sector.

Modernity, Liberalization, and Income Inequality: The "Liberalization Gap." Giovanni Andrea Cornia has surveyed the literature on economic development (and social modernity more generally), market liberalization (or, democratic capitalism), and income inequality among nations during the 1990s.[11] The decade of the 1990s has been characterized by sharp increases in income inequality, not only across nation-states, but within many countries that had previously shown some progress at reducing sharp inequalities. In exploring reasons for this increase, Cornia's analysis draws attention to a pattern that emerges from the residuals reported in Tables 17.12 and 17.14. His findings show that several countries are sharply imbalanced with respect to their degree of social modernity and market liberalization (to whatever extent such liberalization exists within the country). As our findings have shown, some countries have modernity levels much *lower* than their respective degree of market liberalization would predict (for example, Madagascar, India, Spain). Thus, their standardized residual for MODERN (reported as ZRMODCUR) is in the negative range, and some of these residuals are quite sizeable (and therefore, non-typical).

On the face of it, this does not seem all that surprising. These countries, for a variety of reasons, including their civilization and cultural heritage as we have seen in Table 17.14, are lagging behind the typical levels of modernity for countries with similar degrees of market liberalization. This, in any event, is what the standardized residual

(ZRMODCUR) suggests. These countries may be said to be characterized by a "*modernity gap*" (their level of modernity falls below what one would expect given their level of democratic capitalism). This is the usual focus of attention by many students of comparative politics.

Cornia's study draws our attention, however, to countries that are characterized by a different pattern to their residuals as shown in Tables 17.12 and 17.14, as well as Figure 17.3—a pattern that may be of potentially greater interest. These are the countries that have much *higher* levels of modernity than would be expected given their levels of market liberalization. These are not merely the four countries (Russia, Ukraine, Peru, and Colombia) that are generally modern yet also generally authoritarian. Rather, Cornia draws attention to countries that may well be traditional in some absolute sense, yet, much less traditional (and therefore, characterized by much more modern attributes) than one would expect given their degree of market liberalization. These include several Western countries (Canada, Australia, Mexico, and the United States), but also many former colonies and protectorates, as well as countries from Asia, Africa, and the Islamic cultures (for example, Zimbabwe, Tunisia, Malaysia, Turkey, and Indonesia).

Countries with this imbalance between *expected* modernity levels and *observed* market liberalization levels cannot be merely dismissed as lagging behind in terms of development. They may, indeed, be less modern in a relative sense to the typical country of the West. However, this is not what this particular residual highlights. Rather, it identifies those countries that have higher degrees of modernity than we would expect from the model and, in some cases, higher degrees of modernity than would be *typical* for a country at given levels of democratic capitalism. We may therefore describe these countries as being characterized by a "*liberalization gap*" (their level of modernity *exceeds* that which we would expect given their attained level of liberal—or open and competitive—political and economic markets). The "liberalization gap" is, in effect, the mirror image of the "modernity gap."

Why Income Inequality Varies with the "Liberalization Gap." While affluence and social empowerment may account for the size of the "liberalization gap" in countries, we have yet to consider directly why the "liberalization gap" may be associated with rising income inequality across countries. Cornia argues that traditional explanations for income inequality must be supplemented with more relevant explanations. These newer explanations for rising income point directly to the "liberalization" gap as a possible "culprit." There are three interrelated explanations for the higher income inequality among countries with higher degrees of the "liberalization gap."

First, countries characterized by strong "liberalization gaps" are likely to have undergone rapid and often complicated privatization plans, whereby state-owned industries were sold to pay debt and acquire new capital to accommodate their modern society. With less liberalized political and economic markets in these countries, such financial fixes may often be less than efficient and profitable. This has the effect once again of weakening the income earnings of those at the lower end of the income and skill brackets, as they are the most likely to immediately suffer from such inefficient privatization and fiscal reforms. Countries with less defined liberalization gaps (that is, their expected modernity level does not greatly exceed their level of market liberalization, or, alternatively, countries that are characterized by a "modernity gap") are more likely to manage pressures associated with social modernity with liberalized political and economic markets that can more effectively and efficiently manage the capital transfers and property restructuring.

Second, rapidly modernizing social systems often seek capital, either through privatization, or, additionally, through borrowing. Here too, with commercial and capital markets less liberalized—relative to their level of modernity—and with liberal democratic institutions less developed, there is no effective political check to capital reforms. In this circumstance, the ever-present threat of moral hazard, or the propensity of human nature to refrain from cheating if not monitored by accountable and representative public authority, becomes a danger to efficient and profitable capital reform and development. In this manner, the lower skilled and less professional labor within society are the first to see their earning power decline as creditors demand premium rates on loans in order to cover the rising risks of investment. Such premiums often require the states in such imbalanced systems to raise taxes, as well as to close down various production operations (thus raising unemployment and again placing a skewed pressure on income distribution).[12]

Finally, of course, with limited liberal democratic and competitive commercial markets, there is little in the way of effective representation available to lower wage earners to lobby for and legislate income redistribution. Furthermore, lacking sufficiently liberal democratic institutions, as well as competitive capital markets—at least relative to the degree of social modernity within their country—these lower wage earners cannot effectively protect minimum levels of income in the face of the pressures associated with social transformation.[13] Thus, in those countries experiencing higher levels of modernity than the liberal political and economic markets would seem fully capable of managing, we expect severe pressure on existing income balances within the society, which should be reflected in rising income inequality.[14]

To summarize, we expect that in those countries with larger liberalization gaps, we will see larger degrees of income inequality, expressed by the Gini scores for these countries. On the other hand, when the liberalization gap is minimal, that is, in those countries where the pressure for modernity seems to be about what one would expect for a country at its level of liberalization, or, if in fact, where we find no such liberalization gap at all (but rather a modernity gap), we expect income inequality to be generally lower, as reflected in the Gini score for that country. Note that we are not suggesting that democracy or modernity generate income inequality per se. Rather, we are drawing attention to the residual values of modernity, as derived from the regression analysis reported in Table 17.11, and reported in Tables 17.12 and 17.14.

Testing the Relationship Between the Liberalization Gap and Income Inequality. The measure of income inequality—the Gini scores—is represented by the variable ZGINI, or the standardized score for a country's Gini score. These scores reflect the closest approximation to the 1997 figures as are available through the various available sources.[15] Hypothesis 17.2 formalizes our theory:

Hypothesis 17.2: ZGINI varies proportionately with ZRMODCUR across countries

Figure 17.5 reports the linear plot of ZGINI by ZRMODCUR. As expected, income inequality increases across countries in proportion to the degree of a country's liberalization gap ($r^2 = .194$, $F = 11.570$, $p = .001$). Table 17.16 reports the standardized residual scores for ZGINI across the sample (this variable is in CROSSNAT.50 as ZRGINI). Table 17.16 segregates the sample according to whether the value of ZRGINI was greater than 0 (and thus the value ZGINI was greater than expected given the level of the country's liberalization gap), or less than 0 (and thus a country with an income inequality level below what was expected given the degree of the country's liberalization gap).

Implications From Our Theory Refinement: Inequality, Prosperity, and Liberalization. A closer look at Figure 17.5 and Table 17.16 reveals that the majority of the countries above the regression line are African or Latin American countries. These countries have *greater degrees of income inequality* than we would predict from the model. Aside from their geo-civilization cultural heritage, these countries are also among the poorest of the countries within our sample. For instance, consider the standardized scores for the level of human development (ZHUMDEV) among these countries (see Chapter 12 and Table 12.1 for more detail on ZHUMDEV). Uganda (ZHUMDEV = –1.972), Tanzania (–1.865), Madagascar (–1.663), Nigeria (–1.644), and Congo (–1.499) are each characterized with much higher income inequality than would be expected given their respective liberalization gaps, and are also suffering from very low levels of prosperity and social empowerment.

That there is a relationship between higher than expected income levels at various levels of the liberalization gap and a country's overall prosperity and human development should not surprise us. Traditional explanations of income inequality clearly point to poverty and deprivation as crucial factors contributing to the widening gap between the wealthy and the poor portions of the population within the least developed and most impoverished of countries within the world. Within the poorest of the countries, one would expect that very minimal degrees of modernity would result in substantial transfers of income to a few of the most skilled and professional of the labor force. While perhaps not comprising the degrees of wealth and income transfer that one would observe in the more developed and wealthy countries, these transfers in the poorest countries, considering the base of poverty and deprivation throughout their economies, are likely to have dramatic proportional effects and result in signifi-

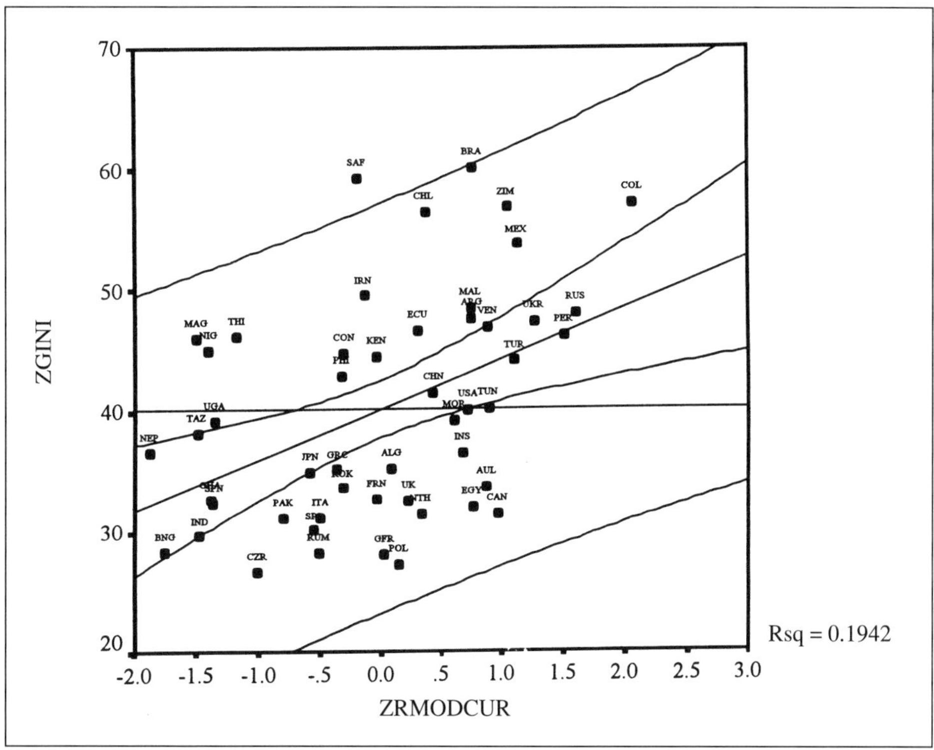

FIGURE 17.5 ZGINI by ZRMODCUR

cant shifts in the overall income distribution within society. Regardless of their overall liberalization gap, which would undoubtedly also be affected by very slight shifts in modernity associated with various reform programs, from a comparative perspective, the income distribution will surely seem exaggerated given their level of modernity and market liberalization.

We may offer initial confirmation of this hypothesis with a simple difference of means test, reported in Table 17.16. Using the standardized residuals (ZRGINI) produced from the regression of ZGINI on ZRMODCUR, we see that the average level of human development (ZHUMDEV) is significantly higher for those twenty-eight countries with lower levels of income inequality than would be expected, given their liberalization gap, than for those twenty-two countries that have higher than expected levels of income inequality, given their liberalization gaps.

Thus, our initial findings suggest a serious risk is posed to the poorest segments of the population within the more impoverished countries of the world when public authority in these countries presses ahead too aggressively with modernity via authoritarian state direction, replete with restricted and closed markets. The poorest segments of the population in these countries are likely to become relatively poorer, in

TABLE 17.16 ZRGINI Scores, Grouped by Size

Countries with Higher Income Inequality Than Expected (ZRGINI > 0), Given Their Degree of a "Liberalization Gap" N = 22		*Countries with Lower Income Inequality Than Expected (ZRGINI < 0), Given Their Degree of a "Liberalization Gap" N = 28*	
COUNTRY	*ZRGINI*	*COUNTRY*	*ZRGINI*
South Africa	2.379	Peru	-0.024
Brazil	2.006	China	-0.056
Chile	1.766	Turkey	-0.075
Zimbabwe	1.471	Ghana	-0.209
Madagascar	1.441	Spain	-0.242
Thailand	1.303	Japan	-0.333
Nigeria	1.274	United States	-0.363
Iran	1.175	Morocco	-0.417
Mexico	1.058	Greece	-0.420
Colombia	1.013	Tunisia	-0.436
Congo	0.690	India	-0.522
Ecuador	0.614	Bangladesh	-0.549
Malaysia	0.614	Algeria	-0.627
Uganda	0.558	Korea	-0.629
Kenya	0.533	Pakistan	-0.677
Argentina	0.518	Indonesia	-0.776
Nepal	0.517	Italy	-0.830
Tanzania	0.502	France	-0.876
Philippines	0.487	Sri Lanka	-0.931
Venezuela	0.357	United Kingdom	-1.019
Ukraine	0.231	Czech	-1.122
Russia	0.142	Romania	-1.181
		Netherlands	-1.201
		Australia	-1.202
		Egypt	-1.350
		Germany	-1.453
		Canada	-1.511
		Poland	-1.618

fact. As our initial findings suggest, if the poorer authoritarian states opt for a political strategy designed to extend modernity through social reorganization, they will surely generate a liberalization gap, which, we suggest further from our elaborated regression and residual analysis, will only extenuate the impoverishment and severe deprivation of the poorest segments of the population within these countries. Figure 17.6 summarizes the logic of our elaborated theory of modernity, taking into account, as it does, the role of liberalized markets and the nature of human development.

A Cautionary Note. Note that we are not suggesting, nor can we infer, that because a country is "poor," it will automatically have more income inequality than we would expect given its "liberalization gap." This would be, as you may recall from Chapter 2

TABLE 17.17 Difference of Means Test, ZRIGINI by Degree of Human Development (ZHUMDEV2)

	Descriptive Statistics		
Countries Grouped According to Degree of Human Development (ZHUMDEV2)	*Mean*	*N*	*Std. Deviation*
Countries With Higher Income Inequality Than Expected (ZRGINI > 0) Given Their Degree of a "Liberalization Gap"	-0.392	22	0.944
Countries With Lower Income Inequality Than Expected (ZRGINI ≤ 0) Given Their Degree of a "Liberatization Gap"	0.308	28	0.947
Total Sample	0	50	1
	Test Statistics		
Difference of Means Test	t	2.599	
	p (1-tail, df = 1,48)	0.006	

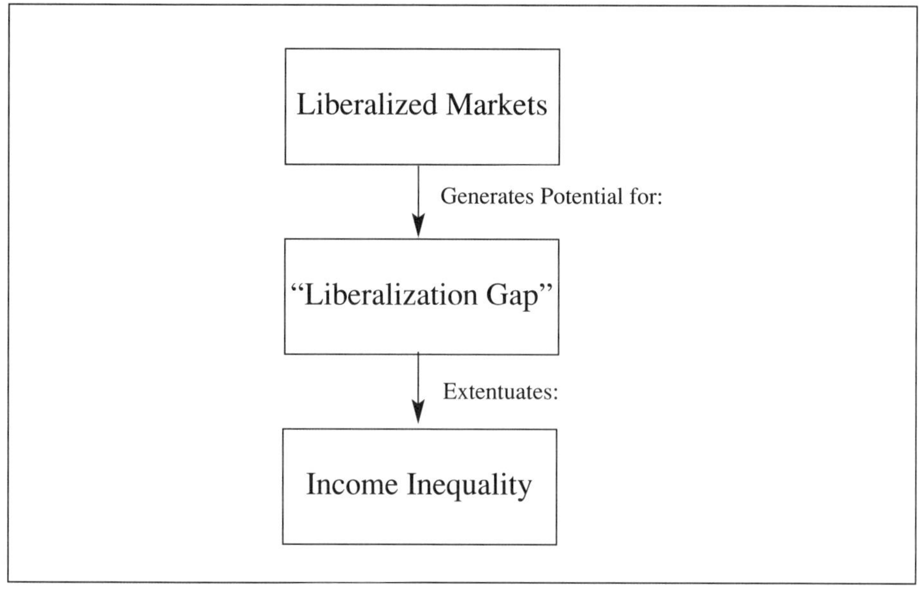

FIGURE 17.6 The Link Between Income Inequality and Liberalized Markets, Following from Modernity and Modified by the Levels of Human Development

(see Endnote 17), an ecological fallacy. Rather, we are concluding that poverty and deprivation are more likely to add income inequality to a country beyond that the liberalization gap within the country would be expected to produce. While policy prescription is not the common objective of students of cross-national analysis, these initial findings clearly suggest that if a normative goal is to reduce income inequality, one must find a way to enhance the extent of liberalized markets within society, as this will reduce the liberalization gap, assuming, of course, that such economic and political reforms are more feasible than simply stopping the process of social transformation associated with modernity in an era of globalization.[16] This, as our data suggest, is undoubtedly more difficult for countries with cultural traditions that run somewhat counter to modernity and liberalization, and, of course, it will be decidedly more difficult for more impoverished countries of the world.

What should be clear to the reader by now is that the regression analysis is not an end-all to the research process, but only one step in an ongoing process of testing, refining, testing again, and refining yet again. The precision associated with regression can often mask to the less experienced researcher the risks we run when we fail to go beyond the basic results of such a powerful statistical tool. Lying beneath the surface of the standard output are the potentials for new questions that may emerge from a closer examination of the residuals. From the residuals, and subsequent re-testing, the seemingly inexplicable and unexpected can be made more comprehensible to those students of comparative politics who are willing to explore and take the time to carefully consider the contours of the portrait provided by the residual error in regression models.

CHAPTER SUMMARY

We have seen that beyond simple hypothesis testing, regression analysis can serve as a critical tool of discovery for the comparativist. By employing variance and standard error measures derived through parameter estimates of the model, the student can go beyond hypothesis testing to basic residual analysis of the countries in the sample. Through such exploratory techniques, we increase our chances of exposing additional important substantive information that extends the range and breadth of our substantive understanding of the political world and can lead to greater refinement of our subsequent hypotheses designed to illuminate comparative political behavior and institutional authority. Indeed, given the nature of their data, comparativists are in a distinctly advantageous position to use confidence intervals and prediction intervals as a part of their regular statistical repertoire. We have demonstrated this in elaborating the empirical relationship between modernity, democracy, market authority, and income inequality within society. Through residual analysis and theory elaboration following from such explorations of the error terms in the initial regression, we have tied liberalization not merely to modernity, but eventually through modernity itself to income inequality, and we have highlighted the risks associated with persistent modernity when the political and economic markets lag too far behind.

Finally, it is important to note that while this text focuses on the basics of bivariate techniques, there are a number of powerful tools at the disposal of the analyst that extend the researchers' power of generalization and offer the promise of greater precision and exactitude.[17] These techniques, such as multiple regression, path analysis, and specialized versions of regression analysis, such as logistic analysis, afford the researcher the opportunity of elaborating theories with more complex and innovative multidimensional models. However, each of these techniques relies upon error estimates and variance measures of bivariate relationships. Without a keen appreciation for the versatility and power of standard bivariate techniques, these more sophisticated techniques cannot be effectively utilized by the student of cross-national analysis.

NOTES

1. Lawrence Mayer, 1996, *Redefining Comparative Politics: Promise Versus Performance* (Newbury Park, Calif.: Sage Publications), p. 48.

2. To produce the 95% c.i. and 95% p.i. bands around the regression line, as shown in Figure 16.3, follow the same steps outlined in Chapter 15 to produce a scatterplot within SPSS 10. Once your plot is produced, use the CHART EDITOR to select your confidence interval and prediction interval bands. This can be achieved by following this sequence (inside the CHART EDITOR): CHART▶OPTIONS▶FIT LINE▶TOTAL▶FIT OPTION▶REGRESSION PREDICTION LINE(S). Select the boxes marked respectively, MEAN (for the mean expected value of Y) and INDIVIDUAL (for prediction intervals). The default confidence range is 95%, though you may select another range if you desire. Within the CHART OPTIONS window, you may also select the MEAN REFERENCE LINE to be included in your graph. Within the CHART EDITOR mode, you may also select the FORMAT menu button and modify the line styles and color, as well as the marker styles and color of your scatterplot. Within the CHART EDITOR, you may then select the EDIT option from the menu and choose COPY CHART. This will write your edited scatterplot to the clipboard within WINDOWS.You may then open a word precessor, such as WordPerfect or Word, and, using the EDIT/PASTE SPECIAL procedure, select SPSS PICTURE and paste the chart to a word processing document. This will be read as a graphic that can be further edited within the word processor. See Marija J. Norušis, 2000, *SPSS© 10.0 Guide to Data Analysis* (Upper Saddle River, N.J.: Prentice Hall), pp. 408–409 for more details on the SPSS options.

3. SPSS 10 offers the student a rich variety of statistical options for residual analysis. To obtain the standardized residuals, predicted value ofY, as well as the upper and lower 95% c.i and 95% p.i. scores for individual cases within your sample, use the regression procedure as described in Demonstration 16.1. Within the LINEAR REGRESSION window, select the SAVE option at the bottom of the window. This allows you to save as variables a number of residual measures. These are divided into five boxes, three of which are immediately relevant to your present needs: *Predicted Values* box, *Prediction Intervals* box, and the *Residuals* box. The *Prediction Intervals* box allows you to select either the standardized or unstandardized predicted value of

Y (if your data are already z-score values, you need not select the standardized check-box). You may also select the standard error estimate of the mean predictions, which when added to the predicted value of Y produces the upper limits for the 95% c.i., and when subtracted, produces the lower bounds of the 95% c.i. for each value of X in the sample. The *Residuals* box also offers you the option of saving the standardized and/or unstandardized residuals for each case in the sample. Finally, by stating the *Prediction Intervals* in the respective box, you will produce the upper and lower 95% c.i. and 95% p.i. for each value of X in your sample. You may also alter the confidence interval if you wish (for example, to 99%). These variables are saved in your database. By following the sequence STATISTICS▶SUMMARIZE▶CASE SUMMARIZE, you may then list these variables for each case in your database for subsequent examination. See Marija J. Norǔsis, 2000, *SPSS: SPSS© 10.0 Guide to Data Analysis* (Upper Saddle River, N.J.: Prentice Hall), pp. 394–406, for more details on the SPSS options. For presentation (such as shown in Table 16.5), you may want to sort the value of the predicted value of Y in ascending order. This may be accomplished within SPSS as well (DATA▶SORT CASES).

4. Ross E. Burkhart, 2000, "Economic Freedom and Democracy: Post-Cold War Tests," *European Journal of Political Research* 37 (March): 237–253. For a comprehensive survey of the relationship between the markets and liberal democracy, see Charles E. Lindblom, 2001, *The Market System: What it Is, How it Works, and What to Make of It* (New Haven: Yale University Press).

5. James Gwartney, Robert Lawson (with Dexter Samida), 1999, *Economic Freedom of the World, 2000* (Fraser Institute), on the web at http://www.fraserinstitute.ca/publications/books/econ_free_2000.

6. To obtain and save standardized residuals within regression analysis using SPSS 10, open the SAVE NEW VARIABLES dialog box within the LINEAR REGRESSION dialog box in SPSS 10. Select standardized residuals, which will be produced and saved as a new variable within your SPSS database (for example, CROSSNAT.50.SAV) when you execute the regression analysis. The variable will appear as the last variable in your DATA EDITOR window. The new variable will be assigned a name by the program. You may, of course, edit that name as you wish within the VARIABLE EDITOR window. We have named the new variable within CROSS NAT.50, which represents the standardized residual for MODERN based on predictions from LIBMARK in our curvilinear model, as ZRMODCUR (Z, for standardized, R for residual, and MODCUR for curvilinear model predictions for the value of MODERN). See Marija J. Norǔsis, 2000, *SPSS© 10.0 Guide to Data Analysis* (Upper Saddle River, N.J.: Prentice Hall), pp. 396–399.

7. Ronald Inglehart, 1997, *Modernization and Postmodernization: Cultural, Economic and Political Change in 43 Societies* (Princeton: Princeton University Press).

8. See Manus I. Midlarsky, ed., 1997, *Inequality, Democracy, and Economic Development* (Cambridge, UK: Cambridge University Press); and Deepak Lal and H. Mynt, 1996, *The Political Economy of Poverty, Equity, and Growth: A Comparative Study* (Oxford: Clarendon/Oxford University Press).

9. See, for instance, Roberto Patricio Korzeniewicz and William C. Smith, May 17, 1999, "Growth, Poverty and Inequality in Latin America: Searching for the High Road," Rights vs. Efficiency Paper #7, Institute for Latin American and Iberian Studies at Colombia University, *Colombia International Affairs Online Working Paper*, on the net at http://www.ciaonet.org. For a brief but insightful overview of the extensive literature on the relationship between liberal

democracy and modernity, see Ethan B. Kapstein and Dimitri Landa, 1999/2000, "Democracy and the Market: the Case of Globalization," Freedom House Working Paper, on the net at http://www.freedomhouse.org/survey/2000/kapstein.html.

10. See Klaus Deininger and Lyn Squire "A New Data Set Measuring Income Inequality," http://www.worldbank.org/html/prdmg/grthweb/dddeisqu.htm and World Bank, *Entering the Twenty-first Century: World Development Report 1999/2000,* Table 5. Gini data can be obtained from World Income Inequality Database, on the net at http://www.undp.org/poverty/initiatives/wider/wiid, and at World Bank Program on Poverty (with various links for data), on the net at http://www.worldbank.org/poverty/data/index.htm. Additionally, the data can be obtained from the World Bank, *World Development Indicators 1999*, CD-ROM. We have used data drawn from the World Bank's *Indicators* CD-ROM.

11. Giovanni Andrea Cornia, "Liberalization, Globalization and Income Distribution," March 1999, Working Paper 157, *World Institute for Development Economics Research*, United Nations University, Helsinki, Finland, on the net at http://www.wider.unu.edu/publications/wp157.pdf.

12. For an insightful look at the implications for imperfections within the capital markets, especially for countries that are likely to be more "modern" than "liberalized," see Thomas Willet, 1998, "International Financial Markets as Sources of Crisis Discipline: The Too Much, Too Late Hypothesis," July 1998, *Center of International Studies*, University of Southern California, Columbia International Affairs Online, Working Papers, on the net at http://www.cc.columbia.edu/sec/dlc/ciao/wps/wit01/wit01.html.

13. For additional insight on this point, see Glenn Rayp, 1999, "Globalisation, Competitiveness, Unemployment, and Social Protection Coordination," in Frans Buelens, ed., *Globalisation and the Nation-State* (Cheltenham, UK: Edward Elgar), pp. 69–88.

14. For an overview of the tensions generated by development, see Sunil Kukreja, 2001, "The Two Faces of Development," in David N. Balaam and Michael Veseth, eds., *Introduction to International Political Economy*, second edition (Upper Saddle River, N.J.: Prentice Hall), pp. 320–345.

15. The sample mean for GINI in CROSSNAT.50 is 40.158, with a standard deviation of 9.225. The variable is normally distributed, with a skew of .476, a K-S statistic of .121 ($p = .066$), and a S-W statistic of .931 ($p = .011$). The minimum value in the sample is 26.6, and the maximum is 60.1.

16. See Philip G. Cerny, 1999, "Reconstructing the Political in a Globalising World: States, Institutions, Actors and Governance," in Frans Buelens, ed., *Globalisation and the Nation-State* (Cheltenham, UK: Edward Elgar), pp. 89–137. The social costs of globalization, especially for labor in wealthy and poor countries, are considered by Jay Mazur, 2000, "Labor's New Internationalism," *Foreign Affairs* 79 (January/February): 79–93.

17. For useful introductions and overviews of these more advanced topics, see William D. Berry and Mitchell S. Sanders, 2000, *Understanding Multivariate Research: a Primer for Beginning Social Scientists* (Boulder: Westview Press); and Alan Agresti and Barbara Finlay, 1997, *Statistical Methods for the Social Sciences,* third edition (Upper Saddle River, N.J.: Prentice Hall).

Index

Note to reader: In the text variable names were often preceded by Z to indicate the z-score for the particular variable and were often followed by a number to indicate a particular study that used the variable. For the sake of simplicity and in order to group all references to the variable in one location I dropped both the Z and number modifiers in the index. For example references to ZPOWER are indexed as POWER and references to AGE18002 are indexed as AGE1800 and so on for all named variables.